THE CHILDREN ACT MANUAL

AUSTRALIA
The Law Book Company
Brisbane * Sydney * Melbourne * Perth

CANADA
Carswell
Ottowa * Toronto * Calgary * Montreal * Vancouver

AGENTS

Steimatzky's Agency Ltd., Tel Aviv

N.M. Tripathi (Private) Ltd., Bombay

Eastern Law House (Private) Ltd., Calcutta

M.P.P. House, Bangalore

Universal Book Traders, Delhi

Aditya Books, Delhi

MacMillan Shuppan KK, Tokyo

Pakistan Law House, Karachi, Lahore

THE CHILDREN ACT MANUAL

Judith Masson
M.A. (Cantab), Ph.D. (Leicester)
Professor of Law, University of Warwick

Michael Morris
LL.B (University College, London),
Solicitor

LONDON
SWEET & MAXWELL
1992

Published in 1992 by
Sweet & Maxwell Limited of
South Quay Plaza, 183 Marsh Wall, London, E14 9FT
Computerset by P.B. Computer Typesetting,
Pickering, North Yorkshire
Printed in Great Britain by Butler & Tanner Ltd., Frome, Somerset

BRITISH LIBRARY CATALOGUING IN PUBLICATION DATA
A Catalogue record for this book
is available from the British Library

ISBN 0 421 469803

All rights reserved.
No part of this publication may be reproduced or transmitted,
in any form or by any means, electronic, mechanical, photocopying,
recording or otherwise or stored in any retrieval system of any
nature, without the written permission of the copyright holder and
the publisher, application for which shall be made to the publisher.

©
Sweet & Maxwell
1992

CONTENTS

Table of Cases vii
Table of Statutes xi
Table of Statutory Instruments xxi
Table of Children Act xxix

PART I
THE CHILDREN ACT 1989 (as amended) 1

PART II
THE COURT RULES 343

The Family Proceeding Rules 1991
(S.I. 1991 No. 1247), Pt IV (as amended) 347
The Family Proceedings Courts (Children Act 1989)
Rules 1991 (S.I. 1991 No. 1395) (as amended) 350

PART III
ADDITIONAL STATUTORY INSTRUMENTS 429

The Children (Admissibility Evidence) Order 1991
(S.I. 1991 No. 1115) 431
The Children (Allocation of Proceedings) Order 1991
(S.I. 1991 No. 1677) 432
The Children (Allocation of Proceedings Appeals)
Order 1991 (S.I. 1991 No. 1801) 452
The Children (Secure Accommodation) Regulations 1991
(S.I. 1991 No. 1505) 452
The Children (Secure Accommodation) (No. 2)
Regulations 1991 (S.I. 1991 No. 2034) 461
The Contact with Children Regulations 1991
(S.I. 1991 No. 891) 462
The Emergency Protection Order (Transfer of
Responsibilities) Regulations 1991 (S.I. 1991 No. 1414) 464
The Family Proceedings Rules 1991
(S.I. 1991 No. 1247) Pts V, VIII and IX in part 466
The Family Proceedings (Costs) Rules 1991
(S.I. 1991 No. 1832) 475
The Family Proceedings Fees Order 1991
(S.I. 1991 No. 2114) 478
The Guardians Ad Litem and Reporting Officers
(Panels) Regulations 1991 (S.I. 1991 No. 2051) 483

Index 491

CONTENTS

Table of Cases vii
Table of Statutes xi
Table of Statutory Instruments xvii
Table of Children Act xxix

PART I
THE CHILDREN ACT 1989 (as amended) 1

PART II
THE COURT RULES 243

The Family Proceeding Rules 1991
(S.I. 1991 No. 1247), Pt IV (as amended) 247
The Family Proceedings Court (Children Act 1989)
Rules 1991 (S.I. 1991 No. 1395) (as amended) 290

PART III
ADDITIONAL STATUTORY INSTRUMENTS 329

The Children (Admissibility of Evidence) Order 1991
(S.I. 1991 No. 1115) 331
The Children (Allocation of Proceedings) Order 1991
(S.I. 1991 No. 1677) 333
The Children (Allocation of Proceedings) (Appeals)
Order 1991 (S.I. 1991 No. 1801) 342
The Children (Secure Accommodation) Regulations 1991
(S.I. 1991 No. 1505) 343
The Children (Secure Accommodation) (No. 2)
Regulations 1991 (S.I. 1991 No. 2034) 351
The Contact with Children Regulations 1991
(S.I. 1991 No. 891) 352
The Emergency Protection Order (Transfer of
Responsibilities) Regulations 1991 (S.I. 1991 No. 1414) 354
The Family Proceedings Rules 1991
(S.I. 1991 No. 1247) Pts V, VIII and IX in part 356
The Family Proceedings (Costs) Rules 1991
(S.I. 1991 No. 1832) 373
The Family Proceedings Fees Order 1991
(S.I. 1991 No. 2114) 376
The Guardians Ad Litem and Reporting Officers
(Panels) Regulations 1991 (S.I. 1991 No. 2051) 382

Index 391

TABLE OF CASES

A. v. Liverpool City Council [1982] A.C. 363; [1981] 2 W.L.R. 948; 125 S.J. 396; [1981] 2
  All E.R. 385; (1981) 79 L.G.R. 62, H.L. 32, 40, 101, 102, 228
Att.-Gen. v. Hammersmith and Fulham London Borough Council, *The Times*,
  December 18, 1979; [144 J.P.N. 38] 67
—— v. Wandsworth L.B.C., *ex p.* Tilley [1981] 1 W.L.R. 854 78
Att.-Gen., *ex rel.* Tilley v. Wandsworth London Borough Council [1981] 1 W.L.R. 854;
  (1981) 125 S.J. 148; [1981] 1 All E.R. 1162; (1980) 78 L.G.R.; (1981) 11 Fam.Law
  119, C.A.; affirming *The Times*, March 21, 1980 .... 51, 53

B., *Re* [1987] A.C. 199 229
——, [1992] 2 F.L.R. 1, C.A. 33
——, [1992] New.L.J. 642 102
——, (A Minor) [1992] 1 F.C.R. 555 362
——, [1992] 1 F.C.R. 25 391
B. (Appeals to Crown Court: Evidence), *Re* [1992] 1 F.C.R. 153 223
B. (A Minor) (Residence Order: ex parte) [1992] 2 F.L.R. 1 43
B. (A Minor) (Wardship: Guardian *ad litem*), *Re*, [1989] 1 F.L.R. 268; [1989] Fam.Law
  152 123
Baker, *Re*, [1962] Ch. 201 112
Bradford City Metropolitan Borough Council v. K., *The Times*, August 18, 1989 223

C, *Re* (unreported) noted in [1992] N.L.J. 832 16
C. (No. 2), *Re The Times*, April 27, 1989 225
C. (A Minor) (Adoption Order: Conditions), *Re* [1988] 2 W.L.R. 474; (1988) 132 S.J.
  334; [1988] 1 All E.R. 705; [1988] F.C.R. 484; [1988] 2 F.L.R. 159; (1988) 152
  L.G.Rev. 771; (1988) 18 Fam.Law 428; (1988) 138 New L.J. 64; (1988) 152 J.P.N.
  430, H.L.; reversing *sub nom.* C. (A Minor) (Adoption: Contract with Sibling)
  [1987] 2 F.L.R. 383; (1988) 18 Fam.Law 13, C.A. 34
C. (A Minor: Care Order), *Re The Times*, August 18, 1992 97
C. (A Minor: Irregularity of Practice), *Re* [1992] Fam.Law 14 30
C. (Parental Rights), *Re* [1992] 1 F.L.R. 1, C.A. 16, 24
Calderdale Borough Council v. H. & P. [1991] 1 F.L.R. 461 .... 33, 47
Cocks v. Thanet District Council [1983] A.C. 286; [1982] 3 W.L.R. 1121; (1982) 126 S.J.
  820; [1982] 3 All E.R. 1135; (1983) 81 L.G.R. 81; (1984) 24 R.V.R. 31, H.L. 66
Croydon London Borough v. A, [1992] 1 F.C.R. 522 .... 32, 221

D. (A Minor), *Re* [1992] 1 All E.R. 892, C.A. 32, 34
D. (A Minor), *Re, sub nom.* D. (A Minor) v. Berkshire County Council [1987] A.C. 317;
  [1986] 3 W.L.R. 1080; (1987) 151 J.P. 313; (1986) 130 S.J. 984; [1987] 1 All E.R. 20;
  (1987) 85 L.G.R. 169; [1987] 1 F.L.R. 422; (1987) 151 L.G.Rev. 268; (1987) 17
  Fam.Law 202; (1986) 136 New L.J. 1184; (1987) 151 J.P.N. 190; (1987) 84 L.S.
  Gaz. 574; [(1987) 84 L.S.Gaz. 15]; H.L.; affirming [1986] 3 W.L.R. 85; (1986) 130
  S.J. 467; [1987] 1 All E.R. 20; (1986) 136 New L.J. 513; (1986) 83 L.S.Gaz. 1720,
  C.A. 96
Dean v. Dean [1987] 1 F.L.R. 517; (1987) 17 Fam.Law 200; (1987) 151 J.P.N. 254; [1987]
  1 F.C.R. 96, C.A. 46
Devon County Council v. Glancy (1985) 1 F.L.R. 20 382
—— v. J and others [1992] 1 F.C.R. 550 403
—— v. S. [1992] 3 All E.R. 793 .... 39, 99
Dipper v. Dipper [1981] Fam. 31; [1980] 3 W.L.R. 626; (1980) 124 S.J. 775; [1980] 2 All
  E.R. 722; (1979) 10 Fam.Law 211, C.A.; [145 J.P.N. 391] 20
Dyson Holdings v. Fox [1976] Q.B. 503; [1975] 3 W.L.R. 744; 119 S.J. 744; [1975] 3 All
  E.R. 1030; 31 P. & C.R. 229; 239 E.G. 39, C.A. 53

F. v. Kent C.C. *The Independent*, August 10, 1992 216
F. v. Wirral Metropolitan Borough Council and Liverpool City Council [1991] Fam.
  69; [1991] 2 W.L.R. 1132; [1991] 2 All E.R. 648; [1991] 2 F.L.R. 114; [1991]
  Fam.Law 299, C.A. 21, 102, 135

Table of Cases

G. v. G. [1985] 1 W.L.R. 647; (1985) F.L.R. 894 .... 221, 404
Gillick v. West Norfolk and Wisbech Area Health Authority and the D.H.S.S. [1986] A.C. 112; [136 New L.J. 75; 1986 S.L.T. 69; 136 New L.J. 184]; [1985] 3 W.L.R. 830; (1985) 129 S.J. 738; [1985] 3 All E.R. 402; [1986] Crim.L.R. 113; (1985) 135 New L.J. 1055; (1985) 82 L.S.Gaz. 3531, H.L.; reversing [1985] 2 W.L.R. 413; (1985) 129 S.J. 42; [1985] 1 All E.R. 533; (1985) 15 Fam.Law 165; (1985) 135 New L.J. 81; (1985) 82 L.S.Gaz. 762, C.A.; reversing [1984] Q.B. 581; [1983] 3 W.L.R. 859; (1983) 127 S.J. 696; (1983) 147 J.P. 888; [1984] 1 All E.R. 365; (1984) 14 Fam.Law 207; (1983) 80 L.S.Gaz. 2678; (1983) New L.J. 888; [(1985) 135 New L.J. 1156; (1987) J.S.W.L. 93] 21, 32, 40, 63, 67, 68, 109, 117, 130, 229, 382, 386
Guevera v. London Borough of Hounslow, *The Times*, April 17, 1987 .... 51, 66

H., *Re*, *The Times*, June 5, 1992 .... 124, 130, 386
H. (Child Orders: Restricting Applications), *Re* [1991] F.C.R. 896 216
H. (A Minor) (Custody), *Re* [1989] Fam.Law 434; [1990] 1 F.L.R. 51; [1990] F.C.R. 353, C.A. 16
H. (Minors) (Local Authority: Parental Rights), *Re* [1989] 1 W.L.R. 551; (1989) 133 S.J. 569; [1989] 2 All E.R. 353; (1989) 87 L.G.R. 548; (1989) 19 Fam.Law 308; [1989] F.C.R. 498; (1989) 153 J.P.N. 643, C.A. 23
H. (Minors) Local Authority: Parental Rights) (No. 3), *Re* [1991] Fam. 151; [1991] 2 W.L.R. 763; [1991] 2 All E.R. 185; (1991) 135 S.J. 16; [1991] 1 F.L.R. 214; 89 L.G.R. 537; [1991] Fam.Law 306; [1991] F.C.R. 361; *The Times*, November 21, 1990, C.A. 23, 24
H. (Minors: Parental Responsibility), *Re*, *The Times*, September 7, 1992 24
H., K., (Minors), *Re*, *The Times*, June 9, 1989 223
H., *Re*, K., *Re* [1989] Fam.Law 388 29
H. v. Hillingdon London Borough Council, *The Times*, July 1, 1992 404
Hopes v. Hopes [1949] P. 227 181

J. v. Berkshire County Council, *The Times*, March 10, 1992 .... 218, 436
J.R. v. Merton London Borough [1992] 2 F.C.R. 185 437
J.S. (A Minor), *Re* [1981] Fam. 22; [1980] 3 W.L.R. 984; (1980) 124 S.J. 881; [1980] 1 All E.R. 1061; (1980) 10 Fam.Law 121, C.A. 23
J. v. C. [1970] A.C. 668; [1969] 2 W.L.R. 540; [1969] 1 All E.R. 788; *sub nom*. C. (An Infant), *Re* (1969) 113 S.J. 164, H.L. 16
J.R. v. Merton London Borough [1992] 2 F.C.R. 174 .... 15, 40, 41

K. (A Minor), *Re* (1978) 122 S.J. 626 22
K. (A Minor) (Ward: Care and Control), *Re* [1990] 1 W.L.R. 431; [1990] 3 All E.R. 795; (1990) 134 S.J. 49; [1990] 2 F.L.R. 64; [1990] Fam.Law 256; (1990) 154 J.P.N. 411; [1990] F.C.R. 553, C.A. 16
K.D., *Re* [1988] A.C. 806; [1988] 2 W.L.R. 398; (1988) 132 S.J. 301; [1988] 1 All E.R. 577; (1988) 18 Fam.Law 288; [1988] 2 F.L.R. 139; [1988] F.C.R. 657; (1988) 152 J.P.N. 558, H.L. 16, 105
Kelly v. Monklands District Council (1985 Court of Session) 62
Krishnan v. London Borough of Sutton [1970] Ch. 181; [1969] 3 W.L.R. 683; 113 S.J. 774; [1969] 3 All E.R. 1367, C.A. 22

L. (A Minor) (Care Proceedings: Wardship) (No. 2), *Re* [1991] 1 F.L.R. 29; [1991] Fam.Law 62 16
Lee v. Lee (1983) 127 S.J. 696; (1984) 12 H.L.R. 68ll 114; (1984) 14 Fam.Law 243; (1983) 80 L.S.Gaz. 2678, C.A. 15
Liddle v. Sunderland Borough Council (1983) 13 Fam.Law 250 .... 66, 67

M., *Re* 1 F.L.R. 1987 400
M., *Re* (A Minor) T.L.R. 4190 392
M. v. C. and Calderdale Borough Council [1992] 2 F.C.R. 141 .... 39, 67
—— v. M. [1973] 2 All E.R. 81 104
—— v. M., *The Times*, August 12, 1992 16
—— v. Westminster City Council [1985] F.L.R. 325; (1985) 15 Fam.Law 93, D.C. 99
M. and H. (Minors), *Re* (Local Authority: Parental Rights) [1988] 3 W.L.R. 485; [1988] 3 All E.R.J.; (1988) 18 Fam.Law 468; [1988] 2 F.L.R. 431; (1988) 152 J.P.N. 818; [1988] L.S.Gaz., September 7, 37, H.L.; affirming [1987] 3 W.L.R. 759; (1987) 131 S.J. 1155; [1987] 85 L.G.R. 844; [1988] 1 F.L.R. 151; (1988) 18 Fam.Law 57; [1988] F.C.R. 97; (1988) 152 J.P.N. 126; (1987) 84 L.S.Gaz. 2360; (1987) 151 L.G.Rev. 1027, C.A. 66, 105

Table of Cases

May v. May [1986] 1 F.L.R 325; (1985) 16 Fam.Law 106, C.A. 16
M'Reight v. M'Reight (1849) 13 1 Eq. 314 22

Newham London Borough v. A.G. [1992] 2 F.C.R. 119 98
Northampton County Council v. H. [1988] 2 W.L.R. 389 222
Nottinghamshire County Council v. Q. [1982] 2 W.L.R. 954 141

O. (A Minor) (Care Order: Education: Procedure), Re [1992] 2 F.L.R. 7 .... 95, 96, 110, 120
O'Reilly v. Mackman; Millbanks v. Secretary of State for the Home Department [1983] 2 A.C. 237; [1982] 3 W.L.R. 1096; (1982) 126 S.J. 820; [1982] 3 All E.R. 1124, H.L.; affirming O'Reilly v. Mackman; Derbyshire v. Same; Dougan v. Same; Millbanks v. Home Office [1982] 3 W.L.R. 604; (1982) 126 S.J. 578; [1982] 3 All E.R. 680; (1982) 79 L.S.Gaz. 1176, C.A.; reversing (1982) 126 S.J. 312 66
Oxfordshire County Council v. R. [1992] 1 F.L.R. 648 .... 454, 458
Oxfordshire C.C. v. R. [1992] 1 F.L.R. 648, sub nom. R. v. X Council, The Times, February 24, 1992 81

P., Re [1986] 1 F.L.R. 272 229
Pasmore v. Oswaldtwistle Urban District Council [1898] A.C. 387 205
Patterson v. Walcot [1984] Fam. 32; [1984] 2 W.L.R. 439; (1984) 128 S.J. 171; (1984) 148 J.P. 161; [1984] 1 All E.R. 866; (1984) 14 Fam.Law 208; (1984) 81 L.S.Gaz. 735, C.A. 46
Practice Direction [1992] 1 F.L.R. 463 220
Practice Note on Sterilisation [1990] 2 F.L.R. 530 21

R., Re [1991] 4 All E.R. 177 229
R. (A Minor) (Wardship: Medical Treatment), Re [1991] 4 All E.R. 177 .... 21, 130
R. v. B. Council, ex p. T. (1991) 2 All E.R. 65 418
—— v. Birmingham Juvenile Court, ex p. Birmingham City Council [1988] 1 W.L.R. 337; (1987) 131 S.J. 1697; [1988] 1 All E.R. 683; (1988) 86 L.G.R. 697; [1988] 1 F.L.R. 424; (1988) 18 Fam.Law 125; (1988) 152 J.P.N. 62; [1988] F.C.R. 175; (1988) 85 L.S.Gaz. 34, C.A.; reversing (1987) 17 Fam.Law 226; (1987) 84 L.S.Gaz. 902; [1987] 2 F.L.R. 80 117
—— v. ——, ex p. G. (1989) 3 All E.R. 336 364
—— v. ——, ex p. S. [1984] Fam. 93 181
—— v. ——, ex p. S. and P. [1984] 1 W.L.R. 618; [1984] 1 All E.R. 393; [1984] F.L.R. 343; (1984) 14 Fam.Law 91 117
—— v. Campbell, The Times, December 10, 1982 223
—— v. Cleveland County Council and Carney, ex p. C.R.E., The Times, August 25, 1992 68
—— v. Cornwall County Council, ex p. Cornwall and Isles of Scilly Galro Panel, The Times, November 20, 1991 383
—— v. ——, ex p. G. [1992] 1 F.L.R. 270 124
—— v. Croydon Juvenile Court, ex p. N. [1987] 151 J.P. 523; [1987] 1 F.L.R. 252; (1987) 17 Fam.Law 199; (1987) 151 J.P.N. 255 116
—— v. G. and Surrey County Council [1984] Fam. 100; [1984] 3 W.L.R. 667; (1984) 128 S.J. 662; [1984] 3 All E.R. 460; (1985) 15 Fam.Law 155; (1984) 81 L.S.Gaz. 2618, C.A. 96
—— v. Hampshire County Council, ex p. K. and Another, The Independent, November 16, 1989 392
—— v. Hayes [1977] 1 W.L.R. 234 223
—— v. Hereford and Worcester County Council, ex p. D. [1992] 1 F.L.R. 448 67
—— v. Hertfordshire County Council, ex p. B.; R. v. Bedfordshire County Council, ex p. C. (1987) 151 J.P.N. 91; (1987) 85 L.G.R. 218 74
—— v. Highgate Justices, ex p. Petrou (1954) 1 All E.R., p. 406 415
—— v. Merton London Borough [1992] 2 F.C.R. 189, C.A. **359**
—— v. Newham London Borough Council, ex p. P. [1990] 1 W.L.R. 482; [1990] 2 All E.R. 19; (1990) 134 S.J. 833; [1990] 1 F.L.R. 404; [1990] Fam.Law 257; 88 L.G.R. 383; [1990] F.C.R. 601; (1990) 154 J.P.N. 693 74
—— v. Norfolk County Council, ex p. M. [1987] 2 All E.R. 359 187
—— v. Northampton Juvenile Court, ex p. Hammersmith and Fulham London Borough (1985) 15 Fam.Law 125 81
—— v. North Yorkshire County Council, ex p. M. [1989] Q.B. 411; (1989) 153 J.P. 390 [1989] 1 All E.R. 143; [1989] 1 F.L.R. 203; [1989] L.S.Gaz. February 1, 42; (1989) 19 Fam.Law 102; [1989] C.O.D. 190; (1989) 153 J.P.N. 288; [1989] F.C.R. 128; (1989) 153 L.G.Rev. 652 67

Table of Cases

R. v. Plymouth Juvenile Court, *ex p.* F. & F. (1987) 1 F.L.R. 169 377
—— v. R. (Child: Surname) [1977] 1 W.L.R. 1256; (1977) 121 S.J. 758; [1978] 2 All E.R. 33, C.A. 102
—— v. Secretary of State for the Environment, *ex p.* Ward [1984] 1 W.L.R. 834 205
—— v. Tower Hamlets London Borough, *ex p.* Monaf; Same v. Same, *ex p.* Ali; Same v. Same, *ex p.* Miah; Same v. Same, *ex p.* Uddin (1988) 20 H.L.R. 529; (1988) 86 L.G.R. 709, C.A.; reversing in part (1987) 19 H.L.R. 577; (1988) 152 L.G.Rev. 329, D.C. 51, 52
—— v. Wallwork (1958) 122 J.P. 299 223
—— v. Wandsworth London Borough Council, *ex p.* P. (1989) 87 L.G.R. 370; [1989] C.O.D. 262; (1989) 153 L.G.Rev. 550; (1989) 153 J.P.N. 803 73
—— v. X Council (A local Authority), *The Times*, February 24, 1992, Family Division 403
R. (B.M.) v. R. (D.N.) [1978] 2 All E.R. 33 102
Ready Mixed Concrete v. Minister of Pensions [1969] 2 Q.B. 497 181
Rice v. Connolly [1966] 2 Q.B. 414 170
Richards v. Richards [1984] A.C. 174; [1983] 3 W.L.R. 173; [1983] 2 All E.R. 807; (1984) 12 H.L.R. 68, 73; 13 Fam.Law 256; (1983) New L.J. 725; (1983) 80 L.S.Gaz. 2134, H.L.; reversing [1983] 2 W.L.R. 633; (1983) 127 S.J. 52; [1983] 1 All E.R. 1017; (1983) 13 Fam.Law 84, C.A. 15, 35
Riley v. Riley (1987) 151 J.P. 650; [1986] 2 F.L.R. 429; (1987) 17 Fam.Law 15; [1987] 1 F.C.R. 65; (1987) 151 J.P.N. 303; (1986) J.P. 439; (1986) 150 J.P.N. 637, C.A. 43

S, *Re* (A Minor), *The Times*, June 23, 1992 388
S. (A Minor) (Adoption or Custodianship), *Re* [1987] Fam. 98; [1987] 2 W.L.R. 977; (1987) 131 S.J. 133; [1987] 2 All E.R. 99; (1987) 151 J.P. 577; (1987) 85 L.G.R. 505; (1987) 17 Fam.Law 238; [1987] 2 F.L.R. 331; [1988] F.C.R. 57; (1988) 152 L.G.Rev. 269; (1987) 151 J.P.N. 239; (1987) 84 L.S.Gaz. 497, C.A. 34
S.W. (A Minor) (Wardship: Jurisdiction), *Re* [1986] 1 F.L.R. 24; (1985) 15 Fam.Law 322 .... 37, 95
Santos v. Santo [1972] Fam. 247 181
Singh v. Sharegin (1984) F.L.R. 114, C.A. 416

T. v. West Glamorgan County Council, *The Times*, October 17, 1989 105
Thompson v. Thompson (1975) [1986] 1 F.L.R. 212 30

W., *Re* [1990] 1 F.L.R. 2031 432
W., *Re*, [1985] 2 All E.R. 301 101
W., *Re* [1992] N.L.J. 1124 .... 130, 229
W., *Re*, *The Times*, May 22, 1992 16
W., *Re* (Minors), (Wardship Evidence) [1990] 1 F.L.R. 203 431
W. v. A. (1980) 124 S.J. 726; *The Times*, July 30, 1980, C.A.; *sub nom.* W. v. A. (Child: Surname) [1981] Fam. 14; [1981] 2 W.L.R. 124; [1981] 1 All E.R. 100; (1980) 11 Fam.Law 22, C.A. 102
—— v. Hertfordshire County Council [1985] 2 All E.R. 301; *sub nom.* W. (A Minor) (Wardship: Jurisdiction), *Re* [1985] A.C. 791; [1985] 2 W.L.R. 892; (1985) 149 J.P. 593; (1985) 129 S.J. 347; (1985) 83 L.G.R. 669; (1985) 15 Fam.Law 326; (1985) 135 New L.J. 483; (1985) 82 L.S.Gaz. 2087, H.L.; affirming (1985) 129 S.J. 269; [1985] 1 All E.R. 1001; (1985) 5 Fam.Law 325; (1985) 135 New L.J. 269; (1985) 82 L.S.Gaz. 924, C.A. 40
—— v. W. (A Minor: Custody Appeal) [1988] 2 F.L.R. 505; (1989) 19 Fam.Law 63, C.A. 30
Wilde v. Wilde (1988) 18 Fam.Law 202; [1988] 2 F.L.R. 83; [1988] F.C.R. 551; (1988) 152 J.P.N. 559, C.A. 15

X (Wardship: Jurisdiction), *Re* [1975] Fam. 47; [1975] 2 W.L.R. 335; *sub nom.* X (A Minor) (Wardship: Restriction on Publication), *Re* [1975] 1 All E.R. 697, C.A. ... 15
X, Y and Z (Wardship Disclosure of Material), *Re* [1991] Fam.Law 318 229

TABLE OF STATUTES

1774	Life Assurance Act (14 Geo. 3, c. 48) 280	1944	Education Act—*cont.* s. 40—*cont.*	
1837	Wills Act (7 Will. 4 & 1 Vict., c. 26) 330		(2) 309	
	s. 1 308		(2A) 309	
1882	Married Women's Property Act (45 & 46 Vict., c. 75)—		(3) 111, 310, 408, 419	
	s. 17 409		(4) 111, 310, 408, 419	
1891	Custody of Children Act (54 & 55 Vict., c. 3) 22, 237, 299		s. 53 282	
			s. 71 210	
1918	Wills (Soldiers and Sailors) Act (7 & 8 Geo. 5, c. 58) 22		(1) (*d*) 310	
			(*e*) 310	
1920	Maintenance Orders (Facilities for Enforcement) Act (10 & 11 Geo. 5, c. 33) 483		s. 76 .... 112, 261	
			s. 95 110	
			s. 99 205	
	Administration of Justice Act (10 & 11 Geo. 5, c. 81)— Pt. II 483		s. 100 282	
			s. 114 (1) 111	
			(1C)–(1E) 310	
1925	Administration of Estates Act (15 & 16 Geo. 5, c. 23) 22		(1D) 111	
		1948	National Assistance Act (11 & 12 Geo. 6, c. 29) 51, 52	
	s. 46 22		s. 21 51	
1933	Children and Young Persons Act (23 & 24 Geo. 5, c. 12) 13, 20, 95, 148, 204, 316		(1) (*a*) 310	
			s. 29 .... 51, 53, 55, 313	
			(1) 55, 311	
	s. 1 22		Children Act (11 & 12 Geo. 6, c. 43)—	
	(1) 309		s. 1 .... 330, 333	
	(2) (*a*) 299		s. 2 .... 330, 334	
	s. 3 (1) 309		s. 29 319	
	s. 4 (1) 309		Nurseries and Child-Minders Regulation Act (11 & 12 Geo. 6, c. 53) 8, 237	
	(2) 309			
	s. 10 (1A) 309			
	s. 11 309	1949	Marriage Act (12, 13 & 14 Geo. 6, c.76) 19	
	s. 17 309			
	s. 23 455		s. 3 .... 19, 341	
	s. 25 (1) 309		(1) 102, 299	
	s. 34 (1) 309		(1A) 37, 299	
	s. 38 223		(1B) 299	
	s. 39 225		Sched. 2 .... 19, 341	
	s. 40 ..... 108, 144, 148, 299, 301, 337	1950	Maintenance Orders Act (14 Geo. 6, c. 37) 482	
	s. 53 .... 201, 454			
	s. 55 214	1951	Reserve and Auxilliary Forces (Protection of Civil Interests) Act (14 & 15 Geo. 6, c. 65)—	
	s. 104 162			
	Foreign Judgments (Reciprocal Enforcement) Act (23 & 24 Geo. 5, c. 13) 483			
			s. 2 (1) (*d*) 311	
1944	Education Act (7 & 8 Geo. 6, c. 31) 22, 172, 210, 234, 235, 263	1953	Births and Deaths Registration Act (1 & 2 Eliz. 2, c. 20) 341	
			s. 10 300	
	s. 29 112		s. 10 (2) 300	
	s. 35 110		(3) 300	
	s. 36 .... 111, 112, 261		s. 10A 300	
	s. 37 .... 96, 109, 112, 214, 261, 310	1954	Mines and Quarries Act (2 & 3 Eliz. 2, c. 70)—	
	(1) 216			
	(2) 111		s. 182 (1) 311	
	s. 39 .... 111, 261, 310	1955	Army Act (3 & 4 Eliz. 2, c. 18)—	
	(2) 111			
	(3A) 310		s. 151 (1A) (*a*) 300, 301	
	(4) 310		Air Force Act (3 & 4 Eliz. 2, c. 19)—	
	s. 40 .... 96, 111			
	(1) 299		s. 151 (1A) 301	

Table of Statutes

1956	Sexual Offences Act (4 & 5 Eliz. 2, c. 69)	26
	s. 19 (3)	301
	s. 20 (2)	301
	s. 21 (3)	301
	s. 28 (3)	301
	(4)	301
	s. 33	26, 301, 323
	s. 38 (1)	324
	(3)	329
	s. 43 (5)	301
	s. 46	301
	s. 46A	301
1957	Naval Discipline Act (5 & 6 Eliz. 2, c. 53)	301
	Affiliation Proceedings Act (5 & 6 Eliz. 2, c. 55)—	
	s. 4	300
1958	Adoption Act (6 & 7 Eliz. 2, c. 5)—	
	s. 22 (2)	291
	s. 37	287
	s. 53	307
	Maintenance Orders Act (6 & 7 Eliz. 2, c. 39)	482
1959	Mental Health Act (7 & 8 Eliz. 2, c. 72)—	
	ss. 8, 9	312
	s. 88	312
1960	Matrimonial Proceedings (Magistrates' Courts) Act (8 & 9 Eliz. 2, c. 48)	325
	s. 2 (1) (e)	330
	(f)	337
	(h)	335
	Administration of Justice Act (8 & 9 Eliz. 2, c. 65)—	
	s. 12 (1)	311
1961	Factories Act (9 & 10 Eliz. 2, c. 34)—	
	s. 176 (1)	311
1962	Education Act (10 & 11 Eliz. 2, c. 12)—	
	s. 9	110
1963	Children and Young Persons Act (c. 37)	51, 301
	s. 3	97
	(1)	324
	s. 23	303
	(5)	337
	s. 25 (5)	338
	s. 53 (3)	237
	s. 106 (2) (a)	342
1964	Administration of Justice Act (c. 42)	297
	s. 38	297
	Perpetuities and Accumulations Act (c. 55)	341
1965	Matrimonial Causes Act (c. 72)	325
1967	Criminal Justice Act (c. 80)—	
	s. 67 (1A) (c)	311
1968	Health Services and Public Health Act (c. 46)	342

1968	Health Services and Public Health Act—cont.	
	s. 60	237
	s. 64 (3) (a)	311
	s. 65 (3) (b)	312
	Social Work (Scotland) Act (c. 49)	94, 237, 278
	s. 1 (2)	234, 256
	s. 2 (2)	312
	s. 5 (2) (c)	312
	s. 16	317
	s. 33 (8)	312
	s. 61	283
	s. 62	180
	s. 71	153
	s. 74 (6)	312
	s. 75 (2)	312
	s. 86 (3)	312
	Civil Evidence Act ([c. 64)	312
	s. 18	223
1969	Family Law Reform Act (c. 49)	21
	s. 6 (3)	239
	s. 7	227, 228
	(2)	323, 324, 330, 331, 332
	(4)	322, 337
	s. 8	21
	s. 20	212, 213
	Children and Young Persons Act (c. 54)	8, 13, 96, 168, 204, 213, 307, 312, 315, 316, 318, 332
	s. 1	213, 302, 312, 324, 330
	(1) (a)	181
	(2)	95, 97, 318
	(a)	95, 96
	(d)	98
	(f)	213
	(3) (b)	336
	(c)	336
	s. 2	312
	(4)	222
	(5)	222
	(9)	222
	(10)	116
	(12)	313
	s. 5 (2)	302
	s. 7 (7)	213, 302
	(a)	213, 340
	(b)	94, 213, 235, 261, 278, 340
	s. 9	312
	ss. 12–12C	303
	s. 12 (2)	302
	s. 12A	64
	(1)	302
	(2)	302
	(3)	214, 302
	s. 12AA	180, 214, 302, 340, 341
	(3)	214
	(6)	214
	(ii)	214
	(7)	214
	(8)	214

Table of Statutes

1969	Children and Young Persons Act—*cont.*	
	s. 12AA—*cont.*	
	(9)	214
	(10)	214
	s. 12C	261
	s. 13	109
	s. 14	48
	s. 14A	108
	s. 15	226, 330
	(1)	213, 340
	s. 16 (8)	226, 313
	s. 20	314
	(3) (*a*)	331
	s. 21 (1)	331
	(2)	336
	(4)	313
	(5)	313
	s. 22 (1)	222
	s. 23	82, 455
	s. 24	453
	s. 25	230, 231, 330
	s. 26	230, 231, 330
	s. 28	338
	(1)	133, 337
	(2)	140, 318
	(3)	140
	(4)	140
	(6)	141, 337, 338
	s. 32	151, 338, 341
	(3)	153
	s. 32A	123
	(1)	123
	s. 32B	123
	s. 34 (7)	309
	(7A)	309
	s. 65	161
	s. 82	161
	s. 107 (1)	309
	s. 124A (2)	64
	Sched. 12, para. 27	338
	Pt. III	312
1970	Administration of Justice Act (c. 31)	312
	Sched. 8	92, 256
	Local Authorities Social Services Act (c. 42)	9, 109, 125, 235
	s. 2	66
	s. 7	9, 13
	s. 7A	485
	s. 7B	86
	Sched. 1	312
	Chronically Sick and Disabled Persons Act (c. 44)	51, 52, 55, 247
	s. 28	313
	s. 28A	313
1971	Guardianship of Minors Act (c. 3)	8, 13, 45, 225, 238, 325
	s. 1	66
	(1)	15
	ss. 3–5	329
	ss. 3–6	26
	s. 5	339

1971	Guardianship of Minors Act—*cont.*	
	s. 6	28
	s. 9	300
	s. 10 (1) (*a*)	318
	(*c*)	318
	s. 13 (1)	328
	Courts Act (c. 23)—	
	Sched. 9, Pt. 1	313
	Attachment of Earnings Act (c. 32)—	
	s. 23	482
	Sched. 1, para. 7	313
	Tribunals and Inquiries Act (c. 62)—	
	Sched. 1, para. 4	313
	Banking and Financial Dealings Act (c. 80)	233, 354
1972	Maintenance Orders (Reciprocal Enforcement) Act (c. 18)	482
	Parliamentary and Other Pensions Act (c. 48)	342
	Local Government Act (c. 70)—	
	s. 101	455
	s. 102 (1)	313
	s. 250 (2)–(5)	201, 202
	Sched. 12A, para. 1 (1) (*b*)	314
1973	Matrimonial Causes Act (c. 18)	13, 46, 325
	ss. 21–33	311
	s. 23	239
	s. 25 (1)	15
	(4)	22
	s. 27	239
	s. 41	17, 304
	s. 42	26
	(1)	318
	(2)	318
	(3)	305, 323, 324
	s. 43 (1)	96, 318, 330
	(5) (*a*)	331
	s. 44	322, 337
	s. 50	474
	s. 52 (1)	34, 39, 305
	s. 63 (4)	46
	s. 96 (3)	323
	Employment of Children Act (c. 24)—	
	s. 2 (2) (*a*)	314
	(2A)	314
	Guardianship Act (c. 29)	8, 19
	s. 2 (2) (*a*)	322, 337
	s. 1 (2)	20
	(3)	33
	s. 2 (2) (*b*)	318, 330
	(3)	335
	(5)	318
	s. 4 (4) (*a*)	331
	Domicile and Matrimonial Proceedings Act (c. 45)	314
	Sched. 1, para. 11 (1), (3)	314

Table of Statutes

1973	Powers of Criminal Courts Act (c. 62)—	
	s. 51 (3) (c)	162
	Sched. 3,	
	para. 3 (2A) (b), (c)	314
	para. 8	260
	para. 18 (1) (b)	260
1974	Rehabilitation of Offenders Act (c. 53)—	
	s. 5	341
	s. 7 (2) (c)	314
	(d)	314
1975	Inheritance (Provision for Family and Dependants) Act (c. 63)—	
	s. 2	245
	Children Act (c. 72)	8, 123, 238, 245, 325
	s. 14	307
	s. 25	307
	s. 33	326
	s. 34 (5)	318, 337
	s. 36	330
	(3) (b)	322, 337
	(5)	335
	s. 37	34
	(1)	34
	s. 41	39
	s. 43 (1)	46, 328
	s. 45 (5)	322
	s. 53 (1A)	293
	s. 68 (4)	341
	(5)	341
	(7)	341
	Sched. 3, para. 13	341
	para. 43	341
	para. 46	342
	para. 47	342
1976	Legitimacy Act (c. 31)	18
	s. 1	19
	s. 2	18, 19
	Adoption Act (c. 136)	12, 34, 176, 211, 228, 295, 296, 308, 435, 437, 438, 439, 441, 487, 488
	s. 1	233, 278, 291
	s. 2	284
	s. 3	288, 294
	s. 6	34
	s. 8	291
	s. 11	284
	s. 12	285, 291, 295, 440
	(3) (b)	286, 293
	s. 14 (1)	285
	(3)	34
	(18)	212
	s. 15 (4)	34
	s. 16	19, 285
	s. 18	19, 101, 107, 228, 285, 286, 293, 307, 440
	(2A)	212
	(7)	212
	s. 19 (2)	285
	s. 20	285
	(3)	212, 291

1976	Adoption Act—cont.	
	s. 20—cont.	
	(3A)	291
	s. 21	286, 307, 434, 480
	s. 22	286
	(1A)	212
	s. 25 (1)	286
	s. 26	336
	(1) (a)	337
	(b)	319
	(2)	335
	s. 27	287
	(1)	286
	(2)	286
	(2A)	286
	s. 28	287
	(1)	286
	(2)	286
	s. 30	287
	s. 31	287
	s. 32	212, 287
	(3A)	288
	s. 33	232
	s. 34 (1)	337
	s. 35	288
	s. 39	19
	s. 51	288, 289
	(1)	294
	s. 51A	212, 289
	s. 55	101, 290, 295
1976	Adoption Act—	
	s. 56	253, 290
	s. 57	290
	(1)	291
	(4)	291
	(5) (b)	291
	s. 57A	212, 290
	(4)	212
	s. 59	291
	s. 60	291
	s. 62 (5) (b)	291
	s. 65	291, 482
	s. 65A	212, 291
	(2)	212
	s. 72 (1)	291
	Sched. 2, para. 1	330
	Sched. 10, para. 4	212
	para. 6 (1)	212
	(3)	212
	para. 8 (3)	212
	para. 10 (1)	212
	para. 18	212
	Domestic Violence and Matrimonial Proceedings Act (c. 50)	13, 30, 34, 479
	Race Relations Act (c. 74)	55, 68
	s. 3 (1)	68
	s. 18	68
	s. 71	68
1977	National Health Service Act (c. 49)	51, 233, 234, 235, 284
	s. 21	51
	s. 76	202
	s. 84	202

1977	National Health Service Act—cont.		1978	Adoption (Scotland) Act—cont
	Sched. 8	51, 53		s. 54 (b) ... 294
	para. 2	305		s. 65 (1) ... 294
	para. 4A	305		National Health Service (Scotland) Act (c. 29) ... 283
1978	Domestic Proceedings and Magistrates Courts Act (c. 22) ... 13, 35, 45, 46, 297, 325			Interpretation Act (c. 30)— s. 7 ... 236
	Pt. 1	239	1979	Justices of the Peace Act (c. 553) ... 244, 297, 308
	s. 2	315		s. 4 ... 433
	(1 (c)	315		s. 2 (1) ... 433
	s. 3 (4)	22		s. 16 (5) ... 297
	ss. 6–8	315		s. 17 (3) ... 297
	s. 8 (2) (a)	319		s. 38 (2) ... 297
	s. 9	322, 337		s. 58 (1) ... 297
	s. 10	330		(5) ... 297
	(1)	319		s. 70 ... 355
	s. 11 (4)	335	1980	Child Care Act (c. 5) ... 8, 13, 19, 53, 66, 238, 340
	s. 14 (3)	316		
	s. 15 (5) (b)	297		s. 1 ... 50, 51, 53, 78
	s. 16 (5) (c)	297		s. 2 ... 60, 330, 333
	s. 19	315		(1) ... 61, 333
	(1) (ii)	319		(c) ... 61
	(3A) (b)	315		(3) ... 51, 71
	s. 20 (12)	315		s. 3 ... 95, 96, 330, 334
	s. 20A	315		(1) (b) (i) ... 96
	s. 21	316		(d) ... 96
	s. 25 (1) (a)	315		(8) ... 96
	(2)	315		s. 5 (2) ... 339
	s. 29 (5)	316		ss. 12A–12G ... 104
	s. 33	328		s. 12B ... 333
	s. 88 (1)	35, 297, 316		s. 12C ... 333
	Adoption (Scotland) Act (c. 28) ... 13, 211, 238, 285, 287			s. 12E ... 107, 333
				s. 13 ... 60, 149, 305
	s. 1	278, 285, 292		s. 14 ... 149
	s. 3	284, 285, 288, 294		s. 15 ... 151, 338
	s. 12	291		s. 16 ... 149, 151, 338
	(1)	295		s. 18 ... 9, 51, 66
	(2)–(4)	294		(1) ... 66
	(3)	295		(3) ... 69
	(4)	295		s. 19 ... 66, 69
	s. 16 (1) (a)	293		s. 21 ... 51
	ss. 18–20	295		(1) ... 71
	s. 18	291, 293, 294		(a) ... 334
	(3)–(5)	293		(2) ... 332, 334
	s. 20 (3)	294		s. 21A ... 80
	(c)	293		(1) ... 82
	s. 21	293		s. 22A ... 334
	s. 23 (4)	291, 293, 294		s. 23 (2) (a) ... 334
	s. 27	287, 293, 295		(5) ... 332
	(2)	295		s. 24 ... 305, 335
	s. 28	287, 293, 295		ss. 27–29 ... 77
	s. 29	293		s. 28 ... 77
	ss. 30–32	295		s. 30 ... 93
	s. 32 (2)	293		s. 31 ... 156, 313, 323
	s. 45	289, 293		s. 32 ... 323
	(2)	291		ss. 35–39 ... 156
	s. 49	295		s. 36 (5) ... 159
	(1)	294		s. 40 ... 158
	(3)	294		s. 42 ... 159
	s. 50 (1)	294		s. 43 ... 160
	s. 53	295		s. 43A ... 161
	(1)	294		s. 44 ... 163
	(2)	294		s. 45 ... 287

Table of Statutes

1980 Child Care Act—cont.
- s. 47 .... 313, 336
- s. 51 .... 313, 316
- s. 53 323
- s. 56 .... 166, 323
- s. 57 323
  - (1)–(6) 166
  - (1) 165
  - (8)–(11) 166
- ss. 57A–57D 166
- s. 59 166
- s. 60 323
- s. 62 338
- s. 64 .... 305, 338, 339
  - (7) 339
- s. 64A 167
- s. 65 .... 305, 330, 339
- s. 68 168
  - (2) 170
  - (5) 170
- s. 69 77
- s. 72 62
- s. 74 200
- s. 75 200
- s. 76 201
- s. 77 205
- s. 78 203
- s. 79 205
- s. 80 203
- s. 82 161
- s. 87 305
- Sched. 4, para. 1 .... 330, 333
- Sched. 5, para. 19 311
  - para. 20 312
  - para. 26 342
- Pt. V 90, 91

Foster Children Act (c. 6) 8, 178, 339
- ss. 4–6 176
- s. 7 (2) 180
- s. 8 .... 178, 323
- s. 9 176
- s. 10 182
  - (3) 182
- s. 11 176
- s. 12 (1) 338
- s. 15 176
- s. 16 183
- s. 19 177

Education Act (c. 20)—
- s. 6 .... 21, 112
- s. 7 .... 112, 261

Magistrates Courts Act (c. 43) 46, 297
- s. 12AA 304
- s. 16 (3) 304
  - (3A) 304
- s. 23 (1) 304
- s. 32 (1A)–(1C) 303
- s. 37 303
- s. 58 .... 91, 92
- s. 59 (3) 242
  - (a)–(d) 242

1980 Magistrates Courts Act—cont.
- s. 59—cont.
  - (4) 242
- s. 62 (5) 316
- s. 63 .... 42, 129
  - (2) 217
  - (3) 45, 46
- s. 64 413
- s. 65 (1)–(3) 298
  - (1) 216
    - (ii) 298
  - (2) 216
    - (a) 298
- s. 66 .... **355**
  - (1) 298
  - (2) 298
- s. 67 .... **355**
  - (1)–(8) 298
- s. 69 224
  - (1)–(4) 298
- s. 70 (2) 298
  - (3) 298
- s. 71 224
  - (1) 298
  - (2) 298
- s. 72 (1) 298
- s. 73 298
- s. 74 (1) 298
- s. 97 420
- s. 121 (8) 298
- s. 127 (1) 183
- s. 128 (7) 303
- s. 144 224
- s. 145 (a) 476
- s. 150 92
  - (1) 245, 256, 298
- Sched. 2, para. 10 46
- Sched. 11, Pt. 1 217

Education (Scotland) Act (c. 44) 198, 235
- s. 6 282

1981 Contempt of Court Act (c. 49)—
- s. 17 417

Supreme Court Act (c. 54)—
- s. 18 (1) (h) (i) 316
  - (ii) 316
- s. 41 (2) 316, 468
  - (2A) 316
  - (3) 463
- s. 51 416
  - (1), (3) 416
  - (6) 416, 475, 476, 477
  - (7) 416
- s. 90 (3) **121**
- Sched. 1, para. 3 298
  - (b) (ii) 316

Armed Forces Act (c. 55)—
- s. 14 (9A) 316

Education Act (c. 60) 55, 88, 235, 247
- s. 3 3–5
- s. 3A 305
- s. 7 172

1981	Education Act—*cont.*		1984	Foster Children (Scotland) Act—*cont.*
	s. 11 (3) (*g*) 171			s. 2 (2) 308
1982	Children's Homes Act (c. 20) 8, 172, 174			s. 7 (1) 308
				Police and Criminal Evidence Act (c. 60)—
	s. 1 323			s. 16 (7) 148
	s. 2 (2) 172			s. 17 (1) (*e*) 148
	ss. 4–8 172			s. 37 (14) 318
	Civil Jurisdiction and Judgements Act (c. 27)—			(15) 64
	s. 2 303			s. 38 (6) 82, 455
	Sched. 4 316			s. 39 (4) 318
	Sched. 5, para. 5 (*a*) 316			Sched. 2 318
1983	Matrimonial Homes Act (c. 19) 15, 30			County Courts Act (c. ?)—
				s. 25 245
	s. 1 35		1985	Surrogacy Arrangements Act (c. 49)—
	(3) 15			s. 1 (2) (*b*) 318
	s. 9 35			Child Abduction and Custody Act (c. 60) 17, 33, 238
1983	Mental Health Act (c. 20) ... 80, 95, 176, 234, 278, 454, 455, 470			
	s. 12 258			s. 9 (9) 318
	s. 27 317			s. 16 108
	s. 28 317			s. 20 (2) (*a*) 318
	s. 116 204			s. 25 (1) (*a*) 108, 259
	s. 131 (2) 317			(*b*) 108, 259
	Pt. III 258			s. 27 (1) 318
	Health and Social Services and Social Security Adjudications Act (c. 41) 53			(4) 318
				Sched. 3, Pt. 1 318
				Housing Act (c. 68) 51, 61, 234
	s. 17 53			s. 59 (1) (*c*) 62
	s. 19 54		1986	Children and Young Persons (Amendment) Act (c. 28) 8
1984	Registered Homes Act (c. 23) ... 166, 172, 198, 210, 234, 282			
				Disabled Persons (Services, Consultation and Representation) Act (c. 33) 55, 247
	s. 1 (4A) 234			
	(5) (*d*) 317			
	(*e*) 317			s. 1 (3) 319
	s. 39 (*a*), (*b*) 317			s. 2 (3) (*a*) 319
	Pt. III 313			(5) 308
	County Courts Act (c. 28)—			(*b*) 319
	s. 97 (1) 482			(*bb*) 319
	Mental Health (Scotland) Act (c. 36)—			(*cc*) 319
				s. 5 (7) (*b*) 319
	s. 10 205			s. 16 319
	s. 54 317			Insolvency Act (c. 45)—
	Child Abduction Act (c. 37) 17, 19, 45			s. 281 (5), (6), (8) 298
				Family Law Act (c. 55) 45, 238
	s. 1 306			s. 1 (1) (*a*) 320, 321, 322
	(2) (*c*)–(*e*) 307			(*b*) 321
	s. 2 .... 152, 153			(*e*) 322
	s. 3 307			(2) 321
	Matrimonial and Family Proceedings Act (c. 42)—			(*c*) 320
				(3)–(5) 320
	s. 12 409			(3) (*a*) 321
	s. 13 .... 409, 483			s. 2 320
	s. 24 .... 409, 483			(2) 321
	s. 33 433			s. 2A 320
	s. 38 435			(4) 322
	(2) (*b*) 318			s. 3 .... 320, 321
	s. 39 435			s. 4 (5) 322
	s. 44 298			s. 6 (3) 321
	Pt. III 35, 483			(3A) 321
	Pt. V 298			(3B) 321
	Foster Children (Scotland) Act (c. 56) 198, 238, 282			(5) 321
	s. 1 308			

1986	Family Law Act—*cont.*		1988	Legal Aid Act—*cont.*	
	s. 6—*cont.*			s. 17	416
	(6)	321		s. 18	416
	(7)	321, 322		s. 27	226
	s. 7	322		s. 28	226
	s. 9	322		s. 30 (1)	226
	s. 10	322		(2)	226
	s. 11 (2) (*a*)	322		Sched. 2, para. 2	308
	s. 13 (5) (*a*)	322		Pt. IV	308
	(6)	321		Education Reform Act (c. 40)—	
	s. 14 (2)	321			
	s. 19 (2)	322		s. 52 (3)	282
	s. 20 (3) (*a*)	322		s. 53 (8)	310
	(6)	322		s. 54 (2)	310
	s. 21 (4) (*a*)	322		s. 58 (5) (*k*)	310
	(5)	321		s. 60	310
	s. 22 (2)	321		s. 61	310
	s. 23 (4) (*a*)	322		s. 110	93
	(5)	322		s. 111	93
	s. 34 (3) (*a*)	322		(5)	93
	s. 32	320		Housing Act (c. 50)—	
	s. 33	148, 225		s. 39	53
	s. 40	320	1990	NHS and Community Care Act (c. 19)—	
	s. 42 (4) (*a*)	322			
	(6)	322		s. 60	186
	(7)	319		s. 66 (1)	64, 76, 200, 206
	s. 56 (1) (*a*)	406		Sched. 9, para. 36 (2)	76
	(*b*)	407		(3)	90
	(2)	407		(4)	200
	s. 57	407		(5)	206
	Pt. 1	148, 319, 320		Human Fertilisation and Embryology Act (c. 37)	13
	Social Security Act (c. 50)	78			
	Pt. II	477		s. 27	19
	Education (No. 2) Act (c. 61)—			s. 28	19
	s. 5 (4)	310		s. 30	19
	s. 15 (2)	310		Courts and Legal Services Act (c. 41)	46
	(6)	310			
	s. 31	310		s. 12 (4)	304
	s. 65 (1)	310		(5)	304
	Sched. 2, para. 7 (6)	310		s. 12B (1)	304
1987	Family Law Reform Act (c. 42)	13, 92, 106		(2)	304
				s. 13 (2)	304
	s. 1	19, 235, 307		s. 23 (2)–(6)	304
	(2)	19		s. 28 (4)	304
	(3)	19		(5)	304
	s. 2 (1) (*f*)	305		s. 32 (1)–(1C)	304
	s. 3	20		(3)	304
	s. 4	23, 24, 300, 324, 325		(4)	304
	s. 18	19		s. 32 (2A)–(4)	304
	(1)	22		s. 34 (1)	304
	s. 27	19		s. 70 (1)	304
	(1)	19		s. 73 (4) (*a*)	304
	Sched.	307		s. 105 (1)	76
1988	Local Government Act (c. 9)—			s. 116	46, 64, 70, 76, 113, 122, 125, 137, 201, 219, 220, 225, 250, 275, 284, 303, 331, 332, 335, 341
	Sched. 1, para. 2 (4)	322			
	Criminal Justice Act (c. 33)—				
	s. 32A	224			
	s. 34	223		s. 125 (7)	125, 201, 238, 259, 331
	Legal Aid Act (c. 34)	226, 342, 476			
				Sched. 10, para. 6	46
	s. 2 (11)	478, 479		Sched. 16, para. 5	304
	s. 15	226		para. 6	92
	(3B)	82		(1)	256

1990 Courts and Legal Services Act—*cont.*	
Sched. 16—*cont.*	
para. 9	306
para. 10 (1)	46
(2)	246
para. 11	64
para. 13	76
para. 14	88
para. 15	90
para. 16	113
para. 17	122
para. 18	125
para. 19	137
para. 20	144, 213
para. 21	201
para. 22	219
para. 23	220
para. 24	225
para. 26	250
para. 29	275
para. 30	284
para. 31	303
para. 32	315
para. 33	331, 332, 335, 341
Sched. 20	125, 201, 238, 259, 331
Broadcasting Act (c. 42)	224
s. 203 (1)	225
Sched. 20, para. 53	225
1991 Maintenance Enforcement Act (c. 17)	46, 92, 256
s. 11 (2)	316
1991 Maintenance Enforcement Act—*cont.*	
Sched. 3	316
Registered Homes (Amendment) Act (c. 20)—	
s. 2	165, 210, 236, 278
(6)	171
Disability Living Allowance and Working Allowance Act (c. 21)	50
s. 7	50, 254
Sched. 3, para. 13	50
para. 14	90
para. 15	254
Child Support Act (c. 48)	8
s. 8	15, 47
Criminal Justice Act (c. 53)—	
s. 10 (2)	302, 303
s. 57	214
s. 59	64
(6A)	318
(6B)	318
s. 60 (3)	82
s. 101 (2)	318
Sched. 11, para. 40	213, 324
Sched. 13	302, 303, 318
Armed Forces Act (c. 62)—	
s. 17 (1)	126
s. 26	301, 331
Sched. 3	301, 331
1992 Social Security (Consequential Provisions) Act—	
Sched. 2, para. 108	50, 254

TABLE OF STATUTORY INSTRUMENTS

1951	Administration of Children's Homes Regulations (S.I. 1951 No. 1217)	156	1983	Secure Accommodation (No. 2) Regulations (S.I. 1983 No. 1808)	461
	Local Authorities and Local Education Authorities (Allocation of Funding) Regulations (S.I. 1951 No. 1472)	93		Guardians Ad Litem and Reporting Officers (Panels) Regulations (S.I. 1983 No. 1908)	489
	Rules of the Supreme Court (S.I. 1965 No. 1776)—		1984	Adoption Rules (S.I. 1984 No. 265)	212
	Order 62	476	1986	Guardians Ad Litem and Reporting Officers (Panels) (Amendment) Regulations (S.I. 1986 No. 3)	489
	Order 58,				
	r. 1	478			
	r. 3 (2)	478			
	Order 67	473		Secure Accommodation (No. 2) Amendment Regulations (S.I. 1986 No. 1591)	453
1970	Justices Clerks Rules (S.I. 1970 No. 231)—				
	Sched., paras. 13–15C	419			
	Magistrates' Courts (Children and Young Persons) Rules (S.I. 1970 No. 1792)	108	1987	Adoption (Northern Ireland) Order	211, 294
				art. 3	278, 285, 294
				art. 4	284, 289
1972	Community Homes Regulations (S.I. 1972 No. 319)	156		art. 12	291, 295
				art. 17	291, 295
	Health and Personal Social Services (Northern Ireland) Order (S.I. 1972 No. 1265)—			art. 18	291, 295
				arts. 28, 29	287, 293
				art. 33	287, 293
	art. 16	256, 289, 294		art. 54	289
1974	Rehabilitation of Offenders Act (Exceptions) Order 1975 (S.I. 1974 No. 1023)	180		(6A), (6B)	294
				(7)	294
				(9)	294
				art. 57	290, 294, 295
				art. 63 (1)	291, 294
1977	Matrimonial Causes Rules (S.I. 1977 No. 1247)	44		Income Support General Regulations (S.I. 1987 No. 1967)—	
1979	Justices' Clerks (Qualifications of Assistants) Rules (S.I. 1979 No. 570)—			reg. 13A	78
				reg. 53 (1)	78
	r. 2 (1)	417		Housing Benefit (General) Regulations (S.I. 1987 No. 1971)	53
1981	Magistrates' Courts (Northern Ireland) Order	151			
	Education (School and Further Education) Regulations (S.I. 1981 No. 879)—			reg. 40 (2)	53
				Sched. 9, para. 28	53
	reg. 10	56		Family Credit (General) Regulations (S.I. 1987 No. 1973)	53
	County Court Rules (S.I. 1981 No. 1687)—				
	Order 13,			reg. 29 (2)	53
	r. 1 (10)	469		Sched. 3, para. 18	53
	Order 37,		1988	Magistrates' Courts (Children and Young Persons) Rules (S.I. 1988 No. 913)	345, 348, 355
	r. 6	469			
	Order 38	476			
	Order 50,			r. 16	376
	r. 5	473		Accommodation of Children (Charge and Central) Regulations (S.I. 1988 No. 2183)	334
1983	Secure Accommodation Regulations (S.I. 1983 No. 652)	453			

Table of Statutory Instruments

1988 Matrimonial Causes (Costs) Rules (S.I. 1988 No. 1328) 476
    r. 15 476
    r. 16 476
Boarding-Out of Children (Foster Placement) Regulations (S.I. 1988 No. 2184) 334

1990 Children's Homes (Control and Discipline) Regulations (S.I. 1990 No. 87) 156
Children (Admissibility of Hearsay Evidence) Order (S.I. 1990 No. 143) 223, 224, 431
Local Authority Social Services (Complaints Procedure) Order (S.I. 1990 No. 2244) 86

1991 Children Act 1989 (Commencement and Transitional Provisions) Order (S.I. 1991 No. 828) 13, 238
    art. 4 .... 331, 332, 333, 336
    Sched. 333, 336
Arrangements for Placement of Children (General) Regulations (S.I. 1991 No. 890) 60, 66, 70, 71, 72, 102, 164, 171, 249, 250, 267, 271, 275, 461
    reg. 2 60
    reg. 3 60
    reg. 5 61
    reg. 7 61
    reg. 8 61
    reg. 9 61
    reg. 10 61
    reg. 11 126
    reg. 13 61
    Scheds. 1–3 60
    Sched. 4 60
        para. 1 60
        para. 2 60
        para. 3 61
        para. 4 61
        para. 5 61
        para. 6 61
        para. 7 61
        para. 8 61
Contact with Children Regulations (S.I. 1991 No. 891) 104, 107, **462**
    reg. 1 .... **462**
    reg. 2 .... 105, 107, **463**
    reg. 3 .... 105, 107, **463**
    reg. 4 .... 105, **463**
    Sched. **464**
Definition of Independent Visitors (Children) Regulations (S.I. 1991 No. 892) 71, 252

1991 Placement of Children with Parents, etc., Regulations (S.I. 1991 No. 893) 70, 73, 102, 106, 117, 250, 327, 332
Representation Procedure (Children) Regulations (S.I. 1991 No. 894) 77, 85, 164, 172, 275, 277
    reg. 12 173
Review of Children's Case Regulations (S.I. 1991 No. 895) 85, 164, 172, 275, 458
    reg. 1 85
    reg. 2 85
    reg. 4 86
        (5) 86
    reg. 5 86
    reg. 6 .... 85, 86
    reg. 7 85
    reg. 8 .... 85, 86
        (1) 86
        (2) 86
    reg. 9 .... 85, 86
    reg. 10 .... 85, 86
    reg. 11 85
    reg. 12 .... 86, 87
Foster Placement (Children) Regulations (S.I. 1991 No. 910) 33, 71, 72, 153, 164, 249, 334
    reg. 3 .... 72, 153
        (1) 153
        (3) 153
        (5) 153
        (6) 72
        (7) 153
        (8) 153
        (9) 154
    reg. 4 .... 72, 153
    reg. 5 73
        (2) 73, 102, 103
    reg. 6 73
    reg. 7 73
    reg. 8 73
    reg. 9 73
    reg. 10 73
    reg. 11 .... 73, 173
        (2)(*b*) 73
        (3)(*b*) 73
    regs. 12–14 73
    reg. 15 73
    reg. 16 73
    regs. 32–34 168
    Sched. 1 72
    Sched. 2 72
        para. 5 73
    Sched. 3 73
Adopted Persons (Contact Register) (Fees) Rules (S.I. 1991 No. 952) 295
Inspection of Premises, Children and Records (Independent Schools) Regulations (S.I. 1991 No. 975) ... 210

Table of Statutory Instruments

1991 Inspection of Premises, Children and Records (Independent Schools) Regulations—*cont.*
    reg. 3 210
    reg. 4 210
Children (Admissibility of Hearsay Evidence) Order (S.I. 1991 No. 1115) 30, 81, 82, 223, **431**, 454
    r. 26 81
    art. 1 .... **431**
    art. 2 .... **431**
    art. 3 .... **431**
Children's Homes Regulations (S.I. 1991 No. 1205) 271
Family Proceedings Rules (S.I. 1991 No. 1247) 128, 219, 221
    r. 2(2)(*a*) 82
    r. 2.5 357
    r. 2.6(4) 479
    r. 2.9 474
    r. 2.45 408
    r. 2.57 474
    r. 3.1 .... 409, 469
    r. 3.2 .... 409, 469
    r. 3.3 469
    r. 3.6 469
    r. 3.8 469
    r. 4 .... 33, 112
    r. 4.1 .... **353**
    r. 4.2 .... **355**, 403
      (2)(*e*) 407
    r. 4.3 .... 358, 373, 464
    r. 4.4 .... 358, 360, 411
      (1)(*b*) 360, 411, 412, 413, 414, 415
      (2) 362
    r. 4.5 .... **363**
      (2) 362
      (3) 363
    r. 4.6 .... **364**, 366, 406, 407, 432, 438
      (1)(*b*) 369
    r. 4.7 .... **367**, 411
      (2) 378
        (*a*) 367
        (*b*) 367
    r. 4.8 .... 348, **370**
      (1)(*b*)(ii) 371
      (4)(*c*) 371
      (8) 371
    r. 4.9 .... **373**
    r. 4.10 .... **373**
      (5) 396
    r. 4.11 .... **378**
      (2)(*a*) 382, 383, 384
      (2A) 124
      (3) 383
      (4) 378
      (8) 372

1991 Family Proceedings Rules—*cont.*
    r. 4.12 .... 372, **383**
      (1)(*a*) 381
    r. 4.13 .... **386**
      (1) 386
    r. 4.14 .... **388**, 391
      (2) **353**
      (3) 386, 387
        (*b*) 387
        (*c*) 387
      (5) 392
    r. 4.15 .... 363, **392**
    r. 4.16 .... **394**
      (5) 401
    r. 4.17 .... **396**, 398
      (1) 374, 396, 398
      (2) 400
    r. 4.18 .... **399**
    r. 4.19 .... **400**
    r. 4.20 .... **401**
    r. 4.21 .... **401**
      (1) 403
      (3) 403
      (4) 403
      (6) 404
    r. 4.22 .... 120, **404**, 405, 406
      (1)(*a*) 404
      (2) 221, 404
        (*a*) 405
        (*b*)–(*d*) 405
      (5) 405
      (6) 405
    r. 4.23 .... **407**
    r. 4.24 .... **407**
    r. 4.25 .... **407**
    r. 4.26 .... **408**
      (2) 408
    r. 4.27 .... 111, **408**
    r. 4.28 .... **408**
    r. 5.1 .... **466**, 468
      (8) 467
      (9) 467
    r. 5.2 .... **467**
    r. 5.3 .... **468**
    r. 5.4 .... **468**
      (1)(*a*), (*b*) **468**
      (2) **468**
    r. 5.5 .... 81, **468**, 469
    r. 5.6 .... **469**
    r. 8.1 .... 403, **469**
      (2) 469
    r. 9.1 .... **470**
    r. 9.2 .... **470**
      (4) 474
      (7) 470
    r. 9.2A 370, 470, **472**, 474
      (1)(*a*) 473
        (*b*)(i) 473
          (ii) 473
      (2) 473
        (*a*) 472

1991 Family Proceedings Rules— cont.

r. 9.2A—cont.
- (3) (b) 473
- (4) 472, 473
- (5) (b) 473
- r. 9.3 .... **474**
- (1) 474
- r. 9.5 .... **474**
- r. 10.21 362
- Appendix 1 .... 348, 358, 360, 402, **408**
- Appendix 2 .... **410**
- Appendix 3 .... 348, 360, 369, 410, **411**

Family Proceedings Court (Children Act 1989) Rules
(S.I. 1991 No. 1395) 16, 219, 221, 345, 347, 350
- r. 1 .... **354**
- r. 2 .... **356**, 400
  - (1) 117
  - (2) 124, 355
    - (c) 253
  - (3) 130
- r. 2 (4) 135
  - (5) 135, 355, 418
- rr. 3–8 358
- r. 3 .... 24, 106, **359**
  - (2) 39
- r. 4 .... 263, **361**, 420
  - (1) (a) 361
  - (b) 361, 422, 423, 424, 425, 426, 427
  - (2) (a) 361
  - (b) 361
  - (3) 473
- r. 5 .... 119, **364**, 365
  - (2) 364
  - (3) 364
- r. 6 .... **368**, 432, 438
  - (2) 389
- r. 7 .... **368**, 422
  - (2) 381
- r. 8 .... 348, 357, **371**
  - (1) (b) (ii) 371
  - (3) (a) (b) 381, 384
  - (4) (a) 384
  - (b) 384
  - (c) 373
  - (8) 373
- r. 9 .... **374**
- rr. 10, 11 123
- rr. 10–19 358
- r. 10 .... 124, 357, **375**, 377, 378, 483
  - (5) 397
  - (7) (a) 123
  - (9) 67
- r. 11 .... 124, 378, **380**, 383, 483
  - (2) 123
  - (a) 381, 383, 385, 386

1991 Family Proceedings Court (Children Act 1989) Rules —cont.

r. 11—cont.
- (3) 385, 391
- (4) 382
  - (b) 222
  - (d) 100
- (8) 374, 387, 399
- r. 12 .... 124, 374, **384**
  - (1) (a) 380, 382
  - (8) 399
- r. 13 .... **387**
  - (1) 386
- rr. 14, 15 100
- r. 14 .... 42, **389**, 392
  - (2) **355**
  - (b) 391
  - (d) 124, 376
  - (3) 419
  - (5) 390, 396
    - (b) 390, 391
- r. 15 .... 16, 42, 363, **393**
  - (1) 391
- r. 16 .... **395**
  - (2) 222
  - (3)–(5) 396
  - (5) 399, 401
- r. 17 .... 17, **397**, 398, 399, 402, 403
  - (1) 377, 397, 399
  - (2) 399, 400
  - (3) 399
  - (4)–(5) 399
- r. 18 .... 117, 134, **399**
  - (3) 398
- r. 19 .... 357, 400
- r. 20 .... 396, **401**
- r. 21 .... 357, 358, **402**, 403
  - (1) 403
  - (2)–(3) 403
  - (2) 402
  - (4) 403
  - (5) 30
  - (6) 30, 404
  - (7) 404
  - (8) 403
- r. 23 .... 29, 357, 358, **416**
  - (1) 229
- r. 24 .... 358, **416**
- r. 25 .... 48, 103, 253, **417**
- r. 26 417
- r. 27 .... 113, 357, 358, **418**
  - (2) 418
  - (5) 114
- r. 28 .... 116, 357, 390, 417, 418
- r. 29 .... **418**
- r. 30 .... 257, **419**
- r. 31 .... 111, 263, **419**
- r. 32 .... 355, **419**
  - (1) 362
- r. 33 .... **420**

Table of Statutory Instruments

1991 Family Proceedings Court (Children Act 1989) Rules —cont.
    r. 34 .... **420**
       (3) 420
    Sched. 1 .... 348, 355, 361, 366, 374, 390, 403, **420**
    Sched. 2 .... 17, 42, 348, 355, 361, 369, 422
       Pt. I 389
    Sched. 3 .... 419, **428**
Emergency Protection Order (Transfer of Responsibilities) Regulations (S.I. 1991 No. 1414) 98, 134, 138, 145, 154, **464**, 465
    reg. 1 .... **465**
    reg. 2 .... **465**
       (c) 465
    reg. 3 .... **465**, 466
    reg. 31 (1) 465
    reg. 4 .... **466**
    reg. 5 .... 145, 153, 465, **466**
Children (Secure Accommodation) Regulations (S.I. 1991 No. 1505) **452**, 462
    reg. 1 .... **454**
    reg. 2 .... **454**
    reg. 3 .... **454**
    reg. 4 .... 80, **454**
    reg. 5 .... 80, **454**, 455, 456
    reg. 6 .... 82, 214, **455**, 459
    reg. 7 .... 80, 82, **456**
    reg. 8 .... 81, **457**
    reg. 9 .... 81, 458, **457**
    regs. 10–12 81
    reg. 10 .... 82, 453, **457**
    reg. 11 .... 82, **458**
    reg. 12 .... 82, **458**
    reg. 13 .... **458**
    reg. 14 .... 81, **459**, 460
    reg. 15 .... 81, **459**, 460
    reg. 16 .... 81, **459**
       (3) 460
    reg. 17 .... 81, **460**
    reg. 18 .... 81, 166, 173, **461**
    reg. 19 .... **461**
Children's Homes Regulations (S.I. 1991 No. 1506) 71, 72, 80, 156, 164, 166, 171, 267, 275, 461
    regs. 2, 3 156
    reg. 4 .... 72, 156
    regs. 5–7 156
    reg. 5 72
    reg. 6 72
    reg. 7 .... 72, 169
    reg. 8 .... 72, 156, 169
    reg. 9 .... 72, 156
    reg. 10 72
    reg. 11 .... 102, 156
    reg. 12 156

1991 Children's Homes Regulations—cont.
    reg. 13 .... 72, 156
    reg. 14 156
    regs. 15, 16 168
    regs. 15–17 .... 72, 156
    reg. 15 169
    reg. 16 .... 126, 169
    reg. 18 .... 72, 156
    reg. 19 .... 72, 156
    reg. 20 72
    reg. 21 .... 72, 156
    reg. 22 .... 72, 156
    reg. 23 156
    reg. 24 156
    regs. 25, 29, 30 157
    reg. 26 157
    regs. 27, 28 157
    regs. 32–34 .... 157, 169
    reg. 33 (3) 169
    Pt. II 153
    Pt. IV 157
    Pt. VII 157
Refuges (Children's Homes and Foster Placements) Regulations (S.I. 1991 No. 1507) 153
Children (Allocation of Proceedings) Order (S.I. 1991 No. 1677) 97, 217, 298, 324, 348, 365, 366, 432
    art. 1 .... **433**
    art. 2 .... **433**
    art. 3 .... 362, 432, **434**
       (1) 434, 436
       (2) 434
          (b) 434
          (e) 434
          (f) 434
          (g) 434
          (i) 434
    art. 4 .... 432, **434**, 437
       (1) 212, 362, 435
       (2) 434
       (3) 434
    arts. 5–13 434
    art. 5 .... **435**
    art. 6 .... **435**
    arts. 7–8 436
    art. 7 .... 435, **436**, 437
       (1) 438
          (a)–(c) 437
          (a) 436
       (2) 436
       (3) 436
       (4) 436
    art. 8 .... **437**
    art. 9 .... **437**, 438
    art. 10 .... **438**
    art. 11 .... **438**, 450
    art. 12 .... 435, **438**
    art. 13 .... 435, **439**

1991 Children (Allocation of Proceedings) Order—*cont.*
  art. 14 .... **439**
  arts. 15–17 .... **438**
  arts. 15–18 .... 436, **437**
  art. 15 .... 432, **439**
  art. 16 .... 432, **439**
  art. 17 .... **440**
    (1) **441**
  art. 18 .... 432, **440**
  art. 19 .... **440**
  art. 20 .... **440**
  art. 21 .... **440**
  art. 22 .... 440, **441**
  Sched. 1 .... 433, **441**
  Sched. 2 ..... 406, 433, 437, 440, **442**
Child Minding and Day Care (Applications for Registration) Regulations (S.I. 1991 No. 1689) 185, **284**
Children (Allocation of Proceedings) (Appeals) Order (S.I. 1991 No. 1801) 217, 220, 221, 298, **452**
  art. 1 .... **452**
  art. 2 .... **452**
Family Proceedings (Costs) Rules (S.I. 1991 No. 1832) 396, **475**, **476**
  r. 1 .... **476**
  r. 3 .... 16, **476**
  r. 14 .... **478**
    (1) **477**
    (2) **477**
  r. 15 .... **476**, **478**
    (1) (*b*) **477**
    (2) **477**
    (3) **477**
    (4) **476**, **477**
    (5) **477**
    (6) **477**
    (7) **477**
  r. 16 .... **477**
  art. 2 .... **475**
Parental Responsibility Agreements Regulations (S.I. 1991 No. 1478) 23, **24**
(S.I. 1991 No. 1880) 212, **295**
Children Act 1989 (Consequential Amendment of Enactments) Order (S.I. 1991 No. 1881) **308**
Legal Aid Act 1988 (Children Act 1989) Order (S.I. 1991 No. 1924) **226**
Children Act 1989 (Commencement No. 2 — Amendment and Transitional Provisions) Order (S.I. 1991 No. 1990) 13, 27, 238, 324, 326, **330**

1991 Family Proceedings Courts (Matrimonial Proceedings, etc.) Rules (S.I. 1991 No. 1991)—
  Sched. 2, para. 8 .... **421**
  reg. 8 .... 357, **391**
Adoption Allowance Regulations (S.I. 1991 No. 2030) 212, **295**
Children (Prescribed Orders — Northern Ireland, Guernsey and Isle of Man) Regulations (S.I. 1991 No. 2032) 152, **231**
  regs. 6, 7 .... **152**
Children (Representations, Placements and Reviews (Miscellaneous Amendments)) Regulations (S.I. 1991 No. 2033) 70, 77, 85, 164, 172, 249, 250, 267, **277**
The Children (Secure Accommodation) (No. 2) Regulations (S.I. 1991 No. 2034) 80, 81, 82, 457, **461**
  reg. 1 .... **462**
  reg. 2 .... 455, **463**
Civil Legal Aid (General) (Amendment) (No. 2) Regulations (S.I. 1991 No. 2036) **226**
Children (Private Arrangements for Fostering) Regulations (S.I. 1991 No. 2050) 176, 178, **281**
  r. 4 .... **176**
  r. 29 (1) **176**
Guardians ad Litem and Reporting Officers (Panels) Regulations (S.I. 1991 No. 2051) 123, 212, 377, **483**, **484**
  reg. 1 .... 124, **484**
  reg. 2 .... **484**
    (1) **490**
  reg. 3 .... 124, **485**
    (*b*) **484**
  reg. 4 .... 484, **485**
  reg. 5 .... 379, 485, **486**
    (2) (*b*) **486**
  reg. 6 .... 124, 485, **486**
  reg. 7 .... 124, **487**
  reg. 8 .... 124, 485, **488**
  reg. 9 .... 124, **488**
    (1) 376, **488**
  reg. 10 .... 124, **489**
    (1) (*a*) **485**
  reg. 11 .... **489**
  Sched. 1 .... **489**
  Sched. 2 .... 485, **490**

1991	Child Minding and Day Care (Registration and Inspection Fees) Regulations (S.I. 1991 No. 2076)	185, 194, 284	1991	Family Proceedings (Amendment) Rules—*cont.*

1991 Child Minding and Day Care (Registration and Inspection Fees) Regulations (S.I. 1991 No. 2076) 185, 194, 284
Disqualification for Caring for Children Regulations (S.I. 1991 No. 2094) ... 175, 180, 186, 187, 271, 284
   reg. 2 180
   reg. 3 .... 166, 180
Magistrates Courts (Costs against Legal Representatives in Civil Proceedings) Rules (S.I. 1991 No. 2096) 42, 100
   reg. 1(2) 73
   reg. 3 73
   reg. 5 73
   reg. 6 73
   reg. 7 73
   reg. 8 74
   reg. 9 .... 73, 74
   reg. 11 74
   reg. 12 .... 73, 74
   reg. 13 .... 73, 106
   Sched. 1 73
   Sched. 2 74
Family Proceedings (Amendment) Rules (S.I. 1991 No. 2113) 219, 221, 356, 361, 369, 470
   reg. 5 354
   reg. 11 365
   reg. 12 365
   reg. 13 380
   reg. 14 469
   reg. 17 472
   reg. 19 410

1991 Family Proceedings (Amendment) Rules—*cont.*
   reg. 20 415
   art. 8 124
Family Proceedings Fees Order (S.I. 1991 No. 2114) 24, **478**
   art. 1 .... **478**
   art. 2 .... **479**
   art. 3 .... 478, **479**
   art. 4 .... **479**
   Sched. **479**
The Child Minding and Day Care (Applications for Registration and Inspection Fees) (Amendment) Regulations (S.I. 1991 No. 2129) 186, 284
Adoption Allowance (Amendment) Regulations (S.I. 1991 No. 2130) 212, 295
Rules of the Supreme Court (Amendment No. 4) (S.I. 1991 No. 2671) 27
1992 Family Proceedings (Amendment) Rules (S.I. 1992 No. 456) 39
   reg. 5 469
   reg. 6 470
   reg. 9 474
   reg. 10 .... 365, 475
   reg. 14 402
   reg. 15 407
   reg. 16 410
Income Support (General Amendment Regulations (S.I. 1992 No. 468)—
   reg. 7 472
   reg. 8 472

TABLE OF CHILDREN ACT

1989 Children Act (as amended) (c.
41) 8, 9, 12, 13, 17, 124, 226,
236, 261, 271, 298, 304, 305,
308, 311, 312, 317, 318, 345,
355, 479
Pt. I 146
Pt. II 173
Pt. III 142, 145, 146, 169, 174,
179, 198, 207
Pts. IV, V 169, 170, 193
Pt. VI 155, 166
Pts. VI, VII 172
Pts. VI–IX, XII 210
Pt. VII 163
Pts. VII–X 145
Pt. VIII 166, 170, 173
Pt. IX 166, 172, 175
Pt. X 183, 186, 199
Pt. XI **198**
Pt. XII 206
s. 1 .... **14**, 39, 51, 53, 105, 216
(1) 24, 41, 48, 82, 114, 128,
133, 152
(2) 15, 16, 30, 99, 116, 345,
378, 380, 399, 435, 436, 437
(3)–(5) 95
(3) ... 15, 16, 17, 23, 26, 97, 105,
118, 329
(a)–(f) 378, 381
(b)–(f) 345
(4) 15, 17, 23, 105
(5) 15, 24, 26, 34, 39, 45, 48,
82, 96, 97, 106, 116, 133, 402
ss. 2–6 9
s. 2 ..... **18**, 21, 23, 26, 31, 38, 42, 44,
101, 133
(1) 18, 28, 39, 43, 44, 50, 60,
101, 118, 127, 133, 185
(2) 18, 19, 23, 24, 26, 28, 44,
50, 60, 101, 127, 133,
185, 326
(3) 18, 19, 325
(4) 325
(5) 19
(6) 19
(7) 19
(8) 17, 19, 20, 22, 32, 101,
130, 325, 326, 327
(9) 19, 20, 24
(10) 19
(11) 20
s. 3 ..... 18, **20**, 21, 23, 24, 26, 31, 38,
42, 44, 101, 133, 187, 227, 234,
353, 355
(1) 21
(2) 21, 54
(4) 22
(5) ... 20, 22, 24, 32, 63, 67, 129,
142

1989 Children Act (as amended)—
cont.
s. 4 ..... 9, 17, **22**, 24, 30, 34, 43, 214,
216, 300
(1) 24, 28, 50, 60, 101, 118,
127, 133, 214, 234, 285, 286,
326
(a) 19, 354, 412, 423, 479
(b) 19, 23
(2) 23, 24, 479
(3) 23, 354, 412, 423, 479
(b) 357, 358
(4) 25
s. 5 ..... 17, 19, 21, **25**, 26, 28, 30, 34,
38, 43, 44, 48, 101, 104, 216, 233,
327, 329, 330
(1) ... 19, 26, 214, 354, 412, 423,
424, 479
(a) (ii) 329
(2) 26
(3)–(5) 28
(3) 26, 214
(4) 26, 214
(5) 26, 27
(6) 26, 28, 44, 50, 60, 65, 70,
85, 101, 118, 127, 133, 137,
140, 167, 168, 174, 176, 178,
185
(7) 27, 39
(8) 19, 39
(9) 27
(10) 26
(11) 13, 22, 27
(12) 13, 27
(13) 26, 27
s. 6 .... 26, **27**, 34
(1) 26, 28
(2) 28
(2)–(4) 28
(3) 28
(5) 28, 29
(6) 28
(7) 28, 354, 412, 423, 479
ss. 7–9 26
s. 7 .... **29**, 48, 110, 123, 138, 353,
355, 357, 358, 377, 388, 389, 390
(1) 16, 29, 30
(b) (ii) 48
(2) 29, 188
(3) 30
(4) 29, 30, 430
(5) 29
(7) 11
ss. 8–10 10
s. 8 .... 9, 15, 16, 17, 20, 22, 24, **30**,
31, 34, 35, 36, 38, 39, 40, 42, 46, 48,
49, 95, 96, 98, 110, 118, 148, 214,
215, 216, 229, 314, 317, 318, 320,
357, 398, 411, 423, 432, 440, 441

1989 Children Act (as amended)—
cont.
s. 8—cont.
(1) 26, 31, 35, 38, 42, 44, 45,
60, 104, 116, 122, 127, 133,
140, 215, 233, 235, 327, 328,
329, 401
(2) 353, 355
(3) 24, 26, 28, 34, 48, 81, 95,
97, 113, 233, 329
(a) 34, 40
(4) 30, 36, 97
(a) 34
(c) 35
(d) 34
(e) 35
(f) 35
s. 9 .... 34, **35**, 49, 63, 95, 96
(1)–(3) 36
(1) 32, 33, 36, 101, 229
(2) 32, 33, 36, 37
(3) 36, 40, 96, 228
(4) 35, 36, 41
(5) 20, 32, 34, 36, 37, 229
(6) 15, 31, 32, 33, 36, 37, 216
(7) 15, 32, 33, 35, 36, 37, 38
s. 10 ..... 34, 36, **37**, 62, 63, 118, 119,
228, 229, 285, 357, 409, 420
(1) 17, 34, 39, 97, 106, 479
(b) 17, 24, 27, 34, 49, 433
(2) 34, 39, 479
(b) 34
(4)–(7) 39
(4) 39, 326, 327
(a) 24
(5) 19, 27, 39, 40, 96,
228, 328
(a) 39
(b) 36, 40
(c) 40
(i) 40, 327
(ii) 40
(iii) 36
(5A) 328
(6) 39
(7) 40
(8) .. 15, 39, 40, 41, 45, 106, 228
(9) 15, 27, 40, 41, 359
(b) 39
(d) 41
(i) 36
(10) 38, 39, 41
s. 11 .... **41**
(1) 42
(3) 42, 43, 357, 387, 415
(4) 33, 42, 43
(5) 33, 42, 43
(6) 32, 42, 43
(7) 15, 31, 32, 38, 42, 43, 45
(c) 43
(d) 120
s. 12 .... 18, 21, 23, 26, 31, 38, 42, **44**
(1) ... 19, 24, 28, 44, 50, 60, 101,
118, 127, 133, 185

1989 Children Act (as amended)
—cont.
s. 12—cont.
(2) 28, 33, 44, 50, 60, 65, 70,
85, 127, 133, 137, 140, 167,
168, 174, 176, 178, 185
(3) 19, 24, 33, 39
(4) 24
s. 13 .... 20, 32, 33, 43, **44**, 45
(1) 45, 354, 412, 423, 479
(2) 33, 45
s. 14 .... 22, **45**, 322, 328, 357, 358,
414
s. 15 .... **46**, 246
(1) 46
(2) 46
s. 16 ...... 9, 17, 34, **47**, 51, 114, 117,
119, 216, 322
(1) 48
(2) 48, 233, 328
(3) 48, 406, 416
(b) 48
(4) 48
(5) 48
(6) 48, 49, 354, 412, 423
(7)–(9) 48
(7) 48
s. 17 .... 10, 11, **49**, 52, 88, 91, 102,
114, 146, 169, 207, 236, 247, 249,
319
(1) 51, 54, 55, 61, 62, 67, 78
(b) 54
(2) 52, 56
(3) 53, 55, 56, 91
(4) 53, 23, 232
(5) 51, 56
(6) 51, 53, 56, 79, 91, 114
(7)–(9) ... 52, 76, 77, 79, 91, 248
(7) 51, 53
(8) 51, 54
(9) 50, 51, 54, 91
(10) 50, 53, 55, 56, 60
(a) 55, 97
(b) 55
(11) 50, 54, 70, 91, 176, 233
s. 18 .... 52, **55**, 91, 114, 185,
190, 191, 192, 194, 197, 200,
233, 247
(1) 51, 56, 66
(3) 51, 56
(4) 56, 58
(5) 56
(6) 145
(7) 56, 57
s. 19 .... 11, 52, **57**, 237, 312
(1) 58
(2) 58
(3) 58
(4) 58
(5) 58, 226
(6) 58
(7) 58
s. 20 .... 10, **58**, 63, 65, 66, 92, 102,
114, 149, 179, 210, 247, 309, 334

Table of Children Act

1989 Children Act (as amended)—
cont.
s. 20—cont.
- (1) 51, 60, 61, 90, 92, 453
- (c) 52, 193
- (2) 61, 92, 250
- (3) 60, 61, 78, 92, 453
- (4) 60, 62, 78
- (5) 60, 62, 78, 80, 453
- (6) 60, 62
- (7) 60, 62, 63
- (8) 22, 23, 60, 62, 80, 212, 286, 287, 455
- (9) 60, 62, 63
- (a) 327
- (10) 20, 60
- (11) 60, 61, 62, 63, 83
- s. 21 .... **63**, 65, 66, 214
- (1) 64, 65, 90
- (2) 118
- (a) 64, 90, 92
- (b) 64, 90, 92
- (c) 64
- (3) 64, 92
- s. 22–24 334
- s. 22 .... 10, **64**, 74, 102, 119, 142, 169, 174, 206, 213, 235, 316
- (1) ... 66, 76, 80, 85, 89, 90, 151, 155, 158, 200
- (2) 65, 67, 85
- (3)–(5) 40, 167
- (3) 36, 66, 67, 71, 92, 106
- (a) 69, 71
- (b) 71
- (4) 61, 62, 66, 67, 68, 135, 457, 459
- (d) 87, 377
- (5) 66, 67, 135
- (6) 69
- (7) 69
- (8) 69
- s. 23 ... 10, 51, 53, **69**, 102, 106, 117, 153, 164, 165, 171, 214, 249, 250, 252, 267, 271, 275, 312, 327, 334
- (1) 71
- (2) 67, 68, 71
- (a) 71, 78, 164, 249
- (c) 169
- (e) 70
- (f) 71, 164, 250
- (3) 35, 70, 72, 85, 169, 234
- (4) 35, 70,, 73, 85, 153, 250
- (c) 327
- (5) 73, 102, 250
- (5A) 70, 73, 74
- (6) 62, 71, 74
- (7) 74, 105
- (8) 71, 74
- s. 24 ...... 10, 12, 52, 65, **74**, 102, 114, 174, 178, 207, 208, 214, 247, 335
- (1) 51, 77, 167
- (2)–(5) 78
- (2) 62, 76, 77, 78
- (c)–(e) 78

1989 Children Act (as amended)—
cont.
s. 24—cont.
- (3) 77, 78
- (4) 77, 78, 169
- (a) 78
- (c) 78
- (5) 77, 78
- (a) 78
- (b) 78
- (6) 77, 78
- (7) 76, 77, 78, 91
- (8)–(10) 79
- (8) 77, 79, 91
- (9) **75**, 77
- (10) 77, 91
- (11) 78
- (12) 77, 78, 79, 169, 174
- (13) 77
- (14) 79
- (15) 79
- s. 25 .... 69, **79**, 99, 123, 156, 166, 203, 226, 266, 331, 354, 355, 356, 357, 375, 407, 414, 417, 426, 434, 453, 454, 455, 457, 460, 462, 480
- (1) 80, 82, 83, 214, 455, 456, 459, 461, 468
- (a) 456
- (b) 456
- (2) 82, 452
- (a) 331
- (4) 82
- (5) 82
- (6) 82
- (7) 83, 452
- (8) 237
- (9) 83
- s. 26 .... 10, 65, **83**, 102, 164, 172, 173, 206, 275, 277, 379
- (1) 85, 114
- (2) 85
- (3)–(8) 86
- (3) 54, 61, 62, 71, 73, 77, 79, 86, 87, 104, 106
- (a)–(d) 86
- (b) 97
- (e) 86
- (4) 86, 87
- (7) 86, 87
- (a) 86
- (8) 86, 87
- s. 27 .... 62, **87**, 207
- (2) 90
- (3) 88
- s. 28 .... **89**
- (4) 89
- s. 29 .... 51, 54, **89**, 257
- (1)–(5) 91
- (1) 54, 56, 90, 91
- (2)–(3) 91
- (2) 54
- (4) 89, 91
- (5) 54, 91
- (6) 91

1989 Children Act (as amended)—
cont.
s. 29—cont.
(7)–(9) 91, 92
(7) 92
(8) 92
(9) 92
s. 30 .... **92**
(1) (a) 94
(b) 95
(2) 60, 91
(3) 93
(4) 93
s. 31 ... 11, 20, 34, 36, 48, 51, 52, 62,
93, 95, 125, 127, 179, 191, 213,
216, 227, 314, 318, 336, 340, 374,
375, 389, 413, 425, 434, 480
(1) 66, 97, 138
(2) ... 95, 97, 112, 113, 115, 116,
118, 146, 213, 228, 229
(b) 95, 96
(3) 66, 95
(4) 95, 97
(5) 98
(6) 98, 101, 134, 138, 145,
154
(7) 96, 98, 145
(8) 95, 99, 101
(9) 38, 80, 95, 99, 101, 125,
127, 133, 137, 138, 140, 144,
145, 192, 227, 234, 374, 375
(10) 55, 80, 95, 97, 99, 127,
133, 137, 227, 233
(11) 95, 99, 101, 104,
105, 108, 113, 116, 117, 118,
120, 122, 137, 144, 151, 215,
231, 232, 235, 260, 318, 329,
337
s. 32 .... **99**, 110, 116
(2) 100
s. 33 .... **100**, 102, 117, 253
(3) ... 19, 74, 101, 137, 140, 151,
167, 168, 174, 176
(b) 101, 106
(4) 101
(5) 101
(6) 19, 102
(a) 68
(7) 20, 103, 123, 354, 356,
357, 412, 416, 423, 434, 480
s. 34 ... 11, 32, 34, 71, **103**, 120, 121,
127, 140, 215, 216, 228, 333, 374,
378, 389, 413, 425, 434, 462, 463
(1) ... 24, 33, 105, 106, 107, 358,
463
(2)–(5) 104
(2) 104, 106, 354, 413, 425,
480
(3) 105, 106, 354, 413, 425,
480
(b) 357, 358
(4) 104, 105, 106, 333, 354,
411, 423, 478
(5) 105, 107

1989 Children Act (as amended)—
cont.
s. 34—cont.
(6) 105, 106, 107, 461
(7) 104, 105, 106, 120
(8) 107
(9) 105, 354, 411, 423, 478
(10) 105, 107
(11) 105, 107
s. 35 ... 101, **108**, 117, 119, 215, 216,
260
(1) (c) 108
s. 36 ... 11, 34, 51, 96, **109**, 215, 233,
309, 340, 434
(1) 110, 354, 412, 424, 480
(2) 110, 263
(3) 110
(4) 110, 111
(5) 110, 111
(6) 110, 111
(7) 110, 111, 263
(8) 89, 110
(9) 110, 310
(10) 111
s. 37 ... **112**, 144, 145, 357, 358, 407,
417, 433
(1) 113, 114, 116, 121, 406,
407, 416, 417, 434
(2) 113, 114
(3) 113, 114
(a)–(c) 315, 405
(4) 113, 114, 116
(5) 111, 113, 114
(b) 113
(6) 113, 114, 145
ss. 38–40 109
s. 38 .... 11, 95, 97, **114**, 116, 129,
215, 216, 373, 389, 405, 435
(1) 113, 116, 117, 120, 357,
389, 417
(2) 116, 117
(3) 116, 117, 119
(4) 116
(5) 116
(6)–(9) 117
(6) 116, 229, 355, 356, 400
(b) 117
(7) 116, 117, 400
(8) 117, 355
(b) .. 354, 356, 413, 425, 480
(9) 117
(10) 117
s. 39 .... **117**, 332
(1) .. 36, 118, 354, 412, 424, 480
(b) 41
(2) 108, 118, 354, 412, 424,
478
(3) 119, 354, 412, 480
(4) 119, 121, 354, 412, 480
(6) 118
s. 40 .... 11, 95, 106, 118, **119**, 221,
229, 406
(1) 120
(2) 120

Table of Children Act

1989 Children Act (as amended)—
cont.
s. 40—*cont.*
(3) 120
(4) 120
(6) 120
s. 41 ..... 12, 119, **120**, 212, 353, 355, 357, 376, 377, 389, 390, 483, 484
    (1) 81, 123
    (2) 122, 124, 125, 377, 379
    (3) 123, 384, 385, 386, 389, 390
    (4) 123
      (b) 383
    (5) 123, 124
    (6) 114, 122, 123, 124, 348, 353, 355, 470, 484
      (b) 114
      (g) 137
    (7) 122, 123, 124, 125, 374, 375
    (8) 123, 124
    (9) 212
    (11) 123, 430
    (12) 123
s. 42 ...... 12, 123, **124**, 156, 375, 481
    (1) 125
s. 43 ..... 11, 64, 80, 97, 99, 105, **126**, 134, 135, 215, 216, 227, 373, 434
    (1) 128, 129, 354, 356, 412, 480
    (2) 127, 144, 233
    (3) 128
    (4) 128, 129
    (5) 128
    (6) 128, 129, 134
    (7) 128
    (8) 117, 128, 130, 134, 135, 229, 260
    (10) 128, 130
    (11) 128, 356
      (a)–(e) 414, 426
    (12) 128, 130, 354, 356, 414, 426, 480
    (13) 128
ss. 44–46 11
s. 44 ... 22, 36, 62, 63, 64, 97, 98, 99, 105, 109, 129, **130**, 139, 141, 170, 179, 193, 194, 210, 215, 216, 227, 228, 232, 233, 354, 355, 375, 402, 403, 434, 480
    (1) 129, 133, 134, 137, 147, 351, 414, 426
      (a) 117, 133, 135, 140
        (i) 133
        (ii) 133
      (b) 128, 129, 133, 134, 144, 145
        (i) 133
      (c) 128, 133
        (i) 134
        (ii) 134
    (2) 133
    (3) 135

1989 Children Act (as amended)—
cont.
s. 44—*cont.*
(4) 127, 133, 137, 140, 144, 147, 149, 151, 154, 167, 168, 174
      (a) 134
      (b) 133, 134
        (i) 132
        (ii) 131, 132
      (c) 138
(5) 133, 135
      (a) 134
      (b) 134
      (c) 134
(6) 133
      (a) 134
      (b) 134
(7) 134, 135, 229
(8) 134
(9) 134, 135, 356
      (b) .. 356, 357, 358, 414, 426
(10) 134
(11) 134, 135
      (b) (i) 135
        (ii) 135
        (iii) 358
(12) 134
(13) 134, 135
(14) 134
(15) 134, 148, 416
(16) 134
s. 45 ... 134, **135**, 227, 232, 354, 375, 434, 480
    (1) 133, 137
    (2) 137
    (3) 141
    (4)–(6) 137
    (4) 138, 154, 414, 426
    (5) 137, 138
    (7) 138
    (8) 137, 154, 412, 426
    (9) 137, 138
    (10) 137
    (11) 137, 138, 141
s. 46 .... 64, 99, 105, 134, 136, **138**, 149, 150, 373, 480
    (1) 136, 140, 141, 148
    (2) 64, 140, 144, 149, 151
    (3) 140
      (b) 140
      (c) (d) 141
      (e) 140, 151
      (f) 140, 141
    (4) 140, 141
    (5) 141
    (6) 140
    (7) 136, 141, 143, 154, 354, 414, 426, 434
    (9) 141, 142
    (10) 141, 142
    (11) 142
s. 47 .... 11, 52, 99, 113, 129, 141, **142–144**, 170

1989 Children Act (as amended)—
cont.
  s. 47—cont.
    (1) 98, 141, 144, 145
      (b) 49, 129, 130, 145
    (2) 144, 145
    (3) 144, 145
      (c) 141
    (4) 113, 128, 134, 144, 145
    (5) 111, 145
    (6) 144, 145
    (7) 144, 145
    (8) 144, 145
    (9)–(11) 88, 145, 146
    (9) 145
    (10) 145
    (11) 144, 145
    (12) 146
  s. 48 ... 134, **146**, 225, 232, 409, 420,
                                  434, 480
    (1) 147, 148
    (2) 148
    (3)–(8) 148
    (3) 148, 157
    (4) 148, 357, 402
    (5) 148
    (6) 148
    (7) 148
    (9)–(10) 148
    (9)–(13) 148, 232
    (9) 148, 170, 179, 194, 209,
            354, 357, 360, 361, 362, 402,
                             403, 414, 426
    (10) 148
    (13) 148
  s. 49 .... **148–149**, 152, 153, 414
    (1) 149, 152
    (2) 149, 151
  s. 50 ... 148, **149–151**, 153, 156, 225,
         238, 338, 353, 355, 373, 402, 403,
                             416, 432, 480
    (1) 151, 152, 354, 414, 426
    (2) 151
    (3) (b) 151
    (4) 151
    (7) 151
    (9) 151
    (11) 151
    (12) 152
    (13) 151, 237
    (14) 151
  s. 51 .... 12, 139, 140, **152**, 212,
                                          466
    (1) 153, 409, 422
    (2) 153, 409, 422
    (3) 153
    (4) 153
    (7) 153
  s. 52 .... **154**
    (3) 98
  s. 53 .... 60, 70, 90, 153, **155**, 164,
         166, 171, 203, 214, 233, 264, 267,
                             271, 275, 313, 322
    (1)–(5) 156

1989 Children Act (as amended)—
cont.
  s. 53—cont.
    (1) 157, 160, 161, 163, 164,
                             165, 168, 171
    (4) 90, 155, 157, 158,
                             160, 161, 163
    (5) 155, 157, 158, 160, 161,
                                          163
  s. 54 .... **157**
    (2) 161
  s. 55 .... **158**
    (1)–(5) 159
    (6) 159, 160, 163
  s. 56 .... **159**
    (3) 161
    (4) (a) 161, 232
  s. 57 .... **160**
    (2) 161
    (3) 161, 232
    (5) 161
  s. 58 .... **161**, 203, 236
    (1)–(4) 163
    (6) 163
  s. 59 .... **163–164**, 167, 339
  s. 60 ..... 70, 153, **165**, 235, 268, 271,
                                          323
    (3) 159, 164, 165, 171, 200,
                             201, 203
    (5) 209
  s. 61 .... **166**, 174, 210
    (1) (c) 77
    (2) 61
  ss. 62–67 194
  s. 62 .... 166, **167**, 174, 232
    (1) 165, 169
    (2) 169
    (3) 168
    (4) 169, 174
    (5) 169, 178
    (6) 169, 170, 179, 194, 211
    (8) 169
    (9) 169, 170
  s. 63 .... 70, 77, 153, 164, 170–171,
         174, 175, 176, 200, 201, 210, 233,
                             234, 323
    (1) 272, 339
    (3)–(7) 172
    (3)–(9) 171
    (3) 172
    (4)–(7) 172
    (4) 172
      (a) 171
      (b) 171
      (c) 171
    (6) 171, 172, 210
    (7) 172
    (8) 171
    (9) 171
    (10) 172, 339
    (11) 172, 275
    (12) 173, 176, 277
  s. 64 .... **173**, 232
    (1) (c) 77

1989	Children Act (as amended)—cont.	
	s. 64—cont.	
	(2)	61
	(4)	166, 168, 174
	s. 65	**174**, 180, 271
	(3)	175
	(4)	175
	s. 66	77, **175**, 200, 234
	(1)–(4)	183
	(1)	171, 176, 178, 180, 182
	(a)	176
	(2)	176
	(3)	176
	(4)	176, 182
	s. 67	78, 166, 176, **177**, 178, 232, 323
	(1)	178
	(3)–(4)	178, 183
	(3)	179, 182
	(5)	178
	s. 68	166, 174, 175, 176, **179**, 182, 186, 187, 271, 279, 284, 308
	(1)	180, 183
	(2)	187
	(3)	180, 182, 183, 187
	(4)	180
	(5)	180
	s. 69	176, 179, **181–182**, 279, 282
	(2)	182, 183
	(3)–(5)	176
	(3)(a)	182
	(b)	182
	(c)	182
	(4)	182
	(5)–(6)	182
	(6)	176
	(7)	182
	s. 70	181, **182**
	(a)(e)	183
	(1)(a)	178
	(d)	180, 197
	(2)	180
	ss. 71–79	11
	s. 71	**183**, 191, 192, 194, 195, 200, 211, 233, 281, 282, 283
	(1)	56, 186
	(a)	187, 188, 190, 196, 197
	(b)	189, 190, 191, 198, 282, 283, 339
	(2)–(3)	185, 190, 191, 192, 194, 197
	(2)	58, 186
	(a)	185, 188, 191, 194, 197
	(b)	185, 190, 191, 192, 197
	(3)	186, 190
	(4)–(6)	186
	(4)	186
	(5)–(6)	186, 187
	(7)–(8)	191
	(7)–(9)	186
	(7)–(10)	187

1989	Children Act (as amended)—cont.	
	s. 71—cont.	
	(7)	197
	(8)–(10)	186
	(8)–(11)	186
	(11)	186, 187
	(12)	185, 188, 190, 191, 194, 197, 233
	(13)–(14)	186
	(13)	185, 187
	(14)	185, 186
	s. 72	62, **187**, 190, 191, 192, 194, 195, 196, 283
	(1)–(2)	188
	(1)	188
	(2)	190
	(3)	188
	(4)	188
	(5)	188
	(6)	188
	ss. 72 & 73	197
	s. 73	**189**, 190, 191, 192, 194, 195, 196, 283
	(2)	190
	(3)	190
	(4)	190
	(5)	190
	(7)–(8)	190
	s. 74	**190**
	(1)–(2)	191
	(2)–(3)	191
	(4)	191
	(b)	191
	(5)	191
	(6)	192
	s. 75	191, **192**, 434
	(1)	192, 193, 357, 361, 403, 426, 427
	(2)	193
	(3)	193
	(4)	193
	(5)	193
	s. 76	**193**, 232, 283
	(1)–(2)	194
	(3)	194
	(4)	186, 194
	(5)	194
	s. 77	190, 192, **194**, 197
	(1)	195, 432
	(2)	187, 188, 191, 195
	(3)–(4)	195
	(5)	195
	(6)	189, 191, 195, 418, 423, 424, 434
	(7)–(8)	196
	(9)	196
	(10)	196
	(11)	196
	s. 78	**196**
	(2)	197
	(3)–(7)	197
	(4)	197
	(5)	197

Table of Children Act

1989 Children Act (as amended)— cont.
s. 78—cont.
- (6) 197
- (7) 197
- (8) 196, 197
- (9) 197
- (10)–(11) 197
- (12) 197
  - (a) 197
  - (b) 197
  - (c) 197
- s. 79 .... 58, **197**
- s. 80 .... 165, **198**, 232
  - (1)–(5) 200
  - (1) 200
    - (c) 165
    - (h) 237
      - (i) 237
  - (2)–(4) 237
  - (4)–(5) 165, 200
  - (5)(a) 237
    - (b) 237
    - (h) 237
  - (6)–(12) 237
  - (6) 165, 200
  - (7) 200
  - (8) 200
  - (11)–(12) 200
- s. 81 .... **201**
  - (1)(d) 201
    - (f) 201
  - (4) 202
  - (5) 201
- s. 82 .... **202–203**
  - (1) 203
  - (2) 203, 236
  - (3) 163, 203
  - (4) 163, 203, 236
  - (5) 163, 201, 203
  - (6) 203, 205
- s. 83 .... **203**
  - (3)–(6) 205
  - (8) 205
  - (9) 202
- s. 84 .... 52, 56, **205**, 228, 232
  - (4) 205
- ss. 85–86 207
- ss. 85–87 145
- s. 85 ... 12, 51, 77, 79, 166, **206**, 208, 209
  - (1) 207
    - (a) 340
  - (2) 207
  - (3) 207
    - (b) 207
  - (4) 207, 211
  - (5) 211
- s. 86 .... 12, 51, 77, 79, 166, **207**, 232
  - (1)–(2) 208
  - (1)(a) 340
  - (3) 208
  - (4)–(8) 208
  - (5) 208, 209

1989 Children Act (as amended)— cont.
s. 86—cont.
- (6)–(8) 208–209
- s. 87 ..... 12, 166, 172, 176, **209**, 232, 310
  - (1) 210
  - (2) 210
  - (3) 210
  - (5)–(6) 210
  - (9) 210
  - (10) 210
- s. 88 .... **211**, 237, 284, 295
  - (2) 13
- s. 89 .... 13, **212**, 236
- s. 90 .... **213**
  - (2) 340
- s. 91 .... 45, **214**, 217, 332, 336
  - (1) 118, 216
  - (2) 32, 33, 106, 216
  - (3) 216
  - (4) 216
  - (5) 216
  - (6) 216
  - (7) 23
  - (8) 23, 216
  - (10) 32, 33, 39, 216
  - (11) 32, 33, 216
  - (12) 216
  - (13) 108, 216
  - (14)–(17) 216
  - (14) 17, 105, 216
  - (15) 118, 128, 216, 357, 358
  - (16) 216
  - (17) 105, 216, 357, 358
- s. 92 .... 12, 97, 106, 196, **216**, 299
  - (1) 217, 434
  - (2) 217
  - (3) 217
  - (4) 217
  - (5) 217
  - (7) 15, 23, 26, 28, 29, 38, 42, 44, 48, 80, 95, 99, 104, 108, 110, 113, 116, 118, 120, 122, 127, 133, 137, 147, 151, 192, 194, 217, 219, 221, 223, 227, 232
  - (9)–(10) 430
- s. 93 .... 107, 117, 154, **218**
  - (2) 219
    - (i) 356
  - (3) 219, 355
- s. 94 ... 11, 12, 81, 95, 109, **219**, 229, 404, 405, 406, 480
  - (1) 120, 220, 221
  - (2) 221
  - (3) 221
  - (4)–(8) 221
  - (6) 221
  - (7) 221
  - (8) 221
  - (9) 221
  - (10) 221
  - (11) 221

1989	Children Act (as amended)— cont.		1989	Children Act (as amended)— cont.	
	s. 94—cont.			s. 105—cont.	
	(14)	228		(1)—cont.	
	s. 95	**221**, 390			164, 165, 167, 168, 171, 174,
	(1)	222			176, 178, 180, 182, 183, 185,
	(2)	222			188, 190, 191, 192, 194, 197,
	(4)	222			200, 201, 203, 205, 206, 207,
	(5)	222			208, 210, 221, 225, 226, 227,
	(6)	222			260, 263, 318, 374, 376
	s. 96	29, 123, 138, **222**, 229		(3)	26, 31, 38, 42, 44, 45, 60, 104
	(1)	223		(4)	65, 76, 80. 85, 89, 90
	(2)	223		(5)	64, 65, 85
	(a)	223		(6)	60, 91, 93, 95, 113, 140, 144
	(b)	223		(7)	60
	(3)–(7)	13, 223, 236		(8)–(10)	186, 195
	(3)	223, 429		(8)	369, 371
	(4)	223, 224		s. 106	**236**
	(5)	224		(2)	163
	(7)	223		s. 107	13, 232, **236**
	s. 97	**224**		s. 108	**236**
	(2)	225		(1)–(3)	237, 238
	(3)	225		(2)	13, 223, 232
	(4)	225, 232		(4)	299
	(5);	225		(5)	308
	(8)	225		(6)	323
	s. 98	**225**		(8)	237, 238
	s. 99	82, **226**, 342		(9)	237, 238
	(2)	227		(ii)	13
	(4)	227		(12)	13
	(5)	226		Pt. III	85, 87, 88
	s. 100	11, 63, 81, 95, 137, **227**, 324		Pt. IV	87
	(1)	228		Pt. V	87, 121
	(2)	32, 37, 228		Pt. IX	72
	(b)	62		Sched. 1	34, 46, 54, 66, 92, 156, 180, 215, 216, 238, 311, 327, 373, 412, 423, 439
	(3)	36, 112, 228, 406		para. 1	22, **238**, 240, 241, 242, 243
	(4)	228, 229		(1)	327, 480
	(5)	228, 229		(2)	246
	s. 101	**230**, 236		(a)–(c)	314
	(1)	231		(a)	240, 244
	(b)	238		(b)	240, 243, 244
	(2)	231, 238		(4)	480
	(4)	216, 231		(7)	46, 246
	(5)	231		para. 2	**239**, 241, 242, 243, 246, 479
	(a)(i)	238		(1)	480
	s. 102	109, 148, 170, 179, 200, 209, **231**, 420, 480		(5)	480
	(1)	354, 357, 360, 361, 362, 403, 414, 426, 427		para. 3	**240**
	(6)	194, 232		(1)	244
	s. 103	**232**		(2)	216, 244
	s. 104	200, **232**, 237		para. 4	**240**
	(3)	53		para. 5	**241**
	(4)	67, 223, 452		(6)	242
	s. 105	50, **233**, 237, 246, 316		para. 6	46, **241**, 246
	(1)	15, 18, 19, 21, 23, 26, 28, 29, 31, 35, 38, 44, 45, 48, 50, 56, 58, 60, 64, 65, 70, 77, 80, 85, 88, 89, 90, 91, 93, 94, 95, 99, 101, 104, 108, 110, 113, 118, 120, 125, 127, 133, 137, 140, 144, 147, 149, 151, 153, 154, 156, 157, 159, 160, 161,		(1)	243
				(5)	480
				(7)	480
				(8)	480
				para. 6A	242, 246

1989 Children Act (as amended)—
cont.
Sched. 1—cont.
para. 7 .... 46, **243**
para. 8 .... **243**
(2) 480
para. 9 .... **243**
para. 10 .... **244**
(2) 480
para. 11 .... **244**, 480
para. 12 .... **245**
para. 13 .... **245**
para. 14 .... **280**
(1) 480
para. 15 ...... 33, 47, 228, **246**, 326
para. 16 .... 46, 233, **246**
(1) 354
Sched. 2 .... 64, 146, 156, 169, **246**
para. 1 .... 52, **246**
(2) 87
para. 2 .... 52, **247**
para. 3 .... 53, 186, **247**
para. 4 .... 52, **247**
para. 5 .... 52, 134, **247**
para. 6 .... 52, 88, **248**
para. 7 .... 52, **248**
para. 8 .... 52, **248**
para. 9 .... 52, 54, **248**
para. 10 .... 52, 179, 207, **249**
para. 11 .... 52, 56, 69, **249**
para. 12 .... **249**
para. 13 .... **250**
para. 14 .... **250**
para. 15 .... 11, 71, 74, 104, 105,
107, **250**
para. 16 .... 71, 105, **251**
para. 17 .... 71, **251**, 452
para. 18 .... 71, **252**
para. 19 ..... 73, 74, 101, 120, **252**,
432
(1) 71, 123, 354, 356, 357,
412, 417, 423, 480
(2) 71
(3)–(5) 71
(3) (c), (d) 407
(6) 71
(7) 71
(8) 71
para. 20 .... 71, **253**
(1) (c) 71
para. 21 .... **254**, 255
(6) 92
para. 22 .... **254**, 255, 256
(5) 54
(7) 255
(8) 255, 418
para. 23 .... **255**, 256, 313, 316,
434
(1) 418, 423, 424
(2) 335, 336, 354
(8) 423, 424
(11) 480
para. 24 .... 237, 238, **256**
para. 25 .... **256**, 257

1989 Children Act (as amended)—
cont.
Sched. 2—cont.
Pt. I 50, 51, 52, 54, 169
Pt. II 65, 71, 102, 169
Pt. III 90, 91, 287, 335
Sched. 3 .... 156, **257**, 336
para. 1 .... 108, 119, 234, **257**, 260
para. 2 .... **257**, 314
para. 3 ... 108, 119, **257**, 314, 336,
480
para. 4 .... 116, **257**, **258**
para. 5 .... 116, **257**, **258**
para. 6 .... 108, **259**, 260
(2) 108
(3) 124, 354, 356, 357, 412,
424
para. 7 .... **259**
para. 8 .... 108, 119, **259**
(1) (b) 232
(2) (b) 232
para. 9 .... **259**
para. 10 260
para. 11 260
para. 12 260
para. 13 261
para. 14 261
para. 15 .... **262**
(2) 354, 412, 413, 424, 425,
480
para. 16 .... **262**
para. 17 .... **262**
(1) 354, 412, 413, 424, 425,
480
para. 18 .... **262**
para. 19 263
para. 20 263
para. 21 263
Pt. I 101, 108, 118, 337
Pt. II 101, 108, 118, 337
Pt. III 110, 111, 117
Sched. 4 .... 155, 156, 166, **263**
para. 1 .... 156, **263**
(1) 232
(9) 267
para. 2 .... 156, **264**
para. 3 .... 156, **265**
(3) 157, 158, 159, 160, 161,
267
para. 4 .... 156, 157, **266**
(1) 452
(2) (d) 452
(i) 452
Pt. I 157, 158, 160, 161, 163
Pt. II 158
Sched. 5 .... 165, **267**
para. 1 .... **267**, 268
para. 2 .... **268**
(2) 269
para. 3 .... **268**
para. 4 .... **269**
para. 5 .... **269**
para. 6 .... 156, **269**
(6) 166

Table of Children Act

1989 Children Act (as amended)—
cont.
Sched. 5—cont.
para. 7 .... 166, 168, 267, **270**
   (1) 452
   (2) (f) 452
   (3) 452
para. 8 .... 166, **271**
Pt. I 166
Sched. 6 .... 171, **271**
para. 1 .... 173, **271**
   (2) 173
   (3) 275
   (10) 172
para. 2 .... 173, 271, **272**, 274
para. 3 .... 173, **272**, 275
   (1) 175, 275
para. 4 .... 173, **272**
paras. 5–7 173
para. 5 .... **273**
   (2) 274
para. 6 .... **273**
para. 7 .... **273**
para. 8 .... 173, 174, **274**
   (3) 175
para. 9 .... 173, **274**
para. 10 .... 272, 273, **274**
   (1) 452
   (2) (j) 452
   (3) 452
Pt. I 172
Pt. II 173
Sched. 7 ..... 156, 171, 172, 173, 176
                  275, 280, 339
para. 1 .... **275**
para. 2 .... 173, 176, **276**, 277
para. 3 .... 173, **276**
para. 4 ...... 87, 173, **276**, 277, 279
   (3) 173
   (5) 173
para. 5 .... 173, 176, **276**
para. 6 .... 73, 86, **277**
para. 8 (1) (e) 173
Sched. 8 .... 72, 176, **277**
paras. 1–5 176
para. 1 .... 176, **277**
   (a) 176
para. 2 .... 176, **277**
   (1) (d) 280
   (2) 176
   (a) 176
paras. 3–5 176
para. 3 .... **277**
para. 4 .... **278**
para. 5 .... **278**
para. 6 ... 176, 181, 182, **278**, 279,
                                              280
   (3) 176
   (4) 176
   (6) 281
para. 7 .... 176, 178, **278**
para. 8 ... 176, 179, 180, 181, 182,
                  278, **279**, 434
   (1) 418, 423, 424

1989 Children Act (as amended)—
cont.
Sched. 8—cont.
para. 8—cont.
   (6) 176
   (8) 176
para. 9 .... 176, 198, **280**
para. 10 .... 176, 182, **280**
para. 11 .... 177, **280**
Sched. 9 .... 185, 186, **281**
para. 1 186
   (4) 186
para. 2 .... 186, 194, 196
   (3) 187, 196
   (3)–(5) 196
   (5) 196
paras. 3–5 186
para. 4 186
para. 6 186
para. 7 .... 186, 190
para. 8 186
Sched. 10 .... 211, **284**
para. 14 (1) 212
para. 20 212
para. 21 212
para. 25 212
para. 29 212
Pt. I 211
Pt. II 13, 211, 212
Sched. 11 .... 97, 217, 229, **295**
para. 2 220
para. 4 (2) 217
Pt. I 12, 357, 366, 430
Sched. 12 .... 213, 237, **299**
para. 1 237
para. 5 .... 37, 102, 341
paras. 7–10 .... 237, 238
para. 16 (1) 341
para. 18 .... 237, 238
paras. 22–25 214
para. 23 .... 11, 64, 340
para. 27 .... 151, 237, 238
para. 30 (a) 237
para. 31 17
para. 32 26
para. 35 .... 13, 106, 236
para. 36 .... 13, 236
para. 37 45
paras. 41–44 237
Sched. 13 .... 237, 263, 308
para. 1 330
para. 5 19
para. 8 111
para. 9 210
para. 10 .... 22, 111
para. 11 51
paras. 18–23 237
para. 21 238
para. 22 238
para. 27 51
para. 32 237
para. 46 .... 237, 238
para. 47 237
para. 50 237

1989 Children Act (as amended)—
cont.
Sched. 13—cont.
para. 53 64
para. 57 .... 33, 108, 237, 238
para. 62 .... 237, 238
para. 63 .... 237, 238
para. 68 (a) 237
(b) 237
(c)–(e) 238
para. 69–71 238
para. 71 237
Sched. 14 ..... 12, 237, 318, 322, **323**
para. 1 .... 237, 418
(1A) 324
(2) 324
para. 2 324
para. 3 .... 26, 324
para. 5 (1) 325, 326, 327, 328, 329
(3) 325, 326, 327, 328
paras. 6–11 325
para. 8 (1)–(5) 327
(2) 329, 330
para. 10 (3) 328
para. 11 (3) 329, 354, 423, 480
(b) 412, 424
(4) 357
paras. 12–14 330
para. 12 330
(1) (a) 329
(i) 329

1989 Children Act (as amended)—
cont.
Sched. 14—cont.
para. 15 180
(1) 324, 325
para. 16 331
(3A) 324
(5) 354, 412, 423, 424
(6A) 324
paras. 18, 25, 26 324
paras. 28–30 238
para. 33 237
para. 34 237
para. 38 (a) 238
Sched. 15 .... 26, 64, 96, 111, 237, 238
Pts. I–V 373, 418
Pt. I 324, 432, 439
Pt. II 306, 324, 432, 439
Pt. III 52, 55, 60, 64, 313, 319, 333, 334, 440
Pt. IV–V 392
Pt. IV 34, 302, 309, 318, 324, 330, 332, 333, 336, 337, 338, 440
Pt. V 34, 301, 440
Pts. VII–IX 51
Pts. VII–X 20
Pt. VIII 339
Pt. IX 339
Pt. X 13, 56, 312, 339, 340
Pt. XII 20

Part I

The Children Act 1989 (As Amended)
(1989 c.41)

CHILDREN ACT 1989 (AS AMENDED)

(1989 c. 41)

Arrangement of Sections

Part I

Introductory

Sect.
1. Welfare of the child.
2. Parental responsibility for children.
3. Meaning of "parental responsibility."
4. Acquisition of parental responsibility by father.
5. Appointment of guardians.
6. Guardians: revocation and disclaimer.
7. Welfare reports.

Part II

Orders With Respect to Children in Family Proceedings

General

8. Residence, contact and other orders with respect to children.
9. Restrictions on making section 8 orders.
10. Power of court to make section 8 orders.
11. General principles and supplementary provisions.
12. Residence orders and parental responsibility.
13. Change of child's name or removal from jurisdiction.
14. Enforcement of residence orders.

Financial relief

15. Orders for financial relief with respect to children.

Family assistance orders

16. Family assistance orders.

Part III

Local Authority Support for Children and Families

Provision of services for children and their families

17. Provision of services for children in need, their families and others.
18. Day care for pre-school and other children.

19. Review of provision for day care, child minding, etc.

Provision of accommodation for children

20. Provision of accommodation for children: general.
21. Provision of accommodation for children in police protection or detention or on remand, etc.

Duties of local authorities in relation to children looked after by them

22. General duty of local authority in relation to children looked after by them.
23. Provision of accommodation and maintenance by local authority for children whom they are looking after.

Advice and assistance for certain children

24. Advice and assistance for certain children.

Secure accommodation

25. Use of accommodation for restricting liberty.

Supplemental

26. Review of cases and inquiries into representations.
27. Co-operation between authorities.
28. Consultation with local education authorities.
29. Recoupment of cost of providing services, etc.
30. Miscellaneous.

PART IV

CARE AND SUPERVISION

General

31. Care and supervision orders.
32. Period within which application for order under this Part must be disposed of.

Care orders

33. Effect of care order.
34. Parental contact, etc., with children in care.

Supervision orders

35. Supervision orders.
36. Education supervision orders.

Powers of court

37. Powers of court in certain family proceedings.
38. Interim orders.
39. Discharge and variation, etc., of care orders and supervision orders.
40. Orders pending appeals in cases about care or supervision orders.

Guardians ad litem

41. Representation of child and of his interests in certain proceedings.
42. Right of guardian ad litem to have access to local authority records.

PART V

PROTECTION OF CHILDREN

43. Child assessment orders.
44. Orders for emergency protection of children.
45. Duration of emergency protection orders and other supplemental provisions.
46. Removal and accommodation of children by police in cases of emergency.
47. Local authority's duty to investigate.
48. Powers to assist in discovery of children who may be in need of emergency protection.
49. Abduction of children in care, etc.
50. Recovery of abducted children, etc.
51. Refuges for children at risk.
52. Rules and regulations.

PART VI

COMMUNITY HOMES

53. Provision of community homes by local authorities.
54. Directions that premises be no longer used for community home.
55. Determination of disputes relating to controlled and assisted community homes.
56. Discontinuance by voluntary organisation of controlled or assisted community home.
57. Closure by local authority of controlled or assisted community home.
58. Financial provisions applicable on cessation of controlled or assisted community home or disposal, etc., of premises.

PART VII

VOLUNTARY HOMES AND VOLUNTARY ORGANISATIONS

59. Provision of accommodation by voluntary organisations.
60. Registration and regulation of voluntary homes.
61. Duties of voluntary organisations.
62. Duties of local authorities.

PART VIII

REGISTERED CHILDREN'S HOMES

63. Children not to be cared for and accommodated in unregistered children's homes.

64. Welfare of children in children's homes.
65. Persons disqualified from carrying on, or being employed in, children's homes.

Part IX

Private Arrangements for Fostering Children

66. Privately fostered children.
67. Welfare of privately fostered children.
68. Persons disqualified from being private foster parents.
69. Power to prohibit private fostering.
70. Offences.

Part X

Child Minding and Day Care for Young Children

71. Registration.
72. Requirements to be complied with by child minders.
73. Requirements to be complied with by persons providing day care for young children.
74. Cancellation of registration.
75. Protection of children in an emergency.
76. Inspection.
77. Appeals.
78. Offences.
79. Application of this Part to Scotland.

Part XI

Secretary of State's Supervisory Functions and Responsibilities

80. Inspection of children's homes, etc., by persons authorised by Secretary of State.
81. Inquiries.
82. Financial support by Secretary of State.
83. Research and returns of information.
84. Local authority failure to comply with statutory duty: default power of Secretary of State.

Part XII

Miscellaneous and General

Notification of children accommodated in certain establishments

85. Children accommodated by health authorities and local education authorities.
86. Children accommodated in residential care, nursing or mental nursing homes.

87. Welfare of children accommodated in independent schools.

Adoption

88. Amendments of adoption legislation.

Paternity tests

89. Tests to establish paternity.

Criminal care and supervision orders

90. Care and supervision orders in criminal proceedings.

Effect and duration of orders, etc.

91. Effect and duration of orders, etc.

Jurisdiction and procedure etc.

92. Jurisdiction of courts.
93. Rules of court.
94. Appeals.
95. Attendance of child at hearing under Part IV or V.
96. Evidence given by, or with respect to, children.
97. Privacy for children involved in certain proceedings.
98. Self-incrimination.
99. Legal aid.
100. Restrictions on use of wardship jurisdiction.
101. Effect of orders as between England and Wales and Northern Ireland, the Channel Islands or the Isle of Man.

Search warrants

102. Power of constable to assist in exercise of certain powers to search for children or inspect premises.

General

103. Offences by bodies corporate.
104. Regulations and orders.
105. Interpretation.
106. Financial provisions.
107. Application to Channel Islands.
108. Short title, commencement, extent, etc.

SCHEDULES

Schedule 1— Financial Provision for Children.
Schedule 2— Local Authority Support for Children and Families.
 Part I— Provision of Services for Families.
 Part II— Children Looked After by Local Authorities.
 Part III— Contributions Towards Maintenance of Children.
Schedule 3— Supervision Orders.
 Part I— General.
 Part II— Miscellaneous.
 Part III— Education Supervision Orders.
Schedule 4— Management and Conduct of Community Homes.

Part I—	Instruments of Management.
Part II—	Management of Controlled and Assisted Community Homes.
Part III—	Regulations.
Schedule 5—	Voluntary Homes.
Part I—	Registration of Voluntary Homes.
Part II—	Regulations as to Voluntary Homes.
Schedule 6—	Registered Children's Homes.
Part I—	Registration.
Part II—	Regulations.
Schedule 7—	Foster Parents: Limits on Number of Foster Children.
Schedule 8—	Privately Fostered Children.
Schedule 9—	Child Minding and Day Care for Young Children.
Schedule 10—	Amendments of Adoption Legislation.
Part I—	Amendments of Adoption Act 1976.
Part II—	Amendments of Adoption (Scotland) Act 1978.
Schedule 11—	Jurisdiction.
Part I—	General.
Part II—	Consequential Amendments.
Schedule 12—	Minor Amendments.
Schedule 13—	Consequential Amendments.
Schedule 14—	Transitionals and Savings.
Schedule 15—	Repeals.

An Act to reform the law relating to children; to provide for local authority services for children in need and others; to amend the law with respect to children's homes, community homes, voluntary homes and voluntary organisations; to make Provision with respect to fostering, child minding and day care for young children and adoption; and for connected purposes. [16th November 1989]

PARLIAMENTARY DEBATES

Hansard, H.L. Vol. 502, cols. 21, 487, 1130, 1147, 1225, 1252, 1341; Vol. 503, cols. 113, 209, 333, 496, 549, 1318, 1409, 1438, 1533; Vol. 504, col. 294; Vol. 505, col. 341; Vol. 512, col. 717; H.C. Vol. 151, col. 1107; Vol. 158, cols. 474, 619, 1288.
The Bill was considered in Standing Committee B from May 9 to June 13, 1989.

INTRODUCTION AND GENERAL NOTE

Introduction
"The most comprehensive and far reaching reform of child law which has come before Parliament in living memory." *Per* Lord Mackay (*Hansard*, H.L. Vol. 502, col. 488).
This Act reforms and brings together the public and private law relating to children. The reforms to private law are those recommended by the Law Commission in their report "Review of Child Law: Guardianship and Custody," Law Com. No. 172. It substantially recasts child care law following many of the recommendations in the Department of Health and Social Security (D.H.S.S.) *Review of Child Care Law* and the White Paper *The Law on Child Care and Family Services* (1987) Cm. 62. It repeals and replaces the Guardianship of Minors Act 1971, the Guardianship Act 1973, much of the Children and Young Persons Act 1969 and all of the Nurseries and Childminders Regulation Act 1948, the Children Act 1975, the Child Care Act 1980, the Foster Children Act 1980, the Children's Homes Act 1982 and the Children and Young Persons (Amendment) Act 1986. The only area of child law to which there are few changes is child support; this is radically reformed by the Child Support Act 1991 which will be implemented in 1993.
The Act is divided into 12 parts, each one relating to a different aspect of child law, but, as the Lord Chancellor repeatedly stated during its passage through Parliament, it must be read as a whole. It is important to note that the provisions of Part I inform the interpretation of the Act generally by stating the principles which the courts must apply

in considering certain cases concerning children—the welfare principle, the non-intervention principle—and defining the rights of parents and guardians. The Schedules contain important details of the private law of child support, local authorities' duties to children in the community and to children they are looking after and the duties of other people and organisations caring for children. Many of the detailed rules which are necessary to bring this law into operation relating to, for example, party status and the jurisdiction of the courts are left to regulations. The Department of Health has also issued 10 volumes of guidance relating to the Act under its powers in the Local Authorities Social Services Act 1970, s.7.

Background

Concern about the state of child care law expressed by the Short Committee led to the setting up of the D.H.S.S. *Review of Child Care Law* in 1984. The law was seen as providing an inadequate framework for child protection and preventive work and failing to facilitate parental involvement in the lives of children accommodated by local authorities. It was also far too complex with a collection of sometimes contradictory provisions in different statutes. *The Review of Child Care Law* (R.C.C.L.) recommended major changes to child care law, many of which were accepted by the Government in the White Paper which followed (Cm. 62). The reports of three child death inquiries concerning Jasmine Beckford, Kimberley Carlile and Tyra Henry strengthened views that the law should be clarified and the powers of social workers increased. The Cleveland crisis and the subsequent inquiry turned attention to control of social work decision-making particularly by strengthening the position of the courts. However, despite the many recommendations in these reports, the Children Act 1989 is largely based on the proposals in the White Paper and the R.C.C.L.

In 1984 the Law Commission started a wide ranging review of private law as part of its family law programme. This provided the opportunity not only to reform the law but also to ensure harmonisation between the public and private law relating to children. Report No. 172, containing the Law Commission's recommendations, was published in 1988.

Overview

The aim of the legislation is to provide a clear and consistent code for the whole of child law which is comprehensible to all who deal with this area; to avoid problems caused by conflicting powers in public and private law and the confusion engendered by conflicting jurisdiction over children's cases. It realigns the balance between families and the State so as to protect families from unwarranted State interference, to emphasise that local authorities have an important role in supporting families in difficulty and to indicate that there is a continuing role for parents when their children are looked after by a local authority. Local authorities cannot by-pass the statutory code by resorting to wardship. The legislation also adjusts the relative power and responsibilities of local authorities and the courts. It will no longer be possible for a court to commit a child into the care of a local authority without a formal application from either the authority or the N.S.P.C.C. Instead, a court concerned about the care of a child will be able to order the local authority to investigate the situation and report back. The High Court will not be able to commit wards to local authority care. Court orders will be needed to retain a child in compulsory care in all cases but local authority decision-making about children in care will not be subject to court direction or review even from the High Court, except in relation to access and emigration.

Private Law

(1) Parental responsibility (ss.2–6)

The "bundle of rights" held by married parents, guardians and those with court orders is labelled "parental responsibility" but not defined in detail in the statute. Unmarried fathers may acquire parental responsibility by a formal agreement under section 4. Parental responsibility can be held by a number of people; parents and guardians do not lose it when others acquire it (except if there is an adoption order), nor when a care order is made, but their freedom to exercise it is restricted. Local authorities acquire parental responsibility whenever a care order is made or they obtain an emergency protection order.

(2) Court orders (ss.8 and 16)

"Section 8" orders can be made in any family proceedings to regulate arrangements about children and the exercise of parental responsibility. These are *residence orders* which replace orders for custody, custodianship, care and control, etc., *contact orders* which replace access orders, *prohibited steps orders*, a type of injunction and *specific issue orders*, where the court decides a particular question about care. There is also a power to make *family assistance orders* which replace supervision orders in family proceedings.

(3) Family proceedings and the right to apply (ss.8–10)

The courts may exercise their powers to grant section 8 orders in a wide range of family disputes whether or not an application has been made. Limitations on applications for court orders are lifted. Parents, step-parents, guardians, long-term carers and people with their consent can apply for "residence" or "contact orders" without leave. Other people, grandparents, foster parents and the child must seek leave. Wardship remains available but no longer has many advantages.

Public Law: Care

The new provisions are based on the concept of partnerships—(1) a partnership between local authorities and parents which supports children who need help within their families, encourages the maintenance of links with the family when children are looked after by the local authority and facilitates reunification of the family. (2) A partnership between local authorities and the children they look after which seeks to involve children in decisions made about them, to value children's individual identity and to ensure that they are prepared for adulthood. (3) A partnership between local authority social services departments, other local authority departments (*e.g.* housing and education), other agencies and the voluntary and independent sectors so that a "seamless service" is provided for children who need help and their families.

(1) Looking after children (ss.20 and 22)

Local authorities are to continue to look after children. Where this is by agreement with the parents, children are "accommodated" by the local authority and the arrangement is voluntary. No notice is required to remove the child; children over 16 years cannot be removed against their will. In all other cases a care order is necessary (s.31). Only children who are committed to care under a care order are referred to as "in care." Children cared for by a local authority in exercise of its functions under the Act are referred to as children "looked after by the local authority" (s.22).

(2) Support for "children in need"

Local authorities owe new duties to "safeguard and promote" the welfare of all "children in need," to provide services to them and to promote their upbringing by their families (s.17). Families cannot be required to accept services unless a care or supervision order is made. The emphasis on agreed service provision is intended to avoid the need for orders.

(3) Duties to children who are looked after

The duty to give "first consideration" to the welfare of a child in care in section 18 of the Child Care Act 1980 is replaced by a duty to "safeguard and promote" the welfare of any child "looked after" by the authority (s.22). There are new duties to consult parents and children, to consider their race, religion, culture and language (s.22), to place children with siblings and near family and home (s.23), to provide a complaints system (s.26), to prepare children to leave care and to advise, etc., people under 21 who have been in care (s.24). There is a new power in the Secretary of State to deal with local authorities who are in default (s.84).

(4) Care and supervision orders (s.31)

The grounds for these are completely recast. Truancy cases will be dealt with by "education supervision orders" (s.36), although prosecution of parents (and in some cases care orders) will continue to be available. Local authorities will be able to appeal against refusal of a care order and the order may be continued pending the appeal (ss.94, 40).

The test for interim care and supervision orders is clarified—the court must be satisfied that there are "reasonable grounds for believing" that the grounds in section 31 exist. New time limits are set—the maximum duration for the first interim order is eight weeks and for subsequent orders four weeks, but there is no limit on the number of subsequent orders.

(5) Investigation and assessment (ss.38, 43 and 47)

The local authority's responsibilities in investigating cases where a child may be harmed are clarified. They have a duty to see the child. Where an assessment is necessary, but the parents refuse to agree, the applicant may seek a "child assessment order" lasting up to seven days (s.43). Courts may order an investigation in any family proceedings (s.38).

(6) Emergency protection (ss.44–46)

There is a new order which may be granted either *ex parte* or *inter partes* in cases where children need to be protected. Emergency protection orders last for eight days, can be extended for seven days, and are subject to review after 72 hours. The test for an emergency protection order appears more stringent—the court, not the applicant, must have "reasonable cause to believe that the child is likely to suffer significant harm"—but an order may be available where access to the child has been unreasonably refused. Police powers to detain children for their protection are limited to 72 hours.

(7) Use of wardship (s.100)

Children may no longer be committed to care in wardship proceedings. Local authorities are restricted severely in their use of wardship and will require leave to make an application.

(8) Contact with children in care (s.34)

Local authorities are under a duty to "endeavour to promote contact" between children looked after by them and a wide range of family members and friends (Sched. 2, para. 15). Care orders will automatically include a provision allowing the child reasonable contact with parents, guardians, etc. Disagreements about contact and its termination go to court.

(9) Juvenile justice

Care orders in criminal proceedings (s.7(7)) are abolished and replaced by supervision orders with a residence requirement (Sched. 12, para. 23).

Public Law: Day Care

(1) Local authority duties

There is a qualified duty to provide day care for under fives and supervised activities for older children who are in need. There is a power to provide for others (s.17). Local authorities must review the day care provision in their area at least every three years (s.19).

(2) Childminding and nurseries (ss.71–79)

Local authorities' powers and duties to register and inspect day care provision are clarified. Registration is now required in relation to care of children under the age of eight years. A new enforcement notice procedure is created to deal with unregistered childminders.

Public Law: Other Care

Local authorities are given new responsibilities for the welfare of children cared for by health authorities or local education authorities (s.85) and for children in residential care homes, nursing homes or mental nursing homes (s.86) and for children in independent boarding schools (s.87). Aftercare must also be provided (s.24). Those providing care must notify the local authority. The Act makes provision for safe houses for runaways (s.51).

Proceedings under the Children Act

A new structure for dealing with cases under this Act and the Adoption Act 1976 is established.

(1) Triple jurisdiction

The family proceedings court (part of the magistrates' court), the county court and the High Court will all be able to hear cases under the Act. Specific courts have been designated care centres or family hearing centres. Appeals in care cases will be heard in the High Court, not the Crown Court (s.94). Comparable rules of procedure and the same rules of evidence will apply throughout the system.

(2) Allocation and transfer

Rules have been made relating to the allocation and transfer of cases. Public law cases will usually start in the family proceedings court but may be transferred to specified county courts or the High Court if appropriate (s.92 and Sched. 11, Pt. I). There are no restrictions on the court in which private law cases are started but most of the advantages of the High Court's inherent jurisdiction are given by the Act to the lower courts.

(3) New procedures

The court rules make substantial changes to the way cases are conducted in the courts, with greater reliance on written materials in the family proceedings court, directions hearings to clarify issues and process and strict timetabling. These are fully discussed in Part II of this book.

(4) The Guardian ad litem Service (ss.41, 42)

The service has been extended to cover a wider range of public law "specified proceedings" including applications for emergency protection orders, secure accommodation orders and appeals. The duties of guardians ad litem have been expanded to include a greater case management role, but the central concepts of representing the child and advising the court remain. Guardians continue to be provided from panels set up by local authorities. Guardians ad litem are given statutory rights of access to case records. Local authorities have no obligations to provide panel guardians for private law cases, children will not usually be parties to these.

(5) New Committees

In order to facilitate co-operation between the different levels of court and ensure a smooth operation of the Act three types of committee have been established: the Children Act Advisory Committee, Family Court Services Committees and Family Court Business Committees (one in each Care Centre).

Transitional Provisions

These are set out in Schedule 14. Existing private law orders will continue to have effect subject to modification-non-custodial parents will have parental responsibility. Existing public law orders or resolutions will be deemed to be care orders.

Commencement

Commencement orders: S.I. 1991 No. 828; S.I. 1991 No. 1990 appointed October 14, 1991 as the date for commencement. Sections 89, 96(3)–(7) and Schedule 12, paragraph 35 which relate to tests to establish paternity, children's evidence and the definition of "parent" in the Child Care Act 1980 came into force on November 16, 1989. Schedule 12, paragraph 36 which empowers local education authorities to pay for special education overseas came into effect on January 16, 1990 (s.108(2)). Section 5(11) and (12) which empowers the High Court to appoint a guardian for a child's property came into force on February 1, 1992. No parts of the Act remain unimplemented but not all of the powers to make regulations have been exercised.

Extent (s.108)

The whole Act applies to England and Wales, Pt. X which relates to nurseries and childminders and other provisions listed in section 108(11), applies to Scotland. The Adoption (Scotland) Act is amended by section 88(2) and Schedule 10, Part II. The provisions listed in section 108(12) apply to Northern Ireland. Parts of the Act may be extended to the Channel Islands by Order (s.107).

ABBREVIATIONS

C.C.A. 1980:	Child Care Act 1980.
C.Y.P.A. 1933:	Children and Young Persons Act 1933.
C.Y.P.A. 1969:	Children and Young Persons Act 1969.
Cleveland Report:	Report of the Inquiry into child abuse in Cleveland 1987 (Cm. 412 1988).
Cm. 62:	The Law on Child Care and Family Services.
D.H.S.S.:	Department of Health and Social Security.
D.P.M.C.A. 1978:	Domestic Proceedings and Magistrates' Courts Act 1978.
D.V.M.P.A. 1976:	Domestic Violence and Matrimonial Proceedings Act 1976.
F.L.R.A. 1987:	Family Law Reform Act 1987.
G.M.A. 1971:	Guardianship of Minors Act 1971.
H.F.E.A. 1990:	Human Fertilisation and Embryology Act 1990.
Law Com. 172:	Law Commission Report No. 172: Review of Child Law: Guardianship and Custody (1988).
GaL Manual:	Manual of Practice Guidance for Guardians ad litem and Reporting Officers (1992).
M.C.A. 1973:	Matrimonial Causes Act 1973.
N.S.P.C.C.:	National Society for the Prevention of Cruelty to Children.
R.C.C.L.:	D.H.S.S. Review of Child Care Law (1985).
Short Committee:	House of Commons Second Report from the Social Services Committee 1983–4: Children in care H.C.P. 360.
Utting Report:	Children in the Public Care, H.M.S.O. (1991).
W.P. 91:	Law Commission Working Paper No. 91, Review of Child Law: Guardianship (1985).
W.P. 96:	Law Commission Working Paper No. 96, Review of Child Law: Custody (1986).

GUIDANCE

The Department of Health has published the following Guidance under its power in the Local Authority Social Services Act 1970, s.7:

Working Together Under the Children Act 1989: a guide to arrangements for interagency co-operation for the protection of children from abuse (1991).

Children Act Guidance and Regulations:

Vol. 1: Court orders.
Vol. 2: Family Support Day Care and Educational Provision for Young Children.
Vol. 3: Family Placement.

Vol. 4: Residential Care.
Vol. 5: Independent Schools.
Vol. 6: Children with disabilities.
Vol. 7: Guardians ad litem and other court related issues.
Vol. 8: Private Fostering and Miscellaneous.
Vol. 9: Adoption issues.
Vol. 10: Index (forthcoming).

Volumes 3–9 also include copies of the relevant regulations. There is considerable duplication between volumes so that each can stand alone in relation to its topic.

The Department of Health and Social Services Inspectorate have also published other material which informs child care practice under the Act:

DH The Care of Children: Principles and Practice in Regulations and Guidance (1989).
DH Patterns and Outcomes in Child Placement (1991).
SSI Inspecting for Quality (1991).
DH The Welfare of Children and Young People in Hospital (1991).
DH Manual of Practice Guidance for Guardians ad litem and Reporting Officers (1992).
DH Manual of Management for GALRO Panel Managers (1992).
DH Working with Child Sexual Abuse — Guidelines for trainers and managers in Social Services Departments (1992).
Home Office & DH Video Recorded Interviews Memorandum of Good Practice (1992).
Parker et al Assessing outcomes in child care (1991).

The Department of Health is continuing to prepare advice and guidance relevant to the Act. A new edition of Reports to the Courts (1987) will be published.

PART I

INTRODUCTORY

Welfare of the child

1.—(1) When a court determines any question with respect to—
  (a) the upbringing of a child; or
  (b) the administration of a child's property or the application of any income arising from it, the child's welfare shall be the court's paramount consideration.

(2) In any proceedings in which any question with respect to the upbringing of a child arises, the court shall have regard to the general principle that any delay in determining the question is likely to prejudice the welfare of the child.

(3) In the circumstances mentioned in subsection (4), a court shall have regard in particular to—
  (a) the ascertainable wishes and feelings of the child concerned (considered in the light of his age and understanding);
  (b) his physical, emotional and educational needs;
  (c) the likely effect on him of any change in his circumstances;
  (d) his age, sex, background and any characteristics of his which the court considers relevant;
  (e) any harm which he has suffered or is at risk of suffering;
  (f) how capable each of his parents, and any other person in relation to whom the court considers the question to be relevant, is of meeting his needs;
  (g) the range of powers available to the court under this Act in the proceedings in question.

(4) The circumstances are that—
  (a) the court is considering whether to make, vary or discharge a section 8 order, and the making, variation or discharge of the order is opposed by any party to the proceedings; or
  (b) the court is considering whether to make, vary or discharge an order under Part IV.

(5) Where a court is considering whether or not to make one or more orders under this Act with respect to a child, it shall not make the order or any of the orders unless it considers that doing so would be better for the child than making no order at all.

DEFINITIONS
"child": ss.9(6), 105(1).
"harm": ss.31(9), 105(1).
"section 8 order": ss.8, 11(7).
"the court": s.92(7).
"upbringing": s.105(1).

GENERAL NOTE
This section lays down general principles for courts dealing with cases involving children. It warns courts that delay is likely to prejudice the welfare of the child (subs. (2)). It re-enacts, with modification (removing the word custody—the concept of custody forms no part of the new code), G.M.A. 1971, s.1(1) and expands the meaning of welfare by providing a checklist (subs. (3)) to assist the courts in specific contested cases (subs. (4)) as recommended in Law Com. 172, para. 3.17. In all cases the court is expressly required to consider whether or not any order should be made (subs. (5)).

Subs. (1)

Any question: It has been suggested that there are some questions relating to children which are not governed by the paramountcy rules: the decision whether or not a book about a child's father should be banned (*Re X* [1975] Fam. 47 *per* Pennycuick J.). Also, a decision to grant leave under section 10(8) or (9), see *J.R.* v. *Merton L.B.* [1992] 2 F.C.R. 174.

In *Richards* v. *Richards* [1984] A.C. 174 the majority of the House of Lords held that a child's welfare was not paramount in any case concerning an exclusion injunction which fell to be decided under the Matrimonial Homes Act 1983, s.1(3). This was extended in *Lee* v. *Lee* (1983) 127 S.J. 696 to exclusion orders sought by an unmarried person but there have been suggestions in the Court of Appeal that in some ouster cases the child's welfare is paramount (*Wilde* v. *Wilde* (1988) 18 Fam. Law 202). The wide power to make residence orders may again encourage the courts to attempt to side-step *Richards* by including a term that one parent must leave the place where the child is living (see the discussion of section 8 orders below). Maintenance is excluded from the definition of upbringing in the Act. Orders relating to maintenance after divorce are also not subject to the test in section 1 but to the requirement in the M.C.A. 1973, s.25(1) to give "first consideration" to welfare. Under the Child Support Act 1991, s.8, the court's jurisdiction to make orders for the maintenance of children is restricted. Most cases of maintenance will be dealt with by the Child Support Agency which is expected to be operational in April 1993.

Upbringing: The Lord Chancellor said this is "a word of general scope" which includes "education and social life while being reared" (*Hansard*, H.L. Vol. 502, col. 1168). It does not include maintenance. The word "custody" has been removed because this concept no longer forms part of child law.

The child's welfare: A child is anyone under the age of 18 years, but the court's power to make orders is restricted by section 9(7) to under 16s unless the case is exceptional. This would seem to put an added gloss on the welfare test. Welfare is not defined but the checklist in subsection (4) indicates some of the issues which may be relevant. Case law will continue to suggest what the judiciary consider to be in children's welfare; psychological and other literature will provide a basis for argument.

Paramount: This does not mean "first and paramount," which Lord Scarman described as a pleonism (*Hansard*, H.L. Vol. 502, col. 1165). "First and paramount" was explained by Lord MacDermott in *J. v. C.* [1970] A.C. 668. The Law Commission noted some confusion from the inclusion of "first" (Law Com. 172, para. 3.13) and proposed a statutory version of the modern accepted interpretation found in cases such as *Re K.D.* [1988] A.C. 806. In the debate the Lord Chancellor explained the new wording as follows (*Hansard*, H.L. Vol. 502, col. 1167): "the welfare of the child should come before and above any other consideration in deciding whether to make an order." Thus the new wording should leave welfare determining decisions and not just heading a list of factors to be considered. The Law Commission also recommended a provision which would indicate how the court should approach cases involving more than one child where the welfare of each conflicted. No such provision was included in the Act so each case must be considered individually without regard to the effect on other children.

Subs. (2)

This may be used to justify a refusal to order reports but is intended to promote prompt action. It may further discourage the practice of adjourning applications generally rather than dismissing them which has been criticised by the Court of Appeal *Re C* [1992] 1 F.L.R. 1. However in *Re C.* (unreported) noted in [1992] N.L.J. 837 Ward J. accepted that delay to allow the completion of an assessment could be beneficial. The Family Proceedings Court (*Children Act* 1989) Rules 1991, r.15 makes provisions for the timetabling of proceedings (see p. 391 below). The Lord Chancellor has stated that legal representatives who do not come with the necessary information can expect "brisk treatment" *per* Lord Mackay [1991] Fam. Law 455; see also the Family Proceedings (Costs) Rules 1991, r.3 (p. 474 below).

Subs. (3)

The value of a checklist was explained in Law Com. 172, para. 3.18. It can guide the courts and help achieve consistency across the country, inform legal advisers and encourage those in dispute to concentrate on the issues which affect their children.

Regard in particular: Other aspects may be considered.

Ascertainable: There is greater emphasis in the Act on consulting children and finding out their views. The courts should not merely suggest that a child is too young to be consulted, nor should they rely on what a parent says the child wants. Guardians ad litem in care proceedings attempt to discover the views of children as young as three years old. The power in section 7(1) to ask for a report from a welfare officer will be very useful, and it will also be important for counsel to be well-versed in the methods used by social workers and others to find out what children want. The court is not constrained by those wishes and should disregard them if the child's welfare so demands *per* Butler-Sloss. L.J., *Re P (Minors)* unreported April 29, 1992, but must do more than pay lipservice to them *M* v. *M The Times* August 12, 1992.

Needs: The emphasis should be on an objective assessment of the needs of the individual child but there is a danger that subjectivity in the form of preferences for particular life-styles might be introduced here, as in *May* v. *May* [1986] 1 F.L.R. 325. Again, it will be important to see the reasons given for identifying particular needs.

Likely effect: Again, evidence should be required.

Any change: There was clear evidence from Eekelaar and Clive, *Custody after divorce* (1977) that the status quo was an extremely important factor in determining custody in the past. Child psychologists have also stressed the importance of stability and continuity for healthy development.

Parents: Increasingly the courts appear to be stressing the value for children of being brought up within their natural families, particularly by parents rather than by other people. *Re K. (A Minor) (Ward: Care and Control)* [1990] 2 F.L.R. 64 (C.A.); *Re L. (A Minor) (Care Proceedings: Wardship) (No. 2.)* [1991] 1 F.L.R. 29; *cf. Re H. (A Minor) (Custody)* [1990] 1 F.L.R. 51. Mothers are prefered for babies, *Re W. The Times* May 22, 1992.

Any other person: There is a power in section 10(1)(b) to make orders in favour of any person even without a formal application, *e.g.* partners of parents.

The range of powers: Under the Act, the range of powers is wider than in the previous law. The court can grant anyone any section 8 order (s.10(1)(b)), even where there has been no application, and make the new "family assistance orders" (s.16). The orders themselves allow the court to direct matters to a greater extent. The court also has a power to prevent further applications under Parts I and II without leave, that is, applications for parental responsibility (s.4), guardianship (s.5) and section 8 orders (s.91(14)).

Subs. (4)

The Law Commission was concerned that the court should not impose its notion of welfare on parties, provided of course, that their proposals were acceptable. This would put too great a burden on the court (Law Com. 172, para. 3.19). The checklist in subs. (3) is only mandated where the court is considering a contested section 8 order, a care order, a supervision or education supervision order, or an order relating to contact with a child in care. However, the Lord Chancellor suggested that the court could refer to it in other cases (*Hansard*, H.L. Vol. 502, col. 1203), but this does not appear clear from the wording. In so far as the checklist contains a definition of welfare, this may be so, but the courts would appear to be free to disregard listed factors or consider others where the checklist is not mandated, *e.g.* in contested applications by unmarried fathers for parental responsibility (s.4) or disputes about guardianship (s.5).

Opposed by any party to the proceedings: The parties to the proceedings are listed in the Family Proceedings Courts (*Children Act* 1989) Rules 1991, r. 7 and Sched. 2, col. iii (see p. 420). Children will not automatically be parties in private law cases concerning their upbringing or property but will be in "specified" (public law) proceedings (see p. 357).

Subs. (5)

This reflects the Law Commission's view that orders were sometimes unnecessary and could discourage parties negotiating arrangements and remaining involved with their children after separation or divorce (see s.10(1)). Accordingly M.C.A. 1973, s.41, has also been amended, see Schedule 12, paragraph 31. However, it has been suggested that this principle of non-intervention may undermine the paramountcy of the child's welfare: Bainham, "The Privatisation of the Public Interest in Children" (1990) 53 M.L.R. 206–221.

This principle applies to all orders under the Children Act but not the making of an adoption order even though a section 8 order may be made in adoption proceedings. In care and related proceedings it requires the court to consider whether an agreement between the parents and the local authority would adequately protect the child; whether the order will provide additional protection or services for the child, and whether such provision is likely to be beneficial to the child.

It is important to note that there are some undesirable consequences of not obtaining an order. Non-parents who look after children without a residence order will not have parental responsibility for the child. This affects their rights in relation to the parents, the local authority and the child. Where a parent has a residence order, the other parent's actions are limited generally by section 2(8) and specifically by section 5 (circumstances when an appointment of a guardian takes effect) and section 13 (covers name change and removal from the jurisdiction). Children may feel less secure if there is no order. If there is a possibility of abduction, the existence of an order will be important for recovery of the child abroad under the Child Abduction and Custody Act 1985. An order is not necessary for removal of the child to be illegal under the Child Abduction Act 1984. Such removal would thus be wrongful under Article 3 of the Hague Convention on International Child Abduction. However, if there is no order the European Convention on Recognition and Enforcement of Custody Decisions will not assist recovery; an order obtained after removal would be sufficient (Art. 12). A court order is not required to operate the port-stop procedure (*per* David Mellor, Minister of Health, Standing Committee B, col. 506). Where abduction is an issue the Lord Chancellor has stated that he sees "no reason why a court would be discouraged by the Act from granting [an order]" Mackay [1991] Fam. Law 457; see also Everall [1992] Fam. Law 164.

Parental responsibility for children

2.—(1) Where a child's father and mother were married to each other at the time of his birth, they shall each have parental responsibility for the child.

(2) Where a child's father and mother were not married to each other at the time of his birth—
  (a) the mother shall have parental responsibility for the child;
  (b) the father shall not have parental responsibility for the child, unless he acquires it in accordance with the provisions of this Act.

(3) References in this Act to a child whose father and mother were, or (as the case may be) were not, married to each other at the time of his birth must be read with section 1 of the Family Law Reform Act 1987 (which extends their meaning).

(4) The rule of law that a father is the natural guardian of his legitimate child is abolished.

(5) More than one person may have parental responsibility for the same child at the same time.

(6) A person who has parental responsibility for a child at any time shall not cease to have that responsibility solely because some other person subsequently acquires parental responsibility for the child.

(7) Where more than one person has parental responsibility for a child, each of them may act alone and without the other (or others) in meeting that responsibility; but nothing in this Part shall be taken to affect the operation of any enactment which requires the consent of more than one person in a matter affecting the child.

(8) The fact that a person has parental responsibility for a child shall not entitle him to act in any way which would be incompatible with any order made with respect to the child under this Act.

(9) A person who has parental responsibility for a child may not surrender or transfer any part of that responsibility to another but may arrange for some or all of it to be met by one or more persons acting on his behalf.

(10) The person with whom any such arrangement is made may himself be a person who already has parental responsibility for the child concerned.

(11) The making of any such arrangement shall not affect any liability of the person making it which may arise from any failure to meet any part of his parental responsibility for the child concerned.

DEFINITIONS
  "child": s.105(1).
  "married ... at the time of his birth": s.2(3).
  "parental responsibility": ss.2, 3, 12.

GENERAL NOTE
  This states the rules relating to the allocation of parental responsibility between parents. It largely re-enacts current law using the term "parental responsibility" in place of "parental rights and duties." If a child's parents were married at the time of his birth (or subsequently if the child is legitimated (see Legitimacy Act 1976, s.2)), both have parental responsibility (subs. (1)), otherwise only the mother has it (subs. (2)).

Parental responsibility can be held by several people concurrently (subs. (5)) and is not lost when another person, or the local authority (see s.33(3)), acquires it (subs. (6)). Each person who has parental responsibility may take action alone to meet it unless there is a statutory requirement to the contrary (subs. (7)), but cannot do anything incompatible with any order under this Act (subs. (8)). The nature of this "independent" parenting is analysed by Bainham in (1990) 53 M.L.R. 206, 210. This section also clarifies the position about agreements between people with parental responsibility and others about the care of children. Parental responsibility cannot be surrendered (subs. (9)), but arrangements can be made for others to meet it, although this does not remove the primary responsibility (subs. (10)).

Subs. (1)

Father and mother: Unmarried fathers are now included within the definition of father, rather than as relatives as they were under the C.C.A. 1980 because of F.L.R.A. 1987, s.1. Step-parents are classed as relatives (s.105(1)).

The position in relation to children born to a married woman as a result of A.I.D. is settled by F.L.R.A. 1987, s.27(1). This provides that the child "shall be treated as a child of the parties to that marriage and not be treated as the child of any other person." It follows that the biological father is not the father in such cases. Where a child is born as a result of embryo implant or donated eggs the birth mother, not the genetic mother, is the legal mother, H.F.E.A. 1990, s.27.

In such cases the mother's husband is treated as the father unless he did not consent to the implant or insemination. The partner of an unmarried woman is treated as the father only where the couple had treatment from a licensed practitioner. Where these provisions do not apply the sperm donor is the child's father unless he did not consent to the use of his sperm or had died before his sperm was used, F.L.R.A. 1986, s.27; H.F.E.A. 1990, s.28. If a child is born to a woman following the donation of gametes by a married woman and/or her husband, the married couple may obtain an order under the H.F.E.A. 1990, s.30, for the child to be treated as their child.

At the time of the birth: This must be interpreted in accordance with the F.L.R.A. 1987, s.1(2)(3). It thus includes: some children of void marriages treated as legitimate (Legitimacy Act 1976, s.1, as amended by F.L.R.A. 1987, s.18); legitimated children (Legitimacy Act 1976, s.2); adopted children (Adoption Act 1976, s.39); children otherwise treated as legitimate.

Each: This means separately (see subss. (5) and (7)).

Subs. (2)

In accordance with the provisions of this Act: An unmarried father can acquire parental responsibility: by obtaining a residence order (s.12(1)); by applying to the court (s.4(1)(a)); by making an agreement with the mother in the "prescribed form" (s.4(1)(b)); by being appointed the child's guardian by the court (s.5(1)); by being appointed the child's guardian by the mother or another guardian (s.5). The appointment as guardian will not take effect while the mother is alive (s.5(8)).

Subs. (3)

See subsection (1) for details of section 1 of the F.L.R.A. 1987.

Natural guardian: The concept of natural guardianship became irrelevant when the Guardianship Act 1973 gave the mother "like powers"; it is now abolished.

Subs. (7)

Consents: The following actions require the consents of more than one person (usually all people with parental responsibility):
 (1) Adoption/freeing for adoption: Adoption Act 1976, ss.16 and 18, but note those who acquire parental responsibility by virtue of a residence order (s.12(3)) or a care order (s.33(6)) do not have the right to consent.
 (2) Removal from the jurisdiction: Child Abduction Act 1984.
 (3) Marriage: Marriage Act 1949, s.3 and Sched. 2, amended by Schedule 13, paragraph 5 of this Act.
 (4) Applications by non-parents for residence orders and contact orders: Children Act 1989, s.10(5).

(5) Name change/removal from the United Kingdom (where a residence order or care order is in force): Children Act 1989, ss.13, 33(7).
(6) Provision of local authority accommodation or the removal of a child from it (but only where a residence order is in force): Children Act 1989, s.20(10).

Subs. (8)

This provision is crucial to the new structure because parental responsibility will only be lost by a parent if the child is adopted. Under the old law many rights were suspended where the child was subject to a care order and, after *Dipper* v. *Dipper* [1981] Fam. 31, the position following a custody order was unclear. Now parents will retain parental responsibility but their actions will be limited if there is an order. The Law Commission recommended this change so that the law would clearly recognise that the responsibility of being a parent continued although what was required of parents changed with change of circumstances. In para. 2.11 of Law Com. 172 they gave this example:

"If the child has to live with one parent and go to a school near his home, it would be incompatible with that order for the other parent to arrange for him to have his hair done in a way which will exclude him from school."

It seems unlikely that this provisions will be enforceable by contempt proceedings unless the order is very specific. Where it is important to have greater clarity a "prohibited steps order" may be necessary (see ss.8, 9(5)).

Subs. (9)

This replaces the provision in section 1(2) of the Guardianship Act 1973 (as amended by the F.L.R.A. 1987, s.3) which allowed agreements between separated parents about the exercise of their rights but prevented enforcement if the court thought this was not for the benefit of the child. The common law position that there can be no surrender is restored but modified to allow delegation. Delegation does not remove primary responsibility but clarifies that the delegated person, for example a nanny, a boarding school or another substitute carer has authority to act. Some delegation arrangements will give rise to further obligations under Parts VII–X and XII which cover different types of substitute care. The position of the person to whom responsibility is not delegated is clarified in section 3(5).

Subs. (11)

Any liability: For example, either under the criminal law (see C.Y.P.A. 1933), or to ensure an adequate standard of care, which is enforceable through care proceedings under section 31 of this Act, or civil liability to the child.

Meaning of "parental responsibility"

3.—(1) In this Act "parental responsibility" means all the rights, duties, powers, responsibilities and authority which by law a parent of a child has in relation to the child and his property.

(2) It also includes the rights, powers and duties which a guardian of the child's estate (appointed, before the commencement of section 5, to act generally) would have had in relation to the child and his property.

(3) The rights referred to in subsection (2) include, in particular, the right of the guardian to receive or recover in his own name, for the benefit of the child, property of whatever description and wherever situated which the child is entitled to receive or recover.

(4) The fact that a person has, or does not have, parental responsibility for a child shall not affect—

(a) any obligation which he may have in relation to the child (such as a statutory duty to maintain the child); or

(b) any rights which, in the event of the child's death, he (or any other person) may have in relation to the child's property.

(5) A person who—
(a) does not have parental responsibility for a particular child; but
(b) has care of the child,

may (subject to the provisions of this Act) do what is reasonable in all the circumstances of the case for the purpose of safeguarding or promoting the child's welfare.

DEFINITIONS
"child": s.105(1).
"guardian": ss.5, 105(1).
"parental responsibility": ss.2, 3, 12.

GENERAL NOTE
This contains the definition, or rather "non-definition" (per Lord Meston, *Hansard*, H.L. Vol. 502, col. 1172), of parental responsibility. Apart from specific points, which will be noted when they occur, the change to "parental responsibility" would seem to be merely a cosmetic one. The Law Commission rejected as impractical a proposal that parental rights and duties should be listed. Therefore it is necessary to return to the common law for a full understanding of the legal position of those with parental responsibility over children, see H. Bevan, *Child Law* (Butterworths, 2nd ed., 1989); S. Cretney and J. Masson, *Principles of Family Law* (Sweet & Maxwell, 5th ed., 1990). The concept of parental responsibility is analysed by J. Eekelaar in " Parental responsibility: State of Nature or Nature of the State" [1991] J.S.W.F.L., pp. 37–50.

Recent case law has clarified that parents may consent to a hysterectomy which was required for therapeutic not merely contraceptive purposes. Sterilisation decisions normally have to be referred to the Courts, see *Practice Note on Sterilisation* [1990] 2 F.L.R. 530. It has also been held that parents may override a child's decision to refuse treatment *Re R (A Minor) (Wardship: Medical Treatment)* [1991] 4 All E.R. 177 because F.L.R.A. 1969, s.8 which enables an over 16 year old to consent, to treatment does not remove the parent's right to give that consent *Re W (a minor) (refusal of medical treatment)* 1992 N.L.J. 1124 *sub nom Re J. The Independent* July 14, 1992. The decision in *Gillick* v. *West Norfolk Area Health Authority* [1986] A.C. 112 limited the power of parents to make decisions for their mature and capable children. The new distinction between a decision and an overriding consent is unconvincing, see Masson [1991] Fam. Law 528.

Although Lord Mackay said in Committee,

"This Bill does nothing to change the underlying principle of *Gillick* which has to be taken into account by all who exercise parental responsibility over a child mature and intelligent enough to take decisions for himself." (*Hansard*, H.L. Vol. 502, col. 1351)

it appears that the Act both removes rights which young people have and fails to establish procedures which will allow them to be fully involved in decision-making where there is a dispute before the courts.

Subs. (1)

Rights: In *F.* v. *Wirral Metropolitan Borough Council and Another* [1991] 2 All E.R. 648, the Court of Appeal held that a parent has no cause of action in negligence against a stranger who interferes with the parent's rights in respect of his relationship with his children.

Subs. (2)

The Law Commission noted that the law relating to rights in the child's estate was confused and uncertain (W.P. 91, para. 2.32). There was authority that a father did not have power to administer the child's property nor to give a valid receipt on the child's behalf (*M'Reight* v. *M'Reight* (1849) 13 I.Eq. 314). Guardians appeared to have these rights. Now anyone with parental responsibility will have them and specific appointments of guardians of the estate of a child will only be permitted in accordance with any rules (s.5(11)).

Subs. (4)

Although the term "parental responsibility" recognises that parents have powers so that they can bring up their children, its use does not remove the liability and rights of those without parental responsibility. Thus, a father without parental responsibility is liable to maintain the child (Sched. 1, para. 1); a step-parent is liable to maintain a child of the family (M.C.A. 1973, s.25(4); D.P.M.C.A. 1978, s.3(4)); anyone with charge of a child may be liable for neglect (C.Y.P.A. 1933, s.1); anyone with care of the child has the liabilities of a parent to see that the child is educated (Education Act 1944 as amended by Sched. 13, para. 10).

All children die intestate except those who make privileged wills under the Wills (Soldiers and Sailors) Act 1918. Devolution of the estate of an intestate minor is covered by the Administration of Estates Act 1925, s.46, and the F.L.R.A. 1987, s.18(1). If the child is unmarried his parents will be entitled to his estate in equal shares.

Subs. (5)

Since a person with parental responsibility cannot act under section 2(8) incompatibly with an order under this Act it would seem to follow that a person without such responsibility is similarly restricted, except for situations where an order would only be binding on someone on whom it had been served (see s.14).

Subject to the provisions of this Act: There are a number of specific restrictions in the Act, namely: section 10: starting proceedings without leave; section 13: changing the child's name or removing him from the jurisdiction; section 20(8): refusing to hand over a child (aged under 16 years) to a parent who wishes to remove him from care.

What is reasonable: The Law Commission suggested that it would be reasonable for someone caring for a child while parents were away to arrange emergency medical treatment but not major elective surgery (Law Com. 172, para. 2.16). The issue is likely to be more complex than that suggests. What is reasonable would also turn on the possibility of contacting the parents for permission, whether the parents were known to have particular views on the matter such as a preference for homoeopathy and the consequences for the child of delaying any action. It was also suggested by the Lord Chancellor that this provision would allow a foster parent to refuse to hand over a child to a parent who was drunk or incapable or, late at night, a child who was asleep (*Hansard*, H.L. Vol. 505, cols. 370–1). This is questionable, particularly when section 20(7) provides that the local authority has no right to retain a child against the wishes of a person with parental responsibility. The lack of clarity here is unfortunate and will no doubt lead to arguments based on the distinct responsibility of the foster parents and the local authority, even to re-running cases such as *Krishnan* v. *London Borough of Sutton* [1970] Ch. 181. Any retention of the child relying on section 3(5) could only be temporary—further action, probably an emergency protection order (s.44) or a prohibited steps order (s.8), would be necessary. A further issue arises as to what redress would exist where unreasonable action has been taken. Habeas corpus would theoretically be available for the recovery of the child (the Custody of Children Act 1891 is repealed by this Act) but it was held in *Re K.* (1978) 122 S.J. 626 that this was the wrong procedure for custody disputes and that wardship should be used. Tort law no longer gives parents an action for the loss of a child's services and there seems to be no other right to damages for them. The child may have a right of action for trespass where a doctor has operated or examined without valid consent.

Acquisition of parental responsibility by father

4.—(1) Where a child's father and mother were not married to each other at the time of his birth—

> (a) the court may, on the application of the father, order that he shall have parental responsibility for the child; or

(b) the father and mother may by agreement ("a parental responsibility agreement") provide for the father to have parental responsibility for the child.

(2) No parental responsibility agreement shall have effect for the purposes of this Act unless—
  (a) it is made in the form prescribed by regulations made by the Lord Chancellor; and
  (b) where regulations are made by the Lord Chancellor prescribing the manner in which such agreements must be recorded, it is recorded in the prescribed manner.

(3) Subject to section 12(4), an order under subsection (1)(a), or a parental responsibility agreement, may only be brought to an end by an order of the court made on the application—
  (a) of any person who has parental responsibility for the child; or
  (b) with leave of the court, of the child himself.

(4) The court may only grant leave under subsection (3)(b) if it is satisfied that the child has sufficient understanding to make the proposed application.

DEFINITIONS
"child": s.105(1).
"parental responsibility": ss.2, 3, 12.
"parental responsibility agreement": s.4(1)(b).
"prescribed": ss.4(2), 105(1).
"the court": s.92(7).

REGULATIONS
The Parental Responsibility Agreements Regulations 1991 (S.I. 1991 No. 1478).

GENERAL NOTE
This section enables an unmarried father to acquire parental responsibility by a court order or an agreement with the mother in the prescribed form. An unmarried father may also obtain parental responsibility in other ways (see the note to s.2(2)). This replaces the more limited provision in the F.L.R.A. 1987, s.4, under which an unmarried father could obtain an order to share the parental rights and duties with the mother. The Law Commission clearly favoured agreements ("judicial proceedings may be unduly elaborate, expensive and unnecessary unless the child's mother objects to the order" (Law Com. 172, para. 2.18)) but agreements and orders may have different effects. Only if there have been court proceedings can issues be *res judicata* (*Re J.S.* [1981] Fam. 22); it would apparently be open to either of the parties to an agreement to contest the issue of paternity at a later date. The welfare test in section 1(1) applies in these proceedings but the checklist in section 1(3) does not (s.1(4)).

Unlike the parental responsibility of married parents, the unmarried father's responsibility may be ended on the application of the child or any person with parental responsibility (subs. (3)). It will also end when the child reaches age 18 (s.91(7), (8)) or is adopted.

Unmarried fathers will be able to obtain orders, even though the child is subject to a care order, as they could obtain orders under F.L.R.A. 1987, s.4 (*Re H* [1989] 2 All E.R. 353, 906; *Re H (No. 3)* [1991] 2 All E.R. 185). Such a father would then qualify as a parent with parental responsibility, but this will not, under the new system, give him automatic rights to remove a child from care, or give him greater rights than the mother of a child in care. It would, however, enable him to remove a child who was only being looked after by the local authority (see s.20(8)). The unmarried father's rights to have contact (access) with his child in care are identical whether or not there is any section 4 order (s.34(1)). An agreement with the mother would seem to have the same consequences.

An order under this section must be made if a residence order is made in favour of a father (s.12(1)). "This is to ensure that a father who is entitled to have the child live with him under a court order will always have parental responsibility for him. If that residence order is later discharged, the parental responsibility order will not come to an end unless the court specifically decides that it should (s.12(4))" *Introduction to the Children Act 1989*, HMSO 1989, para. 2.8.

Subs. (1)

On application of the father: The mother has rights automatically (s.2(2)). The father does not need the mother's consent to make an application.

May order: The court will have to consider whether it is in the child's best interests for the father to have parental responsibility (s.1(1)). The meaning of welfare in this context is not defined. Now that divorced parents who cannot agree nevertheless retain parental responsibility the fact that the mother objects to the father and will not co-operate with him may not be a strong reason for denying an order under section 4. Rather, it justifies the making of a residence order to clarify and determine the rights of both the parents. Recent case law under F.L.R.A. 1987, s.4 supports this view. In *Re H (No. 3)* [1991] 2 All E.R. 185 a parental responsibility order was made but the father's agreement was dispensed with and the children freed for adoption. In *Re C (Parental Rights)* [1992] 1 F.L.R. 1 (C.A.), a section 4 order was made even though parental responsibility could not be exercised because the father had no contact with the child; his application for access was adjourned. See also *Re H (Minors: Parental responsibility) The Times*, September 7, 1992. On an application under section 4 the court can make any section 8 order because these are "family proceedings" (ss.8(3), 10(1)(b)). Having parental responsibility may make the father more willing to support his child but section 4 orders should not be made on the basis of such promises. A person with parental responsibility has considerable power to influence and control the child's life (see ss.2, 3) and it is unlikely to be in a child's interests to have such power held by someone who will not be involved in the child's care. If in the course of proceedings the parents are able to reach agreement it would seem that the court could refuse the order on the basis that it would be better for the matter to be decided by agreement (s.1(5)) but this would leave the father in a weak position because he would not have parental responsibility unless an agreement was made in accordance with subs. (2).

Shall have parental responsibility: The mother still retains it and section 2 applies to deal with conflicts between them. Any disputes can be dealt with by the court on application of either parent (s.10(4)(a)) even if no section 4 order has been made.

Subs. (2)

No parental responsibility agreement shall have effect: However, an informal agreement could still operate as a delegation of responsibility under section 2(9) or indicate what is reasonable for section 3(5).

Regulations: The Parental Responsibility Agreement Regulations 1991 (S.I. 1991 No. 1478) require the application form (three copies) signed by both the mother and the father and witnessed to be sent to the Principal Registry of the Family Division. The copies are stamped, one is filed and one each returned to the parents. There is no fee for making an application but there is a charge for searching the index of agreements and obtaining copies (see Family Proceedings Fees Order 1991 (S.I. 1991 No. 2114)).

Subs. (3)

Section 12(3) provides that an order for parental responsibility under section 4 shall not be brought to an end while a residence order in favour of an unmarried father continues. Where a residence order in favour of an unmarried father ends on the making of a care order the unmarried father retains parental responsibility. The decision to end the order must be made in the child's best interests (s.1(1)).

Any person with parental responsibility: This means the mother, the unmarried father, a guardian, any person who has a residence order or the local authority if there is a care order.

Leave: see the Family Proceedings Courts (*Children Act* 1989) Rules 1991, r. 3 (p. 359 below).

The child: A child can only obtain leave under subsection (4) if he has sufficient understanding to make the proposed application.

Appointment of Guardians

5.—(1) Where an application with respect to a child is made to the court by any individual, the court may by order appoint that individual to be the child's guardian if—
    (a) the child has no parent with parental responsibility for him; or
    (b) a residence order has been made with respect to the child in favour of a parent or guardian of his who has died while the order was in force.

(2) The power conferred by subsection (1) may also be exercised in any family proceedings if the court considers that the order should be made even though no application has been made for it.

(3) A parent who has parental responsibility for his child may appoint another individual to be the child's guardian in the event of his death.

(4) A guardian of a child may appoint another individual to take his place as the child's guardian in the event of his death.

(5) An appointment under subsection (3) or (4) shall not have effect unless it is made in writing, is dated and is signed by the person making the appointment or—
    (a) in the case of an appointment made by a will which is not signed by the testator, is signed at the direction of the testator in accordance with the requirements of section 9 of the Wills Act 1837; or
    (b) in any other case, is signed at the direction of the person making the appointment, in his presence and in the presence of two witnesses who each attest the signature.

(6) A person appointed as a child's guardian under this section shall have parental responsibility for the child concerned.

(7) Where—
    (a) on the death of any person making an appointment under subsection (3) or (4), the child concerned has no parent with parental responsibility for him; or
    (b) immediately before the death of any person making such an appointment, a residence order in his favour was in force with respect to the child,
the appointment shall take effect on the death of that person.

(8) Where, on the death of any person making an appointment under subsection (3) or (4)—
    (a) the child concerned has a parent with parental responsibility for him; and
    (b) subsection (7)(b) does not apply,
the appointment shall take effect when the child no longer has a parent who has parental responsibility for him.

(9) Subsections (1) and (7) do not apply if the residence order referred to in paragraph (b) of those subsections was also made in favour of a surviving parent of the child.

(10) Nothing in this section shall be taken to prevent an appointment under subsection (3) or (4) being made by two or more persons acting jointly.

(11) Subject to any provision made by rules of court, no court shall exercise the High Court's inherent jurisdiction to appoint a guardian of the estate of any child.

(12) Where rules of court are made under subsection (11) they may prescribe the circumstances in which, and conditions subject to which, an appointment of such a guardian may be made.

(13) A guardian of a child may only be appointed in accordance with the provisions of this section.

DEFINITIONS
 "appoint," "appointment": s.5(5).
 "child": s.105(1).
 "guardian of a child": s.5.
 "family proceedings": s.8(3).
 "parental responsibility": ss.2, 3, 12.
 "residence order": ss.8(1), 105(3).
 "signed": s.105(1).
 "the court": s.92(7).

GENERAL NOTE
This section and section 6 simplify and clarify the law of guardianship. They replace G.M.A. 1971, ss.3-6 with provisions recommended by the Law Commission in Law Com. 172.

A guardian of a child can only be appointed by the court in family proceedings, with or without an application (subss. (1), (2) and (13)), by a parent with parental responsibility (subs. (3)) or by an existing guardian (subs. (4)). Two such people may make a joint application (subs. (10)).

Unmarried fathers will be able to make appointments if they have obtained parental responsibility or been appointed as guardian. An appointment must be made by a signed and dated document in writing (subs. (5)); deeds and wills will not be required but will be effective in relation to both existing and new appointments. The child's guardian obtains parental responsibility over him (subs. (6)). Appointments will only be effective if the child has no parent with parental responsibility for him or the deceased person and no other parent had a residence order immediately before death (subss. (7)–(9)). Thus the situation will no longer arise where a surviving parent caring for a child has to co-operate with a guardian appointed by the deceased parent. However, if both parents die, even where only one held a residence order, the guardians they have appointed will both have the power to act. Also, for example, where the parents are dead, the grandfather is the guardian and the child is cared for by an aunt who has a residence order, the grandfather (but not the aunt) may appoint another guardian to act after his death. That guardian will have power alongside the aunt.

The Act also repeals the provisions which allowed the court to make declarations of unfitness under M.C.A. 1973, s.42 or the Sexual Offences Act 1956, s.38 (Sched. 12, para. 32; Sched. 15). Existing declarations ceased to have effect on October 14, 1991 (Sched. 14, para. 3). Such a declaration prevented the person against whom it was made automatically being the child's guardian on the death of a parent.

For details of proceedings, parties, notice, etc., see p. 422 below.

Subs. (1)

May: Section 1(5) applies. The decision and the appointment must be in the child's best interests but the checklist in section 1(3) does not apply.

Individual: Two or more individuals may be appointed (see s.6(1)) but organisations may not be appointed.

No parent with parental responsibility: Married parents always have parental responsibility unless it is removed by an adoption order. Unmarried fathers may acquire parental responsibility (see note on s.2(2)).

Guardian: A guardian for the child can only be appointed under this section (subs. (13)).

Residence order in favour of a parent or guardian: A residence order in favour of anyone else will not preclude an appointment, nor will it prevent an appointment by a parent or guardian being effective immediately the appointor dies (subs. (9)). If there was a residence order in favour of both parents the court can only appoint a guardian following the death of the surviving parent.

Died: Absence overseas, etc., does not permit the appointment of a guardian but it would be possible for a residence order to be made in such circumstances (see s.10(1)(b) and (5)).

Subs. (5)

The document only needs to be witnessed where it is signed at the direction of but not by the appointor; a will which is defective because it is not properly witnessed may be valid for the purpose of appointing a guardian.

Subs. (7)

Take effect: Until the appointment takes effect the guardian has no special powers and will need to seek leave under section 10(9) if he wishes to obtain a section 8 order.

Subs. (11) and (12)

These provisions came into force on February 1, 1991, following the Children Act 1989 (Commencement No. 2, etc.) Order 1991 (S.I. 1991 No. 1990). Appointments are governed by RSC Order 80, rule 13 added by The Rules of the Supreme Court (Amendment No. 4) 1991 (S.I. 1991 No. 2671).

Guardians: revocation and disclaimer

6.—(1) An appointment under section 5(3) or (4) revokes an earlier such appointment (including one made in an unrevoked will or codicil) made by the same person in respect of the same child, unless it is clear (whether as the result of an express provision in the later appointment or by any necessary implication) that the purpose of the later appointment is to appoint an additional guardian.

(2) An appointment under section 5(3) or (4) (including one made in an unrevoked will or codicil) is revoked if the person who made the appointment revokes it by a written and dated instrument which is signed—
    (a) by him; or
    (b) at his direction, in his presence and in the presence of two witnesses who each attest the signature.

(3) An appointment under section 5(3) or (4) (other than one made in a will or codicil) is revoked if, with the intention of revoking the appointment, the person who made it—
    (a) destroys the instrument by which it was made; or
    (b) has some other person destroy that instrument in his presence.

(4) For the avoidance of doubt, an appointment under section 5(3) or (4) made in a will or codicil is revoked if the will or codicil is revoked.

(5) A person who is appointed as a guardian under section 5(3) or (4) may disclaim his appointment by an instrument in writing signed by him and made within a reasonable time of his first knowing that the appointment has taken effect.

(6) Where regulations are made by the Lord Chancellor prescribing the manner in which such disclaimers must be recorded, no such disclaimer shall have effect unless it is recorded in the prescribed manner.

(7) Any appointment of a guardian under section 5 may be brought to an end at any time by order of the court—
- (a) on the application of any person who has parental responsibility for the child;
- (b) on the application of the child concerned, with leave of the court; or
- (c) in any family proceedings, if the court considers that it should be brought to an end even though no application has been made.

DEFINITIONS

"appoint," "appointment": s.5(3)–(5).
"child": s.105(1).
"disclaim," "disclaimer": s.6(5), (6).
"family proceedings": s.8(3).
"guardian": s.5.
"person who has parental responsibility": ss.2(1)(2), 4(1), 5(6), 12(1)(2).
"revocation," "revoke": s.6(2)–(4).
"signed": s.105(1).
"the court": s.92(7).

GENERAL NOTE

This section provides for the revocation, disclaimer and termination of appointments as guardian of a child.

Revocation: can be by a further appointment, except appointment of an additional guardian (subs. (1)), or by a written, signed and dated instrument of revocation (subs. (2)), or by destruction with the intention of revocation except in the case of a will or codicil (subs. (3)), or finally by the revocation of the will or codicil (subs. (4)).

Disclaimer: must be by a written and signed instrument (subss. (5) and (6)).

Termination: is carried out by the court on application of those listed in subsection (7).

Subs. (3)

Destruction of a will or codicil does not necessarily revoke it.

With the intention: Accidental destruction will have no effect.

Subs. (5)

Reasonable time: There is no indication of what period of time is reasonable but it would appear that a decision has to be taken once and for all so that change of circumstances (or change of heart) some time later could not be within a reasonable time. However, it is arguable that a person who decides to disclaim, having heard, after six months, that he has a fatal illness, would have acted within a reasonable time.

Subs. (6)

Prescribed: No regulations have been made.

Subs. (7)

Under the G.M.A. 1971, s.6 anyone could apply to the High Court to have a guardian removed. The Law Commission suggested that this general access should continue and also that local authorities should be able to apply for the removal of a guardian (W.P. No. 91, para. 3.24). This is provided in the case of children in care by paragraph (a). The guardian can apparently apply and avoid the time limit in subsection (5) operating in a way which is contrary to the child's welfare. The court can also end an appointment of its own motion in family proceedings.

Welfare reports

7.—(1) A court considering any question with respect to a child under this Act may—
    (a)   ask a probation officer; or
    (b)   ask a local authority to arrange for—
        (i)   an officer of the authority; or
        (ii) such other person (other than a probation officer) as the authority considers appropriate,
to report to the court on such matters relating to the welfare of that child as are required to be dealt with in the report.

(2) The Lord Chancellor may make regulations specifying matters which, unless the court orders otherwise, must be dealt with in any report under this section.

(3) The report may be made in writing, or orally, as the court requires.

(4) Regardless of any enactment or rule of law which would otherwise prevent it from doing so, the court may take account of—
    (a)   any statement contained in the report; and
    (b)   any evidence given in respect of the matters referred to in the report,
in so far as the statement or evidence is, in the opinion of the court, relevant to the question which it is considering.

(5) It shall be the duty of the authority or probation officer to comply with any request for a report under this section.

DEFINITIONS
  "child": s.105(1).
  "local authority": s.105(1).
  "the court": s.92(7).

GENERAL NOTE

This section enacts the recommendation of the Law Commission (see Law Com. 172, paras. 6.14 *et seq.*). It extends the court's power to call for a welfare report so that it can do so when considering any question with respect to a child under the Act. It removes anomalies that there were different powers to call for reports from different people under different statutes and in different courts (see Law Com. 172, para. 6.16). The probation service and local authorities will be under a duty to provide reports as requested (subs. (5)), but a local authority may delegate the task to someone who is not a member of its staff (subs. (1)), *e.g.* a guardian ad litem. The content of reports may be specified by the court (subs. (1)) or in regulations (subs. (2)); no regulations have yet been made. The court's right to consider reports and evidence about matters in reports regardless of the hearsay rule is clarified. The court may do so if it thinks that it is relevant (subs. (4)). This provision together with section 96 and the order made under it reverse *Re H, Re K* [1989] Fam. Law 388. This section does not remove the rights of the parties to ask the court to order reports and to question the reporter. The duties of the welfare officer and the rights to question him or her are set out in the Family Proceedings Courts (*Children Act* 1989) Rules 1991, r. 13 (see p. 387 below). Like all court documents the report is confidential: r. 23 (see p. 416 below). Guidance on the role of the welfare officers from Association of Chief Probation Officers and the

National Association of Probation Officers will be published soon. The Department of Health will re issue its guidance *Reports to the Court* in an updated form.

Subs. (1)

Any question ... under this Act: The power to order reports when considering the appointment of guardians (s.5) or granting parental responsibility to an unmarried father (s.4) is new. The provision is also wider than it might seem at first because the court may make the new section 8 orders in any "family proceedings" (s.8(4)). A court may thus call for a report *inter alia* in an injunction case under the Domestic Violence and Matrimonial Proceedings Act 1976 or the Matrimonial Homes Act 1983.

May: There is no duty to request a report even if the case is contested. The Lord Chancellor stated that some sort of report would generally be required in most contested cases and there would be some uncontested cases where a court would think a report necessary (*Hansard*, H.L. Vol. 502, col. 1203). In considering whether to request a report the court must give paramount consideration to the child's welfare and have regard to the problems caused by delay (s.1(2)). This may influence the choice of reporter.

Subs. (3)

This clarifies the position about the presentation of reports. Written reports are generally more useful to the parties and their representatives because they can be discussed prior to the hearing but if the court seeks only limited information an oral report may suffice. In exceptional circumstances a judge may receive a confidential report from the welfare officer or see him or her privately; the position in the family proceedings court is unclear (*Re C (A Minor: Irregularity of Practice)* [1992] Fam. Law 14).

Subs. (4)

This provision should be read with section 96 and the Children (Admissibility of Hearsay Evidence) Order 1991 (S.I. 1991 No. 1115): see pp. 223 and 431 below.

The court may: Guidance for guardians ad litem has urged caution when using hearsay in relation to very controversial matters. In *Thompson* v. *Thompson* (1975) [1986] 1 F.L.R. 212 at 217, Buckley L.J. said, "Where a judge has to arrive at crucial findings of fact he should found them upon sworn evidence rather than unsworn report." Where the court decides not to follow the welfare officer's recommendation it should indicate clearly and specifically the reasons for so doing: *W* v. *W (A Minor: Custody Appeal)* [1988] 2 F.L.R. 505 at 511G, *per* Purchas L.J. In exceptional circumstances the court could consider material which was not disclosed to the parties *Re B The Times* July 31, 1992. See also Family Proceedings Courts (Children Act 1989) Rules 1991, r. 17(4)(5) and p. 398 below.

PART II

ORDERS WITH RESPECT TO CHILDREN IN FAMILY PROCEEDINGS

General

Residence, contact and other orders with respect to children

8.—(1) In this Act—

"a contact order" means an order requiring the person with whom a child lives, or is to live, to allow the child to visit or stay with the person named in the order, or for that person and the child otherwise to have contact with each other;

"a prohibited steps order" means an order that no step which could be taken by a parent in meeting his parental responsibility for a child, and which is of a kind specified in the order, shall be taken by any person without the consent of the court;
"a residence order" means an order settling the arrangements to be made as to the person with whom a child is to live; and
"a specific issue order" means an order giving directions for the purpose of determining a specific question which has arisen, or which may arise, in connection with any aspect of parental responsibility for a child.

(2) In this Act "a section 8 order" means any of the orders mentioned in subsection (1) and any order varying or discharging such an order.

(3) For the purposes of this Act "family proceedings" means any proceedings—
  (a) under the inherent jurisdiction of the High Court in relation to children; and
  (b) under the enactments mentioned in subsection (4),
but does not include proceedings on an application for leave under section 100(3).

(4) The enactments are—
  (a) Parts I, II and IV of this Act;
  (b) the Matrimonial Causes Act 1973;
  (c) the Domestic Violence and Matrimonial Proceedings Act 1976;
  (d) the Adoption Act 1976;
  (e) the Domestic Proceedings and Magistrates' Courts Act 1978;
  (f) sections 1 and 9 of the Matrimonial Homes Act 1983;
  (g) Part III of the Matrimonial and Family Proceedings Act 1984.

DEFINITIONS
"child": ss.9(6), 105(1).
"contact order": ss.8(1), 11(7).
"family proceedings": s.8(3)(4).
"parental responsibility": ss.2, 3, 12.
"prohibited steps order": s.8(1).
"residence order": ss.8(1), 105(3).
"section 8 order": ss.8, 11(7).
"single issue order": s.8(1).

GENERAL NOTE
This section, together with sections 9 and 10, forms the heart of the new scheme for the private law relating to children. It enacts the recommendations in Part II of Law Com. 172. Section 8 orders replace orders for custody or care and control and related orders. Although it was suggested in Parliament that this merely amounted to "cosmetic renaming" (*per* Lord Meston, *Hansard*, H.L. Vol. 502, col. 503), a close examination indicates that the courts are getting substantially greater powers to direct what happens to children who are the subject of civil proceedings. Section 8 orders may be made in public law proceedings, guardians ad litem are advised specifically to

consider this but must bear in mind that local authorities cannot be compelled to provide the necessary resources, *Gal Manual*, p.85. Additionally, the making of an order will not remove parental responsibility, although it will restrict the actions of those in whose favour the order is not made (see s.2(8)).

Subs. (1)

A contact order: This order replaces the access order. It requires the person with whom the child is living to allow the child contact with the named person. There is no compulsion on the person who has the benefit of the order to maintain contact, nor can a mature child be required to do so (*Gillick* v. *West Norfolk Area Health Authority* [1986] A.C. 112). If the child visits or stays with someone with parental responsibility (a parent, guardian or a person with a residence order) that person may exercise parental responsibility so far as that is not incompatible with any order under this Act (see s.2(8)). If the child visits or stays with someone without parental responsibility (*e.g.* grandparents) they can take such action as is reasonable (see s.3(5)). Where visits are impractical or undesirable an order can be made to allow receipt of telephone calls or letters. Contact may be terminated by a prohibited steps order. It is likely that orders will usually be for "reasonable contact" which would allow all types of contact. Contact orders cannot be made in respect of children who are in local authority care under a care order (s.9(1)). Contact with children in care is provided for in section 34. Local authorities may not apply for contact orders nor have them made in their favour (s.9(2)). However, an order may be made where the child is only accommodated by the local authority. Although local authorities have wide discretion over the care of children they are accommodating it would be an unwarranted extension of the *Liverpool* principle (*A.* v. *Liverpool City Council* [1982] A.C. 363) to prevent courts from dealing with disputes over contact with such children. The court may only make contact orders in relation to children over 16 years in exceptional circumstances (s.9(7)). Orders only continue in force after the child reaches age 16 years in exceptional circumstances (ss.9(6), 91(10)(11)). If the order is made in favour of a parent it ceases to have any effect if the parents live together for a continuous period of more than six months (s.11(6)). This is so even though the parents are unmarried and the parent with the order is the father and does not have parental responsibility. The making of a care order discharges the order (s.91(2)).

A prohibited steps order: The Law Commission proposed this as part of its aim "to incorporate the most valuable features of wardship into the statutory jurisdictions" (Law Com. 172, para. 4.20). The order differs from the automatic effect of making a child a ward of court in that the actions prohibited or the areas over which control is lost to the court must be specified in the order. When a child is warded "no important step" may be taken without the consent of the court. The new order is clearer but care will need to be taken to consider exactly what decisions should be left to the court. If there is a residence order, removal from the United Kingdom (except for short periods) and name change will automatically require permission under section 13. A prohibited steps order could bar removal where there is no residence order, from a place rather than the jurisdiction, or forbid change of school. A prohibited steps order could be granted to ban further removal from the jurisdiction even though the child had been removed and the other parent was outside the jurisdiction and had no assets there where this would assist proceedings overseas (*Re D (A Minor)* [1992] 1 All E.R. 892 (C.A.)). The order can only relate to action which is within the power of a parent; it cannot therefore be used to prevent one parent from contacting another *Croydon London Borough* v. *A.* [1992] 1 F.C.R. 522. Unlike orders in wardship it does not appear to bind the child nor to give the court control over decisions which the child is entitled to take. Thus an order could stop a person allowing a child to have cosmetic surgery or engage in a dangerous sport but would not be effective to prevent a mature young person making such a decision for himself (see s.11(7) and *Gillick*). There are limitations in section 9(5) on these orders. Prohibited steps orders cannot be made in respect of a child subject to a care order (s.9(1)). They cannot be used to achieve results which could be achieved by a residence order or a contact order. Thus the location of the child's home cannot be the subject of this order but should be specified in detail in a residence order. Nor can they be used to circumvent the restrictions on the wardship jurisdiction in section 100(2), *i.e.* to commit a child to local authority care, to require a child to be accommodated by the local authority or to give the local authority power to make decisions about children. Thus a prohibited steps order cannot be used to prevent a child's removal from care when there is no care order but it could be used to prevent someone visiting the child in the foster home as long as there was no care order (s.9(1)). Prohibited steps orders cannot be made in relation to a child over the age of 16 years unless the circumstances are exceptional (s.9(7)). Similarly, orders only continue in force after the child is 16 in exceptional circumstances (ss.9(6), 91(10)(11)). What is exceptional in relation to this order may be different from the case of contact which is very much a matter for the child by age 16. The making of a care order discharges the order (s.91(2)).

A residence order: The Law Commission was concerned that orders for custody or care and control should be replaced with an order "flexible enough to accommodate a much wider range of situations" (Law Com. 172, para. 4.12) including where the child lived with both parents after their separation. The Lord Chancellor has advised that a residence order confers "rights of custody" for the purposes of the Hague Convention on the Civil Aspects of International Child Abduction. Similarly it should fall within the European Convention on the Recognition and Enforcement of Decisions Concerning the Custody of Children (see [1991] Fam. Law 455, 457 and Everall [1992] Fam. Law 164). Amendments are made to the Child Abduction and Custody Act 1985 which implements these Conventions by Schedule 13, paragraph 57.

The phrase "settling the arrangements" is a broad one and gives the court more scope for including conditions. The Lord Chancellor suggested that this could be used to provide that the child lived with the father only while he remained in a particular neighbourhood (*Hansard*, H.L. Vol. 505, col. 345). A residence order may be made in favour of more than one person (s.11(4)). If these people are not living together it may also specify the periods to be spent in each household. A residence order may be made in favour of an unmarried couple who need not be the child's parents. However, if an order is made in favour of parents, each with parental responsibility, it will cease to have effect if they live together for a continuous period of more than six months (s.11(5)).

The granting of a residence order in favour of any person automatically gives them parental responsibility for the child (s.12(2)). Thus people with residence orders are in the same position as parents or guardians except in relation to matters excluded by the statute. Section 12(3) prevents those with residence orders who are not parents or guardians giving consent to adoption, freeing for adoption and appointing a guardian. Section 13 prevents anyone changing the surname of or removing from the jurisdiction (except for less than a month (s.13(2)) any child who is the subject of a residence order.

A local authority may not apply for a residence order nor have one made in its favour (s.9(2)). However, a residence order may be made in respect of any child, even one subject to a care order (s.9(1)). In this case the residence order discharges the care order (s.9(1)). "Phased return" of a child in care may be achieved by making a residence order which settles arrangements for the child to live temporarily with foster parents with increasing visits to the applicants. There is no provision specifically for "phased return" in the Act. The foster parents would no longer come within the Foster Placement (Children) Regulations 1991 (S.I. 1991 No. 910) but the local authority would have a discretion to provide financial support under Schedule 1, paragraph 15; alternatively the High Court may order a contribution under its inherent jurisdiction (*Calderdale B.C.* v. *H. & P.* [1991] 1 F.L.R. 461). The making of a care order discharges a residence order but the local authority has responsibility in relation to contact with those who held residence orders immediately before a care order was made, *e.g.* s.34(1).

Residence orders end when the child reaches the age of 16 unless the court orders otherwise. Orders in respect of older children or orders to continue after the child is 16 can only be made in exceptional circumstances (ss.9(6), (7) and 91(10)). Such an order might be appropriate in the case of a handicapped child living with non-parents to ensure that the carers retained parental responsibility for the child until age 18 (s.91(11)).

Applications for residence orders may be made *ex parte* in exceptional circumstances *Re B.* [1992] 2 F.L.R. 1 (C.A.). See also the Family Proceedings Rules 1991, r. 4 amended by the Family Proceedings (Amendment) Rules 1992, p. 361 (below).

The enforcement of residence orders is dealt with in section 14.

A specific issue order: Under the Guardianship Act 1973, s.1(3) parents could refer a dispute on any individual question to the court but it was probably more usual for such cases to be dealt with in wardship where the court had control over all major decisions. This new provision extends (s.1(3)) to disputes involving non-parents, including some involving local authorities. The effect is not to give one person a right to take decisions, or to veto them, but to enable the court to give directions. The court could take the disputed decision itself or, alternatively, direct that it should be determined by others. For example, in a case involving medical treatment it could determine that the child should be treated as a specified doctor thought appropriate. Despite section 1(5) the Court of Appeal was prepared to allow an appeal against the refusal of a specific issues order requiring a child to be returned to the jurisdiction which was unenforceable because the person who had removed the child was outside the jurisdiction and had no assets here. The order would assist proceedings overseas and could be granted *ex parte* (*Re D (A Minor)* [1992] 1 All E.R. 892).

The restrictions in section 9 which apply to prohibited steps orders also apply to specific issue orders. However, section 9(5) still leaves scope for local authorities who wish to require a parent to do something, for example to take a child to a doctor or to a school, to seek a specific issue order.

Subs. (3)

The new legislation provides a single system so that all courts dealing with "family proceedings" can make any section 8 order or a family assistance order (s.16). Limitations on applications still continue (see ss.9, 10) but the anomalies which related to the types of orders which could be granted are removed.

"*Family proceedings*":
   (1) Under the *inherent jurisdiction* (s.8(3)(a)), *i.e.* wardship.
   (2) *Part I of the Children Act 1989* (s.8(4)(a)).
       Proceedings for parental responsibility orders (s.4).
       Guardianship proceedings (ss.5, 6).
   (3) *Part II of the Children Act 1989* (s.8(4)(a)).
       Free-standing applications for order (s.10(1)(2)).
       Applications for leave (s.10(2)(b)).
       By the court on its own motion (s.10(1)(b)).
       Applications for financial relief under Schedule 1.
   (4) *Part IV of the Children Act 1989* (s.8(4)(a)).
       Care proceedings (s.31).
       Proceedings re contact with children in care (s.34).
       Proceedings re education supervision orders (s.36).
N.B.: The court does not have this power when it is considering the emergency protection of a child under Part V.
   (5) *M.C.A. 1973* (s.8(4)(b)).
       Divorce, nullity and judicial separation proceedings.
       Applications for financial relief following divorce, etc., or in cases of neglect to maintain (s.27). Section 8 orders may be made even though the child is not "a child of the family" within the M.C.A. 1973, s.52(1) (s.10(1)).
   (6) *D.V.M.P.A. 1976* (s.8(4)(b)).
       Applications for non-molestation orders.
       Applications for exclusion orders, etc., where the parties are unmarried.
The court will thus be able to determine where a child lives and what contact he is to have with the excluded person even if that person is not a parent.
   (7) *Adoption Act 1976* (s.8(4)(d)).
       Adoption proceedings, proceedings for freeing orders.

Under the old law the court could refuse to grant an adoption order and refer the matter back to the divorce court for a custody order or, if the child was not a child of the family, make a custodianship order (Adoption Act 1976, ss.14(3), 15(4); Children Act 1975, s.37). It will now be able to make a residence order instead of an adoption order in any case. The decision whether to grant a residence order or an adoption order will be for the court to make applying the Adoption Act 1976, s.6. In *Re S* [1987] Fam. 98, it was held that a custodianship order could only be made as an alternative to adoption where it was better for the child, but this decision turned on the construction of the Children Act 1975, s.37(1), which has been repealed. Section 1(5) of this Act applies to the making of a section 8 order but not of an adoption order. The court can make a contact order instead of including access conditions in the adoption order (see *Re C* [1988] 2 W.L.R. 474).

(8) *D.P.M.C.A. 1978* (s.8(4)(e)).
Proceedings for financial relief.
Proceedings for injunctions in cases of domestic violence.

The court will thus be able to determine where a child lives and what contact he is allowed to have with the excluded person. Section 8 orders may apparently be made even though the child is not "a child of the family" within the D.P.M.C.A. 1978, s.88(1).

(9) *Sections 1 and 9 of the M.H.A. 1983* (s.8(4)(f)).
Proceedings for exclusion orders and related orders where the parties are married (see *Richards* v. *Richards* [1984] A.C. 174).

(10) *Part III of the Matrimonial and Family Proceedings Act 1984* (s.8(4)(c)).
Proceedings for financial relief after overseas divorce.

Restrictions on making section 8 orders

9.—(1) No court shall make any section 8 order, other than a residence order, with respect to a child who is in the care of a local authority.

(2) No application may be made by a local authority for a residence order or contact order and no court shall make such an order in favour of a local authority.

(3) A person who is, or was at any time within the last six months, a local authority foster parent of a child may not apply for leave to apply for a section 8 order with respect to the child unless—
   (a) he has the consent of the authority;
   (b) he is a relative of the child; or
   (c) the child has lived with him for at least three years preceding the application.

(4) The period of three years mentioned in subsection (3)(c) need not be continuous but must have begun not more than five years before the making of the application.

(5) No court shall exercise its powers to make a specific issue order or prohibited steps order—
   (a) with a view to achieving a result which could be achieved by making a residence or contact order; or
   (b) in any way which is denied to the High Court (by section 100(2)) in the exercise of its inherent jurisdiction with respect to children.

(6) No court shall make any section 8 order which is to have effect for a period which will end after the child has reached the age of 16 unless it is satisfied that the circumstances of the case are exceptional.

(7) No court shall make any section 8 order, other than one varying or discharging such an order, with respect to a child who has reached the age of 16 unless it is satisfied that the circumstances of the case are exceptional.

DEFINITIONS
   "child": ss.9(7), 105(1).
   "contact order": s.8(1).
   "local authority": s.105(1).
   "local authority foster parent": s.23(3)(4).
   "prohibited steps order": s.8(1).
   "relative": s.105(1).
   "residence order": s.8(1).
   "three years": s.9(4).

GENERAL NOTE

This section states the main limitations on the court making the various section 8 orders; particularly it restricts the court's power in relation to children in local authority care (subss. (1)–(3)). It also ensures that the differences in the types of orders are not blurred (sub. (5)). It provides that orders should only continue or be made (but not varied or discharged) in relation to children over 16 in exceptional circumstances (subss. (6) and (7)).

Subs. (1)

The making of a residence order discharges a care order (s.9(1)). Where a child is subject to a care order, anyone with parental responsibility may apply for its discharge without applying for any further order (s.39(1)), but other people can only do so by obtaining a residence order. To seek a residence order they may need the consent of the local authority (ss.9(3), 10(5)(c)(ii)). A residence order will also give the applicant parental responsibility for the child. The courts will not be able to make a residence order in respect of a child subject to a care order when his parents divorce but the issue of the child's residence can be dealt with on the discharge of the care order (s.8(4)).

The court will not be able to direct the local authority how it should treat the child or to control further the parents of a child in care by issuing a prohibited steps or a single issue order. However, in such cases the local authority may, with leave, seek the direction or assistance of the High Court in wardship (s.100(3)). This may be particularly useful in relation to sensitive areas like sterilisation or abortion. In contrast, local authorities may, with leave, apply for prohibited steps orders and specific issue orders in relation to children whom they are accommodating, for example, to get a decision about medical treatment. They may also seek specific issue orders to make a parent take a child for medical treatment in circumstances where an emergency protection order (s.44) would not be available and a child assessment order (s.43) would be inadequate.

Subs. (2)

Local authorities cannot by-pass the need to establish the grounds in section 31 by applying for a residence order rather than a care order. This also applies to the use of contact orders as an alternative to supervision orders.

Subs. (3)

Local authority foster parents and former foster parents who have ceased caring for a child within the last six months are the only group subject to this further restriction on applications for leave to seek section 8 orders. Leave of the court is not required for applications for residence or contact orders by people who have cared for the child for three years (s.10(5)(b)), but is necessary for prohibited steps and single issue orders.

The Law Commission thought that it was inappropriate to allow foster parents the right to apply for orders without restriction because this could undermine the authority's plans (Law Com. 172, para. 4.43). Section 9(3) goes beyond the Commission's recommendations and gives the authority a right of veto. Where it does not apply, or consent is given, the court will have to consider the local authority's plans in any application for leave (s.10(9)(d)(i)). Where children are being accommodated by the authority, the protection of the rights of parents is limited, since the authority can always give its consent, although it must comply with its duty to "safeguard and promote" the child's welfare under section 22(3) in so doing. However, applications for custodianship orders were rare and there is nothing in the legislation which will necessarily make residence orders more attractive to foster parents.

Subs. (4)

This is broader than the definition which applied to custodianship, but an application for a residence order will not prevent the child's removal from the applicant's home (see notes to s.10).

Subs. (5)

This provision prevents local authorities using prohibited steps orders or specific issue orders to get round the restrictions in subsection. (2). Similarly, section 100(2) provides that wardship powers may not be used to subject a child to local authority care or supervision, nor to give a local authority power to make decisions which are part of parental responsibility.

Subs. (6) and (7)

Previously the court's powers to make custody and access orders endured until the child was 18, although they were rarely exercised against the child's wishes. Section 8 orders are now largely restricted to under-16s. Orders may be necessary where a child, through immaturity or handicap, is unable to make decisions for himself, *e.g. Re S.W.* [1986] 1 F.L.R. 24. Orders in wardship will be available until a child is 18 but the changes in the Act will reduce the need for recourse to wardship and a local authority's rights of access to it. The Law Commission suggested that a court considering making an order in relation to a child over 16 years should make the child a party (Law Com. 172, para. 3.25). Where a child lives with a non-parent under a residence order that person's consent is necessary for his marriage under 18. Once the order has expired, the consent of the parents and guardians will be required (Marriage Act 1949, s.3(1A) as amended by Sched. 12, para. 5).

Power of court to make section 8 orders

10.—(1) In any family proceedings in which a question arises with respect to the welfare of any child, the court may make a section 8 order with respect to the child if—

(a) an application for the order has been made by a person who—
  (i) is entitled to apply for a section 8 order with respect to the child; or
  (ii) has obtained the leave of the court to make the application; or
(b) the court considers that the order should be made even though no such application has been made.

(2) The court may also make a section 8 order with respect to any child on the application of a person who—

(a) is entitled to apply for a section 8 order with respect to the child; or
(b) has obtained the leave of the court to make the application.

(3) This section is subject to the restrictions imposed by section 9.

(4) The following persons are entitled to apply to the court for any section 8 order with respect to a child—

(a) any parent or guardian of the child;
(b) any person in whose favour a residence order is in force with respect to the child.

(5) The following persons are entitled to apply for a residence or contact order with respect to a child—

(a) any party to a marriage (whether or not subsisting) in relation to whom the child is a child of the family;
(b) any person with whom the child has lived for a period of at least three years;
(c) any person who—

(i) in any case where a residence order is in force with respect to the child, has the consent of each of the persons in whose favour the order was made;
(ii) in any case where the child is in the care of a local authority, has the consent of that authority; or
(iii) in any other case, has the consent of each of those (if any) who have parental responsibility for the child.

(6) A person who would not otherwise be entitled (under the previous provisions of this section) to apply for the variation or discharge of a section 8 order shall be entitled to do so if—
(a) the order was made on his application; or
(b) in the case of a contact order, he is named in the order.

(7) Any person who falls within a category of person prescribed by rules of court is entitled to apply for any such section 8 order as may be prescribed in relation to that category of person.

(8) Where the person applying for leave to make an application for a section 8 order is the child concerned, the court may only grant leave if it is satisfied that he has sufficient understanding to make the proposed application for the section 8 order.

(9) Where the person applying for leave to make an application for a section 8 order is not the child concerned, the court shall, in deciding whether or not to grant leave, have particular regard to—
(a) the nature of the proposed application for the section 8 order;
(b) the applicant's connection with the child;
(c) any risk there might be of that proposed application disrupting the child's life to such an extent that he should be harmed by it; and
(d) where the child is being looked after by a local authority—
(i) the authority's plans for the child's future; and
(ii) the wishes and feelings of the child's parents.

(10) The period of three years mentioned in subsection (5)(b) need not be continuous but must not have begun more than five years before, or ended more than three months before, the making of the application.

DEFINITIONS
"child": ss.9(7), 105(1).
"child in care of the local authority": s.105(1).
"child of the family": s.105(1).
"contact order": s.8(1).
"guardian": s.5.
"harm": ss.31(9), 105(1).
"local authority": s.105(1).
"parental responsibility": ss.2, 3, 12.
"residence order": ss.8(1), 105(3).
"section 8 order": ss.8, 11(7).
"the court": s.92(7).
"three years": s.10(10).

GENERAL NOTE
This section enacts the Law Commission's proposals for a coherent scheme for determining the circumstances in which section 8 orders may be granted. The court is empowered to grant orders on application or of its own motion in family proceedings.

Power of Court to Make Section 8 Orders

Subsections (4)–(7) list the people who are qualified to apply for the different types of section 8 orders or their variation or discharge without leave. Generally these repeat the previous law relating to applications for custody or access, except that grandparents may no longer make application for contact (access) without leave or the agreement of the parents, etc. Subsection (8) lays down the conditions for granting leave to child applicants, subsection (9) to others. The purpose of the restrictions on making applications is "to protect families from unwarranted interference," *per* the Lord Chancellor (*Hansard*, H.L. Vol. 503, col. 49). Applications for leave may be granted *ex parte* or considered at a hearing: see Family Proceedings Courts (Children Act 1989) Rules 1991, r. 3(2), p. 359 below. A child seeking leave does not need a guardian ad litem or next friend, Family Proceedings Rules 1991, r.9.2A added by Family Proceedings (Amendment) Rules 1992 (1992 S.I. No. 456). There is no replacement for Children Act 1975, s.41; a child may be removed while an application for a residence order is pending but this will not prevent the order being made (subs. 10)).

This section must be read with section 1, which indicates how the court should exercise its discretion.

Subss. (1) and (2)

May: The Law Commission took the view that orders should only be granted where they were necessary (Law Com., para. 3.2):

"No doubt in many, possibly most, uncontested cases an order is needed in the children's own interests, so as to confirm and give stability to the existing arrangements, to clarify the respective roles of the parents, to reassure the parent with whom the child is living and even to reassure the public authorities ... Where a child has a good relationship with both parents the law should seek to disturb this as little as possible. There is always a risk that orders ... deciding upon residence and contact will have the effect of polarising parents' roles ... "

This view was strongly supported by the Lord Chancellor (*Hansard*, H.L. Vol. 502, col. 1226). There are circumstances where orders are desirable (see notes to s.1(5)). Where the Court proposes to make an order which differs from that agreed between the parties it should give them the opportunity to make representations *Devon CC v. S.* [1992] 3 All E.R. 793.

Entitled: For any section 8 order see section 10(4); for residence and contact orders, see section 10(5); for variation or discharge, see section 10(6).

Subs. (4)

Parent: This means the child's mother or father (see notes to s.2(1)). The biological parent of a child freed for adoption is not a parent and must seek leave under section 10(9) for any section 8 order, *M v. C and Calderdale B.C.* [1992] 2 F.C.R. 141.

Guardian: A guardian whose appointment has not yet taken effect under section 5(7) or (8) will need consent under section 10(5) or have to apply for leave under section 10(9). The fact that he has been chosen to be a guardian must be considered under section 10(9)(b).

Any person in whose favour a residence order: A residence order gives a person parental responsibility and thus puts him in the same position as a married parent except where the statute provides otherwise (see s.12(3)).

In force: Residence orders normally expire when the child reaches 16 years (s.91(10)). Where a non-parent wants a residence order to continue beyond age 16 he should either ensure that the initial order states this or apply for its variation before the child reaches 16. If he does not, the order will lapse and he will need to seek leave under section 10(9).

Subs. (5)

The Law Commission, who proposed this provision (Law Com. 172, para. 4.48), stated that its object was "not to provide a qualification for applying ... but to dispense with the requirement of leave where it would be a meaningless formality."

(a) Applications by step-parents and former step-parents. The definition of "child of the family" is the same as in the M.C.A. 1973, s.52(1). It means that the child need not be a child of the applicant or of his spouse or of his former spouse. The step-parent must have been married and with his or her spouse treated the child as a child of their family. The child need not have lived with the couple full time; a "week-end step-parent" may want this arrangement formalised with a contact order. Where the step-parent never married the child's carer he or she must qualify to apply under (b) or (c) or obtain leave from the court.

(b) These applicants could formerly have applied for a custodianship order without the consent of any person (Children Act 1975, s.33(3)(c)). The definition of the three-year period is now more liberal but it cannot start more than five years before the application is made (s.10(10)). Where the child has ceased to live with the applicants proceedings should be started without delay; if more than three months elapse leave will be required under section 10(9).

(c) Applications by others can only be made with the relevant consent:—
 (i) of all those with a residence order;
 (ii) where the child is subject to a care order, of the local authority. When considering whether to give its consent the local authority must comply with its duties under section 22(3)–(5). If the application is by a foster parent who comes within section 10(5)(b), no consent will be required. All other local authority foster parents (and some former foster parents) will require the consent of the authority under section 9(3) or section 10(5)(c)(ii);
 (iii) of the child's parents or guardians. If there is a residence order, parental consent is not required unless the order is in favour of a parent (s.10(5)(c)(i)).

Subs. (7)

No rules have yet been made; grandparents are most likely to benefit if rules are made.

Subs. (8)

This requires children who wish to make applications to show that they are competent to do so. The issue of sufficient understanding to make decisions was discussed by the House of Lords in *Gillick* v. *West Norfolk Area Health Authority* [1986] A.C. 112. In relation to contraception, Lord Scarman stated, "it is not enough that she should understand the nature of the advice which is being given: she must also have sufficient maturity to understand what is involved" (at p. 424). A child applying for a contact order would thus have to want the court to determine the issue of contact and perhaps even have some understanding that involving the court may disturb relationships with carers and may not necessarily achieve the desired aims.

The test of understanding may be different according to the type of application.

Subs. (9)

Applications for leave are not governed by the welfare test in section 1(1) but should be granted if the substantive application is likely to succeed, *JR* v. *Merton B.C.* [1992] 2 F.C.R. 172, reported *sub nom Re A.W. The Independent*, May 13, 1992. Since the substantive application is governed by section 1 the distinction is unclear. It may be advisable for anyone who otherwise needs leave to first seek to obtain agreement to the application from those specified in section 10(5). There may be little to be gained by requiring applicants to go through the leave process if there is a strong possibility that leave will eventually be granted.

Until further restrictions are introduced on the wardship jurisdiction, anyone who has to seek leave for a section 8 application may alternatively consider making an application in wardship. Where a residence order is sought the use of wardship may be inconvenient because of the need to seek the court's directions in relation to major decisions unless the court makes a residence order in wardship (s.8(3)(a)). Wardship is not available to challenge *intra vires* decisions of local authorities (*A* v. *Liverpool City Council* [1982] A.C. 363, *W* v. *Hertfordshire County Council* [1985] 2 All E.R. 301) and thus cannot be used to get over the hurdle of local authority consent under sections 9(3) or 10(5)(c) unless this has been withheld in bad faith.

Leave applications will not themselves be disruptive if they are granted *ex parte* which is possible (see p. 359 below). The Lord Chancellor was adamant that para. (c) was not intended to prejudge the substantive issue (*Hansard*, H.L. Vol. 502, col. 1230), although it seems most unlikely that leave would be granted where there was little chance that the desired order would be granted. The High Court has already faced this difficulty when considering applications to place wards for adoption (see Lowe & White, *Wards of Court* (1986) 14.2.3.).

The Law Commission suggested that the requirement for leave would "scarcely be a hurdle at all to close relatives ... who wish to care for or visit the child" (Law Com. 172, para. 4.4). Closer attention may be paid to those who merely seek to restrict parental action with a prohibited steps or specific issue order. Where the child is being looked after by a local authority the courts seem minded to give special status to the local authority's view point *JR* v. *Merton B.C.* [1992] 2 F.C.R. 172. If the child is sufficiently mature to obtain leave to make his own application under section 10(8), the need to have the local authority's agreement or acquiescence to an application may be avoided. If the child is subject to a care order he will be able to apply for its discharge at any time without establishing that he has any particular understanding under section 39(1)(b), but will be represented by a guardian ad litem who will, if the current rules are repeated, be under an obligation to represent his welfare rather than his wishes. The courts may be more willing to grant leave to relatives, friends or foster parents who wish to care for the child when a discharge application is pending, even where this is opposed by the local authority. Even if leave were not granted under section 10(9), it would still be open for the court to make a residence order in the discharge proceedings.

The welfare principle (s.1(1)) applies to applications for leave as it applies to substantive applications.

Subs. (10)

The definition of three years differs from that in section 9(4); thus a former foster parent might need leave to apply for a residence order but not the authority's consent to that application. The court would still have to consider the authority's plans under section 10(9)(d).

General principles and supplementary provisions

11.—(1) In proceedings in which any question of making a section 8 order, or any other question with respect to such an order, arises, the court shall (in the light of any rules made by virtue of subsection (2)—
    (a) draw up a timetable with a view to determining the question without delay; and
    (b) give such directions as it considers appropriate for the purpose of ensuring, so far as is reasonably practicable, that that timetable is adhered to.

(2) Rules of court may—
    (a) specify periods within which specified steps must be taken in relation to proceedings in which such questions arise; and
    (b) make other provision with respect to such proceedings for the purpose of ensuring, so far as is reasonably practicable, that such questions are determined without delay.

(3) Where a court has power to make a section 8 order, it may do so at any time during the course of the proceedings in question even though it is not in a position to dispose finally of those proceedings.

(4) Where a residence order is made in favour of two or more persons who do not themselves all live together, the order may specify the periods during which the child is to live in the different households concerned.

(5) Where—
    (a) a residence order has been made with respect to a child; and

(b) as a result of the order the child lives, or is to live, with one of two parents who each have parental responsibility for him,

the residence order shall cease to have effect if the parents live together for a continuous period of more than six months.

(6) A contact order which requires the parent with whom a child lives to allow the child to visit, or otherwise have contact with, his other parent shall cease to have effect if the parents live together for a continuous period of more than six months.

(7) A section 8 order may—
- (a) contain directions about how it is to be carried into effect;
- (b) impose conditions which must be complied with by any person—
  - (i) in whose favour the order is made;
  - (ii) who is a parent of the child concerned;
  - (iii) who is not a parent of his but who has parental responsibility for him; or
  - (iv) with whom the child is living,

  and to whom the conditions are expressed to apply;
- (c) be made to have effect for a specified period, or contain provisions which are to have effect for a specified period;
- (d) make such individual, supplemental or consequential provision as the court thinks fit.

DEFINITIONS

"child": s.105(3).
"parental responsibility": ss.2, 3, 12.
"residence order": ss.8(1), 105(3).
"section 8 order": ss.8, 11(7).
"the court": s.92(7).

GENERAL NOTE

This section contains provision for timetabling (subs. (1)) and allows the courts to make section 8 orders even though the proceedings are still continuing (subs. (3)). It also gives further rules relating to "split" residence orders (subs. (4)), the operation of residence and contact orders in favour of parents who cohabit (subss. (5) and (6)) and the contents of section 8 orders (subs. (7)).

Subs. (1)

Timetable: In any case concerning a section 8 order the court should direct the parties to take action within specific times. In doing so it will have to "be realistic and take account of the circumstances, otherwise it simply will not be adhered to," *per* the Lord Chancellor (*Hansard*, H.L. Vol. 503, col. 1347).

Although the section does not so state, such directions will be enforceable through the law of contempt provided that they are sufficiently clear. Magistrates may similarly punish those who disobey their orders (Magistrates' Courts Act 1980, s.63). A penalty of costs may also be imposed in cases of delay. See the Family Proceedings (Costs) Rules 1991 (S.I. 1991 No. 1832), at p. 475 below. For details of timetabling powers see Family Proceedings Courts (Children Act 1989) Rules 1991, rr. 14 and 15 and Sched. 2, col. (ii) (see pp. 388–394 below).

General Principles and Supplementary Provisions

Subs. (3)

The Law Commission envisaged that such a power might be used where a party was continuing to delay proceedings (Law Com. 172, para. 4.58). Where such "interim" orders are made the parties should be aware that it may become difficult to get them changed because of the emphasis on the status quo.

Subs. (4)

This specifically allows the court to make a residence order where the child spends time in two or more homes and thus overrules *Riley* v. *Riley* (1987) 151 J.P. 650. *Guidance*, Vol. 1, para. 2.28 notes, "it is not expected that it will become a common form of order, partly because most children will still need the stability of a single home and partly because in the cases where shared care is appropriate there is less likely to be a need ... for any order at all." Where a child is at boarding school and spends alternate holidays in different homes a shared residence order may be more appropriate than a residence order to one parent and a contact order to the other. If the people concerned are not parents, only the person with a residence order would have parental responsibility; if they are parents, the order made affects the appointment of guardians (s.5).

Subs. (5)

Under the old law only some custody orders lapsed if the parties cohabited (see Law Com. 172, para. 4.13). A residence order only lapses if it is in favour of parents with parental responsibility who cohabit for more than six months. Cohabitation has no effect on a section 4 order granted to an unmarried father by virtue of section 12(1).

Parent: This means mother or father (see note on s.2(1)).

Subs. (6)

This applies even if the unmarried father has not obtained parental responsibility for the child.

Subs. (7)

The directions or conditions will depend on the circumstances of the case and the order sought. The Law Commission considered that these powers would not need to be used frequently (Law Com. 172, para. 4.21–3). Section 13 lists the conditions which apply to all residence orders. Those who do not want to share a residence order or allow contact may be encouraged to do so with conditions relating to their particular anxieties. Conditions can only be imposed on third parties who have parental responsibility or with whom the child is living (para. *(b)*). Conditions need not last as long as the order (s.11(7)(c)).

Directions: For example in a residence order there could be directions that one party return the child *Re B (a minor) (residence order: ex parte)* [1992] 2 F.L.R. 1, 4 or that the child's introduction to his new home should be phased.

Conditions: For example where the child is cared for by someone who will not consent to a blood transfusion, a condition could be made that the carer will inform someone who will consent where a need arise, *e.g.* the terms of a defined contact order.

Residence orders and parental responsibility

12.—(1) Where the court makes a residence order in favour of the father of a child it shall, if the father would not otherwise have parental responsibility for the child, also make an order under section 4 giving him that responsibility.

(2) Where the court makes a residence order in favour of any person who is not the parent or guardian of the child concerned that person shall have parental responsibility for the child while the residence order remains in force.

(3) Where a person has parental responsibility for a child as a result of subsection (2), he shall not have the right—
  (a) to consent, or refuse to consent, to the making of an application with respect to the child under section 18 of the Adoption Act 1976;
  (b) to agree, or refuse to agree, to the making of an adoption order, or an order under section 55 of the Act of 1976, with respect to the child; or
  (c) to appoint a guardian for the child.
 (4) Where subsection (1) requires the court to make an order under section 4 in respect of the father of a child, the court shall not bring that order to an end at any time while the residence order concerned remains in force.

DEFINITIONS
 "child": s.105(1).
 "guardian": s.5.
 "parental responsibility": ss.2, 3, 12.
 "residence order": ss.8(1), 105(3).
 "the court": s.92(7).

GENERAL NOTE
 This section provides that an unmarried father and any person who is not a parent or guardian will have parental responsibility while a residence order exists in his favour. It also clarifies the rights included in parental responsibility for non-parents. Non-parents are not given power in relation to adoption and freeing applications. They cannot appoint a guardian.

Change of child's name or removal from jurisdiction

 13.—(1) Where a residence order is in force with respect to a child, no person may—
  (a) cause the child to be known by a new surname; or
  (b) remove him from the United Kingdom;
without either the written consent of every person who has parental responsibility for the child or the leave of the court.
 (2) Subsection (1)(b) does not prevent the removal of a child, for a period of less than one month, by the person in whose favour the residence order is made.
 (3) In making a residence order with respect to a child the court may grant the leave required by subsection (1)(b), either generally or for specified purposes.

DEFINITIONS
 "child": s.105(1).
 "person who has parental responsibility": ss.2(1), (2), 4(1), 5(6), 12(1)(2).
 "residence order": ss.8(1), 105(3).
 "the court": s.92(7).

GENERAL NOTE
 Section 13 re-enacts with modification the conditions imposed in custody orders under the Matrimonial Causes Rules 1977 relating to name change and removal from the jurisdiction.

Subs. (1)

The child's consent is not required. A child who objects to the proposed step must seek leave under section 10(8) to apply for a prohibited steps order. It follows that a child will only be able to object if he is of sufficient maturity to gain leave, knows his rights and has the skills to obtain them.

In force: See notes on section 91.

No person: The restriction applies to everyone, not just the parties.

United Kingdom: Not, as formerly, the jurisdiction. The Family Law Act 1986 makes orders enforceable throughout the United Kingdom.

Subs. (2)

Although short-term removal by a person with a residence order is not restricted by section 13, it may still pose a substantial threat where that person has substantial links overseas. Removal without the permission of the other parent or the court will still be an offence under the Child Abduction Act 1984 (see Sched. 12, para. 37 for amendments). A prohibited steps order could be sought to preclude any removal or a condition under section 11(7) could be imposed requiring surety for the child's return. The court would need to be satisfied that this was in the child's best interests. A real threat of permanent removal ought to be sufficient (see note on s.1(5)). Section 11 could also be used to ensure that trips were notified in advance with an itinerary and contact addresses.

by: Where the child is going on a school trip the removal is arguably by the school. If so, the exemption does not apply and consent would be required unless the matter had been dealt with by a condition under section 11(7).

Enforcement of residence orders

14.—(1) Where—
  (a) a residence order is in force with respect to a child in
  (b) any other person (including one in whose favour the order is also in force) is in breach of the arrangements settled by that order,

the person mentioned in paragraph (a) may, as soon as the requirement in subsection (2) is complied with, enforce the order under section 63(3) of the Magistrates' Courts Act 1980 as if it were an order requiring the other person to produce the child to him.

(2) The requirement is that a copy of the residence order has been served on the other person.

(3) Subsection (1) is without prejudice to any other remedy open to the person in whose favour the residence order is in force.

DEFINITIONS
  "child": s.105(1).
  "residence order": ss.8(1), 105(3).

GENERAL NOTE

This section enables residence orders to be enforced under the Magistrates' Courts Act 1980, s.63(3), *i.e.* by a penalty of £50 for every day of breach up to a maximum of £2,000 or by imprisonment for up to two months. This provision is required because residence orders are only declaratory and conditions in them are not injunctions. These enforcement provisions previously applied to orders for actual custody or for access under the G.M.A. 1971 and the D.P.M.C.A. 1978 as well as orders for actual custody (custodianship) under the Children Act 1975, s.43(1). The magistrates' court must be satisfied beyond reasonable doubt that the breach has occurred before punishing for disobedience (see *Dean* v. *Dean* [1987] 1 F.L.R. 517). The failure to obey the court order must be wilful (*Patterson* v. *Walcot* [1985] Fam. 32). Other section 8 orders are injunctive in form and are enforceable under Magistrates' Courts Act 1980, s.63(3), see Lowe (1992) 4 J.Ch L. 26, 28. Where a financial penalty is imposed it is enforceable as a fine (Magistrates' Courts Act 1980, s.63(4)).

Under the Contempt of Court Act 1981, s.17, enforcement may be by way of complaint or of the court's own motion. A residence order may be enforced against any person, including a person in whose favour the order is made (subs. (1)), but only after the order has been served on him (subs. (2)). Breach of orders made by the county court or the High Court may be punished as contempt of court.

For procedure see Family Proceedings Courts (Children Act 1989) Rules 1991, r. 24, p. 416 below.

Financial relief

Orders for financial relief with respect to children

15.—(1) Schedule 1 (which consists primarily of the re-enactment, with consequential amendments and minor modifications, of provisions of [section 6 of the Family Law Reform Act 1989] the Guardianship of Minors Acts 1971 and 1973, the Children Act 1975 and of sections 15 and 16 of the Family Law Act 1987) makes provision in relation to financial relief for children.

(2) The powers of a magistrates' court under section 60 of the Magistrates' Courts Act 1980 [and the power of the clerk of a magistrates' court to vary such an order] to revoke, revive or vary an order for the periodical payment of money shall not apply in relation to an order made under Schedule 1.

AMENDMENT

The words in square brackets in subsection (1) were inserted by the Courts and Legal Services Act 1990, s.116, Sched. 16, para. 10(1). The words in square brackets in subsection (2) were inserted by the Maintenance Enforcement Act 1991, Sched. 2, para. 10.

GENERAL NOTE

This section should be read with Schedule 1. The Law Commission explained the reason for this proposal in Law Com. 172, paras. 4.59–69. The aim is to replace the confusing and inconsistent provisions relating to financial relief for children with new provisions with identical rules for making orders regardless of who has a residence order. The new provisions do not replace those in the M.C.A. 1973, nor the D.P.M.C.A. 1978, which the Law Commission could not conveniently assimilate into its scheme. They do not impose the obligation to maintain the child under a court order on any new people—only parents and step-parents (all termed "parents," see Sched. 1, para. 16) can be required to pay. Parents, including unmarried fathers without parental responsibility, guardians and people with a residence order will be able to apply for a whole range of orders for a child but secured orders, settlements and property transfers can only be made in the High Court or county court. Repeated applications for settlements and property transfers by the same person in relation to the same child will still not be possible. Variation, etc., does not come within the Magistrates' Courts Act 1980 but is provided for in Schedule 1, paragraphs 6, 7. The powers in Schedule 1 will be exercisable in respect of wards (para. 1(7) added by the Courts and Legal Services Act, Sched. 10, para. 6). The High Court has claimed wider powers to order support for children under its inherent jurisdiction and could order a local authority to support wards cared for by grandparents (*Calderdale B.C.* v. *T & P* [1991] 1 F.L.R. 461). Had the children merely been subject to residence orders their maintenance would have been a matter for local authority discretion under Schedule 1, paragraph 15.

The Court may not exercise its power to make a maintenance order where a child support officer would have jurisdiction to make a child support assessment, *i.e.* in disputes between parents, Child Support Act 1991, s.8.

Family assistance orders

Family assistance orders

16.—(1) Where, in any family proceedings, the court has power to make an order under this Part with respect to any child, it may (whether or not it makes such an order) make an order requiring—
    (a) a probation officer to be made available; or
    (b) a local authority to make an officer of the authority available,
to advise, assist and (where appropriate) befriend any person named in the order.

(2) The persons who may be named in an order under this section ("a family assistance order") are—
    (a) any parent or guardian of the child;
    (b) any person with whom the child is living or in whose favour a contact order is in force with respect to the child;
    (c) the child himself.

(3) No court may make a family assistance order unless—
    (a) it is satisfied that the circumstances of the case are exceptional; and
    (b) it has obtained the consent of every person to be named in the order other than the child.

(4) A family assistance order may direct—
    (a) the person named in the order; or
    (b) such of the persons named in the order as may be specified in the order,
to take such steps as may be so specified with a view to enabling the officer concerned to be kept informed of the address of any person named in the order and to be allowed to visit any such person.

(5) Unless it specifies a shorter period, a family assistance order shall have effect for a period of six months beginning with the day on which it is made.

(6) Where—
    (a) a family assistance order is in force with respect to a child; and
    (b) a section 8 order is also in force with respect to the child,
the officer concerned may refer to the court the question whether the section 8 order should be varied or discharged.

(7) A family assistance order shall not be made so as to require a local authority to make an officer of theirs available unless—
    (a) the authority agrees; or
    (b) the child concerned lives or will live within their area.

(8) Where a family assistance order requires a probation officer to be made available, the officer shall be selected in accordance with arrangements made by the probation committee for the area in which the child lives or will live.

(9) If the selected probation officer is unable to carry out his duties, or dies, another probation officer shall be selected in the same manner.

DEFINITIONS
"child": s.105(1).
"family assistance order": s.16(1).
"family proceedings": s.8(3).
"guardian": s.5.
"local authority": s.105(1).
"the court": s.92(7).

GENERAL NOTE
Family assistance orders replace supervision orders in custody proceedings. The Law Commission recommended (Law Com. 172, paras. 5.10–5.20) the creation of a new order to remove the need to make the more powerful supervision orders where any social work involvement was intended to be short term, for example, to help the family cope with the immediate problems arising out of separation, etc., to promote arrangements for contact or facilitate co-operation between the parties. However, the Law Commission intended that the courts would still be able to make supervision orders in family proceedings but that recommendation was not enacted. Supervision orders are now only available after proof of the grounds in section 31.

Family assistance orders may only be made in exceptional circumstances and with the agreement of all those involved (except the child) (subss. (3) and (7)). Home Office Circular 65/1991 suggests that these orders should normally be made only after "every other option has been explored." There will usually have been a welfare report under section 7. There is no need for the court to make a section 8 order (subs. (1)), but the supervisor may refer the matter back to court if there is one (subs. (6)). The order lasts for a maximum of six months and cannot be renewed (subs. (5)). The order requires a probation officer or officer of a local authority to be made available (subss. (1), (7)–(9)) and may direct anyone named to keep the officer informed of their or the child's address and permit visits (subs. (4)). It is fundamental to this type of time-limited social work that all those involved should know of its purposes and agree to them. Section 1(5) applies to these orders; *Guidance*, Vol. 1, para. 2.52 notes that it will be "particularly important ... for the court to make plain at the outset why family assistance is needed and what is hoped to be achieved by it."

Subs. (1)
An officer: The officer need not be a social worker; it may be more appropriate for a member of a welfare benefits unit to be appointed in some cases.

Advise, assist, befriend: This was the duty of the supervisor under a supervision order in care proceedings (C.Y.P.A. 1969, s.14).

The Law Commission suggested that, where there has been a report to the court, the report writer should be appointed. This will not be possible if the local authority "subcontracts" reporting work under section 7(1)(b)(ii).

Subs. (2)
Any person with whom the child is living: This rather curious wording is used because no residence order may have been made. However, it is presumably only intended that adults or carers are named, and not the child's siblings, because named people other than the child must consent (s.16(3)(b)).

Subs. (3)
Exceptional: The order must also be in the child's best interests (s.1(1) and (5)).
Consent: May be given orally to the court or in writing and signed (Family Proceedings Courts (Children Act 1989) Rules 1991, r. 25 (see p. 417 below).

Other than the child: It is desirable that the child also supports the making of the order, especially if he will be expected to co-operate with the worker. If the child is adamantly opposed, the order may not be in his best interests.

Subs. (6)
The power of the officer is much less than that which a supervisor had in matrimonial proceedings. He may only refer back issues relating to existing section 8 orders and cannot therefore take steps for the child's committal to care. Where a matter is referred back the court can make any section 8 order (s.10(1)(b)) subject to the restrictions in section 9. The officer would not need to make an application. Where the officer is concerned about the child's well-being he should refer the case to the local authority for investigation under section 47(1)(b).

PART III

LOCAL AUTHORITY SUPPORT FOR CHILDREN AND FAMILIES

Provision of services for children in need, their families and others

17.—(1) It shall be the general duty of every local authority (in addition to the other duties imposed on them by this Part)—
    (a) to safeguard and promote the welfare of children within their area who are in need; and
    (b) so far as is consistent with that duty, to promote the upbringing of such children by their families,
by providing a range and level of services appropriate to those children's needs.

(2) For the purpose principally of facilitating the discharge of their general duty under this section, every local authority shall have the specific duties and powers set out in Part 1 of Schedule 2.

(3) Any service provided by an authority in the exercise of functions conferred on them by this section may be provided for the family of a particular child in need or for any member of his family, if it is provided with a view to safeguarding or promoting the child's welfare.

(4) The Secretary of State may by order amend any provision of Part I of Schedule 2 or add any further duty or power to those for the time being mentioned there.

(5) Every local authority—
    (a) shall facilitate the provision by others (including in particular voluntary organisations) of services which the authority have power to provide by virtue of this section, or section 18, 20, 23 or 24; and
    (b) may make such arrangements as they see fit for any person to act on their behalf in the provision of any such service.

(6) The services provided by a local authority in the exercise of functions conferred on them by this section may include giving assistance in kind or, in exceptional circumstances, in cash.

(7) Assistance may be unconditional or subject to conditions as to the repayment of the assistance or of its value (in whole or in part).

(8) Before giving any assistance or imposing any conditions, a local authority shall have regard to the means of the child concerned and of each of his parents.

(9) No person shall be liable to make any repayment of assistance or of its value at any time when he is in receipt of income support [family credit or disability working allowance] under [Part VII of the Social Security Contributions and Benefits Act 1992].

(10) For the purposes of this Part a child shall be taken to be in need if—

    (a) he is unlikely to achieve or maintain, or to have the opportunity of achieving or maintaining, a reasonable standard of health or development without the provision for him of services by a local authority under this Part;

    (b) his health or development is likely to be significantly impaired, or further impaired, without the provision for him of such services; or

    (c) he is disabled,

and "family," in relation to such a child, includes any person who has parental responsibility for the child and any other person with whom he has been living.

(11) For the purposes of this Part, a child is disabled if he is blind, deaf or dumb or suffers from mental disorder of any kind or is substantially and permanently handicapped by illness, injury or congenital deformity or such other disability as may be prescribed; and in this Part—

    "development" means physical, intellectual, emotional, social or behavioural development; and

    "health" means physical or mental health.

DEFINITIONS
"child": s.105(1).
"child in need": s.17(10).
"development": s.17(11).
"disabled": s.17(11).
"family": s.17(10).
"functions": s.105(1).
"health": s.17(11).
"local authority": s.105(1).
"person who has parental responsibility": ss.2(1)(2), 4(1), 5(6), 12(1)(2).
"services": s.105, Sched. 2, Pt. I.
"voluntary organisation": s.105(1).

AMENDMENT
In subsection (9) the words in square brackets were substituted by the Disability Living Allowance and Working Allowance Act 1991, s.7, Sched. 3, para. 13 and the Social Security (Consequential Provisions) Act 1992, Sched. 2, para. 108.

GENERAL NOTE
This section sets out the general preventive duty which each local authority owes to "children in need" in their area. "In need" is thus a gateway to a range of local authority services including day care and accommodation. The duty is broader than that in the C.C.A. 1980, s.1, which was negative—written in terms of keeping children out of care rather than promoting their welfare—but it is owed to a restricted group of children. It also replaces, as far as children are concerned, the duties

of local authorities under the health and welfare statutes. Consequently National Assistance Act 1948, ss. 21 and 29 are amended by Schedule 13, paragraph 11 to apply to persons over 18 years only; the Chronically Sick and Disabled Persons Act 1970 is extended to "children in need" by Schedule 13, paragraph 27 and the National Health Service Act 1977, s. 21 and Sched. 8 are repealed so far as they applied to children.

In order to comply with the general duty, a local authority must provide services to "children in need" and their families which are appropriate to their needs (subs. (1)). Services may not be imposed under this provision. This can occur only if the authority has obtained an order under section 31 (or possibly under ss.16 or 36). The Lord Chancellor stated that "Partnership with parents based on agreement so far as possible will be the guiding principle" for the provision of services (*Hansard*, H.L. Vol. 502, col. 491). Schedule 2, Part I, expands the section by specifying the action local authorities must take to identify "children in need" and discharge their general duty. In addition, local authorities are under a duty to facilitate the provision of services by others and may delegate provision to others (subs. (5)). Services may include giving assistance in kind or (exceptionally) in cash (subs. (6)). Assistance may be given subject to conditions (subs. (7)) and must be means-tested (subs. (8)). No repayments may be required from a person in receipt of specified social security benefits (subs. (9)). The provisions relating to repayment must be read in conjunction with section 29, which gives further details about liability and recovery.

The Department of Health has issued further Guidance on these provisions, see *Guidance*, Vol. 2; Vol. 6.

Subs. (1)
This provision represents a fundamental shift by providing a statutory framework for all preventive work in child care, not only that designed to help keep children out of care. It recognises both the value of family life and that care may have a positive contribution to make to the welfare of children.

Section 1 of the C.C.A. 1980 (introduced by the Children and Young Persons Act 1963) was couched in similarly general terms and was open to two alternative interpretations. It either created a general duty to provide services to keep children out of care or imposed a specific duty to consider the impact of any decision on individual children who might, in consequence, come into care. In *Att.-Gen., ex rel. Tilley* v. *Wandsworth London Borough Council* [1981] 1 W.L.R. 854 both the High Court and the Court of Appeal held that a specific duty was created. Even so, it was extremely difficult to use court proceedings to enforce the duty in section 1. In *R.* v. *Tower Hamlets London Borough Council, ex p. Monaf* (1988) 20 H.L.R. 529, the Court of Appeal held that the local authority had complete discretion about how the duty should be carried out. Thus section 1 could not impose any greater duty to rehouse an intentionally homeless family than that which existed in the Housing Act 1985. The High Court also refused to find that the C.C.A. 1980, ss. 18 and 21 which specified local authorities' duties to children in care, could found an action in damages (*Guevara* v. *London Borough of Hounslow, The Times*, April 17, 1987).

The C.C.A. 1980, s.2(3) imposed a duty to rehabilitate children in voluntary care where this was consistent with their welfare. The new duty is broader because it is not limited to such children, but would include children in hospitals, in the care of voluntary organisations or in other forms of substitute care like private fostering arrangements. Local authorities have some responsibility for the welfare of such children under Parts VII–IX and sections 85 and 86.

General duty: The addition of the word "general" would suggest that the interpretation of section 1 in the *Tilley* case would no longer apply, but this is far from clear, particularly since the appropriateness of services can only be judged by looking at the individuals who are in need of them. The Secretary of State has power under section 84 to deal with cases where local authorities have defaulted on their duties. The possibilities of using the courts to review local authority decisions or enforce its duties are considered by Sunkin (1992) 4 J.Ch.Law 109.

Other duties:
Section 18(1)(3): day care for some under-fives who are "children in need";
Section 20(1): provision of accommodation for some "children in need";
Sections 22, 23 and 24(1): duties to children looked after by the local authority;

Section 24: duties to some people who have been in care;

Schedule 2, Part I: provision of services in the community.

Welfare: There is no definition of Welfare for Part III. The intention of the Government was to achieve an appropriate balance between the state's powers and those of individual parents. It was guided in its consideration by a number of principles, including that the prime responsibility for the upbringing of children rests with parents and that the state should be ready to help parents to discharge that responsibility, especially where doing so lessened the risk of family breakdown (Cm. 62, para. 5). However, it is well established that the views of individual social workers (and their managers) differ, particularly in relation to the value of the natural family and the consequences of entering local authority care (see Fox, *Two Value Positions in Recent Child Care Law and Practice* (1982) 12 Brit. J. of Social Work 265–290). Even where there is agreement about children's needs there may be no duty on the local authority to satisfy them. For example, the National Child Development Study provides considerable evidence that poverty is associated with poor health, poor educational attainment, employment problems and reception into care for children. Yet section 17 does not require local authorities to take on an income maintenance role, nor is it likely that there would be resources to let local authorities exercise their powers in this way.

So far as is consistent: Where it is not, the authority can offer to accommodate under section 20(1)(c) or take care proceedings under section 31. It could also decide to take no action subject to its duty to prevent neglect and abuse (Sched. 2, para. 4) and its duty to investigate suspected abuse and neglect (s.47).

A range and level of services appropriate: What services are provided and the numbers they can serve would seem largely to be left to the local authority, as under the Court of Appeal decision in *ex p. Monaf*. It will be extremely difficult to show that services are not appropriate. If an authority fails to provide services which are widely accepted as desirable—foster care, residential placements for teenagers or day care for the under-fives (see ss.18 and 19)—or provides a level of services considered inadequate by the Social Services Inspectorate it might be in breach. Action could then be taken under section 84. However, in many areas there is sufficient disagreement to make challenge impossible. *Guidance*, Vol. 2, para. 2.11 states:

"Local authorities are not expected to meet every individual need, but they are asked to identify the extent of need and then make decisions on the priorities for services provision in their area in the context of that information and their statutory duties ... It is important to recognise the benefits of developing packages of services appropriate to the assessed needs of individual children rather than directing them to individual services which may not be appropriate."

And, at paragraph 2.7:

"Good practice requires that the assessment of need should be undertaken in an open way and should involve those caring for the child, the child and other significant persons. Families ... have a right to receive sympathetic support and sensitive intervention in their family's life."

Subs. (2)

The duties in Schedule 2, Part I, are largely qualified, *i.e.* that the local authority shall take reasonable steps or make such provisions as it considers appropriate. The duties include to identify the extent to which there are children in need in their area (para. 1); to prevent children suffering neglect or abuse (para. 4); to provide specific services including advice, activities, home helps (para. 8) and family centres (para. 9) and, where the child is not living with his family, to enable him to live with or be in contact with them (para. 10). The duties to disabled children which came from the National Assistance Act 1948 and the Chronically Sick and Disabled Persons Act 1970 are absolute. Local authorities must open and maintain a register of disabled children (para. 2) and provide services for them (para. 6). Local authorities are also required to provide information about children likely to suffer harm (para. 4) and take reasonable steps to reduce the need to bring various proceedings or take other specific steps in relation to children (para. 7). In providing day care or encouraging people to act as foster parents, the authority must have regard to the ethnic mix of their area (para. 11). The local authority is also empowered to assist alleged abusers to obtain alternative accommodation and may recoup assistance given under section 17(7)–(9) (para. 5).

Provision of Services for Children in Need

Subs. (3)

Family: This is defined in subsection (10) to include "any person with parental responsibility for the child and any other person with whom he has been living." It is not clear whether this adds to a general understanding of family or not. If it does, then relatives with whom the child has not been living, for example, uncles and aunts, or the child's unmarried father, can also receive assistance with a view to safeguarding, etc., the child's welfare. Thus assistance could be given to enable such a person to take over the child's care. If family is more narrowly construed, then such people would either have to obtain parental responsibility by applying to the court (under s.10) or be accepted as local authority foster parents so that they could be assisted through the local authority's duties to children it accommodates under section 23. A wider interpretation of family would appear to be more in keeping with the aims of the legislation.

A member of his family: The assistance may be provided to individuals. This phrase has been interpreted where it appears in the Rent Acts (now Housing Act 1988, s.39) to include the unmarried partner of a tenant (*Dyson Holdings* v. *Fox* [1976] Q.B. 503). Unmarried step-parents with whom the child has been living are clearly included in the definition.

Subs. (4)

The duties in the Schedule can be kept up to date by secondary legislation. Any statutory instrument made under this subsection is subject to the affirmative resolution procedure (s.104(3)).

Amend: The Bill would have permitted the Secretary of State "to modify or repeal" the Schedule but this was considered a "constitutional outrage" by Lord Simon (*Hansard*, H.L. Vol. 502, col. 1295). However, an amendment can go "right up to the edge of repeal", *per* Lord Simon (*Hansard*, H.L. Vol. 505, col. 349). He also stated that no court could possibly find any amendment was in excess of the Secretary of State's powers.

Subs. (6)

The C.C.A. 1980, s.1 permitted local authorities to assist in this way. The Lord Chancellor rejected the notion that there should be a broader power because this "could push local authorities into income maintenance role which is the function of the Social Security System" (*Hansard*, H.L. Vol. 502, col. 1297).

Section 1 payments are disregarded for the purposes of calculating means-tested social security payments and Housing Benefit (Income Support (General) Regulations 1987, reg. 40(2), Sched. 9, para. 28; Family Credit (General) Regulations 1987, reg. 29(2), Sched. 3, para. 18).

Assistance in kind: Both the High Court and the Court of Appeal rejected a narrow interpretation of "assistance in kind" which would have excluded provision of accommodation for a family under the C.C.A. 1980, s.1 (see *Att.-Gen., ex rel. Tilley* v. *Wandsworth London Borough Council* [1981] 1 W.L.R. 854).

Exceptional circumstances: There are two possible interpretations: a restrictive one which requires the circumstances to be exceptional in the life of the individual recipient and another which requires them to be exceptional in the community.

Subs. (7)

The Health and Social Services and Social Security Adjudications Act 1983, s.17, introduced a consistent scheme for charging for services provided by local authorities. That section applied (*inter alia*) to the National Assistance Act 1948, s.29 and the National Health Service Act 1977, Sched. 8, which have both been subsumed in this Act so far as they apply to children. However, there was no power to levy charges in the C.C.A. 1980 except where the child was in care, thus the new power is broader.

Only parents are liable at common law to maintain their children, although stepparents can be required to make contributions for their care in domestic and matrimonial proceedings. Only parents have a duty to maintain their children enforceable in public law. However, non-parents may be given assistance and can be required to pay for it under section 29. If a service were provided to a non-parent for a child under 16, a charge could be levied on the parents or on the recipient. If the recipient has a residence order or is the child's guardian he could seek reimbursement from the parent through an order for financial relief under Schedule 1. Where a service is provided to keep a child out of care it would seem inappropriate for the local authority to impose a condition as to repayment on a non-parent, because such a person would not be liable to support the child if he were being looked after by the local authority.

It is not clear that refusal to accept a condition about repayment or outstanding debts would justify refusal to provide assistance. The Lord Chancellor stated, "The Bill does not provide that failure of parents to comply with any conditions as to assistance renders the child ineligible for other services. The authority's general duty to provide services appropriate to the needs of children in need would remain" (*Hansard*, H.L. Vol. 502, col. 1299). That statement leaves in doubt the position of an individual child (see the discussion of subs. (1)). Conditions about repayment must be lifted where the payee's means are insufficient (see s.29(2)).

Charges may be recovered in the magistrates' court as civil debts (s.29(5)).

Conditions: This might include, for example, interest. The power to charge interest already exists under the comparable Scottish legislation.

Assistance: This would seem to be sufficiently wide to cover any services provided by the local authority under this section or Schedule 2, Part I. However, section 29(1) provides that charges may not be levied for advice, guidance or counselling. It may, however, be difficult to separate this from the provision of some services. For example, a place in a family centre intended to improve parenting skills could be seen as guidance or alternatively training and recreational activities (Sched. 2, para. 9).

Value: There is no set formula for determining the value of a service which could be the cost to the local authority or the benefit of it to the recipient. If it is the benefit this may be impossible to assess. Charges for accommodating children in care are limited to the amount paid to foster parents as a boarding-out allowance (Sched. 2, para. 22(5)). Charges for services are not so limited and could theoretically be higher. If so, this would appear to defeat the general duty in section 17(1)(b). Any dispute about conditions can be referred to the complaints system which must be established under section 26(3).

Subs. (8)

Although non-parents may be charged for services, only parents and children have to be means-tested before assistance is given. Even where the local authority does not wish to impose conditions, it must consider means so that in each case an individual decision is taken. Where the child has funds, his parents, as guardians of his property, (s.3(2)) may have to use them to pay for services. Thus money claimed by child victims from the Criminal Injuries Compensation Scheme may find its way to local authorities assisting them.

Have regard to: Formal means-testing is not required but the authority would need basic information about means.

Subs. (9)

It is not clear whether liability to make repayments is suspended or ended by receipt of benefits. The Department of Health considers that payment is only suspended. Thus when benefit ceases the whole liability resumes. This would create a new benefit trap unless charges were reassessed. This provision is based on one introduced in relation to charges for accommodation by the Health and Social Services and Social Security Adjudications Act 1983, s.19. The rationale for not levying charges for accommodation on parents in receipt of benefit is that there is no provision in the parents' benefit for the child in care. Here the exemption of benefit recipients appears to recognise that they are too poor to contribute. If this is so, suspension would be more logical.

In receipt of: A high proportion, up to 65 per cent., of those who qualify for family credit do not claim it. A local authority could decide not to require repayments from such people but they have no right to be exempted. Arguably, when means testing the authority should identify such people and provide advice about benefits under section 17(1).

Subss. (10) and (11)
These contain the definition of "child in need." Department of Health *Guidance*, Vol. 2, para. 2.4 states,
"The definition of 'need' in the Act is deliberately wide to reinforce the emphasis on preventive support and services to families. It has three categories: a reasonable standard of health or development; significant impairment of health or development; and disablement. It would not be acceptable for the authority to exclude any of these three—for example, by confining services to children at risk of significant harm ... This guidance does not lay down firm criteria or set general priorities because the Act requires each authority to decide their own level and scale of services appropriate to the children in need in their area. However ... a local authority cannot lawfully substitute any other definition for the purposes of Part III."

Children "in need" must be distinguished from children who have special educational needs within the terms of the Education Act 1981. However, there will be children who come within both definitions. Assessments of need for the purposes of this Act may be done alongside other statutory assessments under the 1981 Act, the Chronically Sick and Disabled Persons Act 1970, the Disabled Persons (Services, Consultation and Representation) Act 1986 or any other enactment (Sched. 2, para. 3).

Reasonable standard of health or development: It is not clear how reasonable is to be judged: by the standards of the area, by national standards, or by the standards appropriate for a developed nation. There is a danger that some authorities may accept lower standards in relation to certain groups such as travellers' children, but this is not justified by the legislation and may contravene the Race Relations Act 1976.

Without the provision of services: Children in need remain "in need" even where services are provided. Thus children looked after by local authorities or voluntary organisations can still be "in need" and assistance can be given to their families (*per* the Lord Chancellor (*Hansard*, H.L. Vol. 502, col. 1287)).

Significantly impaired: Section 31(10) defines "significant harm" and requires a comparison between the child and "that which could be reasonably expected of a similar child." Even slight impairment may be significant for the child's long-term development if it affects education or socialisation.

Further impaired: If the child's health development is already impaired, further impairment need not be significant.

Family: See discussion under subsection (3) above.

Disabled: The wording, though different from that in the National Assistance Act 1948, s.29(1), which makes provision for disabled adults, precisely mirrors its content. Thus the same people will qualify for services before and after age 18. All the guidance issued by the Department of Health relating to children with disabilities has been collected together in *Guidance*, Vol. 6.

Blind: Although partially sighted children do not clearly fall within the definition of disabled, they are "children in need" by virtue of section 17(10)(a) or (b) (*per* David Mellor, Minister of Health, Standing Committee B, col. 101, May 16, 1989).

Prescribed: This means prescribed by the Secretary of State. No conditions were prescribed under section 29 of the 1948 Act.

Day care for pre-school and other children

18.—(1) Every local authority shall provide such day care for children in need within their area who are—
 (a) aged five or under; and
 (b) not yet attending schools,
as is appropriate.

(2) A local authority may provide day care for children within their area who satisfy the conditions mentioned in subsection (1)(a) and (b) even though they are not in need.

(3) A local authority may provide facilities (including training, advice, guidance and counselling) for those—
    (a) caring for children in day care; or
    (b) who at any time accompany such children while they are in day care.
(4) In this section "day care" means any form of care or supervised activity provided for children during the day (whether or not it is provided on a regular basis).
(5) Every local authority shall provide for children in need within their area who are attending any school such care or supervised activities as is appropriate—
    (a) outside school hours; or
    (b) during school holidays.
(6) A local authority may provide such care or supervised activities for children within their area who are attending any school even though those children are not in need.
(7) In this section "supervised activity" means an activity supervised by a responsible person.

DEFINITIONS
"child": s.105(1).
"child in need": s.17(10).
"day care": s.18(4).
"local authority": s.105(1).
"supervised activity": s.18(7).

GENERAL NOTE
This section imposes a duty on local authorities to provide specified services for children in need, *i.e.* day care for under-fives who are not attending school (subs. (1)) and supervised activities after school hours and during the holidays for children attending school (subs. (5)). Local authorities should also facilitate the provision of day care, etc., by voluntary organisations and others (s.17(5)). It also empowers local authorities to provide these services for other children (subss. (2) and (6)) and facilities for carers (subs. (3)). Charges can be levied for these services (s.29(1)). The Department of Health has issued guidance on day care, see *Guidance*, Vol. 2.

Subs. (1)
Not yet attending schools: School hours for children of this age may be as short as one and a half hours per day (Education (School and Further Education) Regulations 1981, reg. 10). Attendance is not defined but education law distinguishes between registered pupils and school attendance. Arguably, a child who has a half-time place in a nursery school is not attending school during the rest of the school day. Schools must be distinguished from day nurseries. Local authorities have powers and duties in relation to nurseries under Part X of this Act.
As is appropriate: The authority must have regard to the different racial groups to which children in need in their area belong (Sched. 2, para. 11). Lack of day care provision may be referred to the Secretary of State under section 84.
Facilities may be provided for workers such as childminders, nursery nurses, play leaders and also for parents and other people who bring children to playgroups, etc. (subs. (3)).

Subs. (4)
The definition of "day care" is broad and, unlike section 71(1), not limited to care not on domestic premises. It also covers children cared for by their own families or in their own homes.

Subs. (7)
Responsible person: This is not defined. Arguably, anyone who has charge of children is responsible for them.

Review of provision for day care, child minding, etc.

19.—(1) Every local authority in England and Wales shall review—
   (a) the provisions which they make under section 18;
   (b) the extent to which the services of child minders are available within their area with respect to children under the age of eight; and
   (c) the provision for day care within their area made for children under the age of eight by persons, other than the authority, required to register under section 71(1)(b).

(2) A review under subsection (1) shall be conducted—
   (a) together with the appropriate local education authority; and
   (b) at least once in every review period.

(3) Every local authority in Scotland shall, at least once in every review period, review—
   (a) the provision for day care within their area made for children under the age of eight by the local authority and by persons required to register under section 71(1)(b); and
   (b) the extent to which the services of child minders are available within their area with respect to children under the age of eight.

(4) In conducting any such review, the two authorities or, in Scotland, the authority shall have regard to the provision made with respect to children under the age of eight in relevant establishments within their area.

(5) In this section—
   "relevant establishment" means any establishment which is mentioned in paragraphs 3 and 4 of Schedule 9 (hospitals, schools and other establishments exempt from the registration requirements which apply in relation to the provision of day care); and
   "review period" means the period of one year beginning with the commencement of this section and each subsequent period of three years beginning with an anniversary of that commencement.

(6) Where a local authority have conducted a review under this section they shall publish the result of the review—
   (a) as soon as is reasonably practicable;
   (b) in such form as they consider appropriate; and
   (c) together with any proposals they may have with respect to the matters reviewed.

(7) The authorities conducting any review under this section shall have regard to—
   (a) any representations made to any one of them by any relevant health authority or health board; and
   (b) any other representations which they consider to be relevant.

(8) In the application of this section to Scotland, "day care" has the same meaning as in section 79 and "health board" has the same meaning as in the National Health Service (Scotland) Act 1978.

DEFINITIONS
"childminder": s.71(2).
"day care": s.18(4).
"health authority": s.105(1).
"local authority": s.105(1).
"local education authority": s.105(1).
"relevant establishment": s.19(5).
"review period": s.19(5).

GENERAL NOTE
This section imposes a new duty on local authorities in England and Wales to review the day care they provide and that for children under eight years by childminders and in play groups and nurseries which are required to register with the local authority (subs. (1)). The review must be carried out with the local education authority at least every three years (subss. (2) and (5)) and must take account of other provisions for under-fives in schools and hospitals (subs. (5)). They must also take account of representations by health authorities and others (subs. (7)). The results of the review must be published (subs. (6)). A comparable duty is imposed on Scottish local authorities by subsection (3). For definitions applying to Scotland, see subsection (4) and section 79.

The purpose of the review is so that public and private facilities for under-fives complement each other and to assist planning. The Department of Health has issued Guidance on the Review of Day Care and the contents of the Report, *Guidance*, Vol. 2, Chap. 9.

Subs. (2)
Appropriate local authority: This is not defined for the purposes of this section but presumably means the local education authority operating in the area of the local authority.

Subs. (7)
Other representations: This includes "local voluntary groups, parents and employers" (*per* David Mellor, Minister of Health (Standing Committee B, col. 523, June 13, 1989)). The Minister also suggests that this clause would give local people an opportunity to put pressure on local councillors to give more attention to these services (Standing Committee B, col. 124, May 16, 1989). *Guidance*, Vol. 2, para. 9.8 states, "The purpose of consultation is to enable the organisations and individuals who are interested in services for young children and their families to give the two authorities their views on the existing pattern of services, the need for changes (if any) and for developments and how these might be instituted."

Provision of accommodation for children

Provision of accommodation for children: general

20.—(1) Every local authority shall provide accommodation for any child in need within their area who appears to them to require accommodation as a result of—

(a) there being no person who has parental responsibility for him;

(b) his being lost or having been abandoned; or

(c) the person who has been caring for him being prevented (whether or not permanently, and for whatever reason) from providing him with suitable accommodation or care.

(2) Where a local authority provide accommodation under subsection (1) for a child who is ordinarily resident in the area of another local authority, that other local authority may take over the provision of accommodation for the child within—
> (a) three months of being notified in writing that the child is being provided with accommodation; or
> (b) such other longer period as may be prescribed.

(3) Every local authority shall provide accommodation for any child in need within their area who has reached the age of 16 and whose welfare the authority consider is likely to be seriously prejudiced if they do not provide him with accommodation.

(4) A local authority may provide accommodation for any child within their area (even though a person who has parental responsibility for him is able to provide him with accommodation) if they consider that to do so would safeguard or promote the child's welfare.

(5) A local authority may provide accommodation for any person who has reached the age of 16 but is under 21 in any community home which takes children who have reached the age of 16 if they consider that to do so would safeguard or promote his welfare.

(6) Before providing accommodation under this section, a local authority shall, so far as is reasonably practicable and consistent with the child's welfare—
> (a) ascertain the child's wishes regarding the provision of accommodation; and
> (b) give due consideration (having regard to his age and understanding) to such wishes of the child as they have been able to ascertain.

(7) A local authority may not provide accommodation under this section for any child if any person who—
> (a) has parental responsibility for him; and
> (b) is willing and able to—
>> (i) provide accommodation for him; or
>> (ii) arrange for accommodation to be provided for him,

objects.

(8) Any person who has parental responsibility for a child may at any time remove the child from accommodation provided by or on behalf of the local authority under this section.

(9) Subsections (7) and (8) do not apply while any person—
> (a) in whose favour a residence order is in force with respect to the child; or
> (b) who has care of the child by virtue of an order made in the exercise of the High Court's inherent jurisdiction with respect to children,

agrees to the child being looked after in accommodation provided by or on behalf of the local authority.

(10) Where there is more than one such person as is mentioned in subsection (9), all of them must agree.

(11) Subsections (7) and (8) do not apply where a child who has reached the age of 16 agrees to being provided with accommodation under this section.

DEFINITIONS

"child": s.105(1).
"child in need": ss.17(10), 105(7).
"community home": s.53.
"local authority": s.105(1).
"ordinary residence": ss.30(2), 105(6).
"person with parental responsibility": ss.2(1)(2), 4(1), 5(6), 12(1)(2).
"prescribed": s.105(1).
"residence order": ss.8(1), 105(3).

GENERAL NOTE

This section replaces the C.C.A. 1980, s.2 and the related sections which provided the statutory framework for the voluntary care system. The concept of "provision of accommodation" replaces reception into care. Accommodation has the same status as other services provided under Part III and thus depends on the willingness of the family to accept it. There is no provision to replace the C.C.A. 1980, s.13, so people with parental responsibility cannot be required to give 28 days' notice before removing children from local authority accommodation. The Government remained adamantly opposed to amendments which would undermine the voluntary nature of arrangements for children to be accommodated by local authorities; accommodation by a local authority should equate with that provided in the family.

Local authorities are under a duty to provide accommodation for children in need who satisfy any of the conditions in subsection (1) or subsection (3). They also have the power to provide accommodation for any child and young adults under the age of 21 years (subss. (4) and (5)). Before accommodation is provided, the local authority must ascertain the child's wishes and feelings about this and give due consideration to them (subs. (6)). The voluntary nature of the provision under this section is clear from subsections (7) and (8). Subsection (7) precludes the local authority from providing accommodation for a child under 16 if any person with parental responsibility who is willing and able to provide accommodation for him objects. Subsection (8) states that a person with parental responsibility may remove a child under 16 years at any time. If there is a residence order or an order giving care and control under the inherent jurisdiction of the High Court, these decisions can only be made by a person in whose favour the order was made (subs. (9)). If there is more than one, all must agree (subs. (10)). Those over 16 may themselves decide about going into or remaining in local authority accommodation (subs. (11)).

Department of Health *Guidance*, Vol. 2, para. 3.31 states: "Planning for the child's immediate care and future welfare based on a full assessment of need in partnership with all concerned will be fundamental to the appropriate provision of accommodation."

The Arrangements for Placement of Children (General) Regulations 1991 (S.I. 1991 No. 890) apply to these placements and arrangements between parents, etc., and voluntary organisations or registered children's homes, all termed responsible authorities (reg. 2). Regulation 3 requires the arrangements to be agreed in writing with a person with parental responsibility or, if there is no such person, the child's carer. If the child is over 16 and is accommodated under section 20(11) the agreement must be made with him or her. Unless this is not practicable the agreement should be made before accommodation is provided. The matters to be considered in drawing up the agreement are set out in Schedules 1–3 to the regulations. They include the local authority's immediate and long-term arrangements; the child's state of health, health history and existing arrangements for health surveillance; and the child's educational history and needs. Schedule 4 sets out the matters which must be included in the agreement. These are:

the address where the child will be accommodated and the name of the person responsible for the child there (para. 1);

details of services to be provided for the child (para. 2);

the respective responsibilities of the local authority, the child, the parents and anyone with parental responsibility including any delegation of parental responsibility (paras. 3 and 4);

the arrangements for involving those people in decisions about the child (para. 5);

the arrangements for contact (para. 6); the arrangements for notifying changes (para. 7);

whether section 20(11) applies to the placement (para. 8);

the expected duration of arrangements and the steps which should be taken to bring them to an end.

Regulation 5 requires the arrangements to be notified to a wide range of people and organisations concerned with the child. These include anyone whose wishes and feelings have been sought under sections 22(4), 61(2) or 64(2); anyone who was caring for the child immediately before the arrangements were made and anyone with a contact order. Regulation 7 requires the child to be medically examined and a written assessment provided unless this has been done within the previous three months or a child with sufficient understanding refuses to submit. Regulation 8 requires the authority, etc., to maintain records including a copy of the written agreement, any welfare reports and reports from Reviews. Records must be kept confidential (reg. 9). The local authority must also keep a register of all children placed in their area and any children accommodated by them elsewhere (reg. 10). Where a child has a series of "respite" placements with the same person over a period of one year, each lasting four weeks or less and the total does not exceed 90 days, regulation 13 allows this to be treated as a single placement.

Guidance, Vol. 3, Chap. 2 explains and amplifies the regulations. Paragraph 2.14 states "Agreements between parents and the responsible authority should reflect the fact that parents retain their parental responsibility. The responsible authority's responsibilities . . . should not detract in any way from the parents' continuing parental responsibility. Their continuing involvement with the child and exercise of their responsibility should be the basis of the agreed arrangements; all concerned in the arrangements should be aware of this."

Social workers will need to develop skills in negotiating and drafting written agreements. The Family Rights Group has published useful material: see F.R.G., *Using Written Agreements with Children and Families* (1989); *Working in Partnership with Families Training Programme* (1991) H.M.S.O.

Complaints against the local authority can be referred to its procedure under section 26(3).

Subs. (1)

This re-enacts the C.C.A. 1980, s.2(1) with modifications. The duty is now owed only to children in need but is not limited to those under 17. Over-16s must agree (subs. (11)). The requirement that reception into care must be for the child's welfare in section 2(1)(c) is replaced by the general duty in section 17(1). This duty exists alongside the duties in the Housing Act 1985 to homeless persons. During the Bill's passage through the Lords there were several attempts to restrict the local authority's powers to provide care for children rather than homes for homeless families, but all were unsuccessful.

Subs. (2)

Unless the other authority takes over provision of accommodation the placing authority remains responsible for the child and must comply with all the duties imposed on the responsible authority by the Arrangements Regulations (see above).

Prescribed: This means by the Secretary of State; no period has been prescribed.

Subs. (3)

The law relating to accommodation of 16-year-olds and older children is not clear. Parents appear not to be under a duty to accommodate them; they have the right to live independently. The duty of social services departments towards over-16s in need is narrower since it only arises if the authority considers their welfare is likely to be "seriously prejudiced" without provision of accommodation. Social services departments may thus discharge young people from care or refuse to provide them with accommodation even though they are in need. However, they will owe them duties under section 17(1) and also under section 24(2) if they have been accommodated after the age of 16 years. Housing authorities may accept young people as homeless and with a priority need because they are vulnerable: Housing Act 1985, s.59(1)(c). If so the housing authority will be under a duty to house them. But the *Housing Act Code of Guidance* cautions against automatic acceptance of young people as vulnerable (para. 6.13). Nevertheless, in *Kelly* v. *Monklands D.C.* (1985 Court of Session) Lord Ross stated, "When you find a girl of 16 who has no assets, no income and nowhere to go who has apparently left home because of violence, I am of the opinion that no reasonable authority could fail to conclude that she was vulnerable." Instead of providing housing the housing authority may call on social services to exercise its functions (Housing Act 1985, s.72) and see also section 27 below and Luba, 82 *Childright* 11 (1991).

Subs. (4)

This gives the local authority power to accommodate other children and so allows the service to be provided before a child has been formally accepted as "in need." It provides the authority for respite care schemes which the D.H.S.S. R.C.C.L Chapter 6 was keen to support.

Subs. (5)

This re-enacts the C.C.A. 1980, s.72, removing the provisions which required the community home to be near the child's employment or place of education, etc.

Subs. (6)

This imposes a qualified duty on the local authority to ascertain a child's wishes and give due consideration to them before providing accommodation. Section 22(4) makes similar provision in relation to decisions about other matters. If a child is dissatisfied, he may make a representation or complaint under section 26(3), or, if he is over 16, discharge himself from care (subs. (11)).

Subs. (7)

Where the child's welfare requires him to be looked after by the local authority, and there is an effective objection by someone with parental responsibility, the local authority will have to seek an emergency protection order (s.44) or bring care proceedings under section 31. If there are no grounds for an order the authority cannot seek permission to accommodate the child from the High Court by wardship (s.100(2)(b)).

A person with parental responsibility for a child can object to the local authority accommodating that child and thus prevent it from so doing, but only if he is able and willing to provide accommodation (or make arrangements for this). Thus, if a mother asks for her child to be accommodated, the father's objection will have no effect unless he has parental responsibility (an unmarried father may not, a divorced father will) and he has alternative arrangements for the child's care. If the mother has a residence order and the father has not, her decision to ask the local authority to accommodate her child is effective despite the father's objections because of subsection (9). The father could not prevent the authority from providing accommodation, even if he was able and willing to care for the child. He would need either to persuade the authority to place the child with him by virtue of its duty under sections 17(1) and 23(6) or to obtain a residence order under section 10.

Child: Child under 16—see subsection (11).

Is able and willing: This could be interpreted to invalidate the objection of a homeless or inadequately housed parent. Unless the child was suffering, etc., significant harm and an order was obtained the local authority should not have any rights of compulsion.

Subs. (8)

This provision produced considerable disquiet amongst both statutory and voluntary child care organisations. The repeal of the 28-day notice provision was thought to leave children in care vulnerable to sudden removal and be likely to discourage local authorities from using section 20 rather than compulsory measures. The Lord Chancellor was adamant that provision of accommodation should remain an entirely voluntary matter between the "parents" and local authority as proposed in the White Paper (Cm. 62, para. 22(b)) but suggested two methods of protecting children where removal would be harmful. An emergency protection order could be obtained under section 44. Alternatively, the local authority or the carers might rely on section 3(5), which empowers "persons" without parental responsibility to do "what is reasonable in all the circumstances for the purpose of safeguarding or promoting the child's welfare" (*Hansard*, H.L. Vol. 503, col. 1412; Vol. 505, col. 370). This might justify a refusal to return a child in the middle of the night or to a parent who was incapable, but the relationship between section 3(5) and section 20(8) will need to be clarified by litigation. A foster parent could also make the child a ward of court and seek care and control, although the courts will undoubtedly be concerned that such steps are not taken to avoid the restrictions in sections 9, 10 and 100.

Subs. (9)

See comments on subsection (7) above. Where the parents are divorcing and the child is at risk of coming into care this subsection provides a good justification for making a residence order.

Subs. (11)

This provides that 16- and 17-year-olds have rights to admit themselves to accommodation and to remain there against the wishes of their parents. It does not clearly state that they have a right to discharge themselves accommodation. However, local authorities have no statutory power to detain such children without a care order. The *Gillick* decision recognises that mature young people may make decisions about their own lives except where Parliament has given power to others, so it seems that such young people may "vote with their feet" although they may have extreme difficulty supporting themselves.

Provision of accommodation for children in police protection or detention or on remand, etc.

21.—(1) Every local authority shall make provision for the reception and accommodation of children who are removed or kept away from home under Part V.

(2) Every local authority shall receive, and provide accommodation for, children—
    (a) in police protection whom they are requested to receive under section 46(3)(f);
    (b) whom they are requested to receive under section 38(6) of the Police and Criminal Evidence Act 1984;
    (c) who are—
        (i) on remand under section [16(3A) or] 23(1) of the Children and Young Persons Act 1969; or
        (ii) the subject of a supervision order imposing a residence requirement under section 12AA of that Act,
and with respect to whom they are the designated authority.

(3) Where a child has been—
    (a) removed under Part V; or
    (b) detained under section 38 of the Police and Criminal Evidence Act 1984,
and he is not being provided with accommodation by a local authority or in a hospital vested in the Secretary of State [or otherwise made available pursuant to arrangements made by a District Health

Authority], any reasonable expenses of accommodating him shall be recoverable from the local authority in whose area he is ordinarily resident.

AMENDMENT

In subsection (3) the words in square brackets were inserted by the National Health Service and Community Care Act 1990, s.66(1). The amendment to subsection (2)(c)(i) was made by the Court and Legal Services Act 1990, s.116, Sched. 16, para. 11.

DEFINITIONS

"designated local authority": Sched. 12, para. 23. (C.Y.P.A. 1969, s.124A(2)).
"local authority": s.105(1).
"police protection": s.46(2).

GENERAL NOTE

This section requires local authorities to receive and provide accommodation for certain specified children. These children are first, under subsection (1), children removed or kept away from home under emergency protection orders (s.44) or children being assessed away from home under a child assessment order (s.43); second, under subsection (2)(a), children who have been taken into police protection (s.46); third, under subsection (2)(b), arrested juveniles, *i.e.* those apparently under the age of 17 arrested with or without warrant (Police and Criminal Evidence Act 1984, s.37(15) as amended by the Children Act 1989, Sched. 15). (The obligation to place arrested children in the hands of the local authority has been further clarified and strengthened by amendments to the Police and Criminal Evidence Act 1984, s.38(6) in the Criminal Justice Act 1991, s.59 which replaces Sched. 13, para. 53 of this Act); and finally under subsection (2)(c), children remanded to care or children subject to a supervision order with a residence requirement (see Sched. 12, para. 23 for the text of C.Y.P.A. 1969, s.12AA).

While these children are accommodated they are owed the duties in Part III and Schedule 2 (see s.105(5)).

Duties of local authorities in relation to children looked after by them

General duty of local authority in relation to children looked after by them

22.—(1) In this Act, any reference to a child who is looked after by a local authority is a reference to a child who is—

(a) in their care; or

(b) provided with accommodation by the authority in the exercise of any functions (in particular those under this Act) which stand referred to their social services committee under the Local Authority Social Services Act 1970.

(2) In subsection (1) "accommodation" means accommodation which is provided for a continuous period of more than 24 hours.

(3) It shall be the duty of a local authority looking after any child—

(a) to safeguard and promote his welfare; and
(b) to make such use of services available for children cared for by their own parents as appears to the authority reasonable in his case.

(4) Before making any decision with respect to a child whom they are looking after, or proposing to look after, a local authority shall, so far as is reasonably practicable, ascertain the wishes and feelings of—
(a) the child;
(b) his parents;
(c) any person who is not a parent of his but who has parental responsibility for him; and
(d) any other person whose wishes and feelings the authority consider to be relevant,
regarding the matter to be decided.

(5) In making any such decision a local authority shall give due consideration—
(a) having regard to his age and understanding, to such wishes and feelings of the child as they have been able to ascertain;
(b) to such wishes and feelings of any person mentioned in subsection (4)(b) to (d) as they have been able to ascertain; and
(c) to the child's religious persuasion, racial origin and cultural and linguistic background.

(6) If it appears to a local authority that it is necessary, for the purpose of protecting members of the public from serious injury, to exercise their powers with respect to a child whom they are looking after in a manner which may not be consistent with their duties under this section, they may do so.

(7) If the Secretary of State considers it necessary, for the purpose of protecting members of the public from serious injury, to give directions to a local authority with respect to the exercise of their powers with respect to a child whom they are looking after, he may give such directions to the authority.

(8) Where any such directions are given to an authority they shall comply with them even though doing so is inconsistent with their duties under this section.

DEFINITIONS
"accommodation": s.22(2).
"child looked after by a local authority": ss.22(1), 105(4).
"functions": s.105(5).
"in care": s.105(1).
"local authority": s.105(1).
"person who is not a parent but who has parental responsibility": ss.5(6), 12(2).
"services": s.105(1).

GENERAL NOTE
This section sets out the general duty owed by local authorities to children they are looking after, that is, children subject to care orders and children accommodated under sections 20 and 21. Specific duties are set out in sections 23, 24, 26 and Schedule 2, Part II. The duties owed under this part of the Act are the same whether or not children are

subject to a care order, but local authorities have greater control in relation to children in care because they have parental responsibility in respect of them (s.31(3)). The general duties in subsections (3), (4) and (5) have been taken from the C.C.A. 1980, ss.18 and 19, and amended partly in accordance with the recommendations of the R.C.C.L., paras. 2.18 and 9.3–5. The obligation in C.C.A. 1980, s.18(1) to give "first consideration" to the child's welfare has been amended; local authorities are now required to "safeguard and promote" it (subs. (3)). The old duty was interpreted by Lord Brandon in *M.* v. *H.* [1988] 3 W.L.R. 485 as being no different from giving first and paramount consideration as required by the G.M.A. 1971, s.1. However, the R.C.C.L., para. 2.18, drew a distinction between these two provisions, preferring section 18(1) because it took account of the need for the local authority to consider other children it was looking after. The Government rejected both versions. The wording of the duty is crucial because section 18(1) provided one basis for challenging local authority decisions. In *Liddle* v. *Sunderland Borough Council* (1983) 13 Fam. Law 250, Latey J. quashed a decision to close a children's home because the social services committee had taken the decision without considering its impact on the individual children who lived there. Arguably, the outcome would be the same under the new Act because a local authority which has taken a decision which will affect the welfare of an individual child can hardly be found to have safeguarded or promoted that child's welfare if it has acted in total disregard of it. However, there is no longer a requirement to consider welfare in relation to any decision so it would be possible to determine that a home had to be closed and only as a consequence see how the children's welfare should be promoted. Also, the removal of the word "first" eliminates the priority which Latey J. determined had to be given to children if there was an even balance between them and another client group (at pp. 252–3).

Where a local authority has acted so incompetently that the child's welfare has been seriously prejudiced, it is not clear that there would be a remedy. In *Guevara* v. *London Borough of Hounslow, The Times,* April 17, 1987, the High Court, as a preliminary issue, held that the council was not entitled to immunity, that duties under the 1980 Act could found a claim to damages, but that the proper procedure would have been to apply for judicial review because of the decisions of the House of Lords in *O'Reilly* v. *Mackman* [1983] 2 A.C. 237 and *Cocks* v. *Thanet District Council* [1983] 2 A.C. 286. However, this reasoning has been criticised on the basis that it is for the respondent to show that the plaintiff's choice of procedure is so improper as to be an abuse of process. If a person sought compensation for the care they received as a child, the use of judicial review with an ancillary claim for damages under Ord. 53, r. 7 would seem to be highly artificial, since the decisions taken would be incapable of review (see [1987] J.S.W.L. 374). Where the authority is in default, the Secretary of State may use his powers in section 84 (see below).

The duty in the C.C.A. 1980, s.18(1) to ascertain children's wishes and feelings about decisions and give due consideration to them is extended to parents, people with parental responsibility and other relevant adults (subss. (4) and (5)). There is a new duty to give due consideration to children's race, creed, culture and language (subs. (5)). Local authorities may act inconsistently with their duties where it is necessary to do so to protect members of the public (subs. (6)). The Secretary of State may also issue directions to them in such cases (subs. (7)) with which they must comply (subs. (8)).

The duties in the section are supplemented by the Arrangements for Placement of Children (General) Regulations 1991 (S.I. 1991 No. 890) see above p. 60. The Department of Health has issued detailed guidance on these provisions see *Guidance*, Vols. 3 or 4. It places considerable emphasis on planning the action taken in respect of every child. The need for further changes in residential care is highlighted by the *Utting Report: Children in the Public Care,* H.M.S.O. (1991).

Subs. (1)

Looked after: These children need to be distinguished from those who are "in care," i.e. those subject to care orders (s.31(1)) to whom other duties are also owed (see s.33).

Provided with accommodation: See section 20 for the duties and powers to provide accommodation under the Act. The Local Authority Social Services Act 1970, s.2 and Sched. 1 list the relevant functions. They include provision of accommodation under the previous child care, health and welfare and adoption legislation. Children may also be accommodated by the local authority under section 21. The types of accommodation which can be used are listed in section 23(2) and include placement with relatives. Day care is not accommodation (subs. (2)).

Subs. (3)

Welfare: Views of welfare differ (see note on s.17(1)). Both immediate and long term needs of the child should be considered (*Guidance*, Vol. 3, para. 2.5).

Subs. (4)

This imposes a qualified duty on the local authority to consult before making any decision with respect to a child they are looking after. This duty also applies prior to the child's admission to care in all cases, including those under care proceedings and emergency protection orders. It reflects the view that a child is a "person, not an object of concern" and that the local authority should, where possible, work in partnership with parents (Cm. 62, para. 21).

When there is a guardian ad litem he or she should be consulted and may assist in ascertaining the child's views. In *R. v. North Yorkshire County Council, ex p. M.* [1989] 1 All E.R. 143, Ewbank J. held that the local authority should not have moved a child to an adoptive placement while care proceedings were pending without consulting the guardian ad litem. However, this decision appears to be restricted to periods when there is a current guardian appointment. Guardians ad litem may now be appointed to a case for a specific period, if so they should be consulted even though the case has been heard (Family Proceedings Courts (Children Act 1989) Rules 1991, r. 10(9)).

Any decision with respect to a child: This would appear narrower than the previous wording "relating to." In *Att.-Gen. v. Hammersmith and Fulham London Borough Council, The Times*, December 18, 1979, Dillon J. drew a distinction between a decision "affecting a child" which was not covered by the duty and one "relating to a child," but this was rejected by Latey J. in *Liddle v. Sunderland Borough Council* (1983) 13 Fam. Law 250. Decisions may relate to or affect children without being made in respect of them, for example, a decision to close a library or a park. Decisions relating to the closure of community homes which these cases involved would seem to be made in respect of children because they cannot be made without further decisions about what should happen to the children involved.

Reasonably practicable: It will not be possible to ascertain wishes of: babies (although young children aged three up can express wishes to people skilled in communicating with children): unknown fathers; people who refuse to respond and those whose whereabouts are unknown.

Parents: This includes the unmarried father without parental responsibility. It should not include the biological parent of a child who has been freed for adoption because such a person is not a parent within s.104(4) *M. v. C. and Calderdale B.C.* [1992] 2 F.C.R. 141.

Any other person: *Guidance*, Vol. 3, para. 2.51 suggests consulting the following: the district health authority, the child's G.P., the local authority for the area where the child is to be placed, the local education authority and the child's school, the extended family, a guardian ad litem, a worker in a voluntary agency concerned with the child, former foster parents, the officer in charge of a residential home, a teacher who has been significantly involved with the child, or a community leader. In *R. v. Hereford and Worcester C.C. ex parte D* [1992] 1 F.L.R. 448 the decision to remove a child from a foster home without consulting the foster carer was unfair and quashed by the court.

Subs. (5)

This subsection lists three matters to which the local authority must give due consideration. What is "due consideration" will depend on the circumstances, but the authority must bear in mind the *Gillick* decision which indicates that young people have increasing rights of self-determination as they mature and must also consider the legal status which the person concerned has. Where the child is not in care the local authority does not have parental responsibility and this limits its power to make decisions (see s.3(5)). People consulted under (d) do not have parental responsibility. The local authority must give greater weight to the views of the parent of a mature child or to the views of someone without parental responsibility over those of someone with it where this promotes or safeguards the child's welfare.

Wishes and feelings of the child: *Guidance*, Vol. 3, para. 2.48 states "Children should feel that they have been properly consulted, that their views have been properly considered and that they have participated as partners in the decision-making process. However, they should not be made to feel that the burden of decision-making has fallen totally upon them, nor should they be forced to attend meetings if they choose not to do so."

Religious persuasion, racial origin, cultural and linguistic background: At common law, parents have the right to choose the child's religion, although following the *Gillick* decision the child acquires this right when he is sufficiently mature. Under section 33(6)(a) the authority may not cause a child to be brought up in a different religious persuasion from that to which he would otherwise adhere.

Racial origin is not defined but "racial group" is defined in the Race Relations Act 1976, s.3(1) and has been held to include Sikhs, gypsies and Rastafarians. At first sight there appears to be some conflict between these provisions and those in the Race Relations Act 1976 which make racial discrimination unlawful. However the 1976 Act, s.23(2) exempts arrangements where a person looks after someone as a member of their family (*i.e.* fostering) but this would not allow the local authority to discriminate.

In *R* v. *Cleveland CC and Carney, ex p. CRE, The Times*, August 25, 1992 (C.A.) the court refused a declaration that the local authority had committed an act of unlawful discrimination by transferring a child to another school at the request of the mother. The local education authority was under a mandatory duty under the Education Acts to comply with the parent's request and in so doing could not be tainted by the parent's motives even if these were discriminatory. The 1976 Act, s.18 did not qualify this duty. However, such reasoning would not seemingly be available in relation to a request under section 22(4) because when giving it due consideration the authority would also have regard to the Race Relations Act 1976, particularly section 71. See also CRE *Social Services and Race* (1990).

Guidance, Vol. 3, para. 2.40–42 states as follows: "A child's ethnic origin, cultural background and religion are important factors for consideration. It may be taken as a guiding principle of good practice that, other things being equal and in the great majority of cases, placement with a family of similar ethnic origin and religion is most likely to meet a child's needs as fully as possible and to safeguard his or her welfare most effectively. Such a family is most likely to be able to provide a child with continuity in life and care and an environment which the child will find familiar and sympathetic and in which opportunities will naturally arise to share fully in the culture and way of life of the ethnic group to which he belongs. Where the aim of a placement is to reunite the child with his or her own family, contact and work with the family will in most cases be more comfortable for all and carry a greater chance of success if the foster parents are of similar ethnic origin. Families of similar ethnic origin are also usually best placed to prepare children for life as members of an ethnic minority group in a multi-racial society, where they may meet with racial prejudice and discrimination, and to help them with their development towards independent living and adult life.

These principles should be applied with proper consideration for the circumstances of the individual case. There may be circumstances in which placement with a family of different ethnic origin is the best choice for a particular child. In other cases such a placement may be the best available choice. For example, a child may have formed strong links with prospective foster parents or be related to them. Siblings or step siblings who are not all of the same ethnic origin may need placement together. A child may prefer and need to remain close to school, friends and family even though foster parents of the same ethnic origin cannot be found in the locality. A child with special needs may require carers with particular qualities or abilities, so that choice is limited. The importance of religion as an element of culture should never be overlooked; to some children and families it may be the dominant factor, so that the religion of foster parents, for example, may in some cases be more important than their ethnic origin.

For a child whose parents are of different ethnic groups, placement in a family which reflects as nearly as possible the child's ethnic origins is likely to be the best choice in most cases. But the choice will be influenced by the child's wishes and feelings. In discussing and exploring these with a child, responsible authorities should be ready to help the child with any confusion or misunderstandings about people of different ethnic groups which may have arisen through previous family or placement experience. Children of mixed ethnic origin should be helped to understand and take pride in both or all elements in their cultural heritage and to feel comfortable about their origins. Carers must be able to provide this, with the help and support of others where necessary. This applies equally whether a child is placed with a minority ethnic family or with a white family or a family including members of differing ethnic origins. Where it has not proved possible to make a placement which entirely reflects the child's race and culture, an independent visitor could provide a link with the child's racial and cultural background (if the criteria for appointing an independent visitor apply)."

These issues are as relevant to children in residential care as to children with foster parents. Under Schedule 2, paragraph 11 the local authority has a duty to have regard to ethnic issues when recruiting foster parents.

Subss. (6), (7) and (8)

These provisions were previously found in the C.C.A. 1980, ss.18(3) and 19. They have been amended in accordance with the recommendation of the R.C.C.L. (para. 9.5) to restrict them to "protection from serious injury." The local authority may have to make an application under section 25 to place the child in secure accommodation.

Members of the public: Arguably, this does not include people like social workers who are at risk because of their work. Other children accommodated by the local authority must be protected under section 22(3)(a).

Serious injury: This excludes minor injury and damage to property.

Provision of accommodation and maintenance by local authority for children whom they are looking after

23.—(1) It shall be the duty of any local authority looking after a child—
  (a) when he is in their care, to provide accommodation for him; and
  (b) to maintain him in other respects apart from providing accommodation for him.

(2) A local authority shall provide accommodation and maintenance for any child whom they are looking after by—
  (a) placing him (subject to subsection (5) and any regulations made by the Secretary of State) with—
    (i) a family;
    (ii) a relative of his; or
    (iii) any other suitable person,
on such terms as to payment by the authority and otherwise as the authority may determine;
  (b) maintaining him in a community home;
  (c) maintaining him in a voluntary home;
  (d) maintaining him in a registered children's home;
  (e) maintaining him in a home provided [in accordance with arrangements made] by the Secretary of State under section 82(5) on such terms as the Secretary of State may from time to time determine; or
  (f) making such other arrangements as—
    (i) seem appropriate to them; and
    (ii) comply with any regulations made by the Secretary of State.

(3) Any person with whom a child has been placed under subsection (2)(a) is referred to in this Act as a local authority foster parent unless he falls within subsection (4).

(4) A person falls within this subsection if he is—
  (a) a parent of the child;
  (b) a person who is not a parent of the child but who has parental responsibility for him; or

(c) where the child is in care and there was a residence order in force with respect to him immediately before the care order was made, a person in whose favour the residence order was made.

(5) Where a child is in the care of a local authority, the authority may only allow him to live with a person who falls within subsection (4) in accordance with regulations made by the Secretary of State.

[(5A) For the purposes of subsection (5) a child shall be regarded as living with a person if he stays with the person for a continuous period of more than 24 hours].

(6) Subject to any regulations made by the Secretary of State for the purposes of this subsection, any local authority looking after a child shall make arrangements to enable him to live with—
    (a) a person falling within subsection (4); or
    (b) a relative, friend or other person connected with him,
unless that would not be reasonably practicable or consistent with his welfare.

(7) Where a local authority provides accommodation for a child whom they are looking after, they shall, subject to the provisions of this Part and so far as is reasonably practicable and consistent with his welfare, secure that—
    (a) the accommodation is near his home; and
    (b) where the authority are also providing accommodation for a sibling of his, they are accommodated together.

(8) Where a local authority provide accommodation for a child whom they are looking after and who is disabled, they shall, so far as is reasonably practicable, secure that the accommodation is not unsuitable to his particular needs.

(9) Part II of Schedule 2 shall have effect for the purposes of making further provision as to children looked after by local authorities and in particular as to the regulations that may be made under subsections (2)(a) and (f) and (5).

AMENDMENT

The words in square brackets in subsection (2)(e) and subsection (5A) were inserted by the Courts and Legal Services Act 1990, s.116, Sched. 16, para. 12.

DEFINITIONS

"community home": s.53.
"disabled": s.17(11).
"local authority": s.105(1).
"local authority foster parent": s.23(3), (4).
"person who is not a parent but has parental responsibility": ss.5(6), 12(2).
"registered children's home": s.63.
"relative": s.105(1).
"voluntary home": s.60.

REGULATIONS

Arrangements for Placement of Children (General) Regulations 1991 (S.I. 1991 No. 890) (see notes to s.20). The Placement of Children with Parents, etc. Regulations 1991 (S.I. 1991 No. 893) amended by The Children (Representations, Placements and Reviews) (Miscellaneous Amendments) Regulations 1991 (S.I. 1991 No. 2033). The

Foster Placement (Children) Regulations 1991 (S.I. 1991 No. 910). Children's Homes Regulations 1991 (S.I. 1991 No. 1506).

GENERAL NOTE

This section imposes a duty on local authorities to provide accommodation and to maintain children they are looking after (subs. (1)). It adds four specific but qualified duties: a duty from the C.C.A. 1980, s.21(1) to secure that any accommodation is near his home (subs. (7)(a)); a duty similar to that in C.C.A. 1980, s.2(3) to place the child with relatives or friends (subs. (6)); and two new duties: a duty to accommodate siblings together (subs. (7)(b)) and a duty to secure that accommodation for a disabled child is "not unsuitable to his needs" (subs. (8)). The types of accommodation which can be used are listed in subsection (2). Local authorities are also required to comply with Schedule 2, Part II and regulations under section 23(2)(a), (f) and (5).

Schedule 2, Part II imposes a duty on local authorities to promote contact between children they are looking after and their families (para. 15). It empowers the local authority to make payments to allow such visits (para. 16). Further provision relating to contact for children in care is contained in section 34. Regulations and Department of Health *Guidance* on contact are discussed at p. 104 below. It requires the local authority to appoint an independent visitor (and pay their reasonable expenses) for children they are looking after who are not visited and whose welfare demands it. Mature children may object to the appointment or continuation of a visitor (para. 17 and the Definition of Independent Visitors (Children) Regulations 1991 (S.I. 1991 No. 892)). Guidance about the role of independent visitors is given in *Guidance*, Vol. 3, Chap. 7 and repeated in Vol. 4, Chap. 6. The authority may guarantee apprenticeships for children they are looking after (para. 18). If the local authority wishes a child in care to live outside England and Wales it must obtain the approval of the court which can only be granted under stringent conditions (para. 19(1), (3)–(5)). Where approval is granted the child may be adopted (para. 19(6)). If the court gives its approval the order may be stayed pending an appeal (para. 19(7), (8)). Arrangements may be made for a child who is looked after by the authority but not in care to live outside England and Wales with the consent of everyone with parental responsibility (para. 19(2)). Guidance on these provisions is given in *Guidance*, Vol. 8, para. 1.9 *ff* and Chap. 4. Paragraph 20 sets out the local authority's functions where a child in care dies. The authority may arrange for the child's funeral with the consent (so far as reasonably practicable) of every person with parental responsibility for the child (para. 20(1)(c)). In all cases where a child is looked after the local authority must comply with the Arrangements Regulations 1991 (S.I. 1991 No. 890). In addition the Foster Placement, Children's Homes or Placement with Parents etc. Regulations must be complied with according to the type of placement made.

For a discussion of possible legal action to enforce these duties, see notes to section 22 on p. 66.

Subs. (1)

This duty was formerly found in the C.C.A. 1980, s.21(1).

Maintain: The local authority's duty is arguably no less than that of a parent with adequate, but not unlimited, resources. See also section 22(3)(b).

Subs. (2)

The local authority retains complete discretion over placement but must comply with the duty to safeguard and promote the child's welfare in section 22(3)(a), the provisions in Schedule 2, Part II, and the regulations. Accommodation must be "suitable" because of the duty in section 22(3) (*per* Lord Chancellor (*Hansard*, H.L. Vol. 505, col. 378)).

The local authority also has discretion about whether to pay for the child's care and how much to pay, as under the present law. Disputes can be dealt with under the procedure established under section 26(3).

Placing: Where a voluntary organisation *arranges* the placement the child is still placed by the local authority, and thus the carer is a local authority foster parent. Placements made by voluntary organisations are subject to the Arrangements, Foster Placement and Children's Homes Regulations.

Suitable person: Such a person will have to be approved as a foster parent, see notes to subsection (3) below.

Home: The Children's Homes Regulations 1991, (S.I. 1991 No. 1506) apply to all the types of home listed in this subsection. The primary legislation on community homes is in Part VI and Schedule 4, that on voluntary homes in Part VII and Schedule 5, and that on registered children's homes in Part VIII and Schedule 6.

The regulations require the authority responsible for the home, *i.e.* the local authority, voluntary organisation or person who carries on a registered children's home to compile and maintain a written statement of the purpose and function of the home (reg. 4). The authority must ensure that there are adequate staff (reg. 5) and that individual children are provided with an area in the home which is suitable for their needs (reg. 6). In particular homes must provide facilities where children can meet privately with their parents, solicitor, guardian ad litem, etc. and a payphone where they can make and receive private phone calls (reg. 7). Corporal punishment, deprivation of food or drink, restrictions on communication with their family, distinctive clothing, medication and deprivation of sleep may not be used as methods of discipline. Restriction of liberty can only be used under the terms of section 25. All use of discipline must be recorded (reg. 8). Guidance on permissable control will be issued shortly. The authority responsible for the home must assist with the arrangements for education, training and employment of older children (reg. 9). It shall ensure that each child is enabled to practise their religion (reg. 10) and enable them to purchase their own clothes (reg. 13). Records relating to each child must be kept securely and confidentially; the child's guardian ad litem must be given access to relevant records (regs. 15–17). Parents and people with parental responsibility must be given access to these regulations and guidance (reg. 18) and informed of all significant events relating to the child, *e.g.* the child's serious illness, accident or death and misconduct by staff. Where the home is not run by a local authority, the authority for that area and the registration authority must also be notified (reg. 19). There must be a written procedure for dealing with cases where a child is absent without authority (commonly known as absconding) (reg. 20). Formal procedures must be followed where the officer in charge is absent (reg. 21). The regulations also provide for the regular inspection of homes by the authority which runs them (reg. 22).

The Department of Health has issued detailed guidance about the provision of residential care, *Guidance*, Vol. 4. This stresses the value of residential care but underlines that it must be used appropriately and in a planned way. "Good practice encompasses both the running of the home and individual planning for each child ... Homes must be run so as to be able to respond to each child as an individual ... The institutional needs of the Home should never be allowed to dominate the lives of children and staff." (para. 1.7).

There is some concern that these regulations and guidance will not prevent the development of unacceptable regimes as occurred in Staffordshire (Pindown Report 1991) and Leicestershire. Further proposals are made in the *Utting Report: Children in the Public Care* (1991).

Other arrangements: These include an assortment of placements which are increasingly used for teenagers such as hostels and halfway houses. There are no specific regulations governing such placements but the Arrangements Regulations 1991 apply. Where hostels provide care as well as accommodation they must comply with the Children's Homes Regulations 1991.

Subs. (3)

The Foster Placement (Children) Regulations 1991 (S.I. 1991 No. 910) apply to all placements with foster parents by local authorities or voluntary organisations. They do not apply when a child in care is placed with parents or to placements for adoption. Placements by individuals and other bodies which fall outside these regulations may be controlled by Part IX and Schedule 8 of the Act which relate to private fostering.

The regulations forbid placements (other than "immediate placements") with people who have not been approved as foster parents and set out the minimum requirement for approval (reg. 3 and Sched. 1). The responsible authority must enter into a written foster care agreement with all its foster parents (reg. 3(6) and Sched. 2). Approval must be reviewed annually (reg. 4). In an emergency a local authority may place a child for up to 24 hours with any approved foster parent. Social work staff are sometimes approved so they can act in such cases. Placements with unapproved people who are relatives or friends of the child may be made for up to six weeks where the local authority is satisfied that an immediate placement is necessary, the placement is suitable and a written agreement is made with the carer (reg. 11). The responsible authority must not place a child with a foster parent unless they are satisfied that this is the most suitable way of performing their duty to safeguard and promote the child's welfare and that the selected foster parent is the most suitable. Except in the case of "immediate placements" the authority and the foster parents must make a written agreement about the particular child (reg. 5 and Sched. 3). More limited written agreements must be made for emergency or immediate placements (reg. 11(2)(b), 11(3)(b)). Foster parents must undertake not to use corporal punishment (Sched. 2, para. 5) and to bring up the child in the child's religious persuasion (reg. 5(2)). Foster placements must be supervised with visits after one week then at six week intervals during the first year, thereafter at least every three months. There must be a written report of each visit (reg. 6). Placements must be terminated by the authority if they are no longer the most suitable way of looking after the child. The area authority must remove the child forthwith and notify the responsible authority if continuation of the placement would be detrimental to the child's welfare. No court proceedings are necessary for such a removal from foster parents (reg. 7). Local authorities by agreement in writing, may delegate the provision of their fostering service to a voluntary organisation (reg. 8) but voluntary organisations may not place children outside the United Kingdom, the Channel Isles or the Isle of Man. Placements by local authorities outside England and Wales must comply with Schedule 2, paragraph 19 of the Act (reg. 10). A series of placements lasting under four weeks during a one year period with the same foster parents are treated as a single placement (reg. 9).

Local authorities must keep a register of approved foster parents and case records relating to each of them. Records must be kept confidentially but guardians ad litem must have access where necessary (regs. 12–14). Regulations 15 and 16 set out the local authority's responsibility for overseeing placements made by voluntary organisations who are not acting on behalf of local authorities under regulation 8.

The Department of Health has issued detailed guidance on the provision of fostering services and the role of foster parents, see *Guidance*, Vol. 3, Chaps. 3 and 4. This replaces the previous Code of Practice on Boarding Out. *Guidance* stresses the demands which fostering places on individual foster parents and the support they therefore require from the organisations which use them. The findings of recent research on fostering are outlined in Department of Health, *Patterns and outcomes in child placement* (1991).

People who are refused approval as foster parents or have their approval withdrawn have no specific forms of redress—there is no "right to be a foster parent." However, they must be given opportunities to answer allegations made about them, *R.* v. *Wandsworth L.B.C., ex p. P.* (1989) 87 L.G.R. 370. Complaints by local foster parents including refusals to exempt from the "usual fostering limit" (Sched. 7, para. 6) can be considered under the procedure for dealing with representations under section 26(3).

Subss. (4) and (5)

These placements are governed by the Placement with Parents Regulations 1991 (S.I. 1991 No. 893). These replace the Charge and Control Regulations 1988. The scope of the 1991 regulations is different and apples only to children in care who are placed with parents, guardians or people who had parental responsibility under a residence order immediately before the care order was made (reg. 1(2)). Placements with relatives who fall outside these categories are now foster placements (see above). Placements of young people aged 16 or over are exempt from regulations 3, 6, 7, 9 and 12. There is no authority to restrict the return home of children who are merely accommodated by the local authority.

The purpose of these regulations is to ensure that sufficient consideration is given to all aspects of a child in care's welfare before the decision to place him or her "home on trial" is made. Also to ensure that such placements are adequately supervised. The regulations set out the enquiries which must be made (reg. 3 and Sched. 1). Where the child requires an immediate placement more limited enquiries are permitted (reg. 6). Where a child in care spends periods of less than four weeks with their parents etc. over a year these may be treated as a single placement (reg. 13). Placements of less than 24 hours are not covered by the regulations, see subsection (5A) below. Placement decisions must be made by the Director of Social Services or their nominee (reg. 5). There must be a written agreement about the child's care after the placement (reg. 7

and Sched. 2). Decisions about placements must be notified to a wide range of organisations and individuals (reg. 8). Placements must be supervised with a visit within a week of placement, every six weeks for the first year and thereafter at least every three months (reg. 9). Placements which do not safeguard and promote the child's welfare or are prejudicial to safety must be terminated at once (regs. 11 and 12). Because the child is subject to a care order no further authority is required for the child's removal (s.33(3)). Allegations against those caring for children under these provisions must be investigated fairly R. v. *Hertfordshire C.C. ex parte B.* (1987) 85 L.G.R. 218.

Further guidance on these placements is provided in *Guidance*, Vol. 3, Chap. 5. Results of Department of Health sponsored research into home placements has been published E. Farmer and R. Parker, *Trials and Tribulations*, H.M.S.O. (1991).

Subs. (5A)

This provision incorporates the decision in *R. v. Newham L.B.C., ex p. P* [1990] 2 All E.R. 19 and clarifies that contact visits of 24 hours or more are subject to the regulations.

Subs. (6)

If this person lives outside England and Wales, Schedule 2, paragraph 19 must be complied with.

Subs. (7)

The local authority has wide discretion but must carry out its duties in accordance with section 22.

Near his home: A child's home may be where his parents live or where he used to live; links with both are important and most children return to their home area when they leave care, even if they do not live with their families. There are specific duties about maintaining contact in Schedule 2, paragraph 15. *Guidance*, Vol. 3, para. 4.4. states:

> "A child's need for continuity in life and care should be a constant factor in choice of placement. In most cases, this suggests a need for placement with a family of the same race, religion and culture in a neighbourhood within reach of family, school or day nursery, church, friends and leisure activities. Continuity also requires placement in a foster home which a child can find familiar and sympathetic and not too remote from his own experience in social background, attitudes and expectations, a foster home in which he is most likely to settle down and as far as possible feel 'at home' and free from anxieties. This is equally if not more necessary where it is not possible to place a child near home or where there are special reasons for choosing a placement at a distance."

Sibling: The *Gal Manual* states, "Links with siblings should be jealously preserved and fostered, and guardians should not accept care plans which include the separation of siblings without good reason." (p. 79).

Subs. (8)

This merely underlines that special care needs to be taken with the placement of disabled children. All the relevant guidance has been collected together in *Guidance*, Vol. 6. *Children with Disabilities* (1991).

Advice and assistance for certain children

Advice and assistance for certain children

24.—(1) Where a child is being looked after by a local authority, it shall be the duty of the authority to advise, assist and befriend him with a view to promoting his welfare when he ceases to be looked after by them.

(2) In this Part "a person qualifying for advice and assistance" means a person within the area of the authority who is under 21 and who was, at any time after reaching the age of 16 but while still a child—
  (a) looked after by a local authority;
  (b) accommodated by or on behalf of a voluntary organisation;
  (c) accommodated in a registered children's home;
  (d) accommodated—
      (i) by any health authority or local education authority; or
      (ii) in any residential care home, nursing home or mental nursing home, [or in any accommodation provided by a National Health Service Trust],
for a consecutive period of at least three months; or
  (e) privately fostered,
but who is no longer so looked after, accommodated or fostered.

(3) Subsection (2)(d) applies even if the period of three months mentioned there began before the child reached the age of 16.

(4) Where—
  (a) a local authority know that there is within their area a person qualifying for advice and assistance;
  (b) the conditions in subsection (5) are satisfied; and
  (c) that person has asked them for help of a kind which they can give under this section,
they shall (if he was being looked after by a local authority or was accommodated by or on behalf of a voluntary organisation) and may (in any other case) advise and befriend him.

(5) The conditions are that—
  (a) it appears to the authority that the person concerned is in need of advice and being befriended;
  (b) where that person was not being looked after by the authority, they are satisfied that the person by whom he was being looked after does not have the necessary facilities for advising or befriending him.

(6) Where as a result of this section a local authority are under a duty, or are empowered, to advise and befriend a person, they may also give him assistance.

(7) Assistance given under subsections (1) to (6) may be in kind or, in exceptional circumstances, in cash.

(8) A local authority may give assistance to any person who qualifies for advice and assistance by virtue of subsection (2)(a) by—
  (a) contributing to expenses incurred by him in living near the place where he is, or will be—
      (i) employed or seeking employment; or
      (ii) receiving education or training; or
  (b) making a grant to enable him to meet expenses connected with his education or training.

(9) Where a local authority are assisting the person under subsection (8) by making a contribution or grant with respect to a course of education or training, they may—

(a) continue to do so even though he reaches the age of 21 before completing the course; and

(b) disregard any interruption in his attendance on the course if he resumes it as soon as is reasonably practicable.

(10) Subsections (7) to (9) of section 17 shall apply in relation to assistance given under this section (otherwise than under subsection (8)) as they apply in relation to assistance given under that section.

(11) Where it appears to a local authority that a person whom they have been advising and befriending under this section, as a person qualifying for advice and assistance, proposes to live, or is living, in the area of another local authority, they shall inform that other local authority.

(12) Where a child who is accommodated—

(a) by a voluntary organisation or in a registered children's home;

(b) by any health authority or local education authority; or

(c) in any residential care home, nursing home or mental nursing home, [or in any accommodation provided by a Health Service Trust],

ceases to be so accommodated, after reaching the age of 16, the organisation, authority or (as the case may be) person carrying on the home shall inform the local authority within whose area the child proposes to live.

(13) Subsection (12) only applies, by virtue of paragraph (b) or (c), if the accommodation has been provided for a consecutive period of at least three months.

[(14) Every local authority shall establish a procedure for considering any representations (including any complaint) made to them by a person qualifying for advice and assistance about the discharge of their functions under this Part in relation to him.

(15) In carrying out any consideration of representation under subsection (14), a local authority shall comply with any regulations made by the Secretary of State for the purposes of this subsection.]

AMENDMENT

In subsections (2) and (12) the words in square brackets were added by the National Health Service and Community Care Act 1990, s.66(1), Sched. 9, para. 36(2). Subsections (14) and (15) were added by the Courts and Legal Services Act 1990, s.116, Sched. 16, para. 13.

DEFINITIONS

"assistance": s.24(7).

"child looked after by local authority": ss.22(1), 105(4).

"health authority": s.105(1).

"local authority": s.105(1).

"local education authority": s.105(1).

"mental nursing home": s.105(1).

"nursing home": s.105(1).

"person qualifying for advice and assistance": s.24(2).
"privately fostered": s.66.
"registered children's home": s.63.
"voluntary organisation": s.105(1).

REGULATIONS

Representations Procedure (Children) Regulation 1991 (S.I. 1991 No. 894) as amended by The Children (Representations, Placements and Reviews) (Miscellaneous Amendments) Regulations 1991 (S.I. 1991 No. 2033)

GENERAL NOTE

This section implements many of the recommendations in Chapter 10 of the R.C.C.L. which were intended to remove anomalies and to strengthen local authorities' functions in relation to the preparation for leaving care and the after-care of children cared for away from their families. It replaces the C.C.A. 1980, ss.27–29 and 69. Local authorities now have a duty to advise, assist and befriend all children they are looking after with a view to providing their long-term welfare, not just their welfare during childhood (subs. (1)). They have a duty to advise and befriend people under 21 (not under 18 as previously under C.C.A. 1980, s.28) who, after the age of 16, were looked after by a local authority or accommodated by or on behalf of a voluntary organisation, who request help and satisfy the conditions in subsection (5) (subss. (2) and (4)).

There is also a power to advise and befriend such young people who were cared for in the other establishments listed in subsection (2). All people qualifying for advice can be given assistance (subs. (6)), which may, exceptionally, be in cash (subs. (7)). Financial assistance may also be given to enable a person who was looked after by the local authority after age 16 (not 17 as previously) to be accommodated near their place of work or training, etc., and to meet the costs of training, etc. (subs. (8)). Grants for education or training may continue beyond age 21 (subs. (9)). Subsection (10) imports the provisions about repayment from section 17(7)–(9). Complaints about aftercare services or the lack of them may be made to the local authority's complaints service (see notes on s.26(3) below). In order to facilitate the performance of these duties, local authorities are under a duty to pass information to other local authorities about people they have been advising and befriending (subs. (1)); voluntary organisations, health authorities, N.H.S. Trusts, local education authorities and those who carry on registered homes have a duty to inform local authorities about children who leave their care (subs. (12)). Where care is by a health authority, N.H.S. Trust or local education authority or in a residential care home, nursing home or mental nursing home, the powers and duties only arise if the child was accommodated for more than three consecutive months, which may start before the child reached age 16 (subss. (3) and (13)). Local authorities have other responsibilities to children in such establishments under sections 85 and 86.

The Department of Health has issued Guidance on aftercare, advice and assistance, see *Guidance*, Vol. 3, Chap. 9 repeated in Vol. 4, Chap. 7. Local authorities are expected to provide written statements on their philosophy and practice of preparing young people for leaving care and the provision of aftercare support (para. 9.20). In addition each authority should provide an easy-to-read guide to its services for young people who leave care or accommodation (para. 9.25–6). A senior officer of the authority should be nominated to oversee aftercare provision (para. 9.27).

Subs. (1)

This duty applies to all children, including those who return to their families after brief periods. It imposes an obligation to prepare children for leaving care and for living independently when they grow up, and is thus broader than the duty under the old law which referred to welfare throughout childhood. A comparable duty is placed on voluntary organisations by section 61(1)(c) and on those carrying on registered children's homes by section 64(1)(c).

"Preparation for leaving care must start well before a young person ceases to be looked after or accommodated and is likely to continue until well after he has done so. Preparation for this process should be incorporated in the care plan ... as soon as [the young person] starts to be looked after" *Guidance*, Vol. 3, para. 9.43.

Subss. (2)–(5)

These four subsections set out a further duty (only a power if subsection (2)(c)–(e) applies) to provide aftercare to certain people under 21 who have been in care after the age of 16 years. It may operate as an incentive to discharge children from care shortly before the age of 16, such action may not safeguard and promote their welfare. This duty should be considered alongside the duty in section 20(3) to provide accommodation for certain 16 to 18-year-olds who are in need and the power to provide accommodation to under 21s in section 20(5).

Person qualifying for advice and assistance: As well as the conditions in subsections (2) and (3), the person will have to meet the conditions in subsections (4) and (5), *i.e.* the local authority will have to know about the person (subs. (4)(a)); he must have asked for help of a kind which they can give (subs. (4)(c)); he must satisfy the local authority that he needs advice and befriending (subs. (5)(a)) and, if he was not looked after by the local authority, that the person who looked after him does not have the necessary facilities (subs. (5)(b)).

A local authority: This does not necessarily mean the one in whose area the child now lives. However, a person who requests help from an authority different from the one which looked after him will also have to satisfy the condition in subsection (5)(b). This could mean that authority A would refuse help because authority B 100 miles away could provide it, but this should only be so where authority B has facilities for advising and befriending people outside its area.

Accommodated in a registered children's home: This does not include children placed in such homes by local authorities; they are included in (a) (see s.23(2)(a) for local authority's power to place in such homes).

Privately fostered: Local authorities have a further duty relating to the welfare of such children in section 67 of the Act.

Know: The authority will know if a request is made by or on behalf of the child or if it is informed by another authority under subsection (11), or by another organisation under subsection (12).

Conditions: See "a person qualifying" (above).

Help of a kind . . . : This means help they are able to give. This includes assistance under subsection (7), but the local authority is only under a duty to advise and befriend. Arguably, a request for housing to the Housing Department should trigger this section since accommodation could be provided under subsection (7) as "assistance in kind" (see *Att.-Gen.* v. *Wandsworth London Borough Council, ex p. Tilley* [1981] 1 W.L.R. 854, where the Court of Appeal rejected the view that assistance under the C.C.A. 1980, s.1 did not include accommodation).

They shall: The authority has no duty to help where the conditions are not satisfied except for those under 18 who are in need (s.17(1)). It has a power to help all young people under section 20(4) and (5).

They may: The authority can impose other additional conditions, but must act in accordance with its other duties, particularly under sections 17(1) and 20(3). These duties only apply to under 18s who are in need.

It appears to the authority: The authority has wide discretion.

Subss. (6) and (7)

The local authority only has a power to provide assistance in cash or in kind. It was not intended that they should acquire any income maintenance function for young people ex-care, even though the Social Security Act 1986 appeared to expect that all young people had families to support them. Under the 1986 Act young people faced severe financial problems—under 18s could not generally apply for Income Support; Housing Benefit was paid to them at a reduced rate, and lower benefit rates for single people under 25 presumed that they had a family to rely on (Income Support (General) Regulations 1987, reg. 13A). Attempts were made in the Lords, and during Committee Stage in the Commons, to include amendments to the 1986 Act in the Children Bill but all were unsuccessful. However, a small concession was made which allows some children living away from their families to obtain Income Support at the rate for 18–24 year-olds (see Income Support General Regulations 1987, reg. 13A). Where an authority makes a capital grant to a young person leaving care it will not affect entitlement to benefit, provided that it is under £3,000 (Income Support (General) Regulations 1987, reg. 53(1)). Department of Health *Guidance*, Vol. 3, para. 9.71 encourages local authorities to be proactive in advising young people.

Advice and Assistance for Certain Children

Exceptional circumstances: See note on section 17(6). [This] "refers to the individual young person rather than the general policy of the authority", *Guidance*, Vol. 3, para. 9.71.

Subss. (8)–(10)

Section 17(7)–(9) allows assistance (but not advice, befriending and grants under subsection (8)) to be subject to conditions about repayment. They require assistance to be means-tested, but provide that there is no liability to repay while the person is in receipt of certain benefits. See the discussion of section 17(7)–(9).

Subs. (12)

There are other duties to notify the local authority about such children in sections 85 and 86.

Subss. (14) and (15)

See notes on section 26(3) below.

Secure accommodation

Use of accommodation for restricting liberty

25.—(1) Subject to the following provisions of this section, a child who is being looked after by a local authority may not be placed, and, if placed, may not be kept, in accommodation provided for the purpose of restricting liberty ("secure accommodation") unless it appears—
    (a) that—
        (i) he has a history of absconding and is likely to abscond from any other description of accommodation; and
        (ii) if he absconds, he is likely to suffer significant harm; or
    (b) that if he is kept in any other description of accommodation he is likely to injure himself or other persons.

(2) The Secretary of State may by regulations—
    (a) specify a maximum period—
        (i) beyond which a child may not be kept in secure accommodation without the authority of the court; and
        (ii) for which the court may authorise a child to be kept in secure accommodation;
    (b) empower the court from time to time to authorise a child to be kept in secure accommodation for such further period as the regulations may specify; and
    (c) provide that applications to the court under this section shall be made only by local authorities.

(3) It shall be the duty of a court hearing an application under this section to determine whether any relevant criteria for keeping a child in secure accommodation are satisfied in his case.

(4) If a court determines that any such criteria are satisfied, it shall make an order authorising the child to be kept in secure

accommodation and specifying the maximum period for which he may be so kept.

(5) On any adjournment of the hearing of an application under this section, a court may make an interim order permitting the child to be kept during the period of the adjournment in secure accommodation.

(6) No court shall exercise the powers conferred by this section in respect of a child who is not legally represented in that court unless, having been informed of his right to apply for legal aid and having had the opportunity to do so, he refused or failed to apply.

(7) The Secretary of State may by regulations provide that—
  (a) this section shall or shall not apply to any description of children specified in the regulations;
  (b) this section shall have effect in relation to children of a description specified in the regulations subject to such modifications as may be so specified;
  (c) such other provisions as may be so specified shall have effect for the purpose of determining whether a child of a description specified in the regulations may be placed or kept in secure accommodation.

(8) The giving of an authorisation under this section shall not prejudice any power of any court in England and Wales or Scotland to give directions relating to the child to whom the authorisation relates.

(9) This section is subject to section 20(8).

AMENDMENTS

S.I. 1991 No. 1505 amends the test in section 25(1) in relation to applications relating to certain children (see below).

DEFINITIONS

"child": s.105(1).
"child looked after by a local authority": ss.22(1), 105(4).
"secure accommodation": s.25(1).
"significant harm": ss.31(9)(10), 105(1).
"the court": s.92(7).

REGULATIONS

The Children (Secure Accommodation) Regulations 1991 (S.I. 1991 No. 1505) and The Children (Secure Accommodation) (No. 2.) Regulations 1991 (S.I. 1991 No. 2034).

GENERAL NOTE

This section re-enacts with modifications the C.C.A. 1980, s.21A and sets out the restrictions on the use of secure accommodation which are expanded in the regulations.

Civil Cases

The regulations apply to all children except those who are detained under the Mental Health Act 1983. They cover children accommodated by local education authorities, health authorities, NHS Trusts and in residential care homes, nursing homes and mental nursing homes (reg. 7). Those accommodated under section 20(5) and children subject to residential assessment under a child assessment order (s.43) may not be placed in secure accommodation; secure placement of a child under the age of 13 in a community home requires prior approval of the Secretary of State (regs. 4 and 5).

Secure accommodation may not be provided in voluntary homes or private children's homes (reg. 18). However it may be provided in a wide range of other establishments and where it is the Act and regulations must be complied with. Secure accommodation has been held to include a behaviour modification unit at a hospital where the regime was intended to restrict liberty (*R.* v. *Northampton Juvenile Court, ex p. London Borough of Hammersmith* [1985] 15 Fam. Law 25). The Pindown regime amounted to an unlawful restriction of liberty (*Pindown Report*, para. 12.60). See also *Guidance*, Vol. 4, paras. 8.10 and 8.14, the use of "time-out" facilities must comply with these provisions.

Detention without court authority may not total more than 72 hours in any 28 day period, a first order may last up to three months, subsequent orders up to six months. In calculating the length of an order the period of detention before the order was granted is ignored (regs. 10–12). Community home managers must notify the local authority within 12 hours of placing a child in secure accommodation (reg. 9). Where the local authority plans to seek an order it should notify the child, parents, etc. and the child's independent visitor (reg. 14). Applications for secure accommodation orders are made by the local authority looking after the child (reg. 8); where the child is not looked after but in a hospital, residential school or nursing home, the health authority, NHS Trust, local education authority or person carrying on the home makes the application (reg. 2, No. 2 regs.) Secure accommodation placements must be reviewed after one month and then at three monthly intervals by a review panel which includes a person independent of the local authority. The panel must satisfy itself that the criteria for placement continue to apply, such placement is still necessary and no other accommodation would be appropriate. The child, the family and professionals concerned with the child's care should be consulted and informed about this review (regs. 15 and 16). Local authorities must keep records relating to each child in secure accommodation in a community home (reg. 17).

The Department of Health has issued guidance on the use of secure accommodation (see *Guidance*, Vol. 4, Chap. 8). Because of the safety and security of premises, the skilled staff, the better staffing ratios and the specialist programmes provided, secure accommodation is seen as an important resource for some very troubled (or troublesome) children. "However, restricting the liberty of children is a serious step which must be taken only when there is no appropriate alternative. It must be the 'last resort' in the sense that all else must first have been comprehensively considered and rejected—never because no other placement was available at the time, because of inadequacies in staffing, because the child is simply being a nuisance or runs away . . . , and never as a form of punishment." (para. 8.5). Those proposing a secure placement need to be clear about its aims and objectives; placements should last no longer than is necessary. Local authorities are now under a specific duty to avoid the need for children in their area to be placed in secure accommodation (Sched. 2, para. 7(c)).

Most applications for secure accommodation will continue to be heard in the family proceedings court with appeals against the granting or refusal of accommodation the order to the High Court under section 94. However, these are not "family proceedings" under section 8(3) so the court may not make section 8 orders instead of, or as well as, the order sought. Secure accommodation proceedings concern the "upbringing maintenance or welfare" of a child so the Hearsay Evidence Order (S.I. 1991 No. 1115) applies and hearsay is admissible. The Magistrates must give full reasons for their decision, *Oxfordshire CC* v. *R.* [1992] 1 F.L.R. 648 sub nom *R.* v. *X Council, The Times,* February 24, 1992. Proceedings in the family proceedings court are governed by r. 26 (see p. 415).

Secure accommodation proceedings in the High Court, County Court and family proceedings court are "specified proceedings" so the court must appoint a guardian ad litem unless it is satisfied that this is not necessary in order to safeguard the child's interests (s.41(1)). A guardian ad litem should be able to inform the court about alternative placements for the child and the effect that secure accommodation is likely to have on him or her (see *Childright* 81 (1991)). This may enable the court to operate as an effective check in a way which it has not done previously (see Harris & Timms, *Between Hospital and Prison or thereabouts*, unpublished research commissioned for the Department of Health). Appeals against orders should be listed for an early hearing because of the restriction of liberty involved *Oxfordshire CC* v. *R.*

Wardship may not be used as a route to secure accommodation for children looked after by local authorities (s.100). Applications relating to wards in care under the transitional arrangements should be made to the High Court, *Re C (Minors)* C.A. December 10, 1991 (see 142 N.L.J. 65). Where wardship may be used the new regulations govern the directions (Sched. 14, para. 16(5)) and the child must be a party to the proceedings (Family Proceedings Rules 1991, r. 5.5).

Criminal Cases

The conditions for use of secure accommodation are modified for children who are detained under the Police and Criminal Evidence Act 1984, s.38(6) or remanded under C.Y.P.A. 1969, s.23 and either charged with an offence which carries a prison sentence of 14 years or more for an adult, or charged or convicted of a second or subsequent offence of violence. Such children may not be kept in secure accommodation "unless it appears that any accommodation other than that provided for the purpose of restricting liberty is inappropriate because—
    (a)   the child is likely to abscond from such other accommodation, or
    (b)   the child is likely to injure himself or other people if he is kept in any such other accommodation" (reg. 6).

Other children remanded to care can only be kept in secure accommodation if they satisfy the requirements in the Act. An order for a remanded child to stay in secure accommodation cannot last longer than the period of remand (reg. 13).

Where a child or young person is remanded or committed to secure accommodation in connection with criminal proceedings the case will be dealt with by a youth court or other magistrates court, Criminal Justice Act 1991, s.60(3). These are family proceedings within section 92(2) and the Hearsay Evidence Order (S.I. 1991 No. 1115) applies but are not heard in the family proceedings court. The Children and Young Persons Act 1969, s.23 (as amended) will allow remands to security without applications for secure accommodation orders. Guardians ad litem are only available for secure accommodation proceedings in the family proceedings court.

The Criminal Justice Act 1991, s.61 imposes a duty on each local authority to ensure that they are able to comply with orders remanding children to secure accommodation.

Subs. (1)

Accommodated by the local authority: The regulations extend these provisions to cover children provided with accommodation by health authorities, NHS Trusts, local education authorities, and in residential care homes, nursing homes or mental nursing homes (reg. 7). These applications come under S.I. 1991 No. 2034.

Absconds: "by running away children explicitly reject" the way they are treated in the system. They may have good reasons for do doing, *e.g.* abuse or placement too far from home. The solution may not require further restriction, see *Utting Report*, paras. 3.54 *et seq.*

Significant harm: C.C.A. 1980, s.21A(1) required that the child's "physical, mental or moral welfare" be at risk and it should be compared with what can reasonably be expected of a similar child. The new provision would seem to embrace the same concepts as before, but the addition of "significant" may suggest greater harm than "at risk."

Subs. (2)

The period is 72 hours (reg. 10). Courts may authorise detention for three months with renewals of six months (regs. 11 and 12). The placement need not be continued for the duration of the order (*Guidance*, Vol. 4, para. 8.42). Applications may be made by others (see above).

Subs. (4)

This provision restricts the court's discretion; but section 1(1) and (5) still apply.

Subs. (5)

There is no time limit for "interim" secure accommodation orders. Arguably an interim order should not be made unless a prima facie case relating to the grounds in subsection (1) can be established.

Subs. (6)

Representation must be granted where legal aid is available. Without any means or merits best see Legal Aid Act 1988, s.15(3B) added by section 99 below. A guardian ad litem should also be appointed in civil cases (Family Proceedings Rules, r. 2(2)(a)).

Subs. (7)
Regulations: See notes on subsection (1) above.

Subs. (9)
This makes it clear that a person with parental responsibility can remove a child who is accommodated by the local authority from secure accommodation. Children over 16 who are not in care may also be able to leave (see notes to s.20(11)).

Supplemental

Review of cases and inquiries into representations

26.—(1) The Secretary of State may make regulations requiring the case of each child who is being looked after by a local authority to be reviewed in accordance with the provisions of the regulations.

(2) The regulations may, in particular, make provision—
- (a) as to the manner in which each case is to be reviewed;
- (b) as to the considerations to which the local authority are to have regard in reviewing each case;
- (c) as to the time when each case is first to be reviewed and the frequency of subsequent reviews;
- (d) requiring the authority, before conducting any review, to seek the views of—
  - (i) the child;
  - (ii) his parents;
  - (iii) any person who is not a parent of his but who has parental responsibility for him; and
  - (iv) any other person whose views the authority consider to be relevant,

  including, in particular, the views of those person in relation to any particular matter which is to be considered in the course of the review;
- (e) requiring the authority to consider, in the case of a child who is in their care, whether an application should be made to discharge the care order;
- (f) requiring the authority to consider, in the case of a child in accommodation provided by the authority, whether the accommodation accords with the requirements of this Part;
- (g) requiring the authority to inform the child, so far as is reasonably practicable, of any steps he may take under this Act;
- (h) requiring the authority to make arrangements, including arrangements with such other bodies providing services as it considers appropriate, to implement any decision which they propose to make in the course, or as a result, of the review;
- (i) requiring the authority to notify details of the result of the review and of any decision taken by them in consequence of the review to—
  - (i) the child;
  - (ii) his parents;

(iii) any person who is not a parent of his but who has parental responsibility for him; and
(iv) any other person whom they consider ought to be notified;
(j) requiring the authority to monitor the arrangements which they have made with a view to ensuring that they comply with the regulations.

(3) Every local authority shall establish a procedure for considering any representations (including any complaint) made to them by—
  (a) any child who is being looked after by them or who is not being looked after by them but is in need;
  (b) a parent of his;
  (c) any person who is not a parent of his but who has parental responsibility for him;
  (d) any local authority foster parent;
  (e) such other person as the authority consider has a sufficient interest in the child's welfare to warrant his representations being considered by them,
about the discharge by the authority of any of their functions under this Part in relation to the child.

(4) The procedure shall ensure that at least one person who is not a member or officer of the authority takes part in—
  (a) the consideration; and
  (b) any discussions which are held by the authority about the action (if any) to be taken in relation to the child in the light of the consideration.

(5) In carrying out any consideration of representations under this section a local authority shall comply with any regulations made by the Secretary of State for the purpose of regulating the procedure to be followed.

(6) The Secretary of State may make regulations requiring local authorities to monitor the arrangements that they have made with a view to ensuring that they comply with any regulations made for the purposes of subsection (5).

(7) Where any representation has been considered under the procedure established by a local authority under this section, the authority shall—
  (a) have due regard to the findings of those considering the representation; and
  (b) take such steps as are reasonably practicable to notify (in writing)—
    (i) the person making the representation;
    (ii) the child (if the authority consider that he has sufficient understanding); and
    (iii) such other persons (if any) as appear to the authority to be likely to be affected,
of the authority's decision in the matter and their reasons for taking that decision and of any action which they have taken, or propose to take.

(8) Every local authority shall give such publicity to their procedure for considering representations under this section as they consider appropriate.

DEFINITIONS
"accommodation provided by the local authority": ss.22(2), 105(5).
"child": s.105(1).
"child looked after by the local authority": ss.22(1), 105(4).
"functions": s.105(1).
"in care": s.105(1).
"local authority": s.105(1).
"local authority foster parent": s.23(3)(4).
"person who is not a parent but who has parental responsibility": ss.5(6), 12(2).

REGULATIONS
Review of Children's Cases Regulations 1991 (S.I. 1991 No. 895); Representations Procedure (Children) Regulations 1991 (S.I. 1991 No. 894) as amended by the Children Representations, Placements and Reviews) (Miscellaneous Amendments) Regulations 1991 (S.I. 1991 No. 2033).

GENERAL NOTE
This section provides for two distinct matters. Subsections (1) and (2) deal with "Statutory Reviews"; the remainder of the section provides for local authority systems for handling complaints and representations about the discharge of their functions under Part III. Guidance on both these issues is contained in *Guidance*, Vol. 3, Chaps. 8 and 10 and Vol. 4, Chaps. 3 and 5.

Subss. (1) and (2)
The regulations relating to reviews apply to all children looked after by the local authority and to children accommodated by a voluntary organisation or in a registered children's home. There is no requirement to review other service provision such as day care but *Guidance*, Vol. 2, para. 2.10 states that holding reviews is good practice if the local authority is "significantly involved" with the family. The responsible authority, *i.e.* the local authority, voluntary organisation or person carrying on the home must comply with the regulations (regs. 1 and 2). *Guidance*, Vol. 3, para. 8.3 states, "Any meeting which is convened for the purpose of considering the child's case ... falls within these Regulations. Whether such a meeting is called a planning meeting or a review or a review meeting will not determine whether it is in fact part of a review. This will depend on the purpose for which the meeting is convened." Reviews must take place within four weeks of accommodation being provided, within three months of the first review and then at six monthly intervals. In addition the child must be medically examined every six months before the age of two and thereafter annually. Mature children may refuse medicals (reg. 6). Where a child is repeatedly provided with accommodation at the same place during a year but none of the periods lasts for more than four weeks and the total is 90 days or less the reviews must take place as if there is a single placement (reg. 11). There is no set format for the review but *Guidance* stresses the need to prepare for reviews, by setting an agenda, inviting the appropriate people and choosing a suitable venue (paras. 8.10–8.18). Regulations require the responsible authority to seek and take account of the views of the child, parents, any person with parental responsibility and others whose views are considered relevant, to involve those persons in meetings and to notify them of decisions (reg. 7). *Guidance* suggests that there are few cases where it is not appropriate for the child or the parents to attend and that fears or inhibitions of professionals should not be the reason for excluding them from a review (para. 8.16). Children and parents may need to attend separate parts of a review; children may need a friendly supporter (para. 8.15). Matters to be included or considered within a review are included in the Schedules to the regulations. Amongst these are relevant changes in the child's circumstances; whether an application should be made to discharge a care order or change the child's legal status; arrangements for contact; the appointment of an independent visitor; educational progress; preparation for leaving care; the responsible authority's immediate and long term plans; and the child's health. The responsible authority must make arrangements for decisions to be implemented (regs. 8 and 10). The review process must be monitored (reg. 9).

Regulation 12 (added by S.I. 1991 No. 2033) makes transitional arrangements to ensure the regular review of children already accommodated on October 14, 1991.

Subss. (3)–(8)

This requires each local authority, voluntary organisation and registered children's home (termed responsible authorities) (S.I. 1991 No. 894 (reg. 11)) to set up its own scheme for dealing with representations and complaints, as proposed in Cm. 62, para. 31. Procedures are closely controlled by the regulations made under subs. (6). Complaints procedures were said to have three functions: to enable standards to be maintained, problems to be defused and children to be protected (*per* Lord Meston, (*Hansard*, H.L. Vol. 503, col. 175)). Subsection (3) determines whose representations must be considered within the system. It is clear that complaints may be made about action and, at least by children in need and their parents, about failure to make provision. If the local authority refuses to consider that a child is in need the appropriate remedy is judicial review. See Sunkin (1992) 4 J.Ch.L. 109, 111. Persons outside the scope of section 26(3) may be "qualifying persons" within the local authority complaints procedure set up under the Local Authority Social Services Act 1970, s.7B and S.I. 1990 No. 2244. Subsection (4) requires that the procedure contains an independent element. Subsection (7) provides that the responsible authority shall give due consideration to the findings of its complaints panel and notify the complainant, the child and any other person of its decision and its action. It does not have to follow the recommendation of the panel. Subsection (8) requires the responsible authority to publicise its complaints procedure. Schedule 7, paragraph 6 requires the responsible authority to provide a complaints system in relation to fostering limits and exemptions.

The regulations provide for a two-stage process but authorities may seek to resolve problems informally before a complaint is made. *Guidance*, Vol. 3, para. 10.13–14 supports this approach but suggests that time limits should be set to avoid delaying recourse to the formal process. The process starts when the authority receives a representation or complaint from someone entitled to complain under subsection (3)(a)–(d) or accepts that a person under (3)(e) has sufficient interest to complain (reg. 4(5)). Where the complainant is ineligible *Guidance* recommends that the authority consider whether the substance of the complaint needs to be addressed as if the child had complained (para. 10.40). The complainant must be sent an explanation of the procedure and either offered assistance in using it or advised how to obtain this. If the complaint is made orally the authority must record it in writing and send a copy to the complainant (reg. 4). The authority then appoints an independent person (reg. 5) who considers the complaint with the authority to formulate a response within 28 days. *Guidance* states that the independent person should be allowed to interview the child, the parents and relevant staff and others involved if necessary and be given access to the case record. The independent person should provide written comments to the authority (para. 10.41). The authority must include the independent person in all discussions about action to be taken (reg. 6). Within 28 days the authority must notify the complainant, any person on whose behalf the complaint was made, the independent person and other interested parties of the results of their considerations and their right to refer the matter to a panel (reg. 8(1)). The second stage, reference to a panel, may be activated by the complainant within 28 days of securing the authority's response (reg. 8(2)). The panel, including an independent person (who may be the same person as involved in the first stage) must meet within 28 days to consider any submissions from the complainant and the stage 1 independent person. Complainants have a right to take a supporter to this meeting (reg. 8). The panel must make its recommendation within 24 hours of the meeting and notify the authority, the complainant, the independent person and other interested parties, for example the child's independent visitor. The responsible authority must then consider with the independent person the action it should take (reg. 9). The authority is not required to follow the recommendation of the panel but must give them due regard (subs. (7)(a)).

Regulation 10 requires each authority to monitor the operation of its complaints system and compile an annual report. This should help ensure more responsive service provision.

The experience of one independent person are described by Rubenstein [1992] N.L.J. 866.

Subs. (3)

A procedure: The procedure will have to comply with the rules of natural justice. It will be important that the people involved in hearing complaints have not taken the decisions or action complained about.

Representations (including any complaint): The term representation was chosen by the Government, but they agreed that "complaint" should be added. It is now "clear that there is a statutory right to make a complaint" (*per* Lord Prys-Davies (*Hansard*, H.L. Vol. 503, col. 172)).

Such other persons: The local authority has a similarly wide duty in relation to their wishes and feelings under section 22(4)(d); it could include a guardian ad litem, a teacher, or a grandparent.

Under this part: This means not under Parts IV and V in relation to child protection. There is no provision in the Act for complaints about such action. The care provided to a child and the services (or their refusal) to a family in a case of child abuse would come within Part III. Complaints of maladministration can be referred to the relevant Local Government Ombudsman. Regulation 12 extends the complaints system to cases where a foster parent seeks exemption from the usual fostering limit under Schedule 7, paragraph 4. *Guidance*, Vol. 3, para. 10.9 suggests that authorities extend their complaints system to other matters, for example those relating to groups of children or foster parents.

Subs. (4)

Who is not: Former councillors and former employees can be included, although this would reduce the independence and thus the usefulness of the system. *Guidance* recommends that spouses and cohabitees of those excluded should not be appointed (para. 10.35).

Subs. (7)

This sets out the action which local authorities must take in relation to representations and complaints made under this procedure.

Due regard: The local authority is not required to follow the findings of the panel, but it would seem that they might be vulnerable to judicial review under the Wednesbury rule if any subsequent decision totally disregarded a finding and there had been no change of circumstances.

Such other persons: The local authority has broad discretion but should take care not to generate further complaints.

Subs. (8)

There is a duty to publish details about services under this part in Schedule 2, paragraph 1(2). Although there are differences of opinion about the provision of information to young children in care, it is difficult to see how it might be appropriate not to inform all parents of children looked after and all foster parents.

Co-operation between authorities

27.—(1) Where it appears to a local authority that any authority mentioned in subsection (3) could, by taking any specified action, help in the exercise of any of their functions under this Part, they may request the help of that other authority, specifying the action in question.

(2) An authority whose help is so requested shall comply with the request if it is compatible with their own statutory or other duties and obligations and does not unduly prejudice the discharge of any of their functions.

(3) The [authorities] are—
    (a) any local authority;

(b) any local education authority;
(c) any local housing authority;
(d) any health authority [or National Health Service Trust]; and
(e) any person authorised by the Secretary of State for the purposes of this section.

(4) Every local authority shall assist any local education authority with the provision of services for any child within the local authority's area who has special education needs.

AMENDMENT

The words in square brackets in subsection (3) were substituted by the Court and Legal Services Act 1990, Sched. 16, para. 14.

DEFINITIONS

"functions": s.105(1).
"health authority": s.105(1).
"local authority": s.105(1).
"local education authority": s.105(1).
"local housing authority": s.105(1).
"special education needs": s.105(1).

GENERAL NOTE

This section provides for co-operation between local authorities and other bodies to facilitate the exercise of any local authority powers or duties under Part III. Consultation with the local education authority is provided for in section 28. Consultation in child protection work is provided for in section 47(9)–(11).

Although the Act is primarily addressed to social services departments this provision acknowledges that the services children in need and their families often require may be the responsibility of other authorities. *Guidance* from the Department of Health stresses the need to establish organisational links with the authorities listed here rather than rely on ad hoc arrangements, Volume 2, paragraph 1.13–17 and annex B; Volume 6, Chapters 4, 5, 9 and 10. Annex A and B of Volume 6 contain details of the responsibilities of other authorities to children with disabilities. The statutory *Code of Guidance for Local Authorities on Homelessness* (1991) refers to the right of the social services authority to seek help from the housing authority and notes, "The Secretaries of State are concerned to avoid any possibility that the implementation of the 1989 Act might result in children and young people being sent to and fro between departments or authorities. Each department and authority has a responsibility to those who approach it under its own relevant legislation. However, a corporate policy and clear procedures in respect of collaboration ... will help to ensure co-operation at all levels." (para. 6.16).

Subs. (4)

Children with Special Educational needs within the Education Act 1981 are not necessarily "children in need" within section 17 although most will be. Details of the procedure for making assessments under the Education Act 1981 are contained in Department of Education and Science Circular 22/89 (Welsh Office Circular 54/89). The social services department may need to take part in the assessment which leads to a statement of special educational needs; it may carry out its own assessment at the same time (Sched. 2, para. 3). If the child is disabled the local authority must provide services which facilitate the child's integration (Sched. 2, para. 6).

Consultation with local education authorities

28.—(1) Where—
  (a) a child is being looked after by a local authority; and
  (b) the authority propose to provide accommodation for him in an establishment at which education is provided for children who are accommodated there,
they shall, so far as is reasonably practicable, consult the appropriate local education authority before doing so.

(2) Where any such proposal is carried out, the local authority shall, as soon as is reasonably practicable, inform the appropriate local education authority of the arrangements that have been made for the child's accommodation.

(3) Where the child ceases to be accommodated as mentioned in subsection (1)(b), the local authority shall inform the appropriate local education authority.

(4) In this section "the appropriate local education authority" means—
  (a) the local education authority within whose area the local authority's area falls; or
  (b) where the child has special educational needs and a statement of his needs is maintained under the Education Act 1981, the local education authority who maintain the statement.

DEFINITIONS

"appropriate local education authority": s.28(4).
"child looked after by . . . ": ss.22(1) and 105(4).
"local authority": s.105(1).

GENERAL NOTE

This section imposes new duties on local authorities to consult the appropriate local education authority before they accommodate a child at an establishment which provides education (subs. (1)) and to inform them of the placement (subs. (2)) and when it ends (subs. (3)). It applies to placements in boarding schools and homes which are also schools. Guidance on educational issues for children in residential care is provided in *Guidance*, Vol. 4, paras. 1.105–1.114. The Department of Health is planning to issue further guidance concerning *Community Homes with Education on the Premises*.

The local education authority is required to consult the social services department before applying for an education supervision order by section 36(8).

Recoupment of cost of providing services etc.

29.—(1) Where a local authority provide any service under section 17 or 18, other than advice, guidance or counselling, they may recover from a person specified in subsection (4) such charge for the service as they consider reasonable.

(2) Where the authority are satisfied that that person's means are insufficient for it to be reasonably practicable for him to pay the charge, they shall not require him to pay more than he can reasonably be expected to pay.

(3) No person shall be liable to pay any charge under subsection (1) at any time when he is in receipt of income support [family credit or

disability working allowance] under [Part VII of the Social Security Contributions and Benefits Act 1992].

(4) The persons are—
- (a) where the service is provided for a child under 16, each of his parents;
- (b) where it is provided for a child who has reached the age of 16, the child himself; and
- (c) where it is provided for a member of the child's family, that member.

(5) Any charge under subsection (1) may, without prejudice to any other method of recovery, be recovered summarily as a civil debt.

(6) Part III of Schedule 2 makes provision in connection with contributions towards the maintenance of children who are being looked after by local authorities and consists of the re-enactment with modifications of provisions in Part V of the Child Care Act 1980.

(7) Where a local authority provide any accommodation under section 20(1) for a child who was (immediately before they began to look after him) ordinarily resident within the area of another local authority, they may recover from that other authority any reasonable expenses incurred by them in providing the accommodation and maintaining him.

(8) Where a local authority provide accommodation under section 21(1) or (2)(a) or (b) for a child who is ordinarily resident within the area of another local authority and they are not maintaining him in—
- (a) a community home provided by them;
- (b) a controlled community home; or
- (c) a hospital vested in the Secretary of State [or any other hospital made available pursuant to arrangements made by a District Health Authority],

they may recover from that other authority any reasonable expenses incurred by them in providing the accommodation and maintaining him.

(9) Where a local authority comply with any request under section 27(2) in relation to a child or other person who is not ordinarily resident within their area, they may recover from the local authority in whose area the child or person is ordinarily resident any [reasonable expenses] incurred by them in respect of that person.

AMENDMENT

The words in square brackets in subsection (3) were substituted by the Disability Living Allowance and Working Allowance Act 1991, Sched. 3, para. 14 and the Social Security (Consequential Provisions) Act 1992, Sched 2, para. 108.

The words in square brackets in subsection (8) were added by the National Health Service and Community Care Act 1990, Sched. 9, para. 36(3).

The words in square brackets in subsection (9) were substituted by the Courts and Legal Services Act 1990, Sched. 16, para. 15.

DEFINITIONS

"child looked after by a local authority": ss.22(1), 105(4).
"community home": s.53.
"controlled community home": s.53(4).
"hospital": s.105(1).
"local authority": s.105(1).

"ordinary residence": ss.30(2), 105(6).
"service": s.105(1).

GENERAL NOTE

This section enables local authorities to charge for services (other than advice, guidance or counselling) provided under sections 17 or 18 (subss. (1)–(5)). It should be read with those relating to conditional provision of assistance in sections 17(7)–(9) and 24(10). The rules relating to charging for accommodation formerly in Part V of the C.C.A. 1980, are in Schedule 2, Part III; there have been no substantial amendments (subs. (6)). Guidance on charging is provided in *Guidance*, Vol. 2, paras. 2.38 *et seq*. It states that local authorities "should bear in mind that in some cases parents may accept the provision of services more readily" if they pay for them but does not refer to the research evidence that charging operates as a deterrent and is rarely cost-effective, see FRG, *Parental Contributions for Children* (1984) and Judge & Matthews, *Charging for Social Care* (1980).

Subsections (7)–(9) provide for recoupment of costs between authorities.

Subs. (1)

Any service: This includes assistance in cash or kind, under sections 17(6) and 24(7), but not advice or contributions under section 24(8), etc. Day centre, family centre or nursery placements can be charged for, as can family aides, laundry, etc. Where the service includes advice, there will need to be a discount to ensure that no charge is levied for that.

Subss. (2)–(3)

This requires the local authority to take account of means when levying charges so those of insufficient means are not required to pay more than they can reasonably be expected to. Even though a charge is levied, there is no liability to pay while a person is in receipt of income support, family credit or disability working allowance.

Reasonably expected to pay: As well as the person's resources it will be necessary to consider his expenditure and other debts. It must be unreasonable to expect someone to pay for a service if he risks losing his house and must devote all "spare" resources to arrears on his mortgage or rent.

No person shall be liable: See note to section 17(9).

In receipt of: See note to section 17(9).

Subs. (4)

The only people who are liable for children at common law are parents, and their liability ends when the children reach 16 years.

Provided for a member of the child's family: Some services which are provided for more than one person may present problems. A day nursery placement may appear to be a placement for the child but if it provides a break for the carer, it could be said to be a service for them as well. No problems are created if the child is under 16 and living with parents, since parents will be liable for a service to them and to the child. This is not so if a child is living with relatives, because they have no liability for services for the child.

Member of the child's family: See notes on section 17(3).

Subs. (5)

It will be recovered in the magistrates' court under the Magistrates' Courts Act 1980, s.58.

Subs. (6)

The new provisions for charges for children in care are largely a rewritten revision of those in the C.C.A. 1980, Pt. V "putting more emphasis on reasonableness" (*per* Lord Chancellor (*Hansard*, H.L. Vol. 503, col. 1497)). An authority may only seek contributions if it is reasonable to do so (para. 21(2)). The high cost of collecting contributions may lead to authorities deciding not to try to recover contributions, but paragraph 21(1) appears to require an individual decision in each case. Local authorities may not specify a sum greater than it is reasonably practicable for the contributor to pay (para. 22(5)(b)) and a court making a contribution order must give due regard to the contributor's means (para. 23(3)(b)). The same people—parents and children over 16—can be charged for accommodation provided under section 20 or to children on care orders. The categories of exempt care are the same (para. 21(5) and (7)) and contributors are not liable for any period while they are on Income Support, Family Credit or Disability Working Allowance (para. 21(4)). The two-stage process is retained: the local authority must serve a contributions notice under paragraph 22, to which the contributor may agree. If he does, contributions are now recovered as a civil debt (Magistrates' Courts Act 1980, s.58). Where no agreement is reached, the local authority may apply to the court for an order (para. 23). No order may be made for a sum greater than that specified in the notice (para. 23(3)(a)). Contribution orders made in the magistrates' court are enforceable like magistrates' courts maintenance orders under the Magistrates' Courts Act 1980, s.150 (para. 24). The Lord Chancellor undertook in Parliament to review the provision of legal aid in these proceedings "because I believe it appropriate that it should be available" (Hansard, H.L. Vol. 503, col. 1498). The powers of local authorities to obtain affiliation orders and have existing orders varied in their favour was abolished with affiliation orders by the F.L.R.A. 1987. There are no corresponding powers for local authorities to seek financial relief under Schedule 1 and Schedule 2, paragraph 21(6). The Maintenance Enforcement Act 1991 applies to these proceedings because contribution orders are maintenance orders under the Administration of Justice Act 1970, Sched. 8 as amended by the Courts and Legal Services Act 1990, Sched. 16, para. 6.

There is a new power in the Secretary of State to make regulations about the assessment of contributions, agreements and arrangements for payment (para. 25). There was no indication to Parliament that this power would be exercised.

Subss. (7)–(9)

Where accommodation is provided under section 20(1) (but not where it is provided under section 20(3) to a child in need over the age of 16), or under section 21(2)(a) or (b) but not in any of the facilities listed in subsection (8), the local authority may charge the authority where the child is ordinarily resident. Alternatively, the paying authority may take over the child's care. A decision to move a child can only be made in accordance with section 22(3). Disputes about ordinary residence are determined by the Secretary of State (s.30(2)).

Reasonable expenses: The fact that the "home authority" would not have provided the service does not make it unreasonable.

Miscellaneous

30.—(1) Nothing in this Part shall affect any duty imposed on a local authority by or under any other enactment.

(2) Any question arising under section (20)(2), 21(3) or 29(7) to (9) as to the ordinary residence of a child shall be determined by agreement between the local authorities concerned or, in default of agreement, by the Secretary of State.

(3) Where the functions conferred on a local authority by this Part and the functions of a local education authority are concurrent, the Secretary of State may by regulations provide by which authority the functions are to be exercised.

(4) The Secretary of State may make regulations for determining, as respects any local education authority functions specified in the regulations, whether a child who is being looked after by a local authority is to be treated, for purposes so specified, as a child of parents of sufficient resources or as a child of parents without resources.

Miscellaneous

DEFINITIONS
"functions": s.105(1).
"local authority": s.105(1).
"local education authority": s.105(1).
"ordinary residence": s.105(6).

GENERAL NOTE

Subs. (3)

This re-enacts the C.C.A. 1980, s.30. Regulations already exist (see Local Authorities and Local Education Authorities (Allocation of Funding) Regulations 1951 (S.I. 1951 No. 1472)).

Subs. (4)

This re-enacts the C.C.A. 1980, s.30.

A child of parents of sufficient resources ... : This is not defined in any of the Education Acts 1944–1988. Under the Education Act 1988, s.111, a local authority may levy charges for board and lodging in certain circumstances. If full charges would involve "financial hardship" to the parent, charges may be remitted (s.111(5)). A parent who would suffer financial hardship is presumably one with insufficient resources. There is no comparable provision in relation to charges for "optional extras" under section 110; schools and education authorities have to formulate and keep under review charging and remission policies.

PART IV

CARE AND SUPERVISION

General

Care and supervision orders

31.—(1) On the application of any local authority or authorised person, the court may make an order—
   (a) placing the child with respect to whom the application is made in the care of a designated local authority; or
   (b) putting him under the supervision of a designated local authority or of a probation officer.

(2) A court may only make a care order or supervision order if it is satisfied—
   (a) that the child concerned is suffering, or is likely to suffer, significant harm; and
   (b) that the harm, or likelihood of harm, is attributable to—
      (i) the care given to the child, or likely to be given to him if the order were not made, not being what it would be reasonable to expect a parent to give to him; or
      (ii) the child's being beyond parental control.

(3) No care order or supervision order may be made with respect to a child who has reached the age of 17 (or 16, in the case of a child who is married).

(4) An application under this section may be made on its own or in any other family proceedings.

(5) The court may—
- (a) on an application for a care order, make a supervision order;
- (b) on an application for a supervision order, make a care order.

(6) Where an authorised person proposes to make an application under this section he shall—
- (a) if it is reasonably practicable to do so; and
- (b) before making the application,

consult the local authority appealing to him to be the authority in whose area the child concerned is ordinarily resident.

(7) An application made by an authorised person shall not be entertained by the court if, at the time when it is made, the child concerned is—
- (a) the subject of an earlier application for a care order, or supervision order, which has not been disposed of; or
- (b) subject to—
  - (i) a care order or supervision order;
  - (ii) an order under section 7(7)(b) of the Children and Young Persons Act 1969; or
  - (iii) a supervision requirement within the meaning of the Social Work (Scotland) Act 1968.

(8) The local authority designated in a care order must be—
- (a) the authority within whose area the child is ordinarily resident; or
- (b) where the child does not reside in the area of a local authority,

the authority within whose area any circumstances arose in consequence of which the order is being made.

(9) In this section—

"authorised person" means—
- (a) the National Society for the Prevention of Cruelty to Children and any of its officers; and
- (b) any person authorised by order of the Secretary of State to bring proceedings under this section and any officer of a body which is so authorised;

"harm" means ill-treatment or the impairment of health or development;

"development" means physical, intellectual, emotional, social or behavioural development;

"health" means physical or mental health; and

"ill-treatment" includes sexual abuse and forms of ill-treatment which are not physical.

(10) Where the question of whether harm suffered by a child is significant turns on the child's health or development, his health or development shall be compared with that which could reasonably be expected of a similar child.

(11) In this Act—

"a care order" means (subject to section 105(1)) an order under subsection (1)(a) and (except where express provision to the contrary is made) includes an interim care order made under section 38; and

"a supervision order" means an order under subsection (1)(b) and (except where express provision to the contrary is made) includes an interim supervision order made under section 38.

DEFINITIONS
"authorised person": s.31(9).
"care order": ss.31(11), 105(1).
"child": ss.31(3), 105(1).
"designated local authority": s.31(8).
"development": s.31(9).
"family proceedings": s.8(3).
"harm": s.31(9).
"health": s.31(9).
"ill-treatment": s.31(9).
"local authority": s.105(1).
"ordinary residence": s.105(6).
"significant": s.31(10).
"supervision order": s.31(11).
"the court": s.92(7).

GENERAL NOTE

This section sets out the conditions which must be satisfied before a court grants a care or supervision order. It largely follows the recommendations of the R.C.C.L., Chap. 15 and Cm. 62, paras. 59–60. Compulsory measures of care can only be imposed through care proceedings. Parental rights resolutions and committal to care in matrimonial and other proceedings are abolished; local authorities cannot obtain care orders or any equivalent powers in wardship (s.100) or by section 8 orders (s.9). Thus there is no "safety net" and children can only be protected by an order if the conditions in subsection (2) are satisfied. If the order is refused, the local authority may appeal to the High Court (s.94). If an interim order has been made the child can be kept in care during the appeal period (s.40). Local authorities may apply by commencing care proceedings or in any family proceedings (subs. (4)). The lack of alternatives may affect the way the courts interpret their powers under section 31.

The existing grounds for orders in the C.Y.P.A. 1969, s.1(2) and the C.C.A. 1980, s.3 are replaced by the conditions in subsection (2) and the requirement to satisfy section 1(3)–(5). The court must give paramount consideration to the child's welfare (as defined in the checklist) and may only make an order if it is better than not to do so. The Lord Chancellor stated in his Joseph Jackson memorial lecture ([1989] New L.J. 505) that these conditions should not be regarded as grounds for a care order but the "minimum circumstances" which would justify state intervention in family life.

In general, cases which come within the C.Y.P.A. 1969, s.1(2) or the C.C.A. 1980, s.3 are covered, *i.e.* it will be possible to obtain an order to require a child's placement in care or to prevent the parents from removing him from care as before. However, the administrative procedure is abolished so it will be necessary to satisfy the court in all cases. Moreover, the circumstances listed below pose particular problems—

(1) Orders can only be obtained in respect of people under 17 (or under 16 if they have married). The only interventions to protect a wayward older teenager such as occurred in *Re SW* [1986] 1 F.L.R. 24 would be through criminal proceedings or, if the person was suffering from mental disorder, under the Mental Health Act 1983.

(2) Cases involving "Schedule 1 offenders" (C.Y.P.A. 1933) or previous findings under C.Y.P.A. 1969, s.1(2)(a) no longer receive special consideration although these factors will be relevant to the "likelihood of harm" and "care" in section 31(2)(b).

(3) Truancy is no longer a ground for an order but where non-attendance at school satisfies section 31(2) a care order may be made. In *Re O (a*

minor) (care order: education: procedure), [1992] 2 F.L.R. 7 the High Court upheld a decision by magistrates that a 15-year-old not attending school was, by virtue of that, suffering impairment of development in comparison with 15-year-old attenders. Section 36 provides educational supervision orders as the main intervention to deal with truants; it will still be possible to prosecute parents under the Education Act 1944, s.37, but not to imprison them (s.40 as amended by Sched. 15).

(4) The imposition of the tests in section 1 may, in some cases (particularly cases of moral danger concerning either teenage girls and unsuitable associates or younger children involved in petty crime), lead to courts refusing an order on the ground that it would only exacerbate problems.

(5) Cases under the C.C.A. 1980, s.3, where there was no finding of parental unfitness, may not be covered by the new legislation. These include some cases of abandonment under section 3(1)(b)(i) and cases under section 3(1)(d). There is no equivalent provision to that of "statutory abandonment" which occurred if parents did not notify their address to the local authority for 12 months (C.C.A. 1980, s.3(8)). It will not be possible to get an order where the parent can provide appropriate care. Where the child is "bonded" with a foster parent it is possible that the parent's care might fall within subsection (2)(b) even though it would be adequate for another child. If a care order is not available the foster carers may be able to apply for a residence order under section 10(5) if they have cared for the child for three years or have the necessary consents. The local authority's consent will be required where the child has not lived with the applicants for three years (s.9(3)).

(6) Cases where care orders are sought but it is intended that the child should remain in the family home. In *R. v. G and Surrey County Council* [1984] Fam. 100 the Court of Appeal upheld the making of an order under the M.C.A. 1973, s.43(1) in such a case. The divorced parents were continuing their quarrel over access and the children repeatedly moved from one parent to the other. The court was prepared to find that the exceptional circumstances test in section 43 was satisfied. However, the addition of the requirement in section 1(5), together with the fact that parents retain parental responsibility under a care order, and the wide powers of the supervisor under a supervision order, would suggest that a supervision order would generally be more appropriate in such cases, possibly with prohibited steps or other section 8 orders in addition.

The statute also clearly allows for the protection of some children who were usually dealt with in wardship because of doubts about the scope of the old provisions.

(1) Children at risk: first born, new born babies of mentally ill or severely subnormal parents, drug addicts and other people who seem unable to care; children whose parents are no longer coping (because of mental illness or other problems) but who have not yet been harmed. The decision in *Re D* [1987] A.C. 317, H.L. which allowed the removal under the C.Y.P.A. 1969, s.1(2)(a) of a baby born with foetal drug syndrome did not permit orders in relation to all children local authorities sought to protect.

(2) Children who entered voluntary care after incidents of abuse and neglect who could not be brought before the court under the C.Y.P.A. 1969 because of the lapse of time but against whose parents there was insufficient evidence to ground a parental rights resolution. Emphasis on partnership with parents and avoiding compulsory measures where possible are likely to encourage social workers to use accommodation and service arrangements rather than care or supervision orders. If agreements break down it may be necessary to seek orders months after the original incidents. In such cases the likely significant harm test may be proved by reference to the circumstances surrounding the original incidents and the refusal to continue co-operation. It will be important that the basis of the agreement is made clear from the outset.

Apart from the changes to the grounds, the section largely repeats the provisions of the C.Y.P.A. 1969. Proceedings can only be brought by local authorities and the N.S.P.C.C. (no other people have been authorised by the Secretary of State). Subsection (7) contains new restrictions on applications by authorised persons. There is no procedure equivalent to that in the Children and Young Persons Act 1963, s.3 which enabled parents to force a local authority to take action in relation to a child who is beyond control. A parent who is unable to control his child can only request assistance from the local authority and make a complaint under section 26(3)(b) if it is refused. A child who is beyond parental control arguably comes within the definition of "in need" in section 17(10)(a).

The grounds for intervention are further discussed in Adcock, White and Hollows, *Significant Harm* (1991).

Subs. (1)

On application: This may be in care proceedings or by intervening in any "family proceedings" as defined in section 8(3) (subs. (4)).

The court: Most applications will be heard in the family proceedings court, see notes to section 92, Schedule 11 and the Children (Allocation of Proceedings) Order 1991 (S.I. 1991 No. 1677). There is no power to add any directions to the order specifying rehabilitation or other matters (except contact) *Re C (a Minor: Care Order) The Times*, August 18, 1992.

Subs. (2)

There is no distinction between the grounds for a care or supervision order although the court may continue to be willing to make supervision orders rather than care orders in weaker cases.

In addition to the test here, the court must be satisfied that the order is in the child's welfare as defined in the checklist (s.1(3)) and that it is better to make the order than not (s.1(5)). If the court is not satisfied it may still make a section 8 order because these are family proceedings (ss.8(3) and (4), 10(1)).

This provision will doubtless be the subject of considerable judicial interpretation. Two separate elements which are both contentious have to be established—
  (a) that the child is suffering significant harm, and
  (b) that this is attributable either to the care given to the child or the child being beyond parental control.

Significant: The R.C.C.L. which proposed the new grounds stated at paragraph 15.15—

"having set an acceptable standard of upbringing for the child, it should be necessary to show some substantial deficit in that standard. Minor shortcomings in the health and care provided or minor deficits in physical, psychological or social developments should not give rise to any compulsory intervention unless they are having, or are likely to have, serious and lasting effects upon the child."

What is "significant harm" is explained in subsection (10) for cases of health and development (but not for cases of ill-treatment) by reference to what "could reasonably be expected" of a "similar child" (see below). The R.C.C.L. noted that a child who has been non-accidentally injured or an older sexually abused child "may not have suffered any lasting impairment in his health and development and the resulting emotional damage may be difficult to prove" (para. 15.16). It suggested a form of wording to cover these cases but this has not been included in the Act. It is likely that there will be increased emphasis on medical and psychological evidence to establish significant harm, particularly the emotional damage which may follow from abuse. Evidence or further evidence may be obtained during a child assessment order (s.43), an emergency protection order (s.44) or under an interim order (s.38). Where the harm is ill-treatment, significant is not defined. In these cases ill-treatment may be significant because of its seriousness, *e.g.* a fractured skull; the effect on the child, *e.g.* an eye injury for a partially sighted child; or the nature of the incident, *e.g.* throwing a baby even if no injury resulted. Also reliance may be placed on the likelihood of further significant injuries when there have been a series of insignificant ones.

Is suffering: The fact that there has been harm in the past will not be sufficient unless it is likely that it will be repeated. A local authority which suspects harm and offers to accommodate a child will not necessarily be able to use care proceedings to prevent the child's removal from care after a prolonged period. However, the words "his development is being avoidably prevented" in the C.Y.P.A. 1969, s.1(2), were held not to require that the state persisted at the time of the hearing; *M v. Westminster City Council* [1985] F.L.R. 325.

Is likely to suffer: The R.C.C.L. stated in paragraph 15.18:

"In our view ... 'likely' will place a burden of proof upon local authorities which will be sufficiently difficult for them to discharge, especially in relation to mental or emotional harm and this will prevent unwarranted intervention."

The standard of proof is the civil standard. In the past the courts have balanced the size of the risk against the severity of harm if the event occurs. However, unless the risk establishes that the harm is "likely" the test is not satisfied. The test requires more than a finding that harm may occur on the balance of probabilities *Newham London Borough* v. *AG* [1992] 2 F.C.R. 119.

Attributable to: There has to be a link but not direct causation. For example, harm could be attributable to parental care where the parent failed to ensure that his child did not have contact with someone who was a known child abuser.

Care: Where the child has been accommodated by the local authority for a long time and the parents are not caring for another child it may be difficult to show what their current standard of care is. Reliance on a previously observed care may be sufficient unless the parents are able to point to changes which suggest that they would now care differently.

Reasonable to expect: The need for some children such as those with asthma or brittle bones to receive a higher standard of care is provided for. There was concern during the debate in the House of Lords that this provision might be thought to indicate that different standards of care could be expected from different classes or communities but this was not accepted as a correct interpretation by the Lord Chancellor (*Hansard*, H.L. Vol. 503, col. 354). D.H. *Guidance*, Vol. 1, para. 3.32 endorses this view.

Beyond parental control: This was formerly a ground for an order under C.Y.P.A. 1969, s.1(2)(d). Under the new provision it is only a ground where it produces significant harm or the likelihood of such harm. The word "parental" should include the care of whoever has been entrusted by the parents with the child's care if the parents are not able or willing to exercise effective control themselves.

Subs. (5)

The court may alternatively make any section 8 order subject to the restrictions in section 9 or make no order at all.

Subs. (6)

This contains the additional procedural conditions imposed on action by the N.S.P.C.C. (there are no other authorised persons). If it is reasonably practicable the N.S.P.C.C. must consult the local authority before starting proceedings. Consultation under subsection (6) will automatically bring the local authority's duty to investigate under section 47(1) into play. The local authority may then decide to start care proceedings. If the N.S.P.C.C. has obtained an emergency protection order under section 44, the Emergency Protection Order (Transfer of Responsibilities) Regulations 1991 (S.I. 1991 No. 1414) made under section 52(3) enable the local authority to give notice to the court, the applicant and those notified of the order and take over the order, see p. 462 below. The authority must then be treated as if they had applied for and been granted the order. In other cases the local authority should seek to be made a party under rule 7 of the Family Proceedings Rules see p. 368 below.

Arrangements between the local authorities, the N.S.P.C.C. and others concerned in protecting children should follow *Guidance* from the Department of Health see, *Working Together under the Children Act 1989*, (1991).

Subs. (7)

Restricts applications by the N.S.P.C.C. where:
  (a) there is a local authority application pending, or
  (b) the child is subject to an existing care or supervision order, including a supervision order made in criminal proceedings.

These limitations reflect the view of the R.C.C.L. in paragraph 12.15 that proceedings should usually be brought by the local authority and also current practice. However, there is nothing in the Act to stop the N.S.P.C.C. bringing proceedings where the local authority has agreed to provide accommodation on a voluntary basis following, *e.g.* suspected abuse. It is important that professional rivalries do not interfere with planning for children.

Subs. (8)
If the wrong authority is designated it would need to appeal against the order.
Does not reside: For example a child visiting from outside England and Wales.

Subss. (9) and (10)
The definition of significant harm is constructed like a Russian doll! It also applies to child assessment orders under section 43, emergency protection orders under section 44, the police power to remove a child under section 46, the local authority's duty to investigate under section 47 and detention in secure accommodation under section 25.
Impairment of health or development: This seems wide enough to cover any case of neglect—poor nutrition, low standards of hygiene, poor emotional care or through failure to seek treatment for an illness or condition.
Ill-treatment: The Lord Chancellor explained what was meant (*Hansard*, H.L. Vol. 503, col. 342): "Ill-treatment is not a precise term and would include, for example, instances of verbal abuse or unfairness falling a long way short of significant harm." Such insignificant action could not form the basis of an application but such ill-treatment might produce significant impairment of health in a vulnerable child and thus justify intervention.
Reasonably be expected: This may pose problems if the child already has a handicap and either there is little information about what is normal for such children or the range of development is extremely broad.
A similar child: According to the Lord Chancellor a child with the same physical attributes as the child concerned, not a child of the same background (see *Hansard*, H.L. Vol. 503, col. 354). However, this ignores the fact that social and environmental factors contribute very significantly to what can be achieved.

Period within which application for order under this Part must be disposed of

32.—(1) A court hearing an application for an order under this Part shall (in the light of any rules made by virtue of subsection (2))—
   (a) draw up a timetable with a view to disposing of the application without delay; and
   (b) give such directions as it considers appropriate for the purpose of ensuring, so far as is reasonably practicable, that that timetable is adhered to.
(2) Rules of court may—
   (a) specify periods within which specified steps must be taken in relation to such proceedings; and
   (b) make other provision with respect to such proceedings for the purpose of ensuring, so far as is reasonably practicable, that they are disposed of without delay.

DEFINITIONS
   "care order": ss.31(11), 105(1).
   "supervision order": s.31(11).
   "the court": s.92(7).

GENERAL NOTE
This section should be read with section 1(2) which warns of the dangers of delay. However, it has been recognised *Re C* [1992] N.L.J. 837 that delay may be beneficial where, for example it enables a complete assessment. "Ensuring proper timetabling arrangements is one of the Bill's better reforms" *per* David Mellor, Minister of Health (Standing Committee B, Col. 231, May 23, 1989). The courts have recognised that delay is particularly damaging to children and can lead to a denial of justice. The period for procedural steps should be kept to a minimum. Long hearings may be inappropriate in uncontested care cases. Magistrates should give their decision as soon as possible, *Devon CC v. S.* [1992] 3 All E.R. 793.

A Department of Health Study *The Timetabling of care proceedings before the implementation of the Children Act 1989* (1992) shows firm control by the courts may minimise delay. Directions hearings (r. 14, see p. 389 below) are used to establish the timetable and monitor the progress of each cases. There is an expectation that cases will be completed within 12 weeks. The Lord Chancellor has stated that "brisk treatment can be expected of legal representatives who do not come equipped with the necessary information" to allow dates of hearings to be fixed) [1991] Fam. Law 455–456. A penalty of costs may be imposed on a party who is responsible for delay. See the Family Proceedings (Costs) Rules 1991 (S.I. 1991 No. 1832) p. 475 below.

Subs. (2)

Rules of court: The Family Proceedings Courts (Children Act 1989 Rules 1991 (S.I. 1991 No. 1395) rr. 14 and 15 see below pp. 389–393. Guardians ad litem have responsibility for advising the court about the timing of proceedings under rule 11(4)(d).

Care orders

Effect of care order

33.—(1) Where a care order is made with respect to a child it shall be the duty of the local authority designated by the order to receive the child into their care and to keep him in their care while the order remains in force.

(2) Where—
  (a) a care order has been made with respect to a child on the application of an authorised person; but
  (b) the local authority designated by the order was not informed that that person proposed to make the application,

the child may be kept in the care of that person until received into the care of the authority.

(3) While a care order is in force with respect to a child, the local authority designated by the order shall—
  (a) have parental responsibility for the child; and
  (b) have the power (subject to the following provisions of this section) to determine the extent to which a parent or guardian of the child may meet his parental responsibility for him.

(4) The authority may not exercise the power in subsection (3)(b) unless they are satisfied that it is necessary to do so in order to safeguard or promote the child's welfare.

(5) Nothing in subsection (3)(b) shall prevent a parent or guardian of the child who has care of him from doing what is reasonable in all the circumstances of the case for the purpose of safeguarding or promoting his welfare.

(6) While a care order is in force with respect to a child, the local authority designated by the order shall not—
  (a) cause the child to be brought up in any religious persuasion other than that in which he would have been brought up if the order had not been made; or
  (b) have the right—

(i) to consent or refuse to consent to the making of an application with respect to the child under section 18 of the Adoption Act 1976;
(ii) to agree or refuse to agree to the making of an adoption order, or an order under section 55 of the Act of 1976, with respect to the child; or
(iii) to appoint a guardian for the child.

(7) While a care order is in force with respect to a child, no person may—
(a) cause the child to be known by a new surname; or
(b) remove him from the United Kingdom,

without either the written consent of every person who has parental responsibility for the child or the leave of the court.

(8) Subsection 7(b) does not—
(a) prevent the removal of such a child, for a period of less than one month, by the authority in whose care he is; or
(b) apply to arrangements for such a child to live outside England and Wales (which are governed by paragraph 19 of Schedule 2).

(9) The power in subsection (3)(b) is subject (in addition to being subject to the provisions of this section) to any right, duty, power, responsibility or authority which a parent or guardian of the child has in relation to the child and his property by virtue of any other enactment.

DEFINITIONS
"authorised person": s.31(9).
"care order": ss.31(11), 105(1).
"designated local authority": s.31(8).
"guardian": s.5.
"parental responsibility": ss.2, 3.
"person who has parental responsibility": ss.2(1)(2), 4(1), 5(6), 12(1), 33(3).

GENERAL NOTE
This section sets out the powers and responsibilities of the various parties when a care order is made. The comparable provisions relating to supervision orders are in section 35 and Schedule 3, Parts I and II.

The N.S.P.C.C. is an authorised person (see s.31(9)) and may keep the child in its care until he is received by the local authority but only if the authority was not informed of the application under section 31(6) (subs. (3)).

The parents: Retain parental responsibility for the child but can only exercise it in accordance with: section 2(8), which precludes action incompatible with a court order; subsections (3) and (4), which give the local authority the power to determine, in accordance with the child's welfare, the extent to which the parents may exercise their responsibility; and subsection (5). John Eekelaar strongly criticised the notion that both the parents and the authority should have parental responsibility ([1989] New L.J. 760). He noted that there was no statutory provision allowing the courts to deal with disputes (except over contact) in such cases because specific issue orders are not available (s.9(1)). He suggested that the courts might not follow the decisions in *A* v. *Liverpool City Council* [1982] A.C. 363 and *Re W* [1985] 2 All E.R. 301, which prevented the use of wardship to review the exercise of local authority discretion over children in care because the Act expressly gives the parents parental responsibility alongside the authority. He further suggested that a refusal to exercise wardship in such circumstances could be a breach of Article 6 of the European Convention on Human Rights because parental responsibility is a "civil right" which should be determined through a fair hearing by an independent tribunal. He argued that care orders are made because of parental failure and this should justify the removal of parental responsibility. However, the Government does not seem to have heeded this advice. Section 33 was redrafted to make it clear that "the local authority must be in the driving seat" (*per* David Mellor, Minister of Health, Standing Committee B, Col. 232, May 23, 1989), but parents retain their status. It seems that this has been done to encourage maintenance of links with the family, rehabilitation and perhaps also to justify charging for the child's care. The Arrangement for Placement of Children (General) Regulations 1991 (S.I. 1991 No. 890) apply to placements when a child is in care. The local authority must consult with the parents, etc., but there is no requirement for a written agreement (see notes to ss.20, 22). Whatever limits this section puts on day-to-day decisions by parents it is clear that they still have the right to give or withhold agreement to adoption or freeing for adoption and to appoint a guardian. The parents apparently retain their rights to determine the (immature) child's religion (subs. (6)) They cannot change his name or remove him from the United Kingdom without consent. Parents retain their right to inherit on the child's intestacy.

The Local Authority: This has a duty to receive the child into care and keep him in care while the order is in force. The child can only be accommodated in accordance with section 23 (see notes on s.23 above). He can only live with a parent, a person with parental responsibility, or someone who had a residence order before the care order was made in accordance with regulations made under section 23(5) (see Placement of Children with parents, etc., Regulations 1991 (S.I. 1991 No. 893)). The local authority is also under the duties prescribed in sections 17, 22, 24, 26 and Schedule 2, Part II.

The local authority has parental responsibility (subs. (3)) but cannot change the child's religion, agree to his adoption or freeing for adoption, or appoint a guardian. If the child is mature he may make his own decision about religion and the local authority may support it (David Mellor, Standing Committee B, Col. 234, May 23, 1989). The local authority does have the right to consent to his marriage (see Marriage Act 1949, s.3(1) as amended by Sched. 12, para. 5). It cannot change a child's name (nor allow a foster parent to do so) without the consent of all persons with parental responsibility or the court. A court could only allow name change if it was in the child's welfare. In cases involving remarried parents the courts have been quite unwilling to allow name change without cogent reasons (see *Re W.G.* (1976) 6 Fam. Law 210; *W* v. *A* [1981] Fam. 14) although the Court of Appeal has not always maintained opposition (*R (B.M.)* v. *R (D.N.)* [1978] 2 All E.R. 33). The local authority may remove the child from the United Kingdom without consent for a period of less than one month. Longer periods require the consent of every person with parental responsibility or the court. If the child is to live outside England and Wales, then Schedule 2, paragraph 19, applies and the approval of the court is required. Guidance on placement overseas is given in *Guidance*, Vol. 8, Chap. 4.

A parent who alleges that a local authority has failed to comply with the provisions of this Act should use the procedures and remedies that it provides (*A* v. *Liverpool City Council* [1982] A.C. 363, H.L. and Cases, Part V). The remedy of judicial review is also available. The common law does not afford to a parent a cause of action in negligence against a local authority founded upon the failure by social workers to protect or to avoid injuring a parent's right to, or expectation of, enjoying the company and presence of her child; see *F* v. *Wirral Metropolitan Borough Council* [1991] 2 All E.R. 648, C.A. Guidance on the local authority's responsibilities for children in its care are contained in *Guidance*, Vols. 3 and 4.

The local authority has a duty to take steps to establish the paternity of a child in care where it is in that child's interests to do so *Re B* [1992] N.L.J. 642.

Subss. (3) and (4)

Determine the extent: Details must be recorded in the agreement with the parents made under the Arrangements for Placement of Children (General) Regulations (S.I. 1991 No. 890) or the Placement of Children with Parents, etc., Regulations (S.I. 1991 No. 893) (see notes to ss.20, 23). Where the authority has not restricted the parents' right to consent to medical treatment they cannot allow them to refuse examinations or treatment for the child, see *Guidance*, Vol. 3, para. 2.30.

Subs. (6)

Religious persuasion: *Guidance*, Vol. 4, paras. 1.121 *et seq.* draws attention to the ways in which a child may be helped to follow his religion while in a community home. The Children's Homes Regulations (S.I. 1991 No. 1506) reg. 11 and the Foster Placement

(Children) Regulations (S.I. 1991 No. 910) reg. 5(2) make specific provision in this respect.

Subs. (7)
These are "specified" proceedings so a guardian ad litem should be appointed.
Consent: This must be in writing, see Family Proceedings Courts (Children Act 1989) Rules 1991, r. 25.

Parental contact, etc., with children in care

34.—(1) Where a child is in the care of a local authority, the authority shall (subject to the provisions of this section) allow the child reasonable contact with—
  (a) his parents;
  (b) any guardian of his;
  (c) where there was a residence order in force with respect to the child immediately before the care order was made, the person in whose favour the order was made; and
  (d) where, immediately before the care order was made, a person had care of the child by virtue of an order made in the exercise of the High Court's inherent jurisdiction with respect to children, that person.

(2) On an application made by the authority or the child, the court may make such order as it considers appropriate with respect to the contact which is to be allowed between the child and any named person.

(3) On an application made by—
  (a) any person mentioned in paragraphs (a) to (d) of subsection (1); or
  (b) any person who has obtained the leave of the court to make the application,
the court may make such order as it considers appropriate with respect to the contact which is to be allowed between the child and that person.

(4) On an application made by the authority or the child, the court may make an order authorising the authority to refuse to allow contact between the child and any person who is mentioned in paragraphs (a) to (d) of subsection (1) and named in the order.

(5) When making a care order with respect to a child, or in any family proceedings in connection with a child who is in the care of a local authority, the court may make an order under this section, even though no application for such an order has been made with respect to the child, if it considers that the order should be made.

(6) An authority may refuse to allow the contact that would otherwise be required by virtue of subsection (1) or an order under this section if—
  (a) they are satisfied that it is necessary to do so in order to safeguard or promote the child's welfare; and
  (b) the refusal—
    (i) is decided upon as a matter of urgency; and
    (ii) does not last for more than seven days.

(7) An order under this section may impose such conditions as the court considers appropriate.

(8) The Secretary of State may by regulations make provision as to—

(a) the steps to be taken by a local authority who have exercised their powers under subsection (6);
(b) the circumstances in which, and conditions subject to which, the terms of any order under this section may be departed from by agreement between the local authority and the person in relation to whom the order is made;
(c) notification by a local authority of any variation or suspension of arrangements made (otherwise than under an order under this section) with a view to affording any person contact with a child to whom this section applies.

(9) The court may vary or discharge any order made under this section on the application of the authority, the child concerned or the person named in the order.

(10) An order under this section may be made either at the same time as the care order itself or later.

(11) Before making a care order with respect to any child the court shall—

(a) consider the arrangements which the authority have made, or propose to make, for affording any person contact with a child to whom this section applies; and
(b) invite the parties to the proceedings to comment on those arrangements.

DEFINITIONS

"care order": ss.31(11), 105(1).
"guardian": s.5.
"local authority": s.105(3).
"residence order": ss.8(1), 105(3).
"the court": s.92(7).

REGULATIONS

The Contact with Children Regulations 1991 (S.I. 1991 No. 891).

GENERAL NOTE

This provides for contact (access) between children in care and their families and the only judicial means for dealing with disputes about contact for such children. Disputes may also be referred to the complaints system, established under section 26(3). This section should be read with Schedule 2, paragraph 15, which imposes on the local authority a qualified duty "to endeavour to promote contact" between children who are looked after by the authority, their families and their friends. It replaces the C.C.A. 1980, ss.12A–12G; the D.H.S.S. Code of Practice on Access ceases to have effect but new guidance is provided (*Guidance*, Vol. 3, Chap. 6 and Vol. 4, Chap. 4). This stresses the importance of contact (para. 6.9). Local authorities are no longer empowered to terminate access between children in care and their parents. Decisions about the refusal of contact, its frequency and duration are all made by the court (subsection. (2) to (5)). There is a power in the regulations to agree a variation of arrangements included in court orders.

The legislation reflects the view that contact is "a right of the child" (*per* Wrangham J. in *M.* v. *M.* [1973] 2 All E.R. 81) both in its wording and the fact that children may apply for orders (subss. (2) and (4)).

Local authorities are under a duty to allow a child in care reasonable contact with his parents, guardians or anyone who held a residence order in respect of the child or care under the inherent jurisdiction before the care order was made (subs. (1)) except where subsection (6) applies. The local authority, the child, those listed in subsection (1) and anyone with leave may apply for orders (subs. (3)) allowing contact between the child and a named person and variation or discharge of an order concerning them (subs. (9)). Only the local authority and the child may apply for an order for contact to be refused (subs. (4)). The local authority may refuse to comply with an order for contact under subsection (6) for up to seven days if this is necessary to safeguard the child's welfare as a matter of urgency. Any order may be made, or conditions attached (subs. (7)) by the court of its own motion (subs. (5)). Orders can be made when a care order is made (this includes when an interim order is made (s.31(11)) or later (including in family proceedings) (subss. (5) and (10)). The court must consider the local authority's arrangements for contact when a care order (or interim care order) is made (subs. (11). Details of the proposed arrangements for contact should be included on the application. There is no provision to stay orders pending appeal but the power to imposed conditions (subs. 7) may be used to have this effect. When exercising its powers under the section, the court must apply the welfare principle in section 1, including the checklist in section 1(3) (s.1(4)). Thus the approach to applications may not be very different from that under the previous law, where access was only ordered following a termination by the local authority where there was a substantial chance of rehabilitation (see Millham *et al.*, *Access disputes in Child Care*, Gower (1989) and *Re KD* [1987] 2 F.L.R. 365). However, it would seem that there is an intention to facilitate contact by imposing duties on local authorities to place children near their homes (s.23(7)).

Department of Health *Guidance* states,

"For the majority of children there will be no doubt that their interests will be best served by efforts to sustain or create links with their natural families. Contact in the sense of personal meetings and visits will generally be the most common, and for both families and children, the most satisfactory way of maintaining their relationship ... Contacts, however occasional, may continue to have value for the child even when there is no question of returning to the family ... The first weeks, during which the child is looked after by the local authority are likely to be particularly crucial to the success of the relationship between the parent, the social worker and the child's carers and to the level of future contact between parent and child ... " (paras. 6.9–10).

Limitations on repeated applications are provided in section 91(17) but are less restrictive than under the previous law, which allowed only one bite at the cherry (see T. v. *West Glamorgan County Council*, *The Times*, October 12, 1989). Applications may also be restricted by the leave requirement in section 91(14).

Subs. (1)

This lists the people (other than the local authority or the child) who may apply for contact to a child in care without the leave of the court.

In care: If the child is only accommodated, a dispute can be dealt with by a section 8 contact order. Where the child is subject to a child assessment order (s.43), an emergency protection order (s.44) or in police protection (s.46) those sections contain provisions about contact. The duty in Schedule 2, paragraph 15 applies to all children looked after by the authority. There is also a power in paragraph 16 to contribute towards travel costs, etc.

Subject to the provisions of this section: Contact may be refused under a court order or under subsection (6). A condition could be imposed (under subs. (7)) in an order refusing contact to require the local authority to re-instate it if refusal was no longer necessary for the child's welfare. A provision specifically to this effect was originally included in the Bill but was removed because of drafting difficulties. An agreement may be made between the local authority and anyone with a contact order (S.I. 1991 No. 891, reg. 3) to depart from the terms of the order providing that the child (if he has sufficient understanding) agrees and those listed in regulation 2 who need to know are notified (reg. 4).

Reasonable contact: This phraseology has applied to contact between divorced or separated parents and their children for many years. In those cases the parties are left to work out what is reasonable but can return to the court to have contact defined if they cannot agree. The local authority's view of what is reasonable must safeguard and promote the child's welfare because of the duty in section 22(3). It should reflect not only the child's needs determined by reference to his or her current development but also the importance of maintaining contact in the long term. Unless the contact is satisfying for the adult and the child, arrangements are unlikely to be kept. This will affect the child's chances of returning to his family and the support available to him when he leaves care (see Millham et al. *Lost in Care*, Gower (1986)). If the local authority thinks it is necessary to refuse contact, it may do so but only for seven days in accordance with subsection (6) and the regulations. A court order refusing contact must then be obtained. If the order is refused, contact must be permitted pending an appeal, as section 40 does not apply.

Parents: This includes the unmarried father who has not acquired parental responsibility and thus sidesteps the complications caused by *Re M. and H. (Minors)* [1988] 3 W.L.R. 485 and the error in the drafting of the F.L.R.A 1987. This error is remedied by Schedule 12, paragraph 35 which came into effect on Royal Assent.

Contact: This is not defined for the purposes of this section, but would seem to include all methods of sustaining links between people. It would thus include access visits as well as telephone calls and letters. Any order made would thus be directly comparable with a contact order in section 8. Stays of more than 24 hours must comply with the Placement of Children with Parents, etc., Regulations 1991 (S.I. 1991 No. 893) see notes on section 23 for details. Repeated visits during a year may count as a single placement under regulation 13.

Where there was a residence order: These orders are discharged automatically by the making of a care order (s.91(2)).

Subs. (2)

The child: There is no statutory test of maturity as under section 10(8), but it is difficult to see how a child who does not understand something of the issues can be said to have made an application. A child does not need to have full grasp of the matter because he will probably be represented by a guardian ad litem and a solicitor. The parents could only make an application on the child's behalf if the authority permitted them to under section 33(3)(b).

The court: Most cases will be heard in the family proceedings court see notes on section 92 and the allocation order, p. 432 below.

May make: Section 1(5) applies. The policy that orders should not be made unless they are necessary applies here also (see s.10(1)). Orders will help clarify the situation for the child, the family and the local authority.

Such order as it considers appropriate: An order for reasonable contact will only be appropriate if it appears that the agreement can be reached by the parties. If contact is defined in terms of time, place, duration and frequency a condition can be included under subsection (7) to allow variation in some or all of these matters by agreement. Refusals of contact can only be made in accordance with subsection (4).

That person: A cannot seek orders which will affect B's contact, only A's.

Subs. (3)

There are no conditions for these applications for leave. Applications for leave are governed by rule 3, see p. 359 below. Where the child wishes to maintain the relationship the need for leave may be avoided by the child applying for the order. There may also be advantages in this course of action under the legal aid scheme and because of the attitude of the courts.

To be allowed: Parents and others who want to restrict contact between the child and other people (friends, relatives, etc.), will have to request the authority (or child) to seek such an order. If the authority does not agree the complaints process under section 26(3) will be available because contact is an aspect of looking after children, a local authority service under Part III.

Subs. (4)

If the local authority wishes to refuse contact between the child and a person listed in subsection (1) and that person wants contact, it will need to obtain an order. No such order is required to end contact by others, *e.g.* grandparents, because the authority has no duty to allow reasonable contact with them. However, such a person refused contact can seek leave to obtain an order. A child may refuse to see a person and need not obtain an order unless there is no other way to resist contact.

Subs. (5)

The court may make these orders for contact of its own motion in care proceedings or in any family proceedings relating to the child. No order may be made until there is a care order or an interim care order (subs. (10)).

Subs. (6)

A comparable provision existed under the C.C.A. 1980, s.12E, but the test here seems easier to satisfy, which reflects the fact that it applies to excuse the local authority from complying with an order or its duty under subsection (1). It is no longer necessary to show that a child's welfare is seriously at risk, only that the refusal of contact is necessary "to safeguard or promote the child's welfare." It must be decided upon as a matter of urgency. Regulation 2 of the Contact Regulations (S.I. 1991 No. 891) requires the local authority restricting contact under this provision to notify in writing the child (if of sufficient understanding), the parents and guardians, anyone who held a residence order or care and control in wardship prior to the care order and any other relevant people. An agreement under regulation 3 may be negotiated instead of a restriction under this provision.

Matter of urgency: Where contact has been continuing, it would seem that this test should only be satisfied if an incident has occurred or information has been obtained suggesting that the child is substantially at risk. The decision to place a child for adoption would not justify an emergency refusal, nor would any other change of placement. Although the child's need to settle down has often been given as a reason for refusing contact, there is no evidence that contact with the family damages the child's ability to settle; in fact the most recent evidence is to the contrary (Berridge & Cleaver, *Foster Home Breakdown*, Blackwell (1987)). Where there has been no recent contact with the person it may be easier to justify refusal, at least if there are good reasons for believing that the court would not grant an order. Local authorities will need to take care, however, if lack of past contact is due to a breach of duties they owe under Schedule 2, paragraph 15.

Subs. (8)

The Contact with Children Regulations 1991 (S.I. 1991 No. 891) p. 460 below, require the local authority to notify certain people when it exercises its powers under section 34(6) and empower it to make agreements which vary (or suspend) contact orders. Notifications must be made in writing and state the local authority's decision when it was made, for what reasons, the duration of the variation and the remedies available to dissatisfied persons.

Subs. (10)

Orders may be made at any time after the care order has been made and can thus be made when the child is freed for adoption (Adoption Act 1976, s.18), avoiding the difficulties caused because freeing orders, unlike adoption orders, could not be made subject to conditions.

Subs. (11)

The duty to consider and invite comment does not apply to family proceedings relating to a child in care, *e.g.* where the court considers contact during an (unsuccessful) application for a residence order in respect of a child in care.

Parties: Party status will be determined by rules made under section 93, see p. 367 below. It is quite possible that someone other than a party to the care proceedings will be granted contact. Only if that person has actually applied for an order will they be a party; a person with a contact order would be a party in any subsequent proceedings oabout contact. Views of all interested persons should be canvassed by the guardian ad litem.

Supervision orders

Supervision orders

35.—(1) While a supervision order is in force it shall be the duty of the supervisor—
  (a) to advise, assist and befriend the supervised child;
  (b) to take such steps as are reasonably necessary to give effect to the order; and
  (c) where—
    (i) the order is not wholly complied with; or
    (ii) the supervisor considers that the order may no longer be necessary,
to consider whether or not to apply to the court for its variation or discharge.

(2) Parts I and II of Schedule 3 make further provision with respect to supervision orders.

DEFINITIONS
"supervised child," "supervisor": s.105(1).
"supervision order": s.31(11).
"the court": s.92(7).

GENERAL NOTE
This section sets out the primary duty of the supervisor where the court makes a supervision order (subs. (1)). Details of the terms of supervision orders are found in Schedule 3, Parts I and II. The Act incorporates provisions relating to supervision previously found in the Magistrates' Courts (Children and Young Persons) Rules 1970; it replaces some, but not all, of the provisions in the C.Y.P.A. 1969 dealing with supervision and further amends and clarifies the law. It is particularly important to note that supervision orders will only last for one year from the date on which they were made, unless they are extended (Sched. 3, para. 6). The supervisor may apply to extend it (para. 6(2)) and may seek its variation or discharge (subs. (1)(c) and s.39(2)). The maximum duration for a supervision order is three years. A supervision order cannot continue after the child has reached age 18 (s.91(13)) and is brought to an end if the child's return is ordered or a decision registered under the Child Abduction and Custody Act 1985, ss.16, 25(1)(a)(b) as amended by Schedule 13, paragraph 57.

The Short Committee were concerned that very few supervision orders were made in care cases and suggested that this reflected their perceived ineffectiveness (para. 150). The R.C.C.L. proposed that requirements should be imposed on the parent or any person with whom the child is living. This has been done in Schedule 3, paragraphs 1, 3 and 8. Such people are termed responsible persons and are defined in Schedule 3, paragraph 1. They must provide information to the supervisor and comply with requirements imposed under paragraph 3. Requirements cover taking reasonable steps to ensure that the child complies with the directions of the supervisor or attends for medical examination or treatment. They may also require the responsible person to meet the supervisor and keep him informed of his address.

Requirements may be imposed on the supervised child (para. 2). They can cover where the child lives, meetings with specified people and participation in specified activities. These do not require the child's consent. There is no prescribed remedy for a breach of directions; the supervisor must consider whether to seek variation or discharge under section 35(1)(c). *Guidance*, Vol. 1, para. 3.95 states, "The local authority should at all times respond to non-co-operation in a positive and constructive way designed to regain that co-operation." Under C.Y.P.A. 1969, s.14A, refusal to allow visits or medical examinations were grounds for an order under C.Y.P.A. 1933, s.40 (a place of safety order). There is no similar provision here and the supervisor would have to satisfy the grounds for an emergency protection order in section 44 or a warrant under section 102. Paragraph 4 provides detailed provisions relating to medical and psychiatric examination; paragraph 5 provides for treatment. The court may include a direction requiring the child to submit to a specific examination, such examinations as the supervisor directs or treatment. Children who have sufficient understanding cannot be made subject to such conditions without their consent (paras. 4(4) and 5(5)). This gives effect to the *Gillick* decision which gives mature minors decision-making authority over medical matters (see notes to s.43).

Paragraph 9 replaces C.Y.P.A. 1969, s.13, without any substantial amendment. Children will continue to be supervised by local authority social workers unless paragraph 9(2) applies. Paragraph 11 provides for regulations (none have been made). A supervision order ends existing care or supervision orders (para. 10).

There is provision for interim supervision orders, for discharge and for appeals in sections 38 to 40 and section 94.

Education supervision orders

36.—(1) On the application of any local education authority, the court may make an order putting the child with respect to whom the application is made under the supervision of a designated local education authority.

(2) In this Act "an education supervision order" means an order under subsection (1).

(3) A court may only make an education supervision order if it is satisfied that the child concerned is of compulsory school age and is not being properly educated.

(4) For the purposes of this section, a child is being properly educated only if he is receiving efficient full-time education suitable to his age, ability and aptitude and any special educational needs he may have.

(5) Where a child is—
  (a) the subject of a school attendance order which is in force under section 37 of the Education Act 1944 and which has not been complied with; or
  (b) a registered pupil at a school which he is not attending regularly within the meaning of section 39 of that Act,

then, unless it is proved that he is being properly educated, it shall be assumed that he is not.

(6) An education supervision order may not be made with respect to a child who is in the care of a local authority.

(7) The local education authority designated in an education supervision order must be—
  (a) the authority within whose area the child concerned is living or will live; or
  (b) where—
    (i) the child is a registered pupil at a school; and
    (ii) the authority mentioned in paragraph (a) and the authority within whose area the school is situated agree, the latter authority.

(8) Where a local education authority propose to make an application for an education supervision order they shall, before making the application, consult the social services committee (within the meaning of the Local Authority Social Services Act 1970) of the appropriate local authority.

(9) The appropriate local authority is—
  (a) in the case of a child who is being provided with accommodation by, or on behalf of, a local authority, that authority; and
  (b) in any other case, the local authority within whose area the child concerned lives, or will live.

(10) Part III of Schedule 3 makes further provision with respect to education supervision orders.

DEFINITIONS

"appropriate local authority": s.36(9).
"child": ss.36(3), 105(1).
"designated local education authority": s.36(7).
"education supervision order": s.36(2), Sched. 3, Pt. III.
"local authority": s.105(1).
"local education authority": s.105(1).
"properly educated": s.36(4)(5).
"registered pupil": s.105(1).
"social services committee": s.36(8).
"the court": s.92(7).

GENERAL NOTE

This provides for a new type of order, the "education supervision order" which will be the usual order for dealing with non-attendance at school. Education supervision orders can only be made on application by a local education authority (subs. (1)) in respect of children of compulsory school age (subs. (3)) who are not receiving suitable, efficient full-time education (subs. (4)). A child is deemed to satisfy the conditions for making an education supervision order if either of the conditions in subsection (5) exists. The education supervision order will place the child under the supervision of the designated authority, which will be the authority where the child lives, unless he goes to school elsewhere and the two authorities agree (subs. (7)). The education authority must consult the social services committee of the appropriate authority, *i.e.* the authority accommodating the child or the one for the area where the child lives (subs. (9)), before making the application (subs. (8)). Education supervision orders are not available for children in local authority care (subs. (6)). These are 'family proceedings" the court must apply the tests in section 1 and may seek reports under section 7 or make any section 8 order. They are not "specified proceedings" so there will be no guardian ad litem.

The details of education supervision orders are contained in Schedule 3, Part III (see subs. (10)). Guidance on use of education supervision orders is contained in *Guidance*, Vol. 6, Chap 3.

It seems likely that this order will replace the "Leeds System" for dealing with truants. Under the "Leeds system" care proceedings were started but repeatedly adjourned. During the periods of adjournment attendance was monitored. Orders were not made provided that attendance did not fall below a specified level. The removal of non-attendance as a free standing ground for a care order (but see Re O [1992] 2 F.L.R. 7 and s.32 (above), the timetabling provisions in section 32 and the general doubts about the legality of such repeated adjournments may end that way of dealing with truants. Whether education supervision orders will be successful remains to be seen.

Subss. (3) and (4)

Compulsory school age: This is defined in the Education Act 1944, s.35. A child must attend school from the beginning of the term immediately following his fifth birthday until the age of 16. The upper age limit is affected by the Education Act 1962, s.9, which sets leaving dates and deems a pupil not having attained the age of 16 until the leaving date. The Education Act 1944, s.95 permits the court to presume that a pupil is under or over a specific age where the person bringing the proceedings under the Education Act has been unable, despite reasonable diligence, to find out a child's age.

However, that provision does not apply here, so it will be necessary to show, on the balance of probabilities, that the child is of school age.

Properly educated: This is further explained in subsection (4). The Education Act 1944, s.36 imposes a duty on the parent of every child "to cause him to receive efficient full-time education suitable to his age, ability and aptitude and to any special education needs he may have." A parent who fails in this duty can be served with a school attendance order or prosecuted under Education Act 1944, s.39. Failure to comply with a school attendance order is an offence (s.37(5)), but the parents may no longer be imprisoned (Education Act 1944, s.40 as amended by Sched. 15). It is not necessary for a school attendance order to be in force before the education supervision order procedure is used. However, the court with the criminal case may direct the local authority to institute proceedings for an education supervision order. The direction must be in writing (r. 31; r. 4.27, see p. 416 below). The authority need not comply but must give reasons for the decision to the court within eight weeks (Education Act 1944, s.40(3)(4)). The court may also end the school attendance order when it makes an education supervision order (Education Act 1944, s.40(4), as amended by Sched. 13, para. 8). When there is a dispute about the quality of the education, because the child is being educated otherwise than at school, subsection (5) requires proof of proper education.

Subs. (5)

A school attendance order which has not been complied with: Compliance with a school attendance order requires the parent to cause the child to become a registered pupil at a school named in the order (Education Act 1944, s.37(2)) and to attend that school.

Registered pupil: This is defined in the Education Act 1944, s.114(1). The child's name must appear on the school register.

Attending regularly: The Education Act 1944, s.39 imposes a duty on the parents to secure their child's regular attendance at school, but permits absence with leave for any of the reasons set out in section 39(2): illness, any unavoidable cause, religious observance on days exclusively set aside for such observance by the parent's religious body, lack of suitable arrangements for transport in certain cases where the school is not within walking distance. All these excuses have been the subject of litigation (see *The Law of Education*, Butterworths, 9th Edition).

Subs. (6)

Local authorities are expected to have sufficient skills and resources to ensure that children in care are properly educated. An education supervision order should be otiose.

Subs. (7)

The local education authority must consult the social services committee but does not require its consent to an application for an education supervision order. However, this duty provides a basis to require co-operation and should help to ensure that the local education authority is more fully aware of the child's circumstances. If education problems are evident when the local authority investigates a case it must consult the local education authority under section 47(5).

Subs. (10)

The details of education supervision orders are found in Schedule 3, Part III. The supervisor who may be an educational welfare officer or education social worker (see Department of Education and Science Circular 11/91; Welsh Office Circular 45/91) has a duty to advise, assist and befriend the supervised child and his parents (as defined in the Education Act 1944, s.114(1D) amended by Sched. 13, para. 10). This definition includes everyone with parental responsibility and anyone caring for the child. He may also give them directions which should be confirmed in writing (*Guidance*, Vol. 6 para. 3.34). Failure to comply with a direction is an offence (level 3) (para. 18). Where failure is persistent, the appropriate local authority must be notified and must investigate (para. 19). Before giving directions the supervisor should consult the parents and child particularly to find out their wishes as to the place of the child's education and give due consideration to their wishes (para. 12). Where an education supervision order is in force, the parents' duties under sections the Education Act 1944, ss.29, 36 are replaced by their duty to comply with any directions under the order. The parent and child can be required to keep the supervisor notified of the child's address and allow visits (para. 16). Also, any school attendance order under section 37 ceases to have effect and the 1944 Act, ss.37, 76 and the Education Act 1980, ss.6, 7 cease to apply to the child (para. 13). An education supervision order can exist alongside a supervision order in criminal proceedings but there can be no educational requirement under the C.Y.P.A. 1969, s.12(c) in the criminal supervision order. Failure to comply with a direction under the education supervision order is excluded if compliance would breach the criminal supervision order (paras. 13 and 14). Education supervision orders last for one year and can be extended but not on any occasion for more than three years (para 15). There is no restriction on the number of education supervision orders for any child, but, unless circumstances have changed, the fact that a child is still not being properly educated after the expiry of the education supervision order may suggest that alternative methods of securing attendance are required. Care proceedings may only rarely be available because of the tests in section 31(2). The parents may be prosecuted but the child may not apparently be made a ward of court (*Re Baker* [1962] Ch. 201), at least until the statutory powers have been fully pursued and leave has been obtained (s.100(3)).

Education supervision orders are discharged automatically when the child ceases to be of compulsory school age or by the making of a care order (para. 15(6)). Applications for discharge can be made by the child, a parent, or the local authority (para. 17). Proceedings in the Family Proceedings Court are governed by rule 4 (see p. 361 below). The Secretary of State also has a power to make regulations relating to education supervision orders (para. 20) but none have been made.

Powers of court

Powers of court in certain family proceedings

37.—(1) Where, in any family proceedings in which a question arises with respect to the welfare of any child, it appears to the court that it may be appropriate for a care or supervision order to be made with respect to him, the court may direct the appropriate authority to undertake an investigation of the child's circumstances.

(2) Where the court gives a direction under this section the local authority concerned shall, when undertaking the investigation, consider whether they should—
  (a) apply for a care order or for a supervision order with respect to the child;
  (b) provide services or assistance for the child or his family; or
  (c) take any other action with respect to the child.

(3) Where a local authority undertake an investigation under this section, and decide not to apply for a care order or supervision order with respect to the child concerned, they shall inform the court of—
  (a) their reasons for so deciding;
  (b) any service or assistance which they have provided, or intend to provide, for the child and his family; and
  (c) any other action which they have taken, or propose to take, with respect to the child.

(4) The information shall be given to the court before the end of the period of eight weeks beginning with the date of the direction, unless the court otherwise directs.

(5) The local authority named in a direction under subsection (1) must be—

(a) the authority in whose area the child is ordinarily resident; or
(b) where the child [is not ordinarily resident] in the area of a local authority, the authority within whose area any circumstances arose in consequence of which the direction is being given.

(6) If, on the conclusion of any investigation or review under this section, the authority decide not to apply for a care order or supervision order with respect to the child—
(a) they shall consider whether it would be appropriate to review the case at a later date; and
(b) if they decide that it would be, they shall determine the date on which that review is to begin.

AMENDMENT

In subsection (5)(b) the word in square brackets were substituted by the Courts and Legal Services Act 1990, s.116, Sched. 16, para. 16.

DEFINITIONS

"appropriate authority": s.37(5).
"care order": s.31(11).
"child": s.105(1).
"family proceedings": s.8(3).
"local authority": s.105(1).
"ordinary residence": s.105(6).
"supervision order": s.31(11).
"the court": s.92(7).

GENERAL NOTE

The court's powers in this section replace the powers to commit children to care in matrimonial, guardianship and domestic proceedings. Such committals, made on the grounds of "exceptional circumstances," did not fit with the Government's wish to create a single standard for care orders based on substantial harm, as recommended by the R.C.C.L., paras. 8.20–22 and 15.35–37, Cm. 62 1987 and Law Com. 172, para. 5.1. Nor did it fit with their proposed division of responsibility between local authorities and courts, which was intended to give local authorities greater control over the use of major resources like care. Now the court may only direct a local authority to undertake an investigation of the child's circumstances; it can do so in a wider range of proceedings, family proceedings, which include applications for injunctions in cases of domestic violence (subs. (1)). It is not limited to "children of the family."

Where the court makes a direction, it may make an interim order if there are reasonable grounds for believing that section 31(2) is satisfied (s.38(1)). The court's power to direct investigation exists alongside the local authority's duty to initiate investigation in cases of suspected harm under section 47 and its duty to take reasonable steps to identify children in need under Schedule 2, paragraph 1. A direction under subsection (1) imposes a duty on the authority to consider whether to apply for a care supervision order, to provide services to the child or his family or take any other action (subs. (2)). There is no statutory duty to obtain access to the child as under section 47(4), but it is difficult to see that a proper investigation could be done without seeing him. If the local authority decides not to take action, it must inform the court, within eight weeks (unless otherwise directed (subs. (4)) of the reasons for so doing and any action they have taken (or proposed to take) with respect to the child (subs. (3)). The local authority must also consider whether to review a decision not to take proceedings at a later date and decide when this should be (subs. (6)). The procedure to be followed when a direction is given is set out in rule 27 (see p. 418 below). If the court, having given a direction makes, or is considering whether to make, an interim care order the proceedings become specified proceedings and a guardian ad litem should be appointed, section 41(6).

Subs. (1)

It appears to the court: This is most likely to occur as a result of a welfare officer's report.

May be appropriate: The standard is low. It is not necessary for the court to think that a care order should be made. It may want to ensure that the authority gives full consideration to the child's needs. However, where the court has identified a problem within the family, which may be remedied by social work support, a family assistance order under section 16 may be more appropriate. Family assistance orders cannot be imposed without the consent of the adults concerned. Where this is not forthcoming, and the court considers further action is desirable, this is the only course open to it.

May direct: In making its decision the court must apply section 1(1).

Appropriate authority: This could be a welfare officer or a panel guardian ad litem. A guardian ad litem may only be appointed if the court has made or is considering making an interim care order (s.41(6)(b)).

Subs. (2)

The local authority must investigate, but need only consider the action outlined here. It does not have to take it, but under subsection (3) it will have to explain why it has not applied for a care or supervision order, and the action it has taken.

Services: These may be provided under sections 17, 18, 20 and 24.

Assistance: This may be in cash or in kind (s.17(6)).

Subs. (3)

The report must be in writing, rule 27(5). There appears to be no duty to report back if the local authority has decided to take care proceedings but has not yet done so. Even if an application has been made, it would not necessarily come to the court's attention if it were made to a different court. A decision to apply for a care order in an unspecified time in the future without further action could be unreasonable.

Any other action: Consultations with other bodies, *e.g.* the local education authority about an application for an education supervision order.

Subs. (4)

The court's power would seem to allow it to demand quicker action. Eight weeks would appear to be a reasonable time to complete such an investigation, but no doubt some hard-pressed authorities will seek longer.

Subs. (5)

Circumstances: This will need to be interpreted widely because the direction may not have been made because of any specific occurrence but just general unease. In such a case the appropriate authority would be the one where the relevant adults are living.

Subs. (6)

Again, the local authority has wide discretion, but, having made a decision, must comply with it. The regulations concerning reviews under section 26(1) do not apply to these reviews because the child is not being looked after by the authority.

Interim orders

38.—(1) Where—
    (a) in any proceedings on an application for a care order or supervision order, the proceedings are adjourned; or
    (b) the court gives a direction under section 37(1),

the court may make an interim care order or an interim supervision order with respect to the child concerned.

(2) A court shall not make an interim care order or interim supervision order under this section unless it is satisfied that there are reasonable grounds for believing that the circumstances with respect to the child are as mentioned in section 31(2).

(3) Where, in any proceedings on an application for a care order or supervision order, a court makes a residence order with respect to the child concerned, it shall also make an interim supervision order with respect to him unless satisfied that his welfare will be satisfactorily safeguarded without an interim order being made.

(4) An interim order made under or by virtue of this section shall have effect for such period as may be specified in the order, but shall in any event cease to have effect on whichever of the following events first occurs—
- (a) the expiry of the period of eight weeks beginning with the date on which the order is made;
- (b) if the order is the second or subsequent such order made with respect to the same child in the same proceedings, the expiry, of the relevant period;
- (c) in a case which falls within subsection (1)(a), the disposal of the application;
- (d) in a case which falls within subsection (1)(b), the disposal of an application for a care order or supervision order made by the authority with respect to the child;
- (e) in a case which falls within subsection (1)(b) and in which—
  - (i) the court has given a direction under section 37(4), but
  - (ii) no application for a care order or supervision order has been made with respect to the child,

the expiry of the period fixed by that direction.

(5) In subsection (4)(b) "the relevant period" means—
- (a) the period of four weeks beginning with the date on which the order in question is made; or
- (b) the period of eight weeks beginning with the date on which the first order was made if that period ends later than the period mentioned in paragraph (a).

(6) Where the court makes an interim care order, or interim supervision order, it may give such directions (if any) as it considers appropriate with regard to the medical or psychiatric examination or other assessment of the child; but if the child is of sufficient understanding to make an informed decision he may refuse to submit to the examination or other assessment.

(7) A direction under subsection (6) may be to the effect that there is to be—
- (a) no such examination or assessment; or
- (b) no such examination or assessment unless the court directs otherwise.

(8) A direction under subsection (6) may be—
- (a) given when the interim order is made or at any time while it is in force; and

(b) varied at any time on the application of any person falling within any class of person prescribed by rules of court for the purposes of this subsection.

(9) Paragraphs 4 and 5 of Schedule 3 shall not apply in relation to an interim supervision order.

(10) Where a court makes an order under or by virtue of this section it shall, in determining the period for which the order is to be in force, consider whether any party who was, or might have been, opposed to the making of the order was in a position to argue his case against the order in full

DEFINITIONS

"care order": s.31(11).
"interim care order": s.38.
"interim supervision order": s.38.
"relevant period": s.38(5).
"residence order": s.8(1).
"supervision order": s.31(11).
"the court": s.92(7).

GENERAL NOTE

The R.C.C.L. identified three problems with interim orders. First, the C.Y.P.A. 1969, s.2(10) did not clearly state a ground for making an interim order and the standards applied by courts differed widely. This was remedied by the decision in *R. v. Croydon Juvenile Court, ex p. N.* [1987] 151 J.P. 523, which held that there must be a prima facie case for a care order and the court must exercise its discretion in a judicial manner, giving paramount consideration to the welfare of the child. Second, even though it was rarely possible to process a case within four weeks, the duration of interim orders meant that repeated hearings occurred. Third, there was no power to make an interim supervision order. This section remedies those problems and also clarifies the law relating to medical examinations while an interim order is in force. It departs from the proposals in the R.C.C.L. and Cm. 62 1987 (para. 61) quite markedly in relation to the duration of orders, and it is not clear how easily these generous provisions sit with section 1(2) which aims to minimise delays. This section does not apply to interim orders in other types of family proceedings. Interim orders may be made by a single magistrate under rule 28 (see p. 418 below).

Interim care orders: These can now be made in two situations:—
    (1) When an application for a care or supervision order is adjourned;
    (2) When the court orders an investigation under section 37(1).

In both these cases the court must be satisfied that there are reasonable grounds for believing that the conditions of substantial harm in section 31(2) are satisfied and that it is better to make an order than not, (s.1(5), subss. (1) and (2)).

Interim supervision orders: These can be made as in (1) and (2) above or (3) where the court makes a residence order in care proceedings, unless the child's welfare will be satisfactorily safeguarded without one (subs. (3)).

The maximum duration for orders made under section 38 is set out in subsections (4) and (5). Orders can be made for eight weeks with extensions of four weeks (or longer if the original order was for less than four weeks). There is no limit to the number of interim orders which can be made, but the court will need to comply with the timetabling provisions in section 32. Regardless of the length of the order it will automatically end when the application for the order is disposed of or the period fixed by the court under section 37(4) expires without an application for a care or supervision order being made. When fixing the duration of an interim order, the court is required to consider whether any person who was or might have been opposed to the order would argue his case fully (subs. (10)).

When the court makes an interim order it may make directions about medical or psychiatric examination or an assessment of the child (subs. (6)). Directions may bar such examination or permit it only subject to specific conditions (subs. (7)). Such a direction may be made or varied at any time while the interim order is in force on the application of anyone permitted to apply by the rules made under section 93 (subs. (8)). Where a direction is given, the child may not be examined without his permission if he has sufficient understanding to make decisions about medical matters, as under the *Gillick* test (see notes to s.43(8)). Unless the court's permission is obtained for an examination evidence gained from it may not be admissible, rule 18 (see p. 399 below).

Interim care orders are care orders for the purposes of the Act (s.31(11)). The local authority thus acquires all the powers of parental responsibility except those matters excluded under section 33. It owes duties to the child, who is by virtue of the order in care and who must therefore be accommodated in accordance with section 23. Such a child could only be returned home during the order if the placement complied with the Placement with Parents etc. Regulations 1991 (S.I. 1991 No. 893) (see s.23 above). Similarly, an interim supervision order is a supervision order and the supervisor has functions under section 35 and Schedule 3, Part III, but may not require the child to submit to medical examination or treatment (subs. (9)).

Subs. (1)

Any proceedings: This includes applications for care orders in "family proceedings."

Subs. (2)

Reasonable grounds for believing: The wording is slightly different from that for an emergency protection order under section 44(1)(a), but there appears to be no substantial difference. In *R. v. Birmingham City Council, ex p. Birmingham Juvenile Court* [1988] 1 W.L.R. 337, the Court of Appeal held that the rules which allow a parent to rebut an allegation made against him apply to proceedings for an interim order. This suggests that there may need to be a fairly full hearing of the issue even when the making of the order is not contested.

Subs. (3)

It may be more appropriate to make a family assistance order under section 16. The test in subsection (2) does not have to be satisfied in such cases.

Subss. (6)–(9)

An AIDS test has been ordered under this provision see [1992] N.L.J. 1138. In such cases it is essential that the child is offered skilled counselling before consenting.

A parent who objects to the child's examination or assessment should seek a direction under subsection (7). However, the court will no doubt be mindful that it may have difficulty reaching its decision, particularly in cases of neglect, physical or sexual abuse if medical evidence is lacking. Appeals may be made against directions [1992] N.L.J. 1138, alternatively a variation could be sought.

Rules of court: The Family Proceedings Courts (Children Act 1989) Rules 1991, r. 2(1) specify that the parties to the proceedings and anyone named in the direction under section 38(6)(b) may seek to have the direction varied.

Subs. (10)

If a party were not in a position to argue fully, a short order with substantial court time for a hearing on the return date is appropriate. It does not appear that any restrictions have been imposed to prevent a full airing of the issues for each successive interim order as under *R. v. Birmingham Juvenile Court, ex p. P and S* [1984] F.L.R. 343.

Discharge and variation etc. of care orders and supervision orders

39.—(1) A care order may be discharged by the court on the application of—

    (a) any person who has parental responsibility for the child;

    (b) the child himself; or

(c) the local authority designated by the order.

(2) A supervision order may be varied or discharged by the court on the application of—

(a) any person who has parental responsibility for the child;
(b) the child himself; or
(c) the supervisor.

(3) On the application of a person who is not entitled to apply for the order to be discharged, but who is a person with whom the child is living, a supervision order may be varied by the court in so far as it imposes a requirement which affects that person.

(4) Where a care order is in force with respect to a child the court may, on the application of any person entitled to apply for the order to be discharged, substitute a supervision order for the care order.

(5) When a court is considering whether to substitute one order for another under subsection (4) any provision of this Act which would otherwise require section 31(2) to be satisfied at the time when the proposed order is substituted or made shall be disregarded.

DEFINITIONS

"care order": s.31(11).
"person who has parental responsibility": ss.2(1)(2), 4(1), 5(6), 12(1).
"person entitled to apply for a care order to be discharged": s.39(1).
"person entitled to apply for a supervision order to be discharged": s.39(2).
"supervision order": s.31(11).
"supervisor": s.105(1).
"the court": s.92(7).

GENERAL NOTE

This provision clarifies the law relating to discharge of care or supervision orders and largely implements the recommendations of the R.C.C.L., Ch. 20, about the powers of the court and the grounds for discharge. A care order can also be discharged by the making of a residence order (see s.91(1)). For a full discussion of residence orders, see sections 8 and 10.

Those who may apply for the discharge of a care order are listed in subsection (1); for the variation or discharge of a supervision order in subsections (2) and (3). A person with whom the child is living, *i.e.* "a responsible person" who can be required to comply with the directions of the supervisor under Schedule 3, Parts I and II may seek variation of the order in so far as it affects himself. The test to be applied in discharge proceedings is the welfare test in section 1; the checklist in section 1(3) applies. Thus it is clear that the court must consider not parental fitness but the child's welfare. Despite the virtual abolition of wardship for local authorities, and the defects recognised in the old law, there is no specific power in the court to order a phased return of the child, but this may be achieved by a residence order (see s.8), or possibly using section 40.

There is no longer any power to vary a care order. However, when an application to discharge a care order is made, the court may substitute a supervision order (subs. (4)); the grounds in section 31(2) do not have to be re-proved (subs. (6)), but the tests in section 1 will have to be applied. In contrast, it will now be necessary for the grounds in section 31(2) to be re-proved before a care order can be made.

Section 91(15) restricts a repeated application for the discharge of an order within six months without the leave of the court.

Subs. (1)

An unmarried father without parental responsibility, a person in whose favour a residence order was in force prior to the care order or anyone else without parental responsibility who wishes to end the local authority's care of the child cannot apply for the discharge of the care order under this section but must apply for a residence order under section 10 instead. The local authority considering whether to apply for discharge must comply with its other duties, particularly those in section 22.

The child: There is no statutory restriction on applications by immature minors but the child will be represented by a guardian ad litem under section 41, who may seek to withdraw the application under rule 5 (see p. 364 below).

Subs. (3)

A person with whom the child is living: This means "a responsible person" under Schedule 3, paragraph 1. For the obligations of a responsible person see Schedule 3, paragraphs 3 and 8 and notes to section 35.

Subs. (4)

A supervision order cannot apparently be substituted under this section where someone else seeks to have the care order discharged by applying for a residence order. Nor can an interim supervision order be made under section 38(3). A family assistance order under section 16 could be made.

Orders pending appeals in cases about care or supervision orders

40.—(1) Where—
 (a) a court dismisses an application for a care order; and
 (b) at the time when the court dismisses the application, the child concerned is the subject of an interim care order,
the court may make a care order with respect to the child to have effect subject to such directions (if any) as the court may see fit to include in the order.

(2) Where—
 (a) a court dismisses an application for a care order, or an application for a supervision order; and
 (b) at the time when the court dismisses the application, the child concerned is the subject of an interim supervision order,
the court may make a supervision order with respect to the child to have effect subject to such directions (if any) as the court may see fit to include in the order.

(3) Where a court grants an application to discharge a care order or supervision order, it may order that—
 (a) its decision is not to have effect; or
 (b) the care order, or supervision order, is to continue to have effect but subject to such directions as the court sees fit to include in the order.

(4) An order made under this section shall only have effect for such period, not exceeding the appeal period, as may be specified in the order.

(5) Where—
 (a) an appeal is made against any decision of a court under this section; or
 (b) any application is made to the appellate court in connection with a proposed appeal against that decision,
the appellate court may extend the period for which the order in question is to have effect, but not so as to extend it beyond the end of the appeal period.

(6) In this section "the appeal period" means—
  (a) where an appeal is made against the decision in question, the period between the making of that decision and the determination of the appeal; and
  (b) otherwise, the period during which an appeal may be made against the decision.

DEFINITIONS
"appeal period": s.40(6).
"appellate court": s.94(1).
"care order": s.31(11).
"child": s.105(1).
"interim care order" s.38(1).
"interim supervision order": s.38(1).
"the court": s.92(7).

GENERAL NOTE
This section enables the court to order that a child who is subject to an interim care order remains in care until the determination of any appeal against refusal to make a care order (subs. (1)). Similar powers apply in relation to supervision orders (subs. (2)) and orders for discharge (subs. (3)). The court may include directions as it sees fit, *e.g.* in relation to contact with the parents, or even where the child should reside (subss. (1) to (3)) and may specify a shorter period (subs. (4)). It would appear that this provision could be used to achieve the phased return of the child on the discharge of a care order. The court could, under subsection (3), continue the care order but direct increasing contact with a view to home placement and grant leave to the parents to reapply for discharge after three months.

This section enables the child to be protected while the local authority decides whether to appeal and, if it does, until the appeal is determined. However, its operation is not automatic; the court has the discretion, which it must exercise, giving first consideration to the child's welfare. Where the court refuses to continue a care order, it will not be possible to ward the child. The appellate court will be able to extend an order but not, apparently, revive one which has lapsed pending the appeal. The local authority would have to start fresh proceedings.

A similar power to stay a decision approving the arrangements for a child in care to live abroad is included in Schedule 2, paragraph 19. There is no comparable power to stay the decision to grant a care order, *Re O* [1992] 2 F.L.R. 7. A residence order might be stayed by virtue of section 11(7)(d) and a section 34 contact order under s.34(7).

Subs. (6)
The time limit for appeals against refusal to grant care orders, etc., are set out in the Family Proceedings Rules 1991, r.4.22 (S.I. 1991 No. 1247). Appeals against refusal of a care or supervision order go to the High Court. Notice of appeal must be given within 14 days (seven days in the case of an appeal against an interim order). Where leave to appeal is given the court granting leave may specify the time limits (see p. 404 below).

Guardians ad litem

Representation of child and his interests in certain proceedings

41.—(1) For the purpose of any specified proceedings, the court shall appoint a guardian ad litem for the child concerned unless satisfied that it is not necessary to do so in order to safeguard his interests.

(2) The guardian ad litem shall—

(a) be appointed in accordance with rules of court; and
(b) be under a duty to safeguard the interests of the child in the manner prescribed by such rules.

(3) Where—
(a) the child concerned is not represented by a solicitor; and
(b) any of the conditions mentioned in subsection (4) is satisfied, the court may appoint a solicitor to represent him.

(4) The conditions are that—
(a) no guardian ad litem has been appointed for the child;
(b) the child has sufficient understanding to instruct a solicitor and wishes to do so;
(c) it appears to the court that it would be in the child's best interests for him to be represented by a solicitor.

(5) Any solicitor appointed under or by virtue of this section shall be appointed, and shall represent the child, in accordance with rules of court.

(6) In this section "specified proceedings" means any proceedings—
(a) on an application for a care order or supervision order;
(b) in which the court has given a direction under section 37(1) and has made, or is considering whether to make, an interim care order;
(c) on an application for the discharge of a care order or the variation or discharge of a supervision order;
(d) on an application under section 39(4);
(e) in which the court is considering whether to make a residence order with respect to a child who is the subject of a care order;
(f) with respect to contact between a child who is the subject of a care order and any other person;
(g) under Part V;
(h) on an appeal against—
  (i) the making of, or refusal to make, a care order, supervision order or any order under section 34;
  (ii) the making of, or refusal to make, a residence order with respect to a child who is the subject of a care order; or
  (iii) the variation or discharge, or refusal of an application to vary or discharge, an order of a kind mentioned in subparagraph (i) or (ii);
  (iv) the refusal of an application under section 39(4); or
  (v) the making of, or refusal to make, an order under Part V; or
  (vi) which are specified for the time being, for the purposes of this section, by rules of court.

(7) The Secretary of State may by regulations provide for the establishment of panels of persons from whom guardians ad litem appointed under this section must be selected.

(8) Subsection (7) shall not be taken to prejudice the power of the Lord Chancellor to confer or impose duties on the Official Solicitor under section 90(3) of the Supreme Court Act 1981.

(9) The regulations may, in particular, make provision—
   (a) as to the constitution, administration and procedures of panels;
   (b) requiring two or more specified local authorities to make arrangements for the joint management of a panel;
   (c) for the defrayment by local authorities of expenses incurred by members of panels;
   (d) for the payment by local authorities of fees and allowances for members of panels;
   (e) as to the qualifications for membership of a panel;
   (f) as to the training to be given to members of panels;
   (g) as to the co-operation required of specified local authorities in the provision of panels in specified areas; and
   (h) for monitoring the work of guardians ad litem.
(10) Rules of court may make provision as to—
   (a) the assistance which any guardian ad litem may be required by the court to give to it;
   (b) the consideration to be given by any guardian ad litem, where an order of a specified kind has been made in the proceedings in question, as to whether to apply for the variation or discharge of the order;
   (c) the participation of guardians ad litem in reviews, of a kind specified in the rules, which are conducted by the court.
(11) Regardless of any enactment or rule of law which would otherwise prevent it from doing so, the court may take account of—
   (a) any statement contained in a report made by a guardian ad litem who is appointed under this section for the purpose of the proceedings in question; and
   (b) any evidence given in respect of the matters referred to in the report,
in so far as the statement or evidence is, in the opinion of the court, relevant to the question which the court is considering.
[(12) The Secretary of State may, with the consent of the Treasury, make such grants with respect to expenditure of any local authority—
   (a) in connection with the establishment and administration of guardian ad litem panels in accordance with this section;
   (b) in paying expenses, fees, allowances and in provision of training for members of such panels,
as he considers appropriate.]

AMENDMENT

Subsection (12) was added by the Courts and Legal Services Act 1990, s.116, Sched. 16, para. 17.

DEFINITIONS

"care order": s.31(11).
"guardian ad litem":, "guardian ad litem panel": s.41(2), (7).
"residence order": s.8(1).
"specified proceedings": s.41(6).
"supervision order": s.31(11).
"the court": s.92(7).

REGULATIONS

The Guardians ad litem and Reporting Officers (Panels) Regulations 1991 (S.I. 1991 No. 2051).

GENERAL NOTE

This section provides the new statutory basis for the guardian ad litem service originally introduced by the Children Act 1975 and found in C.Y.P.A. 1969, ss.32A and 32B. It should be read with rules 10 and 11 of the Court Rules (see pp. 375–380 below) and section 42, which sets out the powers of the guardian ad litem to examine certain case records. Further guidance on the role of the guardian ad litem is published by the Department of Health, *Manual of Practice Guidance for Guardians ad litem and Reporting Officers* (1992).

There is no longer any need for the court to order separate representation before it appoints a guardian ad litem. The wording of subsection (1) is more positive than that in the C.Y.P.A. 1969, s.32A(1). The Lord Chancellor indicated that he expected that a guardian would be appointed in almost every case: "We accept that the courts are unlikely to find many cases in which it would be inappropriate to appoint a guardian ad litem" (*Hansard*, H.L. Vol. 503, col. 408). There will clearly be a demand for many more guardians ad litem in some areas. The range of proceedings in which a guardian can be appointed has been widened (subs. 6). This brings a marked increase in involvement of guardians (and requires the setting up of a system of duty guardians). It has not been accepted that guardians should be appointed in other types of "family proceedings." Where no guardian is appointed the court may still obtain a welfare report under section 7.

Guardians will continue to operate with solicitors. Rules of court provide for the guardian to appoint a solicitor (r. 11(2)). If no solicitor has been appointed, the court will be able to do so if any of the conditions in subsection (4) are satisfied (subs. (3), r. 12). Thus if the guardian is appointed sufficiently early he will be able to choose the solicitor for the child but the court will have a power to ensure representation. Where a solicitor is appointed he will have to comply with the court rules when representing the child (subs. (5)).

Guardians ad litem will continue to be appointed to panels managed by local authorities (subs. (7) and S.I. 1991 No. 2051). The Department of Health has issued guidance on panel management, (*Guidance*, Vol. 7 and the *Manual of Practice Management for GALRO Panel Managers* (1992)). The Government did not pursue its heavily criticised scheme for an Office of Child Protection outlined in the Green Paper, *Improvements in Care Proceedings*. However, despite the criticism that the existing system lacks independence it has been made possible by the Court Rules (r. 10(7)(a)) for guardians to be employed by the authority which is making, etc. the application. *Guidance*, vol. 7, para. 2.4 and *Gal Manual*, Ch.11 stress the need for professional independence. Subsection (12) makes provision for specific grants to local authorities for the guardian ad litem service; these could provide a basis for a centrally run service but there appears to be no present intention to establish one. The Official Solicitor retains his role (subs. (8)) but the decrease in wardships, and the fact that guardians will be able to be appointed for proceedings in the county court and the High Court, is likely to have an impact. If a case is started in the magistrates' court and transferred to a higher court the original guardian will continue *cf. Re B (A Minor) (Wardship: Guardian ad litem)* [1989] 1 F.L.R. 268).

Subsection (11) clarifies the position of evidence and reports by the guardian ad litem. It disapplies the hearsay rule and allows the court to take account of any relevant statement. See also section 96, which makes further provision for children's evidence.

Subs. (1)

Specified proceedings: in addition to the proceedings noted in subsection (6) a guardian ad litem may be appointed in
— proceedings under section 25 (secure accommodation) in the family proceedings court
— applications under section 33(7) (to change a child in care's name or remove him from the UK)
— proceedings under Schedule 2, paragraph 19(1) (to allow the placement of a child in care outside England and Wales)

— proceedings under Schedule 3, paragraph 6(3) (to extend a supervision order)
— appeals relating to these proceedings

(S.I. 1991 No. 1395, r. 2(2) and S.I. 1991 No. 2113, art. 8). Rule 14(2)(d) which allows the court to appoint a guardian ad litem otherwise than under section 41(6) does not require the use of a panel guardian. The local authority is under no duty to provide one.

Subs. (2)

See S.I. 1991 No. 1395, rr. 10 and 11.

Subss. (3)–(5)

See S.I. 1991 No. 1395, r. 12. Children with sufficient understanding may instruct their solicitor see *Re H, The Times,* June 5, 1992.

Subs. (7)

The Guardians ad litem and Reporting Officers (Panels) Regulations 1991 (S.I. 1991 No. 2051) require each authority to establish a panel (reg. 1), to appoint a person to administer the panel (reg. 7), to establish a panel committee to liaise with the local authority (reg. 8) and advise on standards and to set up a complaints board to hear complaints about the operation of the panel (reg. 3 and 6). The local authority must pay the guardians ad litem's reasonable expenses incurred in their work on "specified proceedings" within section 41(6) (but not other proceedings under the Children Act 1989) (reg. 9). This power, like its predecessor, does not give the local authority the power to impose arbitrary limits on the amount of work done in individual cases *R v. Cornwall C.C., ex parte G* [1992] 1 F.L.R. 270 although it is clear that the panel managers will have to work within cash limits. The local authority is responsible for identifying and satisfying training needs and monitoring the work of each guardian ad litem (reg. 10).

Subs. (8)

The Lord Chancellor has issued a Direction relating to the duties and functions of the Official Solicitor under the Children Act 1989, see [1991] Fam. Law 492. The Official Solicitor may act as guardian ad litem for the child in "specified proceedings" in the High Court if no one else has been appointed and there are exceptional circumstances which indicate the appointment of the Official Solicitor may be more appropriate. These are (i) a foreign element which is likely to require enquiries outside the jurisdiction; (ii) the likely burden on the guardian ad litem because there are several children involved; (iii) the existence of other High Court proceedings where the Official Solicitor is representing the child and (iv) any other relevant circumstances. The Official Solicitor will also have a role advising panel guardians. The Official Solicitor has indicated in a letter to panel managers that he will offer assistance about the conduct of High Court Proceedings to panel guardians. The Official Solicitor may also be able to assist guardians who seek to arrange for expert opinions about children's welfare.

Where the Official Solicitor is appointed as guardian ad litem he may also act as the child's solicitor unless the mature child wishes to instruct a separate solicitor, the Family Proceedings Rules 1991, r. 4.11(2A).

For a comparison of the work of the Official Solicitor and Panel guardians, see Masson, 1992 J. Ch. Law 58.

Right of guardian ad litem to have access to local authority records

42.—(1) Where a person has been appointed as a guardian ad litem under this Act he shall have the right at all reasonable times to examine and take copies of—

(a) any records of, or held by, a local authority [or authorised person] which were compiled in connection with the

making, or proposed making, by any person of any application under this Act with respect to the child concerned; or [...]
(b) any [...] records of, or held by, a local authority which were compiled in connection with any functions which stand referred to their social services committee under the Local Authority Social Services Act 1970, so far as those records relate to that child; [or
(c) any records of, or held by, an authorised person which were compiled in connection with the activities of that person, so far as those records relate to that child.]

(2) Where a guardian ad litem takes a copy of any record which he is entitled to examine under this section, that copy or any part of it shall be admissible as evidence of any matter referred to in any—
(a) report which he makes to the court in the proceedings in question; or
(b) evidence which he gives in those proceedings.

(3) Subsection (2) has effect regardless of any enactment or rule of law which would otherwise prevent the record in question being admissible in evidence.

[(4) In this section "authorised person" has the same meaning as in section 31.]

AMENDMENTS

The amendments to this section were made by the Courts and Legal Services Act 1990, ss.116, 125(7), Sched. 16, para. 18, Sched. 20.

DEFINITIONS

"authorised person": s.31(9).
"child": s.105(1).
"functions": s.105(1).
"guardian ad litem": s.41(2), (7).
"local authority": s.105(1).

GENERAL NOTE

This section gives a guardian ad litem a right of access to (and to take copies of) records of the local authority or the N.S.P.C.C. relating to the application before the court, or to social work functions performed in relation to the child (subs. (1)). Any copy will be admissible as evidence of any matter referred to in the guardian's evidence or report (subss. (2) and (3)). It should not be evidence of its veracity, only of the fact that the authority had the information. The Rules require the guardian to bring to the court's attention all records and documents which may assist the court (r. 11(9)(b)). This should end the difficulties experienced by some guardians with their investigations of local authority records. It would also allow a guardian ad litem to submit a document (for example the report of a medical examination) which the local authority could not use because of breach of rule 18 which requires leave for medical examinations which are to be used in evidence. The Solicitor-General gave two reasons for this provision: (1) that the guardian must have all the relevant information and it was not sufficient to rely on the local authority's duty to disclose it; and (2) that local authority records could not be open to all the parties because they may be protected by privilege and wide disclosure could interfere with social work on a case (*Hansard*, H.C. Vol. 158, col. 626).

It should be noted that the section does not apply to records held by other bodies such as the health authority or a registered nursing home even though this body may have brought the proceedings. In such cases the guardian may be limited to the records which the child would have access to. The Arrangements for Placement of Children (General) Regulations 1991 (S.I. 1991 No. 890), reg. 11 and the Children's Homes Regulations 1991 (S.I. 1991 No. 1506), reg. 16 make provision for voluntary organisations and people carrying on registered children's homes to give guardians ad litem access to their records and supply copies as requested.

Part V

Protection of Children

GENERAL NOTE

The Armed Forces Act 1991, Pt. III which deals with the protection of the children of service families, is modelled on this part of the Act. It only applies to a child who

"(a) forms part of the family of a person subject to service law serving in a country or territory outside the United Kingdom or of a civilian in a corresponding position; and (b) resides outside the United Kingdom with that family or another such family" (s.17(1) of the 1991 Act).

Children of a service family living within the United Kingdom are subject to civilian law.

Child assessment orders

43.—(1) On the application of a local authority or authorised person for an order to be made under this section with respect to a child, the court may make the order if, but only if, it is satisfied that—

(a) the applicant has reasonable cause to suspect that the child is suffering, or is likely to suffer, significant harm;

(b) an assessment of the state of the child's health or development, or of the way in which he has been treated, is required to enable the applicant to determine whether or not the child is suffering, or is likely to suffer, significant harm; and

(c) it is unlikely that such an assessment will be made, or be satisfactory, in the absence of an order under this section.

(2) In this Act "a child assessment order" means an order under this section.

(3) A court may treat an application under this section as an application for an emergency protection order.

(4) No court shall make a child assessment order if it is satisfied—

(a) that there are grounds for making an emergency protection order with respect to the child; and

(b) that it ought to make such an order rather than a child assessment order.

(5) A child assessment order shall—

(a) specify the date by which the assessment is to begin; and

(b) have effect for such period, not exceeding seven days beginning with that date, as may be specified in the order.

(6) Where a child assessment order is in force with respect to a child it shall be the duty of any person who is in a position to produce the child—

(a) to produce him to such person as may be named in the order; and

(b) to comply with such directions relating to the assessment of the child as the court thinks fit to specify in the order.

(7) A child assessment order authorises any person carrying out the assessment, or any part of the assessment, to do so in accordance with the terms of the order.

(8) Regardless of subsection (7), if the child is of sufficient understanding to make an informed decision he may refuse to submit to a medical or psychiatric examination or other assessment.

(9) The child may only be kept away from home—
  (a) in accordance with directions specified in the order;
  (b) if it is necessary for the purposes of the assessment; and
  (c) for such period or periods as may be specified in the order.

(10) Where the child is to be kept away from home, the order shall contain such directions as the court thinks fit with regard to the contact that he must be allowed to have with other persons while away from home.

(11) Any person making an application for a child assessment order shall take such steps as are reasonably practicable to ensure that notice of the application is given to—
  (a) the child's parents;
  (b) any person who is not a parent of his but who has parental responsibility for him;
  (c) any other person caring for the child;
  (d) any person in whose favour a contact order is in force with respect to the child;
  (e) any person who is allowed to have contact with the child by virtue of an order under section 34; and
  (f) the child,
before the hearing of the application.

(12) Rules of court may make provision as to the circumstances in which—
  (a) any of the persons mentioned in subsection (11); or
  (b) such other person as may be specified in the rules,
may apply to the court for a child assessment order to be varied or discharged.

(13) In this section "authorised person" means a person who is an authorised person for the purposes of section 31.

DEFINITIONS
  "authorised person": ss.31(9), 43(13).
  "child": s.105(1).
  "child assessment order": s.43(2).
  "contact order": s.8(1).
  "emergency protection order": s.44(4).
  "local authority": s.105(1).
  "person ... who has parental responsibility": ss.2(1), (2), 4(1), 5(6), 12(1)(2).
  "significant harm": s.31(9)(10).
  "the court": s.92(7).

GENERAL NOTE
  This section, which was the subject of considerable controversy during the Bill's passage through Parliament, provides for child assessment orders. This provision was added because of concern that the more rigorous requirements for an emergency

protection order could mean that it was impossible to get an emergency protection order where there was fear for the child's safety but no hard evidence. For example, where a child had suddenly ceased to attend a day nursery or family centre in suspicious circumstances, or where neighbours reported repeated screaming. In such cases the first action of the social worker or health visitor should be to attempt to see the child (under s.47(4) there is a duty to do so). If access is refused or the parent refuses or fails to take the child for a medical or other examination which would indicate the child's condition, an application may be made for a child assessment order. However, refusal may provide grounds for an emergency protection order under section 44(1)(b) or (c). That being the case, it is not clear when a child assessment order will be used. Rather, the child assessment order is something which must be considered by the case conference planning intervention. The provisions will provide the background against which professionals concerned with a child's care negotiate with the parents for access to examine or assess the child. Negotiated arrangements may have the advantage of not being as restrictive as orders, for example lasting more than seven days or running over seven non-consecutive days.

Only the local authority or N.S.P.C.C. (subss. (1) and (13)) may apply for a child assessment order. The court may only grant the order if:

(1) the applicant (not the court as for an emergency protection order) has reasonable cause to believe that the child is suffering (or likely to suffer) significant harm;
(2) an assessment is required to determine whether the child is suffering (or likely to suffer) significant harm;
(3) it is unlikely that there would be an assessment without a court order (subs. (1)); and
(4) the grounds for an emergency protection order are not satisfied or it would not be appropriate to make an emergency protection order (subs. (4)).

The court may make an emergency protection order on an application for a child assessment order (subs. (3)). Applications will be made on notice (subs. (11)) and the child will usually be represented by a guardian ad litem.

A child assessment order requires any person who can do so to produce the child for an assessment and comply with the terms of order (subs. (6)); it authorises the child's assessment in accordance with the order (subs. (7)) but does not permit any examination or assessment of a mature child without his permission (subs. (8)). The child may be kept away from home for assessment (but not for protection) in accordance with the court's directions (subs. (1)). The parents retain parental responsibility and the applicant will only be able to take such steps as are permitted by the court without parental consent. Those seeking a child assessment order will need to explain to the court the types of assessment required and how they should be carried out. The order lasts for only seven days but need not begin immediately (subs. (5)). It could be postponed until, *e.g.* a hospital bed became available. If the child is kept away from home, the court must consider contact (subs. (10)). Section 1(1), the welfare principle, applies to these decisions. A child assessment order can be made on any child under 18.

Provision for variation and discharge are made in the Family Proceedings Rules (subs. (12)).

Four advantages have been identified for the child assessment order by Jim Harding, Child Care Director of the N.S.P.C.C.:

(1) *Parental responsibility is retained by parents*: This is although the court may order the child's removal from home, his assessment and even contact with third parties without the parents' consent and against the parents' wishes.
(2) *The child may be seen by the family doctor in a familiar environment*: This is possible but not mandated by the section. The applicant will want to be satisfied that the assessment is thorough and may wish the child to be examined by a specialist paediatrician, etc. It is essential that the assessment is thorough because there can be no further application for a child assessment order within six months (s.91(15)).
(3) *Parents are more likely to co-operate with this type of order and the social work relationship with the family will not be damaged*: Lack of co-operation is a precondition for the order. The order is an "evidence-seeking" order and will be used where there is suspicion, often as a precursor to further proceedings. It will take great social work skill to establish a good relationship with the family in such circumstances.

(4) *The child can be protected in serious but not emergency situations*: This order does not protect the child, it permits assessment. Where protection is required and evidence exists, care proceedings should be started. If there is insufficient evidence and no co-operation in allowing the child to be assessed it may be possible to get an emergency protection order under section 44. Both a child assessment order and an emergency protection order require at least that the applicant has a reasonable cause to suspect that the child is suffering or likely to suffer significant harm.

The Department of Health has issued guidance on the use of child assessment orders, see *Guidance*, Vol. 1, paras. 4.6–4.27. This suggests that the order will usually be most appropriate where harm to the child is long term and cumulative rather than sudden and severe, *e.g.* failure to thrive or sexual abuse (para. 4.9). Applications should always be preceded by an investigation under section 47 which should not be superficial (para. 4.11). Arrangements for the assessment should be prepared before the application is made (para. 4.12). If a serious situation is revealed by the assessment it may be necessary to seek an emergency protection order (s.44). There will be some cases where the assessment indicates impaired health or development but does not identify the problem fully. Further voluntary assessment may need to be arranged; if parents are unwilling to co-operate the authority may need to obtain an interim care or supervision order (s.38). Identified problems should not be ignored and the child's welfare may be adequately safeguarded by the provision of services (paras. 4.21). There should always be substantial efforts to persuade the child's carers to co-operate; professionals should work co-operatively on plans surrounding orders; and the decision to seek an order should be discussed at a case conference (para. 4.23).

Subs. (1)

Reasonable cause to suspect: See section 47(1)(b).

An assessment: This is not a term of art and is used loosely to cover medical and psychiatric testing as well as developmental screening or an opinion formed following observation and discussion by a child care social worker. It may be difficult for any assessment to be carried out where the applicant lacks baseline data, *i.e.* data about the child at an earlier period. The type of assessment which can be carried out will be limited by the duration of the order. It was originally proposed that these orders should last for three months to allow for thorough inter-disciplinary assessment, but the duration was restricted because the grounds for an order are broad. The order does not permit an assessment of the family, only the individual child who is subject to the order. Where a medical or social history forms an essential part of the assessment, the order can require the person who produced the child to answer questions concerning the child. For further details on assessment see Department of Health, *Protecting Children; A guide to social workers undertaking comprehensive assessment* (1988).

In the absence of an order: Courts will need to be careful not to accept, without inquiry, a statement that the parents will agree to the assessment. If the order is refused and the parents fail to co-operate, no further application for a child assessment order (but not an emergency protection order) may be made within six months. Problems may be avoided by adjourning rather than dismissing the application.

Subs. (4)

There are grounds for making an emergency protection order: See section 44(1).

Subs. (6)

The duty of any person ... to produce the child: Failure to comply with a child assessment order may be dealt with under the Magistrates' Courts Act 1980, s.63. However, a simpler (but more Draconian) power of enforcement is found in section 44(1)(b). Refusal to allow access where there was a child assessment order would be unreasonable and thus justify the court making an emergency protection order.

Any person who is in a position to produce the child: A person who is looking after the child but who does not have parental responsibility for him might argue that he is not in such a position. However, he must comply with section 3(5) and a parent cannot lawfully veto the child's production because he cannot exercise parental responsibility in conflict with a court order (s.2(8)). It would thus seem that anyone with the child, including a childminder or teacher, would have to produce him.

Subs. (8)

Comparable provisions apply in relation to emergency protection orders, interim orders and supervision orders. Children who are under 16 but are capable of understanding the nature of medical examination can only be examined with their agreement. All children, including those over 16 can apparently be treated without their consent if a person with parental responsibility, or the High Court exercising its inherent jurisdiction gives consent, *Re W* [1992] N.L.J. 1124 (C.A.); *Re R (a minor) (wardship: medical treatment)* [1991] 4 All E.R. 177 (C.A.). However, it may be difficult, if not impossible for a doctor to treat in some cases where he has no proper opportunity to examine or assess. This may suggest that the recent approach of the Court of Appeal is flawed.

This subsection implements the decision of the House of Lords in *Gillick* v. *West Norfolk Area Health Authority* [1986] A.C. 112. However, it is not exactly clear what a young person must understand in order to establish that he has the maturity to refuse an assessment. Lord Scarman said of the decision to seek contraceptive services, "It is not enough that she should understand the nature of the advice which is being given; she must have sufficient maturity to understand what is involved. There are moral and family questions, especially her relationships with her parents; long term problems associated with the emotional impact of pregnancy and its termination and there are risks to health of sexual intercourse at her age, risks which contraception may diminish but cannot eliminate. It follows that a doctor will have to satisfy himself that she is able to appraise these factors before he can safely proceed on the basis that she has at law capacity to consent to contraceptive treatment" (at p. 189). The level of understanding required to instruct a solicitor is lower than that needed to refuse a psychological assessment, *Re H, The Times* June 5, 1992.

Where an assessment is necessary to establish whether or not the child has been physically, sexually or emotionally abused, there is a further complication. The abuse may have so traumatised a child that although he is mature generally, he is incapable of mature decisions in this aspect of his life. However, doctors must also avoid the view that a child who disagrees is ipso facto immature. The doctor will have to explain the need for the assessment and the consequences of its refusal. Where possible, other avenues of evidence should be explored.

Subs. (10)

As the court thinks fit: As well as considering the child's welfare, the court will have to consider the effect of contact on the assessment process.

Subs. (12)

Rules of Court: See rule 2(3), p. 356 below.

Orders for emergency protection of children

44.—(1) Where any person ("the applicant") applies to the court for an order to be made under this section with respect to a child, the court may make the order if, but only if, it is satisfied that—
    (a) there is reasonable cause to believe that the child is likely to suffer significant harm if—
        (i) he is not removed to accommodation provided by or on behalf of the applicant; or
        (ii) he does not remain in the place in which he is then being accommodated;
    (b) in the case of an application made by a local authority—
        (i) enquiries are being made with respect to the child under section 47(1)(b); and

Orders for Emergency Protection of Children

        (ii) those enquiries are being frustrated by access to the child being unreasonably refused to a person authorised to seek access and that the applicant has reasonable cause to believe that access to the child is required as a matter of urgency; or
  (c) in the case of an application made by an authorised person—
        (i) the applicant has reasonable cause to suspect that a child is suffering, or is likely to suffer, significant harm;
        (ii) the applicant is making enquiries with respect to the child's welfare; and
        (iii) those enquiries are being frustrated by access to the child being unreasonably refused to a person authorised to seek access and the applicant has reasonable cause to believe that access to the child is required as a matter of urgency.

(2) In this section—
  (a) "authorised person" means a person who is an authorised person for the purposes of section 31; and
  (b) "a person authorised to seek access", means—
        (i) in the case of an application by a local authority, an officer of the local authority or a person authorised by the authority to act on their behalf in connection with the enquiries; or
        (ii) in the case of an application by an authorised person, that person.

(3) Any person—
  (a) seeking access to a child in connection with enquiries of a kind mentioned in subsection (1); and
  (b) purporting to be a person authorised to do so,
shall, on being asked to do so, produce some duly authenticated document as evidence that he is such a person.

(4) While an order under this section ("an emergency protection order") is in force it—
  (a) operates as a direction to any person who is in a position to do so to comply with any request to produce the child to the applicant;
  (b) authorises—
        (i) the removal of the child at any time to accommodation provided by or on behalf of the applicant and his being kept there; or
        (ii) the prevention of the child's removal from any hospital, or other place, in which he was being accommodated immediately before the making of the order; and
  (c) gives the applicant parental responsibility for the child.

(5) Where an emergency protection order is in force with respect to a child, the applicant—
  (a) shall only exercise the power given by virtue of subsection (4)(b) in order to safeguard the welfare of the child;

(b) shall take, and shall only take, such action in meeting his parental responsibility for the child as is reasonably required to safeguard or promote the welfare of the child (having regard in particular to the duration of the order); and
(c) shall comply with the requirements of any regulations made by the Secretary of State for the purposes of this subsection.

(6) Where the court makes an emergency protection order, it may give such directions (if any) as it considers appropriate with respect to—
  (a) the contact which is, or is not, to be allowed between the child and any named person;
  (b) the medical or psychiatric examination or other assessment of the child.

(7) Where any direction is given under subsection (6)(b), the child may, if he is of sufficient understanding to make an informed decision, refuse to submit to the examination or other assessment.

(8) A direction under subsection (6)(a) may impose conditions and one under subsection (6)(b) may be to the effect that there is to be—
  (a) no such examination or assessment; or
  (b) no such examination or assessment unless the court directs otherwise.

(9) A direction under subsection (6) may be—
  (a) given when the emergency protection order is made or at any time while it is in force; and
  (b) varied at any time on the application of any person falling within any class of person prescribed by rules of court for the purposes of this subsection.

(10) Where an emergency protection order is in force with respect to a child and—
  (a) the applicant has exercised the power given by subsection (4)(b)(i) but it appears to him that it is safe for the child to be returned; or
  (b) the applicant has exercised the power given by subsection (4)(b)(ii) but it appears to him that it is safe for the child to be allowed to be removed from the place in question,
he shall return the child or (as the case may be) allow him to be removed.

(11) Where he is required by subsection (10) to return the child the applicant shall—
  (a) return him to the care of the person from whose care he was removed; or
  (b) if that is not reasonably practicable, return him to the care of—
    (i) a parent of his;
    (ii) any person who is not a parent of his but who has parental responsibility for him; or
    (iii) such other person as the applicant (with the agreement of the court) considers appropriate.

(12) Where the applicant has been required by subsection (10) to return the child, or to allow him to be removed, he may again

exercise his powers with respect to the child (at any time while the emergency protection order remains in force) if it appears to him that a change in the circumstances of the case makes it necessary for him to do so.

(13) Where an emergency protection order has been made with respect to a child, the applicant shall, subject to any direction given under subsection (6), allow the child reasonable contact with—
- (a) his parents;
- (b) any person who is not a parent of his but who has parental responsibility for him;
- (c) any person with whom he was living immediately before the making of the order;
- (d) any person in whose favour a contact order is in force with respect to him;
- (e) any person who is allowed to have contact with the child by virtue of an order under section 34; and
- (f) any person acting on behalf of any of those persons.

(14) Wherever it is reasonably practicable to do so, an emergency protection order shall name the child; and where it does not name him it shall describe him as clearly as possible.

(15) A person shall be guilty of an offence if he intentionally obstructs any person exercising the power under subsection (4)(b) to remove, or prevent the removal of, a child.

(16) A person guilty of an offence under subsection (15) shall be liable on summary conviction to a fine not exceeding level 3 on the standard scale.

DEFINITIONS
"applicant": 2.44(1).
"authorised person": ss.31(9), 44(2).
"child": s.105(1).
"contact order": s.8(1).
"emergency protection order": ss.44(4), 45(1).
"hospital": s.105(1).
"parental responsibility": ss.2, 3, 44(5).
"person authorised to seek access": s.44(2).
"person who has parental responsibility": ss.2(1)(2), 4(1), 5(6), 12(1)(2).
"significant harm": ss.31(9)(10), 105(1).
"the court": s.92(7).

GENERAL NOTE
This section sets out the grounds for and effect of an emergency protection order, the new order which replaces the place of safety order. Although under subsection (1)(a) the court (not the applicant as before) must be satisfied of the ground, this does not apply to subsection (1)(b) or subsection (1)(c). It appears that these grounds for an emergency protection order may be easier to satisfy than the grounds for a place of safety order in the C.Y.P.A. 1969, s.28(1). However, more emphasis is being placed on the emergency nature of this order; the court will have to be satisfied that the order is necessary and in the child's welfare (s.1(1), (5)).
There are effectively three grounds for the order:—
- (1) reasonable cause to believe that the child is likely to suffer significant harm if not removed (subs. (1)(a)(i));
- (2) reasonable cause, etc., if not kept at current place of accommodation (subs. (1)(a)(ii));
- (3) the applicant has reasonable cause to suspect that a child is suffering or likely to suffer significant harm, is making enquiries (subs. (1)(b)(i) and

(1)(c)(i) and (ii)), and the enquiries are being frustrated by access being unreasonably refused and the applicant has reasonable cause to believe that access is required as a matter of urgency.

The order operates as a direction to anyone who is in a position to do so, to produce the child (subs. (4)(a); see note on section 43(6)). It can be granted in respect of any child under 18. It requires the applicant to comply with regulations (subs. (5)(c)). It gives the applicant the power to remove the child, or prevent his removal, but only where it is necessary to safeguard the child's welfare (subss. (4)(b) and (5)(a)). However, where the child is removed or detained, the applicant is under a duty to return or release him if it is safe to do so (subs. (10)), if possible to the person from whose care he was removed (subs. (11)). The applicant may remove the child once more if this appears necessary (subs. (12)). Thus, a child who is subject to an emergency protection order need not be removed from his home and may be returned during the period of the order. The order enables the applicant to decide whether to remove the child. There is no power under an emergency protection order to order the removal of any adult from the home, but the local authority has a power to assist the perpetrator to obtain alternative accommodation under Schedule 2, paragraph 5.

The order grants the applicant parental responsibility for the child but only permits him to take such action as is reasonably required to safeguard the welfare of the child (subss. (5)(c) and (5)(b)).

The law concerning medical examination and assessment of children under emergency orders is clarified. The applicant's parental responsibility allows him to authorise what is reasonably required to safeguard the child's welfare. This includes examinations made to obtain evidence for care proceedings but leave is required if the results are to be admissible (r.18) and the court may direct or bar examinations (subss. (6)(b), (8) and (9)). Even where an examination or assessment is permitted, it cannot be made if a child with sufficient understanding to make an informed decision objects (subs. (7); see notes on s.43(8)). The agreement of anyone with parental responsibility other than the applicant is not required.

The applicant is required to allow the child reasonable contact with the persons listed in subsection (13). The court may make directions about contact (subss. (6)(a) and (8)).

Where possible, the child should be named (subs. (14)). It is an offence (summary conviction: fine level 3) intentionally to obstruct the child's removal or detention under subsection (4)(b) (subss. (15) and (16)).

The local authority has a duty to provide accommodation for children subject to emergency protection order under section 21.

Emergency protection orders may be sought by any individual and could be used where a child was at risk of significant harm having been removed from home by a parent intending to take the child overseas (particularly to a non-Convention country) or to conceal his whereabouts. In such a case it would replace temporarily an interim residence order or the use of wardship but would bring with it the disadvantages of a local authority investigation under section 47 and possibly further involvement by the local authority taking over the order under the Emergency Protection Order Transfer of Responsibilities Regulations 1991 (S.I. 1991 No. 1414) p. 464 below (see notes to s.31(6) and Whybrow [1992] Fam. Law 94, 124). In most cases an ex parte residence order would be preferable.

This section should be read with sections 43, 45, 46, and 48. Court rules provide for emergency protection orders to be made either *ex parte* (with leave) or on notice (one day). They may be made *ex parte* by a single magistrate (r.2(5)(a)). See p. 357 below.

Guidance is provided in *Guidance*, Vol. 1, paras. 4.28–70 and in *Working together* (1991), para. 3.8 which stresses the need to handle emergency removal of children sensitively.

Subs. (1)

There is ... : It is no longer sufficient for the applicant alone to have a reasonable belief of significant harm, etc., unless subsection (1)(b) applies, he must convince the court. The civil standard of proof applies, but the courts are likely to wish to match the degree of evidence with the seriousness of the order. Where only the applicant has a reasonable belief, a child assessment order may be available (see s.43).

Access: The authorised person has a duty to obtain access under section 47(4), but access is not defined. Being able to see the child, fully clothed, may not be sufficient, since it will not enable any conclusion to be drawn from the enquiries. Social workers have been criticised for not demanding sufficient access to the child (see, *e.g.* Kimberley Carlile Inquiry 1987) and therefore it may be necessary to undress the child. However, refusal to have a child medically examined would not appear to be within this subsection because it is not refusal of access to a person authorised. Where this was the problem the applicant would need to rely on subsection (1)(a) or seek a child assessment order under section 43.

A matter of urgency: This will depend on the nature of the suspicion, the age of the child and the existence of opportunities to see the child, for example at school. The fact that the alleged conduct has occurred for a period already does not prevent access being a matter of urgency.

Being unreasonably refused: The person seeking access may be required to produce evidence of his authority (subs. (3)). It is not clear where it would be reasonable to refuse access to someone who produces such evidence. The excuse that the child was asleep or unwell would probably not be sufficient and access at night may be reasonable in some cases. However, a parent who requires the person to wait or to return at a later time may not have refused access.

Subs. (5)

Only such action as ... : The applicant's parental responsibility is strictly limited; consents given would not be valid if the treatment, etc., was not reasonably required but there appears to be no liability on the applicant or redress for the parents if the provision is not complied with see *F v. Wirral M.B.C.* [1991] 2 W.L.R. 1132 (C.A.). A child who was harmed following permission unlawfully given might have an action in negligence.

Subs. (7)

See note on section 43(8).

Subs. (9)

Varied: See Family Proceedings Courts (Children Act 1989) Rules 1991 (S.I. 1991 No. 1395), r. 2(4), page 356 below.

Subs. (11)

The applicant appears to have free choice between subsections (11)(b)(i) and (11)(b)(ii), but must act in accordance with the child's welfare and should consult the child, etc. (see s.22(4) and (5)). If neither placement seems appropriate, the applicant must seek the court's agreement to another placement, where rule 2(5) applies.

Subs. (13)

The importance of contact at this early stage should be noted see *Guidance*, Vol. 3, para.6.10. The applicant is likely to need to seek directions to establish priorities for contact. Although contact may help the child cope with the crisis of being returned, there is a danger, particularly in sexual abuse cases, that pressure will be put on the child by relatives (not just the perpetrator) to withdraw the allegations.

Solicitors acting for the parents may need to see the child to obtain information about the case. Such interviews are likely to be stressful and it may be appropriate for a social worker or supportive friend to be with the child during visits.

Reasonable contact: It may be reasonable to allow contact only by telephone with some people.

Duration of emergency protection orders and other supplemental provisions

45.—(1) An emergency protection order shall have effect for such period, not exceeding eight days, as may be specified in the order.

(2) Where—

(a) the court making an emergency protection order would, but for this subsection, specify a period of eight days as the period for which the order is to have effect; but
(b) the last of those eight days is a public holiday (that is to say, Christmas Day, Good Friday, a bank holiday or a Sunday),

the court may specify a period which ends at noon on the first later day which is not such a holiday.

(3) Where an emergency protection order is made on an application under section 46(7), the period of eight days mentioned in subsection (1) shall begin with the first day on which the child was taken into police protection under section 46.

(4) Any person who—
(a) has parental responsibility for a child as the result of an emergency protection order; and
(b) is entitled to apply for a care order with respect to the child,

may apply to the court for the period during which the emergency protection order is to have effect to be extended.

(5) On an application under subsection (4) the court may extend the period during which the order is to have effect by such period, not exceeding seven days, as it thinks fit, but may do so only if it has reasonable cause to believe that the child concerned is likely to suffer significant harm if the order is not extended.

(6) An emergency protection order may only be extended once.

(7) Regardless of any enactment or rule of law which would otherwise prevent it from doing so, a court hearing an application for, or with respect to, an emergency protection order may take account of—
(a) any statement contained in any report made to the court in the course of, or in connection with, the hearing; or
(b) any evidence given during the hearing,

which is, in the opinion of the court, relevant to the application.

(8) Any of the following may apply to the court for an emergency protection order to be discharged—
(a) the child;
(b) a parent of his;
(c) any person who is not a parent of his but who has parental responsibility for him; or
(d) any person with whom he was living immediately before the making of the order.

(9) No application for the discharge of an emergency protection order shall be heard by the court before the expiry of the period of 72 hours beginning with the making of the order.

[(10) No appeal may be made against—
(a) the making of, or refusal to make, an emergency protection order;
(b) the extension of, or refusal to extend, the period during which such an order is to have effect;
(c) the discharge of, or refusal to discharge, such an order; or
(d) the giving of, or refusal to give, any direction in connection with such an order.]

(11) Subsection (8) does not apply—
  (a) where the person who would otherwise be entitled to apply for the emergency protection order to be discharged—
    (i) was given notice (in accordance with rules of court) of the hearing at which the order was made; and
    (ii) was present at that hearing; or
  (b) to any emergency protection order the effective period of which has been extended under subsection (5).

(12) A court making an emergency protection order may direct that the applicant may, in exercising any powers which he has by virtue of the order, be accompanied by a registered medical practitioner, registered nurse or registered health visitor, if he so chooses.

AMENDMENT

Subsection (10) was replaced by the Courts and Legal Services Act 1990, s.116 and Sched. 16, para. 19.

DEFINITIONS

"bank holiday": s.105(1).
"care order": s.31(11).
"emergency protection order": s.44(4).
"person who has parental responsibility as a result of an emergency protection order": s.44(1)(4).
"person who is not a parent but has parental responsibility": ss.5(6), 12(2), 33(3).
"significant harm": s.31(9),(10).
"the court": s.92(7).

GENERAL NOTE

This section makes further provision in respect of emergency protection orders, particularly about their duration.

Emergency protection orders last for a maximum of eight days (subs. (1)), except where the last day in a public holiday as defined in subsection (2), when they can extend to the next day which is not a holiday. *Gal Manual*, p.55 is misleading on this point. While the order is in force, a local authority or the N.S.P.C.C. can apply for it to be extended once for up to seven days (subss. (4)–(6)). The court may also grant an extension if it is satisfied that there are reasonable grounds to believe that the child is likely to suffer significant harm if the order is not extended (subs. (5)). An order which has not been extended may be discharged after 72 hours on application of anyone listed in subsection (8) except a person who was given notice and was present at the original hearing (subs. (11)).

There is no appeal against the granting or refusal of an emergency protection order or a direction contained in one (subs. (10)). However, it is possible to challenge the court by judicial review (*per* the Lord Chancellor (Hansard, H.L. Vol. 503, col. 440)). Subsection (12) enables the court to direct that when the applicant exercises any of the powers under the order he may be accompanied by a registered medical practitioner, nurse or health visitor. Section 41(6)(g) makes provision for guardians ad litem in these proceedings.

Subs. (1)

Very short orders (orders for less than 72 hours) will preclude application for discharge under subsection (9) but will impose a heavy burden on the authority to prepare for an extension hearing and care proceedings. A local authority might use judicial review to challenge an unreasonably short order. It could not seek instead to protect the child by wardship because of the restriction in section 100. Informal guidance from the Department of Health *Children Act News No. 2* (1992) notes that the duration of the order should be fixed in relation to the child's best interests, including allowing sufficient time for enquiries.

Subs. (4)

A successful applicant for an emergency protection order gets parental responsibility by virtue of s.44(4)(c). Section 31(1) and (9) states who may apply for a care order (a local authority or the N.S.P.C.C). Other applicants, the police and ordinary citizens cannot apply for any extension, but the Emergency Protection Order (Transfer of Responsibilities) Regulations 1991 (S.I. 1991 No. 1414) allow the local authority to take over responsibility for such a case and apply for an extension, see notes to section 31(6).

Subs. (5)

The test for an extension is the same as that for the original order, but the applicant may need to be prepared to justify intervention more explicitly if the original order was made *ex parte*, because applications for extensions are likely to be heard *inter partes*. Where there is an extension hearing this will provide the only opportunity to challenge the order (subs. (11)).

Subs. (7)

This disapplies the hearsay rule. A comparable but narrower provision exists in relation to reports to the court under section 7 and guardians ad litem's evidence under section 41(11). The matter in question will have to be proved properly when the care order is made but hearsay will still be allowed (see also notes to s.96 and p. 431 below).

Subs. (9)

The hearing may take place at any time after 72 hours. It is open to the court to shorten periods of notice to allow the parents longer to prepare their challenge.

Subs. (11)

Where notice of the original application is given, but the person notified is unable to obtain full legal advice and representation, he may be best advised to stay away from the court and preserve his ability to apply for discharge after 72 hours.

Removal and accommodation of children by police in cases of emergency

46.—(1) Where a constable has reasonable cause to believe that a child would otherwise be likely to suffer significant harm, he may—
    (a) remove the child to suitable accommodation and keep him there; or
    (b) take such steps as are reasonable to ensure that the child's removal from any hospital, or other place, in which he is then being accommodated is prevented.

(2) For the purposes of this Act, a child with respect to whom a constable has exercised his powers under this section is referred to as having been taken into police protection.

(3) As soon as is reasonably practicable after taking a child into police protection, the constable concerned shall—
    (a) inform the local authority within whose area the child was found of the steps that have been, and are proposed to be, taken with respect to the child under this section and the reasons for taking them;

(b) give details to the authority within whose area the child is ordinarily resident ("the appropriate authority") of the place at which the child is being accommodated;
(c) inform the child (if he appears capable of understanding)—
  (i) of the steps that have been taken with respect to him under this section and of the reasons for taking them; and
  (ii) of the further steps that may be taken with respect to him under this section;
(d) take such steps as are reasonably practicable to discover the wishes and feelings of the child;
(e) secure that the case is inquired into by an officer designated for the purposes of this section by the chief officer of the police area concerned; and
(f) where the child was taken into police protection by being removed to accommodation which is not provided—
  (i) by or on behalf of a local authority; or
  (ii) as a refuge, in compliance with the requirements of section 51,
secure that he is moved to accommodation which is so provided.

(4) As soon as is reasonably practicable after taking a child into police protection, the constable concerned shall take such steps as are reasonably practicable to inform—
  (a) the child's parents;
  (b) every person who is not a parent of his but who has parental responsibility for him; and
  (c) any other person with whom the child was living immediately before being taken into police protection,
of the steps that he has taken under this section with respect to the child, the reasons for taking them and the further steps that may be taken with respect to him under this section.

(5) On completing any inquiry under subsection (3)(e), the officer conducting it shall release the child from police protection unless he considers that there is still reasonable cause for believing that the child would be likely to suffer significant harm if released.

(6) No child may be kept in police protection for more than 72 hours.

(7) While a child is being kept in police protection, the designated officer may apply on behalf of the appropriate authority for an emergency protection order to be made under section 44 with respect to the child.

(8) An application may be made under subsection (7) whether or not the authority know of it or agree to its being made.

(9) While a child is being kept in police protection—
  (a) neither the constable concerned nor the designated officer shall have parental responsibility for him; but
  (b) the designated officer shall do what is reasonable in all the circumstances of the case for the purpose of safeguarding or promoting the child's welfare (having regard in particular to the length of the period during which the child will be so protected).

(10) Where a child has been taken into police protection, the designated officer shall allow—
  (a) the child's parents;
  (b) any person who is not a parent of the child but who has parental responsibility for him;
  (c) any person with whom the child was living immediately before he was taken into police protection;
  (d) any person in whose favour a contact order is in force with respect to the child;
  (e) any person who is allowed to have contact with the child by virtue of an order under section 34; and
  (f) any person acting on behalf of any of those persons,
to have such contact (if any) with the child as, in the opinion of the designated officer, is both reasonable and in the child's best interests.

(11) Where a child who has been taken into police protection is in accommodation provided by, or on behalf of, the appropriate authority, subsection (10) shall have effect as if it referred to the authority rather than to the designated officer.

DEFINITIONS

"appropriate authority": s.46(3)(b).
"child": s.105(1).
"contact order": s.8(1).
"designated officer": s.46(3)(e).
"local authority": s.105(1).
"ordinary residence": s.105(6).
"person who is not a parent but has parental responsibility": ss.5(6), 12(2), 33(3), 44(4).
"police protection": s.46(2).
"refuge": s.51.
"significant harm": s.31(9)(10).

GENERAL NOTE

This section replaces the power of a constable to detain a child at risk under the C.Y.P.A. 1969, s.28(2) and reduces the maximum period for police protection from eight days to 72 hours (subs. (6)). The ground for such detention in subsection (1) is comparable to that for an emergency protection order under section 44(1)(a), but the constable, not the court, must have reasonable cause to believe that the child is likely to suffer significant harm. Police action under section 46 may be either removing a child to suitable accommodation (accommodation provided by or on behalf of the local authority or a refuge under section 51 (subs. (3)(f)) or taking reasonable steps to prevent his removal from a hospital or elsewhere (subs. (1)). Local authorities may seek to liaise with the police and protect children by police protection rather than undertake the onerous administrative tasks required for an emergency protection order in a short period. Alternatively, the availability of police protection may provide a safety net where accommodation is used pending care proceedings.

The duties owned by a constable taking action under this section are more onerous than under the C.Y.P.A. 1969, s.28(3) and (4). These additional duties are intended to provide "safeguards which should reduce the stress that may accompany the removal of a child and ensure both that the child does not remain away from home unnecessarily and that contact with the family is maintained" (*per* David Mellor, Minister of Health (Standing Committee B, col. 337, June 6, 1989)). The constable must inform the child and the parent figures listed in subsection (4) of the steps taken, the reasons for them, and what else may be done (subss. (2) and (4)). He must inform the local authority of the reasons for the action and the child's whereabouts and secure that the child is moved to suitable accommodation (subs. (3)). He must inform the child of the action taken and to be taken and discover his wishes and feelings (subs. (3)(c) and (d)). The constable must also ensure that the case is investigated by a designated officer (subs. (3)(c)). The powers and responsibilities of the designated officer are also strengthened; he does not have parental responsibility for the child but may take reasonable action to safeguard the child's welfare (subs. (9)). He must allow the people specified in subsection (1) to have contact with the child. He must release the child when his investigation is completed, unless he considers that the child would be likely to suffer significant harm (subs. (5)). In such a case he may apply for an emergency protection order (subs. (7)).

Although a child who appears capable of understanding must be informed, etc., there is no duty on the police to consult the child or take account of his wishes either in relation to contact under subsection (10) or any other course of action. The police have used their powers to detain a child whose parents have been arrested, to remove children at risk in cases of abuse, etc., or when they find children in unsuitable places, *e.g.* hitch-hiking on the motorway. Police standing orders tell them to return young people under the age of 18 to their parents (*per* Lord Elwyn Jones (*Hansard*, H.L. Vol. 503, col. 444)). The Act requires the local authority to be informed once the child has been taken into police protection; the authority must then investigate under section 47(1). However, this does not apply where a constable is merely returning a missing child home.

There is no statutory provision for review, but judicial review would theoretically be available where duties in the Act were not complied with. There is also the possibility of an action for false imprisonment.

Home Office Circular 54/1991 advised Chief Constables, etc. about police protection.

Subs. (1)

Suitable accommodation: This no longer has to be "a place of safety" but it must be accommodation within subsection (3)(f). "It will clearly not be police premises except for short periods in exceptional circumstances" (Home Office 54/1991). If the child needs medical attention he can presumably be taken to hospital, but an emergency protection order may be necessary because the police do not obtain parental responsibility (see subs. (9)) and cannot consent to treatment except where it is reasonable to safeguard the child, *e.g.* in an emergency.

Subs. (4)

If the parents are informed that the designated officer intends to apply for an emergency protection order, it may be possible for these proceedings to be *inter partes*. This could be the best way of resolving conflicts at an early stage, but the period of 72 hours gives the parents little time to obtain proper representation. See also section 45(11).

Subs. (5)

There is a duty to release unless the condition is satisfied. If it is satisfied, there is no duty on the designated officer to seek an emergency protection order, but notification of the local authority brings its duty to investigate under section 47 into play. The authority must consider whether it should ask the designated officer to apply for an emergency protection order (s.47(3)(c)).

Subs. (7)

The duration of any emergency protection order applied for will be limited by section 45(3); the period of police protection and the emergency protection order cannot together exceed eight days. The local authority may also apply for an emergency protection order while the child is in police protection. It should not be possible for anyone to apply for an emergency protection order to end police protection. In *Nottinghamshire County Council v. Q.* [1982] 2 W.L.R. 954, the Divisional Court held that a parent's application for an interim order under C.Y.P.A. 1969, s.28(6) was an abuse of the process.

On behalf of: Any police officer may seek an order on his own behalf under section 44.

Subs. (9)

The wording of paragraph (b) parallels that in section 3(5) which defines the power of a person who is *in loco parentis*, but the designated officer has a duty to act. This further clouds the effect of parental responsibility because it would seem unrealistic for the officer to be under a duty to obtain medical treatment if his position did not also enable him to consent to it. Although there may be little difficulty over emergency treatment for serious injuries, where investigations are necessary to determine whether the child has been physically or sexually abused an emergency protection order or child assessment order should be sought.

Sub. (10)

Contact may reassure the child or the parents about the situation, but could be used by the parents or someone acting on their behalf to silence the child. It may thus be necessary to find out the child's views before allowing contact and to arrange supervision. The designated officer has to balance the parents' wishes and the child's needs.

Reasonable: What is reasonable must take into account the length of police protection, the circumstances in which the child entered police protection, the child's age, health (emotional and physical) and wishes. Attention should be given to the timing, duration and frequency of visits from parents (or anyone investigating the case), the location and the general arrangements for visits. Where a number of different people wish to visit the child it may be necessary to prioritise claims. Here again the child's wishes will be crucial to his welfare.

Subs. (11)

The officer's duties under subsection (10) fall to the authority if the child is being accommodated by or on behalf of them, but not if he is in a refuge. Where a local authority is accommodating the child it will also be under the duties in Part III and have to consider the wishes and feelings of the child and his parents in accordance with section 22.

Local authority's duty to investigate

47.—(1) Where a local authority—
 (a) are informed that a child who lives, or is found, in their area—
  (i) is the subject of an emergency protection order; or
  (ii) is in police protection; or
 (b) have reasonable cause to suspect that a child who lives, or is found, in their area is suffering, or is likely to suffer, significant harm,
the authority shall make, or cause to be made, such enquiries as they consider necessary to enable them to decide whether they should take any action to safeguard or promote the child's welfare.

(2) Where a local authority have obtained an emergency protection order with respect to a child, they shall make, or cause to be made, such enquiries as they consider necessary to enable them to decide what action they should take to safeguard or promote the child's welfare.

(3) The enquiries shall, in particular, be directed towards establishing—
 (a) whether the authority should make any application to the court, or exercise any of their other powers under this Act, with respect to the child;
 (b) whether, in the case of a child—

Local Authority's Duty to Investigate

  (i) with respect to whom an emergency protection order has been made; and
  (ii) who is not in accommodation provided by or on behalf of the authority,

  it would be in the child's best interests (while an emergency protection order remains in force) for him to be in such accommodation; and

  (c) whether, in the case of a child who has been taken into police protection, it would be in the child's best interests for the authority to ask for an application to be made under section 46(7).

(4) Where enquiries are being made under subsection (1) with respect to a child, the local authority concerned shall (with a view to enabling them to determine what action, if any, to take with respect to him) take such steps as are reasonably practicable—

  (a) to obtain access to him; or
  (b) to ensure that access to him is obtained, on their behalf, by a person authorised by them for the purpose,

unless they are satisfied that they already have sufficient information with respect to him.

(5) Where, as a result of any such enquiries, it appears to the authority that there are matters connected with the child's education which should be investigated, they shall consult the relevant local education authority.

(6) Where, in the course of enquiries made under this section—

  (a) any officer of the local authority concerned; or
  (b) any person authorised by the authority to act on their behalf in connection with those enquiries—
     (i) is refused access to the child concerned; or
     (ii) is denied information as to his whereabouts,

the authority shall apply for an emergency protection order, a child assessment order, a care order or a supervision order with respect to the child unless they are satisfied that his welfare can be satisfactorily safeguarded without their doing so.

(7) If, on the conclusion of any enquiries or review made under this section, the authority decide not to apply for an emergency protection order, a child assessment order, a care order or a supervision order they shall—

  (a) consider whether it would be appropriate to review the case at a later date; and
  (b) if they decide that it would be, determine the date on which that review is to begin.

(8) Where, as a result of complying with this section, a local authority conclude that they should take action to safeguard or promote the child's welfare they shall take that action (so far as it is both within their power and reasonably practicable for them to do so).

(9) Where a local authority are conducting enquiries under this section, it shall be the duty of any person mentioned in subsection (11) to assist them with those enquiries (in particular by providing relevant information and advice) if called upon by the authority to do so.

(10) Subsection (9) does not oblige any person to assist a local authority where doing so would be unreasonable in all the circumstances of the case.

(11) The persons are—
- (a) any local authority;
- (b) any local education authority;
- (c) any local housing authority;
- (d) any health authority [or National Health Service Trust]; and
- (e) any person authorised by the Secretary of State for the purposes of this section.

(12) Where a local authority are making enquiries under this section with respect to a child who appears to them to be ordinarily resident within the area of another authority, they shall consult that other authority, who may undertake the necessary enquiries in their place.

AMENDMENT

The words in square brackets in subs. (11) added by the Courts and Legal Services Act 1990, Sched. 16, para. 20.

DEFINITIONS

"care order": s.31(11).
"child": s.105(1).
"child assessment order": s.43(2).
"emergency protection order": s.44(4).
"health authority": s.105(1).
"local authority": s.105(1).
"local education authority": s.105(1).
"local housing authority": s.105(1).
"ordinary residence ": s.105(6).
"police protection": s.46(2).
"significant harm": s.31 (9)(10).
"supervision order": s.31(11).

GENERAL NOTE

This section imposes duties on local authorities to investigate certain cases of suspected harm. These exist alongside the duty to investigate under section 37 where a court order has been made. The duty to make (or cause to be made) the enquiries which they consider necessary applies where the authority is informed or suspects that there is a child in their area who is subject to an emergency protection order, under police protection or at risk (subs. (1)), or they have obtained an emergency protection order (subs. (2)). Subsection (3) directs the local authority to consider specific courses of action; subsection (4) imposes a qualified duty to see (or have seen) the child concerned. Where investigations are frustrated by unreasonable refusal of access to the child there may be grounds for an emergency protection order under section 44(1)(b). The authority is left with some discretion on how to act but must, of course, act reasonably and without negligence. Once the authority has decided to take action it is under a qualified duty to act (subs. (8)). Where access to the child is denied to the person carrying out the enquiries, the authority must apply for an emergency protection order, a child assessment order, a care order or a supervision order unless it is satisfied that the child's welfare does not require it (subs. (6)).

Ignorance of and failure to use the powers in C.Y.P.A. 1933, s.40 to gain access to Kimberley Carlile which contributed to her death, were heavily criticised by the Inquiry, *A Child in Mind*, Greenwich London Borough Council (1987). The importance of a duty on social workers to take action makes clear what they should do and provides a lever for gaining access to the child. Where the authority decides not to act, it must also decide whether and when to review that decision (subs. (7)).

When carrying out its enquiries under this section the local authority must consult the local education authority where education issues arise. If the child appears to be resident elsewhere the local authority must consult the other authorities who may undertake these enquiries (subs. (2)).

There is a qualified duty (subs. (10)) on the organisations mentioned in subsection (11) to assist the local authority if requested to do so (subs. (9)). This puts on a statutory footing the co-operation already established as good practice. Further guidance on interagency collaboration both in relation to individual cases and generally is provided in the Department of Health booklet *Working Together* (1991).

Subss. (1) and (2)

Reasonable cause to suspect: It would appear that there is a duty to investigate every allegation unless it is thought to be unfounded, or the harm suggested is not significant.

Cause to be made: The primary responsibility is on the local authority but it may "delegate" it. In some areas many initial allegations are dealt with by the N.S.P.C.C. The enquiries will necessarily involve other agencies. See subsections (9) to (11).

Such enquiries: Although the local authority has discretion, it must consider the points in subsection (3), obtain access unless it has sufficient information (subs. (4)) and consult the local education authority in relation to education matters (subs. (5)).

What action she should take: Responsibility for deciding whether to take any action with respect to the child rests with the local authority even where the authority has carried out its inquiries through another agency.

Subs.(3)

Other powers under this Act: This includes their powers (and duties) to children under Part III (particularly in relation to children in need) and powers under Parts VII–X and sections 85–87.

It would be in the child's best interests ... to be in such accommodation: The Emergency Protection Order (Transfer of Responsibilities) Regulations 1991 (S.I. 1991 No. 1414) enable the local authority to take over an emergency protection order except where the child is in a refuge (reg. 5), see notes on section 31(6). The N.S.P.C.C. may still bring proceedings even though the child is accommodated by the local authority (s.31(7)).

Subs. (4)

Person authorised: This is not the same as an authorised person under section 31(9). If the local authority delegates enquiries to other agencies it will also have to authorise their personnel to gain access. Only if access is denied to a person who has been authorised does the duty in subsection (6) apply. Refusal of access to an unauthorised person would also appear entirely reasonable (see s.44(1)(b)).

Subs. (6)

Under this section: The power does not apparently apply to investigations under section 37. However, court-ordered investigation may bring section 47(1)(b) into play; there will then be a duty to gain access and take action if this is denied.

Subs. (7)

A comparable duty to consider reviewing a decision exists in section 37(6).

Subs. (8)

This appears to change a local authority power into a qualified duty to determine that the child is in need. For example, if a local authority find that a six-year-old is being left alone after school, it has a power to provide after-school care under section 18(6). It would not be reasonably practicable for the authority to provide such care if they had already determined not to have such facilities, if there were no vacancies, or if the parents refused to allow the child to attend. In this last case the authority could force attendance through a condition in a supervision order if they could satisfy the test in section 31(2). Where the local authority had no facilities of its own it could still provide advice and guidance to the parents about private facilities. For further details of the local authority's powers see Part III and Schedule 2, Part I (see also notes to s.17).

Subss. (9)–(11)

The list in subsection (11) does not include the police or the probation service. David Mellor explained these omissions on the basis that "police refusal to co-operate on any matter would be indefensible" and that probation officers, as officers of the court "are already under a duty to assist in these matters" (Standing Committee B, col. 342, June 6, 1989). Home Office Circular 54/1991 states that no statutory obligation is placed upon the police "partly on the assumption that the police will always take whatever steps are necessary to assist the local authority in performing its duties ... "

Where doing so would be unreasonable: A problem clearly arises with confidentiality owed by a professional to his client. In Department of Health, *Working Together* (1991), the following guidance was given: "Ethical and statutory codes concerned with confidentiality and data protection are not intended to prevent the exchange of information between different professional staff who have a responsibility for ensuring the protection of children" (para. 3.11). Both the British Medical Association and medical defence societies have expressed the view that a doctor may not only respond to requests for information, he may initiate action by passing on his concerns. The United Kingdom Central Council for Nursing, Midwifery and Health Visiting advises that practitioners should consult with others and be prepared to justify decisions to pass on or withhold confidential information. Local authorities have primary responsibility for child protection and cannot expect other agencies (except the N.S.P.C.C.) to put the same emphasis on child protection work as they do.

Subs. (12)

The duty is on the authority which starts the enquiries; the home authority is empowered but not required to take over the enquiries.

Powers to assist in discovery of children who may be in need of emergency protection

48.—(1) Where it appears to a court making an emergency protection order that adequate information as to the child's whereabouts—

   (a) is not available to the applicant for the order; but
   (b) is available to another person,

it may include in the order a provision requiring that other person to disclose, if asked to do so by the applicant, any information that he may have as to the child's whereabouts.

(2) No person shall be excused from complying with such a requirement on the ground that complying might incriminate him or his spouse of an offence; but a statement or admission made in complying shall not be admissible in evidence against either of them in proceedings for any offence other than perjury.

(3) An emergency protection order may authorise the applicant to enter premises specified by the order and search for the child with respect to whom the order is made.

(4) Where the court is satisfied that there is reasonable cause to believe that there may be another child on those premises with respect to whom an emergency protection order ought to be made, it may make an order authorising the applicant to search for that other child on those premises.

(5) Where—

(a) an order has been made under subsection (4);
(b) the child concerned has been found on the premises; and
(c) the applicant is satisfied that the grounds for making an emergency protection order exist with respect to him,

the order shall have effect as if it were an emergency protection order.

(6) Where an order has been made under subsection (4), the applicant shall notify the court of its effect.

(7) A person shall be guilty of an offence if he intentionally obstructs any person exercising the power of entry and search under subsection (3) or (4).

(8) A person guilty of an offence under subsection (7) shall be liable on summary conviction to a fine not exceeding level 3 on the standard scale.

(9) Where, on an application made by any person for a warrant under this section, it appears to the court—
(a) that a person attempting to exercise powers under an emergency protection order has been prevented from doing so by being refused entry to the premises concerned or access to the child concerned; or
(b) that any such person is likely to be so prevented from exercising any such powers,

it may issue a warrant authorising any constable to assist the person mentioned in paragraph (a) or (b) in the exercise of those powers, using reasonable force if necessary.

(10) Every warrant issued under this section shall be addressed to, and executed by, a constable who shall be accompanied by the person applying for the warrant if—
(a) that person so desires; and
(b) the court by whom the warrant is issued does not direct otherwise.

(11) A court granting an application for a warrant under this section may direct that the constable concerned may, in executing the warrant, be accompanied by a registered medical practitioner, registered nurse or registered health visitor if he so chooses.

(12) An application for a warrant under this section shall be made in the manner and form prescribed by rules of court.

(13) Wherever it is reasonably practicable to do so, an order under subsection (4), an application for a warrant under this section and any such warrant shall name the child; and where it does not name him it shall describe him as clearly as possible.

DEFINITIONS
"applicant": s.44(1).
"child": s.105(1).
"emergency protection order": s.44(4).
"the court": s.92(7).

GENERAL NOTE

This section empowers the court to strengthen the force of an emergency protection order by including an order requiring a person to disclose the child's whereabouts to the applicant (subs. (1)), permitting the applicant to enter premises to search for the child or another child (subss. (3) and (4)) or attaching a warrant to it (subss. (9) and (10)).

Subss. (1) and (2)

Disclosure: A comparable provision exists in the Family Law Act 1986, s.33, which applies to orders under Part I of that Act which includes section 8 orders. The Cleveland Inquiry Report, p. 228, recommended that such a power should exist in child protection cases. It must appear to the court that the person ordered to supply information has it. Failure to comply with the order is contempt of court and may amount to an offence under section 44(15). Self incrimination does not justify refusal to comply, but a person who had abducted a child from care contrary to section 49 could not be prosecuted for that offence relying solely on his statement. This immunity does not apply to an offence of perjury.

Subss. (3)–(8)

Entry and search: There is no automatic power of entry under an emergency protection order but the court may add a power. The police have a right to enter without warrant to save life or limb under the Police and Criminal Evidence Act 1984, s.17(1)(e), which is unaffected by this Act. Where a child is found by the police in these circumstances he may be taken into police protection if section 46(1) is satisfied. No additional test has to be satisfied for an entry power under subsection (3), so this may become a standard form of emergency protection order. However, in cases where there is likely to be resistance, the applicant may be advised either to obtain a warrant under subsection (9) or at least have police assistance available. If there is reasonable cause to believe that another child is on the premises, an emergency protection order can include a power to search for that child (subs. (4)). The second child should be named, if reasonably practicable (subs. (13)). If the second child is found on the premises and the applicant is satisfied of the significant harm test, the power operates as an emergency protection order in respect of him and the applicant may remove him (subs. (5)) but must notify the court (subs. (6)). Obstruction of this power of entry and search is an offence (summary conviction: level 3 fine) (subs. (7)). These powers replace those in C.Y.P.A. 1933, s.40.

Subss. (9)–(13)

Warrants: The applicant for an emergency protection order may apply for a warrant when he applies for the emergency protection order or afterwards, but will have to show that one is needed because he has been prevented from exercising the order by refusal of entry or access to the child or is likely to be so prevented (subs. (9)). A warrant under subsection (9) can only be exercised by the police, but the applicant may accompany the constable unless the court directs otherwise (subs. (10)). There is no longer a duty on the applicant to accompany the constable. If the applicant goes with the constable he may be able to determine whether the child should be removed from the home. However, since there will already be an emergency protection order there is no need for any special form of warrant to authorise removal as there was under the C.Y.P.A. 1933. The court may also direct that the constable be accompanied by a doctor, nurse or health visitor if he wishes. When a constable who is attempting to execute a warrant under this section or section 102 (or a recovery order under s.50) finds the premises unoccupied he should leave a copy of the warrant or order in a prominent place in according with the Police and Criminal Evidence Act, s.16(7) and Home Office Circular 54/1991, para. 35.

Applications for warrants may be made *ex parte* with leave of the court (r. 4(4)(c)); and be heard by a single magistrate (r. 2(5)).

Abduction of children in care etc.

49.—(1) A person shall be guilty of an offence if, knowingly and without lawful authority or reasonable excuse, he—

(a) takes a child to whom this section applies away from the responsible person;

(b) keeps such a child away from the responsible person; or
(c) induces, assists or incites such a child to run away or stay away from the responsible person.

(2) This section applies in relation to a child who is—
(a) in care;
(b) the subject of an emergency protection order; or
(c) in police protection,

and in this section "the responsible person" means any person who for the time being has care of him by virtue of the care order, the emergency protection order, or section 46, as the case may be.

(3) A person guilty of an offence under this section shall be liable on summary conviction to imprisonment for a term not exceeding six months, or to a fine not exceeding level 5 on the standard scale, or to both.

DEFINITIONS

"child": s.105(1).
"emergency protection order": s.44(4).
"in care": s.105(1).
"in police protection": s.46(2).
"responsible person": s.49(2).

GENERAL NOTE

This section re-enacts with modifications the C.C.A. 1980, ss.13, 14, and 16. It makes it an offence (summary conviction: level 5 fine and/or six months' imprisonment) to remove from a responsible person, keep away, or induce to leave, a child who is subject to a care order, an emergency protection order or in police protection (subs. (1)). It does not apply to children who are merely accommodated under section 20 or being assessed under a child assessment order. However Department of Health *Guidance*, Vol. 1, para. 4.90 states that the police should be informed promptly about all children who abscond or are abducted.

Subs. (1)

Without lawful authority or reasonable excuse: This exception is extended to all of the offences in subsection (1).

Recovery of abducted children, etc.

50.—(1) Where it appears to the court that there is reason to believe that a child to whom this section applies—
(a) has been unlawfully taken away or is being unlawfully kept away from the responsible person;
(b) has run away or is staying away from the responsible person; or
(c) is missing,

the court may make an order under this section ("a recovery order").

(2) This section applies to the same children to whom section 49 applies and in this section "the responsible person" has the same meaning as in section 49.

(3) A recovery order—
   (a) operates as a direction to any person who is in a position to do so to produce the child on request to any authorised person;
   (b) authorises the removal of the child by any authorised person;
   (c) requires any person who has information as to the child's whereabouts to disclose that information, if asked to do so, to a constable or an officer of the court;
   (d) authorises a constable to enter any premises specified in the order and search for the child, using reasonable force if necessary.

(4) The court may make a recovery order only on the application of—
   (a) any person who has parental responsibility for the child by virtue of a care order or emergency protection order; or
   (b) where the child is in police protection, the designated officer.

(5) A recovery order shall name the child and—
   (a) any person who has parental responsibility for the child by virtue of a care order or emergency protection order; or
   (b) where the child is in police protection, the designated officer.

(6) Premises may only be specified under subsection (3)(d) if it appears to the court that there are reasonable grounds for believing the child to be on them.

(7) In this section—
   "an authorised person" means—
   (a) any person specified by the court;
   (b) any constable;
   (c) any person who is authorised—
      (i) after the recovery order is made; and
      (ii) by a person who has parental responsibility for the child by virtue of a care order or an emergency protection order,
      to exercise any power under a recovery order; and
   "the designated officer" means the officer designated for the purposes of section 46.

(8) Where a person is authorised as mentioned in subsection (7)(c)—
   (a) the authorisation shall identify the recovery order; and
   (b) any person claiming to be so authorised shall, if asked to do so,
produce some duly authenticated document showing that he is so authorised.

(9) A person shall be guilty of an offence if he intentionally obstructs an authorised person exercising the power under subsection (3)(b) to remove a child.

(10) A person guilty of an offence under this section shall be liable on summary conviction to a fine not exceeding level 3 on the standard scale.

(11) No person shall be excused from complying with any request made under subsection (3)(c) on the ground that complying with it might incriminate him or his spouse of an offence; but a statement or admission made in complying shall not be admissible in evidence against either of them in proceedings for an offence other than perjury.

(12) Where a child is made the subject of a recovery order whilst being looked after by a local authority, any reasonable expenses incurred by an authorised person in giving effect to the order shall be recoverable from the authority.

(13) A recovery order shall have effect in Scotland as if it had been made by the Court of Session and as if that court had had jurisdiction to make it.

(14) In this section "the court," in relation to Northern Ireland, means a magistrates' court within the meaning of the Magistrates' Courts (Northern Ireland) Order 1981.

DEFINITIONS
"authorised person": s.50(7).
"care order": s.31(11).
"child": ss.49(2), 105(1).
"emergency protection order": s.44(4).
"local authority": s.105(1).
"looked after by a local authority": s.22(1).
"person who has parental responsibility by virtue of a care order": s.33(3).
"person who has parental responsibility by virtue of an emergency protection order": s.44(1)(4).
"police protection": s.46(2).
"recovery order": s.50.
"responsible person": s.49(2).
"the court": ss.50(14), 92(7).
"the designated officer": ss.46(3)(e), 50(7).

GENERAL NOTE
This section amends and clarifies the law relating to recovery of children absent from care which is found in C.Y.P.A. 1969, s.32, as amended by Sched. 12, para. 27 and C.C.A. 1980, ss.15 and 16. It only applies to children subject to care orders (including interim orders), emergency protection orders or in police protection (subs. (2)). In other cases the inherent jurisdiction of the High Court and the powers under the Family Law Act 1986, ss.33 and 34, apply. The power to arrest a child absent from care without warrant is supplemented by the power to make a recovery order (subs. (1)), on the application of the person with parental responsibility by virtue of the emergency protection order or care order or the designated officer (subs. (4)). A recovery order directs any person who is able to produce the child; it authorises removal of the child by an authorised person; it requires any person who has information to disclose it to a constable and authorises a constable to search specified premises (subss. (3) and (6)). It is an offence (summary conviction: level 3 fine) intentionally to obstruct an authorised person removing the child (subs. (9)). A person required to provide information cannot refuse on the grounds of self-incrimination but his statement is only admissible in proceedings against him for perjury (subs. (11)). Recovery orders have effect throughout the U.K. (subss. (13)) and (14)).

Guidance on the use of recovery orders is provided in *Guidance*, Vol. 1, paras. 4.90 *et seq*. There is no exemption from the recovery provisions for children in "safe houses" but the Government expects that recovery orders will not be needed. If an order is sought, the organisation running the "safe house" will have to be informed so that they can attend and argue against recovery. If an order is made, it must be obeyed (subs. (9)). If those running the "safe house" wish to take steps to prevent harm to the child, they will be able to seek an emergency protection order, but a child will not be able to be held compulsorily in a "safe house" (*per* David Mellor, Minister of Health (Standing Committee B, col. 542, June 13, 1989)).

Running away from care (or accommodation) is a frequent occurrence—a third of the estimated 43,000 runaways each year are from the care system. NCH, *Runaways, exploding the Myths* (1992); the *Utting Report* (1991) notes that runaways are explicitly rejecting the care system—often because of problems (abuse or distance from home) with their placement. Punishment on return rather than a welcoming atmosphere may encourage running away and make children fearful of returning (paras. 3.54–7).

Subs. (1)

This is wider than section 49(1) in that a recovery order may be made where no offence has been committed.

Unlawfully: This applies if an offence under section 49 of this Act or section 2 of the Child Abduction Act 1984 has been committed.

May make an order: Section 1(1) applies. If the child is in a safe house and satisfactory arrangements can be made between the organisation and the local authority, an order would not be necessary. Where a child repeatedly returns home and is not in danger then an order may be counter-productive.

Subs. (12)

The Children (Prescribed Orders Northern Ireland Guernsey and Isle of Man) Regulations 1991 (S.I. 1991 No. 2032) make provision for the transfer of recovery orders from England and Wales to Northern Ireland or the Isle of Man (and *vice versa*) (regs. 6 and 7). There are currently no comparable provisions relating to the Channel Islands. See also *Guidance*, Vol. 7, paras. 4.13–4.21.

Refuges for children at risk

51.—(1) Where it is proposed to use a voluntary home or registered children's home to provide a refuge for children who appear to be at risk of harm, the Secretary of State may issue a certificate under this section with respect to that home.

(2) Where a local authority or voluntary organisation arrange for a foster parent to provide such a refuge, the Secretary of State may issue a certificate under this section with respect to that foster parent.

(3) In subsection (2) "foster parent" means a person who is, or who from time to time is, a local authority foster parent or a foster parent with whom children are placed by a voluntary organisation.

(4) The Secretary of State may by regulations—
   (a) make provision as to the manner in which certificates may be issued;
   (b) impose requirements which must be complied with while any certificate is in force; and
   (c) provide for the withdrawal of certificates in prescribed circumstances.

(5) Where a certificate is in force with respect to a home, none of the provisions mentioned in subsection (7) shall apply in relation to any person providing a refuge for any child in that home.

(6) Where a certificate is in force with respect to a foster parent, none of those provisions shall apply in relation to the provision by him of a refuge for any child in accordance with arrangements made by the local authority or voluntary organisation.

(7) The provisions are—

(a) section 49;
(b) section 71 of the Social Work (Scotland) Act 1968 (harbouring children who have absconded from residential establishments, etc.), so far as it applies in relation to anything done in England and Wales;
(c) section 32(3) of the Children and Young Persons Act 1969 (compelling, persuading, inciting or assisting any person to be absent from detention, etc.), so far as it applies in relation to anything done in England and Wales;
(d) section 2 of the Child Abduction Act 1984.

DEFINITIONS
"foster parent": s.51(3).
"local authority": s.105(1).
"local authority foster parent": s.23(3), (4).
"registered children's home": s.63.
"voluntary home": s.60.
"voluntary organisation": s.105(1).

REGULATIONS
The Refuges (Children's Homes and Foster Placements) Regulations 1991 (S.I. 1991 No. 1507).

GENERAL NOTE
This section empowers the Secretary of State to issue certificates to voluntary homes, registered homes (subs. (1)) and foster parents (subs. (2)) which will exempt them from the offences, listed in subsection (7), of harbouring, etc., children for whom they are providing a refuge. It is intended to enable "safe houses" legally to provide care for children who are absent from local authority accommodation or from home without permission. There was concern that those running such facilities, notably the Children's Society, could be liable for prosecution, and that criminal liability would lead to children being removed from the refuge, or their whereabouts being discovered. Also, that lack of regulation could lead to inadequate assistance or abuse of this group of vulnerable children.

It will still be possible to obtain a recovery order to remove a child who has run to a safe house under section 50 but not for the local authority to obtain transfer of any emergency protection order (S.I. 1991 No. 1414, reg. 5).

Subs. (4)
The Refuges (Children's Homes and Foster Placements) Regulations 1991 (S.I. 1991 No. 1507) control the conduct of certificated refuges. Refuges which are homes must also comply with Part II of the Children's Homes Regulations 1991 (S.I. 1991 No. 1506) (see notes to s.53). Foster carers who act as refuge providers must comply with the Foster Placement (Children) Regulations 1991 (S.I. 1991 No. 910) (see notes to s.23). Children may not be provided with a refuge unless it appears that they are at risk of harm without it (reg. 3(1)). The provider must inform the designated police officer as soon as possible and within 24 hours of the child's name and last permanent address (if known) and provide a telephone number where the provider may be contacted (reg. 3(3)). He must also provide the names and addresses of the child's parents, etc., or carers (termed responsible persons) within 24 hours of discovery of this (reg. 3(5)). The designated officer has the duty of informing the responsible persons that the child is in a refuge and providing the telephone number; he must not disclose the address (reg. 3(7)). The designated officer must also be notified when the child leaves the refuge (reg. 3(8)). Where the provider breaches regulation 3 or the other relevant regulations, or he or an assistant is convicted of any criminal offence the Secretary of State may withdraw the certificate (reg. 4).

The limits for refuge provision are a period of 14 days or 21 days in any three months (reg. 3(9)).

Rules and regulations

52.—(1) Without prejudice to section 93 or any other power to make such rules, rules of court may be made with respect to the procedure to be followed in connection with proceedings under this Part.

(2) The rules may, in particular make provision—
  (a) as to the form in which any application is to be made or direction is to be given;
  (b) prescribing the persons who are to be notified of—
    (i) the making, or extension, of an emergency protection order; or
    (ii) the making of an application under section 45(4) or (8) or 46(7); and
  (c) as to the content of any such notification and the manner in which, and person by whom, it is to be given.

(3) The Secretary of State may by regulations provide that, where—
  (a) an emergency protection order has been made with respect to a child;
  (b) the applicant for the order was not the local authority within whose area the child is ordinarily resident; and
  (c) that local authority are of the opinion that it would be in the child's best interests for the applicant's responsibilities under the order to be transferred to them, that authority shall (subject to their having complied with any requirements imposed by the regulations) be treated, for the purposes of this Act, as though they and not the original applicant had applied for, and been granted, the order.

(4) Regulations made under subsection (3) may, in particular, make provision as to—
  (a) the considerations to which the local authority shall have regard in forming an opinion as mentioned in subsection (3)(c); and
  (b) the time at which responsibility under any emergency protection order is to be treated as having been transferred to a local authority.

DEFINITIONS

"emergency protection order": s.44(4).
"local authority": s.105(1).

REGULATIONS

The Emergency Protection Order (Transfer of Responsibilities) Regulations 1991 (S.I. 1991 No. 1414)

GENERAL NOTE

The rules relating to applications for emergency protection orders are discussed with S.I. 1991 No. 1414 which empowers local authorities to take over emergency protection orders at p. 134 above.

Part VI

Community Homes

Provision of community homes by local authorities

53.—(1) Every local authority shall make such arrangements as they consider appropriate for securing that homes ("community homes") are available—
  (a) for the care and accommodation of children looked after by them; and
  (b) for purposes connected with the welfare of children (whether or not looked after by them),
and may do so jointly with one or more other local authorities.

(2) In making such arrangements, a local authority shall have regard to the need for ensuring the availability of accommodation—
  (a) of different descriptions; and
  (b) which is suitable for different purposes and the requirements of different descriptions of children.

(3) A community home may be a home—
  (a) provided, managed, equipped and maintained by a local authority; or
  (b) provided by a voluntary organisation but in respect of which a local authority and the organisation—
    (i) propose that, in accordance with an instrument of management, the management, equipment and maintenance of the home shall be the responsibility of the local authority; or
    (ii) so propose that the management, equipment and maintenance of the home shall be the responsibility of the voluntary organisation.

(4) Where a local authority are to be responsible for the management of a community home provided by a voluntary organisation, the authority shall designate the home as a controlled community home.

(5) Where a voluntary organisation are to be responsible for the management of a community home provided by the organisation, the local authority shall designate the home as an assisted community home.

(6) Schedule 4 shall have effect for the purpose of supplementing the provisions of this Part.

DEFINITIONS

  "assisted community home": s.53(5).
  "child looked after by the local authority": s.22(1).
  "community home": s.53.
  "controlled community home": s.53(4).
  "instrument of management": Sched. 4.

"local authority": s.105(1).
"voluntary organisation": s.105(1).

REGULATIONS

The Children's Homes Regulations 1991 (S.I. 1991 No. 1506) issued under the power in Schedule 4, paragraph 4.

GENERAL NOTE

This section imposes a duty on local authorities to ensure that community homes are available for the care and accommodation of children they are looking after and for purposes connected with the welfare of children. Subsections (1) to (5) re-enact with minor drafting amendments C.C.A. 1980, s.31. These provisions are supplemented by Schedule 4 which replaces sections 35–39 of the C.C.A. 1980, ss. 35-39. Paragraphs 1 and 2 permit the Secretary of State to make instruments of management for homes which are assisted or controlled community homes. Paragraph 3 makes further rules about the management, equipment and maintenance of such homes. Paragraph 4 gives the Secretary of State wide powers to make regulations.

The Children's Homes Regulations 1991 (S.I. 1991 No. 1506) apply to community homes, voluntary homes and registered children's homes, referred to collectively as children's homes. They impose obligations on the person or authority responsible for providing the home, termed the responsible authority (regs. 2 and 3). A copy of the regulations and guidance must be kept at each home (reg. 18). They replace the Administration of Children's Homes Regulations 1951, the Community Homes Regulations 1972 and the Children's Homes (Control and Discipline) Regulations 1990.

The responsible authority must compile and maintain a written statement of the purpose and function of the home which must be made available to staff, parents, children and those placing children in the home (reg. 4 and Sched. 1). Homes must be adequately staffed and provide suitable accommodation for each child living there. In particular, homes must have facilities for children to meet privately with parents, relatives, friends, their solicitor, guardian ad litem, independent visitor, etc., and a pay phone where children can make and receive calls in private (regs. 5–7). Certain disciplinary measures are forbidden; these include corporal punishment, deprivation of food, drink or sleep, restrictions of contact or communication with parents, relatives, friends, social worker, guardian ad litem, solicitor or independent visitor and fines. Confining children to their rooms is only permitted in accordance with S.I. 1991 Nos. 1505 and 2034 (see notes on s.25). Disciplinary measures must be recorded within 24 hours of their use (reg. 8). The responsible authority must make provision for storing medicines (reg. 9); for feeding children including cooking facilities for children (reg. 12); and to enable children to purchase clothes (reg. 13). It must give the fire authority written details of the home's location, size and use. It must take adequate fire precautions (reg. 14). It must ensure that each child can practice his religion (reg. 11).

Responsible authorities must maintain confidential records in respect of each child accommodated in their homes (regs. 15 and 17, Scheds. 2 and 3). Most records must be maintained for 75 years; 15 years for children dying under age 18. Guardians ad litem must be allowed access to records (reg. 16 and s.42). The responsible authority must notify the parents, etc., the area local authority and the registration authority of all significant events, e.g. death, serious accident, illness or other harm to a child and misconduct by a member of staff. District Health authorities must also be notified except of misconduct. The Secretary of State must be informed of deaths, misconduct and serious harm (reg. 19). The responsible authority must have a written procedure relating to absence without authority (reg. 19, see also notes on s.50). Regulation 21 sets out the procedure to be followed where the person in charge of a voluntary home or registered home is absent for four weeks or more. Where the person carrying on a voluntary or registered children's home is not the officer in charge he must arrange for monthly visits and written reports on the conduct of the home (reg. 22).

Regulation 23 empowers the Secretary of State to give and revoke directions to a local authority or a voluntary organisation providing an assisted community home to accommodate a child, etc.

Regulation 24 and Schedule 4 set out the requirements for the registration of voluntary homes. Voluntary homes must also provide the information in Schedule 7 as required by Schedule 5, paragraph 6 of the Act.

Part IV of the regulations applies only to registered children's homes. It requires the responsible authority to give information when applying for registration or its cancellation and when there is a change of the person in charge (regs. 25, 29 and 30). It empowers the registering authority to limit the number of children accommodated in the home (reg. 26) and requires it to inspect the home on application, annually and on at least one further occasion each year (regs. 27 and 28).

Part VII sets out the duties of local authorities to visit children in registered children's homes and voluntary homes. Visits must take place within 28 days of notification of placement, 14 days of representations requiring a visit and within seven days of receiving information that a child's welfare is not being safeguarded. Arrangements for further visits are at the local authority's discretion but must occur within six months or 28 days if they have been informed that the child's welfare is not being safeguarded. Each visit should involve seeing the child alone, reading case papers and providing a written report (regs. 32–34).

Guidance on these regulations is contained in *Guidance*, Vol. 4, Chap. 1; for further information on the use of residential care and current policy issues see the *Utting Report*.

Directions that premises be no longer used for community home

54.—(1) Where it appears to the Secretary of State that—
   (a) any premises used for the purposes of a community home are unsuitable for those purposes; or
   (b) the conduct of a community home—
      (i) is not in accordance with regulations made by him under paragraph 4 of Schedule 4; or
      (ii) is otherwise unsatisfactory,

he may, by notice in writing served on the responsible body, direct that as from such date as may be specified in the notice the premises shall not be used for the purposes of a community home.

(2) Where—
   (a) the Secretary of State has given a direction under subsection (1); and
   (b) the direction has not been revoked,

he may at any time by order revoke the instrument of management for the home concerned.

(3) For the purposes of subsection (1), the responsible body—
   (a) in relation to a community home provided by a local authority, is that local authority;
   (b) in relation to a controlled community home, is the local authority specified in the home's instrument of management; and
   (c) in relation to an assisted community home,

is the voluntary organisation by which the home is provided.

DEFINITIONS

"assisted community home": s.53(5).
"community home": s.53(1).
"controlled community home": s.53(4).
"instrument of management": Sched. 4, Pt. I.
"responsible body": s.48(3), Sched. 4, para. 3(3).
"voluntary organisation": s.105(1).

GENERAL NOTE

This re-enacts, with minor drafting amendments, C.C.A. 1980, s.40. It permits the Secretary of State to direct that premises cease to be used as a community home.

Determination of disputes relating to controlled and assisted community homes

55.—(1) Where any dispute relating to a controlled community home arises between the local authority specified in the home's instrument of management and—

(a) the voluntary organisation by which the home is provided; or

(b) any other local authority who have placed, or desire or are required to place, in the home a child who is looked after by them,

the dispute may be referred by either party to the Secretary of State for his determination.

(2) Where any dispute relating to an assisted community home arises between the voluntary organisation by which the home is provided and any local authority who have placed, or desire to place, in the home a child who is looked after by them, the dispute may be referred by either party to the Secretary of State for his determination.

(3) Where a dispute is referred to the Secretary of State under this section he may, in order to give effect to his determination of the dispute, give such directions as he thinks fit to the local authority or voluntary organisation concerned.

(4) This section applies even though the matter in dispute may be one which, under or by virtue of Part II of Schedule 4, is reserved for the decision, or is the responsibility, of—

(a) the local authority specified in the home's instrument of management; or

(b) (as the case may be) the voluntary organisation by which the home is provided.

(5) Where any trust deed relating to a controlled or assisted community home contains provision whereby a bishop or any other ecclesiastical or denominational authority has power to decide questions relating to religious instruction given in the home, no dispute which is capable of being dealt with in accordance with that provision shall be referred to the Secretary of State under this section.

(6) In this Part "trust deed," in relation to a voluntary home, means any instrument (other than an instrument of management) regulating—

(a) the maintenance, management or conduct of the home; or

(b) the constitution of a body of managers or trustees of the home.

DEFINITIONS

"assisted community home": s.53(5).
"child looked after by a local authority": s.22(1).
"controlled community home": s.53(4).
"home": Sched. 4, para. 3(3).
"instrument of management": Sched. 4, Pt. I.

"local authority": s.105(1).
"managers": Sched. 4, para. 3(3).
"trust deed": s.55(6).
"voluntary home": s.60(3).
"voluntary organisation": s.105(1).

GENERAL NOTE

Subsections (1)–(5) re-enact with minor drafting amendments C.C.A. 1980, s.42. They provide for certain disputes relating to controlled or assisted community homes to be determined by the Secretary of State. Subsection (6) re-enacts C.C.A. 1980, s.36(5).

Discontinuance of voluntary organisation of controlled or assisted community home

56.—(1) The voluntary organisation by which a controlled or assisted community home is provided shall not cease to provide the home except after giving to the Secretary of State and the local authority specified in the home's instrument of management not less than two years' notice in writing of their intention to do so.

(2) A notice under subsection (1) shall specify the date from which the voluntary organisation intend to cease to provide the home as a community home.

(3) Where such a notice is given and is not withdrawn before the date specified in it, the home's instrument of management shall cease to have effect on that date and the home shall then cease to be a controlled or assisted community home.

(4) Where a notice is given under subsection (1) and the home's managers give notice in writing to the Secretary of State that they are unable or unwilling to continue as its managers until the date specified in the subsection (1) notice, the Secretary of State may by order—
    (a) revoke the home's instrument of management; and
    (b) require the local authority who were specified in that instrument to conduct the home until—
        (i) the date specified in the subsection (1) notice; or
        (ii) such earlier date (if any) as may be specified for the purposes of this paragraph in the order,
as if it were a community home provided by the local authority.

(5) Where the Secretary of State imposes a requirement under subsection (4)(b)—
    (a) nothing in the trust deed for the home shall affect the conduct of the home by the local authority;
    (b) the Secretary of State may by order direct that for the purposes of any provision specified in the direction and made by or under any enactment relating to community homes (other than this section) the home shall, until the date or earlier date specified as mentioned in subsection (4)(b), be treated as a controlled or assisted community home;
    (c) except in so far as the Secretary of State so directs, the home shall until that date be treated for the purposes of

any such enactment as a community home provided by the local authority; and

(d) on the date or earlier date specified as mentioned in subsection (4)(b) the home shall cease to be a community home.

DEFINITIONS

"assisted community home": s.53(5).
"community home": s.53(1).
"controlled community home": s.53(4).
"home": Sched. 4, para. 3(3).
"instrument of management": Sched. 4, Pt. I.
"local authority": s.105(1).
"managers": Sched. 4, para. 3(3).
"trust deed": s.55(6).
"voluntary organisation" s.105(1).

GENERAL NOTE

This re-enacts with minor drafting amendments C.C.A. 1980, s.43. It requires voluntary organisations providing controlled or assisted community homes to give two years' notice before they stop providing a home.

Closure by local authority of controlled or assisted community home

57.—(1) The local authority specified in the instrument of management for a controlled or assisted community home may give—

(a) the Secretary of State; and

(b) the voluntary organisation by which the home is provided,

not less than two years' notice in writing of their intention to withdraw their designation of the home as a controlled or assisted community home.

(2) A notice under subsection (1) shall specify the date ('the specified date') on which the designation is to be withdrawn.

(3) Where—

(a) a notice is given under subsection (1) in respect of a controlled or assisted community home;

(b) the home's managers give notice in writing to the Secretary of State that they are unable or unwilling to continue as managers until the specified date; and

(c) the managers' notice is not withdrawn,

the Secretary of State may by order revoke the home's instrument of management from such date earlier than the specified date as may be specified in the order.

(4) Before making an order under subsection (3), the Secretary of State shall consult the local authority and the voluntary organisation.

(5) Where a notice has been given under subsection (1) and is not withdrawn, the home's instrument of management shall cease to have effect on—

(a) the specified date; or

(b) where an earlier date has been specified under subsection (3), that earlier date,

and the home shall then cease to be a community home.

DEFINITIONS

"assisted community home": s.53(5).
"controlled community home": s.53(4).
"community home": s.53(1).
"home": Sched. 4, para. 3(3).
"instrument of management": Sched. 4, Pt. I.
"local authority": s.105(1).
"managers": Sched. 4, para. 3(3).
"the specified date": s.57(2).
"voluntary organisation": s.105(1).

GENERAL NOTE

This re-enacts with minor drafting amendments C.C.A. 1980, s.43A. It permits local authorities to withdraw the designation of a community as controlled or assisted and requires them to give two years' notice of their intention to do so.

Financial provisions applicable on cessation of controlled or assisted community home or disposal, etc., of premises

58.—(1) Where—
  (a) the instrument of management for a controlled or assisted community home is revoked or otherwise ceases to have effect under section 54(2), 56(3) or (4)(a) or 57(3) or (5); or
  (b) any premises used for the purposes of such a home are (at any time after 13th January 1987) disposed of, or put to use otherwise than for those purposes,
the proprietor shall become liable to pay compensation ('the appropriate compensation') in accordance with this section.

(2) Where the instrument of management in force at the relevant time relates—
  (a) to a controlled community home; or
  (b) to an assisted community home which, at any time before the instrument came into force, was a controlled community home,
the appropriate compensation is a sum equal to that part of the value of any premises which is attributable to expenditure incurred in relation to the premises, while the home was a controlled community home, by the authority who were then the responsible authority.

(3) Where the instrument of management in force at the relevant time relates—
  (a) to an assisted community home; or
  (b) to a controlled community home which, at any time before the instrument came into force, was an assisted community home,
the appropriate compensation is a sum equal to that part of the value of the premises which is attributable to the expenditure of money provided by way of grant under section 82, section 65 of the Children and Young Persons Act 1969 or section 82 of the Child Care Act 1980.

(4) Where the home is, at the relevant time, conducted in premises which formerly were used as an approved school or were an approved probation hostel or home, the appropriate compensation is a sum equal to that part of the value of the premises which is attributable to the expenditure—

(a) of sums paid towards the expenses of the managers of an approved school under section 104 of the Children and Young Persons Act 1933; or

(b) of sums paid under section 51(3)(c) of the Powers of Criminal Courts Act 1973 in relation to expenditure on approved probation hostels or homes.

(5) The appropriate compensation shall be paid—

(a) in the case of compensation payable under subsection (2), to the authority who were the responsible authority at the relevant time; and

(b) in any other case, to the Secretary of State.

(6) In this section—

"disposal" includes the grant of a tenancy and any other conveyance, assignment, transfer, grant, variation or extinguishment of an interest in or right over land, whether made by instrument or otherwise;

"premises" means any premises or part of premises (including land) used for the purposes of the home and belonging to the proprietor;

"the proprietor" means—

(a) the voluntary organisation by which the home is, at the relevant time, provided; or

(b) if the premises are not, at the relevant time, vested in that organisation, the persons in whom they are vested;

"the relevant time" means the time immediately before the liability to pay arises under subsection (1); and

"the responsible authority" means the local authority specified in the instrument of management in question.

(7) For the purposes of this section an event of a kind mentioned in subsection (1)(b) shall be taken to have occurred—

(a) in the case of a disposal, on the date on which the disposal was completed or, in the case of a disposal which is effected by a series of transactions, the date on which the last of those transactions was completed;

(b) in the case of premises which are put to different use, on the date on which they first begin to be put to their new use.

(8) The amount of any sum payable under this section shall be determined in accordance with such arrangements—

(a) as may be agreed between the voluntary organisation by which the home is, at the relevant time, provided and the responsible authority or (as the case may be) the Secretary of State; or

(b) in default of agreement, as may be determined by the Secretary of State.

(9) With the agreement of the responsible authority or (as the case may be) the Secretary of State, the liability to pay any sum under this section may be discharged, in whole or in part, by the transfer of any premises.

(10) This section has effect regardless of—

(a) anything in any trust deed for a controlled or assisted community home;

Financial Provisions Applicable on Cessation

(b) the provisions of any enactment or instrument governing the disposition of the property of a voluntary organisation.

DEFINITIONS
"appropriate compensation": s.58(1)–(4).
"assisted community home": s.53(5).
"controlled community home": s.53(4).
"community home": s.53(1).
"disposal": s.58(6).
"instrument of management": Sched. 4, Pt. I.
"local authority": s.105(1).
"premises": s.58(6).
"proprietor": s.58(6).
"relevant time": s.58(6).
"responsible authority": s.58(6).
"trust deed": s.55(6).
"voluntary organisation": s.105(1).

GENERAL NOTE
This re-enacts with substantial re-drafting C.C.A. 1980, s.44. It requires proprietors of controlled or assisted community homes which close, to repay any increase in the value of the premises which is attributable to the expenditure of public money ("the appropriate compensation") to the responsible authority or the Secretary of State. As under the 1980 Act, sums repaid to the Secretary of State under this section have to be paid to the Consolidated Fund (s.106(2)). Where a local authority receives a grant to provide secure accommodation somewhere other than in an assisted community home and the secure accommodation ceases to be used, the local authority must repay the grant (s.82(3)). Voluntary organisations can receive grants from the Secretary of State for the establishment, maintenance or improvement of assisted community homes under section 82(4). There is a further power for the Secretary of State to provide special facilities in section 82(5).

PART VII

VOLUNTARY HOMES AND VOLUNTARY ORGANISATIONS

Provision of accommodation by voluntary organisations

59.—(1) Where a voluntary organisation provide accommodation for a child, they shall do so by—
    (a) placing him (subject to subsection (2)) with—
        (i) a family;
        (ii) a relative of his; or
        (iii) any other suitable person,
    on such terms as to payment by the organisation and otherwise as the organisation may determine;
    (b) maintaining him in a voluntary home;
    (c) maintaining him in a community home;
    (d) maintaining him in a registered children's home;
    (e) maintaining him in a home provided by the Secretary of State under section 82(5) on such terms as the Secretary of State may from time to time determine; or
    (f) making such other arrangements (subject to subsection (3)) as seem appropriate to them.

(2) The Secretary of State may make regulations as to the placing of children with foster parents by voluntary organisations and the regulations may, in particular, make provision which (with any necessary modifications) is similar to the provision that may be made under section 23(2)(a).

(3) The Secretary of State may make regulations as to the arrangements which may be made under subsection (1)(f) and the regulations may in particular make provision which (with any necessary modifications) is similar to the provision that may be made under section 23(2)(f).

(4) The Secretary of State may make regulations requiring any voluntary organisation who are providing accommodation for a child—
   (a) to review his case;
   (b) to consider any representations (including any complaint) made to them by any person falling within a prescribed class of person,
in accordance with the provisions of the regulations.

(5) Regulations under subsection (4) may in particular make provision which (with any necessary modifications) is similar to the provision that may be made under section 26.

(6) Regulations under subsection (2) to (4) may provide that any person who, without reasonable excuse, contravenes or fails to comply with a regulation shall be guilty of an offence and liable on summary conviction to a fine not exceeding level 4 on the standard scale.

DEFINITIONS
  "child": s.105(1).
  "community home": s.53(1).
  "registered children's home": s.63.
  "relative": s.105(1).
  "voluntary home": s.60(3).
  "voluntary organisation": s.105(1).

REGULATIONS
  Arrangements for Placement of Children (General) Regulations 1991 (S.I. 1991 No. 890) (see notes to s.23);
  Foster Placement (Children) Regulations 1991 (S.I. 1991 No. 910) (see notes to s.23);
  Representations Procedures (Children) Regulations 1991 (S.I. 1991 No. 894) (see notes to s.26);
  Review of Children's Cases Regulations 1991 (S.I. 1991 No. 895) (see notes to s.26);
  Children (Representations, Placements and Reviews) (Miscellaneous Amendments) Regulations 1991 (S.I. 1991 No. 2033);
  Children's Homes Regulations 1991 (S.I. 1991 No. 1506) (see notes to s.53).

GENERAL NOTE
  This section sets out the powers of voluntary organisations to provide accommodation for children. It imposes equivalent duties on voluntary organisations as are imposed on local authorities by section 23 so that neither the children nor their parents receive a lesser standard of consideration than children looked after by local authorities. Notes on the regulations listed above provide further details of voluntary organisations' responsibilities.

Provision of Accommodation by Voluntary Organisations

Where a placement is arranged by a voluntary organisation for a child looked after by the local authority, the local authority will continue to be responsible for the placement (see ss.23 and 62(1)).

Registration and regulation of voluntary homes

60.—(1) No voluntary home shall be carried on unless it is registered in a register to be kept for the purposes of this section by the Secretary of State.

(2) The register may be kept by means of a computer.

(3) In this Act "voluntary home" means any home or other institution providing care and accommodation for children which is carried on by a voluntary organisation but does not include—

- (a) a nursing home, mental nursing home or residential care home [other than a small home].;
- (b) a school;
- (c) any health service hospital;
- (d) any community home;
- (e) any home or other institution provided, equipped and maintained by the Secretary of State; or
- (f) any home which is exempted by regulations made for the purposes of this section by the Secretary of State.

(4) Schedule 5 shall have effect for the purposes of supplementing the provisions of this Part.

AMENDMENT

The words in square brackets in subsection (3) were added by the Registered Homes (Amendment) Act 1991, s.2.

DEFINITIONS

"child": s.105(1).
"community home": s.53(1).
"health service hospital": s.105(1).
"mental nursing home": s.105(1).
"nursing home": s.105(1).
"residential care home": s.105(1).
"school": s.105(1).
"small home": s.105(1).
"voluntary home": s.60(3).
"voluntary organisation": s.105(1).

GENERAL NOTE

This section requires voluntary homes, defined in subsection (3), to be registered by the Secretary of State, as previously under C.C.A. 1980, s.57(1). Provisions as to registration are included in Schedule 5. The *Utting Report* has recommended that local authority children's homes (Community Homes) are made subject to regulatory inspection by the local authority's independent inspection units. Responsibility for registration and inspection of voluntary homes should be transferred from the Secretary of State and the social services inspectorate to individual local authorities (*Utting* paras. 71–75).

The Secretary of State has a power to inspect premises where children are being accommodated by or on behalf of a voluntary organisation under section 80(1)(c) and the children under section 80(6). There are also powers in relation to other premises (see s.80 below). He may also direct a voluntary organisation to provide information under section 80(4) and (5).

The definition of voluntary home previously found in C.C.A. 1980, s.56, has been clarified. The intention is to provide a coherent code relating to all establishments and private homes (except those provided by the child's family or close relatives) and the care and welfare of all children living there. Where an establishment is a voluntary home the Secretary of State is responsible for registration and inspection. Local authorities are responsible for registration and inspection of registered children's homes (Part VIII of the Act), private foster homes (Part IX of the Act), nursing homes, mental nursing homes and residential care homes (all under the Registered Homes Act 1984). Small homes, *i.e.* those which accommodate fewer than four people are partially exempted from the controls in the 1984 Act but must be registered and inspected as voluntary homes. For advice about inspection of homes see Social Services Inspectorate, *Inspecting for Quality* (1991). Local authorities also have responsibilities for safeguarding the welfare of all children in such homes (ss.62, 64(4), 67 and 86) and in independent schools (s.87) and children accommodated for a consecutive period of at least three months by a local education authority or health authority (s.85). Provision is made for community homes in Part VI and Schedule 4.

Part I of Schedule 5 contains the provisions relating to registration of voluntary homes previously found in C.C.A. 1980, ss.57(1)–(6), 57A–57D and 59. There are minor drafting amendments and the penalty for failure to notify the Secretary of State of the particulars required is now a level 2 offence (Sched. 5, para. 6(6)). Paragraph 7 empowers the Secretary of State to make regulations about voluntary homes and voluntary organisations. This power has been exercised to apply the Children's Homes Regulations 1991 (S.I. 1991 No. 1506) (see notes on s.53 above) and to preclude voluntary homes from providing secure accommodation (S.I. No. 1505, reg. 18) (see notes on s.25 above.)

Paragraph 8 permits the Secretary of State to make regulations disqualifying people from involvement with voluntary homes. This power has been exercised in The Disqualification for Caring for Children Regulations 1991 (S.I. 1991 No. 2094, reg. 3) (see notes on s.68 below.)

The provisions relating to service of notices in C.C.A. 1980, s.57(8)–(11), are now found in section 105(8)–(10).

Duties of voluntary organisations

61.—(1) Where a child is accommodated by, or on behalf of a voluntary organisation, it shall be the duty of the organisation—
    (a) to safeguard and promote his welfare;
    (b) to make such use of the services and facilities available for children cared for by their own parents as appears to the organisation reasonable in his case; and
    (c) to advise, assist and befriend him with a view to promoting his welfare when he ceases to be so accommodated.

(2) Before making any decision with respect to any such child the organisation shall, so far as is reasonably practicable, ascertain the wishes and feelings of—
    (a) the child;
    (b) his parents;
    (c) any person who is not a parent of his but who has parental responsibility for him; and
    (d) any other person whose wishes and feelings the organisation consider to be relevant,
regarding the matter to be decided.

(3) In making any such decision the organisation shall give due consideration—
    (a) having regard to the child's age and understanding, to such wishes and feelings of his as they have been able to ascertain;

(b) to such other wishes and feelings mentioned in subsection (2) as they have been able to ascertain; and
(c) to the child's religious persuasion, racial origin and cultural and linguistic background.

DEFINITIONS
"child": s.105(1).
"person who is not a parent but has parental responsibility": ss.5(6), 12(2), 33(3), 44(4).
"voluntary organisation": s.105(1).

GENERAL NOTE
This section imposes comparable duties on voluntary organisations accommodating children to those required of local authorities under sections 22(3)–(5) and 24(1). This is broader and more specific than the duty in C.C.A. 1980, s.64A, which it replaces. Additional duties are imposed in the regulations, see section 59.

Duties of local authorities

62.—(1) Every local authority shall satisfy themselves that any voluntary organisation providing accommodation—
    (a) within the authority's area for any child; or
    (b) outside that area for any child on behalf of the authority,
are satisfactorily safeguarding and promoting the welfare of the children so provided with accommodation.
(2) Every local authority shall arrange for children who are accommodated within their area by or on behalf of voluntary organisations to be visited, from time to time, in the interests of their welfare.
(3) The Secretary of State may make regulations—
    (a) requiring every child who is accommodated within a local authority's area, by or on behalf of a voluntary organisation, to be visited by an officer of the authority—
        (i) in prescribed circumstances; and
        (ii) on specified occasions or within specified periods; and
    (b) imposing requirements which must be met by any local authority, or officer of a local authority, carrying out functions under this section.
(4) Subsection (2) does not apply in relation to community homes.
(5) Where a local authority are not satisfied that the welfare of any child who is accommodated by or on behalf of a voluntary organisation is being satisfactorily safeguarded or promoted they shall—
    (a) unless they consider that it would not be in the best interests of the child, take such steps as are reasonably practicable to secure that the care and accommodation of the child is undertaken by—
        (i) a parent of his;
        (ii) any person who is not a parent of his but who has parental responsibility for him; or
        (iii) a relative of his; and

(b) consider the extent to which (if at all) they should exercise any of their functions with respect to the child.

(6) Any person authorised by a local authority may, for the purpose of enabling the authority to discharge their duties under this section—
- (a) enter, at any reasonable time, and inspect any premises in which children are being accommodated as mentioned in subsection (1) or (2);
- (b) inspect any children there;
- (c) require any person to furnish him with such records of a kind required to be kept by regulations made under paragraph 7 of Schedule 5 (in whatever form they are held), or allow him to inspect such records, as he may at any time direct.

(7) Any person exercising the power conferred by subsection (6) shall, if asked to do so, produce some duly authenticated document showing his authority to do so.

(8) Any person authorised to exercise the power to inspect records conferred by subsection (6)—
- (a) shall be entitled at any reasonable time to have access to, and inspect and check the operation of, any computer and any associated apparatus or material which is or has been in use in connection with the records in question; and
- (b) may require—
  - (i) the person by whom or on whose behalf the computer is or has been so used; or
  - (ii) any person having charge of, or otherwise concerned with the operation of, the computer, apparatus or material,

to afford him such assistance as he may reasonably require.

(9) Any person who intentionally obstructs another in the exercise of any power conferred by subsection (6) or (8) shall be guilty of an offence and liable on summary conviction to a fine not exceeding level 3 on the standard scale.

DEFINITIONS
"child": s.105(1).
"community home": s.53(1).
"functions": s.105(1).
"local authority": s.105(1).
"person who is not a parent but has parental responsibility": ss.5(6), 12(2), 33(3), 44(4).
"relative": s.105(1).
"voluntary organisation": s.105(1).

REGULATIONS
The Foster Placement (Children) Regulations 1991 (S.I. 1991 No. 910, regs. 32–34); The Children's Homes Regulations 1991 (S.I. 1991 No. 1506, regs. 15 and 16).

GENERAL NOTE
This section specifies the duties of local authorities with respect to children accommodated by voluntary organisations. It also applies, with the exception of subsection (3), to children's homes (see s.64(4)). It re-drafts and expands C.C.A. 1980, s.68.

Local authorities have a duty to satisfy themselves that voluntary organisations providing accommodation within their area are satisfactorily safeguarding and promoting the welfare of the children (subs. (1)). Concern about abuse in residential establishments makes it all the more important for local authorities to undertake their duties effectively. The *Utting Report* provides a useful background to this. Local authorities also have a duty to arrange for such children (except those in community homes (subs. (4)) to be visited in accordance with the regulations. This duty to visit extends to children boarding in non-maintained special schools; in such cases the Department of Health recommends that local authorities follow *Guidance*, Vol. 5, (Vol. 4, para. 1.177). These duties are additional to any they may owe under section 17 and Schedule 2, Part I, to children in need and under section 22 and Schedule 2, Part II to children accommodated in a voluntary home by or on behalf of a local authority. Subsection (5) imposes a qualified duty on the local authority to take action if a child's welfare is not being satisfactorily safeguarded. Where compulsory measures are necessary, the relevant powers are provided by regulations (see subs.(5) below) and Parts IV and V of this Act. Subsection (6) gives the local authority a power to inspect premises, the children themselves and records in order to carry out its duties. Subsection (8) extends this to having access to computer facilities. Subsection (9) provides that it is an offence (summary conviction: level 3 fine) intentionally to obstruct the exercise of the powers in subsections (6) or (8).

Local authorities are also under a duty to provide after-care for children accommodated by voluntary organisations under section 24(4). The voluntary organisation must notify the authority when a child over 16 leaves (s.24(12)).

Subs. (1)

On behalf of the authority: Such a child would be a child looked after by the authority under section 22. The power to accommodate such a child by placing him in a voluntary home is provided in section 23(2)(c). Where the voluntary organisation arranges a foster placement for a child looked after by the local authority, the foster parent is a local authority foster parent under section 23(3). S.I. 1991 No. 910, reg. 8 applies to such arrangements.

Subs. (2)

Visited: Children placed in foster homes by voluntary organisations must be visited within 28 days of placement; within 14 days of representations from the voluntary organisation; within seven days of being informed that the child's welfare is not being safeguarded, etc.; and where welfare is safeguarded at least every six months (reg. 15). The visits must be by an officer of the local authority. The child must be seen on each visit unless he is absent or this is not necessary; arrangements should be made to see absent children. Steps must be taken to discover whether the voluntary organisation is fulfilling its duties (reg. 16). Regulations 15 and 16 do not apply if the local authority has entered into an arrangement under regulation 8 for the voluntary organisation to provide its fostering service. Comparable provisions apply when the child is accommodated in a voluntary home; additionally the visiting officer must read all relevant case papers and write a report (S.I. 1991 No. 1506, regs. 32–34).

Subs. (5)

This limited duty does not apply where the child is being accommodated on behalf of a local authority. In such cases the local authority owes more onerous duties under Part III, particularly section 22. If the child is in need the local authority will have other duties under Schedule 2. If a foster placement appears detrimental, the local authority must remove the child (S.I. 1991 No. 910, reg. 7); no court order is required.

Not satisfied . . . being satisfactorily safeguarded: This is a lower threshold than the "significant harm" test in Parts IV and V.

Unless it would not be in the best interest of the child: This could cover situations where a mature child did not want to leave, where the parents or others were unwilling to provide a home or where any other home would be even less satisfactory. It would also allow a local authority to delay action until a convenient time, *e.g.* the end of the school year. If the child remains in a voluntary home he must be visited again within 28 days (S.I. 1991 No. 1506, reg. 33(3)).

Such steps as are reasonably practicable: This could include searching for the child's family.

Consider the extent . . . : Once the local authority is aware that the child is suffering or is likely to suffer "significant harm" its duty under section 47 arises. It may then seek orders under Parts IV or V.

Subs. (6)

The comparable provision in C.C.A. 1980, s.68(2), was interpreted in *Clarke Hall & Morrison On Children*, para. A 463, as not providing a right of entry without warrant. A warrant could be obtained under section 102 or attached to an emergency protection order under section 48(9).

At any reasonable time: This is not defined. Any time when the children are up could be reasonable. Entry at other times would require an emergency protection order under section 44 and, if entry were refused, a warrant.

Subs. (9)

Intentionally obstructs: The word "intentionally" has been added to the offence in C.C.A. 1980, s.68(5). Anything which makes it more difficult for a person to carry out ohis duty may amount to obstruction. (*Rice v. Connolly* [1966] 2 Q.B. 414).

PART VIII

REGISTERED CHILDREN'S HOMES

Children not to be cared for and accommodated in unregistered children's homes

63.—(1) No child shall be cared for and provided with accommodation in a children's home unless the home is registered under this Part.

(2) The register may be kept by means of a computer.

(3) For the purposes of this Part, "a children's home"—

    (a) means a home which provides (or usually provides or is intended to provide) care and accommodation wholly or mainly for more than three children at any one time; but

    (b) does not include a home which is exempted by or under any of the following provisions of this section or by regulations made for the purposes of this subsection by the Secretary of State.

(4) A child is not cared for and accommodated in a children's home when he is cared for and accommodated by—

    (a) a parent of his;

    (b) a person who is not a parent of his but who has parental responsibility for him; or

    (c) any relative of his.

(5) A home is not a children's home for the purposes of this Part if it is—

    (a) a community home;

    (b) a voluntary home;

    (c) a residential care home, nursing home or mental nursing home [other than a small home];

    (d) a health service hospital;

(e) a home provided, equipped and maintained by the Secretary of State; or
(f) a school (but subject to subsection (6)).

(6) An independent school is a children's home if—
  (a) it provides accommodation for not more than fifty children; and
  (b) it is not approved by the Secretary of State under section 11(3)(a) of the Education Act 1981.

(7) A child shall not be treated as cared for and accommodated in a children's home when—
  (a) any person mentioned in subsection (4)(a) or (b) is living at the home; or
  (b) the person caring for him is doing so in his personal capacity and not in the course of carrying out his duties in relation to the home.

(8) In this Act "a registered children's home" means a children's home registered under this Part.

(9) In this section "home" includes any institution.

(10) Where any child is at any time cared for and accommodated in a children's home which is not a registered children's home, the person carrying on the home shall be—
  (a) guilty of an offence; and
  (b) liable to a fine not exceeding level 5 on the standard scale, unless he has a reasonable excuse.

(11) Schedule 6 shall have effect with respect to children's homes.

(12) Schedule 7 shall have effect for the purpose of setting out the circumstances in which a person may foster more than three children without being treated as carrying on a children's home.

AMENDMENT

The words in square brackets in section 63(5)(c) were added by the Registered Homes (Amendment) Act 1991, s.2(6).

DEFINITIONS

"child": s.105(1).
"children's home": s.63(3)–(9).
"community home": s.53(1).
"health service hospital": s.105(1).
"home": s.63(9).
"independent school": s.105(1).
"mental nursing home": s.105(1).
"nursing home": s.105(1).
"privately fostered child": s.66(1).
"registered children's home": s.63(8).
"residential care home": s.105(1).
"school": s.105(1).
"small home": s.105(1).
"voluntary home": s.60(3).
"voluntary organisation": s.105(1).

REGULATIONS

Children's Homes Regulations 1991 (S.I. 1991 No. 1506) (see notes to s.53);
Arrangements for Placement of Children (General) Regulations 1991 (S.I. 1991 No. 890) (see notes to s.23);

Review of Children's Cases Regulations 1991 (S.I. 1991 No. 895) (see notes to s.26);
Children (Representations, Placements and Reviews) (Miscellaneous Amendments) Regulations 1991 (S.I. 1991 No. 2033);
Representations Procedures (Children) Regulations 1991 (S.I. 1991 No. 894) (see notes to s.26).

GENERAL NOTE

All children's homes as defined in section 63(3)–(7) must now be registered with the local authority and comply with the regulations listed above. These provisions replace the unimplemented Children's Homes Act 1982.

Subss. (4)–(7)

Registered children's homes are those carried on by persons or by organisations which are not non-profit-making. Homes run by local authority and voluntary organisations are not registered children's homes but come under Parts VI and VII of the Act. Residential care homes, caring for four or more people come under the Registered Homes Act 1984, whereas only those with fewer children are regulated by this Act. Where there are three or fewer children, the carers will either be private foster parents (see Pt. IX) or carrying on a children's home which must be registered. Guidance on the distinction between a foster home and a children's home is given in *Guidance*, Vol. 3, para. 4.9. Health Service facilities, and nursing homes and mental nursing homes which have to register with the health authority, are not covered by these provisions. Some schools are also exempt. The Secretary of State has not exercised his power to exempt any homes from the registration requirement (subs. 3).

Children cared for and accommodated by their own families, *i.e.* those listed in subsection (4), are not cared for or accommodated in children's homes. Where the home is a children's home but a child lives there with a parent or person with parental responsibility, or is cared for by someone in a personal capacity, he is not treated as cared for, etc., in a children's home (subs. (7)) and thus the local authority's functions do not affect him.

An independent school: This is defined in the Education Act 1944 as "a school for five or more pupils which is not maintained by a local education authority or a school in respect of which grants are made. ... " Subsection (6) requires independent schools which are not approved to take children who have been statemented under the Education Act 1981, s.7, to register as children's homes if they accommodate not more than 50 children. It does not include non-maintained special schools; these are provided by voluntary organisations and come under sections 61 and 62 (*Guidance*, Vol. 4, para. 1.177). A school which is required to register must continue to register even if the number of pupils changes (Sched. 6, para. 1(10)). Independent boarding schools which are exempted from registering as children's homes are subject to local authority inspection under section 87. *Guidance*, Vol. 4, para. 1.10 notes that schools may have a very different ethos from children's homes even when they are required to register as children's homes. It suggests that local authorities should consider this when exercising their discretion and give close attention to those schools where children spend 52 weeks of the year; where most children have little contact with parents; and where most children are placed by local education authorities or social services departments. See also *Guidance*, Vol. 5, *Independent Schools*.

Subs. (10)

This offence (maximum penalty level 5 fine) is wider than that in the Children's Homes Act 1982, s.2(2), because of the duty to register all children's homes. Also, foster homes which exceed the usual fostering limit are treated as children's homes (see note to Sched. 7).

Reasonable excuse: A person who fails to register and who has exceeded the usual fostering limit temporarily may have an excuse.

Subs. (11)

Schedule 6, Part I contains provisions about registration previously found in the Children's Homes Act 1982, ss.4–8. Children's homes must be registered by the person carrying on the home with the local authority in whose area the home is situated (para.

1(1)). Applications must be made in the prescribed manner (para. 1(2)). The local authority must comply with the requirements of any regulations concerning applications and be satisfied that the home complies with requirements in paragraph 2 and any regulations made under Schedule 6, Part II. Paragraph 3 makes provision for annual review of registration; paragraph 4 for cancellation of registration. Paragraphs 5–7 deal with procedure and paragraph 8 provides for appeals to the Registered Homes Tribunal. If an application is refused or cancelled, no further application may be made for six months (para. 9). Part II empowers the Secretary of State to make regulations; this has been exercised to apply the regulations listed above to registered children's homes and placements in them. Registered children's homes may not provide secure accommodation (S.I. 1991 No. 1505, reg. 18).

Subs. (12)

Schedule 7 limits the number of children who may be fostered by any foster parent (including a private foster parent) to three, "the usual fostering limit" (para. 2), but does not prevent fostering a greater number who are all siblings (para. 3), or where the local authority for the foster parent's home area has given a written exemption (para. 4). "Siblings" is not defined and could include half brothers and sisters, step-brothers and sisters or even children brought up as brother and sister, *e.g.* cousins. Exemptions will apply to named children (para. 4(3)) but regulations may be made to provide for cases of urgency (para. 4(5)). It would seem that emergency placements under S.I 1991 No. 910, reg. 11 can be made even though no exemption has been granted. If the number is exceeded, except where permitted, the person is treated as carrying on a children's home (para. 5) and must comply with Part VIII. Local authorities are required to establish procedures for the consideration of exemptions. The complaints procedure established under section 26 applies, see S.I. 1991 No. 894, reg. 12 (see notes on s.26). Private foster parents may appeal to the court under Schedule 7, paragraph 8(1)(e), against a refusal to grant an exemption. Guidance on the numbers of children in foster homes is provided in *Guidance*, Vol. 3, paras. 4.6 *et seq.*

Welfare of children in children's homes

64.—(1) Where a child is accommodated in a children's home, it shall be the duty of the person carrying on the home to—
(a) safeguard and promote the child's welfare;
(b) make such use of the services and facilities available for children cared for by their own parents as appears to that person reasonable in the case of the child; and
(c) advise, assist and befriend him with a view to promoting his welfare when he ceases to be so accommodated.

(2) Before making any decision with respect to any such child the person carrying on the home shall, so far as is reasonably practicable, ascertain the wishes and feelings of—
(a) the child;
(b) his parents;
(c) any other person who is not a parent of his but who has parental responsibility for him; and
(d) any person whose wishes and feelings the person carrying on the home considers to be relevant,
regarding the matter to be decided.

(3) In making any such decision the person concerned shall give due consideration—
(a) having regard to the child's age and understanding, to such wishes and feelings of his as he has been able to ascertain;

(b) to such other wishes and feelings mentioned in subsection (2) as he has been able to ascertain; and
(c) to the child's religious persuasion, racial origin and cultural and linguistic background.

(4) Section 62, except subsection (4), shall apply in relation to any person who is carrying on a children's home as it applies in relation to any voluntary organisation.

DEFINITIONS

"children's home": s.63.
"child": s.105(1).
"person who is not a parent but has parental responsibility": ss.5(6), 12(2), 33(3), 44(4).

GENERAL NOTE

This section imposes a duty on the person carrying on a children's home (even one which is not registered) to promote the child's welfare, etc. An identical duty exists for voluntary organisations under section 61 and there are comparable duties on local authorities under Part III (see notes on those provisions, especially s.22). Subsection (4) applies section 62 (except s.62(4)) to children's homes. Thus local authorities have duties to satisfy themselves that the children's welfare is being safeguarded and to arrange for children to be visited (see note to s.62). There was no comparable provision under the Children's Homes Act 1982, only a duty to inspect. Where the home is unregistered, it may be impossible for the local authority to carry out its duties. The local authority also has power to provide after-care for children who were accommodated in registered children's homes (s.24). The person carrying on the home must notify the local authority when a child over 16 leaves (s.24(12)).

Persons disqualified from carrying on, or being employed in, children's homes

65.—(1) A person who is disqualified (under section 68) from fostering a child privately shall not carry on, or be otherwise concerned in the management of, or have any financial interest in, a children's home unless he has—
(a) disclosed to the responsible authority the fact that he is so disqualified; and
(b) obtained their written consent.

(2) No person shall employ a person who is so disqualified in a children's home unless he has—
(a) disclosed to the responsible authority the fact that that person is so disqualified; and
(b) obtained their written consent.

(3) Where an authority refuse to give their consent under this section, they shall inform the applicant by a written notice which states—
(a) the reason for the refusal;
(b) the applicant's right to appeal against the refusal to a Registered Homes Tribunal under paragraph 8 of Schedule 6; and
(c) the time within which he may do so.

(4) Any person who contravenes subsection (1) or (2) shall be guilty of an offence and liable on summary conviction to imprisonment for a

term not exceeding six months or to a fine not exceeding level 5 on the standard scale or to both.

(5) Where a person contravenes subsection (2) he shall not be guilty of an offence if he proves that he did not know, and had no reasonable grounds for believing, that the person whom he was employing was disqualified under section 68.

DEFINITIONS
"children's home": s.63.
"responsible authority": Sched. 6, para. 3(1).

GENERAL NOTE
The grounds for disqualification are found in the Disqualification for Caring for Children Regulations 1991 (S.I. 1991 No. 2094) made under section 68, and also apply to disqualification from private fostering. Guidance is provided in *Guidance*, Vol. 8, Chap. 2. Where a person is disqualified, it is always open to him to seek the local authority's written consent. The Department of Health considers that the power to lift a disqualification should only be used in the most exceptional circumstances. Cases should be subject to thorough scrutiny at senior level with legal advice (Vol. 8, para. 2.6–7). If consent is refused, an appeal may be made to the Registered Homes Tribunal (subs. (3)). The offence under subsection (4) will only be committed by an employer who did not know that his employee had committed an offence, if he could reasonably have known. At present local authorities and voluntary organisations can check the credentials of their employees and of people whose homes they register under the Act by arrangement with the police. There is no such provision for private individuals to check.

Subs. (3)
The time within which he may do so: No appeal may be brought more than 28 days after service of the notice (Sched. 6, para. 8(3)).

PART IX

PRIVATE ARRANGEMENTS FOR FOSTERING CHILDREN

Privately fostered children

66.—(1) In this Part—
  (a) "a privately fostered child" means a child who is under the age of sixteen and who is cared for, and provided with accommodation by, someone other than—
    (i) a parent of his;
    (ii) a person who is not a parent of his but who has parental responsibility for him; or
    (iii) a relative of his; and
  (b) "to foster a child privately" means to look after the child in circumstances in which he is a privately fostered child as defined by this section.

(2) A child is not a privately fostered child if the person caring for and accommodating him—
  (a) has done so for a period of less than 28 days; and
  (b) does not intend to do so for any longer period.

(3) Subsection (1) is subject to—
  (a) the provisions of section 63; and
  (b) the exceptions made by paragraphs 1 to 5 of Schedule 8.

(4) In the case of a child who is disabled, subsection (1)(a) shall have effect as if for "sixteen" there were substituted "eighteen".

(5) Schedule 8 shall have effect for the purposes of supplementing the provision made by this Part.

DEFINITIONS

"disabled": ss.17(11), 105(1).
"person who is not a parent ... but has parental responsibility": ss.5(6), 12(2), 33(3), 44(1)(4).
"privately fostered child": s.66(1).
"relative": s.105(1).
"to foster a child privately": s.66(1).

GENERAL NOTE

This section contains the definition of a "privately fostered" child. It must be read with Schedule 7, paragraphs 2 and 5 and also with Schedule 8, paragraphs 1 and 2, which contain the exemptions. Children under 16, and those under 18 who are disabled (subs. (4)), come within the definition and the protection it entails. The definition seeks to exclude children living with their families (subs. (1)(a) and Schedule 8, paragraph 2(a)); children looked after by a local authority (Sched. 8, para. 1) and children whose welfare is secured because of the requirement to register the establishment in which they live and/or the duty of local authorities in respect of children in such establishments (Sched. 8, para. 2). These exceptions do not apply where a child is being cared for in such an establishment by someone living there in a personal capacity who does come within paragraph 1(a) (Sched. 8 para. 2(2)). Children are also exempted from the definition where the local authority has responsibility for their welfare under a supervision order, the Mental Health Act 1983 or the Adoption Act 1976 (Sched. 8, paras. 3–5). Some children accommodated in boarding schools are protected under these provisions rather than section 87. Where independent schools accommodate children in the holidays, Schedule 8, paragraph 9 applies most of the provisions relating to private fostering to them.

Subsection (2) sets down the time condition which excludes arrangements which are planned to and which actually do last for less than 28 days; subsection (3) specifies that any child who falls outside both section 63 and Schedule 8, paragraphs. 1–5, is a privately fostered child.

Schedule 8, paragraph 6, allows the appropriate local authority to impose requirements in circumstances where a person fosters privately or proposes to do so. These requirements are additional to the limit set by Schedule 7 (see s.63(12)). This is a redrafted version of the Foster Children Act 1980, s.9 and the local authority must now give reasons for imposing a requirement (Sched. 8, para. 6(4)). Where a requirement is imposed, the local authority may also prohibit private fostering in accordance with section 69(3) and (5) if the requirement is not complied with in the specified period (s.69(6)). Schedule 8, paragraph 7 replaces the Foster Children Act 1980, ss.4–6. All the duties to notify depend on the regulations (S.I. 1991 No. 2050; see s.67 below). Schedule 8, paragraph 8, provides for appeals. It is wider than the Foster Children Act 1980, s.11, which it replaces, and allows appeals against requirements imposed under Schedule 8, paragraph 6; appeal against the refusal of the local authority to consent to fostering by persons disqualified under section 68 or refusal to grant, etc., an exemption from the fostering limit in Schedule 7; and finally allows appeal against a refusal to cancel a prohibition under section 69. While an appeal is pending, the requirement condition or cancellation of an exemption is not effective (Sched. 8, para. 6(3)). Appeals must still be lodged within 14 days. Appeals can only be made to the family proceedings court and are governed by rule 4 (r. 29(1)). The court may make or vary an exemption or impose a condition (para. 8(6)). Only private foster parents may appeal under this provision (para. 8(8)). Paragraph 10 contains the prohibition against advertising (formerly the Foster Children Act 1980, s.15) but there is no longer a power to make regulations in respect of such advertisements. Paragraph 11 precludes a private foster parent from insuring the life of a privately fostered child; it repeats the Foster Children Act 1980, s.19.

Guidance on private fostering is provided in *Guidance*, Vol. 8, Chap. 1 and is aimed at improving standards in private foster care.

Welfare of privately fostered children

67.—(1) It shall be the duty of every local authority to satisfy themselves that the welfare of children who are privately fostered within their area is being satisfactorily safeguarded and promoted and to secure that such advice is given to those caring for them as appears to the authority to be needed.

(2) The Secretary of State may make regulations—
  (a) requiring every child who is privately fostered within a local authority's area to be visited by an officer of the authority—
    (i) in prescribed circumstances; and
    (ii) on specified occasions or within specified periods; and
  (b) imposing requirements which are to be met by any local authority, or officer of a local authority, in carrying out functions under this section.

(3) Where any person who is authorised by a local authority to visit privately fostered children has reasonable cause to believe that—
  (a) any privately fostered child is being accommodated in premises within the authority's area; or
  (b) it is proposed to accommodate any such child in any such premises,

he may at any reasonable time inspect those premises and any children there.

(4) Any person exercising the power under subsection (3) shall, if so required, produce some duly authenticated document showing his authority to do so.

(5) Where a local authority are not satisfied that the welfare of any child who is privately fostered within their area is being satisfactorily safeguarded or promoted they shall—
  (a) unless they consider that it would not be in the best interests of the child, take such steps as are reasonably practicable to secure that the care and accommodation of the child is undertaken by—
    (i) a parent of his;
    (ii) any person who is not a parent of his but who has parental responsibility for him; or
    (iii) a relative of his; and
  (b) consider the extent to which (if at all) they should exercise any of their functions under this Act with respect to the child.

DEFINITIONS
"functions": s.105(1).
"local authority": s.105(1).
"person who is not a parent...but has parental responsibility": ss.5(6), 12(2).
"privately fostered child": s.66(1).
"relative": s.105(1).

REGULATIONS

The Children (Private Arrangements for Fostering) Regulations 1991 (S.I. 1991 No. 2050).

GENERAL NOTE

This section states the duty of the local authority in respect of private fostering arrangements and replaces the Foster Children Act 1980. It is supplemented by regulations. There is a general duty for the local authority to satisfy itself of the welfare of privately fostered children and a new duty to secure that necessary advice is given to all carers (subs. (1)). Subsections (3) and (4) contain the power to inspect previously in the Foster Children Act 1980, s.8. Subsection (5) states the duty of the local authority in cases where they are not satisfied about the child's welfare. It is identical to section 62(5), which applies to care by voluntary organisations and in children's homes. The duty to notify in Schedule 8, paragraph 7, should ensure that the local authority is aware of many (but probably not all) children to whom it owes these duties. The local authority has power to provide after-care for privately fostered children (see notes to s.24).

The Children (Private Arrangements for Fostering) Regulations 1991, reg. 2(1) lists the matters the local authority must consider when carrying out its functions in section 67 relating to the welfare of privately fostered children; *Guidance*, Vol. 8, Chap. 1 further explains these. Local authorities must arrange for privately fostered children to be visited from time to time. Visits must be made within a week of placement, at six weekly intervals during the first year, every three months thereafter and when reasonably requested by the child or foster parents (reg 3). The child should be seen alone where appropriate; a written report must be made. The regulations also contain details of the required notifications. Prospective foster parents should notify the local authority not less than six and not more than 13 weeks before the placement. Where the child is placed in an emergency, notification must be made within 48 hours. Notification must give details of the child, the carer, the purpose and duration of the placement, the parents, anyone who arranged the placement. Details of offences committed by the carer and any employee or member of his household must be given; changes in address or household composition must also be notified in advance, if possible; otherwise within 48 hours (reg. 4). Former foster parents must notify the local authority within 48 hours of ceasing to care for a child giving details of the person who took over the child's care unless he intends to care for the child within 27 days. In such cases the local authority should be notified if there is a change of plan or the child does not return within 28 days. Deaths of foster children must be notified immediately (reg. 5). Anyone who makes arrangements for private fostering and any parent or person with parental responsibility who knows of the proposed fostering must also notify the authority. Failure to give a required notice is an offence (s.70(1)(a)).

Subs. (1)

Satisfactorily safeguarded: The standards and care in private foster homes are often markedly below what would be acceptable from a local authority foster parent. The local authority can do a number of things in these situations depending on the standard of care and the availability of alternatives. Decisions about unsatisfactory care should not be taken by social workers working alone. Concerns should be discussed with senior managers or the panel which monitors standards and legal advice should be taken. Parents should be informed (*Guidance*, Vol. 8, para. 1.8.13). The authority must exercise its powers under subection (5), but this could mean leaving the child in the foster home. In such cases, providing or arranging for advice may be appropriate. Only if the child is suffering or likely to suffer significant harm can the local authority take compulsory measures of care (ss.31 and 44). If the child is "in need" the authority will have further duties under Part III and Schedule 2, paragraph 10 and could offer to accommodate the child under section 20, or offer other services.

Subs. (3)

This does not give a right of entry without warrant (see note to s.62(6)). A warrant may be obtained under section 102 or if an emergency protection order is obtained under section 48(9).

Persons disqualified from being private foster parents

68.—(1) Unless he has disclosed the fact to the appropriate local authority and obtained their written consent, a person shall not foster a child privately if he is disqualified from doing so by regulations made by the Secretary of State for the purposes of this section.

(2) The regulations may, in particular, provide for a person to be so disqualified where—
 (a) an order of a kind specified in the regulations has been made at any time with respect to him;
 (b) an order of a kind so specified has been made at any time with respect to any child who has been in his care;
 (c) a requirement of a kind so specified has been imposed at any time with respect to any such child, under or by virtue of any enactment;
 (d) he has been convicted of any offence of a kind so specified, or has been placed on probation or discharged absolutely or conditionally for any such offence;
 (e) a prohibition has been imposed on him at any time under section 69 or under any other specified enactment;
 (f) his rights and powers with respect to a child have at any time been vested in a specified authority under a specified enactment.

(3) Unless he has disclosed the fact to the appropriate local authority and obtained their written consent, a person shall not foster a child privately if—
 (a) he lives in the same household as a person who is himself prevented from fostering a child by subsection (1); or
 (b) he lives in a household at which any such person is employed.

(4) Where an authority refuse to give their consent under this section, they shall inform the applicant by a written notice which states—
 (a) the reason for the refusal;
 (b) the applicant's right under paragraph 8 of Schedule 8 to appeal against the refusal; and
 (c) the time within which he may do so.

(5) In this section—
 "the appropriate authority" means the local authority within whose area it is proposed to foster the child in question; and
 "enactment" means any enactment having effect, at any time, in any part of the United Kingdom.

Children Act 1989 (As Amended)

DEFINITIONS

"appropriate authority": s.68(5).
"child": s.105(1).
"enactment": s.68(5).
"local authority": s.105(1).
"to foster a child privately": s.66(1).

REGULATIONS

The Disqualification for Caring for Children Regulations 1991 (S.I. 1991 No. 2094).

GENERAL NOTE

This section disqualifies people in circumstances prescribed in regulations from involvement in private fostering without the consent of the appropriate local authority (subs. (1)). These occupations, etc. come within the Rehabilitation of Offenders Act 1974 (Exceptions) Order 1975 (S.I. 1975 No. 1023). Spent convictions must therefore be disclosed. The disqualification also applies where another person in the same household, or an employee, comes within the regulations (subs. (3)). Where a local authority refuses its consent under subsections (1) or (3) it must give reasons (subs. (4)). Schedule 8, paragraph 8 provides a right of appeal against such a refusal. Fostering in contravention of this provision is an offence (s.70(1)(d)), but if the disqualification does not relate to the foster parent, he has a defence if he did not know and had no reasonable grounds for believing that the other person was disqualified (s.70(2)).

The following are disqualified under S.I. 1991 No. 2094, reg.2 from acting as private foster parents, childminders or day care providers:

(a) parents of children who are or have been subject to care orders;
(b) people who have had children removed from their care under care orders, deemed care orders (Sched. 14, para. 15), supervision orders with a residence requirement (CYPA 1969, s.12AA), approved school or fit person orders and comparable orders under Scottish or Northern Ireland legislation;
(c) (relates to other Scottish orders);
(d) parents against whom parental rights resolutions were made;
(e) people who had children removed under the child protection provisions in adoption legislation;
(f) people against whom orders for removal of private foster children have been made;
(g) Schedule 1 offenders;
(h) people who owned or were otherwise concerned with the management of a voluntary home which has been deregistered or refused registration;
(i) people who owned or were otherwise concerned with a registered children's home which was deregistered or refused registration;
(j) people prohibited from private fostering;
(k) people who have been refused registration as childminders or day care providers or had such registration refused; and
(l) people refused registration or whose registrations have been cancelled under the Social Work (Scotland) Act 1968, s.62.

Such people may not carry on, be otherwise concerned with the management of, or have a financial interest in a voluntary home without the written consent of the Secretary of State. Refusal of consent must be notified in writing with reasons (reg. 3). These provisions are applied to those involved with registered children's homes by section 65. They do not formally apply to local authority employees and foster parents but authorities are advised to have regard to them. Guidance about these regulations is given in *Guidance*, Vol. 8, Chap. 2.

Subs. (3)

Household: The Foster Children Act 1980, s.7(2) used the word "premises," which would seem to be wider than "household." A lodger who cooked and ate separately would probably not be a member of the same household. In divorce law, household has been explained in an abstract sense; it essentially refers to people held together by a particular kind of tie (*Santos* v. *Santo* [1972] Fam. 247 at 262). Thus a married couple have been held to be living in separate households where there has been an end of any life in common (*Hopes* v. *Hopes* [1949] P.227). The explanation of the term household in the C.Y.P.A. 1969, s.1(1)(a) by Arnold P. in *R.* v. *Birmingham Juvenile Court, ex p. S.* [1984] Fam. 93 is not helpful here since it was concerned with whether three people could be considered to be in the same household as another three people when there was only one person in common.

Employed: A non resident person who helped out for a share of fees might not be an employee, only an independent contractor (see *Ready Mixed Concrete* v. *Minister of Pensions* [1969] 2 Q.B. 497). A wide interpretation of employment would protect children but may be considered inappropriate because of the penal liability in section 70.

Power to prohibit private fostering

69.—(1) This section applies where a person—
   (a) proposes to foster a child privately, or
   (b) is fostering a child privately.

(2) Where the local authority for the area within which the child is proposed to be, or is being, fostered are of the opinion that—
   (a) he is not a suitable person to foster a child;
   (b) the premises in which the child will be, or is being, accommodated are not suitable; or
   (c) it would be prejudicial to the welfare of the child for him to be, or continue to be, accommodated by that person in those premises,
the authority may impose a prohibition on him under subsection (3).

(3) A prohibition imposed on any person under this subsection may prohibit him from fostering privately—
   (a) any child in any premises within the area of the local authority; or
   (b) any child in premises specified in the prohibition;
   (c) a child identified in the prohibition, in premises specified in the prohibition.

(4) A local authority who have imposed a prohibition on any person under subsection (3) may, if they think fit, cancel the prohibition—
   (a) of their own motion; or
   (b) on an application made by that person,
if they are satisfied that the prohibition is no longer justified.

(5) Where a local authority impose a requirement on any person under paragraph 6 of Schedule 8, they may also impose a prohibition on him under subsection (3).

(6) Any prohibition imposed by virtue of subsection (5) shall not have effect unless—
   (a) the time specified for compliance with the requirement has expired; and
   (b) the requirement has not been complied with.

(7) A prohibition imposed under this section shall be imposed by notice in writing addressed to the person on whom it is imposed and informing him of—
   (a) the reason for imposing the prohibition;
   (b) his right under paragraph 8 of Schedule 8 to appeal against the prohibition; and

(c) the time within which he may do so.

DEFINITIONS
"child": s.66(4).
"local authority": s.105(1).
"to foster a child privately": s.66(1).

GENERAL NOTE
This section redrafts with some minor amendments the provisions of the Foster Children Act 1980, s.10. It permits the local authority to prohibit an individual from fostering a child privately on any of the grounds in subsection (2). The prohibition may be general (subs. (3)(a)), relate to specific premises (subs. (3)(b)) or apply only to a particular child at a particular place (subs. (3)(c)). Where a prohibition is applied, the local authority may cancel it if it is no longer justified (subs. (4)). A change in circumstances (required by the Foster Children Act 1980, s.10(3)) is no longer necessary. Where a prohibition is imposed the local authority must give reasons. Schedule 8, paragraph 8 provides a right of appeal to be exercised within 14 days. Appeals are heard in the family proceedings court and governed by rule 4 (r. 29(1)). Where a requirement is imposed under Schedule 8, paragraph 6, but not complied with, a prohibition may be added (subss. (5) and (6)). All prohibitions must be notified in writing with reasons (subs. (7)).

Guidance has been given on the use of prohibitions in *Guidance*, Vol. 8, para 1.8.22 ff.

Offences

70.—(1) A person shall be guilty of an offence if—
  (a) being required, under any provision made by or under this Part, to give any notice or information—
    (i) he fails without reasonable excuse to give the notice within the time specified in that provision; or
    (ii) he fails without reasonable excuse to give the information within a reasonable time; or
    (iii) he makes, or causes or procures another person to make, any statement in the notice or information which he knows to be false or misleading in a material particular;
  (b) he refuses to allow a privately fostered child to be visited by a duly authorised officer of a local authority;
  (c) he intentionally obstructs another in the exercise of the power conferred by section 67(3);
  (d) he contravenes section 68;
  (e) he fails without reasonable excuse to comply with any requirement imposed by a local authority under this Part;
  (f) he accommodates a privately fostered child in any premises in contravention of a prohibition imposed by a local authority under this Part;
  (g) he knowingly causes to be published, or publishes, an advertisement which he knows contravenes paragraph 10 of Schedule 8.

(2) Where a person contravenes section 68(3), he shall not be guilty of an offence under this section if he proves that he did not know, and had no reasonable ground for believing, that any person to

whom section 68(1) applied was living or employed in the premises in question.

(3) A person guilty of an offence under subsection (1)(a) shall be liable on summary conviction to a fine not exceeding level 5 on the standard scale.

(4) A person guilty of an offence under subsection (1)(b), (c) or (g) shall be liable on summary conviction to a fine not exceeding level 3 on the standard scale.

(5) A person guilty of an offence under subsection (1)(d) or (f) shall be liable on summary conviction to imprisonment for a term not exceeding six months, or to a fine not exceeding level 5 on the standard scale, or to both.

(6) A person guilty of an offence under subsection (1)(e) shall be liable on summary conviction to a fine not exceeding level 4 on the standard scale.

(7) If any person who is required, under any provision of this Part, to give a notice fails to give the notice within the time specified in that provision, proceedings for the offence may be brought at any time within six months from the date when evidence of the offence came to the knowledge of the local authority.

(8) Subsection (7) is not affected by anything in section 127(1) of the Magistrates' Courts Act 1980 (time limit for proceedings).

DEFINITIONS
"duly authorised officer": s.67(3), (4).
"local authority": s.105(1).
"privately fostered child", "to foster a child privately": s.66(1), (4).

GENERAL NOTE
This section lists the offences for breach of the provisions relating to private fostering. No new offences are created but the level of penalties is different from those in the Foster Children Act 1980, s.16, and there are two new defences. First there is a defence of "reasonable excuse" for the offence of failing to notify or provide information under section 70(1)(a) and (e). Secondly there is a defence that the person "did not know and had no reasonable ground for believing" for the offence in section 68(3) of failing to disclose the offences of a disqualified person who is not the foster parent (subs. (2)).

PART X

CHILD MINDING AND DAY CARE FOR YOUNG CHILDREN

Registration

71.—(1) Every local authority shall keep a register of—
    (a) persons who act as child minders on domestic premises within the authority's area; and
    (b) persons who provide day care for children under the age of eight on premises (other than domestic premises) within that area.
(2) For the purposes of this Part—

(a) a person acts as a child minder if—
  (i) he looks after one or more children under the age of eight, for reward; and
  (ii) the period, or the total of the periods, which he spends so looking after children in any day exceeds two hours; and
(b) a person does not provide day care for children unless the period, or the total of the periods, during which children are looked after exceeds two hours in any day.

(3) Where a person provides day care for children under the age of eight on different premises situated within the area of the same local authority, that person shall be separately registered with respect to each of those premises.

(4) A person who—
  (a) is the parent, or a relative, of a child;
  (b) has parental responsibility for a child; or
  (c) is a foster parent of a child,
does not act as a child minder for the purposes of this Part when looking after that child.

(5) Where a person is employed as a nanny for a child, she does not act as a child minder when looking after that child wholly or mainly in the home of the person so employing her.

(6) Where a person is so employed by two different employers, she does not act as a child minder when looking after any of the children concerned wholly or mainly in the home of either of her employers.

(7) A local authority may refuse to register an applicant for registration under subsection (1)(a) if they are satisfied that—
  (a) the applicant; or
  (b) any person looking after, or likely to be looking after, any children on any premises on which the applicant is, or is likely to be, child minding,
is not fit to look after children under the age of eight.

(8) A local authority may refuse to register an applicant for registration under subsection (1)(a) if they are satisfied that—
  (a) any person living, or likely to be living, at any premises on which the applicant is, or is likely to be, child minding; or
  (b) any person employed, or likely to be employed, on those premises,
is not fit to be in the proximity of children under the age of eight.

(9) A local authority may refuse to register an applicant for registration under subsection (1)(b) if they are satisfied that any person looking after, or likely to be looking after, any children on the premises to which the application relates is not fit to look after children under the age of eight.

(10) A local authority may refuse to register an applicant for registration under subsection (1)(b) if they are satisfied that—
  (a) any person living, or likely to be living, at the premises to which the application relates; or
  (b) any person employed, or likely to be employed, on those premises,
is not fit to be in the proximity of children under the age of eight.

(11) A local authority may refuse to register an applicant for registration under this section if they are satisfied—
  (a) in the case of an application under subsection (1)(a), that any premises on which the applicant is, or is likely to be, child minding; or
  (b) in the case of an application under subsection (1)(b), that the premises to which the application relates, are not fit to be used for looking after children under the age of eight,
whether because of their condition or the condition of any equipment used on the premises or for any reason connected with their situation, construction or size.

(12) In this section—
  "domestic premises" means any premises which are wholly or mainly used as a private dwelling;
  "premises" includes any vehicle.

(13) For the purposes of this Part a person acts as a nanny for a child if she is employed to look after the child by—
  (a) a parent of the child;
  (b) a person who is not a parent of the child but who has parental responsibility for him; or
  (c) a person who is a relative of the child and who has assumed responsibility for his care.

(14) For the purposes of this section, a person fosters a child if—
  (a) he is a local authority foster parent in relation to the child;
  (b) he is a foster parent with whom the child has been placed by a voluntary organisation; or
  (c) he fosters the child privately.

(15) Any register kept under this section—
  (a) shall be open to inspection by members of the public at all reasonable times; and
  (b) may be kept by means of a computer.

(16) Schedule 9 shall have effect for the purpose of making further provision with respect to registration under this section including, in particular, further provision for exemption from the requirement to be registered and provision for disqualification.

DEFINITIONS
  "child": s.71(2), (3).
  "childminder": s.71(2)(a).
  "day care": ss.18, 71(2)(b).
  "domestic premises": s.71(12).
  "fosters": s.71(14).
  "local authority": s.105(1).
  "nanny": s.71(13).
  "parental responsibility": ss.2(1), (2), 5(6), 12(1), (2), 44(1), (4).
  "premises": s.71(12).
  "relative": s.105(1).

REGULATIONS
  Child Minding and Day Care (Applications for Registration) Regulations 1991 (S.I. 1991 No. 1689).
  The Child Minding and Day Care (Registration and Inspection Fees) Regulations 1991 (S.I. 1991 No. 2076).

The Child Minding and Day Care (Applications for Registration and Inspection Fees)(Amendment) Regulations 1991 (S.I. 1991 No. 2129).
The Disqualification for Caring for Children Regulations 1991 (S.I. 1991 No. 2094), see s.68.

GENERAL NOTE

This section should be read with Schedule 9 and the regulations. Subsection (1) requires local authorities to keep two registers: one of childminders (defined in subss. (2) and (4)–(6)) and the other of people providing day care (defined in subss. (2) and (3)). People need only register if they care for children under the age of eight, for more than two hours a day and, in the case of childminders, for reward (subs. (2)). Schedule 9, paragraphs 3–5 exempt most schools, residential homes which are covered by other registration provisions in the Act, and occasional facilities, *i.e.* those available for less than six days in any year. The NHS and Community Care Act 1990, s.60 lifted Crown Immunity from health service bodies. This overrides Schedule 9, paragraph 4. Day-care for under 8's in establishments must now be registered. Parents, relatives, people with parental responsibility, foster parents (subs. (4)) and nannies (including those shared between two families) (subs. (5) and (6)) are not required to register. Registrations must be made in accordance with Schedule 9, paragraph 1, and comply with S.I. 1991 Nos. 1689 and 2129. When a person is registered, he must be issued with a certificate stating his name, address and any requirements imposed on the registration (Sched. 9, para. 6). The local authority is required to register anyone who makes a proper application and pays the prescribed fee (para. 1(4)) unless the provisions of subsections (8) to (11) or Schedule 9, paragraph 2, apply. The authority may refuse to register the applicant if the applicant or any person looking after children on the same premises is not a fit person to look after children under the age of eight years (subss.(7) and (9)), or if any person living or employed at those premises is not a fit person to be in close proximity to such children (subs. (8) and (10)). A person who is disqualified by S.I. 1991 No. 2094 (see notes on s.68 above) may not be registered. Registration may also be refused where the premises or any equipment is unfit (subs. (11)). Local authorities must inspect registered premises at least once a year (s.76(4)) and charge a prescribed fee for this (Schedule 9, paragraph 7). Registration fees have been set at £100 for daycare providers who provide day care for more than four hours each day and £10 for child minders and those providing short, sessional day care; inspection fees are £75 and £7.50, respectively (see regulations above). Schedule 9, paragraph 8 requires any local education authority who could help the local authority with its functions under Part X to do so, if requested.

Guidance on the standards of childminding and day care is provided in *Guidance*, Vol. 2, Chap. 6 and on registration and inspection in *Guidance*, Vol. 8, Chap. 3. The Department of Health has also published a guide to using the law to improve standards, P. Elfer and G. Beasley, *Registration of childminding and Day Care* (1991).

Subs. (1)

This must be read in conjunction with subsections (4) to (6), (13), (14) and Schedule 9, paragraphs 3–5, which list the exceptions.

Subs. (2)

For reward: This is not defined but arguably requires an element of profit. If so, neighbours who care for each other's children on an exchange basis, even if they do so for over two hours, would not need to register, nor would those in baby-sitting schemes. There are no "reward" requirements for day care providers, thus all playgroups taking place outside the home must register.

Subs. (4)

Foster parent: This includes all types of foster parent and children placed with them for fostering (subs. (14)). If a foster parent also acts as a childminder for other children, a second registration will be required (David Mellor, Minister of Health (Standing Committee B, col. 393, June 6, 1989)).

Subss. (5) and (6)

The distinction between a nanny in a nanny-share arrangement and a childminder would seem to be a very fine one, turning on the nature of the contract between the parent and the carer. If A and B jointly employ C, sharing costs and having the control employers have, C will be a nanny. If A employs C and arranges for B's children to be cared for by C, C will be a nanny for A's children and a childminder for B's. If A and B enter into a contract with C to look after their children but do not employ her, she will be a childminder, even if she works in one of their houses.

Subss. (7)–(10)

Not fit to look after children: S.I. 1991 No. 2094 (noted at s. 68 above) applies but local authorities have discretion to refuse to register others, see *Guidance*, Vol. 8, Chap. 2. They will need to be able to justify refusals (s.77(2)) and must act fairly (see *R.* v. *Norfolk County Council, ex p. M.* [1987] 2 All E.R. 359). The fact that someone's name appears on the "at risk" register will not be sufficient to justify a refusal if it results from an unfair and one-sided procedure.

Not fit to be in the proximity of children under the age of eight: Where the person is not involved in the care of the children, the conduct or circumstances justifying refusal to register a childminder or day care provider should be more serious. However, the behaviour need not be culpable, *e.g.* very disturbing or violent behaviour resulting from mental illness or infirmity may be sufficient.

Living at premises: This does not mean household. Where a lodger lived on the premises, *i.e.* not in a separate self-contained flat, his presence could justify refusal to register (*cf.* registration to foster children privately (s.68(3))). A person living in the same household as a disqualified person is automatically disqualified unless they disclose the fact to the local authority and obtain their consent (Sched. 9, para. 2(3)).

Employed: See note to section 68(2).

In these cases the fact that parents are satisfied with the standard of care should not dissuade local authorities from exercising their functions: see Elfer and Beasley (above).

Subs. (11)

The premises . . . are not fit: This requirement covers aspects of safety—fire guards, stair gates, window locks, etc., as well as the size and situation of the premises. Registration could be refused where planning permission had not been obtained or a restrictive covenant precluded use.

Subs. (13)

Assumed responsibility for his care: This concept does not appear elsewhere in the Act. It would seem to require the parent giving up responsibility in practice but not in law (see s.3).

Requirements to be complied with by child minders

72.—(1) Where a local authority register a person under section 71(1)(a), they shall impose such reasonable requirements on him as they consider appropriate in his case.

(2) In imposing requirements on him, the authority shall—
- (a) specify the maximum number of children, or the maximum number of children within specified age groups, whom he may look after when acting as a child minder;
- (b) require him to secure that any premises on which he so looks after any child, and the equipment used in those premises, are adequately maintained and kept safe;
- (c) require him to keep a record of the name and address of—
    - (i) any child so looked after by him on any premises within the authority's area;

(ii) any person who assists in looking after any such child; and

(iii) any person living, or likely at any time to be living, at those premises;

(d) require him to notify the authority in writing of any change in the persons mentioned in paragraph (c)(ii) and (iii).

(3) The Secretary of State may by regulations make provision as to—

(a) requirements which must be imposed by local authorities under this section in prescribed circumstances;

(b) requirements of such descriptions as may be prescribed which must not be imposed by local authorities under this section.

(4) In determining the maximum number of children to be specified under subsection (2)(a), the authority shall take account of the number of other children who may at any time be on any premises on which the person concerned acts, or is likely to act, as a child minder.

(5) Where, in addition to the requirements mentioned in subsection (2), a local authority impose other requirements, those other requirements must not be incompatible with any of the subsection (2) requirements.

(6) A local authority may at any time vary any requirement imposed under this section, impose any additional requirement or remove any requirement.

DEFINITIONS

"child": ss.7(2), 105(1).
"childminder": s.71(2)(a).
"local authority": s.105(1).
"premises": s.71(12).

GENERAL NOTE

This section requires local authorities to impose reasonable requirements on registrations of childminders under section 71(1)(a), relating to first, the maximum number of children within specified age groups, second, the safety of premises and equipment, third, the keeping of records of the children, any assistants and anyone living at the premises and fourth, notification of any changes in the assistants or the occupants of the premises (subss. (1) and (2)). Other requirements may be imposed so long as they are not incompatible with those in subsection (2) or contrary to regulations made under subsection (3) (subs.(5)). Requirements may be varied or removed (subs. (6)). When specifying the number of children, the authority must take account of other children at the premises, *i.e.* the minder's own children and those of others living there (subs. (4)). The Secretary of State is empowered to make regulations imposing or banning specific requirements. No such regulations have been made.

The authority must give reasons for imposing its requirements (s.77(2)) and must act reasonably (subs.(1)) and the Wednesbury principle applies. *Guidance*, Vol. 2, para. 7.37 states that when imposing requirements local authorities should treat each case individually. For further advice on registration requirements see *Guidance*, Vol. 2, Chap. 7 and Elfer and Beasley, *Registration of childminding and day care* (1991).

Requirements to be Complied With by Child Minders

Appeals may be made to the family proceedings court against requirements (s.77(6)). See rules 4 and 29(1) at pp. 361 and 416 below.

Requirements to be complied with by persons providing day care for young children

73.—(1) Where a local authority register a person under section 71(1)(b) they shall impose such reasonable requirements on him as they consider appropriate in his case.

(2) Where a person is registered under section 71(1)(b) with respect to different premises within the area of the same authority, this section applies separately in relation to each registration.

(3) In imposing requirements on him, the authority shall—
  (a) specify the maximum number of children, or the maximum number of children within specified age groups, who may be looked after on the premises;
  (b) require him to secure that the premises, and the equipment used in them, are adequately maintained and kept safe;
  (c) require him to notify the authority of any change in the facilities which he provides or in the period during which he provides them;
  (d) specify the number of persons required to assist in looking after children on the premises;
  (e) require him to keep a record of the name and address of—
    (i) any child looked after on the registered premises;
    (ii) any person who assists in looking after any such child; and
    (iii) any person who lives, or is likely at any time to be living, at those premises;
  (f) require him to notify the authority of any change in the persons mentioned in paragraph (e)(ii) and (iii).

(4) The Secretary of State may by regulations make provision as to—
  (a) requirements which must be imposed by local authorities under this section in prescribed circumstances;
  (b) requirements of such descriptions as may be prescribed which must not be imposed by local authorities under this section.

(5) In subsection (3), references to children looked after are to children looked after in accordance with the provision of day care made by the registered person.

(6) In determining the maximum number of children to be specified under subsection (3)(a), the authority shall take account of the number of other children who may at any time be on the premises.

(7) Where, in addition to the requirements mentioned in subsection (3), a local authority impose other requirements, those other requirements must not be incompatible with any of the subsection (3) requirements.

(8) A local authority may at any time vary any requirement imposed under this section, impose any additional requirement or remove any requirement.

DEFINITIONS

"child": ss.71(2)(3), 105(1).
"children looked after": s.73(5).
"day care": ss.18, 71(2)(b).
"local authority": s.105(1).
"premises": s.71(12).

GENERAL NOTE

This section requires local authorities to impose conditions on the registration of day care providers under section 71(1)(b). It provides comparable power to section 72. The same types of requirement must be imposed as under section 72(2), but additionally the local authority must require the registered person to notify the authority of changes in the facilities offered and specify the number of assistants (subs. (3)). Regulations have been made in exercise of the power in subsection (4) listing the information to be provided with all applications for registration (S.I. 1991 Nos. 1689 and 2129). The local authority also has a power to vary and to impose other requirements (subss. (7) and (8)). Where a day care provider is registered in respect of more than one set of premises under section 71(3), these provisions apply separately to each set of premises (subs. (2)). An appeal may be made to the family proceedings court against the imposition of a requirement under section 77 see pp. 195 and 416 below. Guidance has been provided, see *Guidance*, Vol. 2, Chap 7; Vol. 8, Chap. 3 and Elfer and Beasley, *Registration of childminding and day care* (1991).

Cancellation of registration

74.—(1) A local authority may at any time cancel the registration of any person under section 71(1)(a) if—
  (a) it appears to them that the circumstances of the case are such that they would be justified in refusing to register that person as a child minder;
  (b) the care provided by that person when looking after any child as a child minder is, in the opinion of the authority, seriously inadequate having regard to the needs of that child; or
  (c) that person has—
    (i) contravened, or failed to comply with, any requirement imposed on him under section 72; or
    (ii) failed to pay any annual fee under paragraph 7 of Schedule 9 within the prescribed time.

(2) A local authority may at any time cancel the registration of any person under section 71(1)(b) with respect to particular premises if—
  (a) it appears to them that the circumstances of the case are such that they would be justified in refusing to register that person with respect to those premises;
  (b) the day care provided by that person on those premises is, in the opinion of the authority, seriously inadequate having regard to the needs of the children concerned; or
  (c) that person has—
    (i) contravened, or failed to comply with, any requirement imposed on him under section 73; or
    (ii) failed to pay any annual fee under paragraph 7 of Schedule 9 within the prescribed time.

(3) A local authority may at any time cancel all registrations of any person under section 71(1)(b) if it appears to them that the circumstances of the case are such that they would be justified in refusing to register that person with respect to any premises.

(4) Where a requirement to carry out repairs or make alterations or additions has been imposed on a registered person under section 72 or 73, his registration shall not be cancelled on the ground that the premises are not fit to be used for looking after children if—
  (a) the time set for complying with the requirements has not expired, and
  (b) it is shown that the condition of the premises is due to the repairs not having been carried out or the alterations or additions not having been made.

(5) Any cancellation under this section must be in writing.

(6) In considering the needs of any child for the purposes of subsection (1)(b) or (2)(b), a local authority shall, in particular, have regard to the child's religious persuasion, racial origin and cultural and linguistic background.

DEFINITIONS

"child": ss.71(2), (3), 105(1).
"child minder": s.71(2)(a).
"day care": ss.18, 71(2)(b).
"local authority": s.105(1).
"premises": s.71(12).

GENERAL NOTE

This section empowers local authorities to cancel the registration of childminders and day care providers (subss. (1) and (2)). Cancellations must be notified in writing (subs. (5)) with reasons (s.77(2)) and can be appealed to the family proceedings court (s.77(6)) see pp. 195 and 416 below. Section 75 provides a separate power to obtain a court order cancelling a registration in an emergency. A childminder's registration may be cancelled if, first, circumstances justify refusing to register that person (s.71(7) and (8)), second, the care provided is "seriously inadequate" or third, the childminder has contravened or failed to comply with a requirement imposed under section 72, or failed to pay the annual fee. Comparable grounds justify the cancellation of the registration of a day care provider (subss. (2) and (3)). Registrations may not be cancelled on the grounds that the premises are not fit where repairs, alterations or adaptations to the premises have been required, if the time set for complying has not expired and the condition of the premises is due to this (subs. (4)). Guidance about standards of childminding and day care is provided in *Guidance*, Vol. 2, Chap. 6. Legal action to improve standards is discussed in Elfer and Beasley, *Registration of childminding and day care* (1991).

Subss. (1) and (2)

Seriously inadequate: It is not clear how far down the scale care has to be before it becomes seriously inadequate. Arguably, higher quality care should be required of people registered under section 71, than is required of parents, before a child can be removed under section 31 because, unlike parents, there is no overpowering reason to recognise and protect the status of the childminder or day-care provider. Also, a further intervention is provided in cases of significant harm under section 75. Poor supervision which leads or might lead to minor injuries to the children concerned, poor hygiene, insufficient heat or light, may all produce inadequate care, which could be serious for the children if it continued. Local authorities may find it easier to cancel registrations if they seek to rely on other grounds in addition to that in subsection (4)(b), for example failure to comply with a requirement. Where there is a concern about the quality of care, voluntary assistance could be provided, or even a requirement imposed under sections 72 or 73 in an attempt to raise the standard of care.

Having regard to the needs of that child: Care may not be seriously inadequate for all children on the premises. Regard must be had to the child's religious persuasion, racial origin and cultural and linguistic background in determining his needs (subs. (6)). Although care may not be considered seriously inadequate because it is by a member of a different ethnic group, if the carer is unable to communicate with the child, fails to provide food acceptable to the diet followed by the child, or denigrates the child's cultural heritage, it could be so.

Any annual fee: See S.I. 1991 Nos. 2076 and 2129 and notes on section 71 above.

Protection of children in an emergency

75.—(1) If—
    (a) a local authority apply to the court for an order—
        (i) cancelling a registered person's registration;
        (ii) varying any requirement imposed on a registered person under section 72 or 73; or
        (iii) removing a requirement or imposing an additional requirement on such a person; and
    (b) it appears to the court that a child who is being, or may be, looked after by that person, or (as the case may be) in accordance with the provision for day care made by that person, is suffering, or is likely to suffer, significant harm,

the court may make the order.

(2) Any such cancellation, variation, removal or imposition shall have effect from the date on which the order is made.

(3) An application under subsection (1) may be made ex parte and shall be supported by a written statement of the authority's reasons for making it.

(4) Where an order is made under this section, the authority shall serve on the registered person, as soon as is reasonably practicable after the making of the order—
    (a) notice of the order and of its terms; and
    (b) a copy of the statement of the authority's reasons which supported their application for the order.

(5) Where the court imposes or varies any requirement under subsection (1), the requirement, or the requirement as varied, shall be treated for all purposes, other than those of section 77, as if it had been imposed under section 72 or (as the case may be) 73 by the authority concerned.

DEFINITIONS

    "child": ss.71(2), (3), 105(1).
    "court": s.92(7).
    "day care": ss.18, 71(2)(b).
    "significant harm": s.31(9), (10).

GENERAL NOTE

This section enables local authorities to apply to the family proceedings court for orders cancelling a registration or changing the requirements imposed on a registered person (subs. (1)). *Guidance*, Vol. 2, para. 7.53 advises local authorities to seek legal advice before seeking to exercise this power. The court may make the order if it appears that a child who is being looked after by a registered person is suffering, etc., significant harm. Orders may be made *ex parte* and must be supported by a written statement of the authority's reasons (subs. (3)). Orders have effect from the day when they are made (subs. (2)) and must be served on the registered person with the written reasons as soon as reasonably practicable (subs. (4)). There is no further appeal against a requirement, varied or imposed by the court, under this section (subs. (5)). The order does not give the authority any rights over the child, but they could accommodate him under section 20(1)(c). This power is additional to those under Parts IV and V which might be necessary to protect the carer's own children.

For details of the rules relating to these proceedings see pp. 361 and 424 below.

Subs. (1)

Appears to the court: i.e. on the balance of probabilities. The wording may suggest a lower standard of proof than that for an emergency protection order under section 44 where the court must "be satisfied."

Inspection

76.—(1) Any person authorised to do so by a local authority may at any reasonable time enter—
  (a) any domestic premises within the authority's area on which child minding is at any time carried on; or
  (b) any premises within their area on which day care for children under the age of eight is at any time provided.

(2) Where a local authority have reasonable cause to believe that a child Is being looked after on any premises within their area in contravention of this Part, any person authorised to do so by the authority may enter those premises at any reasonable time.

(3) Any person entering premises under this section may inspect—
  (a) the premises;
  (b) any children being looked after on the premises;
  (c) the arrangements made for their welfare; and
  (d) any records relating to them which are kept as a result of this Part.

(4) Every local authority shall exercise their power to inspect the premises mentioned in subsection (1) at least once every year.

(5) Any person inspecting any records under this section—
  (a) shall be entitled at any reasonable time to have access to, and inspect and check the operation of, any computer and any associated apparatus or material which is, or has been, in use in connection with the records in question; and
  (b) may require—
    (i) the person by whom or on whose behalf the computer is or has been so used; or
    (ii) any person having charge of, or otherwise concerned with the operation of, the computer, apparatus or material, to afford him such reasonable assistance as he may require.

(6) A person exercising any power conferred by this section shall, if so required, produce some duly authenticated document showing his authority to do so.

(7) Any person who intentionally obstructs another in the exercise of any such power shall be guilty of an offence and liable on

summary conviction to a fine not exceeding level 3 on the standard scale.

DEFINITIONS

"child": ss.71(2), (3), 105(1).
"childminder": s.71(2)(a).
"court": s.92(7).
"day care": ss.18, 71(2)(a).
"domestic premises": s.71(12).
"local authority": s.105(1).
"premises": s.71(12).

GENERAL NOTE

This section gives the local authority comparable powers of entry and inspection of premises used for childminding or day care as it has under sections 62 to 67 in relation to voluntary homes, children's homes and premises used for private fostering. It also requires the authority to inspect such premises at least once a year (subs. (4)). Authorised officers of the local authority are empowered to enter premises to inspect the premises (subss. (1) and (2)), any children being looked after there, the arrangements for the welfare of those children and the required records (subs. (3)). Where records are computerised, the assistance of the computer's operator can be required (subs. (5)). An offence is committed by anyone who intentionally obstructs the exercise of the power. Where entry is refused, a warrant can be obtained under section 102(6) or if an emergency protection order is obtained, under section 44 or section 48(9).

See *Guidance*, Vol.2, Chap. 8 for advice about the inspection process.

Subss. (1) and (2)

Any premises may be entered where the local authority has reasonable cause to believe there has been a breach of the registration requirement or any of its terms.

Reasonable time: It would be reasonable to enter at any time when minding or day care was being carried out.

May enter: See discussion of section 62(6).

Subs. (3)

Any child looked after: There is no power to inspect other children, but a social worker could request permission from the person with parental responsibility. If permission were refused, information about the state of the minded children might convince the court of the need to make a child assessment order or an emergency protection order.

Subs. (4)

Guidance, Vol. 2, para 8.1 notes that annual inspection is the minimum requirement; fees may only be charged for an annual inspection (S.I. 1991 No. 2076).

Appeals

77.—(1) Not less than 14 days before—
  (a) refusing an application for registration under section 71;
  (b) cancelling any such registration;
  (c) refusing consent under paragraph 2 of Schedule 9;
  (d) imposing, removing or varying any requirement under section 72 or 73; or

(e) refusing to grant any application for the variation or removal of any such requirement,

the authority concerned shall send to the applicant, or (as the case may be) registered person, notice in writing of their intention to take the step in question ("the step").

(2) Every such notice shall—
- (a) give the authority's reasons for proposing to take the step; and
- (b) inform the person concerned of his rights under this section.

(3) Where the recipient of such a notice informs the authority in writing of his desire to object to the step being taken, the authority shall afford him an opportunity to do so.

(4) Any objection made under subsection (3) may be made in person or by a representative.

(5) If the authority, after giving the person concerned an opportunity to object to the step being taken, decide nevertheless to take it they shall send him written notice of their decision.

(6) A person aggrieved by the taking of any step mentioned in subsection (1) may appeal against it to the court.

(7) Where the court imposes or varies any requirement under subsection (8) or (9) the requirement, or the requirement as varied, shall be treated for all purposes (other than this section) as if it had been imposed by the authority concerned.

(8) Where the court allows an appeal against the refusal or cancellation of any registration under section 71 it may impose requirements under section 72 or (as the case may be) 73.

(9) Where the court allows an appeal against such a requirement it may, instead of cancelling the requirement, vary it.

(10) In Scotland, an appeal under subsection (6) shall be by summary application to the sheriff and shall be brought within 21 days from the date of the step to which the appeal relates.

(11) A step of a kind mentioned in subsection (1)(b) or (d) shall not take effect until the expiry of the time within which an appeal may be brought under this section or, where such an appeal is brought, before its determination.

DEFINITIONS

"notice": ss.77(2), 105(8)–(10).
"the step": s.77(1).

GENERAL NOTE

This section provides appeal rights to those whose application has been refused or cancelled and also rights of appeal against requirements in registration (subs. (1)). For a discussion of the practice relating to such cases under the previous law see Elfer and Beasley, *Registration of childminding and day care* (1991), pp. 4–9. Fourteen days before taking the proposed action ("the step") the local authority must notify the applicant in writing of their intentions, the reasons for them and the applicant's rights of appeal (subs. (2)). Where the applicant informs the authority that he objects to the proposed action, the authority must give him an opportunity to do so (subss. (3) and (4)) and may still decide afterwards to take the action (subs. (5)). A person aggrieved may appeal the court (subs. (6)). The court may impose or vary requirements when granting an appeal (subss. (7) and (8)). A requirement imposed by the court may not be subject to further appeal (subs. (9)). Where the authority is proposing (or refusing) to change the requirements the status quo is maintained until the expiry of the time limit for appealing or the hearing of the appeal (subs. (11)). In Scotland, cases will continue to be heard by the Sheriff (subs. (10)). In England, cases will be heard in the family proceedings court (s.92). For details of procedure see pp. 361 and 418 below. In addition, if the local authority has acted improperly, a case could be made for judicial review.

Offences

78.—(1) No person shall provide day care for children under the age of eight on any premises within the area of a local authority unless he is registered by the authority under section 71(1)(b) with respect to those premises.

(2) If any person contravenes subsection (1) without reasonable excuse, he shall be guilty of an offence.

(3) No person shall act as a child minder on domestic premises within the area of a local authority unless he is registered by the authority under section 71(1)(a).

(4) Where it appears to a local authority that a person has contravened subsection (3), they may serve a notice ("an enforcement notice") on him.

(5) An enforcement notice shall have effect for a period of one year beginning with the date on which it is served.

(6) If a person with respect to whom an enforcement notice is in force contravenes subsection (3) without reasonable excuse he shall be guilty of an offence.

(7) Subsection (6) applies whether or not the subsequent contravention occurs within the area of the authority who served the enforcement notice.

(8) Any person who without reasonable excuse contravenes, or otherwise fails to comply with, any requirement imposed on him under section 72 or 73 shall be guilty of an offence.

(9) If any person—
    (a) acts as a child minder on domestic premises at any time when he is disqualified by regulations made under paragraph 2 of Schedule 9; or
    (b) contravenes any of sub-paragraphs (3) to (5) of paragraph 2,

he shall be guilty of an offence.

(10) Where a person contravenes sub-paragraph (3) of paragraph 2 he shall not be guilty of an offence under this section if he proves that he did not know, and had no reasonable grounds for believing, that the person in question was living or employed in the household.

(11) Where a person contravenes sub-paragraph (5) of paragraph 2 he shall not be guilty of an offence under this section if he proves that he did not know, and had no reasonable grounds for believing, that the person whom he was employing was disqualified.

(12) A person guilty of an offence under this section shall be liable on summary conviction—
    (a) in the case of an offence under subsection (8), to a fine not exceeding level 4 on the standard scale;

(b) in the case of an offence under subsection (9), to imprisonment for a term not exceeding six months, or to a fine not exceeding level 5 on the standard scale, or to both; and

(c) in the case of any other offence, to a fine not exceeding level 5 on the standard scale.

DEFINITIONS
"child": ss.71(2), (3), 105(1).
"childminder": s.71(2)(a).
"day care": ss.18, 71(2)(b).
"domestic premises": s.71(12).
"enforcement notice": s.78(4).
"local authority": s.105(1).
"premises": s.71(12).

GENERAL NOTE
This section lists the offences for failure to comply with this Part and provides a simple enforcement notice procedure where a childminder fails to register. In contrast to proceedings under section 77 the criminal standard of proof applies.
The offences are as follows:
(1) Providing, without reasonable excuse, day care at premises for children under the age of eight without registering with the local authority (subs. (2)). Penalty: fine level 5 (subs. (12)(c)).
(2) Childminding anywhere in breach of an enforcement notice (subs. (6)). Penalty: fine level 5 (subs. (12)(c)).
(3) Failing, without reasonable excuse, to comply with requirements imposed under ss.72 and 73 (subs. (8)). Penalty: fine level 4 (subs. (12)(a)).
(4) Childminding when disqualified (subs. (9)). Penalty: fine level 5 and/or six months' imprisonment (subs. (12)(b)).

All offences are triable summarily (subs. (12)). The defences of lack of knowledge, etc. (subss. (10) and (11)) are new and also apply to the comparable offences under section 70(1)(d), which applies to private fostering.

Enforcement notices can be served on anyone who acts as a childminder without registering (subs. (4)) and are effective for one year (subs. (5)). It is only an offence to carry on unregistered childminding if an enforcement notice has been served, but the offence is committed even if the minding occurs in another area (subs. (7)). Once a notice has been served, a person can only lawfully carry out childminding by registering in accordance with section 71(1)(a). The fact of previous unregistered minding should not mean that the person is necessarily unfit to mind within section 71(7) but may do so. Unregistered minding has in the past been very common, but the standard in such homes has given cause for concern (see B & S Jackson *Child minder—A study in Action Research* (1979) Routledge).

Subss. (3)–(7)
Enforcement notice: The enforcement notice procedure is aimed at protecting the occasional unregistered minder from criminal liability.

Application of this Part to Scotland

79. In the application to Scotland of this Part—
    (a) "the court" means the sheriff;
    (b) "day care" means any form of care or of activity supervised by a responsible person provided for children during the day (whether or not it is provided on a regular basis);

(c) "education authority" has the same meaning as in the Education (Scotland) Act 1980;
(d) "local authority foster parent" means a foster parent with whom a child is placed by a local authority;
(e) for references to a person having parental responsibility for a child there shall be substituted references to a person in whom parental rights and duties relating to the child are vested; and
(f) for references to fostering a child privately there shall be substituted references to maintaining a foster child within the meaning of the Foster Children (Scotland) Act 1984.

GENERAL NOTE

This section amends definitions in Part X so that it may apply to Scotland. S.I. 1991 Nos. 1689, 2076, 2094 and 2129 all apply to Scotland.

PART XI

SECRETARY OF STATE'S SUPERVISORY FUNCTIONS AND RESPONSIBILITIES

Inspection of children's homes etc. by persons authorised by Secretary of State

80.—(1) The Secretary of State may cause to be inspected from time to time any—
  (a) children's home;
  (b) premises in which a child who is being looked after by a local authority is living;
  (c) premises in which a child who is being accommodated by or on behalf of a local education authority or voluntary organisation is living;
  (d) premises in which a child who is being accommodated by or on behalf of a health authority [or National Health Service trust] is living;
  (e) premises in which a child is living with a person with whom he has been placed by an adoption agency;
  (f) premises in which a child who is a protected child is, or will be, living;
  (g) premises in which a privately fostered child, or child who is treated as a foster child by virtue of paragraph 9 of Schedule 8, is living or in which it is proposed that he will live;
  (h) premises on which any person is acting as a child minder;
  (i) premises with respect to which a person is registered under section 71(1)(b);
  (j) residential care home, nursing home or mental nursing home required to be registered under the Registered Homes Act 1984 and used to accommodate children;
  (k) premises which are provided by a local authority and in which any service is provided by that authority under Part III;

(l) independent school providing accommodation for any child.

(2) An inspection under this section shall be conducted by a person authorised to do so by the Secretary of State.

(3) An officer of a local authority shall not be so authorised except with the consent of that authority.

(4) The Secretary of State may require any person of a kind mentioned in subsection (5) to furnish him with such information, or allow him to inspect such records (in whatever form they are held), relating to—
- (a) any premises to which subsection (1) or, in relation to Scotland, subsection (l)(h) or (i) applies;
- (b) any child who is living in any such premises;
- (c) the discharge by the Secretary of State of any of his functions under this Act; or
- (d) the discharge by any local authority of any of their functions under this Act,

as the Secretary of State may at any time direct.

(5) The persons are any—
- (a) local authority;
- (b) voluntary organisation;
- (c) person carrying on a children's home;
- (d) proprietor of an independent school;
- (e) person fostering any privately fostered child or providing accommodation for a child on behalf of a local authority, local education authority, health authority, [National Health Service trust] or voluntary organisation;
- (f) local education authority providing accommodation for any child;
- (g) person employed in a teaching or administrative capacity at any educational establishment (whether or not maintained by a local education authority) at which a child is accommodated on behalf of a local authority or local education authority;
- (h) person who is the occupier of any premises in which any person acts as a child minder (within the meaning of Part X) or provides day care for young children (within the meaning of that Part);
- (i) person carrying on any home of a kind mentioned in subsection (1)(j).

(6) Any person inspecting any home or other premises under this section may—
- (a) inspect the children there; and
- (b) make such examination into the state and management of the home or premises and the treatment of the children there as he thinks fit.

(7) Any person authorised by the Secretary of State to exercise the power to inspect records conferred by subsection (4)—
- (a) shall be entitled at any reasonable time to have access to, and inspect and check the operation of, any computer and any associated apparatus or material which is or has been in use in connection with the records in question; and

(b) may require—
    (i) the person by whom or on whose behalf the computer is or has been so used; or
    (ii) any person having charge of, or otherwise concerned with the operation of, the computer, apparatus or material, to afford him such reasonable assistance as he may require.

(8) A person authorised to inspect any premises under this section shall have a right to enter the premises for that purpose, and for any purpose specified in subsection (4), at any reasonable time.

(9) Any person exercising that power shall, if so required, produce some duly authenticated document showing his authority to do so.

(10) Any person who intentionally obstructs another in the exercise of that power shall be guilty of an offence and liable on summary conviction to a fine not exceeding level 3 on the standard scale.

(11) The Secretary of State may by order provide for subsections (1), (4) and (6) not to apply in relation to such homes, or other premises, as may be specified in the order.

(12) Without prejudice to section 104, any such order may make different provision with respect to each of those subsections.

AMENDMENTS

In subsections (1) and (5) the words in square brackets were inserted by the National Health Service and Community Care Act 1990, s.66(1), Sched. 9, para. 36(4).

DEFINITIONS
"adoption agency": s.105(1).
"child": s.105(1).
"childminder": s.71.
"child . . . looked after by a local authority": s.22(1).
"children's home": s.63.
"day care": ss.18, 71.
"health authority": s.105(1).
"independent school": s.105(1).
"local authority": s.105(1).
"local education authority": s.105(1).
"mental nursing home": s.105(1).
"nursing home": s.105(1).
"privately fostered child": s.66.
"protected child": s.105(1).
"residential care home": s.105(1).
"voluntary home": s.60(3).
"voluntary organisation": s.105(1).

GENERAL NOTE

This section re-enacts C.C.A. 1980, ss.74 and 75 and provides the Secretary of State with powers to inspect premises where children are being cared for by people other than those with parental responsibility or relatives (subs. (1)) and the children therein (subs. (6)). The inspection power is supplemented by powers to direct specified people to give specific information (subss. (4) and (5)), to inspect records (subs. (7)) and to enter (subs. (8)). It is an offence intentionally to obstruct entry (subs. (10)). If entry is refused, a warrant can be obtained under section 102. The Secretary of State may make regulations to exempt premises from the duties in subsections (1), (4) and (6) (subss. (11) and (12)) but has not done so. Inspections by the Social Services Inspectorate (SSI) on behalf of the Secretary of State are likely to be even rarer if the recommendations of the *Utting Report* (1991), para. 4.38 ff are followed. Most inspections will be carried out by local authorities' independent inspection units (IIUs). The SSI will provide guidance and inspect the work of the IIUs.

Inquiries

81.—(1) The Secretary of State may cause an inquiry to be held into any matter connected with—
- (a) the functions of the social services committee of a local authority, in so far as those functions relate to children;
- (b) the functions of an adoption agency;
- (c) the functions of a voluntary organisation, in so far as those functions relate to children;
- (d) a [...] children's home or voluntary home;
- (e) a residential care home, nursing home or mental nursing home, so far as it provides accommodation for children;
- (f) a home provided [in accordance with arrangements made] by the Secretary of State under section 82(5);
- (g) the detention of a child under section 53 of the Children and Young Persons Act 1933.

(2) Before an inquiry is begun, the Secretary of State may direct that it shall be held in private.

(3) Where no direction has been given, the person holding the inquiry may if he thinks fit hold it, or any part of it, in private.

(4) Subsections (2) to (5) of section 250 of the Local Government Act 1972 (powers in relation to local inquiries) shall apply in relation to an inquiry under this section as they apply in relation to a local inquiry under that section.

(5) In this section "functions" includes powers and duties which a person has otherwise than by virtue of any enactment.

AMENDMENTS

The word omitted in subsection (1)(d) was repealed, and the words in square brackets in subsection (1)(f) were inserted, by the Courts and Legal Services Act 1990, ss.116, 125(7), Sched. 16, para. 21, Sched. 20.

DEFINITIONS
"adoption agency": s.105(1).
"child": s.105(1).
"functions": s.81(5).
"local authority": s.105(1).
"mental nursing home": s.105(1).
"nursing home": s.105(1).
"registered children's home": s.63.
"residential care home": s.105(1).
"voluntary home": s.60(3).
"voluntary organisation": s.105(1).

GENERAL NOTE

This section re-enacts with minor amendments C.C.A. 1980, s.76. The scope of the power is broadened to include all homes covered by the Act and also all functions relating to children looked after by voluntary organisations. The power to hold inquiries has not been heavily used; most child death inquiries are held by individual local authorities. The Cleveland Inquiry was held under sections 76 and 84 of the National Health Service Act 1977.

Subs. (4)

Subsections (2) to (5) of section 250 of the Local Government Act: These provisions enable an inquiry to subpoena witnesses to give evidence or to produce documents, take evidence on oath and make orders as to costs.

Financial support by Secretary of State

82.—(1) The Secretary of State may (with the consent of the Treasury) defray or contribute towards—
- (a) any fees or expenses incurred by any person undergoing approved child care training;
- (b) any fees charged, or expenses incurred, by any person providing approved child care training or preparing material for use in connection with such training; or
- (c) the cost of maintaining any person undergoing such training.

(2) The Secretary of State may make grants to local authorities in respect of expenditure incurred by them in providing secure accommodation in community homes other than assisted community homes.

(3) Where—
- (a) a grant has been made under subsection (2) with respect to any secure accommodation; but
- (b) the grant is not used for the purpose for which it was made or the accommodation is not used as, or ceases to be used as, secure accommodation,

the Secretary of State may (with the consent of the Treasury) require the authority concerned to repay the grant, in whole or in part.

(4) The Secretary of State may make grants to voluntary organisations towards—
- (a) expenditure incurred by them in connection with the establishment, maintenance or improvement of voluntary homes which, at the time when the expenditure was incurred—
  - (i) were assisted community homes; or
  - (ii) were designated as such; or
- (b) expenses incurred in respect of the borrowing of money to defray any such expenditure.

(5) The Secretary of State may arrange for the provision, equipment and maintenance of homes for the accommodation of children who are in need of particular facilities and services which—
- (a) are or will be provided in those homes; and
- (b) in the opinion of the Secretary of State, are unlikely to be readily available in community homes.

(6) In this Part—
"child care training" means training undergone by any person with a view to, or in the course of—
- (a) his employment for the purposes of any of the functions mentioned in section 83(9) or in connection with the

adoption of children or with the accommodation of children in a residential care home, nursing home or mental nursing home; or

(b) his employment by a voluntary organisation for similar purposes;

"approved child care training" means child care training which is approved by the Secretary of State; and

"secure accommodation" means accommodation provided for the purpose of restricting the liberty of children.

(7) Any grant made under this section shall be of such amount, and shall be subject to such conditions, as the Secretary of State may (with the consent of the Treasury) determine.

DEFINITIONS

"approved child care training": s.82(6).
"child care training": s.82(6).
"community home", "assisted community home": s.53.
"functions": s.105(1).
"mental nursing home": s.105(1).
"nursing home": s.105(1).
"residential care home": s.105(1).
"secure accommodation": ss.25, 82(6).
"voluntary home": s.60(3).
"voluntary organisation": s.105(1).

GENERAL NOTE

This section re-enacts with minor amendments C.C.A. 1980, ss.78 and 80. It empowers the Secretary of State to make grants as follows: for approved child care training (subs. (1)); to local authorities for secure accommodation (subs. (2)); and to voluntary organisations for voluntary homes (subs. (4)). Grants under subsection (2) may be reclaimed (subs. (3)); grants under subsection (4) may be reclaimed under section 58. The Secretary of State may also arrange for homes to be provided for children who need particular facilities (subs. (5)).

Subs. (5)

Youth Treatment Centres have been established by the Department of Health under this provision "to provide long-term care, control and treatment for a small minority of severely disturbed and anti-social boys and girls between the ages of 12 and 19 whose specialised treatment needs cannot be met satisfactorily in any of the other forms of residential provision" (D.H.S.S. Circular LAC (77)2). A charge becomes payable by a local authority if a child in its care is accommodated at a Youth Treatment Centre.

Research and returns of information

83.—(1) The Secretary of State may conduct, or assist other persons in Research conducting, research into any matter connected with—

(a) his functions, or the functions of local authorities, under the enactments mentioned in subsection (9);

(b) the adoption of children; or
(c) the accommodation of children in a residential care home, nursing home or mental nursing home.

(2) Any local authority may conduct, or assist other persons in conducting, research into any matter connected with—
  (a) their functions under the enactments mentioned in subsection (9);
  (b) the adoption of children; or
  (c) the accommodation of children in a residential care home, nursing home or mental nursing home.

(3) Every local authority shall, at such times and in such form as the Secretary of State may direct, transmit to him such particulars as he may require with respect to—
  (a) the performance by the local authority of all or any of their functions—
    (i) under the enactments mentioned in subsection (9); or
    (ii) in connection with the accommodation of children in a residential care home, nursing home or mental nursing home; and
  (b) the children in relation to whom the authority have exercised those functions.

(4) Every voluntary organisation shall, at such times and in such form as the Secretary of State may direct, transmit to him such particulars as he may require with respect to children accommodated by them or on their behalf.

(5) The Secretary of State may direct the clerk of each magistrates' court to which the direction is expressed to relate to transmit—
  (a) to such person as may be specified in the direction; and
  (b) at such times and in such form as he may direct,
such particulars as he may require with respect to proceedings of the court which relate to children.

(6) The Secretary of State shall in each year lay before Parliament a consolidated and classified abstract of the information transmitted to him under subsections (3) to (5).

(7) The Secretary of State may institute research designed to provide information on which requests for information under this section may be based.

(8) The Secretary of State shall keep under review the adequacy of the provision of child care training and for that purpose shall receive and consider any information from or representations made by—
  (a) the Central Council for Education and Training in Social Work;
  (b) such representatives of local authorities as appear to him to be appropriate; or
  (c) such other persons or organisations as appear to him to be appropriate, concerning the provision of such training.

(9) The enactments are—
  (a) this Act;
  (b) the Children and Young Persons Acts 1933 to 1969;
  (c) section 116 of the Mental Health Act 1983 (so far as it relates to children looked after by local authorities);

(d) section 10 of the Mental Health (Scotland) Act 1984 (so far as it relates to children for whom local authorities have responsibility).

DEFINITIONS
"child care training": s.82(6).
"functions": s.105(1).
"local authority": s.105(1).
"mental nursing home": s.105(1).
"nursing home": s.105(1).
"residential care home": s.105(1).
"voluntary organisation": s.105(1).

GENERAL NOTE
Subsections (1), (2) and (9) re-enact with amendments C.C.A. 1980, s.77. They empower the Secretary of State and local authorities to conduct or assist others in research on child care.
Subsections (3) to (6) re-enact with amendments C.C.A. 1980, s.79. They require local authorities, voluntary organisations and magistrates' court clerks to provide information to the Secretary of State (or another specified person in the case of magistrates' courts) who must lay an abstract of the information before Parliament. Triennial reports to Parliament are no longer required. Subsection (8) requires the Secretary of State to monitor the adequacy of child care training.

Local authority failure to comply with statutory duty: default power of Secretary of State

84.—(1) If the Secretary of State is satisfied that any local authority has failed, without reasonable excuse, to comply with any of the duties imposed on them by or under this Act he may make an order declaring that authority to be in default with respect to that duty.

(2) An order under subsection (1) shall give the Secretary of State's reasons for making it.

(3) An order under subsection (1) may contain such directions for the purpose of ensuring that the duty is complied with, within such period as may be specified in the order, as appear to the Secretary of State to be necessary.

(4) Any such direction shall, on the application of the Secretary of State, be enforceable by mandamus.

GENERAL NOTE
This section provides a new power which will enable the Secretary of State to issue a direction, enforceable by mandamus (subs. (44)), where a local authority is in default of its duties under the Act (subs. (1)). It is envisaged that the power will only be used in "extreme circumstances, but ... it may be necessary to use it ... for example, where a local authority fails to make the requisite provision for a class of children." (*per* Solicitor General (Standing Committee B, col. 492, June 8, 1989)).
A similar power is found in the Education Act 1944, s.99, but the power is rarely used. Ministers seem reluctant to use it and see its value in the threat it provides (see J. Logie *Enforcing statutory duties: The courts and default powers* [1988] J.S.W.L. 185). Where the minister unreasonably refuses to act, it may be possible to challenge his decision by judicial review. Also, although it has been held that the existence of a default power prevents other judicial action (*Pasmore* v. *Oswaldtwistle Urban District Council* [1898] A.C. 387) this does not apply to applications for judicial review (*R.* v. *Secretary of State for the Environment, ex p. Ward* [1984] 1 W.L.R. 834). However, it will be difficult to challenge a

local authority's decisions about its duties under this Act by judicial review (see notes on s.22). Despite this new power, the main method for obtaining redress will be via the complaints procedure in section 26.

PART XII

MISCELLANEOUS AND GENERAL

Notification of children accommodated in certain establishments

Children accommodated by health authorities and local education authorities

85.—(1) Where a child is provided with accommodation by any health authority, [National Health Service trust] or local education authority ("the accommodating authority")—
  (a) for a consecutive period of at least three months; or
  (b) with the intention, on the part of that authority, of accommodating him for such a period,
the accommodating authority shall notify the responsible authority.

(2) Where subsection (1) applies with respect to a child, the accommodating authority shall also notify the responsible authority when they cease to accommodate the child.

(3) In this section "the responsible authority" means—
  (a) the local authority appearing to the accommodating authority to be the authority within whose area the child was ordinarily resident immediately before being accommodated; or
  (b) where it appears to the accommodating authority that a child was not ordinarily resident within the area of any local authority, the local authority within whose area the accommodation is situated.

(4) Where a local authority have been notified under this section, they shall—
  (a) take such steps as are reasonably practicable to enable them to determine whether the child's welfare is adequately safeguarded and promoted while he is accommodated by the accommodating authority; and
  (b) consider the extent to which (if at all) they should exercise any of their functions under this Act with respect to the child.

AMENDMENT

In subsection (1) the words in square brackets were inserted by the National Health Service and Community Care Act 1990, s.66(1), Sched. 9, para. 36(5).

DEFINITIONS
  "child": s.105(1).
  "functions": s.105(1).
  "health authority": s.105(1).

"local authority": s.105(1).
"local education authority": s.105(1).
"the accommodating authority": s.85(1).
"the responsible authority": s.85(3).

GENERAL NOTE

This section imposes new responsibilities on local authorities to safeguard the welfare of children accommodated for more than three consecutive months by health authorities or local education authorities (subs. (4)). Health authorities and local education authorities are under a duty to notify the responsible authority of such children (subs. (1)) and when they cease to accommodate them (subs. (2)). Local authorities have further duties in relation to the after-care of such children under section 24. This follows the recommendations of the R.C.C.L., Chap 11, paras. 8–11, which noted the large number of such children and the concerns expressed that children in long-stay hospitals particularly had no contact with their families.

The Department of Health has issued guidance on sections 85 and 86, see *Guidance*, Vol. 4, para. 1.195–205 and Vol. 6, para. 13.7–13; DH, *The Welfare of Children and Young People in Hospital* (1991) is also relevant.

Subs. (1)

Three months: The Department of Health has stated that school holidays do not count towards this period, see *Guidance*, Vol. 4, para. 1.196, although the reasons for this view have not been made clear.

Subs. (3)

The obligation falls on the authority for the child's home area unless subsection (3)(b) applies, *e.g.* a severely handicapped child who has never lived outside a hospital.

Subs. (4)

Guidance, Vol. 4, para. 1.99 ff states that local authorities should first, within 14 days of being notified, contact the education or health authority, etc. to find out the circumstances of the case. Authorities should find out whether contact between the child and his parents, etc. is adequate and obtain written assurances from the authority that proper parental contact is being established or maintained. Where appropriate the local authority should also contact the parents. If it becomes apparent that contact has ceased, or there are other matters which suggest that the child's welfare is not being safeguarded the authority should arrange to visit the child within 14 days. They have no rights of entry under this provision so visiting must be negotiated with the accommodating authority.

Co-operation between social services, health and education are crucial particularly in the case of children with disabilities where each agency may need to be actively involved with the child and family. Section 27 provides a basis for co-operation; circulars have also been issued—HC (78)28/LAC(78)16 which encourages joint health service and social service review of cases and HN(89)20/HN(FP) (89)(19)/LASSL(89)7 WOC54/89/DES:22/89 which relates to assessments and statements of special educational needs. Further guidance on co-operation and children with disabilities is provided in *Guidance*, Vol. 6.

Their functions: Part III gives local authorities wide scope; Schedule 2, paragraph 10 imposes a duty on local authorities to facilitate reunification and promote contact between separated children and their families. See also notes to section 17.

Children accommodated in residential care, nursing or mental nursing homes

86.—(1) Where a child is provided with accommodation in any residential care home, nursing home or mental nursing home—

(a) for a consecutive period of at least three months; or
(b) with the intention, on the part of the person taking the decision to accommodate him, of accommodating him for such period,

the person carrying on the home shall notify the local authority within whose area the home is carried on.

(2) Where subsection (1) applies with respect to a child, the person carrying on the home shall also notify that authority when he ceases to accommodate the child in the home.

(3) Where a local authority have been notified under this section, they shall—
(a) take such steps as are reasonably practicable to enable them to determine whether the child's welfare is adequately safeguarded and promoted while he is accommodated in the home; and
(b) consider the extent to which (if at all) they should exercise any of their functions under this Act with respect to the child.

(4) If the person carrying on any home fails, without reasonable excuse, to comply with this section he shall be guilty of an offence.

(5) A person authorised by a local authority may enter any residential care home, nursing home or mental nursing home within the authority's area for the purpose of establishing whether the requirements of this section have been complied with.

(6) Any person who intentionally obstructs another in the exercise of the power of entry shall be guilty of an offence.

(7) Any person exercising the power of entry shall, if so required, produce some duly authenticated document showing his authority to do so.

(8) Any person committing an offence under this section shall be liable on summary conviction to a fine not exceeding level 3 on the standard scale.

DEFINITIONS
"child": s.105(1).
"local authority": s.105(1).
"mental nursing home": s.105(1).
"nursing home": s.105(1).
"residential care home": s.105(1).

GENERAL NOTE

This section imposes a duty, comparable to that in section 85, on those carrying on residential care homes, nursing homes and mental nursing homes to notify the local authority about children they are accommodating (subss. (1) and (2)) and on the local authority in whose areas the home is situated to safeguard the children's welfare (subs. (3)). The local authority also has a duty in relation to the after-care of such children under section 24. Failure to notify the authority without reasonable cause is an offence (summary conviction: fine level 3) (subss. (4) and (8)). A person authorised by the local authority has a power of entry to establish whether the section has been complied with (subs. (5)). It is an offence (level 3) to intentionally obstruct such entry (subss. (6) and

(8)). Where entry is refused, a warrant could be obtained under section 102, or, if an emergency protection order was sought, section 48(9).

Guidance has been issued, see notes to section 85 above.

Subs. (5)

A comparable power of entry exists under section 60(5) (see notes to that section).

Welfare of children accommodated in independent schools

87.—(1) It shall be the duty of—
- (a) the proprietor of any independent school which provides accommodation for any child; and
- (b) any person who is not the proprietor of such a school but who is responsible for conducting it,

to safeguard and promote the child's welfare.

(2) Subsection (1) does not apply in relation to a school which is a children's home or a residential care home [other than a small home].

(3) Where accommodation is provided for a child by an independent school within the area of a local authority, the authority shall take such steps as are reasonably practicable to enable them to determine whether the child's welfare is adequately safeguarded and promoted while he is accommodated by the school.

(4) Where a local authority are of the opinion that there has been a failure to comply with subsection (1) in relation to a child provided with accommodation by a school within their area, they shall notify the Secretary of State.

(5) Any person authorised by a local authority may, for the purpose of enabling the authority to discharge their duty under this section, enter at any reasonable time any independent school within their area which provides accommodation for any child.

(6) Any person entering an independent school in exercise of the power conferred by subsection (5) may carry out such inspection of premises, children and records as is prescribed by regulations made by the Secretary of State for the purposes of this section.

(7) Any person exercising that power shall, if asked to do so, produce some duly authenticated document showing his authority to do so.

(8) Any person authorised by the regulations to inspect records—
- (a) shall be entitled at any reasonable time to have access to, and inspect and check the operation of, any computer and any associated apparatus or material which is or has been in use in connection with the records in question; and
- (b) may require—
    - (i) the person by whom or on whose behalf the computer is or has been so used; or
    - (ii) any person having charge of, or otherwise concerned with the operation of, the computer, apparatus or material, to afford him such assistance as he may reasonably require.

(9) Any person who intentionally obstructs another in the exercise of any power conferred by this section or the regulations shall be

guilty of an offence and liable on summary conviction to a fine not exceeding level 3 on the standard scale.

(10) In this section "proprietor" has the same meaning as in the Education Act 1944.

AMENDMENT

The words in square brackets in subs. (2) were inserted by the Registered Homes (Amendment) Act 1991, s.2.

DEFINITIONS
"child": s.105(1).
"children's home": s.63.
"independent school": s.105(1).
"local authority": s.105(1).
"proprietor": s.87(10).
"school": s.105(1).
"residential care home": s.105(1).

REGULATIONS

Inspection of Premises, Children and Records (Independent Schools) Regulations 1991 (S.I. 1991 No. 975).

GENERAL NOTE

This section imposes two new duties: (a) a duty on the proprietors of independent schools which are neither residential care homes nor children's homes (subs. (2)) to safeguard and promote the welfare of children they accommodate (subs. (1)) and (b) a duty on the local authority in whose area the school is situated to take reasonable steps to determine whether the duty is being complied with (subs. (3)).

Where the local authority considers that the proprietors have breached their duty it must inform the Secretary of State, who may send a notice of complaint under the Education Act 1944, s.71 (as amended in Sched. 13, para. 9). This could lead to the closure of the school. Where a child is suffering (or likely to suffer) significant harm, the local authority will be able to take action by removing him under an emergency protection order (s.44) or arranging for him to be accommodated by the local authority with the parents' agreement until they are able to collect him (s.20).

The provision dovetails with those in the Registered Homes Act 1984 and Parts VI–IX and XII of this Act so that the welfare of all children provided with accommodation away from home is safeguarded. This section only applies to independent schools with more than 50 boarders; smaller schools are required to register as children's homes (s.63(6)). Non-maintained special schools are outside section 87 but the local authority has comparable duties under section 61. The local authority has a power to enter premises at any reasonable time and may carry out inspection as permitted by the regulations (subss. (5) and (6)). The regulations do not allow inspection of children of or living with staff members unless they are also pupils (reg.3). All records which contain information concerning a pupil's health, emotional or developmental well-being or welfare may be inspected. The local authority also has a right to obtain the names and qualifications of all staff and volunteers who are responsible for the welfare of children at any time (reg.4). It is an offence (level 3) intentionally to obstruct entry or an inspection permitted by the regulations (subs. (9)).

Guidance has been provided for local authorities and school proprietors on this provision, see *Guidance*, Vol. 5. It is particularly aimed at protecting children at independent schools from inappropriate care or abuse. Proprietors are expected to carry out thorough checks on staff prior to appointment; they may make use of the Department of Health consultancy service which maintains a list of persons whose suitability is in doubt (para. 3.3.1 ff). Guidance is also given on living accommodation, health, contact with family, religious and cultural ethos, personal relations and discipline. Independent schools should have clear and accessible avenues for complaint.

Welfare of Children Accommodated

The Department of Health has also produced training materials to prepare inspectors for their role and schools for inspection, *Inspecting Independent Schools with Boarding: an induction framework for social services inspectors, trainers and managers* (1992).

Subs. (1)
Which provides accommodation: Accommodation outside the curtilage of the school but provided by the school is included. However, where the school merely arranges for children to be boarded with local landladies it does not provide accommodation. If they cared or intended to care for more than 28 days, such people would be private foster parents within Part. IX and have a duty to register with the local authority. The local authority would also have a duty to safeguard the welfare of any children privately fostered. There is no requirement to register as a private foster parent if the children are over 16 unless they are disabled (s.71). However, where the accommodation is provided by the school, the local authority's responsibility will last until the child is 18. The local authority has no special responsibility for day schools but may take action to remove individual children where there are grounds for an emergency protection order.

Subs. (4)
Guidance, Vol. 5, Chap. 4 outlines the notification process. Notifications should be made to the Schools Independent Team at the Department for Education and copied to the Social Services Inspectorate with supporting documents. Failure of the proprietor to safeguard and promote the welfare of a boarding pupil may lead to the school being struck off the Register of Independent Schools. There is a right of appeal to the Independent Schools Tribunal. Vol. 5, para. 4.3.3 states, "A complaint (by the social services department) could not be expected to be sustained unless the SSD's notification states the grounds on which the SSD has formed its opinion... and these grounds can be sustained by reference to the guidance in this circular and the standards expected."

Subs. (5)
Enter at any reasonable time: See section 62(6). Any time when the children are up may be reasonable unless it disrupts the school unduly, *e.g.* the inspection of children during a public exam. *Guidance*, Vol. 5, Chap. 4 suggests that the first visit should be made within 12 months of the implementation of the Act. A second visit should be made a year later to check that the guidance in Vol. 5 has been implemented. Further visits, involving formal inspection should be made at least every two years; other visits should take place as the need arises and at least annually. Written reports should be made of any inspection visits; these should be shown to the proprietor but should not normally be published.

Adoption

Amendments of adoption legislation

88.—(1) The Adoption Act 1976 shall have effect subject to the amendments made by Part I of Schedule 10.

(2) The Adoptlon (Scotland) Act 1978 shall have effect subject to the amendments made by Part II of Schedule 10.

GENERAL NOTE
This section and Schedule 10 amend adoption law. The changes do three things. First, they harmonise U.K. adoption law following the reforms in Northern Ireland introduced by the Adoption (Northern Ireland) Order 1987. This is designed to enable adoption agencies in different parts of the U.K. to work in closer co-operation with one another. Secondly, they make consequential amendments, particularly replacing the terms "parental rights" and "custody." Thirdly, they introduce reforms designed to

improve adoption law. A full review of adoption law is underway and may be expected to lead to further reform in due course. The most significant changes are listed below:

(1) *Age limits*: A parent applicant need only be 18 years (Adoption Act 1976, s.14(18), Sched. 10, para. 4).

(2) *Freeing for adoption*: If parents do not agree, the child must be in care of the local authority (Adoption Act 1976, s.18(2A), Sched. 10, para. 6(1)). The courts must consider whether a non-marital father intends to apply for parental responsibility or a residence order (Adoption Act 1976, s.18(7), Sched. 10, para. 6(3)). Revocation of a freeing order returns parental responsibility to the parents. It does not revive orders under section 8 of this Act. (Adoption Act 1976, s.20(3), Sched. 10, para. 8(3)).

(3) *Notification of intention to adopt*: This cannot be made more than two years before the adoption order (s.22(1A), Sched. 10, para. 10(1)). "Protected child" is redefined to take account of this Act (Pts. VI–IX and XII and the Adoption Act 1976, s.32, para. 18).

(4) *Removal from adoption applicant*: Section 20(8) of this Act does not entitle a parent to remove a child from those who have cared for him for five years (Adoption Act 1976, s.28(2a), Sched. 10, para. 14(1)).

(5) *Access to birth records*: Adoption Act 1976, s.51, is amended to make further provision for counselling and enabling people who were adopted in England or Wales to have access to birth records, even though they now live overseas (Sched. 10, para. 20).

(6) *Adoption contact register*: Adoption Act 1976, s.51A, provides for the Registrar General to establish a register which will enable adopted persons (and their natural relatives) to register their names and addresses and thus facilitate tracing (Sched. 10, para. 21).

(7) *Adoption Allowances*: Adoption Act 1976, s.57A, empowers the Secretary of State to make regulations to replace approval for Schemes under s.57(4). The Adoption Allowance Regulations 1991 (S.I. 1991 No. 2030) and the Adoption Allowance (Amendment) Regulations 1991 (S.I. 1991 No. 2130) came into force on October 14, 1991. (Sched. 10, para. 25).

(8) *Guardians ad litem*: Adoption Act 1976, s.65A empowers the Secretary of State to make regulations about guardian ad litem panels. Section 65A(2) is identical to section 41(9) of this Act, thus panels regulations can apply to guardians under both Acts The Guardians ad litem and Reporting Officers (Panels Regulations) 1991 (S.I. 1991 No. 2051) came into force on October 14, 1991 (see notes to s.41) (Sched. 10, para. 29).

(9) *Scotland*: Part. II of Schedule 10 makes minor amendments to the Adoption (Scotland) Act 1978.

In addition, the Adoption Rules 1984 have been amended by S.I. 1991 No. 1880. Because adoption proceedings are family proceedings the court may make any section 8 order as well as, or instead of an adoption or freeing order. Applications to adopt children in care must be made to the court which made the order see the Children (Allocation of Proceedings) Order 1991, art. 4(1) and p. 434 below. Guidance on the changes to adoption law including the adoption contact register is provided in *Guidance*, Vol. 9.

Paternity tests

Tests to establish paternity

89.—In section 20 of the Family Law Reform Act 1969 (power of court to require use of tests to determine paternity), the following subsections shall be inserted after subsection (1)—

["(1A) An application for a direction under this section shall specify who is to carry out the tests.

(1B) A direction under this section shall]

(a) specify, as the person who is to carry out the tests, the person specified in the application; or

(b) where the court considers that it would be inappropriate to specify that person (whether because to specify him would be incompatible with any provision made by or under regulations made under section 22 of this Act or for any other reason), decline to give the direction applied for."

AMENDMENT

The words in square brackets were substituted by the Courts and Legal Services Act 1990, Sched. 16, para. 20.

GENERAL NOTE

This section amends the Family Law Reform Act 1969, s.20 to take account of developments in blood tests for proof of paternity. There are now two alternative tests: immunological testing, costing under £50, and D.N.A. profiling, costing over £300. Applicants may choose which they prefer but the court will retain its overriding discretion to refuse the order sought.

Criminal care and supervision orders

Care and supervision orders in criminal proceedings

90.—(1) The power of a court to make an order under subsection (2) of section 1 of the Children and Young Persons Act 1969 (care proceedings in [youth courts]) where it is of the opinion that the condition mentioned in paragraph (f) of that subsection ("the offence condition") is satisfied is hereby abolished.

(2) The powers of the court to make care orders—
  (a) under section 7(7)(a) of the Children and Young Persons Act 1969 (alteration in treatment of young offenders etc.); and
  (b) under section 15(1) of that Act, on discharging a supervision order made under section 7(7)(b) of that Act,
are hereby abolished.

(3) The powers given by that Act to include requirements in supervision orders shall have effect subject to amendments made by Schedule 12.

AMENDMENT

The words in square brackets in subsection (1) were substituted by the Criminal Justice Act 1991, Sched. 11, para. 40.

GENERAL NOTE

This section abolishes the power of the court to make a care order in respect of juvenile offenders in care, or criminal proceedings. Guidance on these changes is provided in *Guidance*, Vol. 1, Chap. 6.

C.Y.P.A. 1969, s.1(2)(f), the offence condition, was scarcely used and did not fit with the notion that a care or supervision order should only be made on proof of substantial harm. Its abolition was recommended in the R.C.C.L., para. 15.20. Conduct which led to care proceedings on this ground may still lead to a care order under section 31, but it will be necessary to satisfy the significant harm test in section 31(2). It may be difficult to argue that minor criminal activity, particularly shoplifting or criminal damage, indicates significant harm because it is so widespread; children who steal cars or ride in stolen cars with friends may well be at risk of significant harm.

C.Y.P.A. 1969, s.7(7), care orders in criminal proceedings are abolished and replaced by supervision orders with a residence requirement (six months maximum) under the C.Y.P.A. 1969, s.12AA (see Sched. 12, paras. 22–25). This new sentence can only be imposed where a further serious offence (punishable by imprisonment for someone over 21) is committed by someone already subject to a supervision order with a requirement under the C.Y.P.A. 1969, s.12A(3) or a residence requirement. The court must also be satisfied that the offence is due to the conditions in which the offender was living (C.Y.P.A. 1969, s.12AA(6)). The court will have to have a Social Inquiry Report and consult the local authority (s.12AA(3), (7) and (8)). The offender must be legally represented unless the conditions in C.Y.P.A. 1969, s.12AA(9) and (10) apply.

The intention is to "put another step on the escalator of criminal penalties...to prevent (young offenders) from reaching the point on the escalator which amounts to custody. One can draw a clear distinction. Being required to live in a residential accommodation will not involve the total deprivation of liberty that would be involved in being placed in a custodial institution" (*per* David Mellor, Minister of Health (Standing Committee B, co. 502–3, June 13, 1989)). It is not, however, clear that this will work in practice. The order may be seen to be too lenient and those who might otherwise have been committed to care will be pushed up the tariff to a custodial sentence, thus increasing rather than inhibiting custodial sentences, although the order may be repeated (see C.Y.P.A. 1969, s.12AA(6)(ii) and (7)). It seems unlikely that this disposal will be used in respect of young offenders who are already being looked after by local authorities and will thus add to the disparity in the treatment of the group of disadvantaged young offenders. Such young people may be placed in secure accommodation but only where the conditions in section 25(1) are satisfied; the modified grounds (S.I. 1991 No. 1505, reg. 6) do not apply to such children.

Young offenders subject to orders under C.Y.P.A. 1969, s.12AA are being looked after by the local authority within section 21 of this Act. They are therefore owed the duties in Part III including the duty to provide after-care under section 24. Limited specific guidance has been provided about accommodating such children or making plans relating to them see *Guidance* Vol. 1, para. 6.30. The general provisions apply (see notes to ss.23 and 53). Where a child commits further offences while under a residential supervision order the local authority is not responsible for any financial penalties made against him because they do not have parental responsibility for him (Children and Young Persons Act 1933, s.55 as amended by Criminal Justice Act 1991, s.57).

Effect and duration of orders, etc.

91.—(1) The making of a residence order with respect to a child who is the subject of a care order discharges the care order.

(2) The making of a care order with respect to a child who is the subject of any section 8 order discharges that order.

(3) The making of a care order with respect to a child who is the subject of a supervision order discharges that other order.

(4) The making of a care order with respect to a child who is a ward of court brings that wardship to an end.

(5) The making of a care order with respect to a child who is the subject of a school attendance order made under section 37 of the Education Act 1944 discharges the school attendance order.

(6) Where an emergency protection order is made with respect to a child who is in care, the care order shall have effect subject to the emergency protection order.

(7) Any order made under section 4(1) or 5(1) shall continue in force until the child reaches the age of eighteen, unless it is brought to an end earlier.

(8) Any—

    (a) agreement under section 4; or

    (b) appointment under section 5(3) or (4),

shall continue in force until the child reaches the age of eighteen, unless it is brought to an end earlier.

(9) An order under Schedule 1 has effect as specified in that Schedule.

(10) A section 8 order shall, if it would otherwise still be in force, cease to have effect when the child reaches the age of sixteen, unless it is to have effect beyond that age by virtue of section 9(6).

(11) Where a section 8 order has effect with respect to a child who has reached the age of sixteen, it shall, if it would otherwise still be in force, cease to have effect when he reaches the age of eighteen.

(12) Any care order, other than an interim care order, shall continue in force until the child reaches the age of eighteen, unless it is brought to an end earlier.

(13) Any order made under any other provision of this Act in relation to a child shall, if it would otherwise still be in force, cease to have effect when he reaches the age of eighteen.

(14) On disposing of any application for an order under this Act, the court may (whether or not it makes any other order in response to the application) order that no application for an order under this Act of any specified kind may be made with respect to the child concerned by any person named in the order without leave of the court.

(15) Where an application ("the previous application") has been made for—
    (a) the discharge of a care order;
    (b) the discharge of a supervision order;
    (c) the discharge of an education supervision order;
    (d) the substitution of a supervision order for a care order; or
    (e) a child assessment order,

no further application of a kind mentioned in paragraphs (a) to (e) may be made with respect to the child concerned, without leave of the court, unless the period between the disposal of the previous application and the making of the further application exceeds six months.

(16) Subsection (15) does not apply to applications made in relation to interim orders.

(17) Where—
    (a) a person has made an application for an order under section 34;
    (b) the application has been refused; and
    (c) a period of less than six months has elapsed since the refusal,

that person may not make a further application for such an order with respect to the same child, unless he has obtained the leave of the court.

DEFINITIONS
"care order": s.31(11).
"child assessment order": s.43.
"education supervision order": s.36.
"emergency protection order": s.44.
"interim care order": ss.31(11), 38.
"residence order": s.8(1).
"section 8 order": s.8(1).
"supervision order": ss.31(11), 35.

GENERAL NOTE

This section states the effect and duration of orders:

Section 8 orders: All section 8 orders are discharged by the making of a care order (subs. (2)), or when the child is 16, unless section 9(6) applies (subs. (10)). These orders end at 18 (subs. (11)).

Care orders (s.31): These continue until the child is 18 unless discharged (subs. (12)). Care orders discharge supervision orders (subs. (3)), wardship (subs. (4)), school attendance orders (subs. (5)). Care orders are discharged by the making of a residence order (subs. (1)). Care orders have effect subject to any emergency protection orders made in respect of the child (subs. (6)). They cease to have effect if the child goes to live in Northern Ireland, etc., in accordance with regulations (see s.101(4)). Care orders end at 18 (subs. (12)).

Parental responsibility agreements and orders (s.4) and guardianship appointments (s.5): These continue until the child is 18 unless ended earlier (subs. (8)).

Maintenance orders (Sched. 1): These last until the child is 17 but may last longer where Schedule 1, paragraph 3(2) applies (subs. (9)).

Other orders (ss.16, 34, 35, 38, 43, 44, etc.), end when the child is 18, if not before (subs. 13).

This section also lists the restrictions on further applications, implementing the recommendations in Law Com. 172, para. 6.31 (subss. (14) to (17)). The court has a wide power to order that further applications require leave (subs. (14)). In *Re H (Child Orders: Restricting Applications)* [1991] F.C.R. 896 it was said that this power should be used sparingly and not without a clear basis. Where the child was suffering or likely to suffer because of repeated litigation a restriction should be imposed. Applications for the discharge of care, supervision, education supervision orders, the substitution of a supervision order for a care order, or the making of a child assessment order, all require leave if a previous application has been made within six months (subs. (15)). The same applies where an application has been made unsuccessfully for contact under section 34 (subs. (17)). There are no restrictions in relation to interim orders (subs. (16)).

Subs. (5)

School attendance order: is an order made by a local education authority under the Education Act 1944, s.37(1), requiring parents to have the child registered at and attend a school named in the order.

Subs. (14)

The protection of this provision is only necessary where there is a danger of vindictive or harassing applications by someone such as a parent who does not otherwise require leave. Section 1 applies, so the court will need to be satisfied that it is necessary and in the child's welfare to require leave. In *F v. Kent CC The Independent*, August 10, 1992, Brown P. held that such a restriction was improper in the case of a father who had not been vexatious, frivolous or unreasonable in his application.

Jurisdiction and procedure etc.

Jurisdiction of courts

92.—(1) The name "domestic proceedings", given to certain proceedings in magistrates' courts, is hereby changed to "family proceedings" and the names "domestic court" and "domestic court panel" are hereby changed to "family proceedings court" and "family panel," respectively.

(2) Proceedings under this Act shall be treated as family proceedings in relation to magistrates' courts.

(3) Subsection (2) is subject to the provisions of section 65(1) and (2) of the Magistrates' Courts Act 1980 (proceedings which may be treated as not being family proceedings), as amended by this Act.

(4) A magistrates' court shall not be competent to entertain any application, or make any order, involving the administration or application of—
  (a) any property belonging to or held in trust for a child; or
  (b) the income of any such property.
(5) The powers of a magistrates' court under section 63(2) of the Act of 1980 to suspend or rescind orders shall not apply in relation to any order made under this Act.
(6) Part I of Schedule 11 makes provision, including provision for the Lord Chancellor to make orders, with respect to the jurisdiction of courts and justices of the peace in relation to—
  (a) proceedings under this Act; and
  (b) proceedings under certain other enactments.
(7) For the purposes of this Act "the court" means the High Court, a county court or a magistrates' court.
(8) Subsection (7) is subject to the provision made by or under Part I of Schedule 11 and to any express provision as to the jurisdiction of any court made by any other provision of this Act.
(9) The Lord Chancellor may by order make provision for the principal registry of the Family Division of the High Court to be treated as if it were a county court for such purposes of this Act, or of any provision made under this Act, as may be specified in the order.
(10) Any order under subsection (9) may make such provision as the Lord Chancellor thinks expedient for the purpose of applying (with or without modifications) provisions which apply in relation to the procedure in county courts to the principal registry when it acts as if it were a county court.
(11) Part II of Schedule 11 makes amendments consequential on this section.

DEFINITIONS

"family panel": s.92(1).
"family proceedings": s.92(2).
"family proceedings court": s.92(1).
"specified": Sched. 11, para. 4(2).
"the court": s.92(7).

REGULATIONS

Children (Allocation of Proceedings) Order 1991 (S.I. 1991 No. 1677) and the Children (Allocation of Proceedings) (Appeals) Order 1991 (S.I. 1991 No. 1801); see below, pp. 430–450.

GENERAL NOTE

Under this section that part of the magistrates' court which hears proceedings under this Act will be known as the family proceedings court. This section should be read with Schedule 11. Proceedings which were heard in the domestic court under the Magistrates' Courts Act 1980, s.65(1), (2) (as amended) are now to be heard in the family proceedings court but the court will continue to have no jurisdiction over issues concerning trusts or income arising from trust property (subss. (3) and (4)). Orders made in the magistrates' court can no longer be suspended or rescinded under the Magistrates' Courts Act 1980, s.63(2), and will have to be varied or discharged in accordance with section 91 of this Act (subs. (5)). Other details of jurisdiction are contained in Schedule 11 and the court rules.

The Government indicated that it would expect the majority (75 per cent.) of public law cases to be started in the family proceedings court with transfer to a specified county court (care centre), or even the High Court, in three circumstances: first, if there are other proceedings, for example divorce proceedings, currently being held in the other court; secondly, if the case is complex, *e.g.* it involves contested medical evidence, or thirdly, if transfer could prevent delay (*per* Solicitor General (*Hansard*, H.C., Vol. 158, cols. 549–551)). Magistrates should consider transferring long cases, *J* v. *Berkshire County Council, The Times*, March 10, 1992. Guidance has been issued by the Lord Chancellor's Department and the Home Office (H.O. Circular 45/91) reproduced in Department of Health *Guidance*, Vol. 7, p. 114. For details of the rules relating to allocations see Part II of this book.

Rules of court

93.—(1) An authority having power to make rules of court may make such provision for giving effect to—
    (a) this Act;
    (b) the provisions of any statutory instrument made under this Act; or
    (c) any amendment made by this Act in any other enactment,
as appears to that authority to be necessary or expedient.
  (2) The rules may, in particular, make provision—
    (a) with respect to the procedure to be followed in any relevant proceedings (including the manner in which any application is to be made or other proceedings commenced);
    (b) as to the persons entitled to participate in any relevant proceedings, whether as parties to the proceedings or by being given the opportunity to make representations to the court;
    (c) with respect to the documents and information to be furnished, and notices to be given, in connection with any relevant proceedings;
    (d) applying (with or without modification) enactments which govern the procedure to be followed with respect to proceedings brought on a complaint made to a magistrates' court to relevant proceedings in such a court brought otherwise than on a complaint;
    (e) with respect to preliminary hearings;
    (f) for the service outside the [England and Wales], in such circumstances and in such manner as may be prescribed, of any notice of proceedings in a magistrates' court;
    (g) for the exercise by magistrates' courts, in such circumstances as may be prescribed, of such powers as may be prescribed (even though a party to the proceedings in question [resides] outside England and Wales);
    (h) enabling the court, in such circumstances as may be prescribed, to proceed on any application even though the respondent has not been given notice of the proceedings;
    (i) authorising a single justice to discharge the functions of a magistrates' court with respect to such relevant proceedings as may be prescribed;
    (j) authorising a magistrates' court to order any of the parties to such relevant proceedings as may be prescribed, in such

circumstances as may be prescribed, to pay the whole or part of the costs of all or any of the other parties.

(3) In subsection (2)—

"notice of proceedings" means a summons or such other notice of proceedings as is required; and "given", in relation to a summons, means "served";

"prescribed" means prescribed by the rules; and

"relevant proceedings" means any application made, or proceedings brought, under any of the provisions mentioned in paragraphs (a) to (c) of subsection (1) and any part of such proceedings.

(4) This section and any other power in this Act to make rules of court are not to be taken as in any way limiting any other power of the authority in question to make rules of court.

(5) When making any rules under this section an authority shall be subject to the same requirements as to consultation (if any) as apply when the authority makes rules under its general rule making power.

AMENDMENTS

The words in square brackets in subsection (2) were substituted and inserted by the Courts and Legal Services Act 1990, s.116, Sched. 16, para. 22.

DEFINITIONS

"notice of proceedings": s.93(3).
"prescribed": s.93(3).
"relevant proceedings": s.93(3).
"the court": s.92(7).

RULES OF COURT

The Family Proceedings Rules 1991 (S.I. 1991 No. 1247).
The Family Proceedings (Amendment) Rules 1991 (S.I. 1991 No. 2113).
The Family Proceedings Courts (Children Act 1989) Rules (S.I. 1991 No. 1395).

GENERAL NOTE

This section enables rules of court to be made to govern practice and procedure in proceedings brought under this Act. For full details see the General Note to the Family Proceedings and Courts Rules in Part II of this book and the commentary on the rules below.

Appeals

94.—(1) [Subject to any express provisions to the contrary made by or under this Act, an] appeal shall lie to the High Court against—

(a) the making by a magistrates' court of any order under this Act; or

(b) any refusal by a magistrates' court to make such an order.

(2) Where a magistrates' court has power, in relation to any proceedings under this Act, to decline jurisdiction because it considers that the case can more conveniently be dealt with by another court, no appeal shall lie against any exercise by that magistrates' court of that power.

(3) Subsection (1) does not apply in relation to an interim order for periodical payments made under Schedule 1.

(4) On an appeal under this section, the High Court may make such orders as may be necessary to give effect to its determination of the appeal.

(5) Where an order is made under subsection (4) the High Court may also make such incidental or consequential orders as appear to it to be just.

(6) Where an appeal from a magistrates' court relates to an order for the making of periodical payments, the High Court may order that its determination of the appeal shall have effect from such date as it thinks fit to specify in the order.

(7) The date so specified must not be earlier than the earliest date allowed in accordance with rules of court made for the purposes of this section.

(8) Where, on an appeal under this section in respect of an order requiring a person to make periodical payments, the High Court reduces the amount of those payments or discharges the order—
   (a) it may order the person entitled to the payments to pay to the person making them such sum in respect of payments already made as the High Court thinks fit; and
   (b) if any arrears are due under the order for periodical payments, it may remit payment of the whole, or part, of those arrears.

(9) Any order of the High Court made on an appeal under this section (other than one directing that an application be reheard by a magistrates' court) shall, for the purposes—
   (a) of the enforcement of the order; and
   (b) of any power to vary, revive or discharge orders,
be treated as if it were an order of the magistrates' court from which the appeal was brought and not an order of the High Court.

(10) The Lord Chancellor may by order make provision as to the circumstances in which appeals may be made against decisions taken by courts on questions arising in connection with the transfer, or proposed transfer, of proceedings by virtue of any order under paragraph 2 of Schedule 11.

(11) Except to the extent provided for in any order made under subsection (10), no appeal may be made against any decision of a kind mentioned in that subsection.

AMENDMENT

In subsection (1) the words in square brackets were substituted by the Courts and Legal Services Act 1990, s.116, Sched. 16, para. 23.

REGULATIONS

Children (Allocation of Proceedings) (Appeals) Order 1991 (S.I. 1991 No. 1801)

GENERAL NOTE

This section makes new provision for appeals. Appeals in care proceedings will now be heard by the High Court, not, as previously, the Crown Court. *A Practice Direction* has been issued about appeals from the family proceedings court to the High Court [1992] 1 F.L.R. 463. Appeals should be commenced by filing the documents referred to in rule 4.22(2) of the Family Proceedings Rules 1991 (see p. 402 below). It will be heard by a Family Division judge at the nearest High Court centre, normally sitting in open court.

Appeals do not involve a full rehearing; the parties are not allowed to call fresh evidence unless there are exceptional circumstances. The principles stated in G v. G 1985 1 W.L.R. 647 apply, *Croydon London Borough* v. *A* [1992] 1 F.C.R. 522. Local authorities will have the same rights of appeal as other parties to care proceedings (subs. (1)). There will be no appeal to the High Court from a refusal by the magistrates to exercise jurisdiction because the case could more conveniently be heard elsewhere (subs. (2)), nor will there be an appeal against an interim periodical payments order (subs. (3)). Subsections (4) to (8) set out the powers of the High Court when hearing an appeal. The court has the power to make any order which reflects its conclusions and any necessary consequential orders. Orders in periodical payments appeals may be backdated in accordance with court rules (subss. (6), (7)) and may include orders for repayment or remission of arrears (subs. (8)). Orders made by the appeal court, except orders for rehearing, operate as orders of the original court (subs. (9)). Rules (S.I. 1991 No. 1801) (see p. 450 below) provide for appeals against transfer of cases (subs. (10)). No other appeal may be made on such matters (subs. (11)).

This section should be read with section 40, which deals with the effect of care and supervision orders where appeals are pending.

Attendance of child at hearing under Part IV or V

95.—(1) In any proceedings in which a court is hearing an application for an order under Part IV or V, or is considering whether to make any such order, the court may order the child concerned to attend such stage or stages of the proceedings as may be specified in the order.

(2) The power conferred by subsection (1) shall be exercised in accordance with rules of court.

(3) Subsections (4) to (6) apply where—
   (a) an order under subsection (1) has not been complied with; or
   (b) the court has reasonable cause to believe that it will not be complied with.

(4) The court may make an order authorising a constable, or such person as may be specified in the order—
   (a) to take charge of the child and to bring him to the court; and
   (b) to enter and search any premises specified in the order if he has reasonable cause to believe that the child may be found on the premises.

(5) The court may order any person who is in a position to do so to bring the child to the court.

(6) Where the court has reason to believe that a person has information about the whereabouts of the child it may order him to disclose it to the court.

DEFINITIONS
  "child": s.105(1).
  "the court": s.92(7).

RULES OF COURT
  The Family Proceedings Rules 1991 (S.I. 1991 No. 1247).
  The Family Proceedings (Amendment) Rules 1991 (S.I. 1991 No. 2113).
  The Family Proceedings Courts (Children Act 1989) Rules (S.I. 1991 No. 1395).

GENERAL NOTE

Two distinct philosophies have operated in the Youth court on the one part, and in the county court and the High Court on the other, about the child's attendance at court. In the juvenile court, the child's attendance was required, but he could be excused if he were below the age of five, indisposed, or, in the case of an interim order, legally represented (see C.Y.P.A. 1969, ss.2(9) and 22(1) and *Northampton County Council* v. *H* [1988] 2 W.L.R. 389). In other courts, except in adoption proceedings, the child's attendance was generally considered inappropriate. The court will now have a complete discretion as to whether to order the child's attendance for all or part of any hearing for an order under Parts IV or V (subs. (1)), which must be exercised in accordance with rules of court (subs. (2)).

> "[The] principal reforms on representation of the child and court procedure and practice should make it unnecessary for the child to attend the hearing in many cases"

(*per* Solicitor-General (*Hansard*, H.C., Vol. 158, cols. 630, 631)).

Attendance at proceedings in the family proceedings court is governed by rule 16(2). Proceedings may take place in the absence of the child if he is represented and it is in his interests to do so. The guardian ad litem should advise the court about the child's wishes (r. 11(4)(b)); the child if he is of sufficient understanding, the guardian ad litem and the child's solicitor must be given an opportunity to make representation about the child's attendance (r. 16(2)): see p. 394 below.

Where an order for attendance is not complied with (or there is reasonable cause to believe it will not be), the court may order a constable or other specified person to search premises, take charge of the child and bring him before the court (subs. (4)) or order any person who is in a position to do so to bring the child before the court (subs. (5)), or to disclose information to it (subs. (6)). Those subsections reproduce in a decriminalised form C.Y.P.A. 1969, s.2(4)(5).

Evidence given by, or with respect to, children

96.—(1) Subsection (2) applies where a child who is called as a witness in any civil proceedings does not, in the opinion of the court, understand the nature of an oath.

(2) The child's evidence may be heard by the court if, in its opinion—
  (a) he understands that it is his duty to speak the truth; and
  (b) he has sufficient understanding to justify his evidence being heard.

(3) The Lord Chancellor may by order make provision for the admissibility of evidence which would otherwise be inadmissible under any rule of law relating to hearsay.

(4) An order under subsection (3) may only be made with respect to—
  (a) civil proceedings in general or such civil proceedings, or class of civil proceedings, as may be prescribed; and
  (b) evidence in connection with the upbringing, maintenance or welfare of a child.

(5) An order under subsection (3)—
  (a) may, in particular, provide for the admissibility of statements which are made orally or in a prescribed form or which are recorded by any prescribed method of recording;
  (b) may make different provision for different purposes and in relation to different descriptions of court; and
  (c) may make such amendments and repeals in any enactment relating to evidence (other than in this Act) as the Lord

Chancellor considers necessary or expedient in consequence of the provision made by the order.
(6) Subsection (5)(b) is without prejudice to section 104(4).
(7) In this section—
"civil proceedings" and "court" have the same meaning as they have in the Civil Evidence Act 1968 by virtue of section 18 of that Act; and
"prescribed" means prescribed by an order under subsection (3).

DEFINITIONS
"child": s.105(1).
"civil proceedings": s.96(7).
"prescribed": s.96(7).
"the court": s.92(7).

ORDER
The Children (Admissibility of Hearsay Evidence) Order 1991 (S.I. 1991 No. 1115) (replacing S.I. 1990 No. 143).

GENERAL NOTE
This section makes two major changes to the law of evidence in civil proceedings. First, it allows the unsworn evidence of a child of tender years to be heard if subsection (2) is satisfied. It thus brings civil proceedings in line with criminal proceedings (see C.Y.P.A. 1933, s.38, as amended by Criminal Justice Act 1988, s.34). Secondly, it empowers the Lord Chancellor to make orders overriding the rules relating to hearsay in all or any civil proceedings in respect of evidence about the upbringing, maintenance or welfare of a child (subss. (3) and (4)). It enabled the Lord Chancellor to reverse the effect of *Re H, Re K (Minors), The Times,* June 9, 1989, and *Bradford City Metropolitan Borough Council* v. *K, The Times,* August 18, 1989, which restricted the admissibility of hearsay (particularly of allegations by the child to a third-party witness).

Section 96(3) to (7) came into force on Royal Assent (s.108(2)). It has been held in *Re B (Appeals to Crown Court: Evidence)* [1992] 1 F.C.R. 153 that S.I. 1990 No. 143 applied to appeals in care proceedings to the Crown Court because these were only a stage in civil proceedings in the juvenile court.

Subs. (1)

Understand the nature of an oath: A child may only be sworn if he appreciates the particular nature of the case and realises that taking the oath involves more than the ordinary duty of telling the truth (*per* May L.J. in *R.* v. *Campbell, The Times,* December 10, 1982). The dividing line between children who are normally considered old enough and those normally considered too young lies between the ages of eight and 10 (*R.* v. *Hayes* [1977] 1 W.L.R. 234) and it has been said that it is undesirable for children of five to be called to give evidence (*R.* v. *Wallwork* (1958) 122 J.P. 299), but attitudes are changing (see Spencer [1988] New L.J. 147 and [1989] New L.J. 1309). The admissibility of hearsay may allow the child's evidence to be given by a third party, *e.g.* a social worker to whom a "disclosure" was made.

Subs. (2)

It was suggested that the formulation might prevent hearing the evidence of very young children who, although honest, do not comprehend concepts such as duty and truth. However, the Solicitor-General preferred a novel interpretation which subsumed subsection (2)(a) in (2)(b) (*Hansard,* H.C., Vol. 158, col. 771).

Subss. (4) and (5)

The order applies to all civil proceedings in the High Court, the county court or the family proceedings court in connection with the upbringing, maintenance or welfare of a child. There is no longer any distinction between the three levels of court as there was under S.I. 1990 No. 143. There are no provisions relating to the method of recording. However, guidance is being issued in relation to video recording of children's evidence for criminal proceedings (Criminal Justice Act 1988, s. 32A) and the same recordings are likely to be made for use in either civil or criminal trials: see Home Office, *Video recorded interviews*, *Memorandum of Good Practice*. For further details see p. 431 below.

Privacy for children involved in certain proceedings

97.—(1) Rules made under section 144 of the Magistrates' Courts Act 1980 may make provision for a magistrates' court to sit in private in proceedings in which any powers under this Act may be exercised by the court with respect to a child.

(2) No person shall publish any material which is intended, or likely, to identify—

(a) any child as being involved in any proceedings before a magistrates' court in which any power under this Act may be exercised by the court with respect to that or any other child; or

(b) an address or school as being that of a child involved in any such proceedings.

(3) In any proceedings for an offence under this section it shall be a defence for the accused to prove that he did not know, and had no reason to suspect, that the published material was intended, or likely, to identify the child.

(4) The court or the Secretary of State may, if satisfied that the welfare of the child requires it, by order dispense with the requirements of subsection (2) to such extent as may be specified in the order.

(5) For the purposes of this section—

"publish" includes—

[(a) include in a programme service (within the memory of the Broadcasting Act 1990)] or

(b) cause to be published; and

"material" includes any picture or representation.

(6) Any person who contravenes this section shall be guilty of an offence and liable, on summary conviction, to a fine not exceeding level 4 on the standard scale.

(7) Subsection (1) is without prejudice to—

(a) the generality of the rule making power in section 144 of the Act of 1980; or

(b) any other power of a magistrates' court to sit in private.

(8) [Section 69 (sittings of magistrates' courts for family proceedings) and section 71 (newspaper reports of certain proceedings) of the Act of 1980] shall apply in relation to any proceedings to which this section applies subject to the provisions of this section.

AMENDMENT

In subsection (5) the substitution was by the Broadcasting Act 1990, s.203(1), Sched. 20, para. 53. In subsection (8) the words in square brackets were substituted by the Courts and Legal Services Act 1990, s.116, Sched. 16, para. 24.

DEFINITIONS
"child": s.105(1).
"material": s.97(5).
"publish": s.97(5).
"school": s.105(1).

GENERAL NOTE

This section clarifies the rules relating to the power of magistrates to sit in private and to the publication of material about children involved in civil cases. It will enable children to be given the same privacy in all proceedings in the family proceedings court as they had in the domestic court in proceedings under the G.M.A. 1971. The restriction on reporting children's cases is similar to that in C.Y.P.A. 1933, s.39, which also applied to radio, television and cable broadcasting. It is an offence (level 4) to contravene this section, but there is now a defence for a person who did not know and had no reason to suspect that the published material was intended or likely to identify the child (subs. (3)).

The court or the Secretary of State may permit publication where the welfare of the child requires it (subs. (4)). This might be appropriate to allow full publication to quell rumours or, more commonly, where the child is missing and publication may help those searching for him.

Subss. (2) and (5)

Publish: In defamation proceedings this word has a wide meaning and includes any communication to a third party which is not privileged (see *Winfield and Jolowicz on Tort* (13th ed. 1989) 314 *et seq.*). A similarly wide definition may be appropriate here despite the possibility of a criminal penalty, because of the interests of the child and the availability of the defence in subsection (2). However, the wording of the definition and the recent approach of the High Court to publication in children's cases may suggest a narrower approach (see *Re C (No. 2), The Times*, April 27, 1989).

Self-incrimination

98.—(1) In any proceedings in which a court is hearing an application for an order under Part IV or V, no person shall be excused from—
  (a) giving evidence on any matter; or
  (b) answering any question put to him in the course of his giving evidence,
on the ground that doing so might incriminate him or his spouse of an offence.

(2) A statement or admission made in such proceedings shall not be admissible in evidence against the person making it or his spouse in proceedings for an offence other than perjury.

GENERAL NOTE

This section removes the privilege against self-incrimination in proceedings under Parts IV and V of the Act. In its place it grants the witness indemnity, so that his statements cannot be used for his prosecution except for perjury. Similar provisions exist in relation to disclosure of the child's whereabouts under sections 48 and 50 of this Act and in the Family Law Act 1986, s.33. There should no longer be any reason for delaying care proceedings until the completion of any trial of the alleged perpetrator.

Legal Aid

99.—(1) The Legal Aid Act 1988 is amended as mentioned in subsections (2) to (4).

(2) In section 15 (availability of, and payment for, representation under provisions relating to civil legal aid), for the words "and (3)" in subsection (1) there shall be substituted "to (3B)"; and the following subsections shall be inserted after subsection (3)—

"(3A) Representation under this Part shall not be available—
(a) to any local authority; or
(b) to any other body which falls within a prescribed description,

for the purposes of any proceedings under the Children Act 1989.

(3B) Regardless of subsection (2) or (3), representation under this Part must be granted where a child who is brought before a court under section 25 of the 1989 Act (use of accommodation for restricting liberty) is not, but wishes to be, legally represented before the court."

(3) In section 19(5) (scope of provisions about criminal legal aid), at the end of the definition of "criminal proceedings" there shall be added "and also includes proceedings under section 15 of the Children and Young Persons Act 1969 (variation and discharge of supervision orders) and section 16(8) of that Act (appeals in such proceedings)".

(4) Sections 27, 28 and 30(1) and (2) (provisions about legal aid in care, and other, proceedings in relation to children) shall cease to have effect.

(5) The Lord Chancellor may by order make such further amendments in the Legal Aid Act 1988 as he considers necessary or expedient in consequence of any provision made by or under this Act.

DEFINITION
"child": s.105(1).

GENERAL NOTE
This section makes changes to the Legal Aid Act 1988 to facilitate the granting of legal aid in proceedings brought under this Act. Civil legal aid will be available in care proceedings. Changes in law and procedures were needed to ensure that lack of representation did not inhibit a proper hearing of care, etc., cases and that obtaining representation was not a cause of delay. The Lord Chancellor is given power to make further consequential amendments (subs. (5)).

The Legal Aid Act 1988, s.15 is further amended by the Legal Aid Act 1988 (Children Act 1989) Order (S.I. 1991 No. 1924) and the Civil Legal Aid (General) (Amendment) (No. 2) Regulations 1991 (S.I. 1991 No. 2036). The effect of these amendments is as follows:

Legal Aid is not available for a guardian ad litem. Where the child is giving instructions to his solicitor the court may direct that the guardian is legally represented (r. 11(9)(c)); the cost of that representation falls to the guardian ad litem panel budget and the local authority. Legal aid must be granted without either a means or merits test to the child, to the parents and any person with parental responsibility in "Special Children Act proceedings." These are proceedings under sections 31, 43, 44 and 45. Others who are joined as parties in such proceedings, *e.g.* grandparents or foster carers are subject only to a means test. Legal aid is also available to all such parties in appeals subject to a merits test only.

Civil legal aid will also be available without either a means or a merits test to any child in proceedings under section 25 relating to secure accommodation (subs. (2)). Criminal legal aid will be available in proceedings relating to (criminal) supervision orders under the C.Y.P.A. 1969, s.15 (subs. (4)).

Non-means/non-merits tested cases are dealt with by "self-certificating" by the solicitor which gives immediate effect to the grant of Legal Aid. The form must be received by the Legal Aid Board if work done before issue of the Legal Aid Certificate is to be covered.

Restrictions on use of wardship jurisdiction

100.—(1) Section 7 of the Family Law Reform Act 1969 (which gives the High Court power to place a ward of court in the care, or under the supervision, of a local authority) shall cease to have effect.

(2) No court shall exercise the High Court's inherent jurisdiction with respect to children—
    (a) so as to require a child to be placed in the care, or put under the supervision, of a local authority;
    (b) so as to require a child to be accommodated by or on behalf of a local authority;
    (c) so as to make a child who is the subject of a care order a ward of court; or
    (d) for the purpose of conferring on any local authority power to determine any question which has arisen, or which may arise, in connection with any aspect of parental responsibility for a child.

(3) No application for any exercise of the court's inherent jurisdiction with respect to children may be made by a local authority unless the authority have obtained the leave of the court.

(4) The court may only grant leave if it is satisfied that—
    (a) the result which the authority wish to achieve could not be achieved through the making of any order of a kind to which subsection (5) applies; and
    (b) there is reasonable cause to believe that if the court's inherent jurisdiction is not exercised with respect to the child he is likely to suffer significant harm.

(5) This subsection applies to any order—
    (a) made otherwise than in the exercise of the court's inherent jurisdiction; and
    (b) which the local authority is entitled to apply for (assuming, in the case of any application which may only be made with leave, that leave is granted).

DEFINITIONS
  "local authority": s.105(1).
  "parental responsibility": s.3.
  "significant harm": s.31(9), (10).
  "the court": s.92(7).

GENERAL NOTE

This section completes the new scheme for compulsory measures of care by effectively ending local authorities' use of wardship to remove children from their families or commit them to local authority care. The R.C.C.L. did not recommend changes to wardship but did expect that reform would reduce the need to use it (para. 15.38). The Law Commission canvassed its retention, restriction or abolition (see Working Paper 101 1987, *Wards of Court*) but did not go on to make firm proposals in a report. However, unless some restrictions on the inherent jurisdiction were introduced, it would have been impossible to impose one standard, the "significant harm" test, to justify intervention.

Local authority use of wardship is restricted in three ways. First, the court's powers to commit a child to care in section 7 of the Family Law Reform Act 1969 is abolished (subs. (1)). Secondly, the inherent jurisdiction of the High Court cannot be exercised to require a child to be placed in care, supervised by the local authority, accommodated by the local authority: it cannot be exercised to give the local authority power to make parental decisions in respect of a child, or to make a child subject to a care order a ward (subs. (2)). Finally, if the local authority wishes to apply to the court for an order under the inherent jurisdiction it must obtain leave (subs. (3)) and satisfy the conditions in subsections (4) and (5). Leave will only be granted if the result could not be achieved by the local authority applying for an order other than in wardship and there is reasonable cause to believe that the child will suffer significant harm if the jurisdiction is not exercised.

Apart from these restrictions the inherent jurisdiction remains intact. Anyone other than a local authority who can show sufficient interest will be able to ward any child who is not in local authority care. Where the restrictions in *A* v. *Liverpool City Council* [1982] A.C. 363 and subsection (2) do not apply, wardship can be used to review the decision of a local authority, although an application for judicial review may be required. The High Court can still make orders, *e.g.* injunctions, under its inherent jurisdiction otherwise than in wardship. Where the child is harmed because of the failure of the local authority to act it may be possible to get the Secretary of State to require action under section 84. The distinctions between wardship and the inherent jurisdiction are examined in Parry [1992] J.S.W.F.L. 212.

The removal of wardship will certainly make it more difficult for those local authorities which have relied on it to make some arrangements for children they are looking after.

(1) *Prevention of removal from accommodation*

If section 44 is satisfied, the local authority will be able to obtain an emergency protection order. Where section 31(2) is satisfied it will be able to obtain a care order.

If the child has been with the carers for more than three years they will be able to apply for a residence order without leave (s.10(5)).

If the child has been with the carers for less than three years they will need leave of the court and consent of the authority before making an application for a residence order (ss.9(3) and 10(8)). A local authority which readily gives consent may undermine the confidence of those who need it to accommodate their children. The local authority will be able to support a child under a residence order as they could support those children subject to custodianship orders (Sched. 1, para. 15).

(2) *Facilitating adoption placements*

Contact with the child may be controlled under section 34 but repeated applications for orders may theoretically be made every six months unless they are restricted under section 91(14).

Parental responsibility may be ended by a freeing order under the Adoption Act 1976, s.18, but the child must be in care of the local authority if the order is contested.

The Adoption Act 1976 also provides limited protection for would-be adoption applicants to prevent removal of the child pending an adoption hearing. These supplement the powers to control the child's placement by a care order or residence order. It seems likely that there will be more hearings in such cases but they need not take longer overall.

Where an access condition is appropriate in an adoption order, this could be provided without recourse to wardship by the imposition of a contact under section 10.

In other cases local authority action may be simplified because there will be no need to consult the High Court about plans and because residence orders can be made in favour of third parties under section 10.

(3) *Child abuse cases*

All cases will need to be framed in terms of "significant harm" to the child, not merely to the child's welfare, but hearsay evidence is no longer excluded in the lower courts (see notes to s.96). Sections 40 and 94 enable a child to be protected pending an appeal against refusal to grant or discharge of a care order although these provisions do not apply to all cases (see notes to s.40).

(4) *Disputes with parents and difficult decisions*

Subject to subsections (4) and (5) where the child is in care, the local authority will not be able to submit to the High Court's jurisdiction and have the court make difficult decisions such as whether the child has an abortion (*Re P* [1986] 1 F.L.R. 272). Nor will it be able to have a dispute with parents of a child in care settled by the court.

(5) *Publicity*

Where children are wards of court publicity of information about the child's case is restricted (but not absolute): *Re XY and Z (Wardship Disclosure of Material)* [1991] Fam. Law 318. Although documents are confidential in care proceedings, etc. (r. 23(1)) and restrictions on reporting such proceedings exist it will now be more difficult to restrict publication of information about individual children in care.

Subs. (1)

The High Court will still be able to make a care order but the grounds in section 31(2) will have to be satisfied. Cases will normally start in the magistrates' court and will be transferred to the High Court where appropriate (Sched. 11).

Subss. (2)–(5)

A child who is made a ward in proceedings may be accommodated by the local authority at the request of the current carer with the consent of the court. The High Court may still exercise its inherent jurisdiction without making the child a ward, *e.g.* to grant injunctions against third parties (*per* Solicitor-General (Standing Committee B, col. 488, June 8, 1989)).

If the child is accommodated by the local authority or not being looked after by the local authority, the authority will be able to seek a "prohibited steps" or "specific issue" order but not so as to require a child to enter or remain in local authority accommodation and not to be supervised by the local authority (s.9(5)). Issues about medical treatment over which a parent (or a mature minor) has power could thus be decided by the court. Section 9(1) precludes "prohibited steps" and "specific issue" orders in respect of children in care. Section 8 defines these orders by reference to parental responsibility. Parents do not have a right to make decisions about the medical treatment of mature children under 16 years of age (*Gillick* v. *West Norfolk Area Health Authority* [1986] A.C. 112), nor, apparently, to consent to non-therapeutic treatment (*Re D* [1976] Fam. 185). The court may consent to sterilisation of a minor who is incapable of making the decision (*Re B* [1987] A.C. 199) and could do so without making the child a ward. In *Re R* [1991] 4 All E.R. 177 the Court of Appeal stated *obiter* that the High Court in Wardship could override the decision of a mature minor. In *Re W* [1992] N.L.J. 1124 it held that anyone with parental responsibility could give a valid consent allowing medical treatment to take place against the wishes of any child, even one over the age of 16 years. It seems that it will rarely be necessary for the local authorities to resort to the High Court in relation to medical decisions about children in care. But statutory limits on assessments in sections 38(6), 43(8) and 44(7) may only be overcome (if at all) by the High Court. Where the restriction does not apply the local authority must seek leave. It will have to prove that the child will suffer significant harm without the order and that alternative orders are not available to the authority.

Effect of orders as between England and Wales and Northern Ireland, the Channel Islands or the Isle of Man

101.—(1) The Secretary of State may make regulations providing—
  (a) for prescribed orders which—
    (i) are made by a court in Northern Ireland; and
    (ii) appear to the Secretary of State to correspond in their effect to orders which may be made under any provision of this Act,
  to have effect in prescribed circumstances, for prescribed purposes of this Act, as if they were orders of a prescribed kind made under this Act;
  (b) for prescribed orders which—
    (i) are made by a court in England and Wales; and
    (ii) appear to the Secretary of State to correspond in their effect to orders which may be made under any provision in force in Northern Ireland,
  to have effect in prescribed circumstances, for prescribed purposes of the law of Northern Ireland, as if they were orders of a prescribed kind made in Northern Ireland.

(2) Regulations under subsection (1) may provide for the order concerned to cease to have effect for the purposes of the law of Northern Ireland, or (as the case may be) the law of England and Wales, if prescribed conditions are satisfied.

(3) The Secretary of State may make regulations providing for prescribed orders which—
  (a) are made by a court in the Isle of Man or in any of the Channel Islands; and
  (b) appear to the Secretary of State to correspond in their effect to orders which may be made under this Act,
to have effect in prescribed circumstances for prescribed purposes of this Act, as if they were orders of a prescribed kind made under this Act.

(4) Where a child who is in the care of a local authority is lawfully taken to live in Northern Ireland, the Isle of Man or any of the Channel Islands, the care order in question shall cease to have effect if the conditions prescribed in regulations made by the Secretary of State are satisfied.

(5) Any regulations made under this section may—
  (a) make such consequential amendments (including repeals) in—
    (i) section 25 of the Children and Young Persons Act 1969 (transfers between England and Wales and Northern Ireland); or
    (ii) section 26 (transfers between England and Wales and Channel Islands or Isle of Man) of that Act,
  as the Secretary of State considers necessary or expedient; and
  (b) modify any provision of this Act, in its application (by virtue of the regulations) in relation to an order made otherwise than in England and Wales.

DEFINITION
"care order": s.31(11).

REGULATIONS
The Children (Prescribed Orders—Northern Ireland, Guernsey and Isle of Man) Regulations 1991 (S.I. 1991 No. 2032).

GENERAL NOTE
This section empowers the Secretary of State to make regulations providing that orders made by Northern Ireland courts have effect in England and Wales (subs. (1)) and that orders made by courts in England and Wales have effect in Northern Ireland (subs. (2)); also that care orders shall cease to have effect if the child lawfully goes to Northern Ireland, etc. (subs. (4)). Orders made in courts in the Channel Isles and the Isle of Man may also have the effect prescribed by regulations (subs. (5)). The C.Y.P.A. 1969, ss.25 and 26 can be amended by regulations. These powers have been exercised: see above.

Search warrants

Power of constable to assist in exercise of certain powers to search for children or inspect premises

102.—(1) Where, on an application made by any person for a warrant under this section, it appears to the court—
   (a) that a person attempting to exercise powers under any enactment mentioned in subsection (6) has been prevented from doing so by being refused entry to the premises concerned or refused access to the child concerned; or
   (b) that any such person is likely to be so prevented from exercising any such powers,
it may issue a warrant authorising any constable to assist that person in the exercise of those powers, using reasonable force if necessary.

(2) Every warrant issued under this section shall be addressed to, and executed by, a constable who shall be accompanied by the person applying for the warrant if—
   (a) that person so desires; and
   (b) the court by whom the warrant is issued does not direct otherwise.

(3) A court granting an application for a warrant under this section may direct that the constable concerned may, in executing the warrant, be accompanied by a registered medical practitioner, registered nurse or registered health visitor if he so chooses.

(4) An application for a warrant under this section shall be made in the manner and form prescribed by rules of court.

(5) Where—
   (a) an application for a warrant under this section relates to a particular child; and
   (b) it is reasonably practicable to do so,
the application and any warrant granted on the application shall name the child; and where it does not name him it shall describe him as clearly as possible.

(6) The enactments are—

(a) sections 62, 64, 67, 76, 80, 86 and 87;
(b) paragraph 8(1)(b) and (2)(b) of Schedule 3;
(c) section 33 of the Adoption Act 1976 (duty of local authority to secure that protected children are visited from time to time).

DEFINITION

"the court": s.92(7).

GENERAL NOTE

This section re-enacts the provisions relating to search warrants which may be granted to facilitate the inspection of premises by the Secretary of State, a local authority or any duly authorised person. This power is additional to that to grant warrants in connection with emergency protection orders under section 48. The grounds for a warrant and its provisions are identical to those in section 48(9) to (13) but the provisions in subsection (6) relate to general supervisory powers, not emergency protection. Where a search revealed a child at risk and the local authority wished to remove the child (rather than arrange for the parents to do so), an emergency protection order would be necessary (see notes to ss.44, 45 and 48 above).

General

Offences by bodies corporate

103.—(1) This section applies where any offence under this Act is committed by a body corporate.

(2) If the offence is proved to have been committed with the consent or connivance of or to be attributable to any neglect on the part of any director, manager, secretary or other similar officer of the body corporate, or any person who was purporting to act in any such capacity, he (as well as the body corporate) shall be guilty of the offence and shall be liable to be proceeded against and punished accordingly.

GENERAL NOTE

This section explains where certain officers of a corporate body are involved in committing an offence under the Act, they and the corporate body are liable to be prosecuted.

Regulations and orders

104.—(1) Any power of the Lord Chancellor or the Secretary of State under this Act to make an order, regulations, or rules, except an order under section 54(2), 56(4)(a), 57(3), 84 or 97(4) or paragraph 1(1) of Schedule 4, shall be exercisable by statutory instrument.

(2) Any such statutory instrument, except one made under section 17(4), 107 or 108(2), shall be subject to annulment in pursuance of a resolution of either House of Parliament.

(3) An order under section 17(4) shall not be made unless a draft of it has been laid before, and approved by a resolution of, each House of Parliament.

(4) Any statutory instrument made under this Act may—
  (a) make different provision for different cases;
  (b) provide for exemptions from any of its provisions; and
  (c) contain such incidental, supplemental and transitional provisions as the person making it considers expedient.

Interpretation

105.—(1) In this Act—
  "adoption agency" means a body which may be referred to as an adoption agency by virtue of section 1 of the Adoption Act 1976;
  "bank holiday" means a day which is a bank holiday under the Banking and Financial Dealings Act 1971;
  "care order" has the meaning given by section 31(11) and also includes any order which by or under any enactment has the effect of, or is deemed to be, a care order for the purposes of this Act; and any reference to a child who is in the care of an authority is a reference to a child who is in their care by virtue of a care order;
  "child" means, subject to paragraph 1 6 of Schedule 1, a person under the age of eighteen;
  "child assessment order" has the meaning given by section 43(2);
  "child minder" has the meaning given by section 71;
  "child of the family", in relation to the parties to a marriage, means—
  (a) a child of both of those parties;
  (b) any other child, not being a child who is placed with those parties as foster parents by a local authority or voluntary organisation, who has been treated by both of those parties as a child of their family;
  "children's home" has the same meaning as in section 63;
  "community home" has the meaning given by section 53;
  "contact order" has the meaning given by section 8(1);
  "day care" has the same meaning as in section 18;
  "disabled", in relation to a child, has the same meaning as in section 17(11);
  "district health authority" has the same meaning as in the National Health Service Act 1977;
  "domestic premises" has the meaning given by section 71(12);
  "education supervision order" has the meaning given in section 36;
  "emergency protection order" means an order under section 44;
  "family assistance order" has the meaning given in section 16(2);
  "family proceedings" has the meaning given by section 8(3);
  "functions" includes powers and duties;
  "guardian of a child" means a guardian (other than a guardian of the estate of a child) appointed in accordance with the provisions of section 5;

"harm" has the same meaning as in section 31(9) and the question of whether harm is significant shall be determined in accordance with section 31(10);

"health authority" means any district health authority and any special health authority established under the National Health Service Act 1977;

"health service hospital" has the same meaning as in the National Health Service Act 1977;

"hospital" has the same meaning as in the Mental Health Act 1983, except that it does not include a special hospital within the meaning of that Act;

"ill-treatment" has the same meaning as in section 31(9);

"independent school" has the same meaning as in the Education Act 1944;

"local authority" means, in relation to England and Wales, the council of a county, a metropolitan district, a London Borough or the Common Council of the City of London and, in relation to Scotland, a local authority within the meaning of section 1(2) of the Social Work (Scotland) Act 1968;

"local authority foster parent" has the same meaning as in section 23(3);

"local education authority" has the same meaning as in the Education Act 1944;

"local housing authority" has the same meaning as in the Housing Act 1985;

"mental nursing home" has the same meaning as in the Registered Homes Act 1984;

"nursing home" has the same meaning as in the Act of 1984;

"parental responsibility" has the meaning given in section 3;

"parental responsibility agreement" has the meaning given in section 4(1);

"prescribed" means prescribed by regulations made under this Act;

"privately fostered child" and "to foster a child privately" have the same meaning as in section 66;

"prohibited steps order" has the meaning given by section 8(1);

"protected child" has the same meaning as in Part III of the Adoption Act 1976;

"registered children's home" has the same meaning as in section 63;

"registered pupil" has the same meaning as in the Education Act 1944;

"relative", in relation to a child, means a grandparent, brother, sister, uncle or aunt (whether of the full blood or half blood or by affinity) or step-parent;

"residence order" has the meaning given by section 8(1);

"residential care home" has the same meaning as in the Registered Homes Act 1984 [and "small home" has the meaning given by section 1(4A) of that Act];

"responsible person", in relation to a child who is the subject of a supervision order, has the meaning given in paragraph 1 of Schedule 3;

"school" has the same meaning as in the Education Act 1944 or, in relation to Scotland, in the Education (Scotland) Act 1980;

"service", in relation to any provision made under Part III, includes any facility;

"signed", in relation to any person, includes the making by that person of his mark;

"special educational needs" has the same meaning as in the Education Act 1981;

"special health authority" has the same meaning as in the National Health Service Act 1977;

"specific issue order" has the meaning given by section 8(1);

"supervision order" has the meaning given by section 31(11);

"supervised child" and "supervisor", in relation to a supervision order or an education supervision order, mean respectively the child who is (or is to be) under supervision and the person under whose supervision he is (or is to be) by virtue of the order;

"upbringing", in relation to any child, includes the care of the child but not his maintenance;

"voluntary home" has the meaning given by section 60;

"voluntary organisation" means a body (other than a public or local authority) whose activities are not carried on for profit.

(2) References in this Act to a child whose father and mother were, or (as the case may be) were not, married to each other at the time of his birth must be read with section 1 of the Family Law Reform Act 1987 (which extends the meaning of such references).

(3) References in this Act to—
  (a) a person with whom a child lives, or is to live, as the result of a residence order; or
  (b) a person in whose favour a residence order is in force,
shall be construed as references to the person named in the order as the person with whom the child is to live.

(4) References in this Act to a child who is looked after by a local authority have the same meaning as they have (by virtue of section 22) in Part III.

(5) References in this Act to accommodation provided by or on behalf of a local authority are references to accommodation so provided in the exercise of functions which stand referred to the social services committee of that or any other local authority under the Local Authority Social Services Act 1970.

(6) In determining the "ordinary residence" of a child for any purpose of this Act, there shall be disregarded any period in which he lives in any place—
  (a) which is a school or other institution;
  (b) in accordance with the requirements of a supervision order under this Act or an order under section 7(7)(b) of the Children and Young Persons Act 1969; or
  (c) while he is being provided with accommodation by or on behalf of a local authority.

(7) References in this Act to children who are in need shall be construed in accordance with section 17.

(8) Any notice or other document required under this Act to be served on any person may be served on him by being delivered personally to him, or being sent by post to him in a registered letter or by the recorded delivery service at his proper address.

(9) Any such notice or other document required to be served on a body corporate or a firm shall be duly served if it is served on the secretary or clerk of that body or a partner of that firm.

(10) For the purposes of this section, and of section 7 of the Interpretation Act 1978 in its application to this section, the proper address of a person—

> (a) in the case of a secretary or clerk of a body corporate, shall be that of the registered or principal office of that body;
> (b) in the case of a partner of a firm, shall be that of the principal office of the firm; and
> (c) in any other case, shall be the last known address of the person to be served.

AMENDMENT

The words in square brackets in the definition of "residential care home" were inserted by the Registered Homes (Amendment) Act 1991, s.2.

Financial provisions

106.—(1) Any—
> (a) grants made by the Secretary of State under this Act; and
> (b) any other expenses incurred by the Secretary of State under this Act,

shall be payable out of money provided by Parliament.

(2) Any sums received by the Secretary of State under section 58, or by way of the repayment of any grant made under section 82(2) or (4) shall be paid into the Consolidated Fund.

Application to Channel Islands

107. Her Majesty may by Order in Council direct that any of the provisions of this Act shall extend to any of the Channel Islands with such exceptions and modifications as may be specified in the Order.

GENERAL NOTE

For application of parts to Guernsey, see section 101.

Short title, commencement, extent, etc.

108.—(1) This Act may be cited as the Children Act 1989.

(2) Sections 89 and 96(3) to (7), and paragraph 35 of Schedule 12, shall extent come into force on the passing of this Act and paragraph 36 of Schedule 12 shall come into force at the end of the period of two months beginning with the day on which this Act is passed but

Short Title, Commencement, Extent, Etc.

otherwise this Act shall come into force on such date as may be appointed by order made by the Lord Chancellor or the Secretary of State, or by both acting jointly.

(3) Different dates may be appointed for different provisions of this Act and in relation to different cases.

(4) The minor amendments set out in Schedule 12 shall have effect.

(5) The consequential amendments set out in Schedule 13 shall have effect.

(6) The transitional provisions and savings set out in Schedule 14 shall have effect.

(7) The repeals set out in Schedule 15 shall have effect.

(8) An order under subsection (2) may make such transitional provisions or savings as appear to the person making the order to be necessary or expedient in connection with the provisions brought into force by the order, including—

    (a) provisions adding to or modifying the provisions of Schedule 14; and

    (b) such adaptations—

        (i) of the provisions brought into force by the order; and

        (ii) of any provisions of this Act then in force,

    as appear to him necessary or expedient in consequence of the partial operation of this Act.

(9) The Lord Chancellor may by order make such amendments or repeals, in such enactments as may be specified in the order, as appear to him to be necessary or expedient in consequence of any provision of this Act.

(10) This Act shall, in its application to the Isles of Scilly, have effect subject to such exceptions, adaptations and modifications as the Secretary of State may by order prescribe.

(11) The following provisions of this Act extend to Scotland—
section 19;
section 25(8);
section 50(13);
Part X;
section 80(1)(h) and (i), (2) to (4), (5)(a), (b) and (h) and (6) to (12);
section 88;
section 104 (so far as necessary);
section 105 (so far as necessary);
subsections (1) to (3), (8) and (9) and this subsection;
in Schedule 2, paragraph 24;
in Schedule 12, paragraphs 1, 7 to 10, 18, 27, 30(a) and 41 to 44;
in Schedule 13, paragraphs 18 to 23, 32, 46, 47, 50, 57, 62, 63, 68(a) and (b) and 71;
in Schedule 14, paragraphs 1, 33 and 34;
in Schedule 15, the entries relating to—

    (a) the Custody of Children Act 1891;

    (b) the Nurseries and Child Minders Regulation Act 1948;

    (c) section 53(3) of the Children and Young Persons Act 1963;

    (d) section 60 of the Health Services and Public Health Act 1968;

    (e) the Social Work (Scotland) Act 1968;

(f) the Adoption (Scotland) Act 1978;
(g) the Child Care Act 1980;
(h) the Foster Children (Scotland) Act 1984;
(i) the Child Abduction and Custody Act 1985; and
(j) the Family Law Act 1986.

(12) The following provisions of this Act extend to Northern Ireland—

section 50;

section 101(1)(b), (2) and (5)(a)(i);

subsections (1) to (3), (8) and (9) and this subsection;

in Schedule 2, paragraph 24;

in Schedule 12, paragraphs 7 to 10, 18 and 27;

in Schedule 13, paragraphs 21, 22, 46, 47, 57, 62, 63, 68(c) to (e) and 69 to 71;

in Schedule 14, paragraphs [...] 28 to 30 and 38(a); and

in Schedule 15, the entries relating to the Guardianship of Minors Act 1971, the Children Act 1975, the Child Care Act 1980, and the Family Law Act 1986.

AMENDMENT

The word in subsection (12) was omitted by the Courts and Legal Services Act 1990, s.125(7), Sched. 20.

COMMENCEMENT ORDERS

S.I. 1991 Nos. 828, 1990 (see Introduction).

SCHEDULES

Section 15(1) SCHEDULE 1

FINANCIAL PROVISION FOR CHILDREN

Orders for financial relief against parents

1.—(1) On an application made by a parent or guardian of a child, or by any person in whose favour a residence order is in force with respect to a child, the court may—
    (a) in the case of an application to the High Court or a county court, make one or more of the orders mentioned in sub-paragraph (2);
    (b) in the case of an application to a magistrates' court, make one or both of the orders mentioned in paragraphs (a) and (c) of that sub-paragraph.

(2) The orders referred to in sub-paragraph (1) are—
    (a) an order requiring either or both parents of a child—
        (i) to make to the applicant for the benefit of the child; or
        (ii) to make to the child himself,
    such periodical payments, for such term, as may be specified in the order;
    (b) an order requiring either or both parents of a child—
        (i) to secure to the applicant for the benefit of the child; or
        (ii) to secure to the child himself,
    such periodical payments, for such term, as may be so specified;
    (c) an order requiring either or both parents of a child—

(i) to pay to the applicant for the benefit of the child; or
(ii) to pay to the child himself,
such lump sum as may be so specified;
(d) an order requiring a settlement to be made for the benefit of the child, and to the satisfaction of the court, of property—
(i) to which either parent is entitled (either in possession or in reversion); and
(ii) which is specified in the order;
(c) an order requiring either or both parents of a child—
(i) to transfer to the applicant, for the benefit of the child; or
(ii) to transfer to the child himself,
such property to which the parent is, or the parents are, entitled (either in possession or in reversion) as may be specified in the order.

(3) The powers conferred by this paragraph may be exercised at any time.

(4) An order under sub-paragraph (2)(a) or (b) may be varied or discharged by a subsequent order made on the application of any person by or to whom payments were required to be made under the previous order.

(5) Where a court makes an order under this paragraph—
(a) it may at any time make a further such order under sub-paragraph (2)(a), (b) or (c) with respect to the child concerned if he has not reached the age of eighteen;
(b) it may not make more than one order under sub-paragraph (2)(d) or (e) against the same person in respect of the same child.

(6) On making, varying or discharging a residence order the court may exercise any of its powers under this Schedule even though no application has been made to it under this Schedule.

[(7) Where a child is a ward of court, the court may exercise any of its powers under this Schedule even though no application has been made to it.]

Orders for financial relief for persons over eighteen

2.—(1) If, on an application by a person who has reached the age of eighteen, it appears to the court—
(a) that the applicant is, will be or (if an order were made under this paragraph) would be receiving instruction at an educational establishment or undergoing training for a trade, profession or vocation, whether or not while in gainful employment; or
(b) that there are special circumstances which justify the making of an order under this paragraph,
the court may make one or both of the orders mentioned in sub-paragraph (2).

(2) The orders are—
(a) an order requiring either or both of the applicant's parents to pay to the applicant such periodical payments, for such term, as may be specified in the order;
(b) an order requiring either or both of the applicant's parents to pay to the applicant such lump sum as may be so specified.

(3) An application may not be made under this paragraph by any person if, immediately before he reached the age of sixteen, a periodical payments order was in force with respect to him.

(4) No order shall be made under this paragraph at a time when the parents of the applicant are living with each other in the same household.

(5) An order under sub-paragraph (2)(a) may be varied or discharged by a subsequent order made on the application of any person by or to whom payments were required to be made under the previous order.

(6) In sub-paragraph (3) "periodical payments order" means an order made under—
(a) this Schedule;
(b) section 6(3) of the Family Law Reform Act 1969;
(c) section 23 or 27 of the Matrimonial Causes Act 1973;
(d) Part I of the Domestic Proceedings and Magistrates' Courts Act 1978, for the making or securing of periodical payments.

(7) The powers conferred by this paragraph shall be exercisable at any time.

(8) Where the court makes an order under this paragraph it may from time to time while that order remains in force make a further such order.

Duration of orders for financial relief

3.—(1) The term to be specified in an order for periodical payments made under paragraph 1(2)(a) or (b) in favour of a child may begin with the date of the making of an application for the order in question or any later date but—
    (a) shall not in the first instance extend beyond the child's seventeenth birthday unless the court thinks it right in the circumstances of the case to specify a later date; and
    (b) shall not in any event extend beyond the child's eighteenth birthday.

(2) Paragraph (b) of sub-paragraph (1) shall not apply in the case of a child if it appears to the court that—
    (a) the child is, or will be or (if an order were made without complying with that paragraph) would be receiving instruction at an educational establishment or undergoing training for a trade, profession or vocation, whether or not while in gainful employment; or
    (b) there are special circumstances which justify the making of an order without complying with that paragraph.

(3) An order for periodical payments made under paragraph 1(2)(a) or 2(2)(a) shall, notwithstanding anything in the order, cease to have effect on the death of the person liable to make payments under the order.

(4) Where an order is made under paragraph 1(2)(a) or (b) requiring periodical payments to be made or secured to the parent of a child, the order shall cease to have effect if—
    (a) any parent making or securing the payments; and
    (b) any parent to whom the payments are made or secured,
live together for a period of more than six months.

Matters to which court is to have regard in making orders for financial relief

4.—(1) In deciding whether to exercise its powers under paragraph 1 or 2, and if so in what manner, the court shall have regard to all the circumstances including—
    (a) the income, earning capacity, property and other financial resources which each person mentioned in sub-paragraph (4) has or is likely to have in the foreseeable future;
    (b) the financial needs, obligations and responsibilities which each person mentioned in sub-paragraph (4) has or is likely to have in the foreseeable future;
    (c) the financial needs of the child;
    (d) the income, earning capacity (if any), property and other financial resources of the child;
    (e) any physical or mental disability of the child;
    (f) the manner in which the child was being, or was expected to be, educated or trained.

(2) In deciding whether to exercise its powers under paragraph 1 against a person who is not the mother or father of the child, and if so in what manner, the court shall in addition have regard to—
    (a) whether that person had assumed responsibility for the maintenance of the child and, if so, the extent to which and basis on which he assumed that responsibility and the length of the period during which he met that responsibility;
    (b) whether he did so knowing that the child was not his child;
    (c) the liability of any other person to maintain the child.

(3) Where the court makes an order under paragraph 1 against a person who is not the father of the child, it shall record in the order that the order is made on the basis that the person against whom the order is made is not the child's father.

(4) The persons mentioned in sub-paragraph (1) are—
    (a) in relation to a decision whether to exercise its powers under paragraph 1, any parent of the child;
    (b) in relation to a decision whether to exercise its powers under paragraph 2, the mother and father of the child;

(c) the applicant for the order;
(d) any other person in whose favour the court proposes to make the order.

Provisions relating to lump sums

5.—(1) Without prejudice to the generality of paragraph 1, an order under that paragraph for the payment of a lump sum may be made for the purpose of enabling any liabilities or expenses—
    (a) incurred in connection with the birth of the child or in maintaining the child, and
    (b) reasonably incurred before the making of the order,
to be met.
(2) The amount of any lump sum required to be paid by an order made by a magistrates' court under paragraph 1 or 2 shall not exceed £1000 or such larger amount as the Secretary of State may from time to time by order fix for the purposes of this sub-paragraph.
(3) The power of the court under paragraph 1 or 2 to vary or discharge an order for the making or securing of periodical payments by a parent shall include power to make an order under that provision for the payment of a lump sum by that parent.
(4) The amount of any lump sum which a parent may be required to pay by virtue of sub-paragraph (3) shall not, in the case of an order made by a magistrates' court, exceed the maximum amount that may at the time of the making of the order be required to be paid under sub-paragraph (2), but a magistrates' court may make an order for the payment of a lump sum not exceeding that amount even though the parent was required to pay a lump sum by a previous order under this Act.
(5) An order made under paragraph 1 or 2 for the payment of a lump sum may provide for the payment of that sum by instalments.
(6) Where the court provides for the payment of a lump sum by instalments the court, on an application made either by the person liable to pay or the person entitled to receive that sum, shall have power to vary that order by varying—
    (a) the number of instalments payable;
    (b) the amount of any instalment payable;
    (c) the date on which any instalment becomes payable.

Variation, etc., of orders for periodical payments

6.—(1) In exercising its powers under paragraph 1 or 2 to vary or discharge an order for the making or securing of periodical payments the court shall have regard to all the circumstances of the case, including any change in any of the matters to which the court was required to have regard when making the order.
(2) The power of the court under paragraph 1 or 2 to vary an order for the making or securing of periodical payments shall include power to suspend any provision of the order temporarily and to revive any provision so suspended.
(3) Where on an application under paragraph 1 or 2 for the variation or discharge of an order for the making or securing of periodical payments the court varies the payments required to be made under that order, the court may provide that the payments as so varied shall be made from such date as the court may specify, not being earlier than the date of the making of the application.
(4) An application for the variation of an order made under paragraph 1 for the making or securing of periodical payments to or for the benefit of a child may, if the child has reached the age of sixteen, be made by the child himself.
(5) Where an order for the making or securing of periodical payments made under paragraph 1 ceases to have effect on the date on which the child reaches the age of sixteen, or at any time after that date but before or on the date on which he reaches the age of eighteen, the child may apply to the court which made the order for an order for its revival.
(6) If on such an application it appears to the court that—
    (a) the child is, will be or (if an order were made under this sub-paragraph) would be receiving instruction at an educational establishment or undergoing training for a trade, profession or vocation, whether or not while in gainful employment; or

(b) there are special circumstances which justify the making of an order under this paragraph,

the court shall have power by order to revive the order from such date as the court may specify, not being earlier than the date of the making of the application.

(7) Any order which is revived by an order under sub-paragraph (5) may be varied or discharged under that provision, on the application of any person by whom or to whom payments are required to be made under the revived order.

(8) An order for the making or securing of periodical payments made under paragraph 1 may be varied or discharged, after the death of either parent, on the application of a guardian of the child concerned.

Variation of orders for secured periodical payments after death of parent

[*Variation of orders for periodical payments, etc., made by magistrates' courts*
6A.—(1) Subject to sub-paragraphs (7) and (8), the power of a magistrates' court—
    (a) under paragraph 1 or 2 to vary an order for the making of periodical payments, or
    (b) under paragraph 5(6) to vary an order for the payment of a lump sum by instalments,

shall include power, if the court is satisfied that payment has not been made in accordance with the order, to exercise one of its powers under paragraphs (a) to (d) of section 59(3) of the Magistrates' Courts Act 1980.

(2) In any cases where—
    (a) a magistrates' court has made an order under this Schedule for the making of periodical payments or for the payment of a lump sum by instalments, and
    (b) payments under the order are required to be made by any method of payment falling within section 59(6) of the Magistrates' Courts Act 1980 (standing order, etc.), any person entitled to make an application under this Schedule for the variation of the order (in this paragraph referred to as "the applicant") may apply to the clerk to the justices for the petty sessions area for which the court is acting for the order to be varied as mentioned in sub-paragraph (3).

(3) Subject to sub-paragraph (5), where an application is made under sub-paragraph (2), the clerk, after giving written notice (by post or otherwise) of the application to any interested party and allowing that party, within the period of 14 days beginning with the date of the giving of that notice, an opportunity to make written representations, may vary the order to provide that payments under the order shall be made to the clerk.

(4) The clerk may proceed with an application under sub-paragraph (2) notwithstanding that any such interested party as is referred to in sub-paragraph (3) has not received written notice of the application.

(5) Where an application has been made under sub-paragraph (2), the clerk may, if he considers it inappropriate to exercise his power under sub-paragraph (3), refer the matter to the court which, subject to sub-paragraphs (7) and (8), may vary the order by exercising one of its powers under paragraphs (a) to (d) of section 59(3) of the Magistrates' Court Act 1980.

(6) Subsection (4) of section 59 of the Magistrates' Courts Act 1980 (power of court to order that account be opened) shall apply for the purposes of sub-paragraphs (1) and (5) as it applies for the purposes of that section.

(7) Before varying the order by exercising one of its powers under paragraphs (a) to (d) of section 59(3) of the Magistrates' Court Act 1980, the court shall have regard to any representations made by the parties to the application.

(8) If the court does not propose to exercise its power under paragraph (c) or (d) of subsection (3) of section 59 of the Magistrates' Courts Act 1980, the court shall, unless upon representations expressly made in that behalf by the applicant for the order it is satisfied that it is undesirable to do so, exercise its power under paragraph (b) of that subsection.

(9) None of the powers of the court, or of the clerk to the justices, conferred by this paragraph shall be exercisable in relation to an order under this Schedule for the making of periodical payments, or for the payment of a lump sum by instalments, which is not a qualifying maintenance order (within the meaning of section 59 of the Magistrates' Courts Act 1980).

(10) In sub-paragraphs (3) and (4) "interested party", in relation to an application made by the applicant under sub-paragraph (2), means a person who would be entitled to be a party to an application for the variation of the order made by the applicant under any other provision of this Schedule if such an application were made.]

7.—(1) Where the parent liable to make payments under a secured periodical payments order has died, the persons who may apply for the variation or discharge of the order shall include the personal representatives of the deceased parent.

(2) No application for the variation of the order shall, except with the permission of the court, be made after the end of the period of six months from the date on which representation in regard to the estate of that parent is first taken out.

(3) The personal representatives of a deceased person against whom a secured periodical payments order was made shall not be liable for having distributed any part of the estate of the deceased after the end of the period of six months referred to in sub-paragraph (2) on the ground that they ought to have taken into account the possibility that the court might permit an application for variation to be made after that period by the person entitled to payments under the order.

(4) Sub-paragraph (3) shall not prejudice any power to recover any part of the estate so distributed arising by virtue of the variation of an order in accordance with this paragraph.

(5) Where an application to vary a secured periodical payments order is made after the death of the parent liable to make payments under the order, the circumstances to which the court is required to have regard under paragraph 6(1) shall include the changed circumstances resulting from the death of the parent.

(6) In considering for the purposes of sub-paragraph (2) the question when representation was first taken out, a grant limited to settled land or to trust property shall be left out of account and a grant limited to real estate or to personal estate shall be left out of account unless a grant limited to the remainder of the estate has previously been made or is made at the same time.

(7) In this paragraph "secured periodical payments order" means an order for secured periodical payments under paragraph 1(2)(b).

Financial relief under other enactments

8.—(1) This paragraph applies where a residence order is made with respect to a child at a time when there is in force an order ("the financial relief order") made under any enactment other than this Act and requiring a person to contribute to the child's maintenance.

(2) Where this paragraph applies, the court may, on the application of—
(a) any person required by the financial relief order to contribute to the child's maintenance; or
(b) any person in whose favour a residence order with respect to the child is in force,
make an order revoking the financial relief order, or varying it by altering the amount of any sum payable under that order or by substituting the applicant for the person to whom any such sum is otherwise payable under that order.

Interim orders

9.—(1) Where an application is made under paragraph 1 or 2 the court may, at any time before it disposes of the application, make an interim order—
(a) requiring either or both parents to make such periodical payments, at such times and for such term as the court thinks fit; and
(b) giving any direction which the court thinks fit.

(2) An interim order made under this paragraph may provide for payments to be made from such date as the court may specify, not being earlier than the date of the making of the application under paragraph 1 or 2.

(3) An interim order made under this paragraph shall cease to have effect when the application is disposed of or, if earlier, on the date specified for the purposes of this paragraph in the interim order.

(4) An interim order in which a date has been specified for the purposes of sub-paragraph (3) may be varied by substituting a later date.

Alteration of maintenance agreements

10.—(1) In this paragraph and in paragraph 11 "maintenance agreement" means any agreement in writing made with respect to a child, whether before or after the commencement of this paragraph, which—
    (a)   is or was made between the father and mother of the child; and
    (b)   contains provision with respect to the making or securing of payments, or the disposition or use of any property, for the maintenance or education of the child,

and any such provisions are in this paragraph, and paragraph 11, referred to as "financial arrangements".

(2) Where a maintenance agreement is for the time being subsisting and each of the parties to the agreement is for the time being either domiciled or resident in England and Wales, then, either party may apply to the court for an order under this paragraph.

(3) If the court to which the application is made is satisfied either—
    (a)   that, by reason of a change in the circumstances in the light of which any financial arrangements contained in the agreement were made (including a change foreseen by the parties when making the agreement), the agreement should be altered so as to make different financial arrangements; or
    (b)   that the agreement does not contain proper financial arrangements with respect to the child,

then that court may by order make such alterations in the agreement by varying or revoking any financial arrangements contained in it as may appear to it to be just having regard to all the circumstances.

(4) If the maintenance agreement is altered by an order under this paragraph, the agreement shall have effect thereafter as if the alteration had been made by agreement between the parties and for valuable consideration.

(5) Where a court decides to make an order under this paragraph altering the maintenance agreement—
    (a)   by inserting provision for the making or securing by one of the parties to the agreement of periodical payments for the maintenance of the child; or
    (b)   by increasing the rate of periodical payments required to be made or secured by one of the parties for the maintenance of the child,

then, in deciding the term for which under the agreement as altered by the order the payments or (as the case may be) the additional payments attributable to the increase are to be made or secured for the benefit of the child, the court shall apply the provisions of sub-paragraphs (1) and (2) of paragraph 3 as if the order were an order under paragraph 1(2)(a) or (b).

(6) A magistrates' court shall not entertain an application under sub-paragraph (2) unless both the parties to the agreement are resident in England and Wales and at least one of the parties is resident in the commission area (within the meaning of the Justices of the Peace Act 1979) for which the court is appointed, and shall not have power to make any order on such an application except—
    (a)   in a case where the agreement contains no provision for periodical payments by either of the parties, an order inserting provision for the making by one of the parties of periodical payments for the maintenance of the child;
    (b)   in a case where the agreement includes provision for the making by one of the parties of periodical payments, an order increasing or reducing the rate of, or terminating, any of those payments.

(7) For the avoidance of doubt it is hereby declared that nothing in this paragraph affects any power of a court before which any proceedings between the parties to a maintenance agreement are brought under any other enactment to make an order containing financial arrangements or any right of either party to apply for such an order in such proceedings.

11.—(1) Where a maintenance agreement provides for the continuation, after the death of one of the parties, of payments for the maintenance of a child and that party dies domiciled in England and Wales, the surviving party or the personal representatives of the deceased party may apply to the High Court or a county court for an order under paragraph 10.

(2) If a maintenance agreement is altered by a court on an application under this paragraph, the agreement shall have effect thereafter as if the alteration had been made, immediately before the death, by agreement between the parties and for valuable consideration.

(3) An application under this paragraph shall not, except with leave of the High Court or a county court, be made after the end of the period of six months beginning with the day on which representation in regard to the estate of the deceased is first taken out.

(4) In considering for the purposes of sub-paragraph (3) the question when representation was first taken out, a grant limited to settled land or to trust property shall be left out of account and a grant limited to real estate or to personal estate shall be left out of account unless a grant limited to the remainder of the estate has previously been made or is made at the same time.

(5) A county court shall not entertain an application under this paragraph, or an application for leave to make an application under this paragraph, unless it would have jurisdiction to hear and determine proceedings for an order under section 2 of the Inheritance (Provision for Family and Dependants) Act 1975 in relation to the deceased's estate by virtue of section 25 of the County Courts Act 1984 (jurisdiction under the Act of 1975).

(6) The provisions of this paragraph shall not render the personal representatives of the deceased liable for having distributed any part of the estate of the deceased after the expiry of the period of six months referred to in sub-paragraph (3) on the ground that they ought to have taken into account the possibility that a court might grant leave for an application by virtue of this paragraph to be made by the surviving party after that period.

(7) Sub-paragraph (6) shall not prejudice any power to recover any part of the estate so distributed arising by virtue of the making of an order in pursuance of this paragraph.

Enforcement of orders for maintenance

12.—(1) Any person for the time being under an obligation to make payments in pursuance of any order for the payment of money made by a magistrates' court under this Act shall give notice of any change of address to such person (if any) as may be specified in the order.

(2) Any person failing without reasonable excuse to give such a notice shall be guilty of an offence and liable on summary conviction to a fine not exceeding level 2 on the standard scale.

(3) An order for the payment of money made by a magistrates' court under this Act shall be enforceable as a magistrates' court maintenance order within the meaning of section 150(1) of the Magistrates' Courts Act 1980.

Direction for settlement of instrument by conveyancing counsel

13. Where the High Court or a county court decides to make an order under this Act for the securing of periodical payments or for the transfer or settlement of property, it may direct that the matter be referred to one of the conveyancing counsel of the court to settle a proper instrument to be executed by all necessary parties.

Financial provision for child resident in country outside England and Wales

14.—(1) Where one parent of a child lives in England and Wales and the child lives outside England and Wales with—
  (a) another parent of his;
  (b) a guardian of his; or
  (c) a person in whose favour a residence order is in force with respect to the child,

the court shall have power, on an application made by any of the persons mentioned in paragraphs (a) to (c), to make one or both of the orders mentioned in paragraph 1(2)(a) and (b) against the parent living in England and Wales.

(2) Any reference in this Act to the powers of the court under paragraph 1(2) or to an order made under paragraph 1(2) shall include a reference to the powers which the court has by virtue of sub-paragraph (1) or (as the case may be) to an order made by virtue of sub-paragraph (1).

Local authority contribution to child's maintenance

15.—(1) Where a child lives, or is to live, with a person as the result of a residence order, a local authority may make contributions to that person towards the cost of the accommodation and maintenance of the child.

(2) Sub-paragraph (1) does not apply where the person with whom the child lives, or is to live, is a parent of the child or the husband or wife of a parent of the child.

Interpretation

16.—(1) In this Schedule "child" includes, in any case where an application is made under paragraph 2 or 6 in relation to a person who has reached the age of eighteen, that person.

(2) In this Schedule, except paragraphs 2 and 15, "parent" includes any party to a marriage (whether or not subsisting) in relation to whom the child concerned is a child of the family; and for this purpose any reference to either parent or both parents shall be construed as references to any parent of his and to all of his parents.

AMENDMENT

Paragraph 1(7) was added by the Court and Legal Services Act, Sched. 16, para. 10(2).

Paragraph 6A was added by the Maintenance Enforcement Act 1991, s.6.

DEFINITIONS

"child": s.105, Sched. 1, para. 16.
"parent": Sched. 1, para. 16.

GENERAL NOTE

See notes to section 15.

Sections 17, 23 and 29 **SCHEDULE 2**

LOCAL AUTHORITY SUPPORT FOR CHILDREN AND FAMILIES

PART I

PROVISION OF SERVICES FOR FAMILIES

Identification of children in need and provision of information

1.—(1) Every local authority shall take reasonable steps to identify the extent to which there are children in need within their area.

(2) Every local authority shall—
  (a) publish information—
    (i) about services provided by them under sections 17, 18, 20 and 24; and
    (ii) where they consider it appropriate, about the provision by others (including, in particular, voluntary organisations) of services which the authority have power to provide under those sections; and
  (b) take such steps as are reasonably practicable to ensure that those who might benefit from the services receive the information relevant to them.

Maintenance of a register of disabled children

2.—(1) Every local authority shall open and maintain a register of disabled children within their area.
(2) The register may be kept by means of a computer.

Assessment of children's needs

3. Where it appears to a local authority that a child within their area is in need, the authority may assess his needs for the purposes of this Act at the same time as any assessment of his needs is made under—
  (a) the Chronically Sick and Disabled Persons Act 1970;
  (b) the Education Act 1981;
  (c) the Disabled Persons (Services, Consultation and Representation) Act 1986; or
  (d) any other enactment.

Prevention of neglect and abuse

4.—(1) Every local authority shall take reasonable steps, through the provision of services under Part III of this Act, to prevent children within their area suffering ill-treatment or neglect.
(2) Where a local authority believe that a child who is at any time within their area—
  (a) is likely to suffer harm; but
  (b) lives or proposes to live in the area of another local authority
they shall inform that other local authority.
(3) When informing that other local authority they shall specify—
  (a) the harm that they believe he is likely to suffer; and
  (b) (if they can) where the child lives or proposes to live.

Provision of accommodation in order to protect child

5.—(1) Where—
  (a) it appears to a local authority that a child who is living on particular premises is suffering, or is likely to suffer, ill treatment at the hands of another person who is living on those premises; and
  (b) that other person proposes to move from the premises,
the authority may assist that other person to obtain alternative accommodation.
(2) Assistance given under this paragraph may be in cash.

(3) Subsections (7) to (9) of section 17 shall apply in relation to assistance given under this paragraph as they apply in relation to assistance given under that section.

Provision for disabled children

6. Every local authority shall provide services designed—
   (a) to minimise the effect on disabled children within their area of their disabilities; and
   (b) to give such children the opportunity to lead lives which are as normal as possible.

Provision to reduce need for care proceedings, etc.

7. Every local authority shall take reasonable steps designed—
   (a) to reduce the need to bring—
       (i) proceedings for care or supervision orders with respect to children within their area;
       (ii) criminal proceedings against such children;
       (iii) any family or other proceedings with respect to such children which might lead to them being placed in the authority's care; or
       (iv) proceedings under the inherent jurisdiction of the High Court with respect to children;
   (b) to encourage children within their area not to commit criminal offences; and
   (c) to avoid the need for children within their area to be placed in secure accommodation.

Provision for children living with their families

8. Every local authority shall make such provision as they consider appropriate for the following services to be available with respect to children in need within their area while they are living with their families—
   (a) advice, guidance and counselling;
   (b) occupational, social, cultural or recreational activities;
   (c) home help (which may include laundry facilities);
   (d) facilities for, or assistance with, travelling to and from home for the purpose of taking advantage of any other service provided under this Act or of any similar service;
   (e) assistance to enable the child concerned and his family to have a holiday.

Family centres

9.—(1) Every local authority shall provide such family centres as they consider appropriate in relation to children within their area.

(2) "Family centre" means a centre at which any of the persons mentioned in sub-paragraph (3) may—
   (a) attend for occupational, social, cultural or recreational activities;
   (b) attend for advice, guidance or counselling; or
   (c) be provided with accommodation while he is receiving advice, guidance or counselling.

(3) The persons are—
   (a) a child;
   (b) his parents;
   (c) any person who is not a parent of his but who has parental responsibility for him;
   (d) any other person who is looking after him.

Maintenance of the family home

10. Every local authority shall take such steps as are reasonably practicable, where any child within their area who is in need and whom they are not looking after is living apart from his family—
    (a) to enable him to live with his family; or
    (b) to promote contact between him and his family,
if, in their opinion, it is necessary to do so in order to safeguard or promote his welfare.

Duty to consider racial groups to which children in need belong

11. Every local authority shall, in making any arrangements—
    (a) for the provision of day care within their area; or
    (b) designed to encourage persons to act as local authority foster parents,
have regard to the different racial groups to which children within their area who are in need belong.

GENERAL NOTE
See notes to section 17. For a discussion of legal action to enforce these duties see Sunkin (1992) 4 J.Ch.Law 109.

PART II

CHILDREN LOOKED AFTER BY LOCAL AUTHORITIES

Regulations as to placing of children with local authority foster parents

12. Regulations under section 23(2)(a) may, in particular, make provision—
    (a) with regard to the welfare of children placed with local authority foster parents;
    (b) as to the arrangements to be made by local authorities in connection with the health and education of such children;
    (c) as to the records to be kept by local authorities;
    (d) for securing that a child is not placed with a local authority foster parent unless that person is for the time being approved as a local authority foster parent by such local authority as may be prescribed;
    (e) for securing that where possible the local authority foster parent with whom a child is to be placed is—
        (i) of the same religious persuasion as the child; or
        (ii) gives an undertaking that the child will be brought up in that religious persuasion;
    (f) for securing that children placed with local authority foster parents, and the premises in which they are accommodated, will be supervised and inspected by a local authority and that the children will be removed from those premises if their welfare appears to require it;
    (g) as to the circumstances in which local authorities may make arrangements for duties imposed on them by the regulations to be discharged, on their behalf.

REGULATIONS
See the Foster Placement (Children) Regulations 1991 (S.I. 1991 No. 910); the Arrangements for Placement of Children (General) Regulations 1991 (S.I. 1991 No. 890); the Children (Representations, Placements and Reviews (Miscellaneous Amendments)) Regulations 1991, (S.I. 1991 No. 2033) and the notes to section 23.

Regulations as to arrangements under section 23(2)(f)

13. Regulations under section 23(2)(f) may, in particular, make provision as to—
    (a) the persons to be notified of any proposed arrangements;
    (b) the opportunities such persons are to have to make representations in relation to the arrangements proposed;
    (c) the persons to be notified of any proposed changes in arrangements;
    (d) the records to be kept by local authorities;
    (e) the supervision by local authorities of any arrangements made.

REGULATIONS

S.I. 1991 No. 890 and notes to section 23.

Regulations as to conditions under which child in care is allowed to live with parent, etc.

14. Regulations under section 23(5) may, in particular, impose requirements on a local authority as to—
    (a) the making of any decision by a local authority to allow a child to live with any person falling within section 23(4) (including requirements as to those who must be consulted before the decision is made, and those who must be notified when it has been made);
    (b) the supervision or medical examination of the child concerned;
    (c) the removal of the child, in such circumstances as may be prescribed, from the care of the person with whom he has been allowed to live.
    [(d) the records to be kept by local authorities.]

AMENDMENT

Sub-paragraph (d) was added by the Courts and Legal Services Act 1990, s.116, Sched. 16, para. 26.

REGULATIONS

The Placement of Children with Parents, etc., Regulations 1991 (S.I. 1991 No. 893); S.I. 1991 No. 890; S.I. 1991 No. 2033: see notes to section 23 above.

Promotion and maintenance of contact between child and family

15.—(1) Where a child is being looked after by a local authority, the authority shall, unless it is not reasonably practicable or consistent with his welfare, endeavour to promote contact between the child and—
    (a) his parents;
    (b) any person who is not a parent of his but who has parental responsibility for him; and
    (c) any relative, friend or other person connected with him.

(2) Where a child is being looked after by a local authority—
    (a) the authority shall take such steps as are reasonably practicable to secure that—
        (i) his parents; and
        (ii) any person who is not a parent of his but who has parental responsibility for him,
    are kept informed of where he is being accommodated; and
    (b) every such person shall secure that the authority is kept informed of his or her address.

(3) Where a local authority ("the receiving authority") take over the provision of accommodation for a child from another local authority ("the transferring authority") under section 20(2)—

(a) the receiving authority shall (where reasonably practicable) inform—
    (i) the child's parents; and
    (ii) any person who is not a parent of his but who has parental responsibility for him;
(b) sub-paragraph (2)(a) shall apply to the transferring authority, as well as the receiving authority, until at least one such person has been informed of the change; and
(c) sub-paragraph (2)(b) shall not require any person to inform the receiving authority of his address until he has been so informed.

(4) Nothing in this paragraph requires a local authority to inform any person of the whereabouts of a child if—
    (a) the child is in the care of the authority; and
    (b) the authority has reasonable cause to believe that informing the person would prejudice the child's welfare.

(5) Any person who fails (without reasonable excuse) to comply with sub-paragraph (2)(b) shall be guilty of an offence and liable on summary conviction to a fine not exceeding level 2 on the standard scale.

(6) It shall be a defence in any proceedings under sub-paragraph (5) to prove that the defendant was residing at the same address as another person who was the child's parent or had parental responsibility for the child and had reasonable cause to believe that the other person had informed the appropriate authority that both of them were residing at that address.

Visits to or by children: expenses

16.—(1) This paragraph applies where—
    (a) a child is being looked after by a local authority; and
    (b) the conditions mentioned in sub-paragraph (3) are satisfied.
(2) The authority may—
    (a) make payments to—
        (i) a parent of the child;
        (ii) any person who is not a parent of his but who has parental responsibility for him; or
        (iii) any relative, friend or other person connected with him,
    in respect of travelling, subsistence or other expenses incurred by that person in visiting the child; or
    (b) make payments to the child, or to any person on his behalf, in respect of travelling, subsistence or other expenses incurred by or on behalf of the child in his visiting—
        (i) a parent of his;
        (ii) any person who is not a parent of his but who has parental responsibility for him; or
        (iii) any relative, friend or other person connected with him.
(3) The conditions are that—
    (a) it appears to the authority that the visit in question could not otherwise be made without undue financial hardship; and
    (b) the circumstances warrant the making of the payments.

Appointment of visitor for child who is not being visited

17.—(1) Where it appears to a local authority in relation to any child that they are looking after that—
    (a) communication between the child and—
        (i) a parent of his, or
        (ii) any person who is not a parent of his but who has parental responsibility for him,
    has been infrequent; or
    (b) he has not visited or been visited by (or lived with) any such person during the preceding twelve months,

and that it would be in the child's best interests for an independent person to be appointed to be his visitor for the purposes of this paragraph, they shall appoint such a visitor.

(2) A person so appointed shall—
  (a) have the duty of visiting, advising and befriending the child; and
  (b) be entitled to recover from the authority who appointed him any reasonable expenses incurred by him for the purposes of his functions under this paragraph.

(3) A person's appointment as a visitor in pursuance of this paragraph shall be determined if—
  (a) he gives notice in writing to the authority who appointed him that he resigns the appointment; or
  (b) the authority give him notice in writing that they have terminated it.

(4) The determination of such an appointment shall not prejudice any duty under this paragraph to make a further appointment.

(5) Where a local authority propose to appoint a visitor for a child under this paragraph, the appointment shall not be made if—
  (a) the child objects to it; and
  (b) the authority are satisfied that he has sufficient understanding to make an informed decision.

(6) Where a visitor has been appointed for a child under this paragraph, the local authority shall determine the appointment if—
  (a) the child objects to its continuing; and
  (b) the authority are satisfied that he has sufficient understanding to make an informed decision.

(7) The Secretary of State may make regulations as to the circumstances in which a person appointed as a visitor under this paragraph is to be regarded as independent of the local authority appointing him.

REGULATIONS

The Definition of Independent Visitors (Children) Regulations 1991 (S.I. 1991 No. 892): see notes to section 23 above and *Guidance*, Vol. 4, Chap. 6.

Power to guarantee apprenticeship deeds, etc.

18.—(1) While a child is being looked after by a local authority, or is a person qualifying for advice and assistance, the authority may undertake any obligation by way of guarantee under any deed of apprenticeship or articles of clerkship which he enters into.

(2) Where a local authority have undertaken any such obligation under any deed or articles they may at any time (whether or not they are still looking after the person concerned) undertake the like obligation under any supplemental deed or articles.

Arrangements to assist children to live abroad

19.—(1) A local authority may only arrange for, or assist in arranging for, any child in their care to live outside England and Wales with the approval of the court.

(2) A local authority may, with the approval of every person who has parental responsibility for the child arrange for, or assist in arranging for, any other child looked after by them to live outside England and Wales.

(3) The court shall not give its approval under sub-paragraph (1) unless it is satisfied that—
  (a) living outside England and Wales would be in the child's best interests;
  (b) suitable arrangements have been, or will be, made for his reception and welfare in the country in which he will live;
  (c) the child has consented to living in that country; and
  (d) every person who has parental responsibility for the child has consented to his living in that country.

(4) Where the court is satisfied that the child does not have sufficient understanding to give or withhold his consent, it may disregard sub-paragraph (3)(c) and give its approval if the child is to live in the country concerned with a parent, guardian, or other suitable person.

(5) Where a person whose consent is required by sub-paragraph (3)(d) fails to give his consent, the court may disregard that provision and give its approval if it is satisfied that that person—
    (a) cannot be found;
    (b) is incapable of consenting; or
    (c) is withholding his consent unreasonably.

(6) Section 56 of the Adoption Act 1976 (which requires authority for the taking or sending abroad for adoption of a child who is a British subject) shall not apply in the case of any child who is to live outside England and Wales with the approval of the court given under this paragraph.

(7) Where a court decides to give its approval under this paragraph it may order that its decision is not to have effect during the appeal period.

(8) In sub-paragraph (7) "the appeal period" means—
    (a) where an appeal is made against the decision, the period between the making of the decision and the determination of the appeal; and
    (b) otherwise, the period during which an appeal may be made against the decision.

GENERAL NOTES

See notes to section 33 and *Guidance*, Vol. 8, Chap 6. "There are profound implications for all those involved in a move abroad ... Careful consideration needs to be given to the balance to be struck between gaining a settled family against the loss of familiar people and surroundings (para. 4.8). The local authority must address the contact implications for the child with any parent or person with parental responsibility (para. 4.10)." Applications should be made to the family proceedings court; they are "specified proceedings" so a guardian ad litem should be appointed (r. 2(2)(c)). Consent to removal must be given in writing (r. 25). If an order is granted for the child's removal it will not have effect during the period when an appeal may be made or while an appeal is outstanding. Appeals are made to the High Court and must be filed with 14 days (see pp. 402–403 below).

Death of children being looked after by local authorities

20.—(1) If a child who is being looked after by a local authority dies, the authority—
    (a) shall notify the Secretary of State;
    (b) shall, so far as is reasonably practicable, notify the child's parents and every person who is not a parent of his but who has parental responsibility for him;
    (c) may, with the consent (so far as it is reasonably practicable to obtain it) of every person who has parental responsibility for the child, arrange for the child's body to be buried or cremated; and
    (d) may, if the conditions mentioned in sub-paragraph (2) are satisfied, make payments to any person who has parental responsibility for the child, or any relative, friend or other person connected with the child, in respect of travelling, subsistence or other expenses incurred by that person in attending the child's funeral.

(2) The conditions are that—
    (a) it appears to the authority that the person concerned could not otherwise attend the child's funeral without undue financial hardship; and
    (b) that the circumstances warrant the making of the payments.

(3) Sub-paragraph (1) does not authorise cremation where it does not accord with the practice of the child's religious persuasion.

(4) Where a local authority have exercised their power under sub-paragraph (1)(c) with respect to a child who was under sixteen when he died, they may recover from any parent of the child any expenses incurred by them.

(5) Any sums so recoverable shall, without prejudice to any other method of recovery, be recoverable summarily as a civil debt.

(6) Nothing in this paragraph affects any enactment regulating or authorising the burial, cremation or anatomical examination of the body of a deceased person.

Part III

Contributions Towards Maintenance of Children Looked After by Local Authorities

Liability to contribute

21.—(1) Where a local authority are looking after a child (other than in the cases mentioned in sub-paragraph (7)) they shall consider whether they should recover contributions towards the child's maintenance from any person liable to contribute ("a contributor").

(2) An authority may only recover contributions from a contributor if they consider it reasonable to do so.

(3) The persons liable to contribute are—
    (a) where the child is under 16, each of his parents;
    (b) where he has reached the age of 16, the child himself.

(4) A parent is not liable to contribute during any period when he is in receipt of income support [, family credit or disability working allowance] under the Social Security Contributions and Benefits Act 1992.

(5) A person is not liable to contribute towards the maintenance of a child in the care of a local authority in respect of any period during which the child is allowed by the authority (under section 23(5)) to live with a parent of his.

(6) A contributor is not obliged to make any contribution towards a child's maintenance except as agreed or determined in accordance with this Part of this Schedule.

(7) The cases are where the child is looked after by a local authority under—
    (a) section 21;
    (b) an interim care order;
    (c) section 53 of the Children and Young Persons Act 1933.

Amendment

In paragraph 21(4) the words in square brackets were substituted by the Disability Living Allowance and Disability Working Allowance Act 1991, s.7, Sched. 3, para. 15 and by the Social Security (Consequential Provisions) Act 1992, Sched. 2, para. 108.

Agreed contributions

22.—(1) Contributions towards a child's maintenance may only be recovered if the local authority have served a notice ("a contribution notice") on the contributor specifying—
    (a) the weekly sum which they consider that he should contribute; and
    (b) arrangements for payment.

(2) The contribution notice must be in writing and dated.

(3) Arrangements for payment shall, in particular, include—
    (a) the date on which liability to contribute begins (which must not be earlier than the date of the notice);
    (b) the date on which liability under the notice will end (if the child has not before that date ceased to be looked after by the authority); and
    (c) the date on which the first payment is to be made.

(4) The authority may specify in a contribution notice a weekly sum which is a standard contribution determined by them for all children looked after by them.

(5) The authority may not specify in a contribution notice a weekly sum greater than that which they consider—

Schedule 2

(a) they would normally be prepared to pay if they had placed a similar child with local authority foster parents; and

(b) it is reasonably practicable for the contributor to pay (having regard to his means).

(6) An authority may at any time withdraw a contribution notice (without prejudice to their power to serve another).

(7) Where the authority and the contributor agree—
  (a) the sum which the contributor is to contribute; and
  (b) arrangements for payment.

(whether as specified in the contribution notice or otherwise) and the contributor notifies the authority in writing that he so agrees, the authority may recover summarily as a civil debt any contribution which is overdue and unpaid.

(8) A contributor may, by serving a notice in writing on the authority, withdraw his agreement in relation to any period of liability falling after the date of service of the notice.

(9) Sub-paragraph (7) is without prejudice to any other method of recovery.

Contribution orders

23.—(1) Where a contributor has been served with a contribution notice and has—
  (a) failed to reach any agreement with the local authority as mentioned in paragraph 22(7) within the period of one month beginning with the day on which the contribution notice was served; or
  (b) served a notice under paragraph 22(8) withdrawing his agreement,

the authority may apply to the court for an order under this paragraph.

(2) On such an application the court may make an order ("a contribution order") requiring the contributor to contribute a weekly sum towards the child's maintenance in accordance with arrangements for payment specified by the court.

(3) A contribution order—
  (a) shall not specify a weekly sum greater than that specified in the contribution notice; and
  (b) shall be made with due regard to the contributor's means.

(4) A contribution order shall not—
  (a) take effect before the date specified in the contribution notice; or
  (b) have effect while the contributor is not liable to contribute (by virtue of paragraph 21); or
  (c) remain in force after the child has ceased to be looked after by the authority who obtained the order.

(5) An authority may not apply to the court under sub-paragraph (1) in relation to a contribution notice which they have withdrawn.

(6) Where—
  (a) a contribution order is in force;
  (b) the authority serve another contribution notice; and
  (c) the contributor and the authority reach an agreement under paragraph 22(7) in respect of that other contribution notice,

the effect of the agreement shall be to discharge the order from the date on which it is agreed that the agreement shall take effect.

(7) Where an agreement is reached under sub-paragraph (6) the authority shall notify the court—
  (a) of the agreement; and
  (b) of the date on which it took effect.

(8) A contribution order may be varied or revoked on the application of the contributor or the authority.

(9) In proceedings for the variation of a contribution order, the authority shall specify—
  (a) the weekly sum which, having regard to paragraph 22, they propose that the contributor should contribute under the order as varied; and
  (b) the proposed arrangements for payment.

(10) Where a contribution order is varied, the order—
  (a) shall not specify a weekly sum greater than that specified by the authority in the proceedings for variation; and

(b) shall be made with due regard to the contributor's means.

(11) An appeal shall lie in accordance with rules of court from any order made under this paragraph.

Enforcement of contribution orders etc.

24.—(1) A contribution order made by a magistrates' court shall be enforceable as a magistrates' court maintenance order (within the meaning of section 150(1) of the Magistrates' Courts Act 1980).

(2) Where a contributor has agreed, or has been ordered, to make contributions to a local authority, any other local authority within whose area the contributor is for the time being living may—
  (a) at the request of the local authority who served the contribution notice; and
  (b) subject to the agreement as to any sum to be deducted in respect of services rendered, collect from the contributor any contributions due on behalf of the authority who served the notice.

(3) In sub-paragraph (2) the reference to any other local authority includes a reference to—
  (a) a local authority within the meaning of section 1(2) of the Social Work (Scotland) Act 1968; and
  (b) a Health and Social Services Board established under Article 16 of the Health and Personal Social Services (Northern Ireland) Order 1972.

(4) The power to collect sums under sub-paragraph (2) includes the power to—
  (a) receive and give a discharge for any contributions due; and
  (b) (if necessary) enforce payment of any contributions,
even though those contributions may have fallen due at a time when the contributor was living elsewhere.

(5) Any contribution collected under sub-paragraph (2) shall be paid (subject to any agreed deduction) to the local authority who served the contribution notice.

(6) In any proceedings under this paragraph, a document which purports to be—
  (a) a copy of an order made by a court under or by virtue of paragraph 23; and
  (b) certified as a true copy by the clerk of the court, shall be evidence of the order.

(7) In any proceedings under this paragraph, a certificate which—
  (a) purports to be signed by the clerk or some other duly authorised officer of the local authority who obtained the contribution order; and
  (b) states that any sum due to the authority under the order is overdue and unpaid,
shall be evidence that the sum is overdue and unpaid.

Regulations

25. The Secretary of State may make regulations—
  (a) as to the considerations which a local authority must take into account in deciding—
    (i) whether it is reasonable to recover contributions; and
    (ii) what the arrangements for payment should be;
  (b) as to the procedures they must follow in reaching agreements with—
    (i) contributors (under paragraphs 22 and 23); and
    (ii) any other local authority (under paragraph 23).

GENERAL NOTE

The Maintenance Enforcement Act 1991 applies to these proceedings because contribution orders are maintenance orders within the Administration of Justice Act 1970, Sched. 8 as amended by the Courts and Legal Services Act 1990, Sched. 16, para. 6(1).

Proceedings relating to contributions are governed by rule 30, see p. 416 below and notes to section 29. No regulations have been made under paragraph 25.

Sections 35 and 36

SCHEDULE 3

SUPERVISION ORDERS

PART I

GENERAL

Meaning of "responsible person"

1. In this Schedule, "the responsible person," in relation to a supervised child, means—
   (a) any person who has parental responsibility for the child; and
   (b) any other person with whom the child is living.

Power of supervisor to give directions to supervised child

2.—(1) A supervision order may require the supervised child to comply with any directions given from time to time by the supervisor which require him to do all or any of the following things—
   (a) to live at a place or places specified in the directions for a period or periods so specified;
   (b) to present himself to a person or persons specified in the directions at a place or places and on a day or days so specified;
   (c) to participate in activities specified in the directions on a day or days so specified.
(2) It shall be for the supervisor to decide whether, and to what extent, he exercises his power to give directions and to decide the form of any directions which he gives.
(3) Sub-paragraph (1) does not confer on a supervisor power to give directions in respect of any medical or psychiatric examination or treatment (which are matters dealt with in paragraphs 4 and 5).

Imposition of obligations on responsible person

3.—(1) With the consent of any responsible person, a supervision order may include a requirement—
   (a) that he take all reasonable steps to ensure that the supervised child complies with any direction given by the supervisor under paragraph 2;
   (b) that he take all reasonable steps to ensure that the supervised child complies with any requirement included in the order under paragraph 4 or 5;
   (c) that he comply with any directions given by the supervisor requiring him to attend at a place specified in the directions for the purpose of taking part in activities so specified.
(2) A direction given under sub-paragraph (1)(c) may specify the time at which the responsible person is to attend and whether or not the supervised child is required to attend with him.
(3) A supervision order may require any person who is a responsible person in relation to the supervised child to keep the supervisor informed of his address, if it differs from the child's.

Psychiatric and medical examinations

4.—(1) A supervision order may require the supervised child—
    (a) to submit to a medical or psychiatric examination; or
    (b) to submit to any such examination from time to time as directed by the supervisor.

(2) Any such examination shall be required to be conducted—
    (a) by, or under the direction of, such registered medical practitioner as may be specified in the order;
    (b) at a place specified in the order and at which the supervised child is to attend as a non-resident patient; or
    (c) at—
        (i) a health service hospital; or
        (ii) in the case of a psychiatric examination, a hospital or mental nursing home,
    at which the supervised child is, or is to attend as, a resident patient.

(3) A requirement of a kind mentioned in sub-paragraph (2)(c) shall not be included unless the court is satisfied, on the evidence of a registered medical practitioner, that—
    (a) the child may be suffering from a physical or mental condition that requires, and may be susceptible to, treatment; and
    (b) a period as a resident patient is necessary if the examination is to be carried out properly.

(4) No court shall include a requirement under this paragraph in a supervision order unless it is satisfied that—
    (a) where the child has sufficient understanding to make an informed decision, he consents to its inclusion; and
    (b) satisfactory arrangements have been, or can be, made for the examination.

Psychiatric and medical treatment

5.—(1) Where court which proposes to make or vary a supervision order is satisfied, on the evidence of a registered medical practitioner approved for the purposes of section 12 of the Mental Health Act 1983, that the mental condition of the supervised child—
    (a) is such as requires, and may be susceptible to, treatment; but
    (b) is not such as to warrant his detention in pursuance of a hospital order under Part III of that Act,
the court may include in the order a requirement that the supervised child shall, for a period specified in the order, submit to such treatment as is so specified.

(2) The treatment specified in accordance with sub-paragraph (1) must be—
    (a) by, or under the direction of, such registered medical practitioner as may be specified in the order;
    (b) as a non-resident patient at such a place as may be so specified; or
    (c) as a resident patient in a hospital or mental nursing home.

(3) Where a court which proposes to make or vary a supervision order is satisfied, on the evidence of a registered medical practitioner, that the physical condition of the supervised child is such as requires, and may be susceptible to, treatment, the court may include in the order a requirement that the supervised child shall, for a period specified in the order, submit to such treatment as is so specified.

(4) The treatment specified in accordance with sub-paragraph (3) must be—
    (a) by, or under the direction of, such registered medical practitioner as may be specified in the order;
    (b) as a non-resident patient at such place as may be so specified; or
    (c) as a resident patient in a health service hospital.

(5) No court shall include a requirement under this paragraph in a supervision order unless it is satisfied—
    (a) where the child has sufficient understanding to make an informed decision, that he consents to its inclusion; and

Schedule 3

  (b) that satisfactory arrangements have been, or can be, made for the treatment.

(6) If a medical practitioner by whom or under whose direction a supervised person is being treated in pursuance of a requirement included in a supervision order by virtue of this paragraph is unwilling to continue to treat or direct the treatment of the supervised child or is of the opinion that—
  (a) the treatment should be continued beyond the period specified in the order;
  (b) the supervised child needs different treatment;
  (c) he is not susceptible to treatment; or
  (d) he does not require further treatment,
the practitioner shall make a report in writing to that effect to the supervisor.

(7) On receiving a report under this paragraph the supervisor shall refer it to the court, and on such a reference the court may make an order cancelling or varying the requirement.

PART II

MISCELLANEOUS

Life of supervision order

6.—(1) Subject to sub-paragraph (2) and section 91, a supervision order shall cease to have effect at the end of the period of one year beginning with the date on which it was made.

(2) A supervision order shall also cease to have effect if an event mentioned in section 25(1)(a) or (b) of the Child Abduction and Custody Act 1985 (termination of existing orders) occurs with respect to the child.

(3) Where the supervisor applies to the court to extend, or further extend, a supervision order the court may extend the order for such period as it may specify.

(4) A supervision order may not be extended so as to run beyond the end of the period of three years beginning with the date on which it was made.

7. [Repealed by the Courts and Legal Services Act 1990, s.125(7), Sched. 20]

Information to be given to supervisor etc.

8.—(1) A supervision order may require the supervised child—
  (a) to keep the supervisor informed of any change in his address; and
  (b) to allow the supervisor to visit him at the place where he is living.

(2) The responsible person in relation to any child with respect to whom a supervision order is made shall—
  (a) if asked by the supervisor, inform him of the child's address (if it is known to him); and
  (b) if he is living with the child, allow the supervisor reasonable contact with the child.

Selection of supervisor

9.—(1) A supervision order shall not designate a local authority as the supervisor unless—
  (a) the authority agree; or
  (b) the supervised child lives or will live within their area.

(2) A court shall not place a child under the supervision of a probation officer unless—
  (a) the appropriate authority so request; and

(b) a probation officer is already exercising or has exercised, in relation to another member of the household to which the child belongs, duties imposed on probation officers—
   (i) by paragraphs 8 of Schedule 3 to the Powers of Criminal Courts Act 1973; or
   (ii) by rules under paragraph 18(1)(b) of that Schedule.

(3) In sub-paragraph (2) "the appropriate authority" means the local authority appearing to the court to be the authority in whose area the supervised child lives or will live.

(4) Where a supervision order places a person under the supervision of a probation officer, the officer shall be selected in accordance with arrangements made by the probation committee for the area in question.

(5) If the selected probation officer is unable to carry out his duties, or dies, another probation officer shall be selected in the same manner.

Effect of supervision order on earlier orders

10. The making of a supervision order with respect to any child brings to an end any earlier care or supervision order which—
   (a) was made with respect to that child; and
   (b) would otherwise continue in force.

Local authority functions and expenditure

11.—(1) The Secretary of State may make regulations with respect to the exercise by a local authority of their functions where a child has been placed under their supervision by a supervision order.

(2) Where a supervision order requires compliance with directions given by virtue of this section, any expenditure incurred by the supervisor for the purposes of the directions shall be defrayed by the local authority designated in the order.

DEFINITIONS
"child": s.105(1).
"responsible person": Sched. 3, para. 1.
"supervised child," "supervision": s.105(1).
"supervision order": s.31(11).

GENERAL NOTE
See notes to section 35 and, in relation to the child's consent to medical examinations, see notes to section 43(8). Applications for supervision orders are treated in the same way as applications for care orders. Any application for an extension under paragraph 6 must be heard before the order expires; a temporary extension could be granted pending a full hearing. Applications for extensions are "specified proceedings" and a guardian ad litem should be appointed. Applications for supervision orders are made in the same way as applications for care orders, see pp. 361 and 422 below.

PART III

EDUCATION SUPERVISION ORDERS

Effect of orders

12.—(1) Where an education supervision order is in force with respect to a child, it shall be the duty of the supervisor—

(a) to advise, assist and befriend, and give directions to—
   (i) the supervised child; and
   (ii) his parents,
   in such a way as will, in the opinion of the supervisor, secure that he is properly educated;
(b) where any such directions given to—
   (i) the supervised child; or
   (ii) a parent of his,
   have not been complied with, to consider what further steps to take in the exercise of the supervisor's powers under this Act.

(2) Before giving any directions under sub-paragraph (1) the supervisor shall, so far as is reasonably practicable, ascertain the wishes and feelings of—
   (a) the child; and
   (b) his parents,
including, in particular, their wishes as to the place at which the child should be educated.

(3) When settling the terms of such directions, the supervisor shall give due consideration—
   (a) having regard to the child's age and understanding, to such wishes and feelings of his as the supervisor has been able to ascertain; and
   (b) to such wishes and feelings of the child's parents as he has been able to ascertain.

(4) Directions may be given under this paragraph at any time while the education supervision order is in force.

13.—(1) Where an education supervision order is in force with respect to a child, the duties of the child's parents under sections 36 and 39 of the Education Act 1944 (duty to secure education of children and to secure regular attendance of registered pupils) shall be superseded by their duty to comply with any directions in force under the education supervision order.

(2) Where an education supervision order is made with respect to a child—
   (a) any school attendance order—
      (i) made under section 37 of the Act of 1944 with respect to the child; and
      (ii) in force immediately before the making of the education supervision order,
      shall cease to have effect; and
   (b) while the education supervision order remains in force, the following provisions shall not apply with respect to the child—
      (i) section 37 of that Act (school attendance orders);
      (ii) section 76 of that Act (pupils to be educated in accordance with wishes of their parents);
      (iii) sections 6 and 7 of the Education Act 1980 (parental preference and appeals against admission decisions);
   (c) a supervision order made with respect to the child in criminal proceedings, while the education supervision order is in force, may not include an education requirement of the kind which could otherwise be included under section 12C of the Children and Young Persons Act 1969;
   (d) any education requirement of a kind mentioned in paragraph (c), which was in force with respect to the child immediately before the making of the education supervision order, shall cease to have effect.

Effect where child also subject to supervision order

14.—(1) This paragraph applies where an education supervision order and a Supervision order, or order under section 7(7)(b) of the Children and Young Persons Act 1969, are in force at the same time with respect to the same child.

(2) Any failure to comply with a direction given by the supervisor under the education supervision order shall be disregarded if it would not have been reasonably practicable to comply with it without failing to comply with a direction given under the other order.

Duration of orders

15.—(1) An education supervision order shall have effect for a period of one year, beginning with the date on which it is made.

(2) An education supervision order shall not expire if, before it would otherwise have expired, the court has (on the application of the authority in whose favour the order was made) extended the period during which it is in force.

(3) Such an application may not be made earlier than three months before the date on which the order would otherwise expire.

(4) The period during which an education supervision order is in force may be extended under sub-paragraph (2) on more than one occasion.

(5) No one extension may be for a period of more than three years.

(6) An education supervision order shall cease to have effect on—
    (a) the child's ceasing to be of compulsory school age; or
    (b) the making of a care order with respect to the child;
and sub-paragraphs (1) to (4) are subject to this sub-paragraph.

Information to be given to supervisor etc.

15.—(1) An education supervision order may require the child—
    (a) to keep the supervisor informed of any change in his address; and
    (b) to allow the supervisor to visit him at the place where he is living.

(2) A person who is the parent of a child with respect to whom an education supervision order has been made shall—
    (a) if asked by the supervisor, inform him of the child's address (if it is known to him); and
    (b) if he is living with the child, allow the supervisor reasonable contact with the child.

Discharge of orders

17.—(1) The court may discharge any education supervision order on the application of—
    (a) the child concerned;
    (b) a parent of his; or
    (c) the local education authority concerned.

(2) On discharging an education supervision order, the court may direct the local authority within whose area the child lives, or will live, to investigate the circumstances of the child.

Offences

18.—(1) If a parent of a child with respect to whom an education supervision order is in force persistently fails to comply with a direction given under the order he shall be guilty of an offence.

(2) It shall be a defence for any person charged with such an offence to prove that—
    (a) he took all reasonable steps to ensure that the direction was complied with;
    (b) the direction was unreasonable; or
    (c) he had complied with—
        (i) a requirement included in a supervision order made with respect to the child; or
        (ii) directions given under such a requirement,
    and that it was not reasonably practicable to comply both with the direction and with the requirement or directions mentioned in this paragraph.

(3) A person guilty of an offence under this paragraph shall be liable on summary conviction to a fine not exceeding level 3 on the standard scale.

Schedule 3

Persistent failure of child to comply with directions

19.—(1) Where a child with respect to whom an education supervision order is in force persistently fails to comply with any direction given under the order, the local education authority concerned shall notify the appropriate local authority.

(2) Where a local authority have been notified under sub-paragraph (1) they shall investigate the circumstances of the child.

(3) In this paragraph "the appropriate local authority" has the same meaning as in section 36.

Miscellaneous

20. The Secretary of State may by regulations make provision modifying, or displacing, the provisions of any enactment about education in relation to any child with respect to whom an education supervision order is in force to such extent as appears to the Secretary of State to be necessary or expedient in consequence of the provision made by this Act with respect to such orders.

Interpretation

21. In this Part of this Schedule "parent" has the same meaning as in the Education Act 1944 (as amended by Schedule 13).

DEFINITIONS
"education supervision order": s.36(2).
"local education authority": ss.36(7), 105(1).
"parent": Sched. 3, para. 21.
"school": s.105(1).
"supervised child," "supervision"; s.105(1).

GENERAL NOTE

The use of education supervision orders is discussed in the notes to section 36 above. Guidance has been issued by the Department of Health, see *Guidance*, Vol. 7, Chap. 3. Proceedings are governed by rules 4 and 31, see below pp. 361 and 418. These are not "specified proceedings" so a guardian ad litem is not normally appointed.

Section 53(6) **SCHEDULE 4**

MANAGEMENT AND CONDUCT OF COMMUNITY HOMES

PART I

INSTRUMENTS OF MANAGEMENT

Instruments of management for controlled and assisted community homes

1.—(1) The Secretary of State may by order make an instrument of management providing for the constitution of a body of managers for any [...] home which is designated as a controlled or assisted community home.

(2) Sub-paragraph (3) applies where two or more [...] homes are designated as controlled community homes or as assisted community homes.

(3) If—

(a) those homes are, or are to be, provided by the same voluntary organisation; and

(b) the same local authority is to be represented on the body of managers for those homes,

a single instrument of management may be made by the Secretary of State under this paragraph constituting one body of managers for those homes or for any two or more of them.

(4) The number of persons who, in accordance with an instrument of management, constitute the body of managers for a [...] home shall be such number (which must be a multiple of three) as may be specified in the instrument.

(5) The instrument shall provide that the local authority specified in the instrument shall appoint—

(a) in the case of a [...] home which is designated as a controlled community home, two-thirds of the managers; and

(b) in the case of a [...] home which is designated as an assisted community home, one-third of them.

(6) An instrument of management shall provide that the foundation managers shall be appointed, in such manner and by such persons as may be specified in the instrument—

(a) so as to represent the interests of the voluntary organisation by which the home is, or is to be, provided; and

(b) for the purpose of securing that—

(i) so far as is practicable, the character of the home [...] will be preserved; and

(ii) subject to paragraph 2(3), the terms of any trust deed relating to the home are observed.

(7) An instrument of management shall come into force on such date as it may specify.

(8) If an instrument of management is in force in relation to a [...] home the home shall be (and be known as) a controlled community home or an assisted community home, according to its designation.

(9) In this paragraph—

"foundation managers," in relation to a [...] home, means those of the managers of the home who are not appointed by a local authority in accordance with sub-paragraph (5); and

"designated" means designated in accordance with section 53.

2.—(1) An instrument of management shall contain such provisions as the Secretary of State considers appropriate.

(2) Nothing in the instrument of management shall affect the purposes for which the premises comprising the home are held.

(3) Without prejudice to the generality of sub-paragraph (1), an instrument of management may contain provisions—

(a) specifying the nature and purpose of the home (or each of the homes) to which it relates;

(b) requiring a specified number or proportion of the places in that time (or those homes) to be made available to local authorities and to any other body specified in the instrument; and

(c) relating to the management of that home (or those homes) and the charging of fees with respect to—

(i) children placed there; or

(ii) places made available to any local authority or other body.

(4) Subject to sub-paragraphs (1) and (2), in the event of any inconsistency between the provisions of any trust deed and an instrument of management, the instrument of management shall prevail over the provisions of the trust deed in so far as they relate to the home concerned.

(5) After consultation with the voluntary organisation concerned and with the local authority specified in its instrument of management, the Secretary of State may by order vary or revoke any provision of the instrument.

PART II

MANAGEMENT OF CONTROLLED AND ASSISTED HOMES

3.—(1) The management, equipment and maintenance of a controlled community home shall be the responsibility of the local authority specified in its instrument of management.

(2) The management, equipment and maintenance of an assisted community home shall be the responsibility of the voluntary organisation by which the home is provided.

(3) In this paragraph—

"home" means a controlled community home or (as the case may be) assisted community home; and

"the managers," in relation to a home, means the managers constituted by its instrument of management; and

"the responsible body," in relation to a home, means the local authority or (as the case may be) voluntary organisation responsible for its management, equipment and maintenance.

(4) The functions of a home's responsible body shall be exercised through the managers.

(5) Anything done, liability incurred or property acquired by a home's managers shall be done, incurred or acquired by them as agents of the responsible body.

(6) In so far as any matter is reserved for the decision of a home's responsible body by—

(a) sub-paragraph (8);
(b) the instrument of management;
(c) the service by the body on the managers, or any of them, of a notice reserving any matter,

that matter shall be dealt with by the body and not by the managers.

(7) In dealing with any matter so reserved, the responsible body shall have regard to any representations made to the body by the managers.

(8) The employment of persons at a home shall be a matter reserved for the decision of the responsible body.

(9) Where the instrument of management of a controlled community home so provides, the responsible body may enter into arrangements with the voluntary organisation by which that home is provided whereby, in accordance with such terms as may be agreed between them and the voluntary organisation, persons who are not in the employment of the responsible body shall undertake duties at that home.

(10) Subject to sub-paragraph (11)—

(a) where the responsible body for an assisted community home proposes to engage any person to work at that home or to terminate without notice the employment of any person at that home, it shall consult the local authority specified in the instrument of management and, if that authority so direct, the responsible body shall not carry out its proposal without their consent; and

(b) that local authority may, after consultation with the responsible body, require that body to terminate the employment of any person at that home.

(11) Paragraphs (a) and (b) of sub-paragraph (10) shall not apply—

(a) in such cases or circumstances as may be specified by notice in writing given by the local authority to the responsible body; and

(b) in relation to the employment of any persons or class of persons specified in the home's instrument of management.

(12) The accounting year of the managers of a home shall be such as may be specified by the responsible body.

(13) Before such date in each accounting year as may be so specified, the managers of a home shall submit to the responsible body estimates, in such form as the body may require, of expenditure and receipts in respect of the next accounting year.

(14) Any expenses incurred by the managers of a home with the approval of the responsible body shall be defrayed by that body.

(15) The managers of a home shall keep—
   (a) proper accounts with respect to the home; and
   (b) proper records in relation to the accounts.

(16) Where an instrument of management relates to more than one home, one set of accounts and records may be kept in respect of all the homes to which it relates.

PART III

REGULATIONS

4.—(1) The Secretary of State may make regulations—
   (a) as to the placing of children in community homes;
   (b) as to the conduct of such homes; and
   (c) for securing the welfare of children in such homes.

(2) The regulations may, in particular—
   (a) prescribe standards to which the premises used for such homes are to conform;
   (b) impose requirements as to the accommodation, staff and equipment to be provided in such homes, and as to the arrangements to be made for protecting the health of children in such homes;
   (c) provide for the control and discipline of children in such homes;
   (d) impose requirements as to the keeping of records and giving of notices in respect of children in such homes;
   (e) impose requirements as to the facilities which are to be provided for giving religious instruction to children in such homes;
   (f) authorise the Secretary of State to give and revoke directions requiring—
      (i) the local authority to whom a home is provided or who are specified in the instrument of management for a controlled community home, or
      (ii) the voluntary organisation by which an assisted community home is provided,
   to accommodate in the home a child looked after by a local authority for whom no places are made available in that home or to take such action in relation to a child accommodated in the home as may be specified in the directions;
   (g) provide for consultation with the Secretary of State as to applicants for appointment to the charge of a home;
   (h) empower the Secretary of State to prohibit the appointment of any particular applicant except in the cases (if any) in which the regulations dispense with such consultation by reason that the person to be appointed possesses such qualification as may be prescribed;
   (i) require the approval of the Secretary of State for the provision and use of accommodation for the purpose of restricting the liberty of children in such homes and impose other requirements (in addition to those imposed by section 25) as to the placing of a child in accommodation provided for that purpose, including a requirement to obtain the permission of any local authority who are looking after the child;
   (j) provide that, to such extent as may be provided for in the regulations, the Secretary of State may direct that any provision of regulations under this paragraph which is specified in the direction and makes any such provision as is referred to in paragraph (a) or (b) shall not apply in relation to a particular home or the premises used for it, and may provide for the variation or revocation of any such direction by the Secretary of State.

(3) Without prejudice to the power to make regulations under this paragraph conferring functions on—
   (a) the local authority or voluntary organisation by which a community home is provided; or
   (b) the managers of a controlled or assisted community home,

regulations under this paragraph may confer functions in relation to a controlled or assisted community home on the local authority named in the instrument of management for the home.

AMENDMENT

The words omitted were repealed by the Courts and Legal Services Act 1990, s.125(7), Sched. 20.

DEFINITIONS

"designated": Sched. 4, para. 1(9).
"foundation managers": Sched. 4, para. 1(9).
"home": Sched. 4, para. 3(3).
"the managers": Sched. 4, para. 3(3).
"the responsible body": Sched. 4, para. 3(3).

REGULATIONS

The Arrangements for Placement of Children (General) Regulations 1991 (S.I. 1991 No. 890); The Children (Representations, Placements and Reviews (Miscellaneous Amendments) Regulations 1991 (S.I. 1991 No. 2033), see notes to section 23 and the Children's Homes Regulations 1991 (S.I. 1991 No. 1506), see notes to section 53.

GENERAL NOTES

See notes to section 53.

Section 60(4)   SCHEDULE 5

VOLUNTARY HOMES AND VOLUNTARY ORGANISATIONS

PART I

REGISTRATION OF VOLUNTARY HOMES

General

1.—(1) An application for registration under this paragraph shall—
    (a) be made by the persons intending to carry on the home to which the application relates; and
    (b) be made in such manner, and be accompanied by such particulars, as the Secretary of State may prescribe.

(2) On an application duly made under sub-paragraph (1) the Secretary of State may—
    (a) grant or refuse the application, as he thinks fit; or
    (b) grant the application subject to such conditions as he considers appropriate.

(3) The Secretary of State may from time to time—
    (a) vary any conditions for the time being in force with respect to a voluntary home by virtue of this paragraph; or
    (b) impose an additional condition,
either on the application of the person carrying on the home or without such an application.

(4) Where at any time it appears to the Secretary of State that the conduct of any voluntary home—
    (a) is not in accordance with regulations made under paragraph 7; or

(b) is otherwise unsatisfactory,

he may cancel the registration of the home and remove it from the register.

(5) Any person who, without reasonable excuse, carries on a voluntary home in contravention of—
 (a) section 60; or
 (b) a condition to which the registration of the home is for the time being subject by virtue of this Part,

shall be guilty of an offence.

(6) Any person guilty of such an offence shall be liable on summary conviction to a fine not exceeding—
 (a) level 5 on the standard scale, if his offence is under sub-paragraph (5)(a); or
 (b) level 4, if it is under sub-paragraph (5)(b).

(7) Where the Secretary of State registers a home under this paragraph, or cancels the registration of a home, he shall notify the local authority within whose area the home is situated.

Procedure

2.—(1) Where—
 (a) a person applies for registration of a voluntary home; and
 (b) the Secretary of State proposes to grant his application, the Secretary of State shall give him written notice of his proposal and of the conditions subject to which he proposes to grant the application.

(2) The Secretary of State need not give notice if he proposes to grant the application subject only to conditions which—:
 (a) the applicant specified in the application; or
 (b) the Secretary of State and the applicant have subsequently agreed.

(3) Where the Secretary of State proposes to refuse such an application he shall give notice of his proposal to the applicant.

(4) The Secretary of State shall give any person carrying on a voluntary home notice of a proposal to—
 (a) cancel the registration of the home;
 (b) vary any condition for the time being in force with respect to the home by virtue of paragraph 1; or
 (c) impose any additional condition.

(5) A notice under this paragraph shall give the Secretary of State's reasons for his proposal.

Right to make representations

3.—(1) A notice under paragraph 2 shall state that within 14 days of service of the notice any person on whom it is served may (in writing) require the Secretary of State to give him an opportunity to make representations to the Secretary of State concerning the matter.

(2) Where a notice has been served under paragraph 2, the Secretary of State shall not determine the matter until either—
 (a) any person on whom the notice was served has made representations to him concerning the matter; or
 (b) the period during which any such person could have required the Secretary of State to give him an opportunity to make representations has elapsed without the Secretary of State being required to give such an opportunity; or
 (c) the conditions specified in sub-paragraph (3) are satisfied.

(3) The conditions are that—

(a) a person on whom the notice was served has required the Secretary of State to give him an opportunity to make representations to the Secretary of State;
(b) the Secretary of State has allowed him a reasonable period to make his representations; and
(c) he has failed to make them within that period.

(4) The representations may be made, at the option of the person making them, either in writing or orally.

(5) If he informs the Secretary of State that he desires to make oral representations, the Secretary of State shall give him an opportunity of appearing before, and of being heard by, a person appointed by the Secretary of State.

Decision of Secretary of State

4.—(1) If the Secretary of State decides to adopt the proposal, he shall serve notice in writing of his decision on any person on whom he was required to serve notice of his proposal.

(2) A notice under this paragraph shall be accompanied by a notice explaining the right of appeal conferred by paragraph 5.

(3) A decision of the Secretary of State, other than a decision to grant an application for registration subject only to such conditions as are mentioned in paragraph 2(2) or to refuse an application for registration, shall not take effect—
(a) if no appeal is brought, until the end of the period of 28 days referred to in paragraph 5(3); and
(b) if an appeal is brought, until it is determined or abandoned.

Appeals

5.—(1) An appeal against a decision of the Secretary of State under Part VII shall lie to a Registered Homes Tribunal.

(2) An appeal shall be brought by notice in writing given to the Secretary of State.

(3) No appeal may be brought by a person more than 28 days after service on him of notice of the decision.

(4) On an appeal, the Tribunal may confirm the Secretary of State's decision or direct that it shall not have effect.

(5) A Tribunal shall also have power on an appeal to—
(a) vary any condition for the time being in force by virtue of Part VII with respect to the home to which the appeal relates;
(b) direct that any such condition shall cease to have effect;
(c) direct that any such condition as it thinks fit shall have effect with respect to the home.

Notification of particulars with respect to voluntary homes

6.—(1) It shall be the duty of the person in charge of any voluntary home established after the commencement of this Act to send to the Secretary of State within three months from the establishment of the home such particulars with respect to the home as the Secretary of State may prescribe.

(2) It shall be the duty of the person in charge of any voluntary home (whether established before or after the commencement of this Act) to send to the Secretary of State such particulars with respect to the home as may be prescribed.

(3) The particulars must be sent—
(a) in the case of a home established before the commencement of this Act, in every year, or
(b) in the case of a home established after the commencement of this Act, in every year subsequent to the year in which particulars are sent under sub-paragraph (1),

by such date as the Secretary of State may prescribe.

(4) Where the Secretary of State by regulations varies the particulars which are to be sent to him under sub-paragraphs (1) or (2) by the person in charge of a voluntary home—
- (a) that person shall send to the Secretary of State the prescribed particulars within three months from the date of the making of the regulations;
- (b) where any such home was established before, but not more than three months before, the making of the regulation, compliance with paragraph (a) shall be sufficient compliance with the requirement of sub-paragraph (1) to send the prescribed particulars within three months from the establishment of the home;
- (c) in the year in which the particulars are varied, compliance with paragraph (a) by the person in charge of any voluntary home shall be sufficient compliance with the requirement of sub-paragraph (2) to send the prescribed particulars before the prescribed date in that year.

(5) If the person in charge of a voluntary home fails, without reasonable excuse, to comply with any of the requirements of this paragraph he shall be guilty of an offence.

(6) Any person guilty of such an offence shall be liable on summary conviction to a fine not exceeding level 2 on the standard scale.

PART II

REGULATIONS AS TO VOLUNTARY HOMES

Regulations as to conduct of voluntary homes

7.—(1) The Secretary of State may make regulations—
- (a) as to the placing of children in voluntary homes;
- (b) as to the conduct of such homes; and
- (c) for securing the welfare of children in such homes.

(2) The regulations may, in particular—
- (a) prescribe standards to which the premises used for such homes are to conform;
- (b) impose requirements as to the accommodation, staff and equipment to be provided in such homes, and as to the arrangements to be made for protecting the health of children in such homes;
- (c) provide for the control and discipline of children in such homes;
- (d) require the furnishing to the Secretary of State of information as to the facilities provided for—
  - (i) the parents of children in the homes; and
  - (ii) persons who are not parents of such children but who have parental responsibility for them; and
  - (iii) other persons connected with such children,

  to visit and communicate with the children;
- (e) authorise the Secretary of State to limit the number of children who may be accommodated in any particular voluntary home;
- (f) prohibit the use of accommodation for the purpose of restricting the liberty of children in such homes;
- (g) impose requirements as to the keeping of records and giving of notices with respect to children in such homes;
- (h) impose requirements as to the facilities which are to be provided for giving religious instruction to children in such homes;
- (i) require notice to be given to the Secretary of State of any change of the person carrying on or in charge of a voluntary home or of the premises used by such a home.

(3) The regulations may provide that a contravention of, or failure to comply with, any specified provision of the regulations without reasonable excuse shall be an offence against the regulations.

(4) Any person guilty of such an offence shall be liable to a fine not exceeding level 4 on the standard scale.

Disqualification

8. The Secretary of State may by regulation make provision with respect to the disqualification of persons in relation to voluntary homes of a kind similar to that made in relation to children's home by section 65.

REGULATIONS

The Arrangements for Placement of Children (General) Regulations 1991 (S.I. 1991 No. 890) amended by S.I. 1991 No. 2033, (see notes to s.23); the Children's Homes Regulations 1991 (S.I. 1991 No. 1506) (see notes to s.53) and the Disqualification for Caring for Children Regulations 1991 (S.I. 1991 No. 2094) (see notes to s.68).

GENERAL NOTE

See notes to section 60.

Section 63(11)   SCHEDULE 6

REGISTERED CHILDREN'S HOMES

PART I

REGISTRATION

Application for registration

1.—(1) An application for the registration of a children's home shall be made—
  (a) by the person carrying on, or intending to carry on, the home; and
  (b) to the local authority for the area in which the home is, or is to be, situated.
(2) The application shall be made in the prescribed manner and shall be accompanied by—
  (a) such particulars as may be prescribed; and
  (b) such reasonable fee as the local authority may determine.
(3) In this Schedule "prescribed" means prescribed by regulations made by the Secretary of State.
(4) If a local authority are satisfied that a children's home with respect to which an application has been made in accordance with this Schedule complies or (as the case may be) will comply—
  (a) with such requirements as may be prescribed, and
  (b) with such other requirements (if any) as appear to them to be appropriate,
they shall grant the application, either unconditionally or subject to conditions imposed under paragraph 2.
(5) Before deciding whether or not to grant an application a local authority shall comply with any prescribed requirements.
(6) Regulations made for the purposes of sub-paragraph (5) may, in particular, make provision as to the inspection of the home in question.
(7) Where an application is granted, the authority shall notify the applicant that the home has been registered under this Act as from such date as may be specified in the notice.
(8) If the authority are not satisfied as mentioned in sub-paragraph (4), they shall refuse the application.
(9) For the purposes of this Act, an application which has not been granted or refused within the period of twelve months beginning with the date when it is served

on the authority shall be deemed to have been refused by them, and the applicant shall be deemed to have been notified of their refusal at the end of that period.

(10) Where a school to which section 63(1) applies is registered it shall not cease to be a registered children's home by reason only of a subsequent change in the number of children for whom it provides accommodation.

Conditions imposed on registration

2.—(1) A local authority may grant an application for registration subject to such conditions relating to the conduct of the home as they think fit.

(2) A local authority may from time to time—
> (a) vary any condition for the time being in force with respect to a home by virtue of this paragraph; or
> (b) impose an additional condition,

either on the application of the person carrying on the home or without such an application.

(3) If any condition imposed or varied under this paragraph is not complied with, the person carrying on the home shall, if he has no reasonable excuse, be guilty of an offence and liable on summary conviction to a fine not exceeding level 4 on the standard scale.

Annual review of registration

3.—(1) In this [Schedule] "the responsible authority," in relation to a registered children's home means the local authority who registered it.

(2) The responsible authority for a registered children's home shall, at the end of the period of twelve months beginning with the date of registration, and annually thereafter, review its registration for the purpose of determining whether the registration should continue in force or be cancelled under paragraph 4(3).

(3) If on any such annual review the responsible authority are satisfied that the home is being carried on in accordance with the relevant requirements they shall determine that, subject to sub-paragraph (4), the registration should continue in force.

(4) The responsible authority shall give to the person carrying on the home notice of their determination under sub-paragraph (3) and the notice shall require him to pay to the authority with respect to the review such reasonable fee as the authority may determine.

(5) It shall be a condition of the home's continued registration that the fee is so paid before the expiry of the period of twenty-eight days beginning with the date on which the notice is received by the person carrying on the home.

(6) In this Schedule "the relevant requirements" means any requirements of Part VIII and of any regulation made under paragraph 10, and any conditions imposed under paragraph 2.

Cancellation of registration

4.—(1) The person carrying on a registered children's home may at any time make an application, in such manner and including such particulars as may be prescribed, for the cancellation by the responsible authority of the registration of the home.

(2) If the authority are satisfied, in the case of a school registered by virtue of section 63(6), that it is no longer a school to which that provision applies, the authority shall give to the person carrying on the home notice that the registration of the home has been cancelled as from the date of the notice.

(3) If on any annual review under paragraph 3, or at any other time, it appears to the responsible authority that a registered home is being carried on otherwise than in accordance with the relevant requirements, they may determine that the registration of the home should be cancelled.

(4) The responsible authority may at any time determine that the registration of a home should be cancelled on the ground—

(a) that the person carrying on the home has been convicted of an offence under this Part or any regulations made under paragraph 10; or
(b) that any other person has been convicted of such an offence in relation to the home.

Procedure

5.—(1) Where—
    (a) a person applies for the registration of a children's home; and
    (b) the local authority propose to grant his application,
they shall give him written notice of their proposal and of the conditions (if any) subject to which they propose to grant his application.

(2) The authority need not give notice if they propose to grant the application subject only to conditions which—
    (a) the applicant specified in the application; or
    (b) the authority and the applicant have subsequently agreed.

(3) The authority shall give an applicant notice of a proposal to refuse his application.

(4) The authority shall give any person carrying on a registered children's home notice of a proposal—
    (a) to cancel the registration;
    (b) to vary any condition for the time being in force with respect to the home by virtue of Part VIII; or
    (c) to impose any additional condition.

(5) A notice under this paragraph shall give the local authority's reasons for their proposal.

Right to make representations

6.—(1) A notice under paragraph 5 shall state that within 14 days of service of the notice any person on whom it is served may in writing require the local authority to give him an opportunity to make representations to them concerning the matter.

(2) Where a notice has been served under paragraph 5, the local authority shall not determine the matter until—
    (a) any person on whom the notice was served has made representations to them concerning the matter;
    (b) the period during which any such person could have required the local authority to give him an opportunity to make representations has elapsed without their being required to give such an opportunity; or
    (c) the conditions specified in sub-paragraph (3) below are satisfied.

(3) The conditions are—
    (a) that a person on whom the notice was served has required the local authority to give him an opportunity to make representations to them concerning the matter;
    (b) that the authority have allowed him a reasonable period to make his representations; and
    (c) that he has failed to make them within that period.

(4) The representations may be made, at the option of the person making them, either in writing or orally.

(5) If he informs the local authority that he desires to make oral representations, the authority shall give him an opportunity of appearing before and of being heard by a committee or sub-committee of theirs.

Decision of local authority

7.—(1) If the local authority decide to adopt a proposal of theirs to grant an application, they shall serve notice in writing of their decision on any person on whom they were required to serve notice of their proposal.

(2) A notice under this paragraph shall be accompanied by an explanation of the right of appeal conferred by paragraph 8.

(3) A decision of a local authority, other than a decision to grant an application for registration subject only to such conditions as are mentioned in paragraph 5(2) or to refuse an application for registration, shall not take effect—
- (a) if no appeal is brought, until the end of the period of 28 days referred to in paragraph 8(3); and
- (b) if an appeal is brought, until it is determined or abandoned.

Appeals

8.—(1) An appeal against a decision of a local authority under Part VIII shall lie to a Registered Homes Tribunal.

(2) An appeal shall be brought by notice in writing given to the local authority.

(3) No appeal shall be brought by a person more than 28 days after service on him of notice of the decision.

(4) On an appeal the Tribunal may confirm the local authority's decision or direct that it shall not have effect.

(5) A Tribunal shall also have power on an appeal—
- (a) to vary any condition in force with respect to the home to which the appeal relates by virtue of paragraph 2;
- (b) to direct that any such condition shall cease to have effect; or
- (c) to direct that any such condition as it thinks fit shall have effect with respect to the home.

(6) A local authority shall comply with any direction given by a Tribunal under this paragraph.

Prohibition on further applications

9.—(1) Where an application for the registration of a home is refused, no further application may be made within the period of six months beginning with the date when the applicant is notified of the refusal.

(2) Sub-paragraph (1) shall have effect, where an appeal against the refusal of an application is determined or abandoned, as if the reference to the date when the applicant is notified of the refusal were a reference to the date on which the appeal is determined or abandoned.

(3) Where the registration of a home is cancelled, no application for the registration of the home shall be made within the period of six months beginning with the date of cancellation.

(4) Sub-paragraph (3) shall have effect, where an appeal against the cancellation of the registration of a home is determined or abandoned, as if the reference to the date of cancellation were a reference to the date on which the appeal is determined or abandoned.

PART II

REGULATIONS

10.—(1) The Secretary of State may make regulations—
- (a) as to the placing of children in registered children's homes;
- (b) as to the conduct of such homes; and
- (c) for securing the welfare of the children in such homes.

(2) The regulations may in particular—
- (a) prescribe standards to which the premises used for such homes are to conform;
- (b) impose requirements as to the accommodation, staff and equipment to be provided in such homes;

(c) impose requirements as to the arrangements to be made for protecting the health of children in such homes;
(d) provide for the control and discipline of children in such homes;
(e) require the furnishing to the responsible authority of information as to the facilities provided for—
 (i) the parents of children in such homes;
 (ii) persons who are not parents of such children but who have parental responsibility for them; and
 (iii) other persons connected with such children.
to visit and communicate with the children;
(f) impose requirements as to the keeping of records and giving of notices with respect to children in such homes;
(g) impose requirements as to the facilities which are to be provided for giving religious instruction to children in such homes;
(h) make provision as to the carrying out of annual reviews under paragraph 3;
(i) authorise the responsible authority to limit the number of children who may be accommodated in any particular registered home;
(j) prohibit the use of accommodation for the purpose of restricting the liberty of children in such homes;
(k) require notice to be given to the responsible authority of any change of the person carrying on or in charge of a registered home or of the premises used by such a home;
(l) make provision similar to that made by regulations under section 26.

(3) The regulations may provide that a contravention of or failure to comply with any specified provision of the regulations, without reasonable excuse, shall be an offence against the regulations.

(4) Any person guilty of such an offence shall be liable on summary conviction to a fine not exceeding level 4 on the standard scale.

AMENDMENT

The word in square brackets in paragraph 3(1) was substituted by the Courts and Legal Services Act 1990, s.116, Sched. 16, para. 29.

DEFINITIONS

"prescribed": Sched. 6, para. 1(3).
"the responsible authority": Sched. 6, para. 3(1).

REGULATIONS

The Arrangements for Placement of Children (General) Regulations 1991 (S.I. 1991 No. 890) amended by S.I. 1991 No. 2033 (see notes to s.23); the Children's Homes Regulations 1991 (S.I. 1991 No. 1506) (see notes to s.53); the Representation Procedure (Children) Regulations 1991 (S.I. 1991 No. 894) (see notes to s.26) and the Review of Children's Cases Regulations 1991 (S.I. 1991 No. 895) (see notes to s.26).

GENERAL NOTE

See note on section 63(11).

Section 63(12)

SCHEDULE 7

FOSTER PARENTS: LIMITS ON NUMBER OF FOSTER CHILDREN

Interpretation

1. For the purposes of this Schedule, a person fosters a child if—
 (a) he is a local authority foster parent in relation to the child;

(b) he is a foster parent with whom the child has been placed by a voluntary organisation; or
(c) he fosters the child privately.

The usual fostering limit

2. Subject to what follows, a person may not foster more than three children ("the usual fostering limit").

Siblings

3. A person may exceed the usual fostering limit if the children concerned are all siblings with respect to each other.

Exemption by local authority

4.—(1) A person may exceed the usual fostering limit if he is exempted from it by the local authority within whose area he lives.
(2) In considering whether to exempt a person, a local authority shall have regard, in particular, to—
 (a) the number of children whom the person proposes to foster;
 (b) the arrangements which the person proposes for the care and accommodation of the fostered children;
 (c) the intended and likely relationship between the person and the fostered children;
 (d) the period of time for which he proposes to foster the children; and
 (e) whether the welfare of the fostered children (and of any other children who are or will be living in the accommodation) will be safeguarded and promoted.
(3) Where a local authority exempt a person, they shall inform him by notice in writing—
 (a) that he is so exempted;
 (b) of the children, described by name, whom he may foster; and
 (c) of any condition to which the exemption is subject.
(4) A local authority may at any time by notice in writing—
 (a) vary or cancel an exemption; or
 (b) impose, vary or cancel a condition to which the exemption is subject,
and, in considering whether to do so, they shall have regard in particular to the considerations mentioned in sub-paragraph (2).
(5) The Secretary of State may make regulations amplifying or modifying the provisions of this paragraph in order to provide for cases where children need to be placed with foster parents as a matter of urgency.

Effect of exceeding fostering limit

5.—(1) A person shall cease to be treated as fostering and shall be treated as carrying on a children's home if—
 (a) he exceeds the usual fostering limit; or
 (b) where he is exempted under paragraph 4,—
  (i) he fosters any child not named in the exemption; and

(ii) in so doing, he exceeds the usual fostering limit.

(2) Sub-paragraph (1) does not apply if the children concerned are all siblings in respect of each other.

Complaints etc.

6.—(1) Every local authority shall establish a procedure for considering any representations (including any complaint) made to them about the discharge of their functions under paragraph 4 by a person exempted or seeking to be exempted under that paragraph.

(2) In carrying out any consideration of representations under sub-paragraph (1), a local authority shall comply with any regulations made by the Secretary of State for the purposes of this paragraph.

DEFINITION

"usual fostering limit": Sched. 7, para. 2.

REGULATIONS

The Representation Procedure (Children) Regulations 1991 (S.I. 1991 No. 894) as amended by S.I. 1991 No. 2033, see notes to section 26.

GENERAL NOTE

See notes to section 63(12).

Section 66(5) SCHEDULE 8

PRIVATELY FOSTERED CHILDREN

Exemptions

1. A child is not a privately fostered child while he is being looked after by a local authority.

2.—(1) A child is not a privately fostered child while he is in the care of any person—
   (a) in premises in which any—
       (i) parent of his;
       (ii) person who is not a parent of his but who has parental responsibility for him; or
       (iii) person who is a relative of his and who has assumed responsibility for his care.
       is for the time being living;
   (b) in any children's home;
   (c) in accommodation provided by or on behalf of any voluntary organisation;
   (d) in any school in which he is receiving full-time education;
   (e) in any health service hospital;
   (f) in any residential care home [other than a small home], nursing home or mental nursing home; or
   (g) in any home or institution not specified in this paragraph but provided, equipped and maintained by the Secretary of State.

(2) Sub-paragraph (1)(b) to (g) does not apply where the person caring for the child is doing so in his personal capacity and not in the course of carrying out his duties in relation to the establishment mentioned in the paragraph in question.

3. A child is not a privately fostered child while he is in the care of any person in compliance with—

(a) an order under section 7(7)(b) of the Children and Young Persons Act 1969; or
(b) a supervision requirement within the meaning of the Social Work (Scotland) Act 1968.

4. A child is not a privately fostered child while he is liable to be detained, or subject to guardianship, under the Mental Health Act 1983.

5. A child is not a privately fostered child while—
    (a) he is placed in the care of a person who proposes to adopt him under arrangements made by an adoption agency within the meaning of—
        (i) section 1 of the Adoption Act 1976;
        (ii) section 1 of the Adoption (Scotland) Act 1978; or
        (iii) Article 3 of the Adoption (Northern Ireland) Order 1987; or
    (b) he is a protected child.

AMENDMENT

The words in square brackets in paragraph 2(f) were inserted by the Registered Homes (Amendment) Act 1991, s.2.

Power of local authority to impose requirements

6.—(1) Where a person is fostering any child privately, or proposes to foster any child privately, the appropriate local authority may impose on him requirements as to—
    (a) the number, age and sex of the children who may be privately fostered by him;
    (b) the standard of the accommodation and equipment to be provided for them;
    (c) the arrangements to be made with respect to their health and safety; and
    (d) particular arrangement which must be made with respect to the provision of care for them,
and it shall be his duty to comply with any such requirement before the end of such period as the authority may specify unless, in the case of a proposal, the proposal is not carried out.

(2) A requirement may be limited to a particular child, or class of child.

(3) A requirement (other than one imposed under sub-paragraph (1)(a)) may be limited by the authority so as to apply only when the number of children fostered by the person exceeds a specified number.

(4) A requirement shall be imposed by notice in writing addressed to the person on whom it is imposed and informing him of—
    (a) the reason for imposing the requirement;
    (b) his right under paragraph 8 to appeal against it; and
    (c) the time within which he may do so.

(5) A local authority may at any time very any requirement, impose any additional requirement or remove any requirement.

(6) In this Schedule—
    (a) "the appropriate local authority" means—
        (i) the local authority within whose area the child is being fostered; or
        (ii) in the case of a proposal to foster a child, the local authority within whose area it is proposed that he will be fostered; and
    (b) "requirement," in relation to any person, means a requirement imposed on him under this paragraph.

Regulations requiring notification of fostering etc.

7.—(1) The Secretary of State may by regulations make provisions as to—
    (a) the circumstances in which notification is required to be given in connection with children who are, have been or are proposed to be fostered privately; and
    (b) the manner and form in which such notification is to be given.

(2) The regulations may, in particular—
- (a) require any person who is, or proposes to be, involved (whether or not directly) in arranging for a child to be fostered privately to notify the appropriate authority;
- (b) require any person who is—
  - (i) a parent of a child; or
  - (ii) a person who is not a parent of his but who has parental responsibility for a child,

  and who knows that it is proposed that the child should be fostered privately to notify the appropriate authority;
- (c) require any parent of a privately fostered child, or person who is not a parent of such a child but who has parental responsibility for him, to notify the appropriate authority of any change in his address;
- (d) require any person who proposes to foster a child privately, to notify the appropriate authority of his proposal;
- (e) require any person who is fostering a child privately, or proposes to do so, to notify the appropriate authority of—
  - (i) any offence of which h has been convicted;
  - (ii) any disqualification imposed on him under section 68; or
  - (iii) any prohibition imposed on him under section 69.
- (f) require any person who is fostering a child privately, to notify the appropriate authority of any change in his address;
- (g) require any person who is fostering a child privately, to notify the appropriate authority in writing of any person who begins, or ceases, to be part of his household;
- (h) require any person who has been fostering a child privately, but has ceased to do so, to notify the appropriate authority (indicating, where the child has died, that this is the reason).

Appeals

8.—(1) A person aggrieved by—
- (a) a requirement imposed under paragraph 6;
- (b) a refusal of consent under section 68;
- (c) a prohibition imposed under section 69;
- (d) a refusal to cancel such a prohibition;
- (e) a refusal to make an exemption under paragraph 4 of Schedule 7;
- (f) a condition imposed in such an exemption; or
- (g) a variation or cancellation of such an exemption,

may appeal to the court.

(2) The appeal must be made within 14 days from the date on which the person appealing is notified of the requirement, refusal, prohibition, conditions, variation or cancellation.

(3) Where the appeal is against—
- (a) a requirement imposed under paragraph 6;
- (b) a condition of an exemption imposed under paragraph 4 of Schedule 7; or
- (c) a variation or cancellation of such an exemption,

the requirement, condition, variation or cancellation shall not have effect while the appeal is pending.

(4) Where it allows an appeal against a requirement or prohibition, the court may, instead of cancelling the requirement or prohibition—
- (a) vary the requirement, or allow more time for compliance with it; or
- (b) if an absolute prohibition has been imposed, substitute for it a prohibition on using the premises after such time as the court may specify unless such specified requirements as the local authority had power to impose under paragraph 6 are complied with.

(5) Any requirement or prohibition specified or substituted by a court under this paragraph shall be deemed for the purposes of Part IX (other than this paragraph) to

have been imposed by the local authority under paragraph 6 or (as the case may be) section 69.

(6) Where it allows an appeal against a refusal to make an exemption, a condition imposed in such an exemption or a variation or cancellation of such an exemption, the court may—
    (a) make an exemption;
    (b) impose a condition; or
    (c) vary the exemption.

(7) Any exemption made or varied under sub-paragraph (6), or any condition imposed under that sub-paragraph, shall be deemed for the purposes of Schedule 7 (but not for the purposes of this paragraph) to have been made, varied or imposed under that Schedule.

(8) Nothing in sub-paragraph (1)(e) to (g) confers any right of appeal on—
    (a) a person who is, or would be if exempted under Schedule 7, a local authority foster parent; or
    (b) a person who is, or would be if so exempted, a person with whom a child is placed by a voluntary organisation.

Extension of Part IX to certain school children during holidays

9.—(1) Where a child under 16 who is a pupil at a school which is not maintained by a local education authority lives at the school during school holidays for a period of more than two weeks, Part IX shall apply in relation to the child as if—
    (a) while living at the school, he were a privately fostered child; and
    (b) paragraphs 2(1)(d) and 6 were omitted.

(2) Sub-paragraph (3) applies to any person who proposes to care for and accommodate one or more children at a school in circumstances in which some or all of them will be treated as private foster children by virtue of this paragraph.

(3) That person shall, not less than two weeks before the first of those children is treated as a private foster child by virtue of this paragraph during the holiday in question, give written notice of his proposal to the local authority within whose area the child is ordinarily resident ("the appropriate authority"), stating the estimated number of the children.

(4) A local authority may exempt any person from the duty of giving notice under sub-paragraph (3).

(5) Any such exemption may be granted for a special period or indefinitely and may be revoked at any time by notice in writing given to the person exempted.

(6) Where a child who is treated as a private foster child by virtue of this paragraph dies, the person caring for him at the school shall, not later than 48 hours after the death, give written notice of it—
    (a) to the appropriate local authority; and
    (b) where reasonably practicable, to each parent of the child and to every person who is not a parent of his but who has parental responsibility for him.

(7) Where a child who is treated as a foster child by virtue of this paragraph ceases for any other reason to be such a child, the person caring for him at the school shall give written notice of the fact to the appropriate local authority.

Prohibition of advertisements relating to fostering

10. No advertisement indicating that a person will undertake, or will arrange for, a child to be privately fostered shall be published, unless it states that person's name and address.

Avoidance of insurances on lives of privately fostered children

11. A person who fosters a child privately and for reward shall be deemed for the purposes of the Life Assurance Act 1774 to have no interest in the life of the child.

DEFINITIONS
"requirement": Sched. 8, para. 6(6).
"the appropriate authority": Sched. 8, para. 6(6).

REGULATIONS
The Children (Private Arrangements for Fostering) Regulations 1991 (S.I. 1991 No. 2050).

GENERAL NOTE
See notes to section 66.

Section 71(16) SCHEDULE 9

CHILD MINDING AND DAY CARE FOR YOUNG CHILDREN

Applications for registration

1.—(1) An application for registration under section 71 shall be of no effect unless it contains—
    (a) a statement with respect to the applicant which complies with the requirements of regulations made for the purposes of this paragraph by the Secretary of State; and
    (b) a statement with respect to any person assisting or likely to be assisting in looking after children on the premises in question, or living or likely to be living there, which complies with the requirements of such regulations.

(2) Where a person provides, or proposes to provide, day care for children under the age of eight on different premises situated within the area of the same local authority, he shall make a separate application with respect to each of those premises.

(3) An application under section 71 shall be accompanied by such fee as may be prescribed.

(4) On receipt of an application for registration under section 71 from any person who is acting, or proposes to act, in any way which requires him to be registered under that section, a local authority shall register him if the application is properly made and they are not otherwise entitled to refuse to do so.

Disqualification from registration

2.—(1) A person may not be registered under section 71 if he is disqualified by regulations made by the Secretary of State for the purposes of this paragraph [unless—
    (a) he has disclosed the fact to the appropriate authority; and
    (b) obtained their written consent].

(2) The regulations may, in particular, provide for a person to be disqualified where—
    (a) an order of a prescribed kind has been made at any time with respect to him;
    (b) an order of a prescribed kind has been made at any time with respect to any child who has been in his care;
    (c) a requirement of a prescribed kind has been imposed at any time with respect to such a child, under or by virtue of any enactment;
    (d) he has at any time been refused registration under Part X or any other prescribed enactment or had any such registration cancelled;
    (e) he has been convicted of any offence of a prescribed kind, or has been placed on probation or discharged absolutely or conditionally for any such offence;
    (f) he has at any time been disqualified from fostering a child privately;

(g) a prohibition has been imposed on him at any time under section [69], section 10 of the Foster Children (Scotland) Act 1984 or any other prescribed enactment;
(h) his rights and powers with respect to a child have at any time been vested in a prescribed authority under a prescribed enactment.

(3) A person who lives—
(a) in the same household as a person who is himself disqualified by the regulations; or
(b) in a household at which any such person is employed,

shall be disqualified unless he has disclosed the fact to the appropriate local authority and obtained their written consent.

(4) A person who is disqualified shall not provide day care, or be concerned in the management of, or have any financial interest in, any provision of day care unless he has—
(a) disclosed the fact to the appropriate local authority; and
(b) obtained their written consent.

(5) No person shall employ, in connection with the provision of day care, a person who is disqualified, unless he has—
(a) disclosed to the appropriate local authority the fact that that person is so disqualified; and
(b) obtained their written consent.

(6) In this paragraph "enactment" means any enactment having effect, at any time, in any part of the United Kingdom.

Exemption of certain schools

3.—(1) Section 71 does not apply in relation to any child looked after in any—
(a) school maintained or assisted by a local education authority;
(b) school under the management of an education authority;
(c) school in respect of which payments are made by the Secretary of State under section 100 of the Education Act 1944;
(d) independent school;
(e) grant-aided school;
(f) grant maintained school;
(g) self-governing school;
(h) play centre maintained or assisted by a local education authority under section 53 of the Act of 1944, or by an education authority under section 6 of the Education (Scotland) Act 1980.

(2) The exemption provided by sub-paragraph (1) only applies where the child concerned is being looked after in accordance with provision for day care made by—
(a) the person carrying on the establishment in question as part of the establishment's activities; or
(b) a person employed to work at that establishment and authorised to make that provision as part of the establishment's activities.

(3) In sub-paragraph (1)—
"assisted" and "maintained" have the same meanings as in the Education Act 1944;
"grant maintained" has the same meaning as in section 52(3) of the Education Reform Act 1988; and
"grant-aided school," "self-governing school" and (in relation to Scotland) "independent school" have the same meaning as in the Education (Scotland) Act 1980.

Exemption for other establishments

4.—(1) Section 71(1)(b) does not apply in relation to any child looked after in—
(a) a registered children's home;
(b) a voluntary home;
(c) a community home;
(d) a residential care home, nursing home or mental nursing home required to be registered under the Registered Homes Act 1984;

(e) a health service hospital;
(f) a home provided, equipped and maintained by the Secretary of State; or
(g) an establishment which is required to be registered under section 61 of the Social Work (Scotland) Act 1968.

(2) The exemption provided by sub-paragraph (1) only applies where the child concerned is being looked after in accordance with provision for day care made by—
(a) the department, authority or other person carrying on the establishment in question as part of the establishment's activities; or
(b) a person employed to work at that establishment and authorise to make that provision as part of the establishment's activities.

(3) In this paragraph "a health service hospital" includes a health service hospital within the meaning of the National Health Service (Scotland) Act 1978.

Exemption for occasional facilities

5.—(1) Where day care for children under the age of eight is provided in particular premises on less than six days in any year, that provision shall be disregarded for the purposes of section 71 if the person making it has notified the appropriate local authority in writing before the first occasion on which the premises concerned are so used in that year.

(2) In sub-paragraph (1) "year" means the year beginning with the day on which the day care in question is (after the commencement of this paragraph) first provided in the premises concerned and any subsequent year.

Certificates of registration

6.—(1) Where a local authority register a person under section 71 they shall issue him with a certificate of registration.

(2) The certificate shall specify—
(a) the registered person's name and address;
(b) in a case falling within section 71(1)(b), the address or situation of the premises concerned; and
(c) any requirements imposed under section 72 or 73.

(3) Where, due to a change of circumstances, any part of the certificate requires to be amended, the authority shall issue an amended certificate.

(4) Where the authority are satisfied that the certificate has been lost or destroyed, they shall issue a copy, on payment by the registered person of such fee as may be prescribed.

Fees for annual inspection of premises

7.—(1) Where—
(a) a person is registered under section 71, and
(b) the local authority concerned make an annual inspection of the premises in question under section 76,

they shall serve on that person a notice informing him that the inspection is to be carried out and requiring him to pay to them such fee as may be prescribed.

(2) It shall be a condition of the continued registration of that person under section 71 that the fee is so paid before the expiry of the period of 28 days beginning with the date on which the inspection is carried out.

Co-operation between authorities

8.—(1) Where it appears to a local authority that any local education authority or, in Scotland, education authority could, by taking any specified action, help in the exercise of any of their functions under Part X, they may request the help of that local education authority, or education authority, specifying the action in question.

(2) An authority whose help is so requested shall comply with the request if it is compatible with their own statutory or other duties and obligations and does not unduly prejudice the discharge of any of their functions.

AMENDMENT

The words in square brackets in paragraph 2 were added and substituted by the Courts and Legal Services Act 1990, s.116, Sched. 16, para. 30.

DEFINITIONS

"assisted": Sched. 9, para. 3(3).
"grant aided": Sched. 9, para. 3(3).
"grant maintained," "maintained": Sched. 9, para. 3(3).
"health service hospital": Sched. 9, para. 4(3).
"independent school": Sched. 9, para. 3(3).
"self-governing school": Sched. 9, para. 3(3).
"year": Sched. 9, para. 5(2).

REGULATIONS

Child Minding and Day Care (Applications for Registration) Regulations 1991 (S.I. 1991 No. 1689) and The Child Minding and Day Care (Registration and Inspection Fees) Regulations 1991 (S.I. 1991 No. 2076) amended by S.I. 1991 No. 2129 (see notes to s.71) and The Disqualification for Caring for Children Regulations 1991 (S.I. 1991 No. 2094) (see notes to s.68).

GENERAL NOTES

See notes to section 71.

Section 88   SCHEDULE 10

AMENDMENTS OF ADOPTION LEGISLATION

PART I

AMENDMENTS OF ADOPTION ACT 1976 (C. 36)

1. In section 2 (local authorities' social services) for the words from "relating to" to the end there shall be substituted—
   "(a)   under the Children Act 1989, relating to family assistance orders, local authority support for children and families, care and supervision and emergency protection of children, community homes, voluntary homes and organisations, registered children's homes, private arrangements for fostering children, child minding and day care for young children and children accommodated by health authorities and local education authorities or in residential care, nursing or mental nursing homes or in independent schools; and
   (b)   under the National Health Service Act 1977, relating to the provision of care for expectant and nursing mothers."
2. In section 11 (restrictions on arranging adoptions and placing of children) for subsection (2) there shall be substituted—
   "(2) An adoption society which is—
      (a)   approved as respects Scotland under section 3 of the Adoption (Scotland) Act 1978; or
      (b)   registered as respects Northern Ireland under Article 4 of the Adoption (Northern Ireland) Order 1987,

but which is not approved under section 3 of this Act, shall not act as an adoption society in England and Wales except to the extent that the society considers it necessary to do so in the interests of a person mentioned in section 1 of the Act of 1978 or Article 3 of the Order of 1987."

3.—(1) In section 12 (adoption orders), in subsection (1) for the words "vesting in parental rights and duties relating to a child in" there shall be substituted "giving parental responsibility for a child to."

(2) In subsection (2) of that section for the words "the parental rights and duties so far as they relate" there shall be substituted "parental responsibility so far as it relates."

(3) In subsection (3) of that section for paragraph (a) there shall be substituted—

"(a) the parental responsibility which any person has for the child immediately before the making of the order;

(aa) any order under the Children Act 1989";

and in paragraph (b) for the words "for any period" to the end there shall be substituted "or upbringing for any period after the making of the order."

4. For section 14(1) (adoption by married couple) there shall be substituted—

"(1) An adoption order shall not be made on the application of more than one person except in the circumstances specified in subsections (1A) and (1B).

(1A) An adoption order may be made on the application of a married couple where both the husband and wife have attained the age of 21 years.

(1B) An adoption order may be made on the application of a married couple where—

(a) the husband or the wife—
    (i) is the father or mother of the child; and
    (ii) has attained the age of 18 years:
    and
(b) his or her spouse has attained the age of 21 years."

5.—(1) In section 16 (parental agreement), in subsection (1) for the words from "in England" to "Scotland)" there shall be substituted—

"(i) in England and Wales, section 18;
(ii) in Scotland, under section 18 of the Adoption (Scotland) Act 1978; or
(iii) in Northern Ireland, under Article 17(1) or 18(1) of the Adoption (Northern Ireland) Order 1987."

(2) In subsection (2)(c) of that section for the words "the parental duties in relation to" there shall be substituted "his parental responsibility for."

6.—(1) In section 18 (freeing child for adoption), after subsection (2) there shall be inserted—

"(2A) For the purposes of subsection (2) a child is in the care of an adoption agency if the adoption agency is a local authority and he is in their care."

(2) In subsection (5) of that section, for the words from "the parental rights" to "vest in" there shall be substituted "parental responsibility for the child is given to," and for the words "and (3)" there shall be substituted "to (4)."

(3) For subsections (7) and (8) of that section there shall be substituted—

"(7) Before making an order under this section in the case of a child whose father does not have parental responsibility for him, the court shall satisfy itself in relation to any person claiming to be the father that—

(a) he has no intention of applying for—
    (i) an order under section 4(1) of the Children Act 1989, or
    (ii) a residence order under section 10 of that Act, or
(b) if he did make any such application, it would be likely to be refused.

(8) Subsections (5) and (7) of section 12 apply in relation to the making of an order under this section as they apply in relation to the making of an order under that section."

7. In section 19(2) (progress reports to former parents) for the words "in which the parental rights and duties were vested" there shall be substituted "to which parental responsibility was given."

8.—(1) In section 20 (revocation of section 18 order), in subsections (1) and (2) for the words "the parental rights and duties," in both places where they occur, there shall be substituted "parental responsibility."

(2) For subsection (3) of that section there shall be substituted—

"(3) The revocation of an order under section 18 ("a section 18 order") operates—

(a) to extinguish the parental responsibility given to the adoption agency under the section 18 order;
(b) to give parental responsibility for the child to—
   (i) the child's mother; and
   (ii) where the child's father and mother were married to each other at the time of his birth, the father; and
(c) to revive—
   (i) any parental responsibility agreement,
   (ii) any order under section 4(1) of the Children Act 1989, and
   (iii) any appointment of a guardian in respect of the child (whether made by a court or otherwise),
extinguished by the making of the section 18 order.
(3A) Subject to subsection (3)(c), the revocation does not—
(a) operate to revive—
   (i) any order under the Children Act 1989, or
   (ii) any duty referred to in section 12(3)(b),
extinguished by the making of the section 18 order; or
(b) affect any person's parental responsibility so far as it relates to the period between the making of the section 18 order and the date of revocation of that order."

9. For section 21 (transfer of parental rights and duties between adoption agencies) there shall be substituted—

"**Variation of section 18 order so as to substitute one adoption agency for another**

21.—(1) On an application to which this section applies, an authorised court may vary an order under section 18 so as to give parental responsibility for the child to another adoption agency ('the substitute agency') in place of the agency for the time being having parental responsibility for the child under the order ('the existing agency').

(2) This section applies to any application made jointly by—
(a) the existing agency; and
(b) the would-be substitute agency.

(3) Where an order under section 18 is varied under this section, section 19 shall apply as if the substitute agency had been given responsibility for the child on the making of the order."

10.—(1) In section 22 (notification to local authority of adoption application), after subsection (1) there shall be inserted the following subsections—

"(1A) An application for such an adoption order shall not be made unless the person wishing to make the application has, within the period of two years preceding the making of the application, given notice as mentioned in subsection (1).

(1B) In subsections (1) and (1A) the references to the area in which the applicant or person has his home are references to the area in which he has his home at the time of giving the notice."

(2) In subsection (4) of that section for the word "receives" there shall be substituted "receive" and for the words "in the care of" there shall be substituted "looked after by."

11. In section 25(1) (interim orders) for the words "vesting the legal custody of the child in" there shall be substituted "giving parental responsibility for the child to."

12. In—
(a) section 27(1) and (2) (restrictions on removal where adoption agreed or application made under section 18); and
(b) section 28(1) and (2) (restrictions on removal where applicant has provided home for five years),
for the words "actual custody," in each place where they occur, there shall be substituted "home."

13. After section 27(2) there shall be inserted—

"(2A) For the purposes of subsection (2) a child is in the care of an adoption agency if the adoption agency is a local authority and he is in their care."

14.—(1) After section 28(2) there shall be inserted—

"(2A) The reference in subsections (1) and (2) to any enactment does not include a reference to section 20(8) of the Children Act 1989."

(2) For subsection (3) of that section there shall be substituted—

"(3) In any case where subsection (1) or (2) applies—

(a) the child was being looked after by a local authority before he began to have his home with the applicant or, as the case may be, the prospective adopter, and

(b) the child is still being looked after by a local authority,

the authority which are looking after the child shall not remove him from the home of the applicant or the prospective adopter except in accordance with section 30 or 31 or with the leave of a court."

(3) In subsection (5) of that section—
  (a) for the word "receives" there shall be substituted "receive"; and
  (b) for the words "in the care of another local authority or of a voluntary organisation" there shall be substituted "looked after by another local authority."

15. In section 29 (return of child taken away in breach of section 27 or 28) for subsections (1) and (2) there shall be substituted—

"(1) An authorised court may, on the application of a person from whose home a child has been removed in breach of—
  (a) section 27 or 28,
  (b) section 27 or 28 of the Adoption (Scotland) Act 1978, or
  (c) Article 28 or 29 of the Adoption (Northern Ireland) Order 1987,
order the person who has so removed the child to return the child to the applicant.

(2) An authorised court may, on the application of a person who has reasonable grounds for believing that another person is intending to remove a child from his home in breach of—
  (a) section 27 or 28,
  (b) section 27 or 28 of the Adoption (Scotland) Act 1978, or
  (c) Article 28 or 29 of the Adoption (Northern Ireland) Order 1987,
by order direct that other person not to remove the child from the applicant's home in breach of any of those provisions."

16.—(1) In section 30 (return of children placed for adoption by adoption agencies), in subsection (1) there shall be substituted—
  (a) for the words "delivered into the actual custody of" the words "placed with";
  (b) in paragraph (a) for the words "retain the actual custody of the child" the words "give the child a home"; and
  (c) in paragraph (b) for the words "actual custody" the word "home."

(2) In subsection (3) of that section for the words "in his actual custody" there shall be substituted "with him."

17.—(1) In section 31 (application of section 30 where child not placed for adoption), in subsection (1) for the words from "child," where it first occurs, to "except" there shall be substituted "child—
  (a) who is (when the notice is given) being looked after by a local authority; but
  (b) who was placed with that person otherwise than in pursuance of such arrangements as are mentioned in section 30(1),
that section shall apply as if the child had been placed in pursuance of such arrangements."

(2) In subsection (2) of that section for the words "for the time being in the care of" there shall be substituted "(when the notice is given) being looked after by."

(3) In subsection (3) of that section—
  (a) for the words "remains in the actual custody of" there shall be substituted 'has his home with"; and
  (b) for the words "section 45 of the Child Care Act 1980" there shall be substituted "Part III of Schedule 2 to the Children Act 1989."

(4) At the end of that section there shall be added—

"(4) Nothing in this section affects the right of any person who has parental responsibility for a child to remove him under section 20(8) of the Children Act 1989."

18.—(1) In section 32 (meaning of "protected child"), in subsection (2) for the words "section 37 of the Adoption Act 1958" there shall be substituted—
  "(a) section 32 of the Adoption (Scotland) Act 1978; or
  (b) Article 33 of the Adoption (Northern Ireland) Order 1987."

(2) In subsection (3) of that section for paragraph (a) there shall be substituted—

"(a) he is in the care of any person—
  (i) in any community home, voluntary home or registered children's home;
  (ii) in any school in which he is receiving full-time education;
  (iii) in any health service hospital";
and at the end of that subsection there shall be added—
"(d) he is in the care of any person in any home or institution not specified in this subsection but provided, equipped and maintained by the Secretary of State."
(3) After that subsection there shall be inserted—
"(3A) In subsection (3) 'community home,' 'voluntary home,' 'registered children's home,' 'school' and 'health service hospital' have the same meaning as in the Children Act 1989."
(4) For subsection (4) of that section there shall be substituted—
"(4) A protected child ceases to be a protected child—
  (a) on the grant or refusal of the application for an adoption order;
  (b) on the notification to the local authority for the area where the child has his home that the application for an adoption order has been withdrawn;
  (c) in a case where no application is made for an adoption order, on the expiry of the period of two years from the giving of the notice;
  (d) on the making of a residence order, a care order or a supervision order under the Children Act 1989 in respect of the child;
  (e) on the appointment of a guardian for him under that Act;
  (f) on his attaining the age of 18 years; or
  (g) on his marriage,
whichever first occurs.
(5) In subsection (4)(d) the references to a care order and a supervision order do not include references to an interim care order or interim supervision order."
19.—(1) In section 35 (notices and information to be given to local authorities), in subsection (1) for the words "who has a protected child in his actual custody" there shall be substituted "with whom a protected child has his home."
20.—(1) In section 51 (disclosure of birth records of adopted children), in subsection (1) for the words "subsections (4) and (6)" there shall be substituted "what follows."
(2) For subsections (3) to (7) of that section there shall be substituted—
"(3) Before supplying any information to an applicant under subsection (1), the Registrar General shall inform the applicant that counselling services are available to him—
  (a) if he is in England and Wales—
    (i) at the General Register Office;
    (ii) from the local authority in whose area he is living;
    (iii) where the adoption order relating to him was made in England and Wales, from the local authority in whose area the court which made the order sat;or
    (iv) from any other local authority;
  (b) if he is in Scotland—
    (i) from the regional or islands council in whose area he is living;
    (ii) where the adoption order relating to him was made in Scotland, from the council in whose area the court which made the order sat; or
    (iii) from any other regional or islands council;
  (c) if he is in Northern Ireland—
    (i) from the Board in whose area he is living;
    (ii) where the adoption order relating to him was made in Northern Ireland, from the Board in whose area the court which made the order sat; or
    (iii) from any other Board;
  (d) if he is in the United Kingdom and his adoption was arranged by an adoption society—
    (i) approved under section 3,
    (ii) approved under section 3 of the Adoption (Scotland) Act 1978,

(iii) registered under Article 4 of the Adoption (Northern Ireland) Order 1987,

from that society.

(4) Where an adopted person who is in England and Wales—
    (a) applies for information under—
        (i) subsection (1), or
        (ii) Article 54 of the Adoption (Northern Ireland) Order 1987, or
    (b) is supplied with information under section 45 of the Adoption (Scotland) Act 1978,

it shall be the duty of the persons and bodies mentioned in subsection (5) to provide counselling for him if asked by him to do so.

(5) The persons and bodies are—
    (a) the Registrar General;
    (b) any local authority falling within subsection (3)(a)(ii) to (iv);
    (c) any adoption society falling within subsection (3)(d) in so far as it is acting as an adoption society in England and Wales.

(6) If the applicant chooses to receive counselling from a person or body falling within subsection (3), the Registrar General shall send to the person or body the information to which the applicant is entitled under subsection (1).

(7) Where a person—
    (a) was adopted before November 12, 1975, and
    (b) applies for information under subsection (1),

the Registrar General shall not supply the information to him unless he has attended an interview with a counsellor arranged by a person or body from whom counselling services are available as mentioned in subsection (3).

(8) Where the Registrar General is prevented by subsection (7) from supplying information to a person who is not living in the United Kingdom, he may supply information to any body which—
    (a) the Registrar General is satisfied is suitable to provide counselling to that person, and
    (b) has notified the Registrar General that it is prepared to provide such counselling.

(9) In this section—

"a Board" means a Health and Social Services Board established under Article 16 of the Health and Personal Social Services (Northern Ireland) Order 1972; and

"prescribed" means prescribed by regulations made by the Registrar General."

21. After section 51 there shall be inserted—

"**Adoption Contact Register**

51A.—(1) The Registrar General shall maintain at the General Register Office a register to be called the Adoption Contact Register.

(2) The register shall be in two parts—
    (a) Part I: Adopted Persons; and
    (b) Part II: Relatives.

(3) The Registrar General shall, on payment of such fee as may be prescribed, enter in Part I of the register the name and address of any adopted person who fulfils the conditions in subsection (4) and who gives notice that he wishes to contact any relative of his.

(4) The conditions are that—
    (a) a record of the adopted person's birth is kept by the Registrar General; and
    (b) the adopted person has attained the age of 18 years and—
        (i) has been supplied by the Registrar General with information under section 51; or
        (ii) has satisfied the Registrar General that he has such information as is necessary to enable him to obtain a certified copy of the record of his birth.

(5) The Registrar General shall, on payment of such fee as may be prescribed, enter in Part II of the register the name and address of any person who fulfils the conditions in subsection (6) and who gives notice that he wishes to contact an adopted person.

(6) The conditions are that—
   (a) a record of the adopted person's birth is kept by the Registrar General; and
   (b) the person giving notice under subsection (5) has attained the age of 18 years and has satisfied the Registrar General that—
      (i) he is a relative of the adopted person; and
      (ii) he has such information as is necessary to enable him to obtain a certified copy of the record of the adopted person's birth.

(7) The Registrar General shall, on receiving notice from any person named in an entry in the register that he wishes the entry to be cancelled, cancel the entry.

(8) Any notice given under this section must be in such form as may be determined by the Registrar General.

(9) The Registrar General shall transmit to an adopted person whose name is entered in Part I of the register the name and address of any relative in respect of whom there is an entry in Part II of the register.

(10) Any entry cancelled under subsection (7) ceases from the time of cancellation to be an entry for the purposes of subsection (9).

(11) The register shall not be open to public inspection or search and the Registrar General shall not supply any person with information entered in the register (whether in an uncancelled or a cancelled entry) except in accordance with this section.

(12) The register may be kept by means of a computer.

(13) In this section—
   (a) "relative" means any person (other than an adoptive relative) who is related to the adopted person by blood (including half-blood) or marriage;
   (b) "address" includes any address at or through which the person concerned may be contacted; and
   (c) "prescribed" means prescribed by the Secretary of State."

22.—(1) In section 55 (adoption of children abroad), in subsection (1) after the word "Scotland" there shall be inserted "or Northern Ireland" and for the words "vesting in him the parental rights and duties relating to the child" there shall be substituted "giving him parental responsibility for the child."

(2) In subsection (3) of that section for the words "word (Scotland)' " there shall be substituted "words '(Scotland)' or '(Northern Ireland).' "

23.—(1) In section 56 (restriction on removal of children for adoption outside Great Britain),—
   (a) in subsections (1) and (3) for the words "transferring the actual custody of a child to," in both places where they occur, there shall be substituted "placing a child with"; and
   (b) in subsection (3)(a) for the words "in the actual custody of" there shall be substituted "with."

(2) In subsection (1) of that section—
   (a) for the words from "or under" to "abroad" there shall be substituted "section 49 of the Adoption (Scotland) Act 1978 or Article 57 of the Adoption (Northern Ireland) Order 1987"; and
   (b) for the words "British Islands" there shall be substituted "United Kingdom, the Channel Islands and the Isle of Man."

24.—(1) In section 57 (prohibition on certain payments) in subsection (1)(c), for the words "transfer by that person of the actual custody of a child" there shall be substituted "handing over of a child by that person."

(2) In subsection (3A)(b) of that section, for the words "in the actual custody of" there shall be substituted "with."

25. After section 57 there shall be inserted—

"**Permitted allowances**

57A.—(1) The Secretary of State may make regulations for the purpose of enabling adoption agencies to pay allowances to persons who have adopted, or intend to adopt, children in pursuance of arrangements made by the agencies.

(2) Section 57(1) shall not apply to any payment made by an adoption agency in accordance with the regulations.

(3) The regulations may, in particular, make provision as to—

(a) the procedure to be followed by an agency in determining whether a person should be paid an allowance;
(b) the circumstances in which an allowance may be paid;
(c) the factors to be taken into account in determining the amount of the allowance;
(d) the procedure for review, variation and termination of allowances; and
(e) the information about allowances to be supplied by an agency to any person who is intending to adopt a child.

(4) Any scheme approved under section 57(4) shall be revoked as from the coming into force of this section.

(5) Section 57(1) shall not apply in relation to any payment made—
(a) in accordance with a scheme revoked under subsection (4) or section 57(5)(b); and
(b) to a person to whom such payments were made before the revocation of the scheme.

(6) Subsection (5) shall not apply where any person to whom any payments may lawfully be made by virtue of subsection (5) agrees to receive (instead of such payments) payments complying with regulations made under this section."

26.—(1) In section 59 (effect of determination and orders made in Scotland and overseas in adoption proceedings), in subsection (1) for the words "Great Britain" there shall be substituted "the United Kingdom."

(2) For subsection (2) of that section there shall be substituted—

"(2) Subsections (2) to (4) of section 12 shall apply in relation to an order freeing a child for adoption (other than an order under section 18) as if it were an adoption order; and, on the revocation in Scotland or Northern Ireland of an order freeing a child for adoption, subsections (3) and (3A) of section 20 shall apply as if the order had been revoked under that section."

27. In section 60 (evidence of adoption in Scotland and Northern Ireland), in paragraph (a) for the words "section 22(2) of the Adoption Act 1958" there shall be substituted "section 45(2) of the Adoption (Scotland) Act 1978" and in paragraph (b) for the words from "section 23(4)" to "in force" there shall be substituted "Article 63(1) of the Adoption (Northern Ireland) Order 1987."

28. In section 62(5)(b) (courts), for the words from "section 8" to "child" there shall be substituted—

"(i) section 12 or 18 of the Adoption (Scotland) Act 1978; or
(ii) Article 12, 17 or 18 of the Adoption (Northern Ireland) Order 1987."

29. After section 65 (guardians ad litem and reporting officers) there shall be inserted—

"**Panels for selection of guardians ad litem and reporting officers**

65A.—(1) The Secretary of State may by regulations provide for the establishment of panels of persons from whom guardians ad litem and reporting officers approved under rules made under section 65 must be selected.

(2) The regulations may, in particular, make provision—
(a) as to the constitution, administration and procedures of panels;
(b) requiring two or more specified local authorities to make arrangements for the joint management of a panel;
(c) for the defrayment by local authorities of expenses incurred by members of panels;
(d) for the payment by local authorities of fees and allowances for members of panels;
(e) as to the qualifications for membership of a panel;
(f) as to the training to be given to members of panels;
(g) as to the co-operation required for specified local authorities in the provision of panels in specified areas; and
(h) for monitoring the work of guardians ad litem and reporting officers.

(3) Rules of Court may make provision as to the assistance which any guardian ad litem or reporting officer may be required by the court to give to it."

30.—(1) Section 72(1) (interpretation) shall be amended as follows.

(2) In the definition of "adoption agency" for the words from "section 1" to the end there shall be substituted—

"(a) section 1 of the Adoption (Scotland) Act 1978; and
(b) Article 3 of the Adoption (Northern Ireland) Order 1987."

(3) For the definition of "adoption order" there shall be substituted—

" 'adoption order'—
(a) means an order under section 12(1); and
(b) in sections 12(3) and (4), 18 to 20, 27, 28 and 30 to 32 and in the definition of 'British adoption order' in this subsection includes an order under section 12 of the Adoption (Scotland) Act 1978 and Article 12 of the Adoption (Northern Ireland) Order 1987 (adoption orders in Scotland and Northern Ireland respectively); and
(c) in sections 27, 28 and 30 to 32 includes an order under section 55, section 49 of the Adoption (Scotland) Act 1978 and Article 57 of the Adoption (Northern Ireland) Orders 1987 (orders in relation to children being adopted abroad)."

(4) For the definition of "British adoption order" there shall be substituted—

" 'British adoption order' means—
(a) an adoption order as defined in this subsection, and
(b) an order under any provision for the adoption of a child effected under the law of any British territory outside the United Kingdom."

(5) For the definition of "guardian" there shall be substituted—

" 'guardian' has the same meaning as in the Children Act 1989."

(6) In the definition of "order freeing a child for adoption" for the words from "section 27(2)" to the end there shall be substituted "sections 27(2) and 59 includes an order under—

(a) section 18 of the Adoption (Scotland) Act 1978; and
(b) Articles 17 or 18 of the Adoption (Northern Ireland) Order 1987."

(7) After the definition of "overseas adoption" there shall be inserted—

" 'parent' means, in relation to a child, any parent who has parental responsibility for the child under the Children Act 1989;

'parental responsibility' and 'parental responsibility agreement' have the same meaning as in the Children Act 1989."

(8) After the definition of "United Kingdom national" there shall be inserted—

" 'upbringing' has the same meaning as in the Children Act 1989."

(9) For section 72(1A) there shall be substituted the following subsections—

"(1A) In this Act, in determining with what person, or where, a child has his home, any absence of the child at a hospital or boarding school and any other temporary absence shall be disregarded.

(1B) In this Act, references to a child who is in the care of or looked after by a local authority have the same meaning as in the Children Act 1989."

31. For section 74(3) and (4) (extent) there shall be substituted—

"(3) This Act extends to England and Wales only."

PART II

AMENDMENTS OF ADOPTION (SCOTLAND) ACT 1978 (C. 28)

32. In section 11 (restrictions on arranging of adoptions and placing of children) for subsection (2) there shall be substituted—

"(2) An adoption society which is—
(a) approved as respects England and Wales under section 3 of the Adoption Act 1976; or
(b) registered as respects Northern Ireland under Article 4 of the Adoption (Northern Ireland) Order 1987,

but which is not approved under section 3 of this Act, shall not act as an adoption society in Scotland except to the extent that the society considers it necessary to do so in the interests of a person mentioned in section 1 of that Act or, as the case may be, Article 3 of that Order."

33. For section 14(1) (adoption by married couple) there shall be substituted—

"(1) Subject to section 53(1) of the Children Act 1975 (which provides for the making of a custody order instead of an adoption order in certain cases), an adoption order shall not be made on the application of more than one person except in the circumstances specified in subsections (1A) and (1B).

(1A) An adoption order may be made on the application of a married couple where both the husband and wife have attained the age of 21 years.

(1B) An adoption order may be made on the application of a married couple where—
- (a) the husband or the wife—
  - (i) is the father or mother of the child; and
  - (ii) has attained the age of 18 years; and
- (b) his or her spouse has attained the age of 21 years."

34. In section 16(1)(a) (parental agreement) for the words from "in England" to "revoked," in the second place where it occurs, there shall be substituted—
  - "(i) in Scotland under section 18;
  - (ii) in England and Wales under section 18 of the Adoption Act 1976; or
  - (iii) in Northern Ireland under Article 17(1) or 18(1) of the Adoption (Northern Ireland) Order 1987,

and not revoked."

35. In section 18(5) (effect of order freeing child for adoption) for the words "and (3)" there shall be substituted "to (4)."

36. In section 20(3)(c) (revocation of section 18 order) the words "section 12(3)(b) of the Adoption Act 1976 or of" shall cease to have effect.

37. For section 21 (transfer of parental rights and duties between adoption agencies) there shall be substituted—

"**Variation of section 18 order so as to substitute one adoption agency for another**

21.—(1) On an application to which this section applies an authorised court may vary an order under section 18 so as to transfer the parental rights and duties relating to the child from the adoption agency in which they are vested under the order ('the existing agency') to another adoption agency ('the substituted agency').

(2) This section applies to any application made jointly by the existing agency and the would-be substitute agency.

(3) Where an order under section 18 is varied under this section, section 19 shall apply as if the parental rights and duties relating to the child had vested in the substitute agency on the making of the order."

38. In section 22(4) (notification to local authority of adoption application) for the word "receives" there shall be substituted "receive."

39. In section 29 (return of child taken away in breach of section 27 or 28) after the word "1976" in each place where it occurs there shall be inserted "or Article 28 or 29 of the Adoption (Northern Ireland) Order 1987."

40. In section 32 (meaning of "protected child"), at the end of subsection (2) there shall be added "or Article 33 of the Adoption (Northern Ireland) Order 1987."

41. In section 45 (adopted children register)—
  - (a) for the words from "or an approved" in subsection (5) to the end of subsection (6) there shall be substituted—

"Board or adoption society falling within subsection (6) which is providing counselling for that adopted person.

(6) Where the Registrar General for Scotland furnishes an adopted person with information under subsection (5), he shall advise that person that counselling services are available—
  - (a) if the person is in Scotland—
    - (i) from the local authority in whose area he is living;
    - (ii) where the adoption order relating to him was made in Scotland, from the local authority in whose area the court which made the order sat; or
    - (iii) from any other local authority in Scotland;
  - (b) if the person is in England and Wales—
    - (i) from the local authority in whose area he is living;
    - (ii) where the adoption order relating to him was made in England and Wales, from the local authority in whose area the court which made the order sat; or
    - (iii) from any other local authority in England and Wales;
  - (c) if the person is in Northern Ireland—
    - (i) from the Board in whose area he is living;

(ii) where the adoption order relating to him was made in Northern Ireland, from the Board in whose area the court which made the order sat; or
(iii) from any other Board;
(d) if the person is in the United Kingdom and his adoption was arranged by an adoption society—
(i) approved under section 3;
(ii) approved under section 3 of the Adoption Act 1976; or
(iii) registered under Article 4 of the Adoption (Northern Ireland) Order 1987,
from that society.
(6A) Where an adopted person who is in Scotland—
(a) is furnished with information under subsection (5); or
(b) applies for information under—
(i) section 51(1) of the Adoption Act 1976; or
(ii) Article 54 of the Adoption (Northern Ireland) Order 1987,
any body mentioned in subsection (6B) to which the adopted person applies for counselling shall have a duty to provide counselling for him.
(6B) The bodies referred to in subsection (6A) are—
(a) any local authority falling within subsection (6)(a); and
(b) any adoption society falling within subsection (6)(d) so far as it is acting as an adoption society in Scotland;
(b) in subsection (7)—
(i) for the word "under" there shall be substituted "from a local authority, Board or adoption society falling within";
(ii) for the words "or adoption society which is providing that counselling" there shall be substituted," Board or adoption society"; and
(iii) after the word "authority" where it second occurs there shall be inserted , "Board"; and
(c) after subsection (9) there shall be inserted the following subsection—
"(10) In this section—
'Board" means a Health and Social Services Board established under Article 16 of the Health and Personal Social Services (Northern Ireland) Order 1972; and
"local authority," in relation to England and Wales, means the council of a county (other than a metropolitan county), a metropolitan district, a London borough or the Common Council of the City of London."
42. In section 49 (adoption of children abroad)—
(a) in subsection (1) after the word "Scotland" there shall be inserted "or Northern Ireland"; and
(b) in subsection (3) for the words "word 'England' " there shall be substituted "words '(England)' or '(Northern Ireland).' "
43. In section 50(1) (restriction on removal of children for adoption outside Great Britain) after the word "1976" there shall be inserted "or Article 57 of the Adoption (Northern Ireland) Order 1987."
44. In section 53(1) (effect of determination and orders made in England and Wales and overseas in adoption proceedings)—
(a) in subsection (1) for the words "Great Britain" there shall be substituted "the United Kingdom"; and
(b) for subsection (2) there shall be substituted—
"(2) Subsections (2) to (4) of section 12 shall apply in relation to an order freeing a child for adoption (other than an order under section 18) as if it were an adoption order; and on the revocation in England and Wales or Northern Ireland of an order freeing a child for adoption subsection (3) of section 20 shall apply as if the order had been revoked under that section."
45. In section 54(b) (evidence of adoption in Northern Ireland) for the words from "section 23(4)" to "in force" there shall be substituted "Article 63(1) of the Adoption (Northern Ireland) Order 1987."
46. In section 65(1) (interpretation)—
(a) in the definition of "adoption agency," at the end there shall be added "and an adoption agency within the meaning of Article 3 of the Adoption (Northern Ireland) Order 1987 (adoption agencies in Northern Ireland)";

(b) for the definition of "adoption order" there shall be substituted—
" 'adoption order'—
    (a) means an order under section 12(1); and
    (b) in sections 12 (3) and (4), 18 to 20, 27, 28 and 30 to 32 and in the definition of 'British adoption order' in this subsection includes an order under section 12 of the Adoption Act 1976 and Article 12 of the Adoption (Northern Ireland) Order 1987 (adoption orders in England and Wales and Northern Ireland respectively); and
    (c) in sections 27, 28 and 30 to 32 includes an order under section 49, section 55 of the Adoption Act 1976 and Article 57 of the Adoption (Northern Ireland) Order 1987 (orders in relation to children being adopted abroad);";
(c) for the definition of "British adoption order" there shall be substituted—
" 'British adoption order' means—
    (a) an adoption order as defined in this subsection; and
    (b) an order under any provision for the adoption of a child effected under the law of any British territory outside the United Kingdom;";
(d) in the definition of "order freeing a child for adoption" for the words from "section 27(2)" to the end there shall be substituted "sections 27(2) and 53 includes an order under—
    (a) section 18 of the Adoption Act 1976; and
    (b) Article 17 and 18 of the Adoption (Northern Ireland) Order 1987;".

REGULATIONS

The Adoption Allowance Regulations 1991 (S.I. 1991 No. 2030) as amended by S.I. 1991 No. 2130 and the Adopted Persons (Contact Register) (Fees) Rules 1991 (S.I. 1991 No. 952). The Adoption Rules have also been amended by (S.I. 1991 No. 1880).

GENERAL NOTE

See notes to section 88.

Section 92

SCHEDULE 11

JURISDICTION

PART I

GENERAL

Commencement of proceedings

1.—(1) The Lord Chancellor may by order specify proceedings under this Act or the Adoption Act 1976 which may only be commenced in—
    (a) a specified level of court;
    (b) a court which falls within a specified class of court; or
    (c) a particular court determined in accordance with, or specified in, the order.

(2) The Lord Chancellor may by order specify circumstances in which specified proceedings under this Act or the Adoption Act 1976 (which might otherwise be commenced elsewhere) may only be commenced in—
    (a) a specified level of court;
    (b) a court which falls within a specified class of court; or
    (c) a particular court determined in accordance with, or specified in, the order.

(3) The Lord Chancellor may by order make provision by virtue of which, where specified proceedings with respect to a child under—
- (a) this Act;
- (b) the Adoption Act 1976; or
- (c) the High Court's inherent jurisdiction with respect to children,

have been commenced in or transferred to any court (whether or not by virtue of an order under this Schedule), any other specified family proceedings which may affect, or are otherwise connected with, the child may, in specified circumstances, only be commenced in that court.

(4) A class of court specified in an order under this Schedule may be described by reference to a description of proceedings and may include different levels of court.

Transfer of proceedings

2.—(1) The Lord Chancellor may by order provide that in specified circumstances the whole, or any specified part of, specified proceedings to which this paragraph applies shall be transferred to—
- (a) a specified level of court;
- (b) a court which falls within a specified class of court; or
- (c) a particular court determined in accordance with, or specified in, the order.

(2) Any order under this paragraph may provide for the transfer to be made at any stage, or specified stage, of the proceedings and whether or not the proceedings, or any part of them, have already been transferred.

(3) The proceedings to which this paragraph applies are—
- (a) any proceedings under this Act;
- (b) any proceedings under the Adoption Act 1976;
- (c) any other proceedings which—
  - (i) are family proceedings for the purposes of this Act, other than proceedings under the inherent jurisdiction of the High Court; and
  - (ii) may affect, or are otherwise connected with, the child concerned.

(4) Proceedings to which this paragraph applies by virtue of sub-paragraph (3)(c) may only be transferred in accordance with the provisions of an order made under this paragraph for the purpose of consolidating them with proceedings under—
- (a) this Act;
- (b) the Adoption Act 1976; or
- (c) the High Court's inherent jurisdiction with respect to children.

(5) An order under this paragraph may make such provision as the Lord Chancellor thinks appropriate for excluding proceedings to which this paragraph applies from the operation of any enactment which would otherwise govern the transfer of those proceedings, or any part of them.

Hearings by single justice

3.—(1) In such circumstances as the Lord Chancellor may by order specify—
- (a) the jurisdiction of a magistrates' court to make an emergency protection order;
- (b) any specified question with respect to the transfer of specified proceedings to or from a magistrates' court in accordance with the provisions of an order under paragraph 2,

may be exercised by a single justice.

(2) Any provision made under this paragraph shall be without prejudice to any other enactment or rule of law relating to the functions which may be performed by a single justice of the peace.

General

4.—(1) For the purposes of this Schedule—

(a) the commencement of proceedings under this Act includes the making of any application under this Act in the course of proceedings (whether or not those proceedings are proceedings under this Act); and
(b) there are three levels of court, that is to say the High Court, any county court and any magistrates' court.

(2) In this Schedule "specified" means specified by an order made under this Schedule.

(3) Any order under paragraph 1 may make provision as to the effect of commencing proceedings in contravention of any of the provisions of the order.

(4) An order under paragraph 2 may make provision as to the effect of a failure to comply with any of the provisions of the order.

(5) An order under this Schedule may—
(a) make such consequential, incidental or transitional provision as the Lord Chancellor considers expedient, including provision amending any other enactment so far as it concerns the jurisdiction of any court or justice of the peace;
(b) make provision for treating proceedings which are—
  (i) in part proceedings of a kind mentioned in paragraph (a) or (b) of paragraph 2(3); and
  (ii) in part proceedings of a kind mentioned in paragraph (c) of paragraph 2(3),
as consisting entirely of proceedings of one or other of those kinds, for the purposes of this application of any order made under paragraph 2.

PART II

CONSEQUENTIAL AMENDMENTS

The Administration of Justice Act 1964 (c. 42)

5. In section 38 of the Administration of Justice Act 1964 (interpretation), the definition of "domestic court," which is spent, shall be omitted.

The Domestic Proceedings and Magistrates' Courts Act 1978 (c. 22)

6. In the Domestic Proceedings and Magistrates' Courts Act 1978—
(a) for the words "domestic proceedings," wherever they occur in sections 16(5)(c) and 88(1), there shall be substituted "family proceedings";
(b) for the words "domestic court panel," wherever they occur in section 16(5)(b), there shall be substituted "family panel."

The Justices of the Peace Act 1979 (c. 55)

7. In the Justices of the Peace Act 1979—
(a) for the words "domestic proceedings," wherever they occur in section 16(5), there shall be substituted "family proceedings";
(b) for the words "domestic court," wherever they occur in section 17(3), there shall be substituted "family proceedings court";
(c) for the words "domestic courts," wherever they occur in sections 38(2) and 58(1) and (5), there shall be substituted "family proceedings courts."

The Magistrates' Courts Act 1980 (c. 43)

8. In the Magistrates' Courts Act 1980—

(a) in section 65(1) (meaning of family proceedings), the following paragraph shall be inserted after paragraph (m)—
"(n) the Children Act 1989";
(b) in section 65(2)(a) for the words "and (m)" there shall be substituted "(m) and (n)";
(c) for the words "domestic proceedings," wherever they occur in sections 65(1), (2) and (3), 66(1) and (2), 67(1), (2) and (7), 69(1), (2), (3) and (4), 70(2) and (3), 71(1) and (2), 72(1), 73, 74(1), 121(8) and 150(1), there shall be substituted "family proceedings";
(d) for the words "domestic court panel," wherever they occur in sections 66(2), 67(2), (4), (5), (7) and (8) and 68(1), (2) and (3), there shall be substituted "family panel";
(e) for the words "domestic court panels," wherever they occur in section 67(3), (4), (5) and (6), there shall be substituted "family panels";
(f) for the words "domestic courts," wherever they occur in sections 67(1) and (3) and 68(1), there shall be substituted "family proceedings courts";
(g) for the words "domestic court," wherever they occur in section 67(2) and (5), there shall be substituted "family proceedings court."

The Supreme Court Act 1981 (c. 54)

9. In paragraph 3 of Schedule 1 to the Supreme Court Act 1981 (distribution of business to the Family Division of the High Court), the following sub-paragraph shall be added at the end—
"*(e)* proceedings under the Children Act 1989."

The Matrimonial and Family Proceedings Act 1984 (c. 42)

10. In section 44 of the Matrimonial and Family Proceedings Act 1984 (domestic proceedings in magistrates' courts to include applications to alter maintenance agreements) for the words "domestic proceedings," wherever they occur, there shall be substituted "family proceedings."

The Insolvency Act 1986 (c. 45)

11.—(1) In section 281(5)(b) of the Insolvency Act 1986 (discharge not to release bankrupt from bankruptcy debt arising under any order made in family proceedings or in domestic proceedings), the words "or in domestic proceedings" shall be omitted.
(2) In section 281(8) of that Act (Interpretation), for the definitions of "domestic proceedings" and "family proceedings" there shall be substituted—
"family proceedings" means—
(a) family proceedings within the meaning of the Magistrates' Courts Act 1980 and any proceedings which would be such proceedings but for section 65(1)(ii) of that Act (proceedings for variation of order for periodical payments); and
(b) family proceedings within the meaning of Part V of the Matrimonial and Family Proceedings Act 1984.

DEFINITION
"specified": Sched. 11, para. 4(1).

ORDERS
The Children (Allocation of Proceedings Order 1991 (S.I. 1991 No. 1677) and the Children (Allocation of Proceedings) (Appeals) Order 1991 (S.I. 1991 No. 1801)), see pp. 432 and 452 below.

GENERAL NOTE
See notes to section 92.

Section 108(4) **SCHEDULE 12**

MINOR AMENDMENTS

The Custody of Children Act 1891 (c. 3)

1. The Custody of Children Act 1891 (which contains miscellaneous obsolete provisions with respect to the custody of children) shall cease to have effect.

The Children and Young Persons Act 1933 (c. 12)

2. In section 1(2)(a) of the Children and Young Persons Act 1933 (cruelty to persons under sixteen), after the words "young person" there shall be inserted," or the legal guardian of a child or young person,"
3. Section 40 of that Act shall cease to have effect.

The Education Act 1944 (c. 31)

4. In section 40(1) of the Education Act 1944 (enforcement of school attendance), the words from "or to imprisonment" to the end shall cease to have effect.

The Marriage Act 1949 (c. 76)

5.—(1) In section 3 of the Marriage Act 1949 (consent required to the marriage of a child by common licence or superintendent registrar's certificate), in subsection (1) for the words "the Second Schedule to this Act" there shall be substituted "subsection (1A) of this section."
(2) After that subsection there shall be inserted—
"(1A) The consents are—
  (a) subject to paragraphs (b) to (d) of this subsection, the consent of—
    (i) each parent (if any) of the child who has parental responsibility for him; and
    (ii) each guardian (if any) of the child;
  (b) where a residence order is in force with respect to the child, the consent of the person or persons with whom he lives, or is to live, as a result of the order (in substitution for the consents mentioned in paragraph (a) of this subsection);
  (c) where a care order is in force with respect to the child, the consent of the local authority designated in the order (in addition to the consents mentioned in paragraph (a) of this subsection);
  (d) where neither paragraph (b) nor (c) of this subsection applies but a residence order was in force with respect to the child immediately before he reached the age of sixteen, the consent of the person or persons with whom he lived, or was to live, as a result of the order (in substitution for the consents mentioned in paragraph (a) of this subsection).
(1B) In this section 'guardian of a child,' 'parental responsibility,' 'residence order' and 'care order' have the same meaning as in the Children Act 1989."

The Births and Deaths Registration Act (c. 20)

6.—(1) Sections 10 and 10A of the Births and Deaths Registration Act 1953 (registration of father, and re-registration, where parents not married) shall be amended as follows.

(2) In sections 10(1) and 10A(1) for paragraph (d) there shall be substituted—
"(d) at the request of the mother or that person on production of—
  (i) a copy of a parental responsibility agreement made between them in relation to the child; and
  (ii) a declaration in the prescribed form by the person making the request stating that the agreement was made in compliance with section 4 of the Children Act 1989 and has not been brought to an end by an order of a court; or
(e) at the request of the mother of that person on production of—
  (i) a certified copy of an order under section 4 of the Children Act 1989 giving that person parental responsibility for the child; and
  (ii) a declaration in the prescribed form by the person making the request stating that the order has not been brought to an end by an order of a court; or
(f) at the request of the mother or that person on production of—
  (i) a certified copy of an order under paragraph 1 of Schedule to the Children Act 1989 which requires that person to make any financial provision for the child which is not an order falling within paragraph 4(3) of that Schedule; and
  (ii) a declaration in the prescribed form by the person making the request stating that the order has not been discharged by an order of a court; or
(g) at the request of the mother or that person on production of—
  (i) a certified copy of any of the orders which are mentioned in subsection (1A) of this section which has been made in relation to the child; and
  (ii) a declaration in the prescribed form by the person making the request stating that the order has not been brought to an end or discharged by an order of a court."

(3) After sections 10(1) and 10A(1) there shall be inserted—
"(1A) The orders are—
(a) an order under section 4 of the Family Law Reform Act 1987 that that person shall have all the parental rights and duties with respect to the child;
(b) an order that that person shall have custody or care and control or legal custody of the child made under section 9 of the Guardianship of Minors Act 1971 at a time when such an order could only be made in favour of a parent;
(c) an order under section 9 or 11B of that Act which requires that person to make any financial provision in relation to the child;
(d) an order under section 4 of the Affiliation Proceedings Act 1957 naming that person as putative father of the child."

(4) In section 10(2) for the words "or (d)" there shall be substituted "to (g)."

(5) In section 10(3) for the words from " 'relevant order' " to the end there shall be substituted " 'parental responsibility agreement' has the same meaning as in the Children Act 1989."

(6) In section 10A(2) in paragraphs (b) and (c) for the words "paragraph (d)" in both places where they occur there shall be substituted "any of paragraphs (d) to (g)."

The Army Act 1955 (c. 18)

7. In section 151 of the Army Act 1955 (deductions from pay for maintenance of wife or child), in subsection (1A)(a) for the words "in the care of a local authority in England or Wales" there shall be substituted "being looked after by a local authority in England or Wales (within the meaning of the Children Act 1989)."

8. [Repealed by the Armed Forces Act 1991, s.26, Sched. 3.]

The Air Force Act (c. 19)

9. Section 151(1A) of the Air Force Act 1955 (deductions from pay for maintenance of wife or child) shall have effect subject to the amendment that is set out in paragraph 7 in relation to section 151(1A) of the Army Act 1955.

10. [Repealed by the Armed Forces Act 1991, s.26, Sched. 3.]

The Sexual Offences Act 1956 (c. 69)

11. In section 19(3) of the Sexual Offences Act 1956 (abduction of unmarried girl under eighteen from parent or guardian) for the words "the lawful care or charge of" there shall be substituted "parental responsibility for or care of."

12. In section 20(2) of that Act (abduction of unmarried girl under sixteen from parent or guardian) for the words "the lawful care or charge of" there shall be substituted "parental responsibility for or care of."

13. In section 21(3) of that Act (abduction of defective from parent or guardian) for the words "the lawful care or charge of" there shall be substituted "parental responsibility for or care of."

14. In section 28 of that Act (causing or encouraging prostitution of, intercourse with, or indecent assault on, girl under sixteen) for subsections (3) and (4) there shall be substituted—

"(3) The persons who are to be treated for the purposes of this section as responsible for a girl are (subject to subsection (4) of this section)—
   (a) her parents;
   (b) any person who is not a parent of hers but who has parental responsibility for her; and
   (c) any person who has care of her.

(4) An individual falling within subsection (3)(a) or (b) of this section not to be treated as responsible for a girl if—
   (a) a residence order under the Children Act 1989 is in force with respect to her and he is not named in the order as the person with whom she is to live; or
   (b) a care order under that Act is in force with respect to her."

15. Section 38 of that Act (power of court to divest person of authority over girl or boy in case of incest) shall cease to have effect.

16.—(1) In section 43 of that Act (power to search for and recover woman detained for immoral purposes), in subsection (5) for the words "the lawful care or charge of" there shall be substituted "parental responsibility for or care of."

(2) In subsection (6) of that section, for the words "section forty of the Children and Young Persons Act 1933" there shall be substituted "Part V of the Children Act 1989."

17. After section 46 of that Act there shall be inserted—

"Meaning of 'parental responsibility'
46A. In this Act 'parental responsibility' has the same meaning as in the Children Act 1989."

The Naval Discipline Act 1957 (c. 53)

18. [Repealed by the Armed Forces Act 1991, s.26, Sched. 3.]

The Children and Young Persons Act 1963 (c. 37)

19. Section 3 of the Children and Young Persons Act 1963 (children and young persons beyond control) shall cease to have effect.

The Children and Young Persons Act 1969 (c. 54)

20. In section 5 of the Children and Young Persons Act 1969 (restrictions on criminal proceedings for offences by young persons), in subsection (2), for the words "section 1 of this Act" there shall be substituted "Part IV of the Children Act 1989."

21. [Repealed by the Criminal Justice Act 1991, s.10(2), Sched. 13.]

22. In section 12A of that Act (young offenders) for subsections (1) and (2) there shall be substituted—

"(1) This subsection applies to any supervision order made under section 7(7) of this Act unless it requires the supervised person to comply with directions given by the supervisor under section 12(2) of this Act."

23. After that section there shall be inserted—

"Requirement for young offender to live in local authority accommodation

12AA.—(1) Where the conditions mentioned in subsection (6) of this section are satisfied, a supervision order may impose a requirement ('a residence requirement') that a child or young person shall live for a specified period in local authority accommodation.

(2) A residence requirement shall designate the local authority who are to receive the child or young person and that authority shall be the authority in whose area the child or young person resides.

(3) The court shall not impose a residence requirement without first consulting the designated authority.

(4) A residence requirement may stipulate that the child or young person shall not live with a named person.

(5) The maximum period which may be specified in a residence requirement is six months.

(6) The conditions are that—
  (a) a supervision order has previously been made in respect of the child or young person;
  (b) that order imposed—
    (i) a requirement under section 12A(3) of this Act; or
    (ii) a residence requirement;
  (c) he is found guilty of an offence which—
    (i) was committed while that order was in force;
    (ii) if it had been committed by a person over the age of twenty-one, would have been punishable with imprisonment; and
    (iii) in the opinion of the court is serious; and
  (d) the court is satisfied that the behaviour which constituted the offence was due, to a significant extent, to the circumstances in which he was living,

except that the conditions in paragraph (d) of this subsection does not apply where the condition in paragraph (b)(ii) is satisfied.

(7) For the purposes of satisfying itself as mentioned in subsection (6)(d) of this section, the court shall obtain a social inquiry report which makes particular reference to the circumstances in which the child or young person was living.

(8) Subsection (7) of this section does not apply if the court already has before it a social inquiry report which contains sufficient information about the circumstances in which the child or young person was living.

(9) A court shall not include a residence requirement in respect of a child or young person who is not legally represented at the relevant time in that court unless—
  (a) he has applied for legal aid for the purposes of the proceedings and the application was refused on the ground that it did not appear that his resources were such that he required assistance; or
  (b) he has been informed of his right to apply for legal aid for the purposes of the proceedings and has had the opportunity to do so, but nevertheless refused or failed to apply.

(10) In subsection (9) of this section—
  (a) 'the relevant time' means the time when the court is considering whether or not to impose the requirement; and

(b) 'the proceedings' means—
　　(i) the whole proceedings; or
　　(ii) the part of the proceedings relating to the imposition of the requirement.

(11) A supervision order imposing a residence requirement may also impose any of the requirements mentioned in section 12, 12A, 12B or 12C of this Act.

(12) In this section 'social inquiry report' has the same meaning as in section 2 of the Criminal Justice Act 1982."

24. [Repealed by the Criminal Justice Act 1991, s.10(2), Sched. 13.]

25. [Repealed by the Courts and Legal Service Act 1990, s.116, Sched. 16, para. 31.]

26. For section 23 of that Act (remand to care of local authorities, etc.) there shall be substituted—

"**Remand to local authority accommodation, committal of young persons of unruly character, etc.**

23.—(1) Where a court—
　　(a) remands or commits for trial a child charged with homicide or remands a child convicted of homicide; or
　　(b) remands a young person charged with or convicted of one or more offences or commits him for trial or sentence,

and he is not released on bail, then, unless he is a young person who is certified by the court to be of unruly character, the court shall remand him to local authority accommodation.

(2) A court remanding a person to local authority accommodation shall designate the authority who are to receive him and that authority shall be the authority in whose area it appears to the court that—
　　(a) he resides; or
　　(b) the offence or one of the offences was committed.

(3) Where a person is remanded to local authority accommodation, it shall be lawful for any person acting on behalf of the designated authority to detain him.

(4) The court shall not certify a young person as being of unruly character unless—
　　(a) he cannot safely be remanded to local authority accommodation; and
　　(b) the conditions prescribed by order made by the Secretary of State under this subsection are satisfied in relation to him.

(5) Where the court certifies that a young person is of unruly character, it shall commit him—
　　(a) to a remand centre, if it has been notified that such a centre is available for the reception from the court of such persons; and
　　(b) to a prison, if it has not been so notified.

(6) Where a young person is remanded to local authority accommodation, a court may, on the application of the designated authority, certify him to be of unruly character in accordance with subsection (4) of this section (and on so doing he shall cease to be remanded to local authority accommodation and subsection (5) of this section shall apply).

(7) For the purposes of subsection (6) of this section, "a court" means—
　　(a) the court which remanded the young person; or
　　(b) any magistrates' court having jurisdiction in the place where that person is for the time being,

and in this section "court" and "magistrates' court" include a justice.

(8) This section has effect subject to—
　　(a) section 37 of the Magistrates' Courts Act 1980 (committal to the Crown Court with a view to a sentence of detention in a young offender institution); and
　　(b) section 128(7) of that Act (remands to the custody of a constable for periods of not more than three days),

but section 128(7) shall have effect in relation to a child or young person as if for the reference to three clear days there were substituted a reference to twenty-four hours."

27.—(1) In section 32 of that Act (detention of absentees), for subsection (1A) there shall be substituted the following subsections—

"(1A) If a child or young person is absent, without the consent of the responsible person—
(a) from a place of safety to which he has been taken under section 16(3) of this Act; or
(b) from local authority accommodation—
   (i) in which he is required to live under section 12AA of this Act; or
   (ii) to which he has been remanded under [section 16(3A) or 23(1)] of this Act,

he may be arrested by a constable anywhere in the United Kingdom or Channel Islands without a warrant.

(1B) A person so arrested shall be conducted to—
(a) the place of safety;
(b) the local authority accommodation; or
(c) such other place as the responsible person may direct,

at the responsible person's expense.

(1C) In this section 'the responsible person' means the person who made the arrangements under section 16(3) of this Act or, as the case may be, the authority designated under section 12AA, [16(3B) or 23] of this Act."

(2) In subsection (2B) of that section for the words "person referred to in subsection (1A)(a) or (b) (as the case may be) of this section" there shall be substituted "responsible person."

AMENDMENT

The words in square brackets in paragraph 27 were added by the Courts and Legal Services Act 1990, Sched. 16, para. 5.

28. In section 34(1) of that Act (transitional modifications of Part I for persons of specified ages)—
(a) in paragraph (a), for the words "13(2) or 28(4) or (5)" there shall be substituted "or 13(2)"; and
(b) in paragraph (e), for the words "section 23(2) or (3)" there shall be substituted "section 23(4) to (6)."

29. In section 70(1) of that Act (interpretation)—
(a) after the definition of "local authority" there shall be inserted—
" 'local authority accommodation' means accommodation provided by or on behalf of a local authority (within the meaning of the Children Act 1989)"; and
(b) in the definition of "reside" for "12(4) and (5)" there shall be substituted "12B(1) and (2)."

30. In section 73 of that Act (extent, etc.)—
(a) in subsection (4)(a) for "32(1), (3) and (4)" there shall be substituted "32(1) to (1C) and (2A) to (4)"; and
(b) in subsection (6) for "32(1), (1A)" there shall be substituted "32(1) to (1C)."

The Matrimonial Causes Act 1973 (c. 18)

31. For section 41 of the Matrimonial Causes Act 1973 (restrictions on decrees for dissolution, annulment or separation affecting children) there shall be substituted—

"Restrictions on decrees for dissolution, annulment or separation affecting children

41.—(1) In any proceedings for a decree of divorce or nullity of marriage, or a decree of judicial separation, the court shall consider—
(a) whether there are any children of the family to whom this section applies; and
(b) where there are any such children, whether (in the light of the arrangements which have been, or are proposed to be, made for

their upbringing and welfare) it should exercise any of its powers under the Children Act 1989 with respect to any of them.

(2) Where, in any case to which this section applies, it appears to the court that—

(a) the circumstances of the case require it, or are likely to require it, to exercise any of its powers under the Act of 1989 with respect to any such child;

(b) it is not in a position to exercise that power or (as the case may be) those powers without giving further consideration to the case; and

(c) there are exceptional circumstances which make it desirable in the interests of the child that the court should give a direction under this section,

it may direct that the decree of divorce or nullity is not to be made absolute, or that the decree of judicial separation is not to be granted, until the court orders otherwise.

(3) This section applies to—

(a) any child of the family who has not reached the age of sixteen at the date when the court considers the case in accordance with the requirements of this section; and

(b) any child of the family who has reached that age at that date and in relation to whom the court directs that this section shall apply."

32. In section 42 of that Act, subsection (3) (declaration by court that party to marriage unfit to have custody of children or family) shall cease to have effect.

33. In section 52(1) of that Act (interpretation), in the definition of "child of the family," for the words "has been boarded-out with those parties" there shall be substituted "is placed with those parties as foster parents."

The National Health Service Act 1977 (c. 49)

34. In Schedule 8 to the National Health Service Act 1977 (functions of local social services authorities), the following sub-paragraph shall be added at the end of paragraph 2—

"(4A) This paragraph does not apply in relation to persons under the age of 18."

The Child Care Act 1980 (c. 5)

35. Until the repeal of the Child Care Act 1980 by this Act takes effect, the definition of "parent" in section 87 of that Act shall have effect as if it applied only in relation to Part I and sections 13, 24, 64 and 65 of that Act (provisions excluded by section 2(1)(f) of the Family Law Reform Act 1987 from the application of the general rule in that Act governing the meaning of references to relationships between persons).

The Education Act 1981 (c. 60)

36. The following section shall be inserted in the Education Act 1981, after section 3—

"**Provision outside England and Wales for certain children**

3A.—(1) A local [education] authority may make such arrangements as they think fit to enable any child in respect of whom they maintain a statement under section 7 to attend an establishment outside England and Wales which specialises in providing for children with special needs.

(2) In subsection (1) above "children with special needs" means children who have particular needs which would be special educational needs if those children were in England and Wales.

(3) Where an authority make arrangements under this section with respect to a child, those arrangements may, in particular, include contributing to or paying—

(a) fees charged by the establishment;
(b) expenses reasonably incurred in maintaining him while he is at the establishment or travelling to or from it;
(c) those travelling expenses;
(d) expenses reasonably incurred by any accompanying him while he is travelling or staying at the establishment.

(4) This section is not to be taken as in any way limiting any other powers of a local education authority."

AMENDMENT

The word in square brackets was added by the Courts and Legal Services Act 1990, Sched. 16, para. 9.

The Child Abduction Act 1984 (c. 37)

37.—(1) Section 1 of the Child Abduction Act 1984 (offence of abduction by parent, etc.) shall be amended as follows.

(2) For subsections (2) to (4) there shall be substituted—

"(2) A person is connected with a child for the purposes of this section if—
  (a) he is a parent of the child; or
  (b) in the case of a child whose parents were not married to each other at the time of his birth, there are reasonable grounds for believing that he is the father of the child; or
  (c) he is a guardian of the child; or
  (d) he is a person in whose favour a residence order is in force with respect to the child; or
  (e) he has custody of the child.

(3) In this section 'the appropriate consent,' in relation to a child, means—
  (a) the consent of each of the following—
    (i) the child's mother;
    (ii) the child's father, if he has parental responsibility for him;
    (iii) any guardian of the child;
    (iv) any person in whose favour a residence order is in force with respect to the child;
    (v) any person who has custody of the child; or
  (b) the leave of the court granted under or by virtue of any provision of Part II of the Children Act 1989; or
  (c) if any person has custody of the child, the leave of the court which awarded custody to him.

(4) A person does not commit an offence under this section by taking or sending a child out of the United Kingdom without obtaining the appropriate consent if—
  (a) he is a person in whose favour there is a residence order in force with respect to the child, and
  (b) he takes or sends him out of the United Kingdom for a period of less than one month.

(4A) Subsection (4) above does not apply if the person taking or sending the child out of the United Kingdom does so in breach of an order under Part II of the Children Act 1989."

(3) In subsection (5) for the words from "but" to the end there shall be substituted—

"(5A) Subsection (5)(c) above does not apply if—
  (a) the person who refused to consent is a person—
    (i) in whose favour there is a residence order in force with respect to the child; or
    (ii) who has custody of the child; or
  (b) the person taking or sending the child out of the United Kingdom is, by so acting, in breach of an order made by a court in the United Kingdom."

(4) For subsection (7) there shall be substituted—

"(7) For the purposes of this section—

(a) 'guardian of a child,' 'residence order' and 'parental responsibility' have the same meaning as in the Children Act 1989; and
(b) a person shall be treated as having custody of a child if there is in force an order of a court in the United Kingdom awarding him (whether solely or jointly with another person) custody, legal custody or care and control of the child."

(5) In subsection (8) for the words from "or voluntary organisation" to "custodianship proceedings or" there shall be substituted "detained in a place of safety, remanded to a local authority accommodation or the subject of."

38.—(1) In section 2 of that Act (offence of abduction of child by other persons), in subsection (1) for the words from "Subject" to "above" there shall be substituted "Subject to subsection (3) below, a person, other than one mentioned in subsection (2) below."

(2) For subsection (2) of that section there shall be substituted—

"(2) The persons are—
(a) where the father and mother of the child in question were married to each other at the time of his birth, the child's father and mother;
(b) where the father and mother of the child in question were not married to each other at the time of his birth, the child's mother; and
(c) any other person mentioned in section 1(2)(c) to (e) above.

(3) In proceedings against any person for an offence under this section, it shall be a defence for that person to prove—
(a) where the father and mother of the child in question were not married to each other at the time of his birth—
(i) that he is the child's father; or
(ii) that, at the time of the alleged offence, he believed, on reasonable grounds, that he was the child's father; or
(b) that, at the time of the alleged offence, he believed that the child had attained the age of sixteen."

39. At the end of section 3 of that Act (construction of references to taking, sending and detaining) there shall be added "and
(d) references to a child's parents and to a child whose parents were (or were not) married to each other at the time of his birth shall be construed in accordance with section 1 of the Family Law Reform Act 1987 (which extends their meaning)."

40.—(1) The Schedule to that Act (modifications of section 1 for children in certain cases) shall be amended as follows.

(2) In paragraph 1(1) for the words "or voluntary organisation" there shall be substituted "within the meaning of the Children Act 1989."

(3) For paragraph 2(1) there shall be substituted—
"(1) This paragraph applies in the case of a child who is—
(a) detained in a place of safety under section 16(3) of the Children and Young Persons Act 1969; or
(b) remanded to local authority accommodation under section 23 of that Act."

(4) In paragraph 3(1)—
(a) in paragraph (a) for the words "section 14 of the Children Act 1975" there shall be substituted "section 18 of the Adoption Act 1976"; and
(b) in paragraph (d) for the words "section 25 of the Children Act 1975 or section 53 of the Adoption Act 1958" there shall be substituted "section 55 of the Adoption Act 1976."

(5) In paragraph 3(2)(a)—
(a) in sub-paragraph (i), for the words from "order or," to "Children Act 1975" there shall be substituted "section 18 order or, if the section 18 order has been varied under section 21 of that Act so as to give parental responsibility to another agency", and
(b) in sub-paragraph (ii), for the words "(c) or (e)" there shall be substituted "or (c)."

(6) At the end of paragraph 3 there shall be added—

"(3) Sub-paragraph (2) above shall be construed as if the references to the court included, in any case where the court is a magistrates' court, a reference to any magistrates' court acting for the same area as that court."

(7) For paragraph 5 there shall be substituted—
"5. In this Schedule—
(a) 'adoption agency' and 'adoption order' have the same meaning as in the Adoption Act 1976; and
(b) 'area,' in relation to a magistrates' court, means the petty sessions area (within the meaning of the Justices of the Peace Act 1979) for which the court is appointed."

The Foster Children (Scotland) Act 1984 (c. 56)

41. In section 1 of the Foster Children (Scotland) Act 1984 (definition of foster child)—
(a) for the words "he is— (a)" there shall be substituted "(a) he is"; and
(b) the words "for a period of more than 6 days" and the words from "The period" to the end shall cease to have effect.

42. In section 2(2) of that Act (exceptions to section 1), for paragraph (f) there shall be substituted—
"(f) if he has been in that person's care for a period of less than 28 days and that person does not intend to undertake his care for any longer period."

43. In section 7(1) of that Act (persons disqualified from keeping foster children)—
(a) the word "or" at the end of paragraph (e) shall be omitted; and
(b) after paragraph (f) there shall be inserted "or (g) he is disqualified from fostering a child privately (within the meaning of the Children Act 1989) by regulations made under section 68 of that Act,".

The Disabled Person (Services, Consultation and Representation) Act 1986 (c. 33)

44. In section 2(5) of the Disabled Persons (Services, Consultation and Representation) Act 1986 (circumstances in which authorised representative has right to visit, etc., disabled person), after paragraph (d) there shall be inserted—
"(dd) in accommodation provided by any educational establishment."

The Legal Aid Act (c. 34)

45. In paragraph 2 of Part I of Schedule 2 to the Legal Aid Act 1988 (proceedings in magistrates' courts to which the civil legal aid provisions of Part IV of the Act apply), the following sub-paragraph shall be added at the end—
"(g) proceedings under the Children Act 1989."

Section 108(5)   **SCHEDULE 13**

CONSEQUENTIAL AMENDMENTS

GENERAL NOTE

Further consequential amendments are made in the Children Act 1989 (Consequential Amendment of Enactments) Order 1991 (S.I. 1991 No. 1881).

The Wills Act 1837 (c. 26)

1. In section 1 of the Wills Act 1837 (interpretation), in the definition of "will," for the words "and also to a disposition by will and testament or devise of the custody and tuition of any child" there shall be substituted "and also to an appointment by will of a guardian of a child."

The Children and Young Persons Act 1933 (c. 12)

2. In section 1(1) of the Children and Young Persons Act 1933 (cruelty to persons under sixteen) for the words "has the custody, charge or care of" there shall be substituted "has responsibility for."

3. In the following sections of that Act—
   (a) 3(1) (allowing persons under sixteen to be in brothels);
   (b) 4(1) and (2) (causing or allowing persons under sixteen to be used for begging);
   (c) 11 (exposing children under twelve to risk of burning); and
   (d) 25(1) (restrictions on persons under eighteen going abroad for the purpose of performing for profit),
   for the words "the custody, charge or care of" there shall, in each case, be substituted "responsibility for."

4. In section 10(1A) of that Act (vagrants preventing children from receiving education), for the words from "to bring the child" to the end there shall be substituted "to make an application in respect of the child or young person for an education supervision order under section 36 of the Children Act 1989."

5. For section 17 of that Act (interpretation of Part I) there shall be substituted the following section—

"Interpretation of Part I

17.—(1) For the purposes of this Part of this Act, the following shall be presumed to have responsibility for a child or young person—
   (a) any person who—
       (i) has parental responsibility for him (within the meaning of the Children Act 1989); or
       (ii) is otherwise legally liable to maintain him; and
   (b) any person who has care of him.

(2) A person who is presumed to be responsible for a child or young person by virtue of subsection (1)(a) shall not be taken to have ceased to be responsible for him by reason only that he does not have care of him."

6.—(1) In section 34 of that Act (attendance at court of parent of child or young person charged with an offence, etc.), in subsection (1) after the word "offence" there shall be inserted "is the subject of an application for a care or supervision order under Part IV of the Children Act 1989."

(2) In subsection (7) of that section after the words "Children and Young Persons Act 1969" there shall be inserted "or Part IV of the Children Act 1989."

(3) After subsection (7) of that section there shall be inserted—

"(7A) If it appears that at the time of his arrest the child or young person is being provided with accommodation by or on behalf of a local authority under section 20 of the Children Act 1989, the local authority shall also be informed as described in subsection (3) above as soon as it is reasonably practicable to do so."

7. In section 107(1) of that Act (interpretation)—
   (a) in the definition of "guardian," for the words "charge of or control over" there shall be substituted "care of";
   (b) for the definition of legal guardian shall be substituted—
" 'legal guardian,' in relation to a child or young person, means a guardian of a child as defined in the Children Act 1989."

The Education Act 1944 (c. 31)

8.—(1) Section 40 of the Education Act 1944 (enforcement of school attendance) shall be amended as follows.

(2) For subsection (2) there shall be substituted—

"(2) Proceedings for such offences shall not be instituted except by a local education authority.

(2A) Before instituting such proceedings the local education authority shall consider whether it would be appropriate, instead of or as well as instituting the proceedings, to apply for an education supervision order with respect to the child."

(3) For subsections (3) and (4) there shall be substituted—
"(3) The court—
    (a) by which a person is convicted of an offence against section 37 of this Act; or
    (b) before which a person is charged with an offence under section 39 of this Act,
may direct the local education authority instituting the proceedings to apply for an education supervision order with respect to the child unless the authority, having consulted the appropriate local authority, decide that the child's welfare will be satisfactorily safeguarded even though no education supervision order is made.

(3A) Where, following such a direction, a local education authority decide not to apply for an education supervision order they shall inform the court of the reasons for their decision.

(3B) Unless the court has directed otherwise, the information required under subsection (3A) shall be given to the court before the end of the period of eight weeks beginning with the date on which the direction was given.

(4) Where—
    (a) a local education authority apply for an education supervision order with respect to a child who is the subject of a school attendance order; and
    (b) the court decides that section 36(3) of the Children Act 1989 prevents it from making the order;
the court may direct that the school attendance order shall cease to be in force."

(4) After subsection (4) there shall be inserted—
"(5) In this section—
'appropriate local authority' has the same meaning as in section 36(9) of the Children Act 1989; and
'education supervision order' means an education supervision order under that Act."

9. In section 71 of that Act (complaints with respect to independent schools), the following paragraph shall be added after paragraph (d), in subsection (1)—
"(e) there has been a failure, in relation to a child provided with accommodation by the school, to comply with the duty imposed by section 87 of the Children Act 1989 (welfare of children accommodated in independent schools);".

10. After section 114(1C) of that Act (interpretation) there shall be inserted the following subsections—
"(1D) In this Act, unless the context otherwise requires, 'parent,' in relation to a child or young person, includes any person—
    (a) who is not a parent of his but who has parental responsibility for him, or
    (b) who has care of him,
except for the purposes of the enactments mentioned in subsection (1E) of this section, where it only includes such a person if he is an individual.

(1E) The enactments are—
    (a) sections 5(4), 15(2) and (6), 31 and 65(1) of, and paragraph 7(6) of Schedule 2 to, the Education (No. 2) Act 1986; and
    (b) sections 53(8), 54(2), 58(5)(k), 60 and 61 of the Education Reform Act 1988.

(1F) For the purposes of subsection (1D) of this section—
    (a) 'parental responsibility' has the same meaning as in the Children Act 1989; and
    (b) in determining whether an individual has care of a child or young person any absence of the child or young person at a hospital or boarding school and any other temporary absence shall be disregarded."

The National Assistance Act 1948 (c. 29)

11.—(1) In section 21(1)(a) of the National Assistance Act 1948 (persons for whom local authority is to provide residential accommodation) after the word "persons" there shall be inserted "aged eighteen or over."

(2) In section 29(1) of that Act (welfare arrangements for blind, deaf, dumb and crippled persons) after the words "that is to say persons" and after the words "and other persons" there shall, in each case, be inserted "aged eighteen or over."

The Reserve and Auxiliary Forces (Protection of Civil Interests) Act 1951 (c. 65)

12. For section 2(1)(d) of the Reserve and Auxiliary Forces (Protection of Civil Interests) Act 1951 (cases in which leave of the appropriate court is required before enforcing certain orders for the payment of money), there shall be substituted—
   "(d) an order for alimony, maintenance or other payment made under sections 21 to 33 of the Matrimonial Causes Act 1973 or made, or having effect as if made, under Schedule 1 to the Children Act 1989."

The Mines and Quarries Act 1954 (c. 70)

13. In section 182(1) of the Mines and Quarries Act 1954 (interpretation), in the definition of "parent," for the words from "or guardian" to first "young person" there shall be substituted "of a young person or any person who is not a parent of his but who has parental responsibility for him (within the meaning of the Children Act 1989)."

The Administration of Justice Act 1960 (c. 65)

14. In section 12 of the Administration of Justice Act 1960 (publication of information relating to proceedings in private), in subsection (1) for paragraph (a) there shall be substituted—
   "(a) where the proceedings—
      (i) relate to the exercise of the inherent jurisdiction of the High Court with respect to minors;
      (ii) are brought under the Children Act 1989; or
      (iii) otherwise relate wholly or mainly to the maintenance or upbringing of a minor;".

The Factories Act 1961 (c. 34)

15. In section 176(1) of the Factories Act 1961 (interpretation), in the definition of "parent," for the words from "or guardian" to first "young person" there shall be substituted "of a child or young person or any person who is not a parent of his but who has parental responsibility for him (within the meaning of the Children Act 1989)."

The Criminal Justice Act 1967 (c. 80)

16. In section 67(1A)(c) of the Criminal Justice Act 1967 (computation of sentences of imprisonment passed in England and Wales) for the words "in the care of a local authority" there shall be substituted "remanded to local authority accommodation."

The Health Services and Public Health Act 1968 (c. 46)

17.—(1) In section 64(3)(a) of the Health Services and Public Health Act 1968 (meaning of "relevant enactments" in relation to power of Minister of Health or Secretary of State to provide financial assistance), for sub-paragraph (xix) inserted by paragraph 19 of Schedule 5 to the Child Care Act 1980 there shall be substituted—

"(xx) the Children Act 1989."

(2) In section 65(3)(b) of that Act (meaning of "relevant enactments" in relation to power of local authority to provide financial and other assistance), for sub-paragraph (xx) inserted by paragraph 20 of Schedule 5 to the Child Care Act 1980 there shall be substituted—

"(xxi) the Children Act 1989."

The Social Work (Scotland) Act 1968 (c. 49)

18. In section 2(2) of the Social Work (Scotland) Act 1968 (matters referred to social work committee) after paragraph (j) there shall be inserted—

"(k) section 19 and Part X of the Children Act 1989,".

19. In section 5(2)(c) of that Act (power of Secretary of State to make regulations) for the words "and (j)" there shall be substituted "to (k)."

20. In section 21(3) of that Act (mode of provision of accommodation and maintenance) for the words "section 21 of the Child Care Act 1980" there shall be substituted "section 23 of the Children Act 1989."

21. In section 74(6) of that Act (parent of child in residential establishment moving to England or Wales) for the words from "Children and Young Persons Act 1969" to the end there shall be substituted "Children Act 1989, but as if section 31(8) were omitted."

22. In section 75(2) of that Act (parent of child subject to care order, etc. moving to Scotland), for the words "Children and Young Persons Act 1969" there shall be substituted "Children Act 1989."

23. In section 86(3) of that Act (meaning of ordinary residence for purpose of adjustments between authority providing accommodation and authority of area of residence), the words "the Child Care Act 1980 or" shall be omitted and after the words "education authority" there shall be inserted "or placed with local authority foster parents under the Children Act 1989."

The Civil Evidence Act 1968 (c. 64)

24. [Repealed by the Courts and Legal Services Act 1991, s.116, Sched. 16, para. 2(2).]

The Administration of Justice Act 1970 (c. 31)

25. [Repealed by the Courts and Legal Services Act 1991, s.116, Sched. 16, para. 6(2).]

The Local Authority Social Services Act 1970 (c. 42)

26.—(1) In Schedule 1 to the Local Authority Social Services Act 1970 (enactments conferring functions assigned to social service committee)—
   (a) in the entry relating to the Mental Health Act 1959, for the words "sections 8 and 9" there shall be substituted "section 88"; and
   (b) in the entry relating to the Children and Young Persons Act 1969, for the words "sections 1, 2 and 9" there shall be substituted "section 9."

(2) At the end of that Schedule there shall be added—

"Children Act 1989.
The whole Act, in so far as it confers functions on a local authority within the meaning of that Act.

Welfare reports
Consent to application for residence order in respect of child in care
Family assistance orders.
Functions under Part III of the Act (local authority support for children and families).
Care and supervision.
Protection of children.

Functions in relation to community homes, voluntary homes and voluntary organisations, registered children's homes, private arrangements for fostering children, child minding and day care for young children.
Inspection of children's homes on behalf of Secretary of State.
Research and returns of information.
Functions in relation to children accomodated by health authorities and local education authorities or in residential care, nursing or mental nursing homes or in independent schools."

The Chronically Sick and Disabled Persons Act 1970 (c. 44)

27. After section 28 of the Chronically Sick and Disabled Persons Act 1970 there shall be inserted—

"**Application of Act to authorities having functions under the Children Act 1989**
28A. This Act applies with respect to disabled children in relation to whom a local authority have functions under Part III of the Children Act 1989 as it applies in relation to persons to whom section 29 of the National Assistance Act 1948 applies."

The Courts Act 1971 (c. 23)

28. In Part I of Schedule 9 to the Courts Act 1971 (substitution of references to Crown Court), in the entry relating to the Children and Young Persons Act 1969, for the words "Sections 2(12), 3(8), 16(8), 21(4)(5)" there shall be substituted "Section 16(8)."

The Attachment of Earnings Act 1971 (c. 32)

29. In Schedule 1 to the Attachment of Earnings Act 1971 (maintenance orders to which that Act applies), in paragraph 7, for the words "section 47 or 51 of the Child Care Act 1980" there shall be substituted "paragraph 23 of Schedule 2 to the Children Act 1989."

The Tribunals and Inquiries Act 1971 (c. 62)

30. In Schedule 1 to the Tribunals and Inquiries Act 1971 (tribunals under direct supervision of the Council on Tribunals) for paragraph 4 there shall be substituted—

"**Registration of voluntary homes and children's homes under the Children Act 1989**
4. Registered Homes Tribunals constituted under Part III of the Registered Homes Act 1984."

The Local Government Act 1972 (c. 70)

31.—(1) In section 102(1) of the Local Government Act 1972 (appointment of committees) for the words "section 31 of the Child Care Act 1980" there shall be substituted "section 53 of the Children Act 1989."

(2) In Schedule 12A to that Act (access to information: exempt information), in Part III (interpretation), in paragraph 1(1)(b) for the words "section 20 of the Children and Young Persons Act 1969" there shall be substituted "section 31 of the Children Act 1989" . . .

The Employment of Children Act 1973 (c. 24)

32.—(1) In section 2 of the Employment of Children Act 1973 (supervision by education authorities), in subsection (2)(a) for the words "guardian or a person who has actual custody of" there shall be substituted "any person responsible for."
(2) After that subsection there shall be inserted—

"(2A) For the purposes of subsection (2)(a) above a person is responsible for a child—
    (a) in England and Wales, if he has parental responsibility for the child or care of him; and
    (b) in Scotland, if he is his guardian or has actual custody of him."

The Domicile and Matrimonial Proceedings Act 1973 (c. 45)

33.—(1) In Schedule 1 to the Domicile and Matrimonial Proceedings Act 1973 (proceedings in divorce, etc. stayed by reference to proceedings in other jurisdiction), paragraph 11(1) shall be amended as follows—
    (a) at the end of the definition of "lump sum" there shall be added "or an order made in equivalent circumstances under Schedule 1 to the Children Act 1989 and of a kind mentioned in paragraph 1(2)(c) of that Schedule";
    (b) in the definition of "relevant order," at the end of paragraph (b), there shall be added "or an order made in equivalent circumstances under Schedule 1 to the Children Act 1989 and of a kind mentioned in paragraph 1(2)(a) or (b) of that Schedule";
    (c) in paragraph (c) of that definition, after the word "children)" there shall be inserted "or a section 8 order under the Children Act 1989"; and
    (d) in paragraph (d) of that definition for the words "the custody, care or control" there shall be substituted "care."
(2) In paragraph 11(3) of that Schedule—
    (a) the word "four" shall be omitted; and
    (b) for the words "the custody of a child and the education of a child" there shall be substituted "or any provision which could be made by a section 8 order under the Children Act 1989."

The Powers of Criminal Courts Ct 1973 (c. 62)

34. In Schedule 3 to the Powers of Criminal Courts Act 1973 (the probation and after-care service and its functions), in paragraph 3(2A) after paragraph (b) there shall be inserted—
"and
    (c) directions given under paragraph 2 or 3 of Schedule 3 to the Children Act 1989."

The Rehabilitation of Offenders Act 1974 (c. 53)

35.—(1) Section 7(2) of the Rehabilitation of Offenders Act 1974 (limitations on rehabilitation under the Act) shall be amended as follows.
(2) For paragraph (c) there shall be substituted—
    "(c) in any proceedings relating to adoption, the marriage of any minor, the exercise of the inherent jurisdiction of the High Court with respect to

minors or the provision by any person of accommodation, care or schooling for minors;
  (cc) in any proceedings brought under the Children Act 1989";
(3) For paragraph (d) there shall be substituted—
  "(d) in any proceedings relating to the variation or discharge of a supervision order under the Children and Young Persons Act 1969, or on appeal from any such proceedings."

The Domestic Proceedings and Magistrates' Courts Act 1978 (c. 22)

36. For section 8 of the Domestic Proceedings and Magistrates' Courts Act 1978 (orders for the custody of children) there shall be substituted—

"Restrictions on making of orders under this Act: welfare of children
8. Where an application is made by a party to a marriage for an order under section 2, 6 or 7 of this Act, then, if there is a child of the family who is under the age of eighteen, the court shall not dismiss or make a final order on the application until it has decided whether to exercise any of its powers under the Children Act 1989 with respect to the child."

37. In section 19(3A)(b) (interim orders) for the words "subsections (2) and" there shall be substituted "subsection."

38. For section 20(12) of that Act (variation and revocation of orders for periodical payments) there shall be substituted—
  "(12) An application under this section may be made—
    (a) where it is for the variation or revocation of an order under section 2, 6, 7 or 19 of this Act for periodical payments, by either party to the marriage in question; and
    (b) where it is for the variation of an order under section 2(1)(c), 6 or 7 of this Act for periodical payments to or in respect of a child, also by the child himself, if he has attained the age of sixteen."

39.—(1) For section 20A of that Act (revival of orders for periodical payments) there shall be substituted—

"Revival of orders for periodical payments
20A.—(1) Where an order made by a magistrates' court under this Part of this Act for the making of periodical payments to or in respect of a child (other than an interim maintenance order) ceases to have effect—
  (a) on the date on which the child attains the age of sixteen, or
  (b) at any time after that date but before or on the date on which he attains the age of eighteen,
the child may apply to the court which made the order for an order for its revival.
(2) if on such an application it appears to the court that—
  (a) the child is, will be or (if an order were made under this subsection) would be receiving instruction at an educational establishment or undergoing training for a trade, profession or vocation, whether or not while in gainful employment, or
  (b) there are special circumstances which justify the making of an order under this subsection,
the court shall have power by order to revive the order from such date as the court may specify, not being earlier than the date of the making of the application.
(3) Any order revived under this section may be varied or revoked under section 20 in the same way as it could have been varied or revoked had it continued in being."

40. [Repealed by the Courts and Legal Services Act 1991, s.116, Sched. 16, para. 32.]

41.—(1) In section 25 of that Act (effect on certain orders of parties living together), in subsection (1)(a) for the words "6 or 11(2)" there shall be substituted "or 6."
(2) In subsection (2) of that section—
  (a) in paragraph (a) for the words "6 or 11(2)" there shall be substituted "or 6"; and
  (b) after paragraph (a) there shall be inserted "or."

42. In section 29(5) of that Act (appeals) for the words "sections 14(3), 20 and 21" there shall be substituted "section 20."

43. In section 88(1) of that Act (interpretation)—
    (a) in the definition of "child," for the words from "an illegitimate" to the end there shall be substituted "a child whose father and mother were not married to each other at the time of his birth"; and
    (b) in the definition of "child of the family," for the words "being boarded-out with those parties" there shall be substituted "placed with those parties as foster parents."

The Magistrates' Courts Act 1980 (c. 43)

44. [Repealed by the Maintenance Enforcement Act 1991, s.11(2), Sched. 3.]
(2) For section 62(5) of that Act (payments to children) there shall be substituted—
    "(5) In this section references to the person with whom a child has his home—
    (a) in the case of any child who is being looked after by a local authority (within the meaning of section 22 of the Children Act 1989), are references to that local authority; and
    (b) in any other case, are references to the person who, disregarding any absence of the child at a hospital or boarding school and any other temporary absence, has care of the child."

The Supreme Court Act 1981 (c. 54)

45.—(1) In section 18 of the Supreme Court Act 1981 (restrictions on appeals to Court of Appeal)—
    (a) in subsection (1)(h)(i), for the word "custody" there shall be substituted "residence"; and
    (b) in subsection (1)(h)(ii) for the words "access to," in both places, there shall be substituted "contact with."
(2) In section 41 of that Act (wards of court), the following subsection shall be inserted after subsection (2)—
    "(2A) Subsection (2) does not apply with respect to a child who is the subject of a care order (as defined by section 105 of the Children Act 1989)."
(3) In Schedule 1 to that Act (distribution of business in High Court), for paragraph 3(b)(ii) there shall be substituted—
    (ii) the exercise of the inherent jurisdiction of the High Court with respect to minors, the maintenance of minors and any proceedings under the Children Act 1989, except proceedings solely for the appointment of a guardian of a minor's estate;".

The Armed Forces Act (c. 55)

46. In section 14 of the Armed Forces Act 1981 (temporary removal to, and detention in, place of safety abroad or in the United Kingdom of service children in need of care and control), in subsection (9A) for the words "the Children and Young Persons Act 1933, the Children and Young Persons Act 1969" there shall be substituted "the Children Act 1989."

The Civil Jurisdiction and Judgments Act 1982 (c. 27)

47. In paragraph 5(a) of Schedule 5 to the Civil Jurisdiction and Judgments Act 1982 (maintenance and similar payments excluded from Schedule 4 to that Act) for the words "section 47 or 51 of the Child Care Act 1980" there shall be substituted "paragraph 23 of Schedule 2 to the Children Act 1989."

The Mental Health Act 1983 (c. 20)

48.—(1) For section 27 of the Mental Health Act 1983 (children and young persons in care of local authority) there shall be substituted the following section—

"**Children and young persons in care**

27. Where—
    (a) a patient who is a child or young person is in the care of a local authority by virtue of a care order within the meaning of the Children Act 1989; or
    (b) the rights and powers of a parent of a patient who is a child or young person are vested in a local authority by virtue of section 16 of the Social Work (Scotland) Act 1968,
the authority shall be deemed to be the nearest relative of the patient in preference to any person except the patient's husband or wife (if any)."

(2) Section 28 of that Act (nearest relative of minor under guardianship, etc.) is amended as mentioned in sub-paragraphs (3) and (4).

(3) For subsection (1) there shall be substituted—

"(1) Where—
    (a) a guardian has been appointed for a person who has not attained the age of eighteen years; or
    (b) a residence order (as defined by section 8 of the Children Act 1989) is in force with respect to such a person,
the guardian (or guardians, where there is more than one) or the person named in the residence order shall, to the exclusion of any other person, be deemed to be his nearest relative."

(4) For subsection (3) there shall be substituted—

"(3) In this section 'guardian' does not include a guardian under this Part of this Act."

(5) In section 131(2) of that Act (informal admission of patients aged sixteen or over) for the words from "notwithstanding" to the end there shall be substituted "even though there are one or more persons who have parental responsibility for him (within the meaning of the Children Act 1989)."

The Registered Homes Act 1984 (c. 23)

49.—(1) In section 1(5) of the Registered Homes Act 1984 (requirement of registration) for paragraphs (d) and (e) there shall be substituted—

"(d) any community home, voluntary home or children's home within the meaning of the Children Act 1989."

(2) In section 39 of that Act (preliminary) for paragraphs (a) and (b) there shall be substituted—

"(a) the Children Act 1989."

The Mental Health (Scotland) Act 1984 (c. 36)

50. For section 54 of the Mental Health (Scotland) Act 1984 (children and young persons in care of local authority) there shall be substituted the following section—

"**Children and young persons in care of local authority**

54. Where—
    (a) the rights and powers of a parent of a patient who is a child or young person are vested in a local authority by virtue of section 16 of the Social Work (Scotland) Act 1968; or
    (b) a patient who is a child or young person is in the care of a local authority by virtue of a care order made under the Children Act 1989,
the authority shall be deemed to be the nearest relative of the patient in preference to any person except the patient's husband or wife (if any)."

The Matrimonial and Family Proceedings Act 1984 (c. 42)

51. In section 38(2)(b) of the Matrimonial and Family Proceedings Act 1984 (transfer of family proceedings from High Court to county court) after the words "a ward of court" there shall be inserted "or any other proceedings which relate to the exercise of the inherent jurisdiction of the High Court with respect to minors."

The Police and Criminal Evidence Act 1984 (c. 60)

52. In section 37(14) of the Police and Criminal Evidence Act 1984 (duties of custody officer before charge) after the words "Children and Young Persons Act 1969" there shall be inserted "or in Part IV of the Children Act 1989."
53. [Repealed by the Criminal Justice Act 1991, s.101(2), Sched. 13.]
(2) After that subsection there shall be inserted—
"(6A) [a new subs. 6A is substituted by the Criminal Justice Act 1991, s.59.]
(6B) Where an arrested juvenile is moved to local authority accommodation under subsection (6) above, it shall be lawful for any person acting on behalf of the authority to detain him."
(3) In subsection (8) of that section for the words "Children and Young Persons Act 1969" there shall be substituted "Children Act 1989."
54. In section 39(4) of that Act (responsibilities in relation to persons detained) for the words "transferred to the care of a local authority in pursuance of arrangements made" there shall be substituted "moved to local authority accommodation."
55. In Schedule 2 to that Act (preserved powers of arrest) in the entry relating to the Children and Young Persons Act 1969 for the words "Sections 28(2) and" there shall be substituted "Section."

The Surrogacy Arrangements Act 1985 (c. 49)

56. In section 1(2)(b) of the Surrogacy Arrangements Act 1985 (meaning of "surrogate mother," etc.) for the words "the parental rights being exercised" there shall be substituted "parental responsibility being met."

The Child Abduction and Custody Act 1985 (c. 60)

57.—(1) In section 9(a) and 20(2)(a) of the Child Abduction and Custody Act 1985 (orders with respect to which court's powers suspended), for the words "any other order under section 1(2) of the Children and Young Persons Act 1969" there shall be substituted "a supervision order under section 31 of the Children Act 1989."
(2) At the end of section 27 of that Act (interpretation), there shall be added—
"(4) In this Act a decision relating to rights of access in England and Wales means a decision as to the contact which a child may, or may not, have with any person."
(3) In Part I of Schedule 3 to that Act (orders in England and Wales which are custody orders for the purposes of the Act), for paragraph 1 there shall be substituted—
"1. The following are the orders referred to in section 27(1) of this Act—
  (a) a care order under the Children Act 1989 (as defined by section 31(11) of that Act, read with section 105(1) and Schedule 14);
  (b) a residence order (as defined by section 8 of the Act of 1989); and
  (c) any order made by a court in England and Wales under any of the following enactments—
    (i) section 9(1), 10(1)(a) or 11(a) of the Guardianship of Minors Act 1971;
    (ii) section 42(1) or (2) or 43(1) of the Matrimonial Causes Act 1973;
    (iii) section 2(2)(b), 4(b) or (5) of the Guardianship Act 1973 as applied by section 34(5) of the Children Act 1975;

(iv) section 8(2)(a), 10(1) or 19(1)(ii) of the Domestic Proceedings and Magistrates' Courts Act 1978;
(v) section 26(1)(b) of the Adoption Act 1976."

The Disabled Persons (Services, Consultation and Representation) Act 1986 (c. 33)

58. In section 1(3) of the Disabled Persons (Services, Consultation and Representation) Act 1986 (circumstances in which regulations may provide for the appointment of authorised representatives of disabled persons)—
   (a) in paragraph (a), for the words "parent or guardian of a disabled person under the age of sixteen" there shall be substituted—
      "(i) the parent of a disabled person under the age of sixteen, or
      (ii) any other person who is not a parent of his but who has parental responsibility for him"; and
   (b) in paragraph (b), for the words "in the care of" there shall be substituted "looked after by."

59.—(1) Section 2 of that Act (circumstances in which authorised representative has right to visit, etc., disabled person) shall be amended as follows.

(2) In subsection (3)(a) for the words from second "the" to "by" there shall be substituted "for the words 'if so requested by the disabled person' there shall be substituted 'if so requested by any person mentioned in section 1(3)(a)(i) or (ii).' "

(3) In subsection (5) after paragraph (b) there shall be inserted—
   "(bb) in accommodation provided by or on behalf of a local authority under Part III of the Children Act 1989, or."

(4) After paragraph (c) of subsection (5) there shall be inserted—
   "(cc) in accommodation provided by a voluntary organisation in accordance with arrangements made by a local authority under section 17 of the Children Act 1989, or."

60. In section 5(7)(b) of that Act (disabled persons leaving special education) for the word "guardian" there shall be substituted "other person who is not a parent of his but who has parental responsibility for him."

61.—(1) In section 16 of that Act (interpretation) in the definition of "disabled person," in paragraph (a) for the words from "means" to "applies" there shall be substituted "means—
   "(i) in the case of a person aged eighteen or over, a person to whom section 29 of the 1948 Act applies, and
   (ii) in the case of a person under the age of eighteen, a person who is disabled within the meaning of Part III of the Children Act 1989."

(2) After the definition of "parent" in that section there shall be inserted—
   " 'parental responsibility' has the same meaning as in the Children Act 1989."

(3) In the definition of "the welfare enactments" in that section, in paragraph (a) after the words "the 1977 Act" there shall be inserted "and Part III of the Children Act 1989."

(4) At the end of that section there shall be added—
   "(2) In this Act any reference to a child who is looked after by a local authority has the same meaning as in the Children Act 1989."

The Family Law Act 1986 (c. 55)

62.—(1) The Family Law Act 1986 shall be amended as follows.
(2) Subject to paragraphs 63 to 71, in Part I—
   (a) for the words "custody order," in each place where they occur, there shall be substituted "Part I order";
   (b) for the words "proceedings with respect to the custody of," in each place where they occur, there shall be substituted "Part I proceedings with respect to"; and
   (c) for the words "matters relating to the custody of," in each place where they occur, there shall be substituted "Part I matters relating to."
(3) For section 42(7) (general interpretation of Part I) there shall be substituted—
   "(7) In this Part—

(a) references to Part I proceedings in respect of a child are references to any proceedings for a Part I order or an order corresponding to a Part I order and include, in relation to proceedings outside the United Kingdom, reference to proceedings before a tribunal or other authority having power under the law having effect there to determine Part I matters; and
(b) references to Part I matters are references to matters that might be determined by a Part I order or an order corresponding to a Part I order."

63.—(1) In section 1 (orders to which Part I of the Act of 1986 applies), in subsection (1)—
    (a) for paragraph (a) there shall be substituted—
        "(a) a section 8 order made by a court in England and Wales under the Children Act 1989, other than an order varying or discharging such an order"; and
    (b) for paragraph (d) there shall be substituted the following paragraphs—
        "(d) an order made by a court in England and Wales in the exercise of the inherent jurisdiction of the High Court with respect to children—
            (i) so far as it gives care of a child to any person or provides for contact with, or the education of, a child; but
            (ii) excluding an order varying or revoking such an order;
        (e) an order made by the High Court in Northern Ireland in the exercise of its jurisdiction relating to wardship—
            (i) so far as it gives care and control of a child to any person or provides for the education of or access to a child; but
            (ii) excluding an order relating to a child of whom care or care and control is (immediately after the making of the order) vested in the Department of Health and Social Services or a Health and Social Services Board."

(2) In subsection (2) of that section, in paragraph (c) for "(d)" there shall be substituted "(e)."

(3) For subsections (3) to (5) of that section there shall be substituted—
"(3) In this Part, 'Part I order'—
    (a) includes any order which would have been a custody order by virtue of this section in any form in which it was in force at any time before its amendment by the Children Act 1989; and
    (b) (subject to sections 32 and 40 of this Act) excludes any order which would have been excluded from being a custody order by virtue of this section in any such form."

64. For section 2 there shall be substituted the following sections—

"**Jurisdiction: general**

2.—(1) A court in England and Wales shall not have jurisdiction to make a section 1(1)(a) order with respect to a child in or in connection with matrimonial proceedings in England and Wales unless the condition in section 2A of this Act is satisfied.

(2) A court in England and Wales shall not have jurisdiction to make a section 1(1)(a) order in a non-matrimonial case (that is to say, where the condition in section 2A of this Act is not satisfied) unless the condition in section 3 of this Act is satisfied.

(3) A court in England and Wales shall not have jurisdiction to make a section 1(1)(d) order unless—
    (a) the condition in section 3 of this Act is satisfied, or
    (b) the child concerned is present in England and Wales on the relevant date and the court considers that the immediate exercise of its powers is necessary for his protection.

Jurisdiction in or in connection with matrimonial proceedings

2A.—(1) The condition referred to in section 2(1) of this Act is that the matrimonial proceedings are proceedings in respect of the marriage of the parents of the child concerned and—

(a) the proceedings—
       (i) are proceedings for divorce or nullity of marriage; and
       (ii) are continuing;
   (b) the proceedings—
       (i) are proceedings for judicial separation,
       (ii) are continuing,
   and the jurisdiction of the court is not excluded by subsection (2) below; or
   (c) the proceedings have been dismissed after the beginning of the trial but—
       (i) the section 1(1)(a) order is being made forthwith, or
       (ii) the application for the order was made on or before the dismissal.

(2) For the purposes of subsection (1)(b) above, the jurisdiction of the court is excluded if, after the grant of a decree of judicial separation, on the relevant date, proceedings for divorce or nullity in respect of the marriage are continuing in Scotland or Northern Ireland.

(3) Subsection (2) above shall not apply if the court in which the other proceedings there referred to are continuing has made—
   (a) an order under section 13(6) or 21(5) of this Act (not being an order made by virtue of section 13(6)(a)(i)), or
   (b) an order under section 14(2) or 22(2) of this Act which is recorded as being made for the purpose of enabling Part I proceedings to be taken in England and Wales with respect to the child concerned.

(4) Where a court—
   (a) has jurisdiction to make a section 1(1)(a) order in or in connection with matrimonial proceedings, but
   (b) considers that it would be more appropriate for Part I matters relating to the child to be determined outside England and Wales,
the court may by order direct that, while the order under this subsection is in force, no section 1(1)(a) order shall be made by any court in or in connection with those proceedings."

65.—(1) In section 3 (habitual residence or presence of child concerned) in subsection (1) for "section 2" there shall be substituted "section 2(2)."

(2) In subsection (2) of that section for the words "proceedings for divorce, nullity or judicial separation" there shall be substituted "matrimonial proceedings."

66.—(1) In section 6 (duration and variation of Part I orders), for subsection (3) there shall be substituted the following subsections—

"(3) A court in England and Wales shall not have jurisdiction to vary a Part I order if, on the relevant date, matrimonial proceedings are continuing in Scotland or Northern Ireland in respect of the marriage of the parents of the child concerned.

(3A) Subsection (3) above shall not apply if—
   (a) the Part I order was made in or in connection with proceedings for divorce or nullity in England and Wales in respect of the marriage of the parents of the child concerned; and
   (b) those proceedings are continuing.

(3B) Subsection (3) above shall not apply if—
   (a) the Part I order was made in or in connection with proceedings for judicial separation in England and Wales;
   (b) those proceedings are continuing; and
   (c) the decree of judicial separation has not yet been granted."

(2) In subsection (5) of that section for the words from "variation of" to "if the ward" there shall be substituted "variation of a section 1(1)(d) order if the child concerned."

(3) For subsections (6) and (7) of that section there shall be substituted the following subsections—

"(6) Subsection (7) below applies where a Part I order which is—
   (a) a residence order (within the meaning of the Children Act 1989) in favour of a person with respect to a child,
   (b) an order made in the exercise of the High Court's inherent jurisdiction with respect to children by virtue of which a person has care of a child, or
   (c) an order—
       (i) of a kind mentioned in section 1(3)(a) of this Act,

(ii) under which a person is entitled to the actual possession of a child,

ceases to have effect in relation to that person by virtue of subsection (1) above.

(7) Where this subsection applies, any family assistance order made under section 16 of the Children Act 1989 with respect of the child shall also cease to have effect.

(8) For the purposes of subsection (7) above the reference to a family assistance order under section 16 of the Children Act 1989 shall be deemed to include a reference to an order for the supervision of a child made under—

(a) section 7(4) of the Family Law Reform Act 1969,
(b) section 44 of the Matrimonial Causes Act 1973,
(c) section 2(2)(a) of the Guardianship Act 1973,
(d) section 45(5) or 36(3)(b) of the Children Act 1975, or
(e) section 9 of the Domestic Proceedings and Magistrates' Courts Act 1978;

but this subsection shall cease to have effect once all such orders for the supervision of children have ceased to have effect in accordance with Schedule 14 to the Children Act 1989."

67. For section 7 (interpretation of Chapter II) there shall be substituted—

"Interpretation of Chapter II

7. In this Chapter—
(a) 'child' means a person who has not attained the age of eighteen;
(b) 'matrimonial proceedings' means proceedings for divorce, nullity of marriage or judicial separation;
(c) 'the relevant date' means, in relation to the making or variation of an order—
  (i) where an application is made for an order to be made or varied, the date of the application (or first application, if two or more are determined together), and
  (ii) where no such application is made, the date on which the court is considering whether to make or, as the case may be, vary the order; and
(d) 'section 1(1)(a) order' and 'section 1(1)(d) order' mean orders falling within section 1(1)(a) and (d) of this Act respectively."

68. In each of the following sections—
(a) section 11(2)(a) (provisions supplementary to sections 9 and 10),
(b) section 13(5)(a) (jurisdiction ancillary to matrimonial proceedings),
(c) section 20(3)(a) (habitual residence or presence of child),
(d) section 21(4)(a) (jurisdiction in divorce proceedings, etc.), and
(e) section 23(4)(a) (duration and variation of custody orders),

for "4(5)" there shall be substituted "2A(4)."

69. In each of the following sections—
(a) section 19(2) (jurisdiction in cases other than divorce, etc.),
(b) section 20(6) (habitual residence or presence of child), and
(c) section 23(5) (duration and variation of custody orders), for "section 1(1)(d)" there shall be substituted "section 1(1)(e)."

70. In section 34(3) (power to order recovery of child) for paragraph (a) there shall be substituted—

"(a) section 14 of the Children Act 1989."

71.—(1) In section 42 (general interpretation of Part I), in subsection (4)(a) for the words "has been boarded out with those parties" there shall be substituted "is placed with those parties as foster parents."

(2) In subsection (6) of that section, in paragraph (a) after the word "person" there shall be inserted "to be allowed contact with or."

The Local Government Act 1988 (c. 9)

72. In Schedule 1 to the Local Government Act 1988 (competition) at the end of paragraph 2(4) (cleaning of buildings: buildings to which competition provisions do not apply) for paragraph (c) there shall be substituted—

"(c) section 53 of the Children Act 1989."

Amendments of local Acts

73.—(1) Section 16 of the Greater London Council (General Powers) Act 1981 (exemption from provisions of Part IV of the Act of certain premises) shall be amended as follows.
(2) After paragraph (g) there shall be inserted—
"(gg) used as a children's home as defined in section 63 of the Children Act 1989."
(3) In paragraph (h)—
  (a) for the words "section 56 of the Child Care Act 1980" there shall be substituted "section 60 of the Children Act 1989";
  (b) for the words "section 57" there shall be substituted "section 60"; and
  (c) for the words "section 32" there shall be substituted "section 53."
(4) In paragraph (i), for the words "section 8 of the Foster Children Act 1980" there shall be substituted "section 67 of the Children Act 1989."

74.—(1) Section 10(2) of the Greater London Council (General Powers) Act 1984 (exemption from provisions of Part IV of the Act of certain premises) shall be amended as follows.
(2) In paragraph (d)—
  (a) for the words "section 56 of the Child Care Act 1980" there shall be substituted "section 60 of the Children Act 1989";
  (b) for the words "section 57" there shall be substituted "section 60"; and
  (c) for the words "section 31" there shall be substituted "section 53."
(3) In paragraph (e), for the words "section 8 of the Foster Children Act 1980" there shall be substituted "section 67 of the Children Act 1989."
(4) In paragraph (1) for the words "section 1 of the Children's Homes Act 1982" there shall be substituted "section 63 of the Children Act 1989."

Section 108(6)

SCHEDULE 14

TRANSITIONALS AND SAVINGS

Pending proceedings, etc.

1.—(1) [Subject to sub-paragraphs 1A and (4)], nothing in any provision of this Act (other than the repeals mentioned in sub-paragraph (2)) shall affect any proceedings which are pending immediately before the commencement of that provision.
[(1A) Proceedings pursuant to section 7(2) of the Family Law Reform Act 1969 (committal of wards of court to care of local authority) or in the exercise of the High Court's inherent jurisdiction with respect to children which are pending in relation to a child who has been placed or allowed to remain in the care of a local authority shall not be treated as pending proceedings after 13th October 1992 for the purposes of this Schedule if no final order has been made by that date pursuant to section 7(2) of the 1969 Act or in the exercise of the High Court's inherent jurisdiction in respect of the child's care.]
(2) The repeals are those of—
  (a) section 42(3) of the Matrimonial Causes Act 1973 (declaration by court that party to marriage unfit to have custody of children of family); and
  (b) section 38 of the Sexual Offences Act 1956 (power of court to divest person of authority over girl or boy in cases of incest).
(3) For the purposes of the following provisions of this Schedule, any reference to an order in force immediately before the commencement of a provision of this Act shall be construed as including a reference to an order made after that commencement in proceedings pending before that commencement.
(4) Sub-paragraph (3) is not to be read as making the order in question have effect from a date earlier than that on which it was made.
(5) An order under section 96(3) may make such provision with respect to the application of the order in relation to proceedings which are pending when the order comes into force as the Lord Chancellor considers appropriate.

2. Where, immediately before the day on which Part IV comes into force, there was in force an order under section 3(1) of the Children and Young Persons Act 1963 (order directing a local authority to bring a child or young person before a [youth court] under section 1 of the Children and Young Persons Act 1969), the order shall cease to have effect on that day.

AMENDMENTS

The amendments to this paragraph were made by the Children Act 1989 (Commencement No. 2—Amendment and Transitional Provisions) Order 1991 (S.I. 1991 No. 1990), Sched., para. 1 and the Criminal Justice Act 1991, Sched. 11, para. 40.

GENERAL NOTE

Where proceedings are pending they continue under the pre-Children Act 1989 law. Private law orders made under "old" proceedings will be existing orders (see paras. 5–11) below. Provision is made for public orders in paragraphs 15 (deemed care orders), 18 (access to children in care), 25 and 26 (supervision orders). It will not be possible to have declarations of unfitness made in pending proceedings (para. 1(2))—the power to make these declarations is removed and existing declarations cease to have effect (para. 3). Directions to the local authority to bring care proceedings also ceased to have effect on October 14, 1991 (para. 2) (see also notes to s.31 above).

Sub-para. 1(A)

The use of wardship by local authorities is virtually ended by section 100 and public law wardships are not allowed to continue indefinitely (paras. 1(1A), 16 and 16A). If a child is committed to care under F.L.R.A. 1969, s.7(2), or the inherent jurisdiction, the order is a deemed care order (para. 15(2)) unless proceedings are pending. If proceedings are pending because there has been no final hearing or an application has been made to vary directions, *e.g.* for access (*Re C (A Minor)*) [1992] 1 F.C.R. 169) the child remains a ward of court until October 13, 1992 or a final order is made (if earlier) (para. 1(1A)). Thereafter the child will be subject to a deemed care order (paras. 15, 16(3A)) but existing directions continue (para. 16(5)). Directions relating to secure accommodation cease to operate after April 13, 1992 (para. 16(5)). Applications to vary directions, or which have the effect of varying directions should be made to the High Court because it gave the directions (*Re C* (above) and the Allocation of Proceedings Order 1991 (S.I. 1991 No. 1677)).

CUSTODY ORDERS ETC.

Cessation of declarations of unfitness, etc.

3. Where, immediately before the day on which Parts I and II come into force, there was in force—
    (a) a declaration under section 42(3) of the Matrimonial Causes Act 1973 (declaration by court that party to marriage unfit to have custody of children of family); or
    (b) an order under section 38(1) of the Sexual Offences Act 1956 divesting a person of authority over a girl or boy in a case of incest;
the declaration or, as the case may be, the order shall cease to have effect on that day.

The Family Law Reform Act 1987 (c. 42)

Conversion of orders under section 4

4. Where, immediately before the day on which Parts I and II come into force, there was in force an order under section 4(1) of the Family Law Reform Act 1987 (order

giving father parental rights and duties in relation to a child), then, on and after that day, the order shall be deemed to be an order under section 4 of this Act giving the father parental responsibility for the child.

GENERAL NOTE

Orders to unmarried fathers made under F.L.R.A. 1987, s.4, are deemed to be orders under section 4 of this Act. The unmarried father therefore has parental responsibility which can only be removed by a further order under section 4 or the child's adoption.

Orders to which paragraphs 6 to 11 apply

5.—(1) In paragraphs 6 to 11 "an existing order" means any order which—
    (a) is in force immediately before the commencement of Parts I and II;
    (b) was made under any enactment mentioned in sub-paragraph (2);
    (c) determines all or any of the following—
        (i) who is to have custody of a child;
        (ii) who is to have care and control of a child;
        (iii) who is to have access to a child;
        (iv) any matter with respect to a child's education or upbringing; and;
    (d) is not an order of a kind mentioned in paragraph 15(1).
(2) The enactments are—
    (a) the Domestic Proceedings and Magistrates' Courts Act 1978;
    (b) the Children Act 1975;
    (c) the Matrimonial Causes Act 1973;
    (d) the Guardianship of Minors Acts 1971 and 1973;
    (e) the Matrimonial Causes Act 1965;
    (f) the Matrimonial Proceedings (Magistrates' Courts) Act 1960.
(3) For the purposes of this paragraph and paragraphs 6 to 11 "custody" includes legal custody and joint as well as sole custody but does not include access.

DEFINITIONS

"custody": Sched. 14, para. 5(3).
"existing order": Sched. 14, para. 5(1).

GENERAL NOTE

See below for explanations of the transitional provisions relating to these private law orders.

Parental responsibility of parents

6.—(1) Where—
    (a) a child's father and mother were married to each other at the time of his birth; and
    (b) there is an existing order with respect to the child,
each parent shall have parental responsibility for the child in accordance with section 2 as modified by sub-paragraph (3).
(2) Where—
    (a) a child's father and mother were not married to each other at the time of his birth; and
    (b) there is an existing order with respect to the child,
section 2 shall apply as modified by sub-paragraphs (3) and (4).
(3) The modification is that for section 2(8) there shall be substituted—
    "(8) The fact that a person has parental responsibility for a child does not entitle him to act in a way which would be incompatible with any existing order or any order made under this Act with respect to the child."
(4) The modifications are that—

(a) for the purposes of section 2(2), where the father has custody or care and control of the child by virtue of any existing order, the court shall be deemed to have made (at the commencement of that section) an order under section 4(1) giving him parental responsibility for the child; and

(b) where by virtue of paragraph (a) a court is deemed to have made an order under section 4(1) in favour of a father who has care and control of a child by virtue of an existing order, the court shall not bring the order under section 4(1) to an end at any time while he has care and control of the child by virtue of the order.

DEFINITIONS

"custody order": Sched. 14, para. 5(3).
"existing order": Sched. 14, para. 5(1).

GENERAL NOTE

Existing orders are brought into line with the provisions of the Act relating to parental responsibility. Despite existing orders for custody, etc., both a child's parents will have parental responsibility and the powers in section 2 but neither can exercise it in a way which is incompatible with the order (para. 6(3)). If the parents were not married the father does not have parental responsibility unless he has been granted it by the courts. Orders for custody or care and control operate as if an order under section 4 of this Act had also been made. This gives the man parental responsibility which cannot be removed while the custody, etc., order remains (para. 6(4)).

Persons who are not parents but who have custody or care and control

7.—(1) Where a person who is not the parent or guardian of a child has custody or care and control of him by virtue of an existing order, that person shall have parental responsibility for him so long as he continues to have that custody or care and control by virtue of the order.

(2) Where sub-paragraph (1) applies, [Parts I and II and paragraph 15 of Schedule 1] shall have effect as modified by this paragraph.

(3) The modifications are that—

(a) for section 2(8) there shall be substituted—

"(8) The fact that a person has parental responsibility for a child does not entitle him to act in a way which would be incompatible with any existing order or with any order made under this Act with respect to the child";

(b) at the end of section 10(4) there shall be inserted—

"(c) any person who has custody or care and control of a child by virtue of any existing order"; and

(c) at the end of section 34(1)(c) there shall be inserted—

"(cc) where immediately before the care order was made there was an existing order by virtue of which a person had custody or care and control of the child, that person."

[(d) for paragraph 15 of Schedule 1 there shall be substituted—

"15. Where a child lives with a person as the result of a custodianship order within the meaning of section 33 of the Children Act 1975, a local authority may make contributions to that person towards the cost of the accommodation and maintenance of the child so long as that person continues to have legal custody of that child by virtue of the order.]

AMENDMENTS

The amendments to this paragraph were made by the Children Act 1989 (Commencement No. 2—Amendment and Transitional Provisions) Order 1991 (S.I. 1991 No. 1990).

DEFINITIONS
"custody": Sched. 14, para. 5(3).
"existing order": Sched. 14, para. 5(1).
"residence order": s.8(1).

GENERAL NOTE
Existing orders in favour of people who are neither parents nor guardians operate like residence orders. People with such orders have parental responsibility (para. 7(1)), may apply for any section 8 order (s.10(4) as modified) and obtain financial support under Schedule 1. No one may act incompatibly with the order (s.2(8) as modified).

Persons who have care and control

8.—(1) Sub-paragraphs (2) to (6) apply where a person has care and control of a child by virtue of an existing order, but they shall cease to apply when that order ceases to have effect.
(2) Section 5 shall have effect as if—
  (a) for any reference to a residence order in favour of a parent or guardian there were substituted a reference to any existing order by virtue of which the parent or guardian has care and control of the child; and
  (b) for subsection (9) there were substituted—
"(9) Subsections (1) and (7) do not apply if the existing order referred to in paragraph (b) of those subsections was one by virtue of which a surviving parent of the child also had care and control of him."
(3) Section 10 shall have effect as if for subsection (5)(c)(i) there were substituted—
  "(i) in any case where by virtue of an existing order any person or persons has or have care and control of the child, has the consent of that person or each of those persons."
(4) Section 20 shall have effect as if for subsection (9)(a) there were substituted "who has care and control of the child by virtue of an existing order."
(5) Section 23 shall have effect as if for subsection (4)(c) there were substituted—
  "(c) where the child is in care and immediately before the care order was made there was an existing order by virtue of which a person had care and control of the child, that person."
(6) In Schedule 1, paragraphs 1(1) and 14(1) shall have effect as if for the words "in whose favour a residence order is in force with respect to the child" there were substituted "who has been given care and control of the child by virtue of an existing order."

DEFINITIONS
"custody": Sched. 14, para. 5(3).
"existing order": Sched. 14, para. 5(1).
"residence order": s.8(1).

GENERAL NOTE
This paragraph brings orders for care and control into line with residence orders for the purpose of the appointment of guardians under section 5 (paras. 8(1)(2)); giving consent to applications for residence and contact orders (para. 8(3)) and restrictions on the right to remove children from local authority accommodation (para. 8(4)). Paragraph 8(5) extends the restrictions on placement of children in care to such people, S.I. 1991 No. 893 applies (see s.23 above). Paragraph 8(6) relates to applications for financial support by such people.

Persons who have access

9.—(1) Sub-paragraphs (2) to (4) apply where a person has access by virtue of an existing order.

(2) Section 10 shall have effect as if after subsection (5) there were inserted—
"(5A) Any person who has access to a child by virtue of an existing order is entitled to apply for a contact order."
(3) Section 16(2) shall have effect as if after paragraph (b) there were inserted—
"(bb) any person who has access to the child by virtue of an existing order."
(4) Sections 43(11), 44(13) and 46(10), shall have effect as if in each case after paragraph (d) there were inserted—
"(dd) any person who has been given access to him by virtue of an existing order."

DEFINITIONS
"contact order": s.8(1).
"existing order": Sched. 14, para. 5(3).

GENERAL NOTE
This provision brings existing access orders into line with contact orders under the Act.

Enforcement of certain existing orders

10.—(1) Sub-paragraph (2) applies in relation to any existing order which, but for the repeal by this Act of—
(a) section 13(1) of the Guardianship of Minors Act 1971;
(b) section 43(1) of the Children Act 1975; or
(c) section 33 of the Domestic Proceedings and Magistrates' Courts Act 1978, (provisions concerning the enforcement of custody orders) might have been enforced as if it were an order requiring a person to give up a child to another person.
(2) Where this sub-paragraph applies, the existing order may, after the repeal of the enactments mentioned in sub-paragraph (1)(a) to (c), be enforced under section 14 as if—
(a) any reference to a residence order were a reference to the existing order; and
(b) any reference to a person in whose favour the residence order is in force were a reference to a person to whom actual custody of the child is given by an existing order which is in force.
(3) In sub-paragraph (2) "actual custody," in relation to a child, means the actual possession of his person.

DEFINITIONS
"actual custody": Sched. 14, para. 10(3).
"custody order": Sched. 14, para. 5(3).
"existing order": Sched. 14, para. 5(1).
"residence order": s.8(1).

GENERAL NOTE
This provision allows existing custody, etc. orders to be enforced as residence orders see notes to section 14 above.

Discharge of existing orders

11.—(1) The making of a residence order or a care order with respect to a child who is the subject of an existing order discharges the existing order.
(2) Where the court makes any section 8 order (other than a residence order) with respect to a child with respect to whom any existing order is in force, the existing order shall have effect subject to the section 8 order.

(3) The court may discharge an existing order which is in force with respect to a child—
- (a) in any family proceedings relating to the child or in which any question arises with respect to the child's welfare; or
- (b) on the application of—
  - (i) any parent or guardian of the child;
  - (ii) the child himself; or
  - (iii) any person named in the order.

(4) A child may not apply for the discharge of an existing order except with the leave of the court.

(5) The power in sub-paragraph (3) to discharge an existing order includes the power to discharge any part of the order.

(6) In considering whether to discharge an order under the power conferred by sub-paragraph (3) the court shall, if the discharge of the order is opposed by any party to the proceedings, have regard in particular to the matters mentioned in section 1(3).

DEFINITIONS

"care order": s.31(11).
"existing order": Sched. 14, para. 5(1).
"family proceedings": s.8(3).
"section 8 order": s.8(1).
"residence order": s.8(1).

GENERAL NOTE

Existing orders may be ended in the following ways:
making a care or residence order,
on application by those listed in para. 11(3), and
by the court in any family proceedings.
If the discharge application is opposed the court must have regard to the checklist in s.1(3).

GUARDIANS

Existing guardians to be guardians under this Act

12.—(1) Any appointment of a person as guardian of a child which—
- (a) was made—is
  - (i) under section 3 to 5 of the Guardianship of Minors Act 1971;
  - (ii) under section 38(3) of the Sexual Offences Act 1956; or
  - (iii) under the High Court's inherent jurisdiction with respect to children; and
- (b) has taken effect before the commencement of section 5,

shall (subject to sub-paragraph (2)) be deemed, on and after the commencement of section 5, to be an appointment made and having effect under that section.

(2) Where an appointment of a person as guardian of a child has effect under section 5 by virtue of sub-paragraph (1)(a)(ii), the appointment shall not have effect for a period which is longer than any period specified in the order.

Appointment of guardian not yet in effect

13. Any appointment of a person to be a guardian of a child—
- (a) which was made as mentioned in paragraph 12(1)(a)(i); but
- (b) which, immediately before the commencement of section 5, had not taken effect,

shall take effect in accordance with section 5 (as modified, where it applies, by paragraph 8(2)).

Persons deemed to be appointed as guardians under existing wills

14. For the purposes of the Wills Act 1837 and of this Act any disposition by will and testament or devise of the custody and tuition of any child, made before the commencement of section 5 and paragraph 1 of Schedule 13, shall be deemed to be an appointment by will of a guardian of the child.

GENERAL NOTE

References in paragraphs 12–14 to the commencement of section 5 should be construed as references to the commencement of section 5(1)–(10) and (13) (S.I. 1991 No. 1990, Sched. para. 1C).

Existing appointments of guardians which have taken effect continue (para. 12). Appointments made before the Act will only take effect on the death of the appointer and any surviving parent or guardian (subject to the provisions relating to residence orders or existing orders see s.5 and Sched. 14, para. 8(2)).

CHILDREN IN CARE

Children in compulsory care

15.—(1) Sub-paragraph (2) applies where, immediately before the day on which Part IV comes into force, a person was—
    (a) in care by virtue of—
        (i) a care order under section 1 of the Children and Young Persons Act 1969;
        (ii) a care order under section 15 of that Act, on discharging a supervision order made under section 1 of that Act; or
        (iii) an order or authorisation under section 25 or 26 of that Act;
    (b) [...]
    (c) in care—
        (i) under section 2 of the Child Care Act 1980; or
        (ii) by virtue of paragraph 1 of Schedule 4 to that Act (which extends the meaning of a child in care under section 2 to include children in care under section 1 of the Children Act 1948),
    and a child in respect of whom a resolution under section 3 of the Act of 1980 or section 2 of the Act of 1948 was in force;
    (d) a child in respect of whom a resolution had been passed under section 65 of the Child Care Act 1980;
    (e) in care by virtue of an order under—
        (i) section 2(1)(e) of the Matrimonial Proceedings (Magistrates' Courts) Act 1960;
        (ii) section 7(2) of the Family Law Reform Act 1969;
        (iii) section 43(1) of the Matrimonial Causes Act 1973; or
        (iv) section 2(2)(b) of the Guardianship Act 1973;
        (v) section 10 of the Domestic Proceedings and Magistrates' Courts Act 1978,
    (orders having effect for certain purposes as if the child had been received into care under section 2 of the Child Care Act 1980);
    (f) in care by virtue of an order made, on the revocation of a custodianship order, under section 36 of the Children Act 1975; [...]
    (g) in care by virtue of an order made, on the refusal of an adoption order, under section 26 of the Adoption Act 1976 or any order having effect (by virtue of paragraph 1 of Schedule 2 to that Act) as if made under that section [; or—
    (h) in care by virtue of an order of the court made in exercise by the High Court's inherent jurisdiction with respect to children]

(2) Where this sub-paragraph applies, then, on and after the day on which Part IV commences—
    (a) the order or resolution in question shall be deemed to be a care order;

(b) the authority in whose care the person was immediately before that commencement shall be deemed to be the authority designated in that deemed care order; and

(c) any reference to a child in the care of a local authority shall include a reference to a person who is the subject of such a deemed care order,

and the provisions of this Act shall apply accordingly, subject to paragraph 16.

AMENDMENT

In this paragraph the words omitted were repealed, and the words in square brackets were added by the Courts and Legal Services Act 1990, ss.116, 125(7), Sched. 16, para. 33, Sched. 20, and by the Armed Forces Act 1991, s.26 and Sched. 3.

Modifications

16.—(1) Sub-paragraph (2) only applies where a person who is the subject of a care order by virtue of paragraph 15(2) is a person falling within sub-paragraph (1)(a) [...] of that paragraph.

(2) Where the person would otherwise have remained in care until reaching the age of nineteen, by virtue of—

(a) section 20(3)(a) or 21(1) of the Children and Young Persons Act 1969; or

(b) [repealed by the Armed Forces Act 1991, s.26 and Sched. 3]

This Act applies as if section 91(12) for the word "eighteen" there were substituted "nineteen."

(3) [repealed by the Armed Forces Act 1991, s.26 and Sched. 3]

[(3A) Where in respect of a child who has been placed or allowed to remain in the care of a local authority pursuant to section 7(2) of the Family Law Reform Act 1969 or in the exercise of the High Court's inherent jurisdiction and the child is still in the care of a local authority, proceedings have ceased by virtue of paragraph 1(1A) to be treated as pending, paragraph 15(2) shall apply on 14th October 1992 as if the child was in care pursuant to an order as specified in paragraph 15(1)(e)(ii) or (h) as the case may be.]

(4) [Sub-paragraphs (5) and (6) only apply] where a child who is the subject of a care order by virtue of paragraph 15(2) is a person falling within sub-paragraph (1)(e) to (g) of that paragraph.

(5) [Subject to sub-paragraph (6)] where a court, on making the order, or at any time thereafter, gave directions—

[(a) under section 4(4)(a) of the Guardianship Act 1973;

(b) under section 43(5)(a) of the Matrimonial Causes Act 1973; or

(c) in the exercise of the High Court's inherent jurisdiction with respect to children.]

as to the exercise by the authority of any powers, those directions shall [, subject to the provisions of section 25 of this Act and any regulations made under that section], continue to have effect (regardless of any conflicting provision in this Act) [other than section 25] until varied or discharged by a court under this sub-paragraph.

[(6) Where directions referred to in sub-paragraph (5) are to the effect that a child be placed in accommodation provided for the purpose of restricting liberty then the directions shall cease to have effect upon the expiry of the maximum period specified by regulations under section 25(2)(a) in relation to children of his description, calculated from October 14, 1991.]

AMENDMENTS

The amendments to this paragraph were made by the Children Act 1989 (Commencement and Transitional Provisions) Order 1991 (S.I. 1991 No. 828), art. 4, Sched.; the Courts and Legal Services Act 1990, s.116, Sched. 16, para. 33; the Children Act 1989 (Commencement No. 2—Amendment and Transitional Provisions) Order 1991 (S.I. 1991 No. 1990), Sched. and by the Armed Forces Act 1991, s.26, Sched. 3.

GENERAL NOTE

The orders, etc., listed in paragraph 15(1) are deemed care orders and therefore operate as orders made under section 31 above but subject to the modifications listed in paragraph 16. Such care orders can be discharged by an application under section 39 or for a residence order (s.91). Care orders made under C.Y.P.A. 1969 which would have lasted until the child reached 19 continue to do so (para. 16(2)). Directions, *e.g.* about contact made in the guardianship, matrimonial or inherent jurisdiction continue to operate and can be varied or discharged by the Court. These applications should be made to court which gave the direction, *Re C (A Minor)* [1992] 1 F.C.R. 169, C.A. For an explanation of the position relating to wardship and the inherent jurisdiction, see notes to paragraph 1 above.

[Cessation of wardship where ward in care

16A.—[(1) Where a child who is a ward of court is in care by virtue of—
    (a)   an order under section 7(2) of the Family Law Reform Act 1969; or
    (b)   an order made in the exercise of the High Court's inherent jurisdiction with respect to children,
he shall, on the day on which Part IV commences, cease to be a ward of court.]

[(2) Where immediately before the day on which Part IV commences a child was in the care of a local authority and as the result of an order—
    (a)   pursuant to section 7(2) of the Family Law Reform Act 1969;
    (b)   made in the exercise of the High Court's inherent jurisdiction with respect to children,
continued to be in the care of a local authority and was made a ward of court, he shall on the day on which Part IV commences, cease to be a ward of court.

(3) Sub-paragraphs (1) and (2) do not apply in proceedings which are pending.]

AMENDMENT

This paragraph was inserted by the Courts and Legal Services Act 1990, s.116, Sched. 16, para. 33. Sub-paras. (2) and (3) were inserted by the Children Act 1989 (Commencement No. 2—Amendment and Transitional Provisions) Order 1991, Sched., para. 2.

GENERAL NOTE

See notes to paragraph 1 above.

Children placed with parent, etc., while in compulsory care

17.—(1) This paragraph applies where a child is deemed by paragraph 15 to be in the care of a local authority under an order or resolution which is deemed by that paragraph to be a care order.

(2) If, immediately before the day on which Part III comes into force, the child was allowed to be under the charge and control of—
    (a)   a parent or guardian under section 21(2) of the Child Care Act 1980; or
    (b)   a person who, before the child was in the authority's care, had care and control of the child by virtue of an order falling within paragraph 5,
on and after that day the provision made by and under section 23(5) shall apply as if the child had been placed with the person in question in accordance with that provision.

GENERAL NOTE

Section 23(5) requires the placement of children in care with parents, guardians and those who had parental responsibility before the care order was made to comply with the Placement of Children and Parents, etc., Regulations 1991 (S.I. 1991 No. 893). This provision deems the placement to comply with those regulations.

Orders for access to children in compulsory care

18.—(1) This paragraph applies to any access order—
    (a) made under section 12C of the Child Care Act 1980 (access orders with respect to children in care of local authorities); and
    (b) in force immediately before the commencement of Part IV.

(2) On and after the commencement of Part IV, the access order shall have effect as an order made under section 34 in favour of the person named in the order.

[18A.—(1) This paragraph applies to any decision of a local authority to terminate arrangements for access or to refuse to make such arrangements—
    (a) of which notice has been given under, and in accordance with, section 12B of the Child Care Act 1980 (termination of access); and
    (b) which is in force immediately before the commencement of Part IV.

(2) On and after the commencement of Part IV, a decision to which this paragraph applies shall have effect as a court order made under section 34(4) authorising the local authority to refuse to allow contact between the child and the person to whom notice was given under section 12B of the Child Care Act 1980.]

AMENDMENT

This paragraph was inserted by the Children Act 1989 (Commencement and Transitional Provisions) Order 1991 (S.I. 1991 No. 828), art. 4, Sched.

19.—(1) This paragraph applies where, immediately before the commencement of Part IV, an access order made under section 12C of the Act of 1980 was suspended by virtue of an order made under section 12E of that Act (suspension of access orders in emergencies).

(2) The suspending order shall continue to have effect as if this Act had not been passed.

(3) If—
    (a) before the commencement of Part IV; and
    (b) during the period for which the operation of the access order is suspended, the local authority concerned made an application for its variation or discharge to an appropriate juvenile court, its operation shall be suspended until the date on which the application to vary or discharge it is determined or abandoned.

GENERAL NOTE

Access orders under C.C.A. 1980, s.12C, are deemed to be orders under section 34 and can thus be varied, etc., under that section. Terminations of access under C.C.A. 1980, s.12B, operate as orders terminating contact under section 34(4). Suspensions of access under C.C.A. 1980, s.12E, continue as if the 1989 Act had not been passed. The new provisions are far less restrictive than the old ones; the approach to contact is intended to be more positive so it may be possible for those whose access has been terminated to regain it (see notes to s.34). The limitations in section 91(17) should not restrict an application under section 34 in relation to a case within paragraphs 18–19 because no previous application has been made under section 34.

Children in voluntary care

20.—(1) This paragraph applies where, immediately before the day on which Part III comes into force—
    (a) a child was in the care of a local authority—
        (i)   under section 2(1) of the Child Care Act 1980; or
        (ii) by virtue of paragraph 1 of Schedule 4 to that Act (which extends the meaning of references to children in care under section 2 to include reference to children in care under section 1 of the Children Act 1948); and

(b) he was not a person in respect of whom a resolution under section 3 of the Act of 1980 or section 2 of the Act of 1948 was in force.

(2) Where this paragraph applies, the child shall, on and after the day mentioned in sub-paragraph (1), be treated for the purposes of this Act as a child who is provided with accommodation by the local authority under Part III, but he shall cease to be so treated once he ceases to be so accommodated in accordance with the provisions of Part III.

(3) Where—
    (a) this paragraph applies; and
    (b) the child, immediately before the day mentioned in sub-paragraph (1), was (by virtue of section 21(2) of the Act of 1980) under the charge and control of a person falling within paragraph 17(2)(a) or (b),

the child shall not be treated for the purposes of this Act as if he were being looked after by the authority concerned.

GENERAL NOTE

Children in voluntary care became accommodated under Part III on October 14, 1991. The local authority therefore owed them all the duties it owes to children it is looking after, see notes to sections 20, 22–24.

Boarded out children

21.—(1) Where, immediately before the day on which Part III comes into force, a child in the care of a local authority—
    (a) was—
        (i) boarded out with a person under section 21(1)(a) of the Child Care Act 1980; or
        (ii) placed under the charge and control of a person, under section 21(2) of that Act; and
    (b) the person with whom he was boarded out, or (as the case may be) placed, was not a person falling within paragraph 17(2)(a) or (b),

on and after that day, he shall be treated (subject to sub-paragraph (2)) as having been placed with a local authority foster parent and shall cease to be so treated when he ceases to be placed with that person in accordance with the provisions of this Act.

(2) Regulations made under section 23(2)(a) shall not apply in relation to a person who is a local authority foster parent by virtue of sub-paragraph (1) before the end of the period of twelve months beginning with the day on which Part III comes into force and accordingly that person shall for that period be subject—
    (a) in a case falling within sub-paragraph (1)(a)(i), to terms and regulations mentioned in section 21(1)(a) of the Act of 1980; and
    (b) in a case falling within sub-paragraph (1)(a)(ii), to terms fixed under section 21(2) of that Act and regulations made under section 22A of that Act,

as if that Act had not been repealed by this Act.

GENERAL NOTE

Placements of children in care (voluntary or compulsory) with foster parents had to comply with the Boarding-Out Regulations 1988. Placements with family members had to comply with the Charge and Control Regulations 1988. There are new regulations, the Foster Placement (Children) Regulations 1991 (S.I. 1991 No. 910), see section 23. These will apply from October 14, 1992 for existing placements. Until then the existing regulations will apply. New placements will be subject to the new regulations.

Children in care to qualify for advice and assistance

22. Any reference in Part III to a person qualifying for advice and assistance shall be construed as including a reference to a person within the area of the local authority in

question who is under twenty-one and who was, at any time after reaching the age of sixteen but while still a child—
  (a) a person falling within—
    (i) any of paragraphs (a) to [(h)] of paragraph 15(1); or
    (ii) paragraph 20(1); or
  (b) the subject of a criminal care order (within the meaning of paragraph 36).

AMENDMENT
The amendment to this paragraph was made by the Courts and Legal Services Act 1990, s.116, Sched. 16, para. 33.

GENERAL NOTE
Children subject to deemed care orders, accommodated having been received into voluntary care or subject to criminal care orders benefit from the aftercare provisions in section 24.

Emigration of children in care

23. Where—
  (a) the Secretary of State has received a request in writing from a local authority that he give his consent under section 24 of the Child Care Act 1980 to the emigration of a child in their care; but
  (b) immediately before the repeal of the Act of 1980 by this Act, he has not determined whether or not to give his consent,
section 24 of the Act of 1980 shall continue to apply (regardless of that repeal) until the Secretary of State has determined whether or not to give his consent to the request.

Contributions for maintenance of children in care

24.—(1) Where, immediately before the day on which Part III of Schedule 2 comes into force, there was in force an order made (or having effect as if made) under any of the enactments mentioned in sub-paragraph (2), then, on and after that day—
  (a) the order shall have effect as if made under paragraph 23(2) of Schedule 2 against a person liable to contribute; and
  (b) Part III of Schedule 2 shall apply to the order, subject to the modifications in sub-paragraph (3).
(2) The enactments are—
  (a) section 11(4) of the Domestic Proceedings and Magistrates' Courts Act 1978;
  (b) section 26(2) of the Adoption Act 1976;
  (c) section 36(5) of the Children Act 1975;
  (d) section 2(3) of the Guardianship Act 1973;
  (e) section 2(1)(h) of the Matrimonial Proceedings (Magistrates' Courts) Act 1960,
(provisions empowering the court to make an order requiring a person to make periodical payments to a local authority in respect of a child in care).
(3) The modifications are that, in paragraph 23 of Schedule 2—
  (a) in sub-paragraph (4), paragraph (a) shall be omitted;
  (b) for sub-paragraph (6) there shall be substituted—
"(6) Where—
    (a) a contribution order is in force;
    (b) the authority serve a contribution notice under paragraph 22; and
    (c) the contributor and the authority reach an agreement under paragraph 22(7) in respect of the contribution notice,
the effect of the agreement shall be to discharge the order from the date on which it is agreed that the agreement shall take effect"; and
  (d) at the end of sub-paragraph (10) there shall be inserted—

"and
(e) where the order is against a person who is not a parent of the child, shall be made with due regard to—
  (i) whether that person had assumed responsibility for the maintenance of the child, and, if so, the extent to which and basis on which he assumed that responsibility and the length of the period during which he met that responsibility;
  (ii) whether he did so knowing that the child was not his child;
  (iii) the liability of any other person to maintain the child."

GENERAL NOTE

This paragraph converts orders for the maintenance of children in care listed in paragraph 24(2) to contribution orders within Schedule 2, paragraph 23(2). Although no provisions are set out for payments under C.C.A. 1980, s.47, existing orders will continue unaffected.

SUPERVISION ORDERS

Orders under section 1(3)(b) or 21(2) of the 1969 Act

25.—(1) This paragraph applies to any supervision order—
  (a) made—
   (i) under section 1(3)(b) of the Children and Young Persons Act 1969; or
   (ii) under section 21(2) of that Act on the discharge of a care order made under section 1(3)(c) of that Act; and
  (b) in force immediately before the commencement of Part IV.

(2) On and after the commencement of Part IV, the order shall be deemed to be a supervision order made under section 31 and—
  (a) any requirement of the order that the child reside with a named individual shall continue to have effect while the order remains in force, unless the court otherwise directs;
  (b) any other requirement, imposed by the court, or directions given by the supervisor, shall be deemed to have been imposed or given under the appropriation provisions of Schedule 3.

(3) Where, immediately before the commencement of Part IV, the order had been in force for a period of [six months or more], it shall cease to have effect at the end of the period of six months beginning with the day on which Part IV comes into force unless—
  (a) the court directs that it shall cease to have effect a the end of a different period (which shall not exceed three years);
  (b) it ceases to have effect earlier in accordance with section 91; or
  (c) it would have ceased to have had effect earlier had this Act not been passed.

(4) Where sub-paragraph (3) applies, paragraph 6 of Schedule 3 shall not apply.

(5) Where, immediately before the commencement of Part IV, the order had been in force for less than six months it shall cease to have effect in accordance with section 91 and paragraph 6 of Schedule 3 unless—
  (a) the court directs that it shall cease to have effect at the end of a different period (which shall not exceed three years); or
  (b) it would have ceased to have had effect earlier had this Act not been passed.

AMENDMENT

The words in square brackets were substituted by the Children Act 1989 (Commencement and Transitional Provisions) Order 1991 (S.I. 1991 No. 828), art. 4, Sched.

Schedule 14

Other supervision orders

26.—(1) This paragraph applies to any order for the supervision of a child which was in force immediately before the commencement of Part IV and was made under—
- (a) section 2(1)(f) of the Matrimonial Proceedings (Magistrates' Courts) Act 1960;
- (b) section 7(4) of the Family Law Reform Act 1969;
- (c) section 44 of the Matrimonial Causes Act 1973;
- (d) section 2(2)(a) of the Guardianship Act 1973;
- (e) section 34(5) or 36(3)(b) of the Children Act 1975;
- (f) section 26(1)(a) of the Adoption Act 1976; or
- (g) section 9 of the Domestic Proceedings and Magistrates' Courts Act 1978.

(2) The order shall not be deemed to be a supervision order made under any provision of this Act but shall nevertheless continue in force for a period of one year beginning with the day on which Part IV comes into force unless—
- (a) the court directs that it shall cease to have effect at the end of a lesser period; or
- (b) it would have ceased to have had effect earlier had this Act not been passed.

GENERAL NOTE

There were three types of supervision order under the old law:

(1) *made in care proceedings*

These are deemed supervision orders under section 31(11) and operate as if under the new law but they ceased to have effect on April 14, 1991 (or earlier) if they had been in force for six months or more on October 14, 1991 unless they were extended by the court under paragraph 25(3)(a). Orders which had been in force for less than six months last for a year unless discharged earlier or extended. See notes to section 35 and Schedule 3, Parts I and II.

(2) *made in matrimonial, etc., proceedings*

Supervision orders made in the proceedings listed in paragraph 26(1) have no direct equivalent in the Act. They continue in force until October 14, 1992 unless discharged earlier.

(3) *supervision orders in criminal proceedings*

These can continue to be made and are largely unaffected by the Act.

PLACE OF SAFETY ORDERS

27.—(1) This paragraph applies to—
- (a) any order or warrant authorising the removal of a child to a place of safety which—
  - (i) was made, or issued, under any of the enactment mentioned in sub-paragraph (2); and
  - (ii) was in force immediately before the commencement of Part IV; and
- (b) any interim order made under section 23(5) of the Children and Young Persons Act 1963 or section 28(6) of the Children and Young Persons Act 1969.

(2) The enactments are—
- (a) section 40 of the Children and Young Persons Act 1933 (warrant to search for or remove child);
- (b) section 28(1) of the Children and Young Persons Act 1969 (detention of child in place of safety);
- (c) section 34(1) of the Adoption Act 1976 (removal of protected children from unsuitable surroundings);

(d) section 12(1) of the Foster Children Act 1980 (removal of foster children kept in unsuitable surroundings).

(3) The order or warrant shall continue to have effect as if this Act had not been passed.

(4) Any enactment repealed by this Act shall continue to have effect in relation to the order or warrant so far as is necessary for the purposes of securing that the effect of the order is what it would have been had this Act not been passed.

(5) Sub-paragraph (4) does not apply to the power to make an interim order or further interim order given by section 23(5) of the Children and Young Persons Act 1963 or section 28(6) of the Children and Young Persons Act 1969.

(6) Where, immediately before section 28 of the Children and Young Persons Act 1969 is repealed by this Act, a child is being detained under the powers granted by that section, he may continue to be detained in accordance with that section by subsection (6) shall not apply.

GENERAL NOTE

The above list of short term orders will all have ceased to have effect.

RECOVERY OF CHILDREN

28. The repeal by this Act of subsection (1) of section 16 of the Child Care Act 1980 (arrest of child absent from compulsory care) shall not affect the operation of that section in relation to any child arrested before the coming into force of the repeal.

29.—(1) This paragraph applies where—
  (a) a summons has been issued under section 15 or 16 of the Child Care Act 1980 (recovery of children in voluntary or compulsory care); and
  (b) the child concerned is not produced in accordance with the summons before the repeal of that section by this Act comes into force.

(2) The summons, any warrant issued in connection with it and section 15 or (as the case may be) section 16, shall continue to have effect as if this Act had not been passed.

30. The amendment by paragraph 27 of Schedule 12 of section 32 of the Children and Young Persons Act 1969 (detention of absentees) shall not affect the operation of that section in relation to—
  (a) any child arrested; or
  (b) any summons or warrant issued,
under that section before the coming into force of that paragraph.

GENERAL NOTE

Existing summonses and warrants for the recovery of children absent from care continue to have effect as if the Act had not been passed. New proceedings could also be taken under section 50 but not in relation to children absent from voluntary care or accommodation.

VOLUNTARY ORGANISATIONS: PARENTAL RIGHTS RESOLUTIONS

31.—(1) This paragraph applies to a resolution—
  (a) made under section 64 of the Child Care Act 1980 (transfer of parental rights and duties to voluntary organisations); and
  (b) in force immediately before the commencement of Part IV.

(2) The resolution shall continue to have effect until the end of the period of six months beginning with the day on which Part IV comes into force unless it is brought to an end earlier in accordance with the provisions of the Act of 1980 preserved by this paragraph.

(3) While the resolution remains in force, any relevant provision of, or made under, the Act of 1980 shall continue to have effect with respect to it.

(4) Sub-paragraph (3) does not apply to—
  (a) section 62 of the Act of 1980 and any regulation made under that section (arrangements by voluntary organisations for emigration of children); or

(b) section 65 of the Act of 1980 (duty of local authority to assume parental rights and duties).

(5) Section 5(2) of the Act of 1980 (which is applied to resolutions under Part VI of the Act by section 64(7) of that Act) shall have effect with respect to the resolution as if the reference in paragraph (c) to an appointment of a guardian under section 5 of the Guardianship of Minors Act 1971 were a reference to an appointment of a guardian under section 5 of this Act.

GENERAL NOTE

Parental rights resolutions may no longer be passed. Transfers of parental rights to voluntary organisations under C.C.A. 1980, s.64, ceased to have effect on April 14, 1992. Between October 14, 1991, and that date voluntary organisations had no power to make the arrangements noted in para. 31(4). After April 13, 1991, these children are only accommodated by voluntary organisations; their parents, not the voluntary organisation have parental responsibility for them and the regulations listed in section 59 apply.

FOSTER CHILDREN

32.—(1) This paragraph applies where—
  (a) immediately before the commencement of Part VIII, a child was a foster child within the meaning of the Foster Children Act 1980; and
  (b) the circumstances of the case are such that, had Parts VIII and IX then been in force, he would have been treated for the purposes of this Act as a child who was being provided with accommodation in a children's home and not as a child who was being privately fostered.

(2) If the child continues to be cared for and provided with accommodation as before, section 63(1) and (10) shall not apply in relation to him if—
  (a) an application for registration of the home in question is made under section 63 before the end of the period of three months beginning with the day on which Part VIII comes into force; and
  (b) the application has not been refused or, if it has been refused—
    (i) the period for an appeal against the decision has not expired; or
    (ii) an appeal against the refusal has been made but has not been determined or abandoned.

(3) While section 63(1) and (10) does not apply, the child shall be treated as a privately fostered child for the purposes of Part IX.

GENERAL NOTE

Where children are privately fostered and the "usual fostering limit" (Sched. 7) is exceeded the carer must apply for registration under section 63 (registered children's homes) by January 14, 1992. Providing this is done the offence in section 63(10) will not be committed during the period while the application (or any appeal against refusal) is pending. During this period the child is treated as a privately fostered child and Part IX applies to him or her.

NURSERIES AND CHILD MINDING

33.—(1) Sub-paragraph (2) applies where, immediately before the commencement of Part X, any premises are registered under section 1(1)(a) of the Nurseries and Child-Minders Regulation Act 1948 (registration of premises, other than premises wholly or mainly used as private dwellings, where children are received to be looked after).

(2) During the transitional period, the provisions of the Act of 1948 shall continue to have effect with respect to those premises to the exclusion of Part X.

(3) Nothing in sub-paragraph (2) shall prevent the local authority concerned from registering any person under section 71(1)(b) with respect to the premises.

(4) In this paragraph "the transitional period" means the period ending with—
  (a) the first anniversary of the commencement of Part X; or
  (b) if earlier, the date on which the local authority concerned registers any person under section 71(1)(b) with respect to the premises.

34.—(1) Sub-paragraph (2) applies where, immediately before the commencement of Part X—
    (a) a person is registered under section 1(1)(b) of the Act of 1948 (registration of persons who for reward receive into their homes children under the age of five to be looked after); and
    (b) all the children looked after by him as mentioned in section 1(1)(b) of that Act are under the age of five.
(2) During the transitional period, the provisions of the Act of 1948 shall continue to have effect with respect to that person to the exclusion of Part X.
(3) Nothing in sub-paragraph (2) shall prevent the local authority concerned from registering that person under section 71(1)(a).
(4) In this paragraph "the transitional period" means the period ending with—
    (a) the first anniversary of the commencement of Part X; or
    (b) if earlier, the date on which the local authority concerned registers that person under section 71(1)(a).

GENERAL NOTE

The Nurseries and Child Minders Regulation Act 1948 continues to apply until October 13, 1992. During this period existing establishments and providers must be registered under Part X of the Act. Registrations under Part X will be effective from the date on which they are made.

CHILDREN ACCOMMODATED IN CERTAIN ESTABLISHMENTS

35. In calculating, for the purposes of section 85(1)(a) or 86(1)(a), the period of time for which a child has been accommodated any part of that period which fell before the day on which that section came into force shall be disregarded.

GENERAL NOTE

See notes to sections 85 and 86.

CRIMINAL CARE ORDERS

36.—(1) This paragraph applies where, immediately before the commencement of section 90(2) there was in force an order ("a criminal care order") made—
    (a) under section 7(7)(a) of the Children and Young Persons Act 1969 (alteration in treatment of young offenders, etc.); or
    (b) under section 15(1) of that Act, on discharging a supervision order made under section 7(7)(b) of that Act.
(2) The criminal care order shall continue to have effect until the end of the period of six months beginning with the day on which section 90(2) comes into force unless it is brought to an end earlier in accordance with—
    (a) the provisions of the Act of 1969 preserved by sub-paragraph (3)(a); or
    (b) this paragraph.
(3) While the criminal care order remains in force, any relevant provisions—
    (a) of the Act of 1969; and
    (b) of the Child Care Act 1980,
shall continue to have effect with respect to it.
(4) While the criminal care order remains in force, a court may, on the application of the appropriate person, make—
    (a) a residence order;
    (b) a care order or a supervision order under section 31;
    (c) an education supervision order under section 36 (regardless of subsection (6) of that section); or
    (d) an order falling within sub-paragraph (5),
and shall, on making any of those orders, discharge the criminal care order.
(5) The order mentioned in sub-paragraph (4)(d) is an order having effect as if it were a supervision order of a kind mentioned in section 12AA of the Act of 1969 (as inserted by paragraph 23 of Schedule 12), that is to say, a supervision order—

(a) imposing a requirement that the child shall live for a specified period in local authority accommodation; but
(b) in relation to which the conditions mentioned in [subsection (6)] of section 12AA are not required to be satisfied.

(6) The maximum period which may be specified in an order made under sub-paragraph (4)(d) is six months and such an order may stipulate that the child shall not live with a named person.

(7) Where this paragraph applies, section 5 of the Rehabilitation of Offenders Act 1974 (rehabilitation periods for particular sentences) shall have effect regardless of the repeals in it made by this Act.

(8) In sub-paragraph (4) "appropriate person" means—
(a) in the case of an application for a residence order, any person (other than a local authority) who has the leave of the court;
(b) in the case of an application for an education supervision order, a local education authority; and
(c) in any other case, the local authority to whose care the child was committed by the order.

AMENDMENT

The words in square brackets were substituted by the Courts and Legal Services Act 1990, s.116, Sched. 16, para. 33.

DEFINITION

"appropriate person": Sched. 14, para. 36(8).

GENERAL NOTE

Criminal care orders can no longer be made. Existing orders ceased to have effect no later than April 14, 1992.

MISCELLANEOUS

Consents under the Marriage Act 1949 (c. 76)

37.—(1) In the circumstances mentioned in sub-paragraph (2), section 3 of and Schedule 2 to the Marriage Act 1949 (consents to marry) shall continue to have effect regardless of the amendment of that Act by paragraph 5 of Schedule 12.
(2) The circumstances are that—
(a) immediately before the day on which paragraph 5 of Schedule 12 comes into force, there is in force—
(i) an existing order, as defined in paragraph 5(1); or
(ii) an order of a kind mentioned in paragraph 16(1); and
(b) section 3 of and Schedule 2 to the Act of 1949 would, but for this Act, have applied to the marriage of the child who is the subject of the order.

The Children Act 1975 (c. 72)

38. The amendments of other enactments made by the following provisions of the Children Act 1975 shall continue to have effect regardless of the repeal of the Act of 1975 by this Act—
(a) section 68(4), (5) and (7) (amendments of section 32 of the Children and Young Persons Act 1969); and
(b) in Schedule 3—
(i) paragraph 13 (amendments of Births and Deaths Registration Act 1953);
(ii) paragraph 43 (amendment of Perpetuities and Accumulations Act 1964);

(iii) paragraphs 46 and 47 (amendments of Health Services and Public Health Act 1968); and
(iv) paragraph 77 (amendment of Parliamentary and Other Pensions Act 1972).

The Child Care Act 1980 (c. 5)

39. The amendment made to section 106(2)(a) of the Children and Young Persons Act 1963 by paragraph 26 of Schedule 5 to the Child Care Act 1980 shall continue to have effect regardless of the repeal of the Act of 1980 by this Act.

Legal aid

40. The Lord Chancellor may by order make such transitional and saving provisions as appear to him to be necessary or expedient, in consequence of any provision made by or under this Act, in connection with the operation of any provisions of the Legal Aid Act 1988 (including any provision of that Act which is amended or repealed by this Act).

GENERAL NOTE
See notes to section 99.

PART II

THE COURT RULES

The Family Proceedings Rules 1991
 (S.I. 1991 No. 1247), Pt. IV

The Family Proceedings Courts (Children Act 1989) Rules 1991
 (S.I. 1991 No. 1395)

THE FAMILY PROCEEDINGS RULES 1991 PART IV
THE FAMILY PROCEEDINGS COURTS
(CHILDREN ACT 1989) RULES 1991

GENERAL NOTE

A wide range of rules, regulations and orders have been made under The Children Act. By no means all are included in this volume, those selected being the most relevant to the busy practitioner or Guardian ad Litem. Detailed commentary is provided upon the two main sets of Rules: the Family Proceedings Rules (S.I. 1991 No. 1247), Part IV and their Magistrates' Courts equivalent, The Family Proceedings Courts (Children Act 1989) Rules (S.I. 1991 No. 1395). Brief annotations of Parts V, VIII (r. 8.1) and IX (rr. 9.1, 9.2, 9.2A, 9.3 and 9.5) and the remaining regulations and orders as listed are set out in Part III. There is extensive cross referencing between the Rules themselves and with The Children Act 1989 as together they are all intended, as a whole, to reform child law (see Part I). There is also extensive reference to explanatory Home Office circulars and to guidance issued by the Department of Health in particular Volume 1, *Court Orders* and Volume 7, *Guardians ad Litem and other Court related issues*.

The Rules replace the Magistrates' Courts (Children & Young Persons) Rules 1988 in the Public Law arena as well as fitting in with the Private Law structure at all Court levels. The Rules continue the process of formalising, clarifying and tidying up Child Care law.

The Rules are the engine room of the legislation: they enable the welfare principles and objectives of The Children Act to be carried through into everyday practice. The principles of the Act are the principles of the Rules, for example the Act stresses the importance of the wishes and feelings of the child, the Rules detail how children are to be heard.

The Act enjoins courts to have particular regard to children's needs, any proposed changes in the circumstances, particular characteristics, actual or potential harm, together with an assessment of potential carers (checklist s.1(3) b—f). The Rules stipulate how, when, by whom and in what circumstances all of this data is to be gathered and presented to the courts. The avoidance of delay (s.1(2)) features with great prominence in the Rules, most notably at rule 14 and in the Allocation Order.

At a different level, there are clear administrative objectives behind the Rules such as the need for flexibility, the most effective use of court resources, and the pre-eminence of documentation both by parties in presenting cases and by courts in recording findings and decisions.

The Rules cover both public and private law proceedings and taken together, apply to all three levels of courts dealing with children's cases: Family Proceedings Courts, County Courts and the Family Division of the High Court.

FAMILY PROCEEDINGS RULES 1991

(S.I. 1991 No. 1247)

ARRANGEMENT OF RULES

PART IV

PROCEEDINGS UNDER THE CHILDREN ACT 1989

4.1 Interpretation and application
4.2 Matters prescribed for the purposes of the Act of 1989
4.3 Application for leave to commence proceedings
4.4 Application
4.5 Withdrawal of application
4.6 Transfer
4.7 Parties
4.8 Service
4.9 Answer to application
4.10 Appointment of guardian ad litem
4.11 Powers and duties of guardian ad litem
4.12 Solicitor for child
4.13 Welfare officer
4.14 Directions
4.15 Timing of proceedings
4.16 Attendance at directions appointment and hearing
4.17 Documentary evidence
4.18 Expert evidence—examination of child
4.19 Amendment
4.20 Oral evidence
4.21 Hearing
4.22 Appeals
4.23 Confidentiality of documents
4.24 Notification of consent
4.25 Secure accommodation—evidence
4.26 Investigation under section 37
4.27 Direction to local education authority to apply for education supervision order
4.28 Transitional provision
    APPENDIX 1— Forms
    APPENDIX 3— Part IV applications—notice and respondents

GENERAL NOTE

These two key sets of Rules operate in tandem. The Family Proceedings Courts (Children Act 1989) Rules 1991 (FPC) govern the work of the Family Proceedings Courts, that is courts at magistrates' court level; Part IV of the Family Proceedings

Rules 1991 (FPR) deals with the work of the county courts and High Court. Part IV of the FPR specifically covers Children Act proceedings; the remaining parts rework the now repealed Matrimonial Causes Rules 1977. The most relevant provisions (covering wardship and appeals) are included in Part III of this volume at p. 464. The first 21 rules run in parallel and cover the same items: for example, the provisions for service of documents are dealt with at rule 4.8 (FPR) and rule 8 (FPC). For ease of reference, therefore, rr. 1 to 21 are set out and dealt with together with differences highlighted where they occur. The final parts of both sets of Rules are annotated separately.

Both the FPR and the FPC end with three appendices and three schedules respectively. Appendices 1 and 3 (FPR) and Schedules 1 and 2 (FPC) are included. Appendix 1 and Schedule 2 give details of court forms. Appendix 3 and Schedule 2 supply identical details of service periods, respondents and persons to be given notice all set out in tabular form. Appendix 2 and Schedule 3 which respectively supply contents of divorce petitions and minor amendments of the Justices' Clerk's Rules 1970 are not reproduced here.

The Rules operate chronologically from commencement of proceedings through pre-hearing requirements, hearings and thereafter to appeals. The Rules replace the Magistrates' Courts (Children & Young Persons) Rules 1988 in the public law arena, as well as fitting in with the private law structure at all court levels. The terms public and private law when applied to children's cases are terms to be used with care, and do not appear as such in the legislation. With the greater flexibility of The Children Act many cases will have elements of both. By and large, public law cases are known as "specified proceedings" as defined in section 41(6), rule 4.2 and rule 2. This is a very important definition and full commentary is set out together with rule 4.2 and rule 2 at pp. 355–358.

Major changes

The Rules introduce major changes to the ways in which courts are to deal with children's cases of which the most significant are set out below:

1. *Written applications*

All proceedings in all jurisdictions are commenced by written application in the forms prescribed in Schedule 1 and Appendix 1. In particular, the complaint/summons procedure at magistrates' court level is abolished in children's civil proceedings (r. 4.4, r. 4).

2. *Ex parte applications*

Certain applications can be made *ex parte* (notably prohibited steps orders, specific issue orders and emergency protection orders). In Family Proceedings Courts, leave of a court clerk is required. Emergency protection orders therefore, can no longer be granted by a magistrate without liaison with the court, a lesson drawn from the Cleveland report, although the enactment goes further than Butler-Sloss LJ recommended—see the *Report of the Inquiry into Child Abuse in Cleveland* (1987), HMSO, Cm. 412, at p. 252.

3. *Commencement of proceedings*

The Children Act structure does not create a Family Court as such but provides concurrent jurisdiction for children's cases. Straightforward cases are expected to be dealt with in the Family Proceedings Courts, with the more complex proceedings being heard in the county or High Court. The details as to where a case should be commenced are set out in the Children (Allocation of Proceedings) Order 1991 (S.I. 1991 No. 1677) (see p. 432). Essentially, most public law cases are to be commenced in Family Proceedings Courts whilst private law applicants generally have a choice of jurisdiction.

4. *Transfer*

Once issued, on application or of its own motion, the court can transfer proceedings to another Family Proceedings Court or to a county court with provisions for further transfers thereafter. See also the Children (Allocation of Proceedings) Order 1991 (S.I.

1991 No. 1677) at p. 432. For details of commencement and transfer of proceedings, see rule 4.6 and rule 6.

5. Parties

Certain listed persons are automatic respondents. Anyone may seek leave to be joined or cease to be a respondent (r. 4.7, appendix 3; r. 7, Sched. 2).

6. Service

Responsibility for service of documents supplied by a party rests with that party and not with the court. There are detailed provisions concerning the service of application forms and other documents (r. 4.4; r. 8).

7. Guardians ad litem

Children involved in public law cases will continue to have independent representation by guardians ad litem and children's solicitors. There is a strong presumption of appointment of a guardian ad litem in specified proceedings (r. 4.10; r. 10).

The powers and duties of guardians are set out in detail, the overall impact of which is to strengthen the guardian's position with wide responsibilities throughout the proceedings (r. 4.11; r. 11). Children's Solicitors may be appointed by guardians or by the court (r. 4.12; r. 12).

8. Directions hearings

Courts may (but almost invariably will) convene directions hearings, such a procedure being an innovation of Family Proceedings Court level. Presided over by court clerks, magistrate(s), district judges or judges, courts at directions hearings have wide powers to keep cases moving and ensure readiness for substantive hearings by dealing with all procedural matters at an early stage (r. 4.14; r. 14). Directions given are to be followed. There are potential penalties for default lying in costs (r. 22) and/or exclusion of evidence if the timetable for disclosure has not been followed (r. 4.17(3); r. 17(3)).

9. Attendance

Attendance of parties is required; the courts may proceed in the absence either of the applicant or a respondent, but not in the absence of both (r. 4.16; r. 16).

10. Disclosure

In all proceedings other than section 8 cases, parties must disclose in advance the substance of their evidence in statement (not affidavit) form whether or not specifically directed to do so. There is to be disclosure in section 8 proceedings if the court so directs (r. 4.17; r. 17). Documents can be amended with leave of the court (r. 4.19; r. 19).

11. Examination of children

Court leave is required for the results of expert examination of children to be adduced as evidence in proceedings.

12. Conduct of hearings

There are detailed provisions concerning the conduct of court hearings. The court must state its findings of fact and reasons for its decisions whether or not the proceedings are contested (r. 4.21; r. 21).

13. Single justices and court clerks
Single justices and court clerks are both given substantial powers, the latter in particular being accorded a quasi-judicial role (r. 2(5); r. 28 and r. 32).

THE FAMILY PROCEEDINGS COURTS (CHILDREN ACT 1989) RULES 1991

(1991 No. 1395)

ARRANGEMENT OF RULES

PART I

INTRODUCTORY

1. Citation, commencement and interpretation
2. Matters prescribed for the purposes of the Act of 1989

PART II

General

3. Application for leave to commence proceedings
4. Application
5. Withdrawal of application
6. Transfer of proceedings
7. Parties
8. Service
9. Answer to application
10. Appointment of guardian ad litem
11. Powers and duties of guardian ad litem
12. Solicitors for child
13. Welfare officer
14. Directions
15. Timing of proceedings
16. Attendance at directions appointment and hearing
17. Documentary evidence
18. Expert evidence—examination of child
19. Amendment
20. Oral evidence
21. Hearing

PART III

Miscellaneous

22. Costs
23. Confidentiality of documents
24. Enforcement of residence order
25. Notification of consent
26. Secure accommodation
27. Investigation under section 37
28. Limits on the power of a justices' clerk or a single justice to make an order under section 11(3) or secton 38(1)

29. Appeals to a family proceedings court under section 77(6) and paragraph 8(1) of Schedule 8
30. Contribution orders
31. Direction to local education authority to apply for education supervision order
32. Delegation by justices' clerk
33. Application of section 97 of the Magistrates' Courts Act 1980
34. Consequential and minor amendments, savings and transitionals

SCHEDULES

1. Forms
2. Respondents and notice
3. Consequential and minor amendments

THE FAMILY PROCEEDINGS RULES 1991
(S.I. 1991 NO. 1247) PART IV

THE FAMILY PROCEEDINGS COURTS
(CHILDREN ACT 1989) RULES 1991
(S.I. 1991 NO. 1395)

PART IV

PROCEEDINGS UNDER THE CHILDREN ACT 1989

4.1. Interpretation and application

(1) In this Part of these rules, unless a contrary intention appears—
"a section or schedule referred to means the section or schedule so numbered in the Act of 1989;
"a section 8 order" has the meaning assigned to it by section 8(2);
"application" means an application made under or by virtue of the Act of 1989 or under these rules, and "applicant" shall be construed accordingly;
"child", in relation to proceedings to which this Part applies—
   (a) means, subject to sub-paragraph (b), a person under the age of 18 with respect to whom the proceedings are brought, and
   (b) where the proceedings are under Schedule 1, also includes a person who has reached the age of 18;
"directions appointment" means a hearing for directions under rule 4.14(2);
"emergency protection order" means an order under section 44;
"guardian ad litem" means a guardian ad litem, appointed under section 41, of the child with respect to whom the proceedings are brought;
"leave" includes permission and approval;
"note" includes a record made by mechanical means;
"parental responsibility" has the meaning assigned to it by section 3;
"recovery order" means an order under section 50;
"specified proceedings" has the meaning assigned to it by section 41(6) and rule 4.2(2); and
"welfare officer" means a person who has been asked to prepare a welfare report under section 7.

(2) Except where the contrary intention appears, the provisions of this Part apply to proceedings in the High Court and the county courts—

(a) on an application for a section 8 order;
(b) on an application for a care order or a supervision order;
(c) on an application under section 4(1)(a), 4(3), 5(1), 6(7), 13(1), 16(6), 33(7), 34(2), 34(3), 34(4), 34(9), 36(1), 38(8)(b), 39(1), 39(2), 39(3), 39(4), 43(1), 43(12), 44, 45, 46(7), 48(9) [, 50(1) or 102(1)];
(d) under Schedule 1, except where financial relief is also sought by or on behalf of an adult;
(e) on an application under paragraph 19(1) of Schedule 2;
(f) on an application under paragraph 6(3), 15(2) or 17(1) of Schedule 3;
(g) on an application under paragraph 11(3) or 16(5) of Schedule 14; or
(h) under section 25.

AMENDMENT

The words in square brackets were substituted by the Family Proceedings (Amendment) Rules 1991 (S.I. 1991 No. 2113), reg. 5 (October 14, 1991).

PART I

INTRODUCTORY

Citation, commencement and interpretation

1.—(1) These Rules may be cited as the Family Proceedings Courts (Children Act 1989) Rules 1991 and shall come into force on 14th October 1991.

(2) Unless a contrary intention appears—

a section or schedule referred to means the section or schedule in the Act of 1989,

"application" means an application made under or by virtue of the Act of 1989 or under these Rules, and "applicant" shall be construed accordingly,

"business day" means any day other than—

(a) a Saturday, Sunday, Christmas Day or Good Friday; or
(b) a bank holiday, that is to say, a day which is, or is to be observed as, a bank holiday, or a holiday, under the Banking and Financial Dealings Act 1981, in England and Wales,

"child"

(a) means, in relation to any relevant proceedings, subject to sub-paragraph (b), a person under the age of 18 with respect to whom the proceedings are brought, and
(b) where paragraph 16(1) of Schedule 1 applies, also includes a person who has reached the age of 18;

"contribution order" has the meaning assigned to it by paragraph 23(2) of Schedule 2, "court" means a family proceedings court constituted in accordance with sections 66 and 67 of the Magistrates' Courts Act 1980 or, in respect of those proceedings prescribed in rule 2(5), a single justice who is a member of a family panel,

"directions appointment" means a hearing for directions under rule 14(2),

"emergency protection order" means an order under section 44,

"file" means deposit with the justices' clerk,

"form" means a form in Schedule 1 to these Rules with such variation as the circumstances of the particular case may require,

"guardian ad litem" means a guardian ad litem, appointed under section 41, of the child with respect to whom the proceedings are brought,

"justices' clerk" has the meaning assigned to it by section 70 of the Justices of the Peace Act 1979 and includes any person who performs a justices' clerk's functions by virtue of rule 32,

"leave" includes approval,

"note" includes a record made by mechanical means,

"parental responsibility" has the meaning assigned to it by section 3,

"parties" in relation to any relevant proceedings means the respondents specified for those proceedings in the third column of Schedule 2 to these Rules, and the applicant,

"recovery order" means an order under section 50,

"relevant proceedings" has the meaning assigned to it by section 93(3),

"section 8 order" has the meaning assigned to it by section 8(2),

"specified proceedings" has the meaning assigned to it by section 41(6) and rule 2(2),

"the 1981 rules" means the Magistrates' Courts Rules 1981,

"the Act of 1989" means the Children Act 1989,

"welfare officer" means a person who has been asked to prepare a welfare report under section 7.

GENERAL NOTE

The word "form" is given a flexible definition in respect of FPC applications. A substantial amount of information is required for most Children Act applications. The element of flexibility is not permissive of inaccuracy or incompleteness, but to enable parties to supply additional information if necessary.

4.2. Matters prescribed for the purposes of the Act of 1989

(1) The parties to proceedings in which directions are given under section 38(6), and any person named in such a direction, form the prescribed class for the purposes of section 38(8) (application to vary directions made with interim care or interim supervision order).

(2) The following proceedings are specified for the purposes of section 41 in accordance with subsection (6)(i) thereof—

    (a) proceedings under section 25;

(b) applications under section 33(7);
(c) proceedings under paragraph 19(1) of Schedule 2;
(d) applications under paragraph 6(3) of Schedule 3;
[(e) appeals against the determination of proceedings of a kind set out in sub-paragraphs (a) to (d).]

(3) The applicant for an order that has been made under section 43(1) and the persons referred to in section 43(11) may, in any circumstances, apply under section 43(12) for a child assessment order to be varied or discharged.

(4) The following persons form the prescribed class for the purposes of section 44(9) (application to vary directions)—
    (a) the parties to the application for the order in respect of which it is sought to vary the directions;
    (b) the guardian ad litem;
    (c) the local authority in whose area the child concerned is ordinarily resident;
    (d) any person who is named in the directions.

AMENDMENT

The words in square brackets were substituted by the Family Proceedings (Amendment) Rules 1991 (S.I. 1991 No. 2113), reg. 8 (October 14, 1991).

Matters prescribed for the purposes of the Act of 1989

2.—(1) The parties to proceedings in which directions are given under section 38(6), and any person named in such a direction, form the prescribed class for the purposes of section 38(8)(b) (application to vary directions made with interim care or interim supervision order).

(2) The following proceedings are specified for the purposes of section 41 in accordance with subsection (6)(i) thereof—
    (a) proceedings [in a family proceedings court] under section 25;
    (b) applications under section 33(7);
    (c) proceedings under paragraph 19(1) of Schedule 2;
    (d) applications under paragraph 6(3) of Schedule 3.

(3) The applicant for an order that has been made under section 43(1) and the persons referred to in section 43(11) may, in any circumstances, apply under section 43(12) for a child assessment order to be varied or discharged.

(4) The following persons form the prescribed class for the purposes of section 44(9)(b) (application to vary directions)—
    (a) the parties to the application for the order in respect of which it is sought to vary the directions;
    (b) the guardian ad litem;
    (c) the local authority in whose area the child concerned is ordinarily resident;
    (d) any person who is named in the directions.

(5) The following proceedings are prescribed for the purposes of section 93(2)(i) as being proceedings with respect to which a single justice may discharge the functions of a family proceedings court, that is to say, proceedings—

(a) where an ex parte application is made, under sections 10, 44(1), 48(9), 50(1), 75(1) or 102(1),
(b) subject to rule 28, under sections 11(3) or 38(1),
(c) under sections 4(3)(b), 7, 14, 34(3)(b), 37, 41, 44(9)(b) and (11)(b)(iii), 48(4), 91(15) or (17), or paragraph 11(4) of Schedule 14,
(d) in accordance with any Order made by the Lord Chancellor under Part I of Schedule 11, and
(e) in accordance with rules 3 to 8, 10 to 19, 21, 22, or 27.

DEFINITIONS
"child": s.105(1), r. 4.1(2); r. 1(2).
"child assessment order": s.43(2).
"guardian ad litem": s.41(2).
"local authority": s.105(1).
"specified proceedings": s.41(6), r. 4.2(2); r. 2(2).

AMENDMENT
The words in square brackets were substituted by the Family Proceedings Courts (Matrimonial Proceedings, etc.) Rules 1991 (S.I. 1991 No. 1991), reg. 8 (October 14, 1991).

GENERAL NOTE
The Rule extends the meaning of specified proceedings (para. 2) sets out the powers of single justices (para. 5) and gives details as to who may apply to vary directions given on the making of interim care or supervision orders (para. 1), child assessment orders (para. 3) and emergency protection orders (para. 4).

Para. 2
In general terms specified proceedings are public law proceedings. The detailed definition of specified proceedings at section 41(b) is extended by this paragraph. The main practical importance is that in specified proceedings the child automatically has party status with the potential availability of a guardian ad litem and solicitor. The Rule extends the definition to include secure accommodation applications (s.25), applications to remove a child subject to a care order from the United Kingdom or change the name of a child in care (s.33(7)), applications for children in care to live outside England and Wales (Sched. 2, para. 19(1)), applications to extend supervision orders (Sched. 3, para. 6(3)) and appeals against any of the above.

Specified proceedings and public law proceedings are not, however, synonymous terms. The definition of specified proceedings has not been extended to include applications by local authorities or prohibited steps orders or specific issues orders under section 8. Also, "private" emergency protection order applications, *i.e.* applications by individuals and not by local authorities or the NSPCC, are specified proceedings. These two areas have caused confusion and difficulties in the immediate post-implementation period. Party status, and representation by a solicitor and guardian ad litem are available to children subject to "private" emergency protection order applications, whereas they are not when local authorities make section 8 applications. Further confusion surrounds the availability of guardian ad litems in section 8 applications, see commentary in respect of rule 4.10 and rule 10 at p. 374–5.

Para. 5
At Family Proceedings Court level there is an additional rule 2.5 setting out the powers of a single justice. It was expected that the Children Act would bring a substantial extra workload to magistrates' courts. In order to ease that burden and keep cases moving, both court clerks and single justices are given substantial powers. In so far as single justices are concerned, they are as follows:

(a) hearing *ex parte* applications with the leave of the court clerk;
(b) making repeat and identical interim section 8 or interim care/supervision orders (for details see r. 28 at p. 418);
(c) giving leave to bring certain proceedings:
  (i) to a child to bring an application to discharge a parental responsibility order or agreement (s.4(3)(b)) and to a child to discharge an section 8 order;
  (ii) to anyone who is not given the right to do so in section 34(1), to bring an application for contact between a child in care and the applicant (s.34(3)(b));
  (iii) to bring an application within six months of a previous application (s.91(15) and (17));
(d) ordering a court welfare officer report (s.7) or ordering a local authority to investigate a child's circumstances (s.37);
(e) enforcing a residence order (s.14); see also rule 24 at p. 416;
(f) appointing a guardian and/or a solicitor to represent a child in specified proceedings;
(g) dealing with certain aspects of emergency protection orders: giving or varying a direction attached to an emergency protection order or agreeing to an application that a child subject to an emergency protection order be placed in the care of a named person(s) (s.44(9)(b) and s.44(11)(b)(iii));
(h) dealing with applications to transfer proceedings;
(i) exercising the powers given to a court under rules 3–8, 10–19, 21, 22 or 27.

It ought to be remembered that certain functions are specifically reserved to court clerks, see commentary to rule 32.

4.3. Application for leave to commence proceedings

(1) Where the leave of the court is required to bring any proceedings to which this Part applies, the person seeking leave shall file—

(a) a written request for leave setting out the reasons for the application; and
(b) a draft of the application for the making of which leave is sought in the appropriate form in Appendix 1 to these rules or, where there is no such form, in writing, together with sufficient copies for one to be served on each respondent.

(2) On considering a request for leave filed under paragraph (1), the court shall—

(a) grant the request, whereupon the proper officer shall inform the person making the request of the decision, or
(b) direct that a date be fixed for the hearing of the request, whereupon the proper officer shall fix such a date and give such notice as the court directs to the person making the request and such other persons as the court requires to be notified, of the date so fixed.

(3) Where leave is granted to bring proceedings to which this Part applies the application shall proceed in accordance with rule 4.4; but paragraph (1)(a) of that rule shall not apply.

(4) In the case of a request for leave to bring proceedings under Schedule 1, the draft application under paragraph (1) shall be accompanied by a statement setting out the financial details which the person seeking leave believes to be relevant to the request and containing a declaration that it is true to the maker's best knowledge

and belief, together with sufficient copies for one to be served on each respondent.

PART II

GENERAL

Application for leave to commence proceedings

3.—(1) Where the leave of the court is required to bring any relevant proceedings, the person seeking leave shall file—
  (a) a written request for leave setting out the reasons for the application; and
  (b) a draft of the application for the making of which leave is sought in the appropriate form in Schedule 1 to these Rules or, where there is no such form, in writing, together with sufficient copies for one to be served on each respondent.

(2) On considering a request for leave filed under paragraph (1), the court shall—
  (a) grant the request, whereupon the justices' clerk shall inform the person making the request of the decision, or
  (b) direct that a date be fixed for a hearing of the request, whereupon the justices' clerk shall fix such a date and give such notice as the court directs to the person making the request and to such other persons as the court requires to be notified, of the date so fixed.

(3) Where leave is granted to bring any relevant proceedings, the application shall proceed in accordance with rule 4; but paragraph (1)(a) of that rule shall not apply.

DEFINITIONS
  "court": s.92(7).
  "justices' clerk": r. 1(2).
  "relevant proceedings": s.93(3).

GENERAL NOTE
  Applications for leave to bring proceedings will be commonplace. The open door policy of the Children Act enables anyone to bring a section 8 application in respect of any child. The requirement of leave is a brake upon a potential eruption of child litigation. In so far as section 8 applications are concerned, rule 3 should be read in conjunction with section 10(9) which sets out mainly child-centred factors the courts consider when deciding to grant leave, particularly the applicant's connection with the child and the risk of disruption to the child's life as a result of the application (see p. 38). In such applications the child's welfare is not the paramount consideration: that question only arose when the court heard the substantive application, see *JR* v. *Merton London Borough* [1992] 2 F.C.R. 189, C.A.
  In procedural terms an applicant for leave to bring any Children Act application should file his application in the prescribed form with sufficient copies for each respondent, together with a written request for leave. The court can grant leave with or without a hearing, but there must be a hearing to refuse an application.

4.4. Application

(1) Subject to paragraph (4), an applicant shall—
- (a) file the application in respect of each child in the appropriate form in Appendix 1 to these rules or, where there is no such form, in writing, together with sufficient copies for one to be served on each respondent, and
- (b) serve a copy of the application, endorsed in accordance with paragraph (2)(b), on each respondent such number of days prior to the date fixed under paragraph (2)(a) as is specified for that application in column (ii) of Appendix 3 to these rules.

(2) On receipt of the documents filed under paragraph (1)(a) the proper officer shall—
- (a) fix the date for a hearing or a directions appointment, allowing sufficient time for the applicant to comply with paragraph (1)(b),
- (b) endorse the date so fixed upon the copies of the application filed by the applicant, and
- (c) return the copies to the applicant forthwith.

(3) The applicant shall, at the given time as complying with paragraph (1)(b), give written notice of the proceedings, and of the date and place of the hearing or appointment fixed under paragraph (2)(a), to the persons set out for the relevant class of proceedings in [column (iv)] of Appendix 3 to these rules.

(4) An application for—
- (a) a [section 8 order],
- (b) an emergency protection order,
- (c) a warrant under section 48(9), [...]
- (d) a recovery order, [or
- (e) a warrant under section 102(1)]

may be made ex parte in which case the applicant shall—
- (i) file the application in respect of each child in the appropriate form in Appendix 1 to these rules—
  - (a) where the application is made by telephone, within 24 hours after the making of the application, or
  - (b) in any other case, at the time when the application is made, and
- (ii) in the case of an application for a [section 8 order] or an emergency protection order, serve a copy of the application on each respondent within 48 hours after the making of the order.

(5) Where the court refuses to make an order on an ex parte application it may direct that the application be made inter partes.

(6) In the case of proceedings under Schedule 1, the application under paragraph (1) shall be accompanied by a statement setting out the financial details which the applicant believes to be relevant to the application and containing a declaration that it is true to the maker's best knowledge and belief, together with sufficient copies for one to be served on each respondent.

AMENDMENT

The words in square brackets were substituted by the Family Proceedings Rules 1991 (S.I. 1991 No. 2113), reg. 9, (October 14, 1991) and the Family Proceedings (Amendment No. 2) Rules 1992 (S.I. 1992 No. 2067), rr. 6 and 9 (October 5, 1992).

Application

4.—(1) Subject to paragraph (4), an applicant shall—
    (a) file the application in respect of each child in the appropriate form in Schedule 1 to these Rules or where there is no such form, in writing, together with sufficient copies for one to be served on each respondent, and
    (b) serve a copy of the application, endorsed in accordance with paragraph (2)(b), on each respondent such minimum number of days prior to the date fixed under paragraph (2)(a) as is specified in relation to that application in column (ii) of Schedule 2 to these Rules.

(2) On receipt of the documents filed under paragraph (1)(a), the justices' clerk shall—
    (a) fix the date, time and place for a hearing or a directions appointment, allowing sufficient time for the applicant to comply with paragraph (1)(b),
    (b) endorse the date, time and place so fixed upon the copies of the application filed by the applicant, and
    (c) return the copies to the applicant forthwith.

(3) The applicant shall, at the same time as complying with paragraph (1)(b), give written notice of the proceedings, and of the date, time and place of the hearing or appointment fixed under paragraph (2)(a) to the persons set out in relation to the relevant class of proceedings in column (iv) of Schedule 2 to these Rules.

(4) An application for—
    (a) a [section 8 order],
    (b) an emergency protection order,
    (c) a warrant under section 48(9),
    (d) a recovery order, or
    (e) a warrant under section 102(1),

may, with leave of the justices' clerk, be made ex parte in which case the applicant shall—
    (i) file with the justices' clerk or the court the application in respect of each child in the appropriate form in Schedule 1 to these Rules at the time when the application is made or as directed by the justices' clerk, and
    (ii) in the case of an application for a prohibited steps order, or a specific issue order, under section 8 or an emergency protection order, and also in the case of an application for an order under section 75(1) where the application is ex parte, serve a copy of the application on each respondent within 48 hours after the making of the order.

(5) Where the court refuses to make an order on an ex parte application it may direct that the application be made inter partes.

(6) In the case of proceedings under Schedule 1, the application under paragraph (1) shall be accompanied by a statement setting out

the financial details which the applicant believes to be relevant to the application and containing a declaration that it is true to the maker's best knowledge and belief, together with sufficient copies for one to be served on each respondent.

DEFINITIONS
"child": s.102(1), r. 4.1(2), r. 1(2).
"court": s.92(7).
"directions appointment": r. 4(1)(2), r. 1(2).
"emergency protection orders": s.44(4).
"justices' clerk": r. 1(2).
"prohibited steps order": s.8(1).
"recovery order": s.50.
"specific issue order": s.8(1).

AMENDMENT
The words in square brackets were substituted by the Family Proceedings Courts (Miscellaneous Amendments) Rules 1992 (S.I. 1992 No. 2068), Sched., para. 1 (October 5, 1992).

GENERAL NOTE
Rule 4 sets out the procedure for commencing Children Act applications in all jurisdictions. The complaint/summons procedure formerly in use in magistrates' courts children's cases is abolished "in line with the promotion of less adversarial procedures" (Home Office Circular 48/1991). The aim is to entirely dissociate children's cases from the criminal jurisdiction of magistrates' courts.

Applications are to be issued in writing in the prescribed form, if any (see FPR, appendix 1; FPC, Sched. 1 at pp. 408–410 and 420–422). There is to be one application form per child and a copy for each respondent. Applicants must therefore work out in advance the identity of automatic respondents, see rule 4.7 and rule 7 at pp. 367–368.

Upon receipt of the application, the court will fix a hearing date and return the papers indorsed with the court details including case number to the applicant for service upon respondents.

Applicants are also required to give notice of proceedings to certain other persons listed at appendix 3 and Schedule 2 to the Rules (r. 7 at p. 368).

The forms to be completed by applicants are lengthy, detailed and designed to be child centred. Applications can be issued without completed forms with good reason and, where necessary, even more information can be supplied. Addresses of applicants can be omitted from the forms in cases of difficulty (FPR, r. 10.21), although the court must be informed of the actual address.

Paragraph 4 deals with *ex parte* applications of which there are only the five listed. The two warrants referred to are a police warrant to enforce an emergency protection order (s.48(9)) and a police search warrant (s.102(1)). The position concerning *ex parte* applications, particularly for residence orders, had caused considerable confusion. However the rule has been amended by the F.P. (Amendment No. 2) Rules 1992 with the effect that any s.8 order can be sought *ex parte*. Furthermore the Court of Appeal has now made it clear that all Children Act applications can be made *ex parte* where necessary, *Re B (A Minor)* [1992] 1 F.C.R. 555: "In my judgment the Act cannot be read as being constrained by the rules to preclude an ex parte application", per Butler-Sloss L.J.

There are variations in powers between the jurisdictions in respect of *ex parte* applications.

Family Proceedings Courts
At Family Proceedings Court level, *ex parte* applications cannot proceed without the leave of a court clerk. In this and other rules the words employed are "justices' clerk," but effectively, any court clerk may so act (r. 32(1)). The imposition of an additional hurdle, in the granting of emergency protection orders in particular, is a major change from the pre-Children Act law. An emergency protection order or other *ex parte* order granted by a magistrate alone without leave will be invalid.

Guidance, Vol. I, para. 4.46 indicates that emergency protection orders in particular will usually be heard *ex parte*, but should, if possible, be made to a court if one is available. Emergency protection order applications will almost always be made to Family Proceedings Courts (see the Children (Allocation and Proceedings) Order 1991, arts. 3 and 4(1), commentary p. 435). Magistrates' courts have established procedures to enable emergency applications to be made by social workers and others. There is typically a duty clerk system covering out-of-hours work, and the clerk will have details of available magistrates.

County and High Courts—FPR

Ex parte applications in the county and High Courts do not require leave. In such proceedings there is provision for applications to be made by telephone. It must be assumed that this procedure is only available in cases of extreme urgency, particularly out of court hours and/or in rural areas when applicants would need to undertake a substantial journey to locate a judge in person. The written application form must be submitted within 24 hours of a telephone application or, in any case, when the application is made.

Both jurisdictions

Ex parte orders must be served upon each respondent within 48 hours. In cases of difficulty, applications can be made under rule 4.15 and rule 15 to extend this or any other time period specified by the rules. Emergency protection orders are accompanied by explanatory notes for parents and others giving details about what will happen to the child and what they can do next.

Para. 5

Courts can direct that *ex parte* applications can be heard *inter partes*. Where an emergency protection order is heard *inter partes* a subsequent challenge is not possible by a person who had notice and attended the application hearing (see s.45(11)).

4.5. Withdrawal of application

(1) An application may be withdrawn only with leave of the court.

(2) Subject to paragraph (3), a person seeking leave to withdraw an application shall file and serve on the parties a written request for leave setting out the reasons for the request.

(3) The request under paragraph (2) may be made orally to the court if the parties and either the guardian ad litem or the welfare officer are present.

(4) Upon receipt of a written request under paragraph (2) the court shall—
- (a) if—
    - (i) the parties consent in writing,
    - (ii) the guardian ad litem has had an opportunity to make representations, and
    - (iii) the court thinks fit,

    grant the request, in which case the proper officer shall notify the parties, the guardian ad litem and the welfare officer of the granting of the request, or
- (b) direct that a date be fixed for the hearing of the request in which case the proper officer shall give at least 7 days' notice to the parties, the guardian ad litem and the welfare officer, of the date fixed.

Withdrawal of application

5.—(1) An application may be withdrawn only with leave of the court.

(2) Subject to paragraph (3), a person seeking leave to withdraw an application shall file and serve on the parties a written request for leave setting out the reasons for the request.

(3) The request under paragraph (2) may be made orally to the court if the parties and, if appointed, the guardian ad litem or the welfare officer are present.

(4) Upon receipt of a written request under paragraph (2), the court shall—
- (a) if—
  - (i) the parties consent in writing,
  - (ii) any guardian ad litem has had an opportunity to make representations, and
  - (iii) the court thinks fit,

  grant the request; in which case the justices' clerk shall notify the parties, the guardian ad litem and the welfare officer of the granting of the request; or
- (b) the justices' clerk shall fix a date for the hearing of the request and give at least 7 days' notice to the parties, the guardian ad litem and the welfare officer of the date fixed.

DEFINITIONS

"court": s.92(7).
"GAL": s.41(2).
"justices' clerk": r. 1(2).
"parties": r. 4(1)(2), r. 1(2).
"welfare officer": r. 4(1)(2), r. 1(2).

GENERAL NOTE

The withdrawal of any Children Act application is a judicial decision not, as under the former law, a power reserved to applicants. The law had been moving in this direction in care proceedings, *R.* v. *Birmingham Juvenile Court, ex p. G* (1989) 3 All E.R. 336, but in other proceedings this is a substantial development. The central theme of the Children Act is that courts must be active in exercising their duty to do what is best for the child and therefore courts and not the parties are in charge. Rule 5 provides an example of this theme.

Requests to withdraw applications may be made either verbally in court with all parties including a guardian ad litem or a court welfare officer present, or in writing. A written request can be granted without a hearing if all parties agree. The guardian ad litem does not have to agree as such, merely be given an opportunity to make representations. Even if there is all-party agreement the court may still refer the withdrawal request for adjudication on seven days' notice.

4.6. Transfer [...]

(1) Where an application is made, in accordance with the provisions of [the Allocation Order], to a county court for an order transferring proceedings from a magistrates' court following the refusal of the magistrates' court to order such a transfer, the applicant shall—
- (a) file the application in Form CHA58, together with a copy of the certificate issued by the magistrates' court, and
- (b) serve a copy of the documents mentioned in sub-paragraph (a) personally on all parties to the proceedings

which it is sought to have transferred, within 2 days after receipt by the applicant of the certificate.

(2) Within 2 days after receipt of the documents served under paragraph (1)(b), any party other than the applicant may file written representations.

(3) The court shall, not before the fourth day after the filing of the application under paragraph (1), unless the parties consent to earlier consideration, consider the application and either—
    (a) grant the application, whereupon the proper officer shall inform the parties of that decision, or
    (b) direct that a date be fixed for the hearing of the application, whereupon the proper officer shall fix such a date and give not less than 1 day's notice to the parties of the date so fixed.

(4) Where proceedings are transferred from a magistrates' court to a county court in accordance with the provisions of [the Allocation Order], the county court shall consider whether to transfer those proceedings to the High Court in accordance with that Order and either—
    (a) determine that such an order need not be made,
    (b) make such an order,
    (c) order that a date be fixed for the hearing of the question whether such an order should be made, whereupon the proper officer shall give such notice to the parties as the court directs of the date so fixed, or
    (d) invite the parties to make written representations, within a specified period, as to whether such an order should be made; and upon receipt of the representations the court shall act in accordance with sub-paragraph (a), (b) or (c).

(5) The proper officer shall notify the parties of an order transferring the proceedings from a county court or from the High Court made in accordance with the provisions of [the Allocation Order].

[(6) Before ordering the transfer of proceedings from a county court to a magistrates' court in accordance with the Allocation Order, the county court shall notify the magistrates' court of its intention to make such an order and invite the views of the clerk to the justices on whether such an order should be made.

(7) An order transferring proceedings from a county court to a magistrates' court in accordance with the Allocation Order shall—
    (a) be in form CHA66, and
    (b) be served by the court on the parties.

(8) In this rule "the Allocation Order" means the Children (Allocation of Proceedings) Order 1991 or any Order replacing that Order.]

AMENDMENTS

The words in square brackets were deleted by the Family Proceedings (Amendment) Rules 1991 (S.I. 1991 No. 2113), reg. 11 (October 14, 1991).

The words in square brackets were substituted by the Family Proceedings (Amendment) Rules 1991 (S.I. 1991 No. 2113), reg. 10 (October 14, 1991).

Paragraphs (6), (7) and (8) were added by the Family Proceedings (Amendment) Rules 1991 (S.I. 1991 No. 2113), reg. 12 (October 14, 1991).

Transfer of proceedings

6.—(1) Where, in any relevant proceedings, the justices' clerk or the court receives a request in writing from a party that the proceedings be transferred to another family proceedings court or to a county court, the justices' clerk or court shall issue a certificate in the appropriate form in Schedule 1 to these Rules, granting or refusing the request in accordance with any Order made by the Lord Chancellor under Part I of Schedule 11.

(2) Where a request is granted under paragraph (1), the justices' clerk shall send a copy of the certificate—
   (a) to the parties,
   (b) to any guardian ad litem, and
   (c) to the family proceedings court or to the county court to which the proceedings are to be transferred.

(3) Any consent given or refused by a justices' clerk in accordance with any Order made by the Lord Chancellor under Part I of Schedule 11 shall be recorded in writing by the justices' clerk at the time it is given or refused or as soon as practicable thereafter.

(4) Where a request to transfer proceedings to a county court is refused under paragraph (1), the person who made the request may apply in accordance with rule 4.6 of the Family Proceedings Rules 1991 for an order under any Order made by the Lord Chancellor under Part I of Schedule 11.

GENERAL NOTE

These two rules are inevitably slightly different as they view transfers from different jurisdictional standpoints. They should be read in conjunction with the Children (Allocation of Proceedings) Order 1991 (S.I. 1991 No. 1677) (see p. 432). The Allocation Order deals with the grounds for transfers, whereas these Rules deal with the procedure. Together they form the machinery of concurrent jurisdiction: more complex cases are dealt with by the county or High Court, with most cases remaining at Family Proceedings Court level. The aim is to achieve smooth transfers up, down and across the jurisdictions.

There are to be standard file covers and a nationwide system of file and case reference numbers to enable courts to keep track of cases. Each court has its own reference number, and also included in the case reference number is the year in which the case is commenced and the number of the application. For example, if the application in question is the 20th filed in the Nottingham Family Proceedings Court in 1992, the number will be FPC/2568/92/20. The complete file including the standard file cover and case number will be sent to the receiving court if there is a transfer. Requests for transfer are to be made in writing to the court currently holding the case. Transfers can be ordered on application at a hearing or a directions hearing, or without either. The court can order a transfer of its own initiative. The grant or refusal of a request to transfer is to be recorded in writing with notification to the parties.

FPR, Paras. 1–3

These paragraphs deal with the procedure for appeals against refusals by a Family Proceedings Court to transfer to a county court. Any party may apply to transfer the case, and appeals against refusal require rapid action. The tight timetable is triggered unusually: the date of transfer is irrelevant. The clock starts running upon the date of receipt of the Certificate of Refusal by the applicant for a transfer (who is not necessarily the applicant in the proceedings as a whole). Within two days the applicant must file in the county court the Certificate of Refusal together with Form CHA 58, Application for Reconsideration of a Refusal to Transfer. Within the same two days, copies of the same documents must be served upon all parties who themselves then have two days after receipt to file written representations.

After four days of receipt of the documents, the county court can either grant the application or direct that there be a hearing with a minimum of one day's notice to the parties.

Rule 4.6 is therefore a clear example of the expectation that courts will keep cases moving and not spend undue time upon procedural details. The timetable can be foreshortened with the parties' consent (para. 3).

Para. 4

Upon receipt of a case transferred up, county courts must automatically consider transfer to the High Court. The decision can be taken without consultation with the parties or on the basis of written representations, or at a hearing.

Paras. 6–8

The last three paragraphs were added by the Family Proceedings (Amendment) Rules 1991 (S.I. 1991 No. 2113) and deal with transfers or retransfers from the county court back to the Family Proceedings Courts. The criteria are set out in the Children (Allocation of Proceedings) Order at p. 432. Consultation between the courts is necessary. Local liaison between courts on the general questions of allocation is likely to take place to prevent cases undertaking epic journeys.

4.7. Parties

(1) The respondents to proceedings to which this Part applies shall be those persons set out in the relevant entry in [column (iii)] of Appendix 3 to these rules.

(2) In proceedings to which this Part applies, a person may file a request in writing that he or another person—

(a) be joined as a party, or
(b) cease to be a party.

(3) On considering a request under paragraph (2) the court shall, subject to paragraph (4)—

(a) grant it without a hearing or representations, save that this shall be done only in the case of a request under paragraph (2)(a), whereupon the proper officer shall inform the parties and the person making the request of that decision, or

(b) order that a date be fixed for the consideration of the request, whereupon the proper officer shall give notice of the date so fixed, together with a copy of the request—

  (i) in the case of a request under paragraph (2)(a), to the applicant, and
  (ii) in the case of a request under paragraph (2)(b), to the parties, or

(c) invite the parties or any of them to make written representations, within a specified period, as to whether the request should be granted; and upon the expiry of the period the court shall act in accordance with sub-paragraph (a) or (b).

(4) Where a person with parental responsibility requests that he be joined under paragraph (2)(a), the court shall grant his request.

(5) In proceedings to which this Part applies the court may direct—

(a) that a person who would not otherwise be a respondent under these rules be joined as a party to the proceedings, or

(b) that a party to the proceedings cease to be a party.

AMENDMENT

The words in square brackets were substituted by the Family Proceedings (Amendment No. 2) Rules 1992 (S.I. 1992 No. 2067), r. 7 (October 5, 1992).

Parties

7.—(1) The respondents to relevant proceedings shall be those persons set out in the relevant entry in column (iii) of Schedule 2 to these Rules.

(2) In any relevant proceedings a person may file a request in writing that he or another person—

(a) be joined as a party, or
(b) cease to be a party.

(3) On considering a request under paragraph (2) the court shall, subject to paragraph (4)—

(a) grant it without a hearing or representations, save that this shall be done only in the case of a request under paragraph (2)(a), whereupon the justices' clerk shall inform the parties and the person making the request of that decision, or

(b) order that a date be fixed for the consideration of the request, whereupon the justices' clerk shall give notice of the date so fixed, together with a copy of the request—

  (i) in the case of a request under paragraph (2)(a), to the applicant, and

  (ii) in the case of a request under paragraph (2)(b), to the parties, or

(c) invite the parties or any of them to make written representations, within a specified period, as to whether the request should be granted; and upon the expiry of the period the court shall act in accordance with sub-paragraph (a) or (b).

(4) Where a person with parental responsibility requests that he be joined under paragraph (2)(a), the court shall grant his request.

(5) In any relevant proceedings the court may direct—

(a) that a person who would not otherwise be a respondent under these Rules be joined as a party to the proceedings, or

(b) that a party to the proceedings cease to be a party.

GENERAL NOTE

Details of applicants are set out in the main body of the Act in the relevant sections for each application. Respondent status is dealt with by the Rules. Rules 4.7 and 7 should be read in conjunction with Appendix 3 (FPR) and Schedule 2 (FPC), which cover the same ground by tabulating each Children Act section under which an application can be issued, minimum notice periods, automatic respondents, and persons to whom notice is to be given. In the early editions of the rules the last two columns were inverted in the two sets of rules. This trap for the unwary has been removed by the Amendment (No. 2) Rules, later editions are therefore uniform. At any time during a case, any person may apply in writing for party status, and likewise, a party may lose that status on their own application or on the application of another party. Again flexibility and the open door policy are clearly in evidence.

There are further elements of flexibility in the definitions of respondents to the various applications, but parental responsibility is an important factor: persons with parental responsibility must always be joined as respondents if they so request (para. 4). Certain categories of persons are automatic respondents in all applications, those being:

1. every person whom the applicant believes to have parental responsibility for the child;
2. where the child is the subject of a care order, every person whom the applicant believes to have parental responsibility immediately before the making of the care order;
3. in the case of an application to extend, vary or discharge an order, the parties to the proceedings leading to the order which it is sought to have extended, varied or discharged.
4. in specified proceedings, the child.

As well as the above, various other persons qualify as automatic respondents in each particular application, full details of which are set out in Appendix 3 and Schedule 2 at pp. 411–415 and 422–428.

Respondent status can be conferred by the Court without a hearing, but any decision concerning the proposed termination of a respondent's status, must be either at a hearing or on the basis of written representations from the parties (para. 3).

Rule 7 does not refer to the second class citizens of the Children Act: persons who are not automatic respondents but must be given notice (see para. 3 of r. 4.4 and r. 4), they are detailed in the columns of Appendix 3 and Schedule 2. Whilst it is clear that the columns need to be checked when issuing any Children Act application to ensure that notice is given to the persons listed, it is, nevertheless, not entirely clear as to what degree of detail is to be supplied. A copy of the application form is not necessary but details of the applicant, child, nature of the application, together with the court details and date, time and place of the hearing, would seem to be the bare essentials.

The purpose of the notice provision is to enable people who do not qualify as respondents but are concerned with the child, to be kept informed, and to thereby be able to seek leave to be joined as respondents if they so choose, without turning every Children Act case into multi party action.

Persons to be given notice in all cases are:
1. the Local Authority providing accommodation for the child;
2. persons caring for the child at the time when proceedings are commenced (this will often include foster parents, grandparents and other relatives);
3. the person providing a refuge under section 51 if the child is so accommodated.

GENERAL NOTE

It should be noted that in section 8 applications, certain categories of people have been promoted by the Amendment (No. 2) Rules 1992. Persons believed by the applicant to be named in existing court orders, parties to pending proceedings and those with whom the child has lived for at least three years prior to the application are non-automatic respondents and not merely entitled to notice as before.

In certain situations, there will be no automatic respondents at all and nobody will need to be given notice, *e.g.* a single mother applying for a prohibited steps order against a boyfriend whom she discovers to have a history of child abuse. Even if the boyfriend is the father of the child, in the absence of his having parental responsibility, he will not be an automatic respondent. Nor would he be entitled to notice. If he is a person with whom the child had lived at least three years prior to the application, he would however become a respondent. Of course the court could join him as a respondent on its own initiative or his application. If the boyfriend were not the father, the father would only become a respondent if he had parental responsibility. Commentators have expressed concern that many Children Act cases will be swamped with parties, there are also likely to be a sizeable number of one party cases.

4.8. Service

(1) Subject to the requirement in rule 4.6(1)(b) of personal service, where service of a document is required under this Part (and not by a provision to which section 105(8) (Service of notice or other document under the Act) applies) it may be affected—
    (a) if the person to be served is not known by the person serving to be acting by solicitor—
        (i) by delivering it to him personally, or
        (ii) by delivering it at, or by sending it by first-class post to, his residence or his last known residence, or
    (b) if the person to be served is known by the person serving to be acting by solicitor—
        (i) by delivering the document at, or sending it by first-class post to, the solicitor's address for service,
        (ii) where the solicitor's address for service includes a numbered box at a document exchange, by leaving the document at that document exchange or at a document exchange which transmits documents on every business day to that document exchange, or
        (iii) by sending a legible copy of the document by facsimile transmission to the solicitor's office.

(2) In this rule "first-class post" means first-class post which has been pre-paid or in respect of which pre-payment is not required.

(3) Where a child who is a party to proceedings to which this Part applies is required by these rules or other rules of court to serve a document, service shall be effected by—
    (a) the solicitor acting for the child, or
    (b) where there is not such solicitor, the guardian ad litem, or
    (c) where there is neither such a solicitor nor a guardian ad litem, the court.

(4) Service of any document on a child [who is not prosecuting or defending the proceedings concerned without a next friend or guardian ad litem under rule 9.2A] shall, subject to any direction of the court, be effected by service on—
    (a) the solicitor acting for the child, or
    (b) where there is no such solicitor, the guardian ad litem, or
    (c) where there is neither such a solicitor nor a guardian ad litem, with leave of the court, the child.

(5) Where the court refuses leave under paragraph (4)(c) it shall give a direction under paragraph (8).

(6) A document shall, unless the contrary is proved, be deemed to have been served—
    (a) in the case of service by first-class post, on the second business day after posting, and
    (b) in the case of service in accordance with paragraph (1)(b)(ii), on the second business day after the day on which it is left at the document exchange.

(7) At or before the first directions appointment in, or hearing of, proceedings to which this Part applies the applicant shall file a statement that service of—
> (a) a copy of the application has been effected on each respondent, and
> (b) notice of the proceedings has been effected under rule 4.4(3);

and the statement shall indicate—
> > (i) the manner, date, time and place of service, or
> > (ii) where service was effected by post, the date, time and place of posting.

For rule 4.8(8), there shall be substituted the following—
[(8) In proceedings to which this Part applies, where these rules or other rules of court require a document to be served, the court may, without prejudice to any power under rule 4.14, direct that—
> (a) the requirement shall not be apply;
> (b) the time specified by the rules for complying with the requirement shall be abridged to such extent as may be specified in the direction;
> (c) service shall be effected in such manner as may be specified in the direction.]

AMENDMENT

The words in square brackets were substituted by the Family Proceedings (Amendment) Rules 1992 (S.I. 1992 No. 456), reg. 4 (April 1, 1992) and the Family Proceedings (Amendment No. 2) Rules 1992 (S.I. 1992 No. 2067), r. 19 (October 5, 1992).

Service

8.—(1) Where service of a document is required by these Rules (and not by a provision to which section 105(8) (service of notice or other document under the Act) applies) it may be effected—
> (a) if the person to be served is not known by the person serving to be acting by solicitor—
> > (i) by delivering it to him personally, or
> > (ii) by delivering it at, or by sending it by first-class post to, his residence or his last known residence, or
> (b) if the person to be served is known by the person serving to be acting by solicitor—
> > (i) by delivering the document at, or sending it by first-class post to, the solicitor's address for service,
> > (ii) where the solicitor's address for service includes a numbered box at a document exchange, by leaving the document at that document exchange or at a document exchange which transmits documents on every business day to that document exchange, or
> > (iii) by sending a legible copy of the document by facsimile transmission to the solicitor's office.

(2) In this rule, "first-class post" means first-class post which had been pre-paid or in respect of which pre-payment is not required.

(3) Where a child who is a party to any relevant proceedings is required by these Rules to serve a document, service shall be effected by—

    (a) the solicitor acting for the child,
    (b) where there is no such solicitor, the guardian ad litem, or
    (c) where there is neither such a solicitor nor a guardian ad litem, the justices' clerk.

(4) Service of any document on a child shall, subject to any direction of the justices' clerk or the court, be effected by service on—

    (a) the solicitor acting for the child,
    (b) where there is no such solicitor, the guardian ad litem, or
    (c) where there is neither such a solicitor nor a guardian ad litem, with leave of the justices' clerk or the court, the child.

(5) Where the justices' clerk or the court refuses leave under paragraph (4)(c), a direction shall be given under paragraph (8).

(6) A document shall, unless the contrary is proved, be deemed to have been served—

    (a) in the case of service by first-class post, on the second business day after posting, and
    (b) in the case of service in accordance with paragraph (1)(b)(ii), on the second business day after the day on which it is left at the document exchange.

(7) At or before the first directions appointment in, or hearing of, relevant proceedings, whichever occurs first, the applicant shall file a statement that service of—

    (a) a copy of the application has been effected on each respondent, and
    (b) notice of the proceedings has been effected under rule 4(3);

and the statement shall indicate—

        (i) the manner, date, time and place of service, or
        (ii) where service was effected by post, the date, time and place of posting.

[(8) In any relevant proceedings, where these rules require a document to be served, the court or the justices' clerk may, without prejudice to any power under rule 14, direct that—

    (a) the requirement shall not apply;
    (b) the time specified by the rules for complying with the requirement shall be abridged to such extent as may be specified in the direction;
    (c) service shall be effected in such a manner as may be specified in the direction.]

AMENDMENT

Subsection 8 was substituted by the Family Proceedings Courts (Miscellaneous Amendments) Rules 1992 (S.I. 1992 No. 2068), Sched., para. 2 (October 5, 1992).

GENERAL NOTE

Responsibility for service rests with the parties: each party must file their various documents with the court and serve copies upon all other parties. The court itself only has responsibility for serving reports of guardians ad litem and court welfare officers, directions and orders (other than *ex parte* orders).

For applications under Parts I–V of the Children Act, service can be either personal or by first-class post. The latter will be the norm, though the former may be specifically ordered by the court in certain cases. If the person to be served is "known by the person serving to be acting by Solicitor," service may be to the solicitor's office by personal delivery, by first-class post, by document exchange, or by fax. Fax transmissions are required to be legible.

The expression "known to be acting by a solicitor" contains potential for difficulty. Guidance in the form of case law or practice directions will be needed if solicitors are to avoid having their post bag swelled with documents for former clients, while parties and others remain ignorant of developments in their childrens' cases. The Rule assumes a degree of Solicitor/Client loyalty which is not universal.

Paras. 3–5

These provisions deal with the requirements of service of documents on behalf of and upon children. In specified proceedings, children will be parties and in such cases there is a difficult balancing exercise between the child's right to know and the need to avoid bombarding children with formal and potentially upsetting paperwork. Service upon the child's solicitor, or if none, the GAL is sufficient. The solicitor or GAL thereafter, has a duty to explain the contents to the child if of sufficient understanding (rr. 4.12 and 12, rr. 4.11(8) and 11(8)). In very few cases in which there is neither solicitor nor guardian, service can only be effected upon the child with the leave of the court and can be dispensed with altogether (paras. 4(c) and 8).

Para. 7

The applicant is required to prove service by filing a statement (not affidavit) of service, including all the details of service: confirmation that copies have been sent to respondents, notice given to those entitled and in particular, the date, time and place of posting for service should be set out.

Para. 8

There is power to dispense with service: this power is likely to be exercised in cases in which it is demonstrated that respondents have disappeared, or in cases of service upon children, that the children are either too young to be served or likely to be distressed by the contents of the documents in question. The Amendment (No. 2) Rules 1992 give courts the power to shorten service periods where appropriate. This provision provides a welcome element of flexibility. There is also a specific power to dispense with service.

4.9. Answer to application

(1) Within 14 days of service of an application for a section 8 order, each respondent shall file, and serve on the parties, an answer to the application in Form CHA10A.

(2) Within 14 days after service of an application under Schedule 1, each respondent shall file, and serve on the parties, an answer to the application in Form CHA13A.

(3) Following service of an application to which this Part applies, other than an application under rule 4.3 or for a section 8 order, a respondent may, subject to paragraph (4), file a written answer, which shall be served on the other parties.

(4) An answer under paragraph (3) shall, except in the case of an application under section 25, 31, 34, 38, 43, 44, 45, 46, 48 or 50, be

filed, and served, not less than two days before the date fixed for the hearing of the application.

Answer to application

9.—(1) Within 14 days of service of an application for a section 8 order, each respondent shall file and serve on the parties an answer to the application in the appropriate form in Schedule 1 to these Rules.

(2) Within 14 days of service of an application under Schedule 1, each respondent shall file and serve on the parties an answer to the application in the appropriate form in Schedule 1 to these Rules.

4.10. Appointment of guardian ad litem

(1) As soon as practicable after the commencement of specified proceedings, or the transfer of such proceedings to the court, the court shall appoint a guardian ad litem unless—
- (a) such an appointment has already been made by the court which made the transfer and is subsisting, or
- (b) the court considers that such an appointment is not necessary to safeguard the interests of the child.

(2) At any stage in specified proceedings a party may apply, without notice to the other parties unless the court directs otherwise, for the appointment of a guardian ad litem.

(3) The court shall grant an application under paragraph (2) unless it considers such an appointment not to be necessary to safeguard the interests of the child, in which case it shall give its reasons; and a note of such reasons shall be taken by the proper officer.

(4) At any stage in specified proceedings the court may, of its own motion, appoint a guardian ad litem.

(5) The proper officer shall, as soon as practicable, notify the parties and any welfare officer of an appointment under this rule or, as the case may be, of a decision not to make such an appointment.

(6) Upon the appointment of a guardian ad litem the proper officer shall, as soon as practicable, notify him of the appointment and serve on him copies of the application and of documents filed under rule 4.17(1).

(7) A guardian ad litem appointed from a panel established by regulations made under section 41(7) shall not—
- (a) be a member, officer or servant of a local authority which, or an authorised person (within the meaning of section 31(9)) who, is a party to the proceedings, unless he is employed by such an authority solely as a member of a panel of guardians ad litem and reporting officers;
- (b) be, or have been, a member, officer or servant of a local authority or voluntary organisation (within the meaning of section 105(1)) who has been directly concerned in that capacity in arrangements relating to the care, accommodation or welfare of the child during the five years prior to the commencement of the proceedings;

(c) be a serving probation officer (except that a probation officer who has not in that capacity been previously concerned with the child or his family and who is employed part-time may, when not engaged in his duties as a probation officer, act as a guardian ad litem).

(8) When appointing a guardian ad litem the court shall consider the appointment of anyone who has previously acted as guardian ad litem of the same child.

(9) The appointment of a guardian ad litem under this rule shall continue for such time as specified in the appointment or until terminated by the court.

(10) When terminating an appointment in accordance with paragraph (9), the court shall give its reasons in writing for so doing.

(11) Where the court appoints a guardian ad litem in accordance with this rule or refuses to make such an appointment, the court or the proper officer shall record the appointment or refusal in Form CHA30.

Appointment of guardian ad litem

10.—(1) As soon as practicable after the commencement of specified proceedings or the transfer of such proceedings to the court, the justices' clerk or the court shall appoint a guardian ad litem unless—
(a) such an appointment has already been made by the court which made the transfer and is subsisting, or
(b) the justices' clerk or the court considers that such an appointment is not necessary to safeguard the interests of the child.

(2) At any stage in specified proceedings a party may apply, without notice to the other parties unless the justices' clerk or the court otherwise directs, for the appointment of a guardian ad litem.

(3) The justices' clerk or the court shall grant an application under paragraph (2) unless it is considered that such an appointment is not necessary to safeguard the interests of the child, in which case reasons shall be given; and a note of such reasons shall be taken by the justices' clerk.

(4) At any stage in specified proceedings the justices' clerk or the court may appoint a guardian ad litem even though no application is made for such an appointment.

(5) The justices' clerk shall, as soon as practicable, notify the parties and any welfare officer of an appointment under this rule or, as the case may be, of a decision not to make such an appointment.

(6) Upon the appointment of a guardian ad litem the justices' clerk shall, as soon as practicable, notify him of the appointment and serve on him copies of the application and of documents filed under rule 17(1).

(7) A guardian ad litem appointed from a panel established by regulations made under section 41(7) shall not—
(a) be a member, officer or servant of a local authority which, or an authorised person (within the meaning of section 31(9)) who, is a party to the proceedings unless he is

employed by such an authority solely as a member of a panel of guardians ad litem and reporting officers;
(b) be, or have been, a member, officer or servant of a local authority or voluntary organisation (within the meaning of section 105(1)) who has been directly concerned in that capacity in arrangements relating to the care, accommodation or welfare of the child during the five years prior to the commencement of the proceedings;
(c) be a serving probation officer (except that a probation officer who has not in that capacity been previously concerned with the child or his family and who is employed part-time may, when not engaged in his duties as a probation officer, act as a guardian ad litem).

(8) When appointing a guardian ad litem, the justices' clerk or the court shall consider the appointment of anyone who has previously acted as guardian ad litem of the same child.

(9) The appointment of a guardian ad litem under this rule shall continue for such time as is specified in the appointment or until terminated by the court.

(10) When terminating an appointment in accordance with paragraph (9), the court shall give reasons in writing for so doing, a note of which shall be taken by the justices' clerk.

(11) Where the justices' clerk or the court appoints a guardian ad litem in accordance with this rule or refuses to make such an appointment, the justices' clerk shall record the appointment or refusal in the appropriate form in Schedule 1 to these Rules.

DEFINITIONS

"Local Authority": s.105(1).
"panel of GALs": s.41(7), reg. 2(1), Galro Panels Regs.
"voluntary organisation": s.105(1).

GENERAL NOTE

Rules 10 and 11 concern the appointment, powers and duties of guardians ad litem, and they should be read together and in conjunction with sections 41 and 42 and the GALRO Panels Regulations. (see p. 483). Comparison between rules 10 and 11 and the pre-Children Act Law (Magistrates' Courts Children & Young Persons Rules 1988, r. 16) is instructive: guardians now have an enhanced role. Essentially, the guardian's portfolio has been expanded. Whereas formerly, a guardian was the writer of a report to which serious attention must be given, under the Children Act the guardian becomes the Court's chief child care advisor at every stage, and in respect of all issues in care cases. *Guidance*, Vol. 7, para. 2.2:

> "Guardians ad litem are ... charged with playing a full and active role in advising the Court on issues of case management, in addition to the role they always had of representing the interests of the child, and advising the Courts from a social work perspective. They have a pro-active role with regard to the conduct of proceedings including timetabling and offering advice to the Courts on the range of orders available."

And further in the Manual of Practice Guidance for Guardians at Litem and Reporting Officers (Department of Health) at p.3:

> "The crucial importance of the guardian ad litem's role is that it stands at the interface between the conflicting rights and powers of courts, local authorities, and natural and substitute parents in relation to the child. The guardian has to safeguard the child's interests, to ensure the most positive outcome possible for the child. The guardian also has to make a judgement between the potentially

conflicting demands of children's rights, children's rescue, the autonomy of the family and the duty of the state."

Rule 10 deals only with specified proceedings. The question has arisen as to whether guardians can be appointed in non-specified proceedings, in particular in section 8 applications by Local Authorities. Rule 14(2)(d) appears to create the possibility of such an appointment with the words "the appointment of a guardian whether under section 41 *or otherwise*", see p. 389. Had such a widening of guardian ad litem availability been the intention, it would be expected that the details would be located in rule 10 and not in rule 14 which deals with directions. It is clear that the Local Authority is not obliged to pay for guardians in non-specified proceedings (GALRO Panels Regulations 1991, art. 9(1), art. 1 at pp. 484 and 488). Where there are linked Private and Public Law cases involving different children in a same family, the person acting as guardian ad litem could be requested to provide a court welfare report under section 7 if the court appointed the Local Authority and the Local Authority delegated the task to the guardian. In such case rule 13, not rules 10 and 11 would apply. However, courts have been appointing guardians in non-specified proceedings and clarification is needed.

Non-panel guardian ad litem can be appointed in an entirely different capacity as a next friend in county and High Court proceedings (see Pt. IX of FPR). It is probably this provision to which rule 14(2)(d) is referring.

The lack of guardians in private law cases can lead to potential difficulties, *e.g.* in an application for a residence order concerning a child formerly subject to care proceedings. However, there is nothing to stop the guardian's report from the previous proceedings being made available to the Court, or even a former guardian ad litem acting as a witness.

For information concerning the role of the Official Solicitor in High Court cases, see commentary upon section 41 at p. 123.

Para. 1

There is a strong presumption of appointment as early as possible in specified proceedings. The presumption of appointment as set out in rule 10 is a direct repetition of section 41(1) and is much stronger than under the old law (for purposes of comparison, see *R. v. Plymouth Juvenile Court, ex p. F & F* [1987] 1 F.L.R. 169).

Para. 3

Reasons for non-appointment must be given to the parties and a note taken by the court. Given the strength of the presumption of appointment, it is difficult to envisage what reasons there could ever be. Delay was amongst the more common factors influencing courts against appointment under the pre-Children Act regime, particularly in areas of scarcity of guardians ad litem. However, it is clearly envisaged that the GALRO Panels will operate within the context of the avoidance of delay principle, thereby theoretically eliminating delay as a reason for proceeding without a guardian. Other situations could include long running cases with numerous applications over a period of years reserved to a particular Judge. The guardian may leave the panel and the Judge, who is sufficiently familiar with the case to proceed without a fresh incumbent being appointed. Such situations would be very rare.

Para. 7

Whilst the management of GALRO Panels remains in the hands of Local Authorities, there are numerous additional safeguards to bolster the independence of the guardian's position. See commentary upon the GALRO Panels Regulations at p. 483. Guardians may now be employed by the Local Authorities into whose cases they will be inquiring. However, paragraph 7 seeks to ensure independence by dis-barring the appointment of anyone as a guardian who is:

1. a member, officer or servant of the Local Authority which is a party to the proceedings (unless the employment by the Local Authority is solely in the capacity of a guardian ad litem);

2. likewise, in respect of the NSPCC where that organisation is bringing proceedings;

3. the person who has had previous official child care involvement with the child during the five years prior to commencement of proceedings;

4. full-time Probation Officer;

5. a part-time Probation Officer who has had official involvement with the child or the child's family.

Even if the guardian does not come within one of the above categories, if there is any risk of their position being seen to be other than one of total independence, they should seek guidance from the court (for further details see *Guidance*, Vol. 7, pp. 10–11).

Para. 8

Continuity can be a great benefit both in avoiding repetitious enquiries and thereby acting expeditiously. There are also less specific benefits in terms of "feel" of cases over a period of time. The court is therefore required to actively consider re-appointing a former guardian ad litem of the same child in subsequent proceedings. Although the rule does not say so, it would seem to be helpful for courts to try to appoint a guardian who has acted for a child of the same family.

Paras. 9 and 10

Termination of a guardian's appointment in a specific case is solely within the authority of the court. No specific criteria for termination are provided, merely a requirement for reasons to be given and noted by the court. Courts can terminate of their own initiative or on application by a party. Termination altogether as a guardian from the panel is within the province of Local Authorities (see GALRO Panels Regs., reg. 5, p. 486).

The guardian's ad litem appointment is now time limited and may continue after the completion of the case. The guardian has responsibilities relating to appeals and may wish to make representations on behalf of the child under section 26 (see p. 83). It may also be appropriate for the Local Authority to consult the guardian about decisions under section 22(4)(d). It may be particularly helpful to have a guardian involved in relation to potential disputes over contact if the Court orders reasonable contact under section 34.

4.11. Powers and duties of guardian ad litem

(1) In carrying out his duty under section 41(2), the guardian ad litem shall have regard to the principle set out in section 1(2) and the matters set out in section 1(3)(a) to (f) as if for the word "court" in that section there were substituted the words "guardian ad litem."

(2) The guardian ad litem shall—
    (a) appoint a solicitor to represent the child unless such a solicitor has already been appointed, and
    (b) give such advice to the child as is appropriate having regard to his understanding and, subject to rule 4.12(1)(a), instruct the solicitor representing the child on all matters relevant to the interests of the child, including possibilities for appeal, arising in the course of the proceedings.

[(2A) Where the guardian ad litem is the Official Solicitor, paragraph 2(a) shall not require him to appoint a solicitor for the child if he intends to act as the child's solicitor in the proceedings, unless—
    (a) the child wishes to instruct a solicitor direct; and
    (b) the Official Solicitor or the court considers that he is of sufficient understanding to do so.]

(3) Where it appears to the guardian ad litem that the child—
    (a) is instructing his solicitor direct, or
    (b) intends to, and is capable of, conducting the proceedings on his own belief,

he shall so inform the court and thereafter—
- (i) shall perform all of his duties set out in this rule, other than duties under paragraph (2)(a) and such other duties as the court may direct,
- (ii) shall take such part in the proceedings as the court may direct, and
- (iii) may, with leave of the court, have legal representation in his conduct of those duties.

(4) The guardian ad litem shall, unless excused by the court, attend all directions appointments in and hearing of the proceedings and shall advise the court on the following matters—
- (a) whether the child is of sufficient understanding for any purpose including the child's refusal to submit to a medical or psychiatric examination or other assessment that the court has power to require, direct or order;
- (b) the wishes of the child in respect of any matter relevant to the proceedings, including his attendance at court;
- (c) the appropriate forum for the proceedings;
- (d) the appropriate timing of the proceedings or any part of them;
- (e) the options available to it in respect of the child and the suitability of each such option including what order should be made in determining the application;
- (f) any other matter concerning which the court seeks his advice or concerning which he considers that the court should be informed.

(5) The advice given under paragraph (4) may, subject to any order of the court, be given orally or in writing and if the advice be given orally, a note of it shall be taken by the court or the proper officer.

(6) The guardian ad litem shall, where practicable, notify any person whose joinder as a party to those proceedings would be likely, in the guardian ad litem's opinion, to safeguard the interests of the child, of that person's right to apply to be joined under rule 4.7(2) and shall inform the court—
- (a) of any such notification given,
- (b) of anyone whom he attempted to notify under this paragraph but was unable to contact, and
- (c) of anyone whom he believes may wish to be joined to the proceedings.

(7) The guardian ad litem shall, unless the court otherwise directs, not less than seven days before the date fixed for the final hearing of the proceedings, file a written report advising on the interests of the child; and the proper officer shall, as soon as practicable, serve a copy of the reports on the parties.

(8) The guardian ad litem shall serve and accept service of documents on behalf of the child in accordance with rule 4.8(3)(b) and (4)(b) and, where the child has not himself been served, and has sufficient understanding, advise the child of the contents of any document so served.

(9) The guardian ad litem shall make such investigations as may be necessary for him to carry out his duties and shall, in particular—
- (a) contact or seek to interview such persons as he thinks appropriate or as the court directs,

(b) if he inspects records of the kinds referred to in section 42, bring to the attention of the court and such other persons as the court may direct all such records and documents which may, in his opinion, assist in the proper determination of the proceedings, and
(c) obtain such professional assistance as is available to him which he thinks appropriate or which the court directs him to obtain.

(10) In addition to his duties under other paragraphs of this rule, the guardian ad litem shall provide to the court such other assistance as it may require.

(11) A party may question the guardian ad litem about oral or written advice tendered by him to the court under this rule.

AMENDMENT

Paragraph (2A) was added by the Family Proceedings (Amendment) Rules 1991 (S.I. 1991 No. 2113), reg. 13 (October 14, 1991).

Powers and duties of guardian ad litem

11.—(1) In carrying out his duty under section 41(2), the guardian ad litem shall have regard to the principle set out in section 1(2) and the matters set out in section 1(3)(a) to (f) as if for the word "court" in that section there were substituted the words "guardian ad litem."

(2) The guardian ad litem shall—
(a) appoint a solicitor to represent the child, unless such a solicitor has already been appointed, and
(b) give such advice to the child as is appropriate having regard to his understanding and, subject to rule 12(1)(a), instruct the solicitor representing the child on all matters relevant to the interests of the child, including possibilities for appeal, arising in the course of the proceedings.

(3) Where it appears to the guardian ad litem that the child—
(a) is instructing his solicitor direct, or
(b) intends to, and is capable of, conducting the proceedings on his own belief,

he shall so inform the court through the justices' clerk and thereafter—
(i) shall perform all of his duties set out in this rule, other than duties under paragraph (2)(a) and such other duties as the justices' clerk or the court may direct,
(ii) shall take such part in the proceedings as the justices' clerk or the court may direct, and
(iii) may, with leave of the justices' clerk or the court, have legal representation in his conduct of those duties.

(4) The guardian ad litem shall, unless excused by the justices' clerk or the court, attend all directions appointments in, and hearing of, the proceedings and shall advise the justices' clerk or the court on the following matters—
(a) whether the child is of sufficient understanding for any purpose including the child's refusal to submit to a

medical or psychiatric examination or other assessment that the court has power to require, direct or order;
- (b) the wishes of the child in respect of any matter relevant to the proceedings, including his attendance at court;
- (c) the appropriate forum for the proceedings;
- (d) the appropriate timing of the proceedings or any part of them;
- (e) the options available to it in respect of the child and the suitability of each such option including what order should be made in determining the application;
- (f) any other matter concerning which the justices' clerk or the court seeks his advice or concerning which he considers that the court should be informed.

(5) The advice given under paragraph (4) may, subject to any order of the court, be given orally or in writing; and if the advice be given orally, a note of it shall be taken by the justices' clerk or the court.

(6) The guardian ad litem shall, where practicable, notify any person whose joinder as a party to those proceedings would be likely, in the guardian ad litem's opinion, to safeguard the interests of the child, of that person's right to apply to be joined under rule 7(2) and shall inform the justices' clerk or the court—
- (a) of any such notification given,
- (b) of anyone whom he attempted to notify under this paragraph but was unable to contact, and
- (c) of anyone whom he believes may wish to be joined to the proceedings.

(7) The guardian ad litem shall, unless the justices' clerk or the court otherwise directs, not less than seven days before the date fixed for the final hearing of the proceedings, file a written report advising on the interests of the child; and the justices' clerk shall, as soon as practicable, serve a copy of the reports on the parties.

(8) The guardian ad litem shall serve and accept service of documents on behalf of the child in accordance with rule 8(3)(b) and (4)(b) and, where the child has not himself been served, and has sufficient understanding, advise the child of the contents of any document so served.

(9) The guardian ad litem shall make such investigations as may be necessary for him to carry out his duties and shall, in particular—
- (a) contact or seek to interview such persons as he thinks appropriate or as the court directs,
- (b) if he inspects records of the kinds referred to in section 42, bring to the attention of the court, through the justices' clerk, and such other persons as the justices' clerk or the court may direct, all such records and documents which may, in his opinion, assist in the proper determination of the proceedings, and
- (c) obtain such professional assistance as is available to him which he thinks appropriate or which the justices' clerk or the court directs him to obtain.

(10) In addition to his duties under other paragraphs of this rule, the guardian ad litem shall provide to the justices' clerk and the court such other assistance as it may require.

(11) A party may question the guardian ad litem about oral or written advice tendered by him to the justices' clerk or the court under this rule.

GENERAL NOTE

The Rule sets out guardians' duties in detail ranging from instructing a solicitor through to advising the court at every stage of proceedings. The guardian is a vital cog to be consulted by the court for guidance on most, if not all, issues in care cases from commencement to appeal. Guided by the same principles as the court, in attendance at every hearing, with full access to documents and considering procedural as well as substantial issues, the guardian is decidedly the court's own child care advisor. In addition, the guardian retains the traditional role of representing the best interests of the child. Courts are required to listen to a guardian's advice: the decision in *Devon C.C.* v. *Glancy* (1985) 1 F.L.R. 20 is therefore likely to remain good law. If magistrates fail to follow advice received from a guardian without good reason, an appeal should ordinarily be allowed.

Para. 2

The Rule retains the element of flexibility on the question of whether childrens' solicitors are appointed by courts or guardians ad litem. There are varying local practices. Rule 11(2)(a) and rule 4.11(2)(a) permit appointments by guardians if a solicitor has not already been appointed by the court.

To some extent local practice has been determined by the availability of guardians: in areas of shortage resulting in delays before guardians were appointed, courts have felt it necessary to set on a solicitor for the child so that the child's interests can be at least partially represented. Where guardians are able to start work instantly, courts have sometimes preferred to allow them to choose their own legal working partners. There is no definitive guidance. Local negotiation and co-operation will need to continue to avoid difficulties.

Guardians ad litem give instructions to solicitors and the solicitor should accept their instructions in the absence of conflict with the child as set out at paragraph 3. This part of rule 11 should be read in conjunction with rule 4.12(1)(a) and rule 12(1)(a), and together they concern the rare but difficult question of conflict between child and guardian. Detailed commentary is set out at rule 12, p. 385. Guardians are required to form a view as to a child's capability and intentions as regard conflict. Little official guidance is available other than the *Gillick* principle set out by Lord Scarman in *Gillick* v. *West Norfolk Area Health Authority* [1986] A.C. 112: "It is not enough that she should understand the nature of the advice which is being given: she must also have sufficient maturity to understand what is involved" (p. 424).

Those words clearly echo beyond contraceptive advice from doctors, and may well be relevant as to the advice of guardians ad litem to children in care cases. Not many distressed adolescents or even younger children, will have sufficient maturity to understand the often far reaching repercussions of what is involved in care cases. Many guardians and solicitors find the *Gillick* test too restrictive and would argue that it does not strictly apply to Children Act proceedings. The higher courts are likely to take heed of *Gillick* should the issue of conflict ever become the subject of litigation in its own right. Whatever their applicability, Lord Scarman's words are helpful guidance in the very difficult situations of conflict between children and guardians.

It falls to the guardian to inform the court where a conflict is declared. Thereafter, guardians may themselves be represented. However, legal aid is not available and Local Authorities are not manifesting enthusiasm at the prospect of paying guardians' solicitors fees. The Department of Health's view is that guardians who have obtained the court's leave for separate representation will be able to claim their reasonable legal expenses from local authorities (*Manual of Practice Guidance* at p.26).

Paragraph 4.(5) put succinctly means that the guardian ad litem should be on hand to advise the court about anything relevant to the proceedings, including the five topics referred to at (a)–(e).

The corollary is that a court should consult its guardian ad litem about any significant steps throughout the proceedings. A court can seek a written opinion from the guardian without the necessity of a hearing. Guardians may therefore be required to provide interim reports of a general or specific nature.

Para. 6

This provision is illustrative of the breadth of the guardian's new role as advisor to the court: if in the course of investigations guardians unearth useful or willing potential respondents, the court should be so advised with a view to joinder.

Para. 7

Amongst their new duties, guardians ad litem are still to fulfil their central task of preparing a report. The report was the central element of the guardian's role: it is now one of many but remains a crucial function. There is as yet no statutory guidance on the form or content of reports. The Department of Health has issued a *Manual of Practice Guidance* to be read alongside the Green Guide for Guardians *ad litem*. The purpose of the report is "advising on the interests of the child." Guardians must resolve for themselves the layout and emphasis of their reports. There is officially no two-stage process in Children Act care cases and therefore the guardian's report may fulfil a slightly different function and in particular may help to identify the issues of agreement and conflict. Local Authorities remain in charge of GALRO Panels, but may not intervene to influence the time spent on cases by guardians ad litem (*R.* v. *Cornwall C.C., ex p. Cornwall & Isles of Scilly Galro Panel*) *The Times*, November 20, 1991.

Guardians' reports must be lodged not less than seven days before the final hearing unless the court orders otherwise. The court is responsible for distribution of the reports to the parties.

Para. 8

Either the solicitor for the child or the guardian ad litem or both are to advise the child in respect of the contents of any documents in the proceedings, according to the child's level of understanding (see r. 4.12(2) and r. 12(2), pp. 383 and 384).

Paras. 9 and 10

General guidance is given as to the guardian's ad litem investigations in terms of interviewing and inspecting records and obtaining expert assistance. Paragraphs 9(a) and 10 clearly envisage a degree of direction by courts to guardians. Courts can direct a guardian to interview named persons. Guardians are, however, chiefly of value for their experience and independent judgment: they should be given scope to proceed as they consider appropriate.

4.12. Solicitor for child

(1) A solicitor appointed under section 41(3) or in accordance with rule 4.11(2)(a) shall represent the child—
   (a) in accordance with instructions received from the guardian ad litem (unless the solicitor considers, having taken into account the views of the guardian ad litem and any direction of the court under rule 4.11(3), that the child wishes to give instructions which conflict with those of the guardian ad litem and that he is able, having regard to his understanding, to give such instructions on his own behalf in which case he shall conduct the proceedings in accordance with instructions received from the child), or
   (b) where no guardian ad litem has been appointed for the child and the condition in section 41(4)(b) is satisfied, in accordance with instructions received from the child, or
   (c) in default of instructions under (a) or (b), in furtherance of the best interests of the child.

(2) A solicitor appointed under section 41(3) or in accordance with rule 4.11(2)(a) shall serve and accept service of documents on behalf

of the child in accordance with rule 4.8(3)(a) and (4)(a) and, where the child has not himself been served and has sufficient understanding, advise the child of the contents of any document so served.

(3) Where the child wishes an appointment of a solicitor under section 41(3) or in accordance with rule 4.11(2)(a) to be terminated, he may apply to the court for an order terminating the appointment; and the solicitor and the guardian ad litem shall be given an opportunity to make representations.

(4) Where the guardian ad litem wishes an appointment of a solicitor under section 41(3) to be terminated, he may apply to the court for an order terminating the appointment; and the solicitor and, if he is of sufficient understanding, the child, shall be given an opportunity to make representations.

(5) When terminating an appointment in accordance with paragraph(3) or (4), the court shall give its reasons for so doing, a note of which shall be taken by the court or the proper officer.

(6) Where the court appoints a solicitor under section 41(3) or refuses to make such an appointment, the court or the proper officer shall record the appointment or refusal in form CHA31.

Solicitor for child

12.—(1) A solicitor appointed under section 41(3) or in accordance with rule 11(2)(a) shall represent the child—
   (a) in accordance with instructions received from the guardian ad litem (unless the solicitor considers, having taken into account the views of the guardian ad litem and any direction of the court under rule 11(3), that the child wishes to give instructions which conflict with those of the guardian ad litem and that he is able, having regard to his understanding, to give such instructions on his own behalf in which case he shall conduct the proceedings in accordance with instructions received from the child), or
   (b) where no guardian ad litem has been appointed for the child and the condition in section 41(4)(b) is satisfied, in accordance with instructions received from the child, or
   (c) in default of instructions under (a) or (b), in furtherance of the best interests of the child.

(2) A solicitor appointed under section 41(3) or in accordance with rule 11(2)(a) shall serve and accept service of documents on behalf of the child in accordance with rule 8(3)(a) and (4)(a) and, where the child has not himself been served and has sufficient understanding, advise the child of the contents of any document so served.

(3) Where the child wishes an appointment of a solicitor under section 41(3) or in accordance with rule 11(2)(a) to be terminated, he may apply to the court for an order terminating the appointment; and the solicitor and the guardian ad litem shall be given an opportunity to make representations.

(4) Where the guardian ad litem wishes an appointment of a solicitor under section 41(3) to be terminated, he may apply to the court for an order terminating the appointment; and the solicitor and,

if he is of sufficient understanding, the child, shall be given an opportunity to make representations.

(5) When terminating an appointment in accordance with paragraph (3) or (4), the court shall give reasons for so doing, a note of which shall be taken by the justices' clerk.

(6) Where the justices' clerk or the court appoints a solicitor under section 41(3) or refuses to make such an appointment, the justices' clerk shall record the appointment or refusal in the appropriate form in Schedule 1 to these Rules and serve a copy on the parties and, where he is appointed, on the solicitor.

GENERAL NOTE

The Rule deals with appointment of solicitors to represent children. Such an appointment can only be made in specified proceedings and can be by either the guardian ad litem or the court. Childrens' solicitors are a new feature in the county and High Court. The Rule deals with two particular areas of difficulty for childrens' solicitors:
1. where instructions from the child conflict with those of the guardian ad litem; and
2. termination of appointment.

As with the previous law, there is again no guidance as to precisely how a solicitor representing the child should carry out his or her work: the Rule is specific only as to taking instructions from the guardian ad litem and/or child, and advising the child as to the contents of documents served in the proceedings. There is no pre Children Act caselaw. There are now two useful books containing guidance for children's solicitors: King and Young, *The Child as Client* (Family Law) and Liddle, *Acting for Children* (The Law Society).

Solicitors are expected to rely upon their professional judgment and commonsense as to how they should proceed. The central issues of practice for most cases, including whether and how often to see the child, what to discuss when and if the child is seen, attendance upon witnesses including experts, and presentation in court, are all within the discretion of the solicitor in discussion with the guardian.

There is no requirement in the Rules that a child's solicitor must be appointed from the renamed Children Panel, which is a specialist panel of solicitors maintained by the Law Society. However, it is the almost universal practice of courts and guardians ad litem to appoint only panel members.

Membership of the Law Society's Children Panel is open to all solicitors with practising certificates subject to certain minimum criteria, including three years' qualification, relevant experience and training, satisfactory completion of an interview, and completion of a strict undertaking to conduct cases personally.

Para. 1(a)

The child's solicitor is clearly required to act in accordance with the instructions of the guardian ad litem. It is not open to the solicitor to reject such instructions and/or simply proceed with the case independently. All matters of significance should be referred to the guardian for guidance. If there is fundamental disagreement between guardian and solicitor as to the conduct of the case, that disagreement should be referred to the court with a view to one or the other, probably the solicitor, retiring from the case.

Occasionally the guardian and child are in conflict, *e.g.* in a sexual abuse case in which the guardian's recommendation is for a care order for the child whilst the child, whether acknowledging the abuse or not, wishes to remain at or return home where the perpetrator may live. The question as to whether or not a conflict exists is for the solicitor to determine. It is not a decision for the guardian ad litem, the child or the court. The solicitor should consult with the guardian and should probably inform the court, although the guardian is required to do so. Conflict need be not only fundamental, but also on an important issue and continuing.

The difficult issue for the solicitor is that a view must be taken of the child's ability to give instructions, having regard to his understanding. Clearly, pre-school children cannot possibly have the necessary degree of understanding, whatever that may be, whilst older adolescents must usually be deemed to understand the issues. The areas of difficulty are in the middle range. Experience tends to suggest that sadly some seven- to 11-year-olds understand all too clearly the issues with which the court will grapple, and the likely long term implications for themselves of the various options; equally obviously, there are older children who understand very little. Thus it is a matter of careful judgment in the individual case. Case law is of limited guidance (see comments upon the *Gillick* case at rule 11(3) at p. 380) and *In re H (a minor)* [1992] 2 F.C.R. 330, a case concerning a grossly disturbed 15 year old boy. It was held that "it put the case a bit high to suggest that any child of 15 years had sufficient understanding to instruct a solicitor ... a child had to have sufficient understanding *within rationality* to instruct a solicitor. Significantly Thorpe J. held that as the solicitor failed to take his instructions exclusively from the child, the child had not been properly represented—a legitimate ground for appeal. If experts were already involved in the case the problem should be referred to them. In practice, many guardians themselves often urge solicitors to accept the child's conflicting view on the basis that children caught up in difficult cases need to be heard clearly by the court.

Para. 1(b) and (c)

It is envisaged that there will be very few cases without a guardian ad litem. In the absence of a guardian, instructions are to be taken from the child if the child has sufficient understanding and wishes to instruct a solicitor. If there is neither a guardian nor instructions from the child, the solicitor must exercise his own judgment and act in accordance with the best interests of the child.

Para. 2

The only specific duty of the child's solicitor (which is also the duty of the guardian ad litem, r. 11(8)), is the duty to advise the child of the contents of documents served in the proceedings. The child's solicitor would appear to be first in line for service and presumably, therefore, it could be argued that the child's solicitor is the first in line to explain the contents of the documents. A better approach however, would be to regard such explanation to be for negotiation between the solicitor and guardian. Again a judgment needs to be taken of the child's level of understanding. This is a new requirement but not a surprising one given the proliferation of documents as compared to the pre-Children Act cases.

Few children will wish or benefit from a line by line approach to the task. Sensitivity is the key requirement. Information is likely to be set out in documents, the full explanation of which may be more damaging than the allegations themselves. Solicitors should obviously consult closely with GALs and consider the documents very carefully before embarking upon this task.

Paras. 3–6

The rule devotes almost as much space to the disposal of solicitors from cases as it does to appointment. Either the guardian or the child may apply for dismissal, solicitors are allowed to be heard and both appointment and dismissal must be noted in writing by the court. Many solicitors may take the view that resignation is the preferable departure route.

["Welfare officer

4.13.—(1) Where the court has directed that a written report be made by a welfare officer, the report shall be filed at or by such time as the court directs or, in the absence of such a direction, at least 14 days before a relevant hearing; and the proper officer shall, as soon as practicable, serve a copy of the report on the parties and any guardian ad litem.

(2) In paragraph (1), a hearing is relevant if the proper officer has given the welfare officer notice that his report is to be considered at it.

(3) After the filing of a report by a welfare officer, the court may direct that the welfare officer attend any hearing at which the report is to be considered; and
   (a) except where such a direction is given at a hearing attended by the welfare officer, the proper office shall inform the welfare officer of the direction; and
   (b) at the hearing at which the report is considered any party may question the welfare officer about his report.
(4) This rule is without prejudice to any power to give directions under rule 4.14.".]

["Welfare officer

13.—(1) Where the court or a justices' clerk has directed that a written report be made by a welfare officer, the report shall be filed at or by such time as the court or justices' clerk directs or, in the absence of such a direction, at least 14 days before a relevant hearing; and the justices' clerk shall, as soon as practicable, serve a copy of the report on the parties and any guardian ad litem.
(2) In paragraph (1), a hearing is relevant if the justices' clerk has given the welfare officer notice that his report is to be considered at it.
(3) After the filing of a written report by a welfare officer, the court or the justices' clerk may direct that the welfare officer attend any hearing at which the report is to be considered; and
   (a) except where such a direction is given at a hearing attended by the welfare officer, the justices' clerk shall inform the welfare officer of the direction; and
   (b) at the hearing at which the report is considered any party may question the welfare officer about his report.
(4) This rule is without prejudice to the court's power to give directions under rule 14.".]

DEFINITION
Rule 4.1(1), Rule 1.

AMENDMENTS
Rule 4.13 was substituted by the Family Proceedings (Amendment No. 2) Rules 1992 (S.I. 1992 No. 2067), r. 12 (October 5, 1992). Rule 13 was substituted by the Family Proceedings Courts (Miscellaneous Amendments) Rules 1992 (S.I. 1992 No. 2068), Sched., para. 3 (October 5, 1992).

GENERAL NOTE
The court welfare officer's role remains that of author of report and is therefore relatively untouched by the Children Act. In theory, a welfare officer could be appointed in care proceedings, but it is envisaged that a guardian ad litem would be the more usual appointment because of their more wide ranging responsibilities. There is nothing to prevent both being appointed in the same case, particularly where various different types of proceedings are consolidated. However, this is envisaged to be very unusual:
   " . . . this would undoubtedly lead to an unnecessary duplication of effort as the guardian ad litems role includes consideration of all the options including the

making of private law orders, and it should be viewed as an exceptional arrangement" (Home Office circular 48/1991).

The Court of Appeal confirmed this view, see *In re S (A Minor) The Times*, June 23, 1992. It was held to be inappropriate to direct the making of a court welfare officer's report where a guardian ad litem had already prepared a report for the court.

4.14. Directions

(1) In this rule, "party" includes the guardian ad litem and, where a request or a direction concerns a report under section 7, the welfare officer.

(2) In proceedings to which this Part applies the court may, subject to paragraph (3), give, vary or revoke directions for the conduct of the proceedings, including—
- (a) the timetable for the proceedings;
- (b) varying the time within which or by which an act is required, by these rules or by other rules of court, to be done;
- (c) the attendance of the child;
- (d) the appointment of a guardian ad litem, whether under section 41 or otherwise, or of a solicitor under section 41(3);
- (e) the service of documents;
- (f) the submission of evidence including experts' reports;
- (g) the preparation of welfare reports under section 7;
- (h) the transfer of the proceedings to another court;
- (i) consolidation with other proceedings.

(3) Directions under paragraph (2) may be given, varied or revoked either—
- (a) of the court's own motion having given the parties notice of its intention to do so, and an opportunity to attend and be heard or to make written representations,
- (b) on the written request of a party specifying the direction which is sought, filed and served on the other parties, or
- (c) on the written request of a party specifying the direction which is sought, to which the other parties consent and which they or their representatives have signed.

(4) In an urgent case the request under paragraph (3)(b) may, with the leave of the court, be made—
- (a) orally, or
- (b) without notice to the parties, or
- (c) both as in sub-paragraph (a) and as in sub-paragraph (b).

(5) On receipt of a written request under paragraph (3)(b) the proper officer shall fix a date for the hearing of the request and give not less than two days' notice to the parties of the date so fixed.

(6) On considering a request under paragraph (3)(c) the court shall either—
- (a) grant the request, whereupon the proper officer shall inform the parties of the decision, or
- (b) direct that a date be fixed for the hearing of the request, whereupon the proper officer shall fix such a date and give not less than two days' notice to the parties of the date so fixed.

(7) A party may apply for an order to be made under section 11(3) or, if he is entitled to apply for such an order, under section 38(1) in accordance with paragraph (3)(b) or (c).

(8) Where a court is considering making, of its own motion, a section 8 order, or an order under section 31, 34 or 38, the power to give directions under paragraph (2) shall apply.

(9) Directions of a court which are still in force immediately prior to the transfer of proceedings to which this Part applies to another court shall continue to apply following the transfer, subject to any changes of terminology which are required to apply those directions to the court to which the proceedings are transferred, unless varied or discharged by directions under paragraph (2).

(10) The court or the proper officer shall take a note of the giving, variation or revocation of a direction under this rule and serve, as soon as practicable, a copy of the note on any party who was not present at the giving, variation or revocation.

Directions

14.—(1) In this rule, "party" includes the guardian ad litem and, where a request or a direction concerns a report under section 7, the welfare officer.

(2) In any relevant proceedings the justices' clerk or the court may, subject to paragraph (5), give, vary or revoke directions for the conduct of the proceedings, including—

    (a) the timetable for the proceedings;
    (b) varying the time within which or by which an act is required, by these Rules, to be done;
    (c) the attendance of the child;
    (d) the appointment of a guardian ad litem, whether under section 41 or otherwise, or of a solicitor under section 41(3);
    (e) the service of documents;
    (f) the submission of evidence including experts' reports;
    (g) the preparation of welfare reports under section 7;
    (h) the transfer of the proceedings to another court in accordance with any Order made by the Lord Chancellor under Part I of Schedule II;
    (i) consolidation with other proceedings.

and the justices' clerk shall, on receipt of an application, or where proceedings have been transferred to his court, consider whether such directions need to be given.

(3) Where the justices' clerk or a single justice who is holding a directions appointment considers, for whatever reason, that it is inappropriate to give a direction on a particular matter, he shall refer the matter to the court which may give any appropriate direction.

(4) Where a direction is given under paragraph (2)(h), a certificate shall be issued in the appropriate form in Schedule 1 to these Rules and the justices' clerk shall follow the procedure set out in rule 6(2).

(5) Directions under paragraph (2) may be given, varied or revoked either—

(a) of the justices' clerk or the court's own motion having given the parties notice of its intention to do so and an opportunity to attend and be heard or to make written representations,
(b) on the written request of a party specifying the direction which is sought, filed and served on the other parties, or
(c) on the written request of a party specifying the direction which is sought, to which the other parties consent and which they or their representatives have signed.

(6) In an urgent case the request under paragraph (5)(b) may, with the leave of the justices' clerk or the court, be made—
(a) orally, or
(b) without notice to the parties, or
(c) both as in sub-paragraph (a) and as in sub-paragraph (b).

(7) On receipt of a request under paragraph (5)(b) the justices' clerk shall fix a date for the hearing of the request and give not less than two days' notice to the parties of the date so fixed.

(8) On considering a request under paragraph (5)(c) the justices' clerk or the court shall either—
(a) grant the request, whereupon the justices' clerk shall inform the parties of the decision, or
(b) direct that a date be fixed for the hearing of the request, whereupon the justices' clerk shall fix such a date and give not less than two days' notice to the parties of the date so fixed.

(9) Subject to rule 28, a party may request, in accordance with paragraph 5(b) or (c), that an order be made under section 11(3) or, if he is entitled to apply for such an order, under section 38(1), and paragraphs (6), (7) and (8) shall apply accordingly.

(10) Where, in any relevant proceedings, the court has power to make an order of its own motion, the power to give directions under paragraph (2) shall apply.

(11) Directions of the justices' clerk or a court which are still in force immediately prior to the transfer of relevant proceedings to another court shall continue to apply following the transfer, subject to any changes of terminology which are require to apply those directions to the court to which the proceedings are transferred, unless varied or discharged by directions under paragraph (2).

(12) The justices' clerk or the court shall [record] the giving, variation or revocation of a direction under this rule [in the appropriate form in Schedule 1 to these Rules] and serve, as soon as practicable, a copy of [the form] on any party who was not present at the giving, variation or revocation.

AMENDMENT

The words in square brackets were substituted by the Family Proceedings Courts (Matrimonial Proceedings, etc.) Rules 1991 (S.I. 1991 No. 1991), reg. 8, (October 14, 1991)

DEFINITIONS

"directions appointment": rr. 4.14(2), 14(2)

GENERAL NOTE

The importance of directions hearings in childrens' cases is stressed in the *Guidance*, HO circular 48/1991, at para. 60:

"The directions appointment is intended to be an informal preliminary hearing and is a major procedural development introduced by these rules. Its purposes are to clarify the central issues of a case and to ensure the case's efficient disposal. Central to this is the need to control the case timetable."

And at para. 62:

" ... the directions appointment is ... pivotal to the satisfactory disposal of cases ..."

Thus the two main purposes of directions hearings are to maintain the court's grip on cases particularly in order to keep them moving, and to deal with all the preliminary and procedural issues. Substantive hearings can therefore concentrate on the main issues. Few, if any, final wardship or care hearings ever began without problems of the emergence of new evidence or the non-disclosure of old evidence, or missing witnesses or some other procedural or evidential complication. All such matters should now have been resolved at an earlier stage at a directions hearing. Flexibility is the key: if a problem occurs at any stage before the hearing, it should be referred for the court's consideration at a directions hearing without the necessity of waiting for the next pre-arranged hearing date.

It is important to note that directions hearings are different from the traditional hearing before a District Judge. Firstly, they will be held in all three jurisdictions representing an innovation for Magistrates' Courts. Secondly, there are a wider range of powers (see para. 2), and thirdly, the directions given under pre-Children Act law are often regarded as little more than a general interest: rule 14 directions are to be followed with penalties particularly in costs and, in the case of statements filed late, there is the risk that the evidence contained therein will be excluded (see r. 17.3 at p. 396).

Para. 2

The list is not exhaustive, other matters such as the admissibility of certain evidence or the attendance of a party can be raised.

(a) The list starts with timetabling thereby stressing the central purpose of directions hearings.

(b) Rule 14(2)(b) gives rise to difficulty and seems to permit an abbreviation of time limits, whereas rule 15(1) refers specifically only to lengthening time limits. The most obvious example thrown up on the immediate post-implementation period, has been the 21-day service period in section 8 proceedings. Rule 14(2)(b) would seem to permit a reduction of that and other service periods. Butler-Sloss L.J. provides clarification *In re B (A Minor)* [1992] 1 F.C.R. No. 25 at p. 559:

"The 21 days for a residence order is the standard. The standard can always be abridged if the requirements of the children require the case to be heard very quickly."

(c) Attendance of the child. Section 95 deals with attendance of children in Parts IV and V of the Children Act. The court may order the child to attend all or part of the proceedings. The issue should at least be considered at directions hearings, and it is expected that the child's own views will be relevant if of sufficient understanding. However, rule 14(2)(c) does not apply to Parts IV and V: children may be ordered to attend any Children Act proceedings although most courts will take a lot of convincing that a child's attendance is worthwhile in other than exceptional circumstances.

(d) There is provision for appointment of a guardian ad litem "under section 41 or otherwise." It has been suggested that the words "or otherwise" indicate that guardians ad litem may be appointed in non-specified proceedings but this is not clear (see commentary on r. 11 at p. 382).

(e) The service of documents will be an often used direction and one with which courts are familiar: time scales will be set out for the exchange of witness statements (not affidavits, see r. 17 at p. 396). The timetable must be complied with.

(f) Documents other than witness statements are included, *e.g.* medical or social work reports, chronologies, statements made to the Police, copy letters, etc.

Clearly, each party can organise, file and serve their own evidence, but what of access to documents held by other parties which they do not choose to disclose, such as social work records or reports unfavourable to the party commissioning them?

The word "discovery" is not used: there is still no specific power for courts to order discovery and inspection of documents. There was, however, no power under the old law: *Re M (A Minor)* T.L.R. 4190. In that case the Court of Appeal considered a father's application for discovery of social work records in wardship proceedings. It would seem likely that the decision in *Re M* will be persuasive in Children Act cases, *per* Lord Justice Butler-Sloss:

> "Disclosure of documents chronicling the continuing discussions and concerns of the Local Authority over a period of time, might be very damaging to the welfare of the child in the potential souring of relations between Social Workers and the family ... in some cases the disclosure of documents might have serious repercussions for the child himself. Sources of valuable information might require to be protected ... "

Nevertheless, the court held that certain documents might need to be disclosed. There was held to be no absolute rule against disclosure, no absolute immunity of Local Authorities from disclosure. Applications could be made for disclosure of specific documents. "Old" caselaw provides such an example in *R. v. Hampshire C.C., ex p. K and Another, The Independent,* November 16, 1989, a case which concerned the disclosure of a police surgeon's report prepared before proceedings were commenced. The court ordered that it be disclosed.

Parties cannot, therefore, simply seek discovery and inspection of social work and analogous records in a general sense. Specific documents can be ordered to be disclosed on application. The question of how parties become aware of the existence of potentially useful documents is unresolved. Perhaps the guardian's increased right of access to Local Authority records will assist (see s.42 at p. 124).

(h) Upon receipt of a case transferred from another court, the receiving court must consider whether any directions should be given. This is likely to mean that there will be a directions hearing shortly after the transfer of the case.

Para. 5 FPR; para. 7 FPC

Once given, directions can be varied or revoked. Directions can be given by a court at a hearing, at a directions hearing, of the court's own motion on notice, at the written request of parties on two days' notice, or in writing by consent. Flexible and creative use of directions is called for.

Para. 9 FPR; para. 11 FPC

Directions accompany a transferred case until altered by the receiving court.

Para. 10 FPR; para. 12 FPC

Directions must be recorded in writing by the court.

4.15. Timing of proceedings

(1) Where these rules or other rules of court provide a period of time within which or by which a certain act is to be performed in the course of proceedings to which this Part applies, that period may not be extended otherwise than by direction of the court under rule 4.14.

(2) At the—
   (a) transfer to a court of proceedings to which this Part applies,
   (b) postponement or adjournment of any hearing or directions appointment in the course of proceedings to which this Part applies, or
   (c) conclusion of any such hearing or directions appointment other than one at which the proceedings are determined, or so soon thereafter as is practicable,

the court or the proper officer shall—
  (i) fix a date upon which the proceedings shall come before the court again for such purposes as the court directs, which date shall, where paragraph (a) applies, be as soon as possible after the transfer, and
  (ii) give notice to the parties, the guardian ad litem or the welfare officer of the date so fixed.

Timing of proceedings

15.—(1) Any period of time fixed by these Rules, or by any order or direction, for doing any act shall be reckoned in accordance with this rule.

(2) Where the period, being a period of seven days or less, would include a day which is not a business day, that day shall be excluded.

(3) Where the time fixed for filing a document with the justices' clerk expires on a day on which the justices' clerk's office is closed, and for that reason the document cannot be filed on that day, the document shall be filed in time if it is filed on the next day on which the justices' clerk's office is open.

(4) Where these rules provide a period of time within which or by which a certain act is to be performed in the course of relevant proceedings, that period may not be extended otherwise than by a direction of the justices' clerk or the court under rule 14.

(5) At the—
  (a) transfer to a court of relevant proceedings,
  (b) postponement or adjournment of any hearing or directions appointment in the course of relevant proceedings, or
  (c) conclusion of any such hearing or directions appointment other than one at which the proceedings are determined, or so soon thereafter as is practicable,
the justices' clerk or the court shall—
  (i) fix a date upon which the proceedings shall come before the justices' clerk or the court again for such purposes as the justices' clerk or the court directs, which date shall, where paragraph (a) applies, be as soon as possible after the transfer, and
  (ii) give notice to the parties and to the guardian ad litem or the welfare officer of the date so fixed.

GENERAL NOTE

Para. 1
The court has power to extend any time period fixed by the legislation: presumably a power to be used sparingly.

Para. 2 FPR; para. 4 FPC
The court must always fix the next hearing date, that particular procedure representing a change in practice for the county and High Courts.

4.16. Attendance at directions appointment and hearing

(1) Subject to paragraph (2), a party shall attend a directions appointment of which he has been given notice in accordance with rule 4.14(5) unless the court otherwise directs.

(2) Proceedings or any part of them shall take place in the absence of any party, including the child, if—
- (a) the court considers it in the interests of the child, having regard to the matters to be discussed or the evidence likely to be given, and
- (b) the party is represented by a guardian ad litem or solicitor;

and when considering the interests of the child under sub-paragraph (a) the court shall give the guardian ad litem, the solicitor for the child and, if he is of sufficient understanding, the child an opportunity to make representations.

(3) Subject to paragraph (4), where at the time and place appointed for a hearing or directions appointment the applicant appears but one or more of the respondents do not, the court may proceed with the hearing or appointment.

(4) The court shall not begin to hear an application in the absence of a respondent unless—
- (a) it is proved to the satisfaction of the court that he received reasonable notice of the date of the hearing; or
- (b) the court is satisfied that the circumstances of the case justify proceeding with the hearing.

(5) Where, at the time and place appointed for a hearing or directions appointment one or more of the respondents appear but the applicant does not, the court may refuse the application or, if sufficient evidence has previously been received, proceed in the absence of the applicant.

(6) Where at the time and place appointed for a hearing or directions appointment neither the applicant nor any respondent appears, the court may refuse the application.

(7) Unless the court otherwise directs, a hearing of, or directions appointment in, proceedings to which this Part applies shall be in chambers.

Attendance at directions appointment and hearing

16.—(1) Subject to paragraph (2), a party shall attend a directions appointment of which he has been given notice in accordance with rule 14(5) unless the justices' clerk or the court otherwise directs.

(2) Relevant proceedings shall take place in the absence of any party including the child, if—
- (a) the court considers it in the interests of the child, having regard to the matters to be discussed or the evidence likely to be given, and
- (b) the party is represented by a guardian ad litem or solicitor;

and when considering the interests of the child under sub-paragraph (a) the court shall give the guardian ad litem, solicitor for the child and, if he is of sufficient understanding, the child, an opportunity to make representations.

(3) Subject to paragraph (4) below, where at the time and place appointed for a hearing or directions appointment the applicant appears but one or more of the respondents do not, the justices' clerk or the court may proceed with the hearing or appointment.

(4) The court shall not begin to hear an application in the absence of a respondent unless—
- (a) it is proved to the satisfaction of the court that he received reasonable notice of the date of the hearing; or
- (b) the court is satisfied that the circumstances of the case justify proceeding with the hearing.

(5) Where, at the time and place appointed for a hearing or directions appointment, one or more respondents appear but the applicant does not, the court may refuse the application or, if sufficient evidence has previously been received, proceed in the absence of the applicant.

(6) Where at the time and place appointed for a hearing or directions appointment neither the applicant nor any respondent appears, the court may refuse the application.

(7) Unless the court considers it expedient in the interests of the child, it shall hear any relevant proceedings in private when only the officers of the court, the parties, their legal representatives and such other persons as specified by the court may attend.

GENERAL NOTE

Because directions hearings are so important, parties are required to attend all hearings, unless the court directs otherwise. Home Office circular 48/1991 at para. 62:

"In this context 'party' is interchangeable with the party's legal representative. If a legal representative attends, he should be someone conversant with the case with full authority to act."

There may be costs penalties in non-attendance both for parties (see commentary on r.22) and for legal representatives (see commentary on the Family Proceedings (Costs) Rules 1991 (S.I. 1991 No. 1832) at p. 475).

The court can proceed with a hearing of the case notwithstanding the absence of either applicant or a respondent, but not in the absence of all the parties. The court is to take a more dominating role but there are limits: at least one party needs to be present for a hearing or directions hearing to take place.

Paras. 2 and 7

Notwithstanding the importance of all parties attending, the court can direct that any party, including the child, can be excluded if to do so would be in the child's best interests and the party is represented. It is difficult to see how courts will exercise this power *vis-à-vis* parties other than the child. The Rule is clearly drafted on the basis that any party, that is the child and/or any other, may be excluded. The exclusion of someone sufficiently important either to have automatic respondent status, or to have been accorded that status by the court, must surely be a very exceptional step. Clearly, parties need to be able to hear and meet allegations made. In any event, even if the evidence is adjudged to be too sensitive for the ears of the party in question, that party's solicitor remains in the hearing and will need to take instructions. If such a situation arises, it may be more expedient to proceed in accordance with paragraph 7, *i.e.* in Chambers or in private, in the absence of all parties.

The power of exclusion is more likely to be exercised in respect of the child who may be excluded from "proceedings or any part of them." As always in childrens' cases, great sensitivity will be required of courts in exercising their powers of exclusion.

Paras. 3–5

It is likely that in some cases there will be substantial numbers of parties whose degree of interest in the proceedings, together with their attention to punctuality, may vary as cases take their course. Paragraphs 3–5 permit courts to proceed with hearings or directions hearings in the absence of a respondent if that person has been given notice, and to proceed is considered justifiable. The court may even proceed without the applicant "if sufficient evidence has previously been received." Both provisions are examples of the avoidance of delay principle. Practitioners may find it prudent to draw these provisions to their client's attention at the outset.

Paragraph 5 is intriguing: it should be read together with rule 20 concerning note taking by the court or court clerk. It is clearly envisaged that a hearing will take place in which a Judge or Magistrate will make orders on the basis of evidence heard and noted from another Judge or other Magistrates. Continuity of judiciary in childrens' cases can be of immense value for this reason alone.

4.17. Documentary evidence

(1) Subject to paragraphs (4) and (5), in proceedings to which this Part applies a party shall file and serve on the parties, any welfare officer and any guardian ad litem of whose appointment he has been given notice under rule 4.10(5)—

    (a) written statements of the substance of the oral evidence which the party intends to adduce at a hearing of, or a directions appointment in, those proceedings, which shall—

        (i) be dated,

        (ii) be signed by the person making the statement, [...]

        (iii) contain a declaration that the maker of the statement believes it to be true and understands that it may be placed before the court; and

        ["(iv) show in the top right hand corner of the first page—

            (a) the initials and surname of the person making the statement,

            (b) the number of the statement in relation to the maker,

            (c) the date on which the statement was made, and

            (d) the party on whose behalf it is filed; and".]

    (b) copies of any documents, including experts' reports, upon which the party intends to rely at a hearing of, or a directions appointment in, those proceedings,

at or by such time as the court directs or, in the absence of a direction, before the hearing or appointment.

(2) A party may, subject to any direction of the court about the timing of statements under this rule, file and serve on the parties a statement which is supplementary to a statement served under paragraph (1).

(3) At a hearing or a directions appointment a party may not, without the leave of the court—

    (a) adduce evidence, or

    (b) seek to rely on a document,

in respect of which he has failed to comply with the requirements of paragraph (1).

(4) In proceedings for a section 8 order a party shall—
  (a) neither file nor serve any document other than as required or authorised by these rules, and
  (b) in completing a form prescribed by these rules, neither give information, nor make a statement, which is not required or authorised by that form,
without the leave of the court.

(5) In proceedings for a section 8 order no statement or copy may be filed under paragraph (1) until such time as the court directs.

AMENDMENTS

The words in square brackets were substituted by the Family Proceedings (Amendment No. 2) Rules 1992 (S.I. 1992 No. 2067), r. 20 (October 5, 1992).

Documentary Evidence

17.—(1) Subject to paragraphs (4) and (5), in any relevant proceedings a party shall file and serve on the parties, any welfare officer and any guardian ad litem of whose appointment he has been given notice under rule 10(5)—
  (a) written statements of the substance of the oral evidence which the party intends to adduce at a hearing of, or a directions appointment in, those proceedings, which shall—
    (i) be dated,
    (ii) be signed by the person making the statement, [...]
    (iii) contain a declaration that the maker of the statement believes it to be true and understands that it may be placed before the court, and
    ["(iv) show in the top right hand corner of the first page—
      (a) the initials and surname of the person making the statement,
      (b) the number of the statement in relation to the maker,
      (c) the date on which the statement was made, and
      (d) the party on whose behalf it is filed; and".]
  (b) copies of any documents, including, subject to rule 18(3), experts' reports, upon which the party intends to rely, at a hearing of, or a directions appointment in, those proceedings,
at or by such time as the justices' clerk or the court directs or, in the absence of a direction, before the hearing or appointment.

(2) A party may, subject to any direction of the justices' clerk or the court about the timing of statements under this rule, file and serve on the parties a statement which is supplementary to a statement served under paragraph (1).

(3) At a hearing or a directions appointment a party may not, without the leave of the justices' clerk, in the case of a directions appointment, or the court—
  (a) adduce evidence, or
  (b) seek to rely on a document,
in respect of which he has failed to comply with the requirements of paragraph (1).

(4) In proceedings for a section 8 order a party shall—
  (a) neither file nor serve any document other than as required or authorised by these Rules, and
  (b) in completing a form prescribed by these Rules, neither give information, nor make a statement, which is not required or authorised by that form,
without the leave of the justices' clerk or the court.

(5) In proceedings for a section 8 order, no statement or copy may be filed under paragraph (1) until such time as the justices' clerk or the court directs.

DEFINITIONS
"file": r.1(2), FPC.
"s.8 Order": s.8(2).

AMENDMENT
The words in square brackets were substituted by the Family Proceedings Courts (Miscellaneous Amendments) Rules 1992 (S.I. 1992 No. 2068), Sched., r. 4 (October 5, 1992).

GENERAL NOTE
Rules 4.17 and 17 are essentially about disclosure of evidence. As against care cases under the old law, the changes are vast. Whereas formerly, there was disclosure only of guardians ad litem and social work reports, together with medical reports, there is now to be full revelation of all parties cases in advance. Likewise, disclosure becomes a feature of private law cases in all jurisdictions. The difference is that there is to be no disclosure in section 8 proceedings unless ordered by the court: in all other proceedings, statements must be served in advance of the hearing at which they are to be used. Documentation is therefore a very important feature of Children Act proceedings.

The reason behind rule 17 is twofold: to enable parties to prepare their cases properly and to enable magistrates in particular to read the evidence before the commencement of hearings. The hearing should thereby be better able to deal with the issues in the case and become less of a guessing game for all concerned.

In care cases practitioners need to note in particular that the disclosure provisions apply to parents and other respondents, as well as to local authorities. Whilst not all parties may wish to have their cases disclosed to all other parties, there would appear to be no choice.

Evidently, rule 17 is about disclosure and is not particularly concerned with shortening hearings. It is not clear whether parties should repeat the contents of their statements in full in court when giving evidence, or merely confirm the truth of the contents. The former would appear to be wholly pointless as all parties will have had the sight of the documents, and even the child should have been advised as to the contents where necessary (r. 11(8) and r. 12(8)). In the absence of clear guidance, each court will presumably develop its own local practices.

Para. 1
The form of disclosure is by a written statement (not affidavit). The statement must be signed, dated and declared as being true with the maker's knowledge that it may be placed before a court. Formalities are thereby kept to a minimum. It would be good practice to number paragraphs for ease of reference and cross reference in court.

There is no requirement to disclose minutiae. The Rule requires "the substance of the oral evidence" to be in written form. It is expected that neither lengthy tomes nor one page denials or platitudes will find favour with courts.

Experts reports are to be disclosed, together with any other documents which parties will seek to use in court including, for example, height or weight charts, school attendance records, letters of confession. All will have to be neatly bundled, filed and served.

Para. 2

Supplementary statements may be served, most usually with a view to updating developments. Amendment of statements is dealt with at rule 19.

Para. 3

This paragraph provides the sanction. If a statement is not served in advance or not served in accordance with a direction, the evidence in the statement cannot be used without the leave of the court. Parties are clearly, therefore, well advised to comply with directions to ensure that even without directions, statements are filed and served before hearings. Whilst courts will obviously be reluctant to exclude important evidence, for procedural reasons, there will be times when the courts enforce section 1(2) and penalise the dilatory.

Paras. 4, 5

Whilst in care and many other Children Act proceedings, there is a clear interest in disclosure to enable allegations to be answered, different principles apply to most section 8 proceedings. It is felt that reconciliation or conciliation between the parties may be hindered by peppery statements.

No statements or documents are therefore to be filed and served in section 8 proceedings unless the court specifically so directs. Many such proceedings will be relatively straightforward, thereby not requiring the exchange of statements or documents at all.

4.18. Expert evidence—examination of child

(1) No person may, without the leave of the court, cause the child to be medically or psychiatrically examined, or otherwise assessed, for the purpose of the preparation of expert evidence for use in the proceedings.

(2) An application for leave under paragraph (1) shall, unless the court otherwise directs, be served on all parties to the proceedings and on the guardian ad litem.

(3) Where the leave of the court has not been given under paragraph (1), no evidence arising out of an examination or assessment to which that paragraph applies may be adduced without the leave of the court.

Expert evidence—examination of child

18.—(1) No person may, without the leave of the justices' clerk or the court, cause the child to be medically or psychiatrically examined, or otherwise assessed, for the purpose of the preparation of expert evidence for use in the proceedings.

(2) An application for leave under paragraph (1) shall, unless the justices' clerk or the court otherwise directs, be served on all parties to the proceedings and on the guardian ad litem.

(3) Where the leave of the justices' clerk or the court has not been given under paragraph (1), no evidence arising out of an examination or assessment to which that paragraph applies may be adduced without the leave of the court.

GENERAL NOTE

Rule 18 is of wide application and is probably part of the Cleveland inheritance. It is one example amongst many, of the court being in charge of the proceedings not just of hearings. The Rule should be read together with section 38(6), (7) and rules 4.2 and 2, see pp. 115 and 355–357.

Who is an expert is a matter for the court to decide and a witness' status as an expert can be challenged by another party to the proceedings. Essentially, an expert witness is someone with special skill outside the knowledge and experience of the court. All assessments of any kind must be approved by the court, otherwise the results cannot be used for the purposes of expert evidence.

Expert examination for therapeutic as opposed to forensic purposes, does not require leave of the court. There are, however, often elements of both present in an assessment, although the distinction is valid (see comments of Latey J. in *Re M* 1 F.L.R. 1987, p. 294). If an assessment is intended to assist the child without any bearing upon the proceedings, there is no requirement for leave, but if such an assessment produces unexpected evidence, retrospective leave can be sought to adduce it (para. 3).

4.19. Amendment

(1) Subject to rule 4.17(2), a document which has been filed or served in proceedings to which this Part applies, may not be amended without the leave of the court which shall, unless the court otherwise directs, be requested in writing.

(2) On considering a request for leave to amend a document the court shall either—

    (a) grant the request, whereupon the proper officer shall inform the person making the request of that decision, or

    (b) invite the parties or any of them to make representations, within a specified period, as to whether such an order should be made.

(3) A person amending a document shall file it and serve it on those persons on whom it was served prior to amendment; and the amendments shall be identified.

Amendment

19.—(1) Subject to rule 17(2), a document which has been filed or served in any relevant proceedings may not be amended without the leave of the justices' clerk or the court which shall, unless the justices' clerk or the court otherwise directs, be requested in writing.

(2) On considering a request for leave to amend a document the justices' clerk or the court shall either—

    (a) grant the request, whereupon the justices' clerk shall inform the person making the request of that decision, or

    (b) invite the parties or any of them to make representations, within a specified period, as to whether such an order should be made.

(3) A person amending a document shall file it with the justices' clerk and serve it on those persons on whom it was served prior to amendment; and the amendments shall be identified.

4.20. Oral evidence

The court or the proper officer shall keep a note of the substance of the oral evidence given at a hearing of, or directions appointment in, proceedings to which this Part applies.

Oral evidence

20. The justices' clerk or the court shall keep a note of the substance of the oral evidence given at a hearing of, or directions appointment in, relevant proceedings.

GENERAL NOTE

It is important that a clear legible note be taken of any evidence given, and that the notes be available for future reference. The notes may be needed at a later stage in the same proceedings in particular in the subsequent absence of the applicant, see rules 4.16(5) and 16(5), or in future proceedings concerning the same child or parties. Home Office Circular 48/1991 stipulates that notes of evidence should be made available to any of the parties on request.

4.21. Hearing

(1) The court may give directions as to the order of speeches and evidence at a hearing, or directions appointment, in the course of proceedings to which this Part applies.

(2) Subject to directions under paragraph (1), at a hearing of, or directions appointment in, proceedings to which this Part applies, the parties and the guardian ad litem shall adduce their evidence in the following order—
   (a) the applicant,
   (b) any party with parental responsibility for the child,
   (c) other respondents,
   (d) the guardian ad litem,
   (e) the child, if he is a party to the proceedings and there is no guardian ad litem.

(3) After the final hearing of proceedings to which this Part applies, the court shall deliver its judgment as soon as is practicable.

(4) When making an order or when refusing an application, the court shall state any findings of fact and the reasons for the court's decision.

(5) An order made in proceedings to which this Part applies shall be recorded, by the court or the proper officer, either in the appropriate form in Appendix 1 to these rules or, where there is no such form, in writing.

(6) Subject to paragraph (7), a copy of an order made in accordance with paragraph (5) shall, as soon as practicable after it has been made, be served by the proper officer on the parties to the proceedings in which it was made [and] on any person with whom the child is living.

(7) Within 48 hours after the making ex parte of—
   (a) a [section 8 order], or
   (b) an order under section 44, 48(4), 48(9) or 50,
the applicant shall serve a copy of the order in the appropriate form in Appendix 1 to these Rules on—

(i) each party,
(ii) any person who has actual care of the child or who had such care immediately prior to the making of the order, and
(iii) in the case of an order referred to in sub-paragraph (b), the local authority in whose area the child lives or is found.

(8) At a hearing of, or directions appointment in, an application which takes place outside the hours during which the court office is normally open, the court or the proper officer shall take a note of the substance of the proceedings.

AMENDMENT

The word in square brackets was inserted by the Family Proceedings (Amendment) Rules 1992 (S.I. 1992 No. 456), reg. 14 (April, 1992) and the Family Proceedings (Amendment No. 2) Rules 1992 (S.I. 1992 No. 2067), r. 10 (October 5, 1992).

Hearing

21.—(1) Before the hearing, the justice or justices who will be dealing with the case shall read any documents which have been filed under rule 17 in respect of the hearing.

(2) The justices' clerk at a directions appointment, or the court at a hearing or directions appointment, may give directions as to the order of speeches and evidence.

(3) Subject to directions under paragraph (2), at a hearing of, or directions appointment in, relevant proceedings, the parties and the guardian ad litem shall adduce their evidence in the following order—
(a) the applicant,
(b) any party with parental responsibility for the child,
(c) other respondents,
(d) the guardian ad litem,
(e) the child if he is a party to the proceedings and there is no guardian ad litem.

(4) After the final hearing of relevant proceedings, the court shall make its decision as soon as is practicable.

(5) Before the court makes an order or refuses an application or request, the justices' clerk shall record in writing—
(a) the names of the justice or justices constituting the court by which the decision is made, and
(b) in consultation with the justice or justices the reasons for the court's decision and any findings of fact.

(6) When making an order or when refusing an application, the court, or one of the justices constituting the court by which the decision is made, shall state any findings of fact and the reasons for the court's decision.

(7) After the court announces its decision, the justices' clerk shall as soon as practicable—
(a) make a record of any order made in the appropriate form in Schedule 1 to these Rules or, where there is no such form, in writing; and

(b) subject to paragraph (8), serve a copy of any order made on the parties to the proceedings and on any person with whom the child is living.

(8) Within 48 hours after the making of an order under section 48(4) or the making, ex parte, of—
   (a) a [section 8 order], or
   (b) an order under section 44, 48(9), 50 [or] 75(1) [...],
the applicant shall serve a copy of the order in the appropriate form in Schedule 1 to these Rules on—
   (i) each party,
   (ii) any person who has actual care of the child, or who had such care immediately prior to the making of the order, and
   (iii) in the case of an order referred to in sub-paragraph (b), the local authority in whose area the child lives or is found.

DEFINITIONS

"Section 8 Order", see section 8(2).

AMENDMENT

The words in square brackets were substituted by the Family Proceedings Courts (Miscellaneous Amendments) Rules 1992 (S.I. 1992 No. 2068), Sched., paras. 1 and 5.

GENERAL NOTE

General guidance is provided by rule 21 as to the conduct of hearings.

Para. 1 FPC

Magistrates, but not Judges, must have read all rule 17 documents before starting to hear the case. Careful consideration will therefore need to be given to presentation in the form of bundles of numbered documents.

Paras. 1, 2 FPR; paras. 2, 3 FPC

The court may regulate its own procedure in advance or at the start of hearings. Witness inconvenience can therefore be minimised. In the absence of any specific direction, the evidence is to be heard in the order set out at FPR, para. 2, FPC, para. 3.

Para. 3 FPR; para. 4 FPC

There is no obligation upon the court to announce its decision immediately: the enjoinder against delay is as applicable to courts in giving judgment as it is to parties throughout the proceedings. A delay of more than seven days is considered highly undesirable (Home Office Circular 48/1991, at para. 74) and 10 days definitely too long (*Devon C.C.* v. *J and others* [1992] 1 F.C.R. 550).

Para. 4, FPR; para. 6 FPC

Courts must state their findings of fact and reasons for their decision. This provision is applicable in public and private cases, contested or uncontested proceedings, and in all jurisdictions. It is applicable to interim orders (*W (Minors)* v. *Hertfordshire C.C.*, The Times, September 14, 1992). The reasons must be more than "meagre"—*R.* v. *X Council (A Local Authority)*, The Times, 24 February 1992, Family Division. The case concerned a secure accommodation application but was applicable to all Children Act proceedings. Mr. Justice Douglas Brown:

"His Lordship had sympathy with Justices who were not professional Judges, and had to give reasons after a complex case. It was better to adjourn and give decision and reasons later, and on the later date it was only necessary for one Justice to sit."

Proper findings of fact and reasons must be given. Any defect in this regard cannot be rectified later by sending extended reasons to an appellate court (*H.* v. *Hillingdon L.B.C., The Times,* July 1, 1992). It would seem likely that the section 1 principles will feature prominently in judgments.

Para. 6, FPR; para. 7 FPC

The court must serve copy orders upon all parties and upon any non-party with whom the child is living. If courts decide to make no order (s.1(5)) the parties must also be given written notification of that adjudication.

Family Proceedings Rules

["Attachment of penal notice to section 8 order

4.21.A CCR Order 29, rule 1 (committal for breach of order or undertaking) shall apply to section 8 orders as if for paragraph (3) of that rule there were substituted the following:—

"(3) In the case of a section 8 order (within the meaning of section 8(2) of the Children Act 1989(**a**)) enforceable by committal order under paragraph (1), the judge or the district judge may, on the application of the person entitled to enforce the order, direct that the proper officer issue a copy of the order, indorsed with or incorporating a notice as to the consequences of disobedience, for service in accordance with paragraph (2); and no copy of the order shall be issued with any such notice indorsed or incorporated save in accordance with such a direction.".]

AMENDMENT

This whole rule was inserted by the Family Proceedings (Amendent No. 2) Rules 1992 (S.I. 1992 No. 2067), r. 13 (October 5, 1992).

GENERAL NOTE

Enforcement of Children Act orders, particularly section 8 orders, has proved problematic in the first year of the Act. This new rule which has been added in by the Amendment (No. 2) Rules 1992 should go some way towards clarifying the position: penal notices can be attached to section 8 orders. Enforcement at FPC level is still difficult, see p. 414.

FPR, 4.22. Appeals

(1) Where an appeal lies—
    (a) to the High Court under section 94, or
    (b) from any decision of a district judge to the judge of the court in which the decision was made,
it shall be made in accordance with the following provisions; and references to "the court below" are references to the court from which, or person from whom, the appeal lies.

(2) The appellant shall file and serve on the parties to the proceedings in the court below, and on any guardian ad litem—

(a) notice of the appeal in writing, setting out the grounds upon which he relies;
(b) a certified copy of the summons or application and of the order appealed against, and of any order staying its execution;
(c) a copy of any notes of evidence;
(d) a copy of any reasons given for the decision.

["(2A) In relation to an appeal to the High Court under section 94, the documents required to be filed by paragraph (2) shall,—
    (a) where the care centre listed in column (ii) of Schedule 2 to the Children (Allocation of Proceedings) Order 1991(c) against the entry in column (i) relating to the petty sessions area or London commission area in which the court below is situated—
        (i) is the principle registry, or
        (ii) has a district registry in the same place,
    be filed in that registry, and
    (b) in any other case, be filed in the district registry, being in the same place as a care centre within the meaning of article 2(c) of the said Order, which is nearest to the court below.".]

(3) The notice of appeal shall be filed and served in accordance with paragraph (2)(a)—
    (a) within 14 days after the determination against which the appeal is brought, or
    (b) in the case of an appeal against an order under section 38(1), within seven days after the making of the order, or
    (c) with the leave of the court to which, or judge to whom, the appeal is to be brought, within such other time as that court or judge may direct.

(4) The documents mentioned in paragraph (2)(b) to (d) shall, subject to any direction of the court to which, or judge to whom, the appeal is to be brought, be filed and served as soon as practicable after the filing and service of the notice of appeal under paragraph (2)(a).

(5) Subject to paragraph (6), a respondent who wishes—
    (a) to contend on the appeal that the decision of the court below should be varied, either in any event or in the event of the appeal being allowed in whole or in part, or
    (b) to contend that the decision of the court below should be affirmed on grounds other than those relied upon by that court, or
    (c) to contend by way of cross-appeal that the decision of the court below was wrong in whole or in part,
shall, within 14 days of receipt of notice of the appeal, file and serve on all other parties to the appeal a notice in writing, setting out the grounds upon which he relies.

(6) No notice under paragraph (5) may be filed or served in an appeal against an order under section 38.

(7) In the case of an appeal mentioned in paragraph (1)(a), an application to—

(a) withdraw the appeal,
(b) have the appeal dismissed with the consent of all the parties, or
(c) amend the grounds of appeal,

may be heard by a district judge.

(8) An appeal of the kind mentioned in paragraph (1)(a) shall, unless the President otherwise directs, be heard and determined by a single judge.

AMENDMENT

Subsection (2A) was inserted by the Family Proceedings (Amendment No. 2) Rules 1992 (S.I. 1992 No. 2067), r. 4 (October 5, 1992).

GENERAL NOTE

Appeals against the making or refusing to make an order by Magistrates lie to the High Court, (s.94, p. 219); appeals from decisions of the county or High Court may lie to the Court of Appeal; appeals against decisions of District Judges in the county court may lie to a Judge (Part VIII, r. 8.1). Anyone who had party status in the original proceedings may appeal.

Rule 4.22 sets out the procedure on appeal from the county and High Court to the Court of Appeal. Procedural details in respect of appeals from decisions of Family Proceedings Courts are dealt with by a Practice Direction. The Practice Direction essentially adopts the rule 4.22 procedure.

PRESIDENTS DIRECTION JANUARY 31, 1992 CHILDREN ACT 1989

APPEALS FROM MAGISTRATES' COURTS

Appeals from Magistrates' Courts to the High Court under section 94 of the Children Act 1989 are made in accordance with the provisions of Rule 4.22 of The Family Proceedings Rules 1991.

Such appeal should be commenced by filing the documents referred to in Rule 4.22(2) in the Registry, which is also a care centre, nearest to the Court in which the order appealed from was made. This will usually be the care centre listed against the entry in column (I) of Schedule 2 to the Children (Allocation of Proceedings) Order 1991 (S.I. 1677 No. 1991) for the petty sessions area or London commission area in which the Magistrates' Court is located. The appeal will be heard and determined by a High Court Judge of the Family Division who will normally sit in open Court. The hearing will take place as directed at the nearest convenient High Court centre.

GENERAL NOTE

In line with the other procedural steps under the Children Act, there are tight time limits with flexibility (paras. 3 and 5). Substantial amounts of documents are required to be filed and served (paras. 2 and 4).

The Rule should be read together with section 94 which deals with appeals and section 40 concerning orders pending appeals in certain situations (see pp. 119 and

219). There are no appeals against emergency protection order adjudication; transfer decisions have their own separate appeal mechanism (see r. 4.6 at p. 364).

Overall, the new appeal system is a vast improvement on the muddled state of the law which preceded it. Formerly, certain parties could not appeal at all and different rules of evidence applied in the appellate court as against the Court of First Instance. Moving from procedure to substance however, the appellate courts are still going to hesitate before interfering with the decisions of the courts below in many situations (*G v. G* [1985] F.L.R. 894). The application of *E. v. E.* to Children Act cases has been specifically confirmed by the decision in *Croydon L.B.C. v. A. & Others* [1992] 3 All E.R. 788:—

"An appeal under the 1989 Act is not a full rehearing in which fresh evidence can be called unless there are exceptional circumstances. Furthermore in matters of discretion the appellate Court will not interfere with justices' exercise of their discretion except on the accepted principles relating to unreasonableness."

Appeals are specified proceedings and therefore a guardian ad litem and child's solicitor can be appointed (FPR, r. 4.2(2)(e)).

FPR, 4.23. Confidentiality of documents

(1) Notwithstanding any rule of court to the contrary, no document, other than a record of an order, held by the court and relating to proceedings to which this Part applies shall be disclosed, other than to—
  (a) a party,
  (b) the legal representative of a party,
  (c) the guardian ad litem,
  (d) the Legal Aid Board, or
  (e) a welfare officer,
without leave of the judge or district judge.

(2) Nothing in this rule shall prevent the notification by the court or the proper officer of a direction under section 37(1) to the authority concerned.

FPR, 4.24. Notification of consent

Consent for the purpose of—
  (a) section 16(3), [or]
[. . .]
  (c) paragraph 19(3)(c) or (d) of Schedule 2,
shall be given either—
  (i) orally in court, or
  (ii) in writing to the court signed by the person giving his consent.

AMENDMENT

The words in square brackets were added and deleted by the Family Proceedings (Amendment) Rules 1992 (S.I. 1992 No. 456), reg. 15 (April, 1, 1992).

FPR, 4.25. Secure accommodation—evidence

In proceedings under section 25, the court shall, if practicable, arrange for copies of all written reports before it to be made available before the hearing to—
  (a) the applicant;
  (b) the parent or guardian of the child;

(c) any legal representative of the child;
(d) the guardian ad litem; and
(e) the child, unless the court otherwise directs;

and copies of such reports may, if the court considers it desirable, be shown to any person who is entitled to notice of the proceedings in accordance with these rules.

FPR, 4.26. Investigation under section 37

(1) This rule applies where a direction is given to an appropriate authority by the High Court or a county court under section 37(1).

(2) On giving a direction the court shall adjourn the proceedings and the court or the proper officer shall record the direction in writing.

(3) A copy of the direction recorded under paragraph (2) shall, as soon as practicable after the direction is given, be served by the proper officer on the parties to the proceedings in which the direction is given and, where the appropriate authority is not a party, on that authority.

(4) When serving the copy of the direction on the appropriate authority the proper officer shall also serve copies of such of the documentary evidence which has been, or is to be, adduced in the proceedings as the court may direct.

(5) Where a local authority informs the court of any of the matters set out in section 37(3)(a) to (c) it shall do so in writing.

FPR, 4.27. Direction to local education authority to apply for education supervision order

(1) For the purpose of section 40(3) and (4) of the Education Act 1944 a direction by the High Court or a county court to a local education authority to apply for an education supervision order shall be given in writing.

(2) Where, following such a direction, a local education authority informs the court that they have decided not to apply for an education supervision order, they shall do so in writing.

FPR, 4.28. Transitional provision

Nothing in any provision of this Part of these rules shall affect any proceedings which are pending (within the meaning of paragraph 1 of Schedule 14 to the Act of 1989) immediately before these rules come into force.

APPENDIX 1

FORMS

M1   Statement of Information for a Consent Order
M2   General Heading of Proceedings

M3	Certificate with Regard to Reconciliation
M4	Statement of Arrangements for Children
M5	Notice of Proceedings
M6	Acknowledgment of Service
M7	Affidavit by Petitioner in Support of Petition.
M8	Notice of Application for Decree Nisi to be made Absolute
M9	Certificate of Making Decree Nisi Absolute (Divorce)
M10	Certificate of Making Decree Nisi Absolute (Nullity)
M11	Notice of Application for Ancillary Relief
M12	Notice of Application under Rule 2.45
M13	Notice of Intention to Proceed with Application for Ancillary Relief Made in [Petition or] Answer
M14	Notice of Allegation in Proceedings for Ancillary Relief
M15	Notice of Request for Periodical Payments Order at Same Rate as Order for Maintenance Pending Suit
M16	Request for Issue of Judgment Summons
M17	Judgment Summons
M18	Notice of Appointment to Hear Representations Before Child is Committed to Care of Local Authority
M19	Originating Application on Ground of Failure to Provide Reasonable Maintenance
M20	Notice of Application Under Rule 3.1 or 3.2
M21	Originating Application for Alteration of Maintenance Agreement during Parties' Lifetime
M22	Originating Application for Alteration of Maintenance Agreement after Death of One of the Parties
M23	Originating Summons Under Section 17 of the Married Women's Property Act 1882 or Section 1 of the Matrimonial Homes Act 1967
M24	Notice to be Indorsed on Document Served in Accordance with Rule 9.3
M25	Ex Parte Originating Summons Under Section 13 of the Matrimonial and Family Proceedings Act 1984
M26	Originating Summons Under Section 12 of the Matrimonial and Family Proceedings Act 1984
M27	Originating Summons Under Section 24 of the Matrimonial and Family Proceedings Act 1984
M28	Notice of Proceedings and Acknowledgment of Service
M29	Declaration as to Marital Status Under Section 56(1)(a) of the Family Law Act 1986
M30	Declaration as to Parentage Under Section 56(1)(a) of the Family Law Act 1986
M31	Declaration as to Legitimacy or Legitimation Under Section 56(1)(b) and (2) of the Family Law Act 1986
[M32	Declaration as to an Adoption Effected Overseas Under Section 57 of the Family Law Act 1986]
[M33	Application for registration of Maintenance Order in a Magistrates' Court]
CHA1	Application for a Parental Responsibility Order
CHA2	Parental Responsibility Order
CHA3	Application for the appointment of a guardian
CHA4	Order for the appointment of a guardian
CHA5	Application for the termination of an appointment of a guardian
CHA6	Order terminating the appointment of a guardian
[CHA7	Contact/Residence Order]
CHA8	Prohibited Steps Order
CHA9	Specific Issue Order
CHA10	Application for a Contact Order, Prohibited Steps Order, Residence Order or Specific Issue Order
CHA10A	Respondent's Answer to Section 10 Application
CHA10D	Section 10 Application made by Petitioner or Respondent in divorce proceedings
CHA11	Application to change child's surname
CHA11A	Application to remove child from the jurisdiction of the UK

CHA12	Order authorising change of child's surname/removal of child from the jurisdiction of the UK
CHA13	Application for Financial Provision
CHA13A	Respondent's Answer to Application for Financial Provision
CHA14	Statement of Means
[CHA15	Application for variation/discharge of an order for Financial Provision for Children]
CHA16	Family Assistance Order
[CHA17	Application for Authority to Hold a Child in Secure Accommodation]
CHA18	Order authorising child to be held in secure accommodation
CHA19	Application for a care/supervision Order
CHA20	Order for the care/supervision of a child
CHA21	Application for contact with a child in care
CHA22	Order allowing contact with a child in care
CHA23	Application for permission to refuse contact with a child in care
CHA24	Order refusing contact with a child in care
CHA25	Application for an Education Supervision Order
CHA26	Education Supervision Order
CHA27	Interim Care/Supervision Order
CHA28	Application to discharge Care/Supervision Order, vary Supervision Order or substitute Supervision Order for a Care Order
CHA29	Order discharging Care/Supervision Order, varying Supervision Order or substituting Supervision Order for a Care Order
CHA30	Order making or refusing the appointment of a guardian ad litem
[CHA31	Order making or refusing the appointment of a solicitor]
CHA32	Application for a Child Assessment Order
CHA33	Child Assessment Order
CHA34	Application for an Emergency Protection Order
CHA35	Emergency Protection Order
CHA36	Application to vary Emergency Protection Order directions
CHA37	Order varying Emergency Protection Order directions
CHA38	Application to extend Emergency Protection Order
CHA39	Order extending an Emergency Protection Order
CHA40	Application to discharge an Emergency Protection Order
CHA41	Order discharging an Emergency Protection Order
CHA42	Order authorising search for another child
CHA43	Application for a Warrant under Section 48
CHA44	Warrant under Section 48
CHA45	Application for Recovery Order
CHA46	Recovery Order
CHA47	Order that a child attend proceedings
CHA47A	Order to a person to bring a child to court
CHA48	Order to a person to disclose whereabouts of a child
CHA49	Application to further extend a Supervision Order
CHA50	Order further extending a Supervision Order
CHA51	Application extending an Education Supervision Order
CHA52	Order extending an Education Supervision Order
CHA53	Application discharging an Education Supervision Order
CHA54	Order discharging an Education Supervision Order
CHA55	Application to vary or discharge certain order or directions
CHA56	General Order Form
[CHA57	Refusal of Order]
CHA58	Application for Reconsideration of Refusal to Transfer
CHA59	Form for the disclosure of addresses
[CHA66	Certificate of Transfer to Magistrates' Court]
[CHA67	Order following Reconsideration of a Refusal to Transfer]
[CHA68	Direction to undertake an investigation]
[CHA69	Directions]

AMENDMENT

The words in square brackets were substituted by the Family Proceedings (Amendment) Rules 1991 (S.I. 1991 No. 2113), reg. 19 (October 14, 1991), the Family Proceedings (Amendment) Rules 1992 (S.I. 1992 No. 456) reg. 16 (April 1, 1992) and the Family Proceedings (Amendment No. 2) Rules 1992 (S.I. 1992 No. 2067), rr. 11 and 17 (October 5, 1992).

APPENDIX 2

CONTENTS OF PETITION

(*Unless otherwise directed under rule 2.3*)

[*Not reproduced*]

APPENDIX 3

Rules 4.4 and 4.7

NOTICES AND RESPONDENTS

(i) Provision under which proceedings brought	(ii) Minimum number of days prior to hearing or directions appointment for service under rule 4.4(1)(b)	(iii) Respondents	(iv) Persons to whom notice is to be given
All applications	See separate entries below.	Subject to separate entries below:— every person whom the applicant believes to have parental responsibility for the child; where the child is the subject of a care order, every person whom the applicant believes to have had parental responsibility immediately prior to the making of the care order; in the case of an application to extend, vary or discharge an order, the parties to the proceedings leading to the order which it is sought to have extended, varied or discharged; in the case of specified proceedings, the child.	Subject to separate entries below:— local authority providing accommodation for the child; persons who are caring for the child at the time when the proceedings are commended; in the case of proceedings brought in respect of a child who is alleged to be staying in a refuge which is certified under section 51(1) or (2), the person who is providing the refuge.

(i) Provision under which proceedings brought	(ii) Minimum number of days prior to hearing or directions appointment for service under rule 4.4(1)(b)	(iii) Respondents	(iv) Persons to whom notice is to be given
Section 4(1)(a), 4(3), 5(1), 6(7), 8, 13(1), 16(6), 33(7), Schedule 1, paragraph 19(1) of Schedule 2, or paragraph 11(3) or 16(5) of Schedule 14.	14 days	As for all applications above, and: in the case of proceedings under Schedule 1, those persons whom the applicant believes to be interested in or affected by the proceedings; in the case of an application under paragraph 11(3)(b) or 16(5) of Schedule 14, any person, other than the child, named in the order or directions which it is sought to discharge or vary.	As for "all applications" above, and: in the case of an application for a section 8 order, every person whom the applicant believes— (i) to be named in a court order with respect to the same child, which has not ceased to have effect, (ii) to be a party to pending proceedings in respect of the same child, or (iii) to be a person with whom the child has lived for at least 3 years prior to the application, unless, in a case to which (i) or (ii) applies, the applicant believes that the court order or pending proceedings are not relevant to the application; in the case of an application under paragraph 19(1) of Schedule 2, the parties to the proceedings leading to the care order; in the case of an application under section 5(1), the father of the child if he does not have parental responsibility.

(i) Provision under which proceedings brought	(ii) Minimum number of days prior to hearing or directions appointment for service under rule 4.4(1)(b)	(iii) Respondents	(iv) Persons to whom notice is to be given
Section 36(1), 39(1), 39(2), 39(3), 39(4), 43(1), or paragraph 6(3), 15(2) or 17(1) of Schedule 3.	7 days	As for "all applications" above and: in the case of an application under section 39(2) or (3), the supervisor; in the case of proceedings under paragraph 17(1) of Schedule 3, the local education authority concerned; in the case of proceedings under section 36 or paragraph 15(2) or 17(1) of Schedule 3, the child.	As for "all applications" above and: in the case of an application for an order under section 43(1)— (i) every person whom the applicant believes to be a parent of the child, (ii) every person whom the applicant believes to be caring for the child, (iii) every person in whose favour a contact order is in force with respect to the child, and (iv) every person who is allowed to have contact with the child by virtue of an order under section 34.
Section 31, 34(2), 34(3), 34(4), 34(9) or 38(8)(b).	3 days	As for "all applications" above, and: in the case of an application under section 34, the person whose contact with the child is the subject of the application.	As for "all applications" above, and: in the case of an application under section 31— (i) every person whom the applicant believes to be a party to pending relevant proceedings in respect of the same child, and

(i) Provision under which proceedings brought	(ii) Minimum number of days prior to hearing or directions appointment for service under rule 4.4(1)(b)	(iii) Respondents	(iv) Persons to whom notice is to be given
			(ii) every person whom the applicant believes to be a parent without parental responsibility for the child.
Section 43(12)	2 days	As for "all applications" above.	Those of the persons referred to in section 43(11)(a) to (e) who were not party to the application for the order which it is sought to have varied or discharged.
Section 25, 44(1), 44(9)(b), 45(4), 45(8), 46(7), 48(9), 50(1) or 102(1)	1 day	As for "applications" above and: in the case of an application under section 44(9)(b)— (i) the parties to the application for the order in respect of which it is sought to vary the directions; (ii) any person who was caring for the child prior to the making of the order, and (iii) any person whose contact with the child is affected by the direction which it is sought to have varied;	Except for applications under section 102(1), as for "all applications" above, and: in the case of an application under section 44(1), every person whom the applicant believes to be a parent of the child; in the case of an applicant under section 44(9)(b)— (i) the local authority in whose area the child is living, and (ii) any person whom the applicant believes to be affected by the direction which it is sought to have varied;

(i)	(ii)	(iii)	(iv)
Provision under which proceedings brought	Minimum number of days prior to hearing or directions appointment for service under rule 4.4(1)(b)	Respondents	Persons to whom notice is to be given
		in the case of an application under section 50, the person whom the applicant alleges to have effected or to have been or to be responsible for the taking or keeping of the child.	in the case of an applicant under section 102(1), the person referred to in section 102(1) and any person preventing or likely to prevent such a person from exercising powers under enactments mentioned in subsection (6) of that section.]

AMENDMENT

Appendix 3 was substituted by the Family Procedings (Amendment No. 2) Rules 1992 (S.I. 1992 No. 2067), r.8 (October 5, 1992).

PART III

MISCELLANEOUS

Family Proceedings Courts (Children Act 1989) Rules

Costs

FPC, 22.—(1) In any relevant proceedings, the court may, at any time during the proceedings in that court, make an order that a party pay the whole or any part of the costs of any other party.

(2) A party against whom the court is considering making a costs order shall have an opportunity to make representations as to why the order should not be made.

GENERAL NOTE

There is specific provision for orders for costs against any party only in the Family Proceedings Court Rules. The victim has the right to make representations. Obvious examples for likely orders would be failure to attend hearings or failure to file documents in time. If a case is transferred, an order for costs travels with it.

In line with the Magistrates' Courts Act 1980, s.64, the amount of the costs ordered must be specified, should be such sum as the court considers just and reasonable, and should be recoverable as a civil debt. The amount must not exceed the proper costs incurred and not be a penalty in the guise of costs, see *R. v. Highgate Justices, ex p. Petrou* [1954] 1 All E.R., p. 406.

Many parties to Children Act proceedings will be legally aided and sections 17 and 18 of the Legal Aid Act 1988 should be borne in mind. Essentially, section 17 limits the legally aided party's liability under an order for costs by stipulating that the amount payable should be reasonable having regard to all the circumstances, and in particular, the financial resources and conduct of all parties. Unassisted parties may recover costs against the Legal Aid Board in certain very limited circumstances as set out in section 18 of the Legal Aid Act, *i.e.* that an order for costs would have been made in the proceedings if the party had not been legally aided, that the proceedings were instituted by the legally aided party, and that the court is satisfied that the unassisted party will suffer severe financial hardship unless the order is made, and in any case, that the court is satisfied that it is just and equitable in all the circumstances of the case that provision for the costs should be made out of public funds. Such awards are likely to be very rare in children cases.

Rule 22 deals with orders for costs against the parties themselves. Reference should be made to the Family Proceedings (Costs) Rules for orders for costs against legal representatives, see p. 475.

There is no equivalent rule in the Family Proceedings Rules concerning awards of costs in Children Act cases in the county or High Courts. It would seem, therefore, that the general civil law applies which is set out in the Supreme Court Act 1981 s.51, as amended by the Courts and Legal Services Act 1990, s.4. The legislation provides that costs shall be at the discretion of the court with the court having full power to determine by whom and to what extent, the costs are to be paid (s.51(1)(3)). There are wasted costs provisions in respect of legal representatives (s.51(6)(7)) (see commentary in respect of Family Proceedings (Costs) Rules at p. 475).

The normal civil principle that as a starting point costs will follow the event should be tempered by the consideration that it is unusual to order costs in childrens' cases see (*Singh* v. *Sharegin* [1984] F.L.R. 114, Court of Appeal).

Confidentiality of documents

FPC, 23.—(1) No document, other than a record of an order, held by the court and relating to relevant proceedings shall be disclosed, other than to—
   (a) a party,
   (b) the legal representative of a party,
   (c) the guardian ad litem,
   (d) the Legal Aid Board, or
   (e) a welfare officer,
without leave of the justices' clerk or the court.

(2) Nothing in this rule shall prevent the notification by the court or the justices' clerk of a direction under section 37(1) to the authority concerned.

Enforcement of residence order

FPC, 24. Where a person in whose favour a residence order is in force wishes to enforce it he shall file a written statement describing the alleged breach of the arrangements settled by the order, whereupon the justices' clerk shall fix a date, time and place for a hearing of the proceedings and give notice, as soon as practicable, to the person wishing to enforce the residence order and to any person whom it is alleged is in breach of the arrangements settled by that order, of the date fixed.

DEFINITIONS
   "residence order": s.8(1).

General Note

Enforcement of orders in children's cases has been problematic, particularly at Magistrates' Court level. If problems are anticipated, the higher courts are likely to be the more suitable venue with their wider powers. Rule 4.21.A. inserted by the Amendment (No. 2) Rules 1992 enables District Judges and Justices to attach a penal notice to section 8 orders, see p. 402. If enforcement becomes a problem during proceedings, an application for transfer can be made.

Rule 24 deals specifically with enforcement of residence orders and fits with section 14 (see p. 45). A procedure is set out which although straightforward, may be too cumbersome for many parties in situations of crisis. A mother whose children have remained overlong with their father for a period of contact extended unilaterally, will look askance at the procedure described in the rule.

There is no specific provision for enforcement of other section 8 orders, and therefore Contempt of Court Act 1981, s.17, is applicable: there are penalties of payments per day of default or imprisonment (see notes to s.14, p. 45). Magistrates' have understandably always regarded both powers as being only suitable for cases of last resort.

Sections 44(15), 49 and 50 deal with enforcement of Emergency Protection Orders and care orders by invoking the criminal jurisdiction (see pp. 133, 148 and 149).

Notification of consent

FPC, 25. Consent for the purposes of—
    (a)   section 16(3), [or]
[. . . .]
    (c)   paragraph 19(1) of Schedule 2,
shall be given either—
    (i)   orally in court, or
    (ii)   in writing to the justices' clerk or the court and signed by the person giving his consent.

Amendment

The words in square brackets were substituted by the Family Proceedings Courts (Miscellaneous Amendments) Rules 1992 (S.I. 1992 No. 2068), Sched., r. 6 (October 5, 1992).

Secure accommodation

FPC, 26. In proceedings under section 25, the justices' clerk shall, if practicable, arrange for copies of all written reports before the court to be made available before the hearing to—
    (a)   the applicant,
    (b)   the parent or guardian of the child,
    (c)   any legal representative of the child,
    (d)   the guardian ad litem, and
    (e)   the child, unless the justices' clerk or the court otherwise directs;
and copies of such reports may, if the court considers it desirable, be shown to any person who is entitled to notice of the proceedings in accordance with these Rules.

General Note

This Rule should be read in conjunction with section 25 and the Secure Accommodations Regulations at pp. 79 and 452.

Investigation under section 37

FPC, 27.—(1) This rule applies where a direction is given to an appropriate authority by a family proceedings court under section 37(1).

(2) On giving a direction the court shall adjourn the proceedings and the justices' clerk or the court shall record the direction [in the appropriate form in Schedule 1 to these Rules].

(3) A copy of the direction recorded under paragraph (2) shall, as soon as practicable after the direction is given, be served by the justices' clerk on the parties to the proceedings in which the direction is given and, where the appropriate authority is not a party, on that authority.

(4) When serving the copy of the direction on the appropriate authority the justices' clerk shall also serve copies of such of the documentary evidence which has been, or is to be, adduced in the proceedings as the court may direct.

(5) Where a local authority informs the court of any of the matters set out in section 37(3)(a) to (c) it shall do so in writing.

Limits on the power of a justices' clerk or a single justice to make an order under section 11(3) or section 38(1)

FPC, 28. A justices' clerk or single justice shall not make an order under section 11(3) or section 38(1) unless—
  (a) a written request for such an order has been made to which the other parties and any guardian ad litem consent and which they or their representatives have signed,
  (b) a previous such order has been made in the same proceedings, and
  (c) the terms of the order sought are the same as those of the last such order made.

GENERAL NOTE

Whereas rule 2(5) deals with the powers of a single Magistrate, rule 28 gives details of one of the powers given to single Magistrates as well as to Court Clerks: to make repeat interim section 8 and interim care and/or supervision orders. In care proceedings in particular under the old law, monthly five-minute attendances in interim care orders were sometimes little more than rubber stamping exercises. Rule 28 allows parties to submit written agreement to the making of the repeat order on the basis that all parties consent, and the order is in indentical terms to the order it is proposed should be replaced.

Appeals to a family proceedings court under section 77(6) and paragraph 8(1) of Schedule 8

FPC, 29.—(1) An appeal under section 77(6) or paragraph 8(1) of Schedule 8 shall be by application in accordance with rule 4.

(2) An appeal under section 77(6) shall be brought within 21 days from the date of the step to which the appeal relates.

GENERAL NOTES
This Rule does not apply to proceedings under Parts I to V of the Children Act. See commentary on section 77 at p. 195 and Schedule 8 at p. 279.

Contribution orders

FPC, 30.—(1) An application for a contribution order under paragraph 23(1) of Schedule 2 shall be accompanied by a copy of the contribution notice served in accordance with paragraph 22(1) of that Schedule and a copy of any notice served by the contributor under paragraph 22(8) of that Schedule.

(2) Where a local authority notifies the court of an agreement reached under paragraph 23(6) of Schedule 2, it shall do so in writing through the justices' clerk.

(3) An application for the variation or revocation of a contribution order under paragraph 23(8) of Schedule 2 shall be accompanied by a copy of the contribution order which it is sought to vary or revoke.

Direction to local education authority to apply for education supervision order

FPC, 31.—(1) For the purposes of section 40(3) and (4) of the Education Act 1944, a direction by a magistrates' court to a local education authority to apply for an education supervision order shall be given in writing.

(2) Where, following such a direction, a local education authority informs the court that they have decided not to apply for an education supervision order, they shall do so in writing.

Delegation by justices' clerk

FPC, 32.—(1) In this rule, "employed as a clerk in court" has the same meaning as in rule 2(1) of the Justices' Clerks (Qualifications of Assistants) Rules 1979.

(2) Anything authorised to be done by, to or before a justices' clerk under these Rules, or under paragraphs 13 to 15C of the Schedule to the Justices' Clerks Rules 1970 as amended by Schedule 3 to these Rules, may be done instead by, to or before a person employed as a clerk in court where that person is appointed by the magistrates' courts committee to assist him and where that person has been specifically authorised by the justices' clerk for that purpose.

(3) Any authorisation by the justices' clerk under paragraph (2) shall be recorded in writing at the time the authority is given or as soon as practicable thereafter.

GENERAL NOTE
Put simply, the rule makes the words "Court Clerk" synonymous with "Justices' Clerk" throughout the rules.

Court clerks are given a quasi-judicial role by the Rules. Their powers are listed below, and taken together, there is a significant shift in function which if considered successful, may have substantial implications for future legislation in other areas of Magistrates' Court work.

The administrative functions of court clerks include fixing directions and hearing dates, serving reports of guardians ad litem and court welfare officers, serving directions and orders (except *ex parte* orders which should be served by the applicant), issuing certificates of transfer or refusal to transfer cases, recording directions, findings of fact and decisions, and noting evidence.

Their quasi-judicial functions include the following:

(1) giving leave for *ex parte* applications;

(2) giving, varying or revoking directions and presiding over directions hearings (but see r. 14(3) where either the Court Clerk or a single Magistrate can refer a decision about a direction to the Court if that is felt to be the more appropriate way forward);

(3) transferring proceedings to another Family Proceedings Court or to a county court;

(4) appointing a guardian ad litem and a child's solicitor;

(5) making repeat interim section 8 and interim care and/or supervision orders.

Court clerks have been given these powers to enable cases to be kept moving with the necessary degree of flexibility, and so that Magistrates' Courts sittings are not overwhelmed by Children Act business.

Application of section 97 of the Magistrates' Courts Act 1980

FPC, 33. Section 97 of the Magistrates' Courts Act 1980 shall apply to relevant proceedings in a family proceedings court as it applies to a hearing of a complaint under that section.

MCA, s.97, enables Magistrates to issue a witness summons to compel the attendance of a witness likely to be able to give material evidence, that witness being a person who will not attend voluntarily. This procedure can be used in Children Act cases. Failure to attend in answer to a witness summons can result in the issue of a witness warrant. Failure to give evidence on attendance can result in up to one month's imprisonment or a substantial fine (to be increased to a maximum of £2,500 by the Criminal Justice Act 1991, Sched. 4).

This power can be used to compel the attendance of a child who is a party to care proceedings, but should not be used if the summons would be so inimical to the child's welfare, that it outweighed the legitimate interest to the person seeking it, or where, in any event, the child would not be permitted to give evidence. (See *R. v. B Council, ex p. T* (1991) 2 All E.R. 65 where a stepfather attempted to compel a Magistrates' Court to issue a witness summons against stepdaughter allegedly sexually abused by him so that she could be cross-examined).

Consequential and minor amendments, savings and transitionals

FPC, 34.—(1) Subject to paragraph (3) the consequential and minor amendments in Schedule 3 to these Rules shall have effect.

(2) Subject to paragraph (3), the provisions of the 1981 rules shall have effect subject to these Rules.

(3) Nothing in these Rules shall affect any proceedings which are pending (within the meaning of paragraph 1 of Schedule 14 to the Act of 1989) immediately before these Rules come into force.

SCHEDULE 1

FORMS

1. Application for a Parental Responsibility Order.
2. Parental Responsibility Order.

3. Application for the appointment of a guardian.
4. Order for the appointment of a guardian.
5. Application for the termination of an appointment of a guardian.
6. Order terminating the appointment of a guardian.
7. Contact/Residence Order.
8. Prohibited Steps Order.
9. Specific Issue Order.
10. Application for a Contact Order, Prohibited Steps Order, Residence Order or Specific Issue Order.
10A. Respondent's Answer to Section 10 Application.
11. Application to change child's surname.
11A. Application to remove child from the jurisdiction of the UK.
12. Order authorising change of child's surname/removal of child from the jurisdiction of the UK.
13. Application for Financial Provision.
13A. Respondent's Answer to Application for Financial Provision.
14. Statement of Means.
[15. Application for [Variation] [Discharge] of an order for Financial Provision for Children.]
16. Family Assistance Order.
[17. Application for Authority to Hold Child in Secure Accommodation.]
18. Order authorising child to be held in secure accommodation.
19. Application for a Care/Supervision Order.
20. Order for the care/supervision of a child.
21. Application for contact with a child in care.
22. Order allowing contact with a child in care.
23. Application for permission to refuse contact with a child in care.
24. Order refusing contact with a child in care.
25. Application for an Education Supervision Order.
26. Education Supervision Order.
27. Interim Care/Supervision Order.
28. Application to discharge Care/Supervision Order, vary Supervision Order or substitute Supervision Order for a Care Order.
29. Order discharging Care/Supervision Order, varying Supervision Order or substituting Supervision Order for a Care Order.
30. Order making or refusing the appointment of a guardian ad litem.
31. Order making or refusing the appointment of a solicitor.
32. Application for a Child Assessment Order.
33. Child Assessment Order.
34. Application for an Emergency Protection Order.
35. Emergency Protection Order.
36. Application to vary Emergency Protection Order directions.
37. Order varying Emergency Protection Order directions.
38. Application to extend Emergency Protection Order.
39. Order extending an Emergency Protection Order.
40. Application to discharge an Emergency Protection Order.
41. Order discharging an Emergency Protection Order.
42. Order authorising search for another child.
43. Application for a Warrant under Section 48.
44. Warrant under Section 48.
45. Application for Recovery Order.
46. Recovery Order.
47. Order that a child attend proceedings.
47A. Order to a person to bring a child to court.
48. Order to a person to disclose whereabouts of a child.
49. Application to further extend a Supervision Order.
50. Order further extending a Supervision Order.
51. Application to extend an Education Supervision Order.
52. Order extending an Education Supervision Order.
53. Application to discharge an Education Supervision Order.
54. Order discharging an Education Supervision Order.
55. Application to vary or discharge an order or direction.
56. General Order Form.

57. Refusal of Order.
59. Form for the disclosure of address.
60. Application concerning registration of child minders or providers of day care.
61. Order concerning registration of child minders or providers of day care.
[62. Application for a Warrant under Section 102.]
[63. Warrant under Section 102.]
64. Certificate of Transfer.
65. Refusal to Transfer Proceedings.
[68. Direction to undertake an investigation.]
[69. Directions.]

AMENDMENT

The words in square brackets were substituted by the Family Proceedings Courts (Matrimonial Proceedings, etc.) Rules 1991 (S.I. 1991 No. 1991), Sched. 2, para. 8 (October 14, 1991).

Schedule 2

Rules 4 and 7

RESPONDENTS AND NOTICE

(i) Provision under which proceedings brought	(ii) Minimum number of days prior to hearing or directions appointment for service under rule 4(1)(b)	(iii) Respondents	(iv) Persons to whom notice is to be given
All applications.	See separate entries below.	Subject to separate entries below, every person whom the applicant believes to have parental responsibility for the child; where the child is the subject of a care order, every person whom the applicant believes to have had parental responsibility immediately prior to the making of the care order;	Subject to separate entries below, the local authority providing accommodation for the child; persons who are caring for the child at the time when the proceedings are commenced;

FPC, Schedule 2

(i) Provision under which proceedings brought	(ii) Minimum number of days prior to hearing or directions appointment for service under rule 4(1)(b)	(iii) Respondents	(iv) Persons to whom notice is to be given
Section 4(1)(a), 4(3), 5(1), 6(7), [8], 13(1), 16(6), 33(7), 77(6), [Schedule 1], paragraph 19(1), 23(1) or 23(8) of Schedule 2, paragraph 8(1) of Schedule 8, or paragraph 11(3) or 16(5) of Schedule 14.	14 days.	in the case of an application to extend, vary or discharge an order, the parties to the proceedings leading to the order which it is sought to have extended, varied or discharged; in the case of specified proceedings, the child. Except for proceedings under section 77(6), Schedule 2, or paragraph 8(1) of Schedule 8, as for 'all applications' above, and— in the case of an application under paragraph 11(3)(b) or 16(5) of Schedule 14, any person, other than the child, named in the order or directions which it is sought to discharge or vary; in the case of proceedings under section 77(6), the local authority against whose decision the appeal is made; [in the case of proceedings under Schedule 1, those persons whom the applicant believes to be interested in or affected by the proceedings;]	in the case of proceedings brought in respect of a child who is alleged to be staying in a refuge which is certificated under section 51(1) or (2), the person who is providing the refuge. As for 'all applications' above, and— in the case of an application under paragraph 19(1) of Schedule 2, the parties to the proceedings leading to the care order; in the case of an application under section 5(1), the father of the child if he does not have parental responsibility.

(i) Provision under which proceedings brought	(ii) Minimum number of days prior to hearing or directions appointment for service under rule 4(1)(b)	(iii) Respondents	(iv) Persons to whom notice is to be given
		in the case of an application under paragraph 23(1) of Schedule 2, the contributor; in the case of an application under paragraph 23(8) of Schedule 2— (i) if the applicant is the local authority, the contributor, and (ii) if the applicant is the contributor, the local authority. In the case of an application under paragraph 8(1) of Schedule 8, the local authority against whose decision the appeal is made. ["in the case of an application for a section 8 order, every person whom the applicant believes— (i) to be named in a court order with respect to the same child, which has not ceased to have effect, (ii) to be a party to pending proceedings in respect of the same child, or	

(i) *Provision under which proceedings brought*	(ii) *Minimum number of days prior to hearing or directions appointment for service under rule 4(1)(b)*	(iii) *Respondents*	(iv) *Persons to whom notice is to be given*
		(iii) to be a person with whom the child has lived for at least three years prior to the application, unless, in a case to which (i) or (ii) applies, the applicant believes that the court order or pending proceedings are not relevant to the application.".]	
Section 36(1), 39(1), 39(2), 39(3), 39(4), 43(1), or paragraph 6(3), 15(2) or 17(1) of Schedule 3.	7 days.	As for 'all applications' above, and— in the case of an application under section 39(2) or (3), the supervisor; in the case of proceedings under paragraph 17(1) of Schedule 3, the local education authority concerned; in the case of proceedings under section 36 or paragraph 15(2) or 17(1) of Schedule 3, the child.	As for 'all applications' above, and— in the case of an application for an order under section 43(1)— (i) every person whom the applicant believes to be a parent of the child, (ii) every person whom the applicant believes to be caring for the child, (iii) every person in whose favour a contact order is in force with respect to the child, and (iv) every person who is allowed to have contact with the child by virtue of an order under section 34.

(i) Provision under which proceedings brought	(ii) Minimum number of days prior to hearing or directions appointment for service under rule 4(1)(b)	(iii) Respondents	(iv) Persons to whom notice is to be given
Section 31, 34(2), 34(3), 34(4), 34(9) or 38(8)(b).	3 days	As for 'all applications' above, and— in the case of an application under section 34, the person whose contact with the child is the subject of the application.	As for 'all applications' above, and— in the case of an application under section 31— (i) every person whom the applicant believes to be a party to pending relevant proceedings in respect of the same child, and (ii) every person whom the applicant believes to be a parent without parental responsibility for the child
Section 43(12).	2 days.	As for 'all applications' above.	Those of the persons referred to in section 43(11)(a) to (e) who were not party to the application for the order which it is sought to have varied or discharged.
Section, 25, 44(1), 44(9)(b), 45(4), 45(8), 46(7), 48(9), 50(1), 75(1) or 102(1).	1 day.	Except for applications under section 75(1) or 102(1), as for 'all applications' above, and— in the case of an application under section 44(9)(b)	As for 'all applications' above, and— in the case of an application under section 44(1), every person whom the applicant believes to be a parent of the child; in the case of an application under section 44(9)(b)—

(i) Provision under which proceedings brought	(ii) Minimum number of days prior to hearing or directions appointment for service under rule 4(1)(b)	(iii) Respondents	(iv) Persons to whom notice is to be given
		(i) the parties to the application for the order in respect of which it is sought to vary the directions; (ii) any person who was caring for the child prior to the making of the order; and (iii) any person whose contact with the child is affected by the direction which it is sought to have varied; in the case of an application under section 50, the person whom the applicant alleges to have effected or to have been or to be responsible for the taking or keeping of the child; in the case of an application under section 75(1), the registered person; in the case of an application under section 102(1), the person referred to in section 102(1) and any person preventing or likely to prevent such a person from exercising powers under enactments mentioned in subsection (6) of that section.	(i) the local authority in whose area the child is living, and (ii) any person whom the applicant believes to be affected by the direction which it is sought to have varied.

428 Part II

AMENDMENT

The words in square brackets were substituted by the Family Proceedings Courts (Miscellaneous Amendments) Rules 1992 (S.I. 1992 No. 2068), Sched., para. 9 (October 5, 1992).

SCHEDULE 3 Rule 34(1)

CONSEQUENTIAL AND MINOR AMENDMENTS

[*not reproduced*]

PART III

ADDITIONAL STATUTORY INSTRUMENTS

The Children (Admissibility of Hearsay Evidence) Order 1991
(S.I. 1991 No. 1115)

The Children (Allocation of Proceedings) Order 1991
(S.I. 1991 No. 1677)

The Children (Allocation of Proceedings Appeals) Order 1991
(S.I. 1991 No. 1801)

The Children (Secure Accommodation) Regulations 1991
(S.I. 1991 No. 1505)

The Children (Secure Accommodation) (No. 2) Regulations 1991
(S.I. 1991 No. 2034)

The Contact with Children Regulations 1991
(S.I. 1991 No. 891)

The Emergency Protection Order (Transfer of Responsibilites) Regulations 1991
(S.I.) 1991 No. 1414

The Family Proceedings Rules 1991
(S.I. 1991 No. 1247)
Pts. V, VIII and IX in part

The Family Proceedings (Costs) Rule 1991
(S.I. 1991 No. 1832)

The Family Proceedings Fees Order 1991
(S.I. 1991 No. 2114)

The Galro Panels Regulations 1991
(S.I. 1991 No. 2051)

THE CHILDREN (ADMISSIBILITY OF HEARSAY EVIDENCE) ORDER 1991

(S.I. 1991 No. 1115)

Made by the Secretary of State under ss.96(3) and 104 of the Children Act 1989.

Citation and commencement

1. This Order may be cited as the Children (Admissibility of Hearsay Evidence) Order 1991 and shall come into force on 14th October 1991.

Admissibility of hearsay evidence

2. In civil proceedings before the High Court or a county court and in family proceedings in a magistrates' court, evidence given in connection with the upbringing, maintenance or welfare of a child shall be admissible notwithstanding any rule of law relating to hearsay.

Revocation

3. The Children (Admissibility of Hearsay Evidence) Order 1990 is revoked.

GENERAL NOTE

The order replaces the previous Children Act Hearsay Order (S.I. 1990 No. 143) the new order being of even wider ambit. Hearsay evidence is admissible in all Children Act proceedings in all jurisdictions if it is evidence given in connection with the upbringing maintenance or welfare of a child. At first sight, the order and its predecessor are almost revolutionary, however they achieve little more than the legitimisation of common practice. Hearsay evidence was always admissible in Wardship proceedings and often managed to sneak its way in to other children's proceedings.

Admissibility of hearsay evidence attracted particular attention as local authorities tried to persuade courts to admit evidence of disclosures of abuse made by children to third parties, such as teachers or foster parents. There will now be no difficulty as to admissibility, the focus switching to credibility of the evidence and the weight to be attached to it.

The order is not limited to what is sometimes termed first hand hearsay. If a neighbour finds young children unattended, tells a Police Officer who reports the matter to a social worker, the social worker can give the evidence. However, a note of caution is sounded in the wardship case of *Re W (Minors), (Wardship Evidence)* [1990] 1 F.L.R. 203 which is likely to be followed in Children Act proceedings. Butler-Sloss L.J. gave the judgment of the Court of Appeal including the following:

"I cannot imagine that any Judge would allow a grave allegation against a parent to be proved solely by hearsay, at any rate in a case in which direct evidence could be produced ... unless uncontroversial it (hearsay evidence) had to be regarded with grave caution."

Hearsay evidence is as admissible in Children Act proceedings as it is in wardship, and therefore courts hearing Children Act cases are likely to consider themselves bound by *Re W*.

The Hearsay Order should be read together with sections 7(4) and 41(11) (admissibility of evidence in the reports of guardians ad litem and court welfare officers), see pp. 29 and 122.

THE CHILDREN (ALLOCATION OF PROCEEDINGS) ORDER 1991)

(S.I. 1991 No. 1677)

Made by the Lord Chancellor under s.92(9) (10) and Sched. 11, Pt. 1 to the Children Act 1989.

GENERAL NOTE

The Children Act structure does not create a Family Court as such but concurrent jurisdiction in children's cases is an interesting development and an important aspect of the Act. DoH *Guidance*, Vol. 1 at para. 1.13:

"The Children Act creates a concurrent system of jurisdiction for a wide range of family proceedings in new Magistrates' Family Proceedings Courts, County Courts and the High Court. Rules governing the allocation and transfer of cases either vertically between the various tiers or horizontally within tiers, will ensure that cases are directed to the most appropriate Court."

The Allocation Order should be read in conjunction with Home Office Circular 45/91 reprinted in full in Volume 7 of the DoH *Guidance*. The Allocation Order sets out details of where cases should be commenced, together with relevant considerations for transfer. Rules 4.6 and 6 deal with the transfer procedures.

The Allocation Order applies to adoption as well as Children Act proceedings.

The majority of public law cases are expected to be heard in the Family Proceedings Courts; private law applicants are still able to choose their court subject to legal aid considerations if applicable. Wherever commenced, cases are likely to be transferred on the varying basis of complexity, consolidation or urgency. Some cases may make strange journeys around the country and/or up, down or across the jurisdictions.

Hearings at Magistrates' Courts level will be in the Family Proceedings Courts (except secure accommodation applications which will be in Magistrates' Courts). County courts are divided into Divorce County Courts, Family Hearing Centres and Care Centres. Lists of each are set out in the Schedules to the Order. A county court designated as a Divorce County Court may hear and determine all applications under Parts I and II of The Children Act including Schedule 1 applications. Contested section 8 applications are the exception: they must be heard in a Family Hearing Centre. County courts designated as Care Centres can hear all Children Act proceedings (arts. 15, 16 and 18).

Commencement

Articles 3 and 4 of the order deal with commencement. Applicants should consult articles 3 and 4. If the case contemplated is listed in article 3 (which are broadly public law cases), the application must start at Family Proceedings Court level. If not, and if the application contemplated is not caught by article 4, the applicant may choose the court in which the launch his case.

There are four exceptions to the general principle that public law cases must start at Family Proceedings Court level:

(1) applications by Local Authorities under section 8 for prohibited steps orders or specific issue orders are not in the article 3 list and therefore may be commenced in any court;

(2) if care proceedings are issued following a section 37 direction, the court which directed the investigation should hear the case (art. 3(2));

(3) all proceedings concerning the same child should be consolidated: if there are current proceedings in another court, that court should hear the public law application also (art. 3(3));

(4) applications which in effect extend, vary or discharge an existing order, should be made to the court making the original order (art. 4).

This latter situation was considered by the Court of Appeal in *Re C* (1992) FCR, p. 478. The case considered the definition of pending proceedings under Schedule 14 as well as the Allocation Order, and in respect of the latter, concluded that:

"An application (*e.g.* for contact) made under the 1989 Act the determination of which might have the effect of varying or discharging the Wardship order made before the Act came into force, should be made to the Court which made the earlier order and not to the Family Proceedings Court" (Butler-Sloss L.J.).

That the child was no longer a ward was therefore irrelevant: the High Court made the original order and therefore to the High Court should be addressed any subsequent application the effect of which may vary or alter that original order.

Citation, commencement and interpretation

1.—(1) This Order may be cited as the Children (Allocation of Proceedings) Order 1991 and shall come into force on 14th October 1991.

(2) In this Order, unless the context otherwise requires—

"child"—
   (a) means, subject to sub-paragraph (b), a person under the age of 18 with respect to whom proceedings are brought, and
   (b) where the proceedings are under Schedule 1, also includes a person who has reached the age of 18;

"London commission area" has the meaning assigned to it by section 2(1) of the Justices of the Peace Act 1979;

"petty sessions area" has the meaning assigned to it by section 4 of the Justices of the Peace Act 1979; and

"the Act" means the Children Act 1989, and a section, Part or Schedule referred to by number alone means the section, Part or Schedule so numbered in that Act.

Classes of county court

2. For the purposes of this Order there shall be the following classes of county court:
   (a) divorce county courts, being those courts designated for the time being as divorce county courts by an order under section 33 of the Matrimonial and Family Proceedings Act 1984;
   (b) family hearing centres, being those courts set out in Schedule 1 to this Order;
   (c) care centres, being those courts set out in column (ii) of Schedule 2 to this Order.

COMMENCEMENT OF PROCEEDINGS

Proceedings to be commenced in magistrates' court

3.—(1) Subject to paragraphs (2) and (3) and to article 4, proceedings under any of the following provisions shall be commenced in a magistrates' court:
  (a) section 25 (use of accommodation for restricting liberty);
  (b) section 31 (care and supervision orders);
  (c) section 33(7) (leave to change name of or remove from United Kingdom child in care);
  (d) section 34 (parental contact);
  (e) section 36 (education supervision orders);
  (f) section 43 (child assessment orders);
  (g) section 44 (emergency protection orders);
  (h) section 45 (duration of emergency protection orders, etc.);
  (i) section 46(7) (application for emergency protection order by police officer);
  (j) section 48 (powers to assist discovery of children, etc.);
  (k) section 50 (recovery orders);
  (l) section 75 (protection of children in an emergency);
  (m) section 77(6) (appeal against steps taken under section 77(1));
  (n) section 102 (powers of constable to assist, etc.);
  (o) paragraph 19 of Schedule 2 (approval of arrangements to assist child to live abroad);
  (p) paragraph 23 of Schedule 2 (contribution orders);
  (q) paragraph 8 of Schedule 8 (certain appeals);
  (r) section 21 of the Adoption Act 1976.

(2) Notwithstanding paragraph (1) and subject to paragraph (3), proceedings of a kind set out in sub-paragraph (b), (e), (f), (g), (i) or (j) or paragraph (1), and which arise out of an investigation directed, by the High Court or a county court, under section 37(1), shall be commenced—
  (a) in the court which directs the investigation, where that court is the High Court or a care centre, or
  (b) in such care centre as the court which directs the investigation may order.

(3) Notwithstanding paragraphs (1) and (2), proceedings of a kind set out in sub-paragraph (a) to (k), (n) or (o) of paragraph (1) shall be made to a court in which are pending other proceedings, in respect of the same child, which are also of a kind set out in those sub-paragraphs.

Application to extend, vary or discharge order

4.—(1) Subject to paragraphs (2) and (3), proceedings under the Act, or under the Adoption Act 1976—
  (a) to extend, vary or discharge an order, or
  (b) the determination of which may have the effect of varying or discharging an order,

shall be made to the court which made the order.

(2) Notwithstanding paragraph (1), an application for an order under section 8 which would have the effect of varying or discharging an order made, by a county court, in accordance with section 10(1)(b) shall be made to divorce county court.

(3) Notwithstanding paragraph (1), an application to extend, vary or discharge an order made, by a county court, under section 38, or for an order which would have the effect of extending, varying or discharging such an order, shall be made to a care centre.

(4) A court may transfer proceedings made in accordance with paragraph (1) to any other court in accordance with the provisions of articles 5 to 13.

TRANSFER OF PROCEEDINGS

GENERAL NOTE
Articles 5–13 of the Order deal with transfer of proceedings. Cases may be transferred six ways: from one Magistrates' Court to another (art. 6), from a Magistrates' Court to a county court (arts. 7 and 8), from a county court to another county court (art. 10), from a county court back to Magistrates' Court (art. 11) and from the county court to the High Court (art. 12) and back again (art. 13). The common grounds for transfers in all of these various directions are what is in the best interests of the child having regard to the avoidance of delay principle.

More extensive and detailed grounds are set out at article 7 concerning cases started in the Family Proceedings Court because they are on the article 3 list (*i.e.* mainly public law cases), as to when they should be transferred to the county court. In particular, additional grounds of complexity and consolidation are set out with a list of factors for Courts to consider in judging complexity.

Disapplication of enactments about transfer

5. Sections 38 and 39 of the Matrimonial and Family Proceedings Act 1984 shall not apply to proceedings under the Act or under the Adoption Act 1976.

Transfer from one magistrates' court to another

6. A magistrates' court (the "transferring court") shall transfer proceedings under the Act or under the Adoption Act 1976 to another magistrates' court (the "receiving court") where—
   (a) having regard to the principle set out in section 1(2), the transferring court considers that the transfer is in the interest of the child—
      (i) because it is likely significantly to accelerate the determination of the proceedings,
      (ii) because it would be appropriate for those proceedings to be heard together with other family proceedings which are pending in the receiving court, or
      (iii) for some other reason, and
   (b) the receiving court, by its justices' clerk (as defined by rule 1(20 of the Family Proceedings Courts (Children Act 1989) Rules 1991), consents to the transfer.

Transfer from magistrates' court to county court by magistrates' court

7.—(1) Subject to paragraphs (2), (3) and (4) and to articles 15 to 18, a magistrates' court may, upon application by a party or of its own motion, transfer to a county court proceedings of any of the kinds mentioned in article 3(1) where it considers it in the interests of the child to do so having regard, first, to the principle set out in section 1(2) and, secondly, to the following questions:
> (a) whether the proceedings are exceptionally grave, important or complex, in particular—
>> (i) because of complicated or conflicting evidence about the risks involved to the child's physical or moral well-being or about other matters relating to the welfare of the child;
>> (ii) because of the number of parties;
>> (iii) because of a conflict with the law of another jurisdiction;
>> (iv) because of some novel and difficult point of law; or
>> (v) because of some question of general public interest;
>
> (b) whether it would be appropriate for those proceedings to be heard together with other family proceedings which are pending in another court; and
> (c) whether transfer is likely significantly to accelerate the determination of the proceedings, where—
>> (i) no other method of doing so, including transfer to another magistrates' court, is appropriate, and
>> (ii) delay would seriously prejudice the interests of the child who is the subject of the proceedings.

(2) Notwithstanding paragraph (1), proceedings of the kind mentioned in sub-paragraph (g) to (j), (l), (m), (p) or (q) or article 3(1) shall not be transferred from a magistrates' court.

(3) Notwithstanding paragraph (1), proceedings of the kind mentioned in sub-paragraph (a) or (n) of article 3(1) shall only be transferred from a magistrates' court to a county court in order to be heard together with other family proceedings which arise out of the same circumstances as gave rise to the proceedings to be transferred and which are pending in another court.

(4) Notwithstanding paragraphs (1) and (3), proceedings of the kind mentioned in article 3(1)(a) shall not be transferred from a magistrates' court which is not a family proceedings court within the meaning of section 92(1).

GENERAL NOTE

The article 7(1)(a) ground of exceptional gravity, importance or complexity, is not without its difficulties: many cases could be said to come within the definition. It is, however, clearly envisaged that the majority of care cases should remain at Family Proceedings Court level (The Lord Chancellors Department has indicated that it anticipates perhaps only 25 per cent. of care cases being dealt with by the higher courts). A case which is very difficult at the contested interim stage should be transferred up, and then returned once the issues have become clearer and perhaps more straightforward, see *Re H (A Minor) (Care Proceedings)* [1992] 2 F.C.R. 332. Few cases benefit from too many courts spoiling the broth.

In *J. v. Berkshire C.C. The Times,* 10 March, 1992, the court expressed the view that long cases (in that case a care case spanning eight days), should be transferred upwards.

Additional factors said to favour the High Court are set out in *JR* v. *Merton London Borough* [1992] 2 F.C.R. 185 and include:
(1) Complexity of issues.
(2) Nature of the evidence to be adduced.
(3) Highly charged atmosphere between the parties.
(4) Novelty of the procedure and principles to be applied.
(5) Possible length of hearing (10 days).
In *Re H* [1992] 2 F.C.R. 332, there is further guidance. The case was one in which:
" ... an able intelligent adolescent was demonstrating the capacity to blight his prospects of achievement as a consequence of grossly disturbed behaviour ... [this] was a class of case more appropriately dealt with by a Judge of the Family Division ... ".
This article also sets out the proceedings which cannot be transferred at all: in particular applications for emergency protection orders and linked applications (*i.e.* ss.44–46). It may be, however, that emergency protection orders which have the effect of varying or discharging an existing county or High Court Order should be directed to the court making the original Order. Likewise, considerations of consolidation or a section 37 Direction case giving rise to an emergency protection order may mean such applications are made to the higher courts (Art. 4(1), Art. 3(2)(3)). Secure accommodation applications can only be transferred on the basis of consolidation.

8. Subject to articles 15 to 18, a magistrates' court may transfer to a county court proceedings under the Act or under the Adoption Act 1976, being proceedings to which article 7 does not apply, where, having regard to the principle set out in section 1(2), it considers that in the interests of the child the proceedings can be dealt with more appropriately in that county court.

GENERAL NOTE

Article 8 deals with cases not on the article 3 list (*i.e.* mainly private law cases), and their transfer from a Family Proceedings Court to a county court. If the case is not caught by articles 3 or 4, the applicant has free choice for commencement: the grounds for transfer are therefore much narrower than article 7 transfers. The only ground for a transfer is "having regard to the principle set out in s.1(2) (avoidance of delay), the court considers in the interests of the child, the proceedings can be dealt with more appropriately in a County Court." Complexity is not specifically expressed to be a ground for transfer. Article 4 cases therefore seem to be left with the worst of both worlds: no choice of venue, and if the venue is to be a Family Proceedings Court, there are very narrow grounds for transfer therefrom. Few county courts can hear applications more quickly than Magistrates', thus article 8 transfers may become collectors' items.

Transfer from magistrates' court following refusal of magistrates' court to transfer

9.—(1) Where a magistrates' court refuses to transfer proceedings under article 7, a party to those proceedings may apply to the care centre listed in column (ii) of Schedule 2 to this Order against the entry in column (i) for the petty sessions area or London commission area in which the magistrates' court is situated for an order under paragraph (2).

(2) Upon hearing an application under paragraph (1) the court may transfer the proceedings to itself where, having regard to the principle set out in section 1(2) and the questions set out in article 7(1)(a) to (c), it considers it in the interests of the child to do so.

(3) Upon hearing an application under paragraph (1) the court may transfer the proceedings to the High Court where, having regard to the principle set out in section 1(2), it considers—
    (a) that the proceedings are appropriate for determination in the High Court, and

(b) that such determination would be in the interests of the child.

GENERAL NOTE

Article 9 links with rules 4.6 and 6, and deals with the transfer procedure from Magistrates' Court to county court in respect of article 7 cases which the court has refused to transfer. There is no equivalent procedure for article 8 (*i.e.* mainly private law) refusals: if the Family Proceedings Court declines an application to transfer any proceedings other than those listed in article 3(1), there is nothing the parties can do about it. See p. 366 for the detailed procedure on transfer and appeals against refusals to transfer in commentary at FPR, r. 4.6, FPC, r. 6.

Transfer from one county court to another

10. Subject to articles 15 to 17, a county court (the "transferring court") shall transfer proceedings under the Act or under the Adoption Act 1976 to another county court (the "receiving court") where—
   (a) the transferring court, having regard to the principle set out in section 1(2), considers the transfer to be in the interests of the child, and
   (b) the receiving court is—
      (i) of the same class or classes, within the meaning of article 2, as the transferring court, or
      (ii) to be presided over by a judge or district judge who is specified by directions under section 9 of the Court and Legal Services Act 1990 for the same purposes as the judge or district judge presiding over the transferring court.

Transfer from county court to magistrates' court by county court

11. A county court may transfer to a magistrates' court before trial proceedings which were transferred under article 7(1) where the county court, having regard to the principle set out in section 1(2) and the interests of the child, considers that the criterion cited by the magistrates' court as the reason for transfer—
   (a) in the case of the criterion in article 7(1)(a), does not apply,
   (b) in the case of the criterion in article 7(1)(b), no longer applies, because the proceedings with which the transferred proceedings were to be heard have been determined,
   (c) in the case of the criterion in article 7(1)(c), no longer applies.

Transfer from county court to High Court by county court

12. A county court may transfer proceedings under the Act or the Adoption Act 1976 to the High Court where, having regard to the principle set out in section 1(2), it considers—
   (a) that the proceedings are appropriate for determination in the High Court, and

(b) that such determination would be in the interests of the child.

Transfer from High Court to county court

13. Subject to articles 15, 16 and 18, the High Court may transfer to a county court proceedings under the Act or the Adoption Act 1976 where, having regard to the principle set out in section 1(2), it considers that the proceedings are appropriate for determination in such a court and that such determination would be in the interests of the child.

ALLOCATION OF PROCEEDINGS TO PARTICULAR COUNTY COURTS

Commencement

14. Subject to articles 18, 19 and 20 and to rule 2.40 of the Family Proceedings Rules 1991 (Application under Part I or II of the Children Act 1989 where matrimonial cause is pending), an application under the Act or under the Adoption Act 1976 which is to be commenced in a county court shall be commenced in a divorce county court.

Proceedings under Part I or II or Schedule 1

15.—(1) Subject to paragraph (3), where an application under Part I or II or Schedule 1 is to be transferred from a magistrates' court to a county court, it shall be transferred to a divorce county court.

(2) Subject to paragraph (3), where an application under Part I or II or Schedule 1, other than an application for an order under section 8, is to be transferred from the High Court to a county court, it shall be transferred to a divorce county court.

(3) Where an application under Part I or II or Schedule 1, other than an application for an order under section 8, is to be transferred to a county court for the purpose of consolidation with other proceedings, it shall be transferred to the court in which those other proceedings are pending.

Orders under section 8 of the Children Act 1989

16.—(1) An application for an order under section 8 in a divorce county court, which is not also a family hearing centre, shall, if the court is notified that the application will be opposed, be transferred for trial to a family hearing centre.

(2) Subject to paragraph (3), where an application for an order under section 8 is to be transferred from the High Court to a county court it shall be transferred to a family hearing centre.

(3) Where an application for an order under section 8 is to be transferred to a county court for the purpose of consolidation with other proceedings, it may be transferred to the court in which those

other proceedings are pending whether or not it is a family hearing centre; but paragraph (1) shall apply to the application following the transfer.

Application for adoption or freeing for adoption

17.—(1) Subject to article 22, proceedings in a divorce county court, which is not also a family hearing centre, under section 12 or 18 of the Adoption Act 1976 shall, if the court is notified that the proceedings will be opposed, be transferred for trial to a family hearing centre.

(2) Where proceedings under the Adoption Act 1976 are to be transferred from a magistrates' court to a county court, they shall be transferred to a divorce county court.

Applications under Part III, IV or V

18.—(1) An application under Part III, IV or V, if it is to be commenced in a county court, shall be commenced in a care centre.

(2) An application under Part III, IV or V which is to be transferred from the High Court to a county court shall be transferred to a care centre.

(3) An application under Part III, IV or V which is to be transferred from a magistrates' court to a county court shall be transferred to the care centre listed against the entry in column (i) of Schedule 2 to this Order for the petty sessions area or London commission area in which the relevant magistrates' court is situated.

Principal Registry of the Family Division

19. The principal registry of the Family Division of the High Court shall be treated, for the purposes of this Order, as if it were a divorce county court, a family hearing centre and a care centre listed against every entry in column (i) of Schedule 2 to this Order (in addition to the entries against which it is actually listed).

Lambeth and Woolwich County Courts

20. Notwithstanding articles 14, 16 and 17, an application for an order under section 8 or under the Adoption Act 1976 may be commenced and tried in Lambeth County Court or in Woolwich County Court.

MISCELLANEOUS

Contravention of provision of this Order

21. Where proceedings are commenced or transferred in contravention of a provision of this Order, the contravention shall not have the effect of making the proceedings invalid; and no appeal shall lie against the determination of proceedings on the basis of such contravention alone.

GENERAL NOTE

Erroneous transfers do not invalidate the proceedings nor form the basis of an appeal.

Transitional provision—proceedings under Adoption Act 1976

22. Proceedings under the Adoption Act 1976 which are commenced in a county court prior to the coming into force of this Order may, notwithstanding article 17(1), remain in that court for trial.

SCHEDULES

SCHEDULE 1

Article 2

FAMILY HEARING CENTRES

Midland and Oxford Circuit

Birmingham County Court
Coventry County Court
Derby County Court
Leicester County Court
Lincoln County Court
Mansfield County Court
Northampton County Court
Nottingham County Court
Oxford County Court
Peterborough County Court
Stafford County Court
Stoke-on-Trent County Court
Telford County Court
Walsall County Court
Wolverhampton County Court
Worcester County Court

Northern Circuit

Blackburn County Court
Bolton County Court
Carlisle County Court
Lancaster County Court
Liverpool County Court
Manchester County Court
Stockport County Court

South Eastern Circuit

Brighton County Court
Bow County Court
Brentford County Court
Bromley County Court
Cambridge County Court
Canterbury County Court
Chelmsford County Court
Chichester County Court
Colchester and Clacton County Court
Croydon County Court
Edmonton County Court
Guildford County Court
Hitchin County Court
Ilford County Court
Ipswich County Court
Kingston-upon-Thames County Court
Luton County Court
Maidstone County Court
Medway County Court
Milton Keynes County Court
Norwich County Court
Reading County Court
Romford County Court
Slough County Court
Southend County Court
Wandsworth County Court
Watford County Court
Willesden County Court

Part III

FAMILY HEARING CENTRES

North Eastern Circuit

Barnsley County Court
Bradford County Court
Darlington County Court
Dewsbury County Court
Doncaster County Court
Durham County Court
Halifax County Court
Harrogate County Court
Huddersfield County Court
Keighley County Court
Kingston-upon-Hull County Court
Leeds County Court
Newcastle-upon-Tyne County Court
Pontefract County Court
Rotherham County Court
Scarborough County Court
Sheffield County Court
Skipton County Court
Sunderland County Court
Teesside County Court
Wakefield County Court
York County Court

Wales and Chester Circuit

Aberystwyth County Court
Caernarfon County Court
Cardiff County Court
Carmarthen County Court
Chester County Court
Crewe County Court
Haverfordwest County Court
Llangefni County Court
Macclesfield County Court
Methyr Tydfil County Court
Newport (Gwent) County Court
Rhyl County Court
Swansea County Court
Warrington County Court
Welshpool and Newtown County Court
Wrexham County Court

Western Circuit

Basingstoke County Court
Bournemouth County Court
Bristol County Court
Exeter County Court
Gloucester County Court
Plymouth County Court
Portsmouth County Court
Southampton County Court
Swindon County Court
Taunton County Court
Truro County Court

SCHEDULE 2

Article 2

CARE CENTRES

(i) Petty Sessions Areas	(ii) Care Centres

Midland and Oxford Circuit

Abingdon	Oxford County Court
Aldridge and Brownhills	Wolverhampton County Court
Alfreton and Belper	Derby County Court
Ashby-De-La-Zouch	Leicester County Court
Atherstone and Coleshill	Coventry County Court
Barton-on-Humber	Lincoln County Court
Bewdley and Stourport	Worcester County Court
Bicester	Oxford County Court
Birmingham	Birmingham County Court
Boston	Lincoln County Court

(i)
Petty Sessions Areas

(ii)
Care Centres

Midland and Oxford Circuit

Bourne and Stamford	Lincoln County Court
Bridgenorth	Telford County Court
Brigg	Lincoln County Court
Bromsgrove	Worcester County Court
Burton-upon-Trent	Stoke-on-Trent County Court
Caistor	Lincoln County Court
Cannock	Wolverhampton County Court
Cambridge	Peterborough County Court
Cheadle	Stoke-on-Trent County Court
Chesterfield	Derby County Court
City of Hereford	Worcester County Court
Congleton	Stoke-on-Trent County Court
Corby	Northampton County Court
Coventry	Coventry County Court
Crewe and Nantwich	Stoke-on-Trent County Court
Daventry	Northampton County Court
Derby and South Derbyshire	Derby County Court
Didcot and Wantage	Oxford County Court
Drayton	Telford County Court
Dudley	Wolverhampton County Court
East Retford	Nottingham County Court
East Oxfordshire	Oxford County Court
Eccleshall	Stoke-on-Trent County Court
Elloes	Lincoln County Court
Ely	Peterborough County Court
Epworth and Goole	Lincoln County Court
Gainsborough	Lincoln County Court
Glossop	Derby County Court
Grantham	Lincoln County Court
Grimsby and Cleethorpes	Lincoln County Court
Halesowen	Wolverhampton County Court
Henley	Oxford County Court
High Peak	Derby County Court
Huntingdon	Peterborough County Court
Ikeston	Derby County Court
Kettering	Northampton County Court
Kidderminster	Worcester County Court
Leek	Stoke-on-Trent County Court
Leicester (City)	Leicester County Court
Leicester (County)	Leicester County Court
Lichfield	Stoke-on-Trent County Court
Lincoln District	Lincoln County Court
Loughborough	Leicester County Court
Louth	Lincoln County Court
Ludlow	Telford County Court
Lutterworth	Leicester County Court
Malvern Hills	Worcester County Court
Mansfield	Nottingham County Court
Market Bosworth	Leicester County Court
Market Harborough	Leicester County Court
Market Rasen	Lincoln County Court
Melton and Belvoir	Leicester County Court
Mid-Warwickshire	Coventry County Court
Mid-Worcestershire	Worcester County Court
Newark and Southwell	Nottingham County Court
Newcastle-under-Lyme	Stoke-on-Trent County Court

(i) **Petty Sessions Areas** (ii) **Care Centres**

Midland and Oxford Circuit

Newmarket	Peterborough County Court
	Ipswich County Court
Northampton	Northampton County Court
North Herefordshire	Worcester County Court
North Oxfordshire and Chipping Norton	Oxford County Court
North Witchford	Peterborough County Court
Nottingham	Nottingham County Court
Nuneaton	Coventry County Court
Oswestry	Telford County Court
Oxford	Oxford County Court
Peterborough	Peterborough County Court
Pirehill North	Stoke-on-Trent County Court
Redditch	Worcester County Court
Rugby	Coventry County Court
Rugeley	Wolverhampton County Court
Rutland	Leicester County Court
Scunthorpe	Lincoln County Court
Seisdon	Wolverhampton County Court
Sleaford	Lincoln County Court
Shrewsbury	Telford County Court
Solihull	Birmingham County Court
South Herefordshire	Worcester County Court
South Warwickshire	Coventry County Court
Spilsby and Skegness	Lincoln County Court
Stoke-on-Trent	Stoke-on-Trent County Court
Stone	Stoke-on-Trent County Court
Stourbridge	Wolverhampton County Court
Sutton Coldfield	Birmingham County Court
Tamworth	Stoke-on-Trent County Court
Telford	Telford County Court
Toseland	Peterborough County Court
Towcester	Northampton County Court
Uttoxeter	Stoke-on-Trent County Court
Vale of Evesham	Worcester County Court
Warley	Wolverhampton County Court
Walsall	Wolverhampton County Court
Wellingborough	Northampton County Court
West Bromwich	Wolverhampton County Court
West Derbyshire	Derby County Court
Wisbech	Peterborough County Court
Witney	Oxford County Court
Wolds	Lincoln County Court
Wolverhampton	Wolverhampton County Court
Woodstock	Oxford County Court
Worcester City	Worcester County Court
Worksop	Nottingham County Court

Northern Circuit

Appleby	Carlisle County Court
Ashton-under-Lyne	Manchester County Court
Barrow with Bootle	Lancaster County Court
Blackburn	Blackburn County Court
Blackpool	Lancaster County Court
Bolton	Manchester County Court

(i) Petty Sessions Areas	(ii) Care Centres

Northern Circuit

Burnley	Blackburn County Court
Bury	Manchester County Court
Carlisle	Carlisle County Court
Chorley	Blackburn County Court
Darwen	Blackburn County Court
Eccles	Manchester County Court
Fylde	Lancaster County Court
Hyndburn	Blackburn County Court
Kendal and Lonsdale	Lancaster County Court
Keswick	Carlisle County Court
Knowsley	Liverpool County Court
Lancaster	Lancaster County Court
Leigh	Manchester County Court
Liverpool	Liverpool County Court
Manchester	Manchester County Court
Middleton and Heywood	Manchester County Court
North Lonsdale	Lancaster County Court
North Sefton	Liverpool County Court
Oldham	Manchester County Court
Ormskirk	Liverpool County Court
Pendle	Blackburn County Court
Penrith and Alston	Carlisle County Court
Preston	Blackburn County Court
Ribble Valley	Blackburn County Court
Rochdale	Manchester County Court
Rossendale	Blackburn County Court
St. Helens	Liverpool County Court
Salford	Manchester County Court
South Lakes	Lancaster County Court
South Ribble	Blackburn County Court
South Sefton	Liverpool County Court
South Tameside	Manchester County Court
Stockport	Manchester County Court
Trafford	Manchester County Court
West Allerdale	Carlisle County Court
Whitehaven	Carlisle County Court
Wigan	Liverpool County Court
Wigton	Carlisle County Court
Wirral	Liverpool County Court
Wyre	Lancaster County Court

North Eastern Circuit

Bainton Beacon	Kingston-upon-Hull County Court
Barnsley	Sheffield County Court
Batley and Dewsbury	Leeds County Court
Berwick-upon-Tweed	Newcastle-upon-Tyne County Court
Beverley	Kingston-upon Hull County Court
Blyth Valley	Newcastle-upon-Tyne County Court
Bradford	Leeds County Court
Brighouse	Leeds County Court
Calder	Leeds County Court
Chester-le-Street	Newcastle-upon-Tyne County Court
Claro	York County Court
Coquetdale	Newcastle-upon-Tyne County Court

446   Part III

(i)　　　　　　　　　　　　　　(ii)
Petty Sessions Areas　　　　　　Care Centres

North Eastern Circuit

Darlington	Teesside County Court
Derwentside	Newcastle-upon-Tyne County Court
Dickering	Kingston-upon-Hull County Court
Doncaster	Sheffield County Court
Durham	Newcastle-upon-Tyne County Court
Easington	Sunderland County Court
Easingwold	York County Court
Gateshead	Newcastle-upon-Tyne County Court
Hartlepool	Teesside County Court
Holme Beacon	Kingston-upon-Hull County Court
Houghton-le-Spring	Sunderland County Court
Howdenshire	Kingston-upon-Hull County Court
Huddersfield	Leeds County Court
Keighley	Leeds County Court
Kingston-upon-Hull	Kingston-upon-Hull County Court
Langbaurgh East	Teesside County Court
Leeds	Leeds County Court
Middle Holderness	Kingston-upon-Hull County Court
Morley	Leeds County Court
Morpeth Ward	Newcastle-upon-Tyne County Court
Newcastle-upon-Tyne	Newcastle-upon-Tyne County Court
Northallerton	Teesside County Court
North Holderness	Kingston-upon-Hull County Court
North Tyneside	Newcastle-upon-Tyne County Court
Pontefract	Leeds County Court
Pudsey and Otley	Leeds County Court
Richmond	Teesside County Court
Ripon Liberty	York County Court
Rotherham	Sheffield County Court
Ryedale	York County Court
Scarborough	York County Court
Sedgefield	Newcastle-upon-Tyne County Court
Selby	York County Court
Sheffield	Sheffield County Court
Skyrack and Wetherby	Leeds County Court
South Holderness	Kingston-upon-Hull County Court
South Hunsley Beacon	Kingston-upon-Hull County Court
South Tyneside	Sunderland County Court
Staincliffe	Leeds County Court
Sunderland	Sunderland County Court
Teesdale and Wear Valley	Newcastle-upon-Tyne County Court
Teesside	Teesside County Court
Todmorden	Leeds County Court
Tynedale	Newcastle-upon-Tyne County Court
Wakefield	Leeds County Court
Wansbeck	Newcastle-upon-Tyne County Court
Whitby Strand	Teesside County Court
Wilton Beacon	Kingston-upon-Hull County Court
York	York County Court

South Eastern Circuit

Ampthill	Luton County Court
Arundel	Brighton County Court
Ashford and Tenterden	Medway County Court

(i) Petty Sessions Areas	(ii) Care Centres

South Eastern Circuit

Aylesbury	Milton Keynes County Court
Barnet	Principal Registry of the Family Division
Barking and Dagenham	Principal Registry of the Family Division
Basildon	Chelmsford County Court
Battle and Rye	Brighton County Court
Beccles	Ipswich County Court
Bedford	Luton County Court
Bexhill	Brighton County Court
Bexley	Principal Registry of the Family Division
Biggleswade	Luton County Court
Bishop's Stortford	Watford County Court
Brent	Principal Registry of the Family Division
Brentwood	Chelmsford County Court
Brighton	Brighton County Court
Bromley	Principal Registry of the Family Division
Buckingham	Milton Keynes County Court
Burnham	Milton Keynes County Court
Cambridge	Peterborough County Court
Canterbury and St. Augustine	Medway County Court
Chelmsford	Chelmsford County Court
Chertsey	Guildford County Court
Cheshunt	Watford County Court
Chichester and District	Brighton County Court
Chiltern	Milton Keynes County Court
Colchester	Chelmsford County Court
Crawley	Brighton County Court
Cromer	Norwich County Court
Crowborough	Brighton County Court
Croydon	Principal Registry of the Family Division
Dacorum	Watford County Court
Dartford	Medway County Court
Diss	Norwich County Court
Dorking	Guilford County Court
Dover and East Kent	Medway County Court
Downham Market	Norwich County Court
Dunmow	Chelmsford County Court
Dunstable	Luton County Court
Ealing	Principal Registry of the Family Division
Eastbourne	Brighton County Court
East Dereham	Norwich County Court
Ely	Peterborough County Court
Enfield	Principal Registry of the Family Division
Epping and Ongar	Chelmsford County Court
Epsom	Guildford County Court
Esher and Walton	Guildford County Court
Fakenham	Norwich County Court
Farnham	Guildford County Court
Faversham and Sittingbourne	Medway County Court
Felixstowe	Ipswich County Court
Folkestone and Hythe	Medway County Court
The Forest	Reading County Court
Freshwell and South Hinckford	Chelmsford County Court
Godstone	Guildford County Court
Guildford	Guildford County Court
Gravesham	Medway County Court
Great Yarmouth	Norwich County Court

(i) Petty Sessions Areas

(ii) Care Centres

South Eastern Circuit

Hailsham	Brighton County Court
Halstead and Hedingham	Chelmsford County Court
Harlow	Chelmsford County Court
Harrow Gore	Principal Registry of the Family Division
Haringey	Principal Registry of the Family Division
Harwich	Chelmsford County Court
Hastings	Brighton County Court
Havering	Principal Registry of the Family Division
Hertford and Ware	Watford County Court
Hillingdon	Principal Registry of the Family Division
Horsham	Brighton County Court
Hounslow	Principal Registry of the Family Division
Hove	Brighton County Court
Hunstanton	Norwich County Court
Huntingdon	Peterborough County Court
Ipswich	Ipswich County Court
King's Lynn	Norwich County Court
Kingston-upon-Thames	Principal Registry of the Family Division
Leighton Buzzard	Luton County Court
Lewes	Brighton County Court
Lowestoft	Ipswich County Court
Luton	Luton County Court
Maidenhead	Reading County Court
Maidstone	Medway County Court
Maldon and Witham	Chelmsford County Court
Margate	Medway County Court
Medway	Medway County Court
Merton	Principal Registry of the Family Division
Mid-Hertfordshire	Watford County Court
Mid-Sussex	Brighton County Court
Mildenhall	Ipswich County Court
Milton Keynes	Milton Keynes County Court
Newham	Principal Registry of the Family Division
Newmarket	Ipswich County Court or Peterborough County Court
North Hertfordshire	Watford County Court
North Walsham	Norwich County Court
North Witchford	Peterborough County Court
Norwich	Norwich County Court
Peterborough	Peterborough County Court
Ramsgate	Medway County Court
Reading and Sonning	Reading County Court
Redbridge	Principal Registry of the Family Division
Reigate	Guildford County Court
Richmond-upon-Thames	Principal Registry of the Family Division
Risbridge	Ipswich County Court
Rochford and Southend-on-Sea	Chelmsford County Court
Saffron Walden	Chelmsford County Court
St Albans	Watford County Court
St Edmundsbury	Ipswich County Court
Saxmundham	Ipswich County Court
Sevenoaks	Medway County Court
Slough	Reading County Court
South Mimms	Watford County Court
Staines and Sunbury	Guildford County Court
Stevenage	Watford County Court
Steyning	Brighton County Court
Stow	Ipswich County Court

(i)
Petty Sessions Areas

(ii)
Care Centres

South Eastern Circuit

Sudbury and Cosford	Ipswich County Court
Sutton	Principal Registry of the Family Division
Swaffham	Norwich County Court
Tendring	Chelmsford County Court
Thetford	Norwich County Court
Thurrock	Chelmsford County Court
Tonbridge and Malling	Medway County Court
Toseland	PeterboroughCounty Court
Tunbridge Wells and Cranbrook	Medway County Court
Waltham Forest	Principal Registry of the Family Division
Watford	Watford County Court
West Berkshire	Reading County Court
Windsor	Reading County Court
Wisbech	Peterborough County Court
Woking	Guildford County Court
Woodbridge	Ipswich County Court
Worthing	Brighton County Court
Wycombe	Milton Keynes County Court
Wymondham	Norwich County Court

Wales and Chester Circuit

Ardudwy-is-Artro	Caernarfon/Llangefni County Court
Ardudwy-uwch-Artro	Caernarfon/Llangefni County Court
Bangor	Caernarfon/Llangefni County Court
Bedwellty	Newport (Gwent) County Court
Berwyn	Rhyl County Court
Brecon	Merthyr Tydfil County Court
Caernarfon and Gwyrfai	Caernarfon/Llangefni County Court
Cardiff	Cardiff County Court
Carmarthen North	Swansea County Court
Carmarthen South	Swansea County Court
Ceredigion Ganol	Swansea County Court
Chester	Chester County Court
Cleddau	Swansea County Court
Colwyn	Rhyl County Court
Congleton	Stoke-on-Trent County Court
Conwy and Llandudno	Caernarfon/Llangefni County Court
Crewe and Nantwich	Stoke-on-Trent County Court
Cynon Valley	Merthyr Tydfil County Court
De Ceredigion	Swansea County Court
Dinefwr	Swansea County Court
Dyffryn Clywd	Rhyl County Court
East Gwent	Newport (Gwent) County Court
Eifionydd	Caernarfon/Llangefni County Court
Ellesmere Port and Neston	Chester County Court
Estimaner	Caernarfon/Llangefni County Court
Flint	Rhyl County Court
Gogledd Ceredigion	Swansea County Court
Gogledd Preseli	Swansea County Court
Halton	Warrington County Court
Hawarden	Rhyl County Court
Llandrindod Wells	Merthyr Tydfil County Court
Llanelli	Swansea County Court
Lliw Valley	Swansea County Court

(i) Petty Sessions Areas	(ii) Care Centres

Wales and Chester Circuit

Lower Rhymney Valley	Cardiff County Court
Macclesfield	Warrington County Court
Machynlleth	Merthyr Tydfil County Court
Merthyr Tydfil	Merthyr Tydfil County Court
Miskin	Merthyr Tydfil County Court
Mold	Rhyl County Court
Nant Conwy	Caernarfon/Llangefni County Court
Neath	Swansea County Court
Newcastle and Ogmore	Cardiff County Court
Newport	Newport (Gwent) County Court
Newton	Merthyr Tydfil County Court
North Anglesey	Caernarfon/Llangefni County Court
Penllyn	Caernarfon/Llangefni County Court
Port Talbot	Swansea County Court
Pwellheli	Caernarfon/Llangefni County Court
Rhuddlan	Rhyl County Court
South Anglesey	Caernarfon/Llangefni County Court
South Pembrokeshire	Swansea
Swansea	Swansea County Court
Talybont	Caernarfon/Llangefni County Court
Upper Rhymney Valley	Merthyr Tydfil County Court
Vale of Glamorgan	Cardiff County Court
Vale Royal	Chester County Court
Warrington	Warrington County Court
Welshpool	Merthyr Tydfil County Court
Wrexham Maelor	Rhyl County Court
Ystradgynlais	Swansea County Court

Western Circuit

Alton	Portsmouth County Court
Andover	Portsmouth County Court
Axminster	Taunton County Court
Barnstaple	Taunton County Court
Basingstoke	Portsmouth County Court
Bath and Wansdyke	Bristol County Court
Bideford and Great Torrington	Taunton County Court
Blandford and Sturminster	Bournemouth County Court
Bodmin	Truro County Court
Bournemouth	Bournemouth County Court
Bristol	Bristol County Court
Bridport	Bournemouth County Court
Cheltenham	Bristol County Court
Christchurch	Bournemouth County Court
Cirencester, Fairford and Tetbury	Bristol County Court
Cullompton	Taunton County Court
Dorchester	Bournemouth County Court
Droxford	Portsmouth County Court
Dunheved and Stratton	Truro County Court
Eastleigh	Portsmouth County Court
East Penwith	Truro County Court
East Powder	Truro County Court
Exeter	Plymouth County Court
Exmouth	Plymouth County Court
Falmouth and Kerrier	Truro County Court
Fareham	Portsmouth County Court

(i) Petty Sessions Areas	(ii) Care Centres

Western Circuit

(i)	(ii)
Forest of Dean	Bristol County Court
Gloucester	Bristol County Court
Gosport	Portsmouth County Court
Havant	Portsmouth County Court
Honiton	Taunton County Court
Hythe	Bournemouth County Court
Isle of Wight	Portsmouth County Court
Isles of Scilly	Truro County Court
Kennet	Bristol County Court
Kingsbridge	Plymouth County Court
Long Ashton	Bristol County Court
Lymington	Bournemouth
Mendip	Taunton County Court
North Avon	Bristol County Court
North Cotswold	Bristol County Court
North Wiltshire	Bristol County Court
Odiham	Portsmouth County Court
Okehampton	Plymouth County Court
Penwith	Truro County Court
Petersfield	Portsmouth County Court
Plymouth	Plymouth County Court
Plympton	Plymouth County Court
Portsmouth	Portsmouth County Court
Poole	Bournemouth County Court
Pydar	Truro County Court
Ringwood	Bournemouth County Court
Romsey	Bournemouth County Court
Salisbury	Bournemouth County Court
Sedgemoor	Taunton County Court
Shaftesbury	Bournemouth County Court
Sherborne	Bournemouth County Court
Southampton	Portsmouth County Court
South East Cornwall	Plymouth County Court
South Gloucestershire	Bristol County Court
South Molton	Taunton County Court
South Somerset	Taunton County Court
Swindon	Bristol County Court
Taunton Deane	Taunton County Court
Tavistock	Plymouth County Court
Teignbridge	Plymouth County Court
Tewkesbury	Bristol County Court
Tiverton	Taunton County Court
Torbay	Plymouth County Court
Totnes	Plymouth County Court
Totton and New Forest	Bournemouth County Court
Truro and South Powder	Truro County Court
Wareham and Swanage	Bournemouth County Court
West Somerset	Taunton County Court
Weston-Super-Mare	Bristol County Court
West Wiltshire	Bristol County Court
Weymouth and Portland	Bournemouth County Court
Wimborne	Bournemouth County Court
Winchester	Portsmouth County Court
Wonford	Plymouth County Court

(i)	(ii)
London Commission Area	Care Centre
Inner London Area and City of London	Principal Registry of the Family Division

CHILDREN (ALLOCATION OF PROCEEDINGS) (APPEALS) ORDER 1991

(S.I. 1991 No. 1801)

Citation, commencement and interpretation

1. (1) This Order may be cited as the Children (Allocation of Proceedings) (Appeals) Order 1991 and shall come into force on 14th October 1991.
(2) In this Order—
"district judge" includes an assistance district judge and a deputy district judge; and
"circuit judge" means any person who is capable of sitting as a judge for a county court district and who is allocated to hear appeals permitted by this Order in accordance with directions given under section 9 of the Courts and Legal Services Act 1990.

Appeals

2. Where a district judge orders the transfer of proceedings to a magistrates' court in accordance with article 11 of the Children (Allocation of Proceedings) Order 1991 an appeal may be made against that decision—
 (a) to a judge of the Family Division of the High Court, or
 (b) except where the order was made by a district judge or deputy district judge of the principal registry of the Family Division, to a circuit judge.

CHILDREN (SECURE ACCOMMODATION) REGULATIONS 1991

(S.I. 1991 No. 1505)

Made by the Secretary of State under Children Act 1989, ss.25(2), (7), 104(4), Sch. 4, para. 4(1), (2)(d), (i), Sch. 5, para. 7(1), (2)(f), (3), Sch. 6, para. 10(1), (2)(j), (3).

S.I. 1991 No. 1505

ARRANGEMENT OF REGULATIONS

REGULATIONS
1. Citation and commencement
2. Interpretation
3. Approval by Secretary of State of secure accommodation in a community home
4. Placement of a child aged under 13 in secure accommodation in a community home
5. Children to whom section 25 of the Act shall not apply
6. Detained and remanded children to whom section 25 of the Act shall have effect subject to modifications
7. Children to whom section 25 of the Act shall apply and have effect subject to modifications
8. Applications to court
9. Duty to give information of placement in community homes
10. Maximum period in secure accommodation without court authority
11. Maximum initial period of authorisation by a court
12. Further periods of authorisation by a court
13. Maximum periods of authorisation by court for remanded children
14. Duty to inform parents and others in relation to children in secure accommodation in a community home
15. Appointment of persons to review placement in secure accommodation in a community home
16. Review of placement in secure accommodation in a community home
17. Records to be kept in respect of a child in secure accommodation in a community home
18. Voluntary homes and registered children's homes not to be used for restricting liberty
19. Revocation of Secure Accommodation (No. 2) Regulations 1983 and the Amendment Regulations

DEFINITIONS
"the Act": reg. 2(1).
"child": s.105(1).
"community home": s.53.
"court": s.92(7).
"independent visitor": reg. 2(1), Sched. 2, para. 17.
"local authority": s.105(1).
"parental responsibility": s.3.
"person who is not a parent but who has parental responsibility": ss.5(6), 12(2).
"secure accommodation": reg. 2(1), s.25.
"voluntary home": s.60.

GENERAL NOTE
These regulations (and the (No. 2) Regulations) (see p. 461 below) replace the Secure Accommodation Regulations 1983 (S.I. 1983 No. 652) and the Secure Accommodation (No. 2) Amendment Regulations 1986 (S.I. 1986 No. 1591). They must be read together with section 25 of the Act. The Act and regulations limit the circumstances in which and the duration for which a child may be placed in secure accommodation. Placements for more than 72 hours, or totalling more than 72 hours in any 28-day period, require court authority (reg. 10). Applications are made to the family proceedings court; these are classed as Family Proceedings and thus the Hearsay

Evidence Order (S.I. 1991 No. 1115) applies. Magistrates should give full reasons for their decisions: *Oxfordshire C.C. v. R* [1992] 1 F.L.R. 648. Children under 13 may not be placed in secure accommodation in a community home without the prior approval of the Secretary of State (reg. 4). Secure accommodation in community homes (but not hospitals nor schools) must be approved by the Secretary of State (reg. 3). Voluntary homes and registered children's homes may not provide secure accommodation (reg. 18). Guidance on the use of secure accommodation is contained in *Guidance*, Vol. 4, Chap. 8.

Citation and commencement

1. These Regulations may be cited as the Children (Secure Accommodation) Regulations 1991 and shall come into force on 14th October 1991.

Interpretation

2. (1) In these Regulations, unless the context otherwise requires—
"the Act" means the Children Act 1989;
"independent visitor" means a person appointed under paragraph 17 of Schedule 2 to the Act;
"secure accommodation" means accommodation which is provided for the purpose of restricting the liberty of children to whom section 25 of the Act (use of accommodation for restricting liberty) applies.

(2) Any reference in these regulations to a numbered regulations shall be construed as a reference to the regulation bearing that number in these Regulations, and any reference in a regulation to a numbered paragraph is a reference to the paragraph bearing that number in that regulation.

Approval by Secretary of State of secure accommodation in a community home

3. Accommodation in a community home shall not be used as secure accommodation unless it has been approved by the Secretary of State for such use and approval shall be subject to such terms and conditions as he sees fit.

Placement of a child aged under 13 in secure accommodation in a community home

4. A child under the age of 13 years shall not be placed in secure accommodation in a community home without the prior approval of the Secretary of State to the placement of that child [and such approval shall be subject to such terms and conditions as he sees fit].

AMENDMENT
The words in square brackets were inserted by the Children (Secure Accommodation) Amendment Regulations 1992 (S.I. 1992 No. 2117), reg. 2 (October 1, 1992).

Children to whom section 25 of the Act shall not apply

5. (1) Section 25 of the Act shall not apply to a child who is detained under any provision of the Mental Health Act 1983 or in respect of whom an order has been made under section 53 of the

Children and Young Persons Act 1933 (punishment of certain grave crimes).

(2) Section 25 of the Act shall not apply to a child—
  (a) to whom section 20(5) of the Act (accommodation of persons over 16 but under 21) applies and who is being accommodated under that section,
  (b) in respect of whom an order has been made under section 43 of the Act (child assessment order) and who is kept away from home pursuant to that order.

GENERAL NOTE

Detained under any provision of the Mental Health Act 1983: Children who are compulsory patients may be detained in accordance with that Act and no court authority is required for the use of secure accommodation nor do the grounds in Children Act 1989, s.25(1) apply. If a child is a "voluntary patient" having been placed by a parent (or the local authority if subject to a care order) he or she is not detained under the Mental Health Act 1983 and the Act and regulations apply. If the child is not looked after by a local authority the application should be made by the health authority or National Health Service Trust (S.I. 1991 No. 2034, reg. 2).

Under section 53: Children convicted of grave crimes may have their liberty restricted by nature of their conviction and sentence; no further court authority is required.

Para. (2)

Use of secure accommodation is not permissible in any circumstances for children accommodated in community homes after the age of 16 under section 20(5). This would not preclude the use of secure accommodation for over-16s who are in care or are accommodated under section 20(3) because their welfare is seriously prejudiced. However, children who are not in care may leave secure accommodation by discharging themselves from accommodation (s.20(1)). Secure accommodation may not be used in respect of a child subject to an assessment under a child assessment order. It may be used where there is an agreement to assess but parents could discharge the child under section 20(8).

Detained and remanded children to whom section 25 of the Act shall have effect subject to modifications

6.—(1) Subject to regulation 5, section 25 of the Act shall have effect subject to the modification specified in paragraph (2) in relation to children who are being looked after by a local authority and are of the following descriptions—
  (a) children detained under section 38(6) of the Police and Criminal Evidence Act 1984 (detained children), and
  [(b) children remanded to local authority accommodation under section 23 of the Children and Young Persons Act 1969 (remand to local authority accommodation) but only if—
    (i) the child is charged with or has been convicted of a violent or sexual offence, or of an offence punishable in the case of an adult with imprisonment for a term of 14 years or more, or
    (ii) the child has a recent history of absconding while remanded to local authority accommodation, and is charged with or has been convicted of an imprisonable offence alleged or found to have been committed while he was remanded."]

(2) The modification referred to in paragraph (1) is that, for the words "unless it appears" to the end of subsection (1), there shall be substituted the following words—

"unless it appears that any accommodation other than that provided for the purpose of restricting liberty is inappropriate because—
  (a) the child is likely to abscond from such other accommodation, or
  (b) the child is likely to injure himself or other people if he is kept in any such other accommodation."

AMENDMENT

The words in square brackets in subsection (1)(b) were substituted by the Children (Secure Accommodation) Amendment Regulations 1992 (S.I. 1992 No. 2117), reg. 2 (October 1, 1992).

GENERAL NOTE

This replaces the words in section 25(1) in respect of children who are detained or remanded and charged or convicted with offences of violence. In these cases it is not necessary to establish that the child will suffer significant harm if he absconds or is kept in other accommodation. Where these grounds do not apply secure accommodation could be authorised by the court if it was satisfied of the terms in section 25(1). For a further discussion of these cases see notes to section 25 above.

Children to whom section 25 of the Act shall apply and have effect subject to modifications

7.—(1) Subject to regulation 5 and paragraphs (2) and (3) of this regulation section 25 of the Act shall apply (in addition to children looked after by a local authority)—

  (a) to children, other than those looked after by a local authority, who are accommodated by health authorities, National Health Service trusts established under section 5 of the National Health Service and Community Care Act 1990 or local education authorities, and
  (b) to children, other than those looked after by a local authority, who are accommodated in residential care homes, nursing homes or mental nursing homes.

(2) in relation to the children of a description specified in paragraph (1)(a) section 25 of the Act shall have effect subject to the following modifications—

  (a) for the words "who is being looked after by a local authority" in subsection (1) there shall be substituted the words "who is being provided with accommodation by a health authority, a National Health Service trust established under section 5 of the National Health Service and Community Care Act 1990 or a local education authority."
  (b) for the words "local authorities" in subsection (2)(c) there shall be substituted the words "health authorities, National Health Service trusts or local education authorities."

(3) In relation to the children of a description specified in paragraph (1)(b), section 25 of the Act shall have effect subject to the following modifications—
- (a) for the words "who is being looked after by a local authority" in subsection (1) there shall be substituted the words "who is being provided with accommodation in a residential care home, a nursing home or a mental nursing home"; and
- (b) for the words "local authorities" in subsection (2)(c) there shall be substituted the words "persons carrying on residential care homes, nursing homes or mental nursing homes."

GENERAL NOTE

The requirements of the Act and these regulations now clearly apply to children in health and education settings including some parts of the private sector—residential care homes, nursing homes and mental nursing homes. Applications in respect of these children are governed by the No. 2 Regulations (S.I. 1991 No. 2034) and are made by the health authority, Health Service Trust, local education authority or the person who carries on the residential care home, etc., unless the child is looked after by a local authority.

Applications to court

8. Subject to section 101 of the Local Government Act 1972, applications to a court under section 25 of the Act in respect of a child shall be made only by the local authority which are looking after that child.

GENERAL NOTE

Where the child is not looked after by the local authority, it is not responsible and may not make the application to the court (S.I. 1991 No. 2034).

The court: Applications are made to the family proceedings court and are specified proceedings so a guardian ad litem should be appointed.

Duty to give information of placement in community homes

9. Where a child is placed in secure accommodation in a community home which is managed by an authority other than that which are looking after him the local authority which manage that accommodation shall inform the authority which are looking after him that he has been placed there, within 12 hours of his being placed there, with a view to obtaining their authority to continue to keep him there if necessary.

GENERAL NOTE

The duty to inform allows the local authority to consider the case and to decide whether to make an application for further secure placement. If an application is intended those listed in regulation 14 should be informed. The decision to place in secure accommodation is a decision within section 22(4) and thus the authority must consult relevant people (including the child) and consider their wishes and feelings.

Maximum period in secure accommodation without court authority

10. (1) Subject to paragraphs (2) and (3), the maximum period beyond which a child to whom section 25 of the Act applies may not be kept in secure accommodation without the authority of a court is an aggregate of 72 hours (whether or not consecutive) in any period of 28 consecutive days.

(2) Where authority of a court to keep a child in secure accommodation has been given, any period during which the child has been kept in such accommodation before the giving of that authority shall be disregarded for the purposes of calculating the maximum period in relation to any subsequent occasion on which the child is placed in such accommodation after the period authorised by the court has expired.

(3) Where a child is in secure accommodation at any time between 12 midday on the day before and 12 midday on the day after a public holiday or a Sunday, and
> (a) during that period the maximum period specified in paragraph (1) expires, and
> (b) the child had, in the 27 days before the day on which he was placed in secure accommodation, been placed and kept in such accommodation for an aggregate of more than 48 hours,

the maximum period does not expire until 12 midday on the first day, which is not itself a public holiday or a Sunday, after the public holiday or Sunday.

Maximum initial period of authorisation by a court

11. Subject to regulations 12 and 13 the maximum period for which a court may authorise a child to whom section 25 of the Act applies to be kept in secure accommodation is three months.

Further periods of authorisation by a court

12. Subject to regulation 13 a court may from time to time authorise a child to whom section 25 of the Act applies to be kept in secure accommodation for a further period not exceeding 6 months at any one time.

GENERAL NOTE

Even where secure placement is authorised the child should not be kept there if the grounds no longer apply. There is no stated maximum period of detention if an interim order is made but proceedings should be heard without delay and take note of the serious nature of restrictions of liberty: *Oxfordshire C.C.* v. *R* [1992] 1 F.L.R. 648.

Maximum periods of authorisation by court for remanded children

13. (1) The maximum period for which a court may from time to time authorise a child who has been remanded to local authority accommodation under section 23 of the Children and Young Persons Act 1969 to be kept in secure accommodation (whether the period is an initial period or a further period) is the period of the remand.

(2) Any period of authorisation in respect of such a child shall not exceed 28 days on any one occasion without further court authorisation.

GENERAL NOTE
This limitation would seem to apply even if the secure placement were authorised under section 25(1) rather than regulation 6.

Duty to inform parents and others in relation to children in secure accommodation in a community home

14. Where a child to whom section 25 of the Act applies is kept in secure accommodation in a community home and it is intended that an application will be made to a court to keep the child in that accommodation, the local authority which are looking after the child shall if practicable inform of that intention as soon as possible—
    (a) his parents,
    (b) any person who is not a parent of his but who has parental responsibility for him,
    (c) the child's independent visitor, if one has been appointed, and
    (d) any other person who that local authority consider should be informed.

GENERAL NOTE
See notes on section 22(4). It may be appropriate to inform the child's guardian ad litem and others such as teachers who have substantial knowledge of the child. The child's behaviour may be a response to the lack of consultation and only be exacerbated by a secure placement.

Appointment of persons to review placement in secure accommodation in a community home

15. Each local authority looking after a child in secure accommodation in a community home shall appoint at least three persons, [at least one of whom is neither a member nor an officer of the local authority] by or on behalf of which the child is being looked after, who shall review the keeping of the child in such accommodation for the purposes of securing his welfare within one month of the inception of the placement and then at intervals not exceeding three months where the child continues to be kept in such accommodation.

AMENDMENT
The words in square brackets were substituted by the Children (Secure Accommodation) Amendment Regulations 1992 (S.I. 1992 No. 2117), reg. 2 (October 1, 1992).

Review of placement in secure accommodation in a community home

16.—(1) The persons appointed under regulation 15 to review the keeping of a child in secure accommodation shall satisfy themselves as to whether or not—
    (a) the criteria for keeping the child in secure accommodation continue to apply;
    (b) the placement in such accommodation in a community home continues to be necessary; and
    (c) any other description of accommodation would be appropriate for him,
and in doing so shall have regard to the welfare of the child whose case is being reviewed.

(2) In undertaking the review referred to in regulation 15 the persons appointed shall, if practicable, ascertain and take into account the wishes and feelings of—
   (a) the child,
   (b) any parent of his,
   (c) any person not being a parent of his but who has parental responsibility for him,
   (d) any other person who has had the care of the child, whose views the persons appointed consider should be taken into account,
   (e) the child's independent visitor if one has been appointed, and
   (f) the local authority managing the secure accommodation in which the child is placed if that authority are not the authority who are looking after the child.

(3) The local authority shall, if practicable, inform all those whose views are required to be taken into account under paragraph (2) of the outcome of the review ["what action, if any, the local authority propose to take in relation to the child in the light of the review, and their reasons for taking or not taking such action."]

AMENDMENT

The words in square brackets were substituted by the Children (Secure Accommodation) Amendment Regulations 1992 (S.I. 1992 No. 2117) reg. 2.

GENERAL NOTE

These reviews are additional to those which must occur under the Reviews of Children's Cases Regulations 1991 (S.I. 1991 No. 895) (see notes to s.26 above). The recommendation of the review panel is not decisive although an authority which ignores it may be acting irrationally and have its decision quashed by judicial review. Department of Health *Guidance*, Vol. 4, para. 8.56 requires the authority to review the placement immediately the review panel has concluded that it should not continue.

Records to be kept in respect of a child in secure accommodation in a community home

17. Whenever a child is placed in secure accommodation in a community home the local authority which manage that accommodation shall ensure that a record is kept of—
   (a) the name, date of birth and sex of that child,
   (b) the care order or other statutory provision by virtue of which the child is in the community home and in either case particulars of any other local authority involved with the placement of the child in that home,
   (c) the date and time of his placement in secure accommodation, the reason for his placement, the name of the officer authorising the placement and where the child was living before the placement,
   (d) all those informed by virtue of regulation 9, 14 or 16(3) in their application to the child,
   (e) court orders made in respect of the child by virtue of section 25 of the Act,

(f) reviews undertaken in respect of the child by virtue of regulation 15,
(g) the date and time of any occasion on which the child is locked on his own in any room in the secure accommodation other than his bedroom during usual bedtime hours, the name of the person authorising this action, the reason for it and the date on which and time at which the child ceases to be locked in that room, and
(h) the date and time of his discharge and his address following discharge from secure accommodation,

and the Secretary of State may require copies of these records to be sent to him at any time.

GENERAL NOTE

These records are additional to those required under the Children's Homes Regulations 1991 (S.I. 1991 No. 1506) and the Arrangements for Placement of Children (General) Regulations 1991 (S.I. 1991 No. 890) (see s.23 above).

Voluntary homes and registered children's homes not to be used for restricting liberty

18.—(1) The use of accommodation for the purpose of restricting the liberty of children in voluntary homes and registered children's homes is prohibited.

(2) The contravention of, or failure to comply with the provisions of paragraph (1), without reasonable excuse, shall be an offence against these Regulations.

Revocation of Secure Accommodation (No. 2) Regulations 1983 and the Amendment Regulations

19. The Secure Accommodation (No. 2) (Amendment) Regulations 1986 are hereby revoked.

CHILDREN (SECURE ACCOMMODATION) (NO. 2) REGULATIONS 1991

(S.I. 1991 NO. 2034)

Made by the Secretary of State under the Children (Secure Accommodation) (No. 2) Regulations 1991.

DEFINITION

"looked after by a local authority": s.22(1)

GENERAL NOTE

These regulations make provision for applications for placement in secure accommodation in respect of children who are not looked after by a local authority. For details of the restrictions on use of secure accommodation see section 25(1) and the Children (Secure Accommodation) Regulations 1991, above, pp. 79 and 452.

Citation and commencement

1.—(1) These Regulations may be cited as the Children (Secure Accommodation) (No. 2) Regulations 1991 and shall come into force on 14th October 1991 immediately after the Children (Secure Accommodation) Regulations 1991.

Applications to court—special cases

2.—(1) Applications to a court under section 25 of the Children Act 1989 in respect of a child provided with accommodation by a health authority, a National Health Service trust established under section 5 of the National Health Service and Community Care Act 1990 or a local education authority shall, unless the child is looked after by a local authority, be made only by the health authority, National Health Service trust or local education authority providing accommodation for the child.

(2) Applications to a court under section 25 of the Children Act 1989 in respect of a child provided with accommodation in a residential care home, nursing home or mental nursing home shall, unless the child is looked after by a local authority, be made only by the person carrying on the home in which accommodation is provided for the child.

CONTACT WITH CHILDREN REGULATIONS 1991

(S.I. 1991 No. 891)

GENERAL NOTE

The Regulations fit in with section 34 concerning contact between children subject to care orders and other named persons. See commentary on section 34 at p. 104. Local authorities are required to notify the persons listed in article 2 in writing of their decision to refuse contact with the child. It will be seen that the child is to be notified if of sufficient understanding, together with parents and others closely concerned. As to who comes within item (f) is a decision for local authorities: foster parents, siblings and other close relatives are all likely candidates depending upon the circumstances of individual cases. The Schedule sets out what information is to be notified including, in particular, the reasons for the decision to refuse contact and remedies available if there is dissatisfaction about the decision.

Citation, commencement and interpretation

1.—(1) These Regulations may be cited as the Contact with Children Regulations 1991, and shall come into force on 14th October 1991.

(2) Any notice required under these Regulations is to be given in writing and may be sent by post.

(3) In these Regulations unless the context requires otherwise—
  (a) any reference to a numbered section is to the section in The Children Act 1989 bearing that number;
  (b) any reference to a numbered regulation is to the regulation in these Regulations bearing that number; and

(c) any reference to a Schedule is to the Schedule to these Regulations.

Local authority refusal of contact with child

2. Where a local authority has decided under section 34(6) to refuse contact with a child that would otherwise be required by virtue of section 34(1) or a court order, the authority shall, as soon as the decision has been made, notify the following persons in writing of those parts of the information specified in the Schedule as the authority considers those persons need to know—
   (a) the child, if he is of sufficient understanding;
   (b) the child's parents;
   (c) any guardian of his;
   (d) where there was a residence order in force with respect to the child immediately before the care order was made, the person in whose favour the order was made;
   (e) where immediately before the care order was made, a person had care of the child by virtue of an order made in the exercise of the High Court's inherent jurisdiction with respect to children, that person; and
   (f) any other person whose wishes and feelings the authority consider to be relevant.

Departure from terms of court order on contact under section 34

3. The local authority may depart from the terms of any order under section 34 (parental contact etc with children in care) by agreement between the local authority and the person in relation to whom the order is made and in the following circumstances and subject to the following condition—
   (a) where the child is of sufficient understanding, subject to agreement also with him; and
   (b) a written notification shall be sent to the persons specified in regulation 2 containing those parts of the information specified in the Schedule as the authority considers those persons need to know, within seven days of the agreement to depart from the terms of the order.

GENERAL NOTE

This article permits local authorities to negotiate agreements to vary or suspend section 34 contact orders. The agreement to do so must be ratified by the child if of sufficient understanding, and communicated in writing to the persons listed at article 2 within seven days of the date of the agreement. Clearly such agreements will have to be on a formal basis.

Notification of variation or suspension of contact arrangements

4. Where a local authority varies or suspends any arrangements made (otherwise than under an order made under section 34) with a

view to affording any person contact with a child in the care of that local authority, written notification shall be sent to those persons specified in regulation 2 containing those parts of the information specified in the Schedule as the authority considers those persons need to know, as soon as the decision is made to vary or suspend the arrangements.

GENERAL NOTE

This article deals with variation or suspension of voluntary contact arrangements made "with a view to affording any person contact with a child in care," and requires the same article 2 persons to be afforded written notification in the terms of the Schedule. It can only be assumed that variation or suspension of voluntary contact arrangements made other than with a view to affording someone else contact are not covered by the regulations.

SCHEDULE

Regulations 2, 3 and 4

INFORMATION TO BE CONTAINED IN WRITTEN NOTIFICATION

1. Local authority's decision.
2. Date of the decision.
3. Reasons for the decision.
4. Duration (if applicable).
5. Remedies available in case of dissatisfaction.

EMERGENCY PROTECTION ORDER (TRANSFER OF RESPONSIBILITIES) REGULATIONS 1991

(S.I. 1991 No. 1414)

Made by the Secretary of State under the Emergency Protection Order (Transfer of Responsibility) Regulations 1991.

DEFINITIONS

"child": s.105(1).
"emergency protection order": s.44.
"local authority": s.105(1).
"refuge": s.51.

GENERAL NOTE

These regulations allow the local authority where the child is ordinarily resident to take over emergency protection orders which have been applied for by other applicants, *e.g.* other local authorities, the NSPCC or private individuals. It does not allow transfer if the child is in a refuge and the carer has decided that the child will remain there for the duration of the order (reg. 5). When the local authority takes over the order it, rather than the applicant, has parental responsibility and must make the decisions about whether the child should be returned to or removed from home (s.44(10), (12))). Before giving the notices required by regulation 3 to achieve a transfer, the local authority must consider the matters in regulations 2(1) and 3(1).

Citation and commencement

1. These Regulations may be cited as the Emergency Protection Order (Transfer of Responsibilities) Regulations 1991 and shall come into force on 14th October 1991.

Transfer of responsibilities under emergency protection orders

2. Subject to regulation 5 of these Regulations, where—
 (a) an emergency protection order has been made with respect to a child;
 (b) the applicant for the order was not the local authority within whose area the child is ordinarily resident; and
 (c) that local authority are of the opinion that it would be in the child's best interests for the applicant's responsibilities under the order to be transferred to them,
that authority shall (subject to their having complied with the requirements imposed by regulation 3(1) of these Regulations) be treated, for the purposes of the Children Act 1989, as though they and not the original applicant had applied for, and been granted, the order.

Requirements to be complied with by local authorities

3. (1) In forming their opinion under regulation 2(c) of these Regulations the local authority shall consult the applicant for the emergency protection order and have regard to the following considerations—
 (a) the ascertainable wishes and feelings of the child having regard to his age and understanding;
 (b) the child's physical, emotional and educational needs for the duration of the emergency protection order;
 (c) the likely effect on him of any change in his circumstances which may be caused by a transfer of responsibilities under the order;
 (d) his age, sex, family background;
 (e) the circumstances which gave rise to the application for the emergency protection order;
 (f) any directions of a court and other orders made in respect of the child;
 (g) the relationship (if any) of the applicant for the emergency protection order to the child, and
 (h) any plans which the applicant may have in respect of the child.

(2) The local authority shall give notice, as soon as possible after they form the opinion referred to in regulation 2(c), of the date and time of the transfer to—
 (a) the court which made the emergency protection order,

(b) the applicant for the order, and
(c) those (other than the local authority) to whom the applicant for the order gave notice of it.

(3) A notice required under this regulation shall be given in writing and may be sent by post.

GENERAL NOTE

Notices may be sent by post but the transfer is only effective from the time that notice is given to the applicant (reg. 4).

When responsibility under emergency protection order transfers

4. The time at which responsibility under any emergency protection order is to be treated as having been transferred to a local authority shall be the time stated as the time of transfer in the notice given in accordance with regulation 3 of these Regulations by the local authority to the applicant for the emergency protection order or the time at which notice is given to him under that regulation, whichever is the later.

Exception for children in refuges

5. These Regulations shall not apply where the child to whom the emergency protection order applies is in a refuge in respect of which there is in force a Secretary of State's certificate issued under section 51 of the Children Act 1989 (refuges for children at risk) and the person carrying on the home or, the foster parent providing the refuge, having taken account of the wishes and feelings of the child, has decided that the child should continue to be provided with the refuge for the duration of the order.

THE FAMILY PROCEEDINGS RULES 1991

(S.I. 1991 NO. 1247)

PART V

WARDSHIP

5.1. Application to make a minor a ward of court

(1) An application to make a minor a ward of court shall be made by originating summons and, unless the court otherwise directs, the plaintiff shall file an affidavit in support of the application when the originating summons is issued.

(2) Rule 4.3 shall, so far as applicable, apply to an application by a local authority for the leave of the court under section 100(3) of the Act of 1989.

(3) Where there is no person other than the minor who is a suitable defendant, an application may be made ex parte to a district judge for leave to issue either an ex parte originating summons or an originating summons with the minor as defendant thereto; and, except where such leave is granted, the minor shall not be made a defendant to an originating summons under this rule in the first instance.

(4) Particulars of any summons issued under this rule in a district registry shall be sent by the proper officer to the principal registry for recording in the register of wards.

(5) The date of the minor's birth shall, unless otherwise directed, be stated in the summons, and the plaintiff shall—

    (a) on issuing the summons or before or at the first hearing thereof lodge in the registry out of which the summons issued a certified copy of the entry in the Register of Births or, as the case may be, in the Adopted Children Register relating to the minor, or

    (b) at the first hearing of the summons apply for directions as to proof of birth of the minor in some other manner.

(6) The name of each party to the proceedings shall be qualified by a brief description, in the body of the summons, of his interest in, or relation to, the minor.

(7) Unless the court otherwise directs, the summons shall state the whereabouts of the minor or, as the case may be, that the plaintiff is unaware of his whereabouts.

(8) Upon being served with the summons, every defendant other than the minor shall forthwith lodge in the registry out of which the summons issued a notice stating the address of the defendant and the whereabouts of the minor or, as the case may be, that the defendant is unaware of his whereabouts and, unless the court otherwise directs, serve a copy of the same upon the plaintiff.

(9) Where any party other than the minor changes his address or becomes aware of any change in the whereabouts of the minor after the issue or, as the case may be, service of the summons, he shall, unless the court otherwise directs, forthwith lodge notice of the change in the registry out of which the summons issued and serve a copy of the notice on every other party.

(10) The summons shall contain a notice to the defendant informing him of the requirements of paragraphs (8) and (9).

(11) In this rule any reference to the whereabouts of a minor is a reference to the address at which and the person with whom he is living and any other information relevant to the question where he may be found.

5.2. Enforcement of order by tipstaff

The power of the High Court to secure, through an officer attending upon the court, compliance with any direction relating to a ward of court may be exercised by an order addressed to the tipstaff.

5.3. Where minor ceases to be a ward of court

(1) A minor who, by virtue of section 41(2) of the Supreme Court Act 1981, becomes a ward of court on the issue of a summons under rule 5.1 shall cease to be a ward of court—
  (a) if an application for an appointment for the hearing of the summons is not made within the period of 21 days after the issue of the summons, at the expiration of that period;
  (b) if an application for such an appointment is made within that period, on the determination of the application made by the summons unless the court hearing it orders that the minor be made a ward of court.

(2) Nothing in paragraph (1) shall be taken as affecting the power of the court under section 41(3) of the said Act to order that any minor who is for the time being a ward of court shall cease to be a ward of court.

(3) If no application for an appointment for the hearing of a summons under rule 5.1 is made within the period of 21 days after the issue of the summons, a notice stating whether the applicant intends to proceed with the application made by the summons must be left at the registry in which the matter is proceeding immediately after the expiration of that period.

5.4. Adoption of minor who is a ward of court

(1) An application for leave—
  (a) to commence proceedings to adopt a minor who is a ward or
  (b) to commence proceedings to free such a minor for adoption,
may be made ex parte to a district judge.

(2) Where a local authority has been granted leave to place a minor who is a ward with foster parents with a view to adoption it shall not be necessary for an application to be made for leave under paragraph (1)(a) or (b) unless the court otherwise directs.

(3) If the applicant for leave under paragraph (1)(a) or (b), or a local authority which has applied for leave as referred to in paragraph (2), or a foster parent so requests, the district judge may direct that any subsequent proceedings shall be conducted with a view to securing that the proposed adopter is not seen by or made known to any respondent or prospective respondent who is not already aware of his identity except with his consent.

(4) In paragraphs (1) and (3) "proceedings" mean proceedings in the High Court or in a county court.

[5.5. Orders for use of secure accommodation

No order shall be made with the effect of placing or keeping a minor in secure accommodation, within the meaning of section 25(1) of the Act of 1989 [unless the minor has been made a party to the summons.]

AMENDMENT

The words in square brackets were substituted by the Family Proceedings (Amendment) Rules 1992 (S.I. 1992 No. 456), reg. 5 (April 1, 1992).

5.6. Notice to provider of refuge

Where a child is staying in a refuge which is certified under section 51(1) or 51(2) of the Act of 1989, the person who is providing that refuge shall be given notice of any application under this Part of these rules in respect of that child.]

AMENDMENT

Rules 5.5 and 5.6 in the square brackets were substituted by the Family Proceedings (Amendment) Rules 1991 (S.I. 1991 No. 2113), reg. 14 (October 14, 1991).

PART VIII

APPEALS

8.1. Appeals from district judges

(1) Except where paragraph (2) applies, any party may appeal from an order or decision made or given by the district judge in family proceedings in a county court to a judge on notice; and in such a case—
    (a) CCR Order 13 rule 1(10) (which enables the judge to vary or rescind an order made by the district judge in the course of proceedings), and
    (b) CCR Order 37 rule 6 (which gives a right of appeal to the judge from a judgment or final decision of the district judge),
shall not apply to the order or decision.

(2) Any order or decision granting or varying an order (or refusing to do so)—
    (a) on an application for ancillary relief, or
    (b) in proceedings to which rules 3.1, 3.2, 3.3, 3.6 or 3.8 apply,
shall be treated as a final order for the purposes of CCR Order 37, rule 6.

(3) On hearing an appeal to which paragraph (2) above applies, the judge may exercise his own discretion in substitution for that of the district judge.

(4) Unless the court otherwise orders, any notice under this rule must be issued within 14 days of the order or decision appealed against and served not less than 14 days before the day fixed for the hearing of the appeal.

(5) Appeals under this rule shall be heard in chambers unless the judge otherwise directs.

(6) Unless the court otherwise orders, an appeal under this rule shall not operate as a stay of proceedings on the order or decision appealed against.

PART IX

DISABILITY

9.1 Interpretation and application of Part IX

(1) In this Part—
"patient" means a person who, by reason of mental disorder within the meaning of the Mental Health Act 1983, is incapable of managing and administering his property and affairs;
"person under disability" means a person who is a minor or a patient;
"Part VII" means Part VII of the Mental Health Act 1983.

(2) So far as they relate to minors [who are the subject of applications], the provisions of this Part of these rules shall not apply to proceedings which are specified proceedings within the meaning of section 41(6) of the Children Act 1989 and, with respect to proceedings which are dealt with together with specified proceedings, this Part shall have effect subject to the said section 41 and Part IV of these rules.

[(3) Rule 9.2A shall apply only to proceedings under the Act of 1989 or the inherent jurisdiction of the High Court with respect to minors.]

AMENDMENTS

The words in square brackets were substituted by the Family Proceedings (Amendment) Rules 1991 (S.I. 1991 No. 2113) (October 14, 1991). Paragraph (3) was inserted by the Family Proceedings (Amendment) Rules 1992 (S.I. 1992 No. 456) reg. 6 (April 1, 1992).

9.2 Person under disability must sue by next friend etc.

(1) [Except where rule 9.2A or any other rule otherwise provides, a person under disability may begin and prosecute any family proceedings only by his next friend and may defend any such proceedings only] by his guardian ad litem and, except as otherwise provided by this rule, it shall not be necessary for a guardian ad litem to be appointed by the court.

(2) No person's name shall be used in any proceedings as next friend of a person under disability unless he is the Official Solicitor or the documents mentioned in paragraph (7) have been filed.

(3) Where a person is authorised under Part VII to conduct legal proceedings in the name of a patient or on his behalf, that person shall, subject to [paragraph (2)], be entitled to be next friend or

guardian ad litem of the patient in any family proceedings to which his authority extends.

(4) Where a person entitled to defend any family proceedings is a patient and there is no person authorised under Part VII to defend the proceedings in his name or on his behalf, then—

(a) the Official Solicitor shall, if he consents, be the patient's guardian ad litem, but at any stage of the proceedings an application may be made on not less than four days' notice to the Official Solicitor, for the appointment of some other person as guardian;

(b) in any other case, an application may be made on behalf of the patient for the appointment of a guardian ad litem;

and there shall be filed in support of any application under this paragraph the documents mentioned in paragraph (7).

(5) Where a petition, answer, originating application or originating summons has been served on a person whom there is reasonable ground for believing to be a person under disability and no notice of intention to defend has been given, or answer or affidavit in answer filed, on his behalf, the party at whose instance the document was served shall, before taking any further steps in the proceedings, apply to a district judge for directions as to whether a guardian ad litem should be appointed to act for that person in the cause, and on any such application the district judge may, if he considers it necessary in order to protect the interests of the person served, order that some proper person be appointed his guardian ad litem.

(6) [Except where a minor is prosecuting or defending proceedings under rule 9.2A, no] notice of intention to defend shall be given, or answer or affidavit in answer filed, by or on behalf of a person under disability unless the person giving the notice or filing the answer or affidavit—

(a) is the Official Solicitor or, in a case to which paragraph (4) applies, is the Official Solicitor or has been appointed by the court to be guardian ad litem; or

(b) in any other case, has filed the documents mentioned in paragraph (7).

(7) The documents referred to in paragraphs (2), (4) and (6) are—

(a) a written consent to act by the proposed next friend or guardian ad litem;

(b) where the person under disability is a patient and the proposed next friend or guardian ad litem is authorised under Part VII to conduct the proceeding in his name or on his behalf; an office copy; sealed with the seal of the Court of Protection, of the order or other authorisation made or given under Part VII; and

(c) except where the proposed next friend or guardian ad litem is authorised as mentioned in sub-paragraph (b), a certificate by the solicitor acting for the person under disability—

(i) that he knows or believes that the person to whom the certificate relates is a minor or patient, stating (in the case of a patient) the grounds of his knowledge or belief and, where the person under disability is a

patient, that there is no person authorised as aforesaid, and
(ii) that the person named in the certificate as next friend or guardian ad litem has no interest in the cause or matter in question adverse to that of the person under disability and that he is a proper person to be next friend or guardian.

AMENDMENT
The words in square brackets were substituted by the Income Support (General) Amendment Regulations 1992 (S.I. 1992 No. 468) regs. 7 and 8 and by the Family Proceedings (Amendment) Rules 1991 (S.I. 1991 No. 2113) reg. 17 (October 14, 1991).

[9.2A Certain minors may sue without next friend etc.

(1) Where a person entitled to begin, prosecute or defend any proceedings to which this rule applies, is a minor to whom this Part applies, he may, subject to paragraph (4), begin, prosecute or defend, as the case may be, such proceedings without a next friend or guardian ad litem—
(a) where he has obtained the leave of the court for that purpose; or
(b) where a solicitor—
(i) considers that the minor is able, having regard to his understanding, to give instructions in relation to the proceedings; and
(ii) has accepted instructions from the minor to act for him in the proceedings and, where the proceedings have begun, is so acting.
(2) A minor shall be entitled to apply for the leave of the court under paragraph 1 (a) without a next friend or guardian ad litem either—
(a) by filing a written request for leave setting out the reasons for the application, or
(b) by making an oral request for leave at any hearing in the proceedings.
(3) On considering a request for leave filed under paragraph (2)(a), the court shall either—
(a) grant the request, whereupon the proper officer shall communicate the decision to the minor and, where the leave relates to the prosecution or defence of existing proceedings, to the other parties to those proceedings, or
(b) direct that the request be heard ex parte, whereupon the proper officer shall fix a date for such a hearing and give to the minor making the request such notice of the date so fixed as the court may direct.
(4) Where a minor has a next friend or guardian ad litem in proceedings and the minor wishes to prosecute or defend the remaining stages of the proceedings without a next friend or guardian ad litem, the minor may apply to the court for leave for that purpose and for the removal of the next friend or guardian ad litem; and

paragraph (2) shall apply to the application as if it were an application under paragraph (1)(a).

(5) On considering a request filed under paragraph (2) by virtue of paragraph (4), the court shall either—
- (a) grant the request, whereupon the proper officer shall communicate the decision to the minor and next friend or guardian ad litem concerned and to all other parties to the proceedings, or
- (b) direct that the request be heard, whereupon the proper officer shall fix a date for such a hearing and give to the minor and next friend or guardian ad litem concerned such notice of the date so fixed as the court may direct;

provided that the court may act under sub-paragraph (a) only if it is satisfied that the next friend or guardian ad litem does not oppose the request.

(6) Where the court is considering whether to
- (a) grant leave under paragraph (1)(a), or
- (b) grant leave under paragraph (4) and remove a next friend or guardian ad litem,

it shall grant the leave sought and, as the case may be, remove the next friend or guardian ad litem if it considers that the minor concerned has sufficient understanding to participate as a party in the proceedings concerned or proposed without a next friend or guardian ad litem.

(7) Where a request for leave is granted at a hearing fixed under paragraph (3)(b) (in relation to the prosecution or defence of proceedings already begun) or (5)(b), the proper officer shall forthwith communicate the decision to the other parties to the proceedings.

(8) The court may revoke any leave granted under paragraph (1)(a) where it considers that the child does not have sufficient understanding to participate as a party in the proceedings concerned without a next friend or guardian ad litem.

(9) Without prejudice to any requirement of CCR Order 50, rule 5 or RSC Order 67, where a solicitor is acting for a minor in proceedings which the minor is prosecuting or defending without a next friend or guardian ad litem by virtue of paragraph (1)(b) and either of the conditions specified in paragraph (1)(b)(i) and (ii) cease to be fulfilled, he shall forthwith so inform the court.

(10) Where—
- (a) the court revokes under paragraph (8), or
- (b) either of the conditions specified in paragraph (1)(b)(i) or (ii) is no longer fulfilled,

the court may, if it considers it necessary in order to protect the interests of the minor concerned, order that some proper person be appointed his next friend or guardian ad litem.

(11) Where a minor is of sufficient understanding to begin, prosecute or defend proceedings without a next friend or guardian ad litem—
- (a) he may nevertheless begin, prosecute or defend them by his next friend or guardian ad litem; and
- (b) where he is prosecuting or defending proceedings by his next friend or guardian ad litem, the respective powers

and duties of the minor and next friend or guardian ad litem, except those conferred or imposed by this rule, shall not be affected by the minor's ability to dispense with a next friend or guardian ad litem under the provisions of this rule.]

AMENDMENT

This regulation was inserted by the Family Proceedings (Amendment) Rules 1992 (S.I. 1992 No. 456) reg. 9 (April 1, 1992).

9.3 Service on person under disability

(1) Where a document to which rule 2.9 applies is required to be served on a person [...], it shall be served—
- (a) in the case of a minor who is not also a patient, on his father or guardian or, if he has no father or guardian, on the person with whom he resides or in whose care he is;
- (b) in the case of a patient—
    - (i) on the person (if any) who is authorised under Part VII to conduct in the name of the patient or on his behalf the proceedings in connection with which the document is to be served, or
    - (ii) if there is no person so authorised, on the Official Solicitor if he has consented under rule 9.2(4) to be the guardian ad litem of the patient, or
    - (iii) in any other case, on the person with whom the patient resides or in whose care he is: Provided that the court may order that a document which has been, or is to be, served on the person under disability or on a person other than one mentioned in sub-paragraph (a) or (b) shall be deemed to be duly served on the person under disability.

(2) Where a document is served in accordance with paragraph (1) it shall be indorsed with a notice in Form M24; and after service has been effected the person at whose instance the document was served shall, unless the Official Solicitor is the guardian ad litem of the person under disability or the court otherwise directs, file an affidavit by the person on whom the document was served stating whether the contents of the document were, or its purport was, communicated to the person under disability and, if not, the reasons for not doing so.

AMENDMENT

The words in square brackets were omitted by the Family Proceedings (Amendment No. 2) Rules 1992 (S.I. 1992 No. 2067), r. 21 (October 5, 1992).

9.5 Separate representation of children

(1) Without prejudice to [rules 2.57 and 9.2A], if in any family proceedings it appears to the court that any child ought to be separately represented, the court may appoint—
- (a) the Official Solicitor, or
- (b) some other proper person,

(provided, in either case, that he consents) to be the guardian ad litem of the child, with authority to take part in the proceedings on the child's behalf.

(2) An order under paragraph (1) may be made by the court of its own motion or on the application of a party to the proceedings or of the proposed guardian ad litem.

(3) The court may at any time direct that an application be made by a party for an order under paragraph (1) and may stay the proceedings until the application has been made.

(4) Unless otherwise directed, on making an application for an order under paragraph (1) the applicant shall—
    (a) unless he is the proposed guardian ad litem, file a written consent by the proposed guardian to act as such;
    (b) unless the proposed guardian ad litem is the Official Solicitor, file a certificate by a solicitor that the proposed guardian has no interest in the proceedings adverse to that of the child and that he is a proper person to be a guardian.

(5) Unless otherwise directed, a person appointed under this rule or rule 2.57 to be the guardian ad litem of a child in any family proceedings shall be treated as a party for the purpose of any provision of these rules requiring a document to be served on or notice to be given to a party to the proceedings.

AMENDMENT

The words in square brackets were substituted by the Family Proceedings (Amendment) Rules 1992 (S.I. 1992 No. 456) reg. 10 (April 1, 1992).

FAMILY PROCEEDINGS (COSTS) RULES 1991

(S.I. 1991 No. 1832)

GENERAL NOTE

These Rules operate at county and High Court level and deal with two separate important matters. First, Children Act proceedings are fastened into the taxation of costs system (art. 2) and secondly, there is provision for payment of costs by legal representatives. Legal representatives (so phrased as to include solicitors and others) are personally liable in costs if the court so decides.

The Rules fit in with section 51(6) of the Supreme Court Act 1981 as amended by section 4 of the Courts and Legal Services Act 1990 which stipulates that:

" ... the Court may disallow or order the Legal or other representative concerned to meet the whole of any wasted costs or such part of them, as may be determined by rules of Court."

Wasted costs are defined in section 51(7) as being:

"costs incurred by a party—(a) as a result of any improper unreasonable or negligent act or omission on the part of any legal or other representative, or any employee of a such a representative:– or (b) which in the light of any such act or omission occurring after they were incurred, the Court considers it unreasonable to expect that party to pay."

Costs may be ordered either directly by a judge or a judge may ask a district judge to make inquiries and report back. The district judge can also be asked to deal with the matter without reporting back. Additionally district judges can activate their powers of ordering costs without a referral from a judge when they deal with cases on taxation. There is a show cause provision unless the criteria of article 15(5) apply.

It is likely that most orders for costs will be on the basis of unacceptable delay, the costs rules being the teeth of the avoidance of delay principle in so far as lawyers are concerned.

The equivalent provision in the Family Proceedings Courts, to which the costs rules do not apply, is set out at Magistrates' Courts Act 1980, s.145(a), inserted by the Courts and Legal Services Act 1990, s.112. The power to disallow or order wasted costs to be paid is in exactly the same terms as section 51(6) and (7) as set out above.

All tiers of courts, therefore, in Children Act proceedings have wide powers to disallow and/or order payment of costs by lawyers.

1. (1) These rules may be cited as the Family Proceedings (Costs) Rules 1991 and shall come into force on 14th October 1991.

(2) In these rules, the "principal rules" means the Family Proceedings Rules 1991, and expressions used in these rules have the same meanings as in those rules.

2. (1) Subject to the following provisions of this rule, these rules shall apply for the taxation of costs in family proceedings instituted before, on or after 14th October 1991.

(2) The Matrimonial Causes (Costs) Rules 1988 (except rule 10 and Schedule 2), with the modifications specified in rule 3 below, shall have effect as if those rules were part of these rules and shall apply for the taxation of costs in proceedings—
  (a) under the Children Act 1989; or
  (b) of any kind (and whenever commenced) with respect to which rules made under section 50 of the Matrimonial Causes Act 1973 applied immediately before the commencement of these rules.

(3) The taxation of costs in all family proceedings other than those mentioned in paragraph (2) above shall be taxed—
  (a) where the proceedings are in the High Court, in accordance with RSC Order 62; and
  (b) where the proceedings are in a county court, in accordance with CCR Order 38.

(4) These rules shall not apply to the extent that regulations made under the Legal Aid Act 1988 determine the amount of costs payable to legal representatives in relation to family proceedings.

3. For rules 15 and 16 of the Matrimonial Causes (Costs) Rules 1988, as applied by these rules, there shall be deemed to be substituted the following—

"Personal liability of legal representative for costs

15. (1)(a) Where the court decides to make an order under section 51(6) of the Supreme Court Act 1981 disallowing wasted costs or ordering a legal representative to meet such costs or part of them, it shall, subject to paragraph (4), specify in the order the costs which are to be so disallowed or met, and make such other order as it thinks fit;
  (b) before proceeding under sub-paragraph (a), the court may direct a district judge to inquire into the matter and report to the court.

(2) When conducting an inquiry pursuant to a direction under paragraph (1)(b), the district judge shall have all the powers and duties of the court under paragraphs (6) and (7) of this rule; and references in those paragraphs and paragraphs (4) and (5) to the court include references to the district judge.

(3) Instead of proceeding under paragraph (1) of this rule the court may refer the matter to a district judge, in which case the district judge shall deal with the matter under paragraphs (2) and (3) of rule 16.

(4) No order may be made under the said section 51(6) unless the court has given the legal representative a reasonable opportunity to appear and show cause why an order should not be made.

(5) The court shall not be obliged to give the legal representative a reasonable opportunity to show cause where proceedings fail, cannot conveniently proceed or are adjourned without useful progress being made because the legal representative—
  (a) fails to attend in person or by a proper representative;
  (b) fails to deliver any document for the use of the court, which ought to have been delivered or to be prepared with any proper evidence or account, or
  (c) otherwise fails to proceed.

(6) The court may, except in proceedings in a county court or in proceedings in the principal registry which are treated as pending in a county court, direct the Official Solicitor to attend and take such part in any proceedings or inquiry under this rule as the court may direct and the court shall make such order as to the payment of the Official Solicitor's costs as it thinks fit.

(7) The court may direct that notice of any proceedings or order against a legal representative under this rule be given to his client in such manner as may be specified in the direction.

Powers of district judges in relation to misconduct, neglect, etc.

16. (1) Where, whether or not on a reference by the court under rule 14(2), it appears to the district judge when taxing a bill of costs that any thing has been done, or that any omission has been made, unreasonably or improperly by or on behalf of any party in the taxation proceedings or in the proceedings which gave rise to the taxation proceedings, he may exercise the powers conferred on the court by rule 14(1).

(2) Where, whether or not on a reference by the court under rule 15(3), it appears to the district judge that costs have been wasted in the taxation proceedings or in the proceedings which gave rise to the taxation proceedings, he may, subject to paragraph (3) of this rule, exercise the powers conferred on the court by section 51(6) of the Supreme Court Act 1981.

(3) In relation to the exercise by a district judge of the powers of the court under the said section 51(6), paragraphs (4) to (7) of rule 15 shall apply as if for references to the court there were substituted references to the district judge.

(4) Where a party entitled to costs—

(a) fails without good reason to commence or conduct proceedings for the taxation of those costs in accordance with these rules or any direction, or
(b) delays lodging a bill of costs for taxation,

the district judge may—
   (i) disallow all or part of the costs of taxation that he would otherwise have awarded that party; and
   (ii) after taking into account all the circumstances, including any prejudice suffered by any other party as a result of such failure or delay, as the case may be, and any additional interest payable under section 17 of the Judgments Act 1838 because of the failure or delay, allow the party so entitled less than the amount he would otherwise have allowed on taxation of the bill or may wholly disallow the costs.

(5) In exercising his powers under this rule the district judge shall have all the powers available to the court in the exercise of its discretion under rules 14 and 15.

(6) An appeal shall lie from the exercise by a district judge of the powers conferred by this rule—
   (a) except in proceedings in a county court or in proceedings in the principal registry which are treated as pending in a county court, to a judge in chambers, and RSC Order 58, rule 1 (as modified, in the case of an appeal from a district judge, by Order 58, rule 3(2) shall apply to such an appeal as it applies to an appeal from a master;
   (b) in proceedings in a county court or in proceedings in the principal registry which are treated as pending in a county court, to a judge in accordance with rule 8.1 of the principal rules."

FAMILY PROCEEDINGS FEES ORDER 1991

(S.I. 1991 No. 2114)

GENERAL NOTE

Article 3 creates exemptions from payment of court fees. No application or taxation fees are payable in family proceedings in which the applicant is in receipt of Income Support, Family Credit or is legally aided within the meaning of the Legal Aid Act 1988, s.2(11). Section 2(11) of the 1988 Act defines a legally assisted person as a person who receives advice and assistance or representation under the Act, *i.e.* anyone who has any Legal Aid Certificate or is receiving Green Form advice and assistance. This exemption applies in all jurisdictions.

1. (1) This Order may be cited as the Family Proceedings Fees Order 1991 and shall come into force on 14th October 1991.

(2) In this Order, unless a contrary intention appears—
   a rule or form referred to by number alone means the rule or form so numbered in the Family Proceedings Rules 1991;
   expressions also used in the Family Proceedings Rules 1991 have the same meaning as in those Rules.

2. Subject to articles 3 and 4, the fees specified in the Schedule to this Order shall be taken in family proceedings in the High Court or in a county court.

3. No fee shall be payable under this Order where the person who would otherwise be liable to pay—
   (a) is a legally assisted person within the meaning of section 2(11) of the Legal Aid Act 1988;
   (b) is in receipt of income support or family credit under Part II of the Social Security Act 1986;
   (c) is a person who is not a beneficiary of a trust fund in court of a value of more than £50,000 and who is—
       (i) under the age of eighteen, or
       (ii) a person for whose financial relief an order under paragraph 2 of Schedule 1 to the Children Act 1989 is in force or is being applied for.

4. Where it appears to the Lord Chancellor that the payment of any fee prescribed by this Order would, owing to the exceptional circumstances of the particular case, involve undue hardship, he may reduce or remit the fee in that case.

SCHEDULE

Article 2

FEES TO BE TAKEN IN FAMILY PROCEEDINGS

Action for which or stage at which fee taken	Fee

Part I—Fees to be taken in the High Court and in the county courts

1. *Commencement of proceedings*

(a) On filing an application or originating application, or on sealing an originating summons or a summons, to commence family proceedings, other than proceedings mentioned elsewhere in this Schedule;	£15
(b) on presenting any petition, other than a second petition with leave granted under rule 2.6(4);	£40
(c) on applying for an injunction under the Domestic Violence and Matrimonial Proceedings Act 1976 (c. 50).	£30

2. *Proceedings under the Children Act 1989 (c. 41)*
   (1) On filing an application or requesting leave under the following provisions of the Children Act 1989—

Parental responsibility, guardians, section 8 orders etc.

(a) section 4(1)(a), or (3), 5(1), 10(1) or (2);	£30
(b) section 6(7), or 13(1);	£20

Action for which or stage at which fee taken	Fee
Financial provision for children	
(c) paragraph 1(1), 2(1), 6(5) or 14(1) of Schedule 1;	£30
(d) paragraph 1(4), 2(5), 5(6), 6(7), 6(8), 8(2), 10(2), or 11 of Schedule 1;	£20
Secure accommodation	
(e) Section 25;	No fee
Care, supervision, etc.	
(f) section 31;	£50
(g) section 33(7), 38(8)(b), 39(1), (2), (3) or (4), paragraph 6 of Schedule 3 or paragraph 11(3) of Schedule 14;	£20
Contact with child in care	
(h) section 34(2), (3), (4) or (9);	£20
Placement abroad	
(i) paragraph 19(1) of Schedule 2;	£20
Education supervision	
(j) section 36(1);	£50
(k) paragraph 15(2) or 17(1) of Schedule 3;	£20
Child assessment order	
(l) section 43(1);	£50
Emergency protection	
(m) section 43(12);	£20
(n) section 44, 45, 46 or 48;	No fee
Recovery of Children	
(o) section 50;	No fee
Miscellaneous	
(p) section 102.	£20
(2) On commencing an appeal under section 94 of, or paragraph 23(11) of Schedule 2 to, the Children Act 1989.	£15
3. *Adoption and wardship applications*	
(a) On commencing proceedings under the Adoption Act 1976 (c. 36) other than under section 21 thereof;	£30
(b) on commencing proceedings under section 21 of the Adoption Act 1976;	£20
(c) on applying for the exercise by the High Court of its inherent jurisdiction with respect to children.	£50
4. *Applications for ancillary relief* On filing a notice in Form M11 or M13 except where the terms of any agreement as to the order which the court is to be asked to make are set out in the notice or the notice is filed for dismissal purposes only.	£20

Action for which or stage at which fee taken	Fee

5. *Applications in proceedings*
On any application in family proceedings (including an application to a county court to transfer to it family proceedings in a magistrates' court), except where separately listed in this Schedule or where it is for an order by consent. £15

6. *Appeal from a district judge*
On filing a notice of appeal from a district judge to a judge. £15

7. *Searches*
   (a) On making a search in the central index of decrees absolute kept at the Principal Registry of the Family Division for any specified period of ten calendar years or, if no such period is specified, for the ten most recent years, and, if appropriate, providing a certificate of decree absolute. £5
   (b) On making a search in the central index of parental responsibility agreements kept at the Principal Registry of the Family Division in accordance with regulations made under section 4(2) of the Children Act 1989 (c. 41) and, if appropriate, providing a copy of an agreement. £5

8. *Copies of documents*
   (a) On making a personal application for a copy of any document (other than a welfare officer's report), whether or not issued as an office copy, per page—
       (i) typewritten; 50p
       (ii) carbon or photographic. 25p
   (b) (i) On making a postal application for a copy of any document (other than a welfare officer's report) in the Principal Registry of the Family Division and, where appropriate, for being supplied with photographic copies of the first four pages; £1
       (ii) for each page after the fourth. 25p

9. *Taxation*
   (a) On the taxation of costs or expenses, for every £1, and any balance of less than £1, allowed. 5p, but no fee is payable where costs are allowed without taxation. The district judge may in any case before taxation require a deposit of the amount of fees which would be payable if the bill or the expenses were allowed by him at the full amount thereof.
   (b) On the withdrawal of a bill of costs which has been lodged for taxation. Such fee (not exceeding the amount which would have been payable under Fee No. 9 (a) if the bill had been allowed in full) as may be reasonable having regard to the amount of work done in the court office.

Action for which or stage at which fee taken	Fee

10. *Registration of maintenance orders*
On an application for a maintenance order to be—
    (a) registered under the Maintenance Orders Act 1950 (14 Geo. 6 c. 37) or the Maintenance Orders Act 1958 (6 & 7 Eliz. 2 c. 39);   £5
    (b) sent abroad for enforcement under the Maintenance Orders (Reciprocal Enforcement) Act 1972 (c. 18).   £10

Part II—Fees to be taken in the county courts only

11. *Service*
On a request for service by a bailiff, where service by post will not be used, of any document except—
    (a) an order for a debtor to attend an adjourned hearing of a judgment summons;
    (b) an interpleader summons under an execution;
    (c) an order made under section 23 of the Attachment of Earnings Act 1971 (c. 32) (Enforcement Provisions); or
    (d) an order for a debtor to attend an adjourned oral examination as to his means,
per person to be served or, where personal service is not required, per address to be served.   £5

12. *Enforcement*
On an application for the enforcement of a judgment or order—
    (a) by the issue of a warrant of execution against goods other than a warrant to enforce payment of a court fee or to enforce an order for the payment of a fine, for every £1, and any balance of less than £1, for which the warrant issues;   15p, but with a mimimum fee of £5 and a maximum fee of £38.
    (b) by the examination of a debtor as to his means or as to other matters;   £12
    (c) by entering garnishee proceedings;   £12
    (d) by an application for an order charging the land or securities of a judgment debtor; or   £12
    (e) by the issue of a judgment summons.   £12

13. *Sale*
    (a) For removing or taking steps to remove goods to a place of deposit and keeping them there (including feeding and caring for any animals);   The reasonable expenses incurred.
    (b) for advertising a sale by public auction under section 97(1) of the County Courts Act 1984 (c. 28);   The reasonable expenses incurred.
    (c) for the appraisement of goods, for every £1, and any balance of less than £1, of the appraised value;   5p
    (d) for the sale of goods (including advertisements, catalogues, sale and commission and delivery of goods), for every £1, and any balance of less than £1, realised; and   15p
    (e) where an execution is withdrawn, satisfied or stopped before a sale takes place—
        (i) where the goods have been appraised, for every £1, and any balance of less than £1, of the appraised value;   10p
        (ii) where the goods have not been appraised.   The reasonable expenses incurred.

Action for which or stage at which fee taken	Fee
Part III—Fees to be taken in the High Court only	
14. *Examination*	
On the examination of a witness before trial.	£5
15. *Directions for trial*	
On an application for directions for trial in a defended cause.	£30
16. *Enforcement*	
(a) On sealing a writ of execution;	£6
(b) on an application to examine a judgment debtor before an officer of the court;	£12
(c) on the issue of a judgment summons;	£12
(d) on an application for a garnishee order *nisi*, for a charging order *nisi* or for the appointment of a receiver by way of equitable execution; and	£12
(e) on issuing a certified copy of a judgment or order for the purposes of Part II of the Administration of Justice Act 1920 (10 (11 Geo. 5 c. 81) or the Foreign Judgments (Reciprocal Enforcement) Act 1933 (23 & 24 Geo. 5 c. 13).	£10
17. *Registration of maintenance orders*	
On an application to transmit a maintenance order abroad under the Maintenance Orders (Facilities for Enforcement) Act 1920 (10 & 11 Geo. 5 c. 33).	£10
18. *Financial relief after overseas divorce etc.*	
On sealing an originating summons in proceedings under Part III of the Matrimonial and Family Proceedings Act 1984 (c. 42)—	
(a) under section 24;	£15
(b) under section 13, where an application has not already been made by the same person under section 24.	£15

GUARDIANS AD LITEM AND REPORTING OFFICERS (PANELS) REGULATIONS 1991

(S.I. 1991 No. 2051)

Enabling powers made by the Secretary of State under The Children Act 1989

GENERAL NOTE

Panels of guardians ad litem and reporting officers were latterly a feature of care and adoption proceedings, having been established by the GALRO Regulations 1983. The new regulations fit with sections 41 and 42 of the Children Act and rules 10 and 11 (FPR and FPC). GALROs are organised into panels on a local basis managed and paid for by Local Authorities. The regulations endeavour to instal administrative devices in panel management to maximise guardians' independence from their local authority paymasters.

The situation is still not ideal: almost by definition, independence of guardians ad litem cannot be absolute as they are linked closely with the applicant in most care cases. On an individual basis, guardians' independence has rarely been challenged. The overwhelming majority of guardians act with a refreshing sense of independence. The problem has always been in the realms of perception: justice must be seen to be done. Flash points have occurred notably in the Cornwall case which was resolved in favour of guardians' independence (see commentary on r. 11 at p. 382).

Detailed guidance to the regulations is provided in Volume 7 of Department of Health *Guidance* at Chap. 2. There is a restatement of the commitment to independence at paragraph 2.4:

> "The right of children to separate and independent representation in public law hearings is a central tenet of The Children Act. It is essential that Galro's in reaching their judgments about the welfare of each child, should continue to be independent of the Local Authority or other organisation providing the service. Arrangements for the management of the panel and the day to day work of the Galro must take full account of this requirement within the existing legal framework of ultimate accountability residing with the Local Authority."

The importance of guardians' independence is given considerable prominence in the Department of Health *Practice Manual*, at Chapter 11.

Citation, commencement and interpretation

1. (1) These Regulations may be cited as the Guardians Ad Litem and Reporting Officers (Panels) Regulations 1991 and shall come into force on 14th October 1991.

(2) In these Regulations, unless the context otherwise requires—

"complaints board" means a board established under regulation 3(a) of these Regulations;

"panel" means a panel established under regulation 2(1) of these Regulations;

"panel committee" means a committee established under regulation 3(b) of these Regulations;

"relevant proceedings" means specified proceedings as defined in section 41(6) of the Children Act 1989 or proceedings on an application for any order referred to in section 65 of the Adoption Act 1976.

Panels of guardian ad litem and reporting officers

2. (1) Each local authority shall establish a panel of persons in accordance with regulation 4 of these Regulations in respect of their area.

(2) Guardians ad litem and reporting officers appointed under section 41 of the Children Act 1989 for the purposes of relevant proceedings or under rules made under section 65 of the Adoption Act 1976 must be selected from the panel established in respect of the

local authority's area in which the court is situated (unless selected from another local authority's panel established under these Regulations).

(3) Each local authority shall ensure that so far as possible the number of persons appointed to the panel established in respect of their area is sufficient to provide guardian ad litem and reporting officers for all relevant proceedings in which guardians ad litem and reporting officers may be appointed and which may be heard in their area.

GENERAL NOTE

Each local authority is to establish a GALRO Panel and ensure that there are sufficient suitably qualified GALROs to service the requirements of the courts in specified proceedings (arts. 1 and 2). There is therefore no obligation upon local authorities to supply guardians ad litem for non-specified proceedings.

Complaints boards and panel committees

3. For the purpose of assisting them with matters concerning the membership of panels, the administration and procedures of panels and the monitoring of the work of guardians ad litem and reporting officers in relevant proceedings, each local authority shall establish—
   (a) a board ("complaints board") in accordance with Schedule 1 to these Regulations, which shall have the functions conferred on them by regulations 5 and 6 of these Regulations;
   (b) a committee ("panel committee") in accordance with Schedule 2 to these Regulations, which shall have the functions conferred on it by regulations 8 and 10(1)(a) of these Regulations.

Appointments to panels

4. (1) The local authority in respect of whose area the panel is established shall appoint persons to be members of the panel.

(2) The local authority shall decide whether the qualifications and experience of any person who they propose to appoint to the panel are suitable for the purposes of that person's appointment as a guardian ad litem or a reporting officer who they propose to appoint to the panel.

(3) The local authority shall in respect of any person whom they propose to appoint to the panel—
   (a) interview each such person,
   (b) consult the panel committee, and
   (c) obtain the names of at least two persons who can provide a reference in writing for the persons whom they propose to appoint and take up those references.

(4) The local authority shall notify in writing any person who is appointed to a panel of the appointment which shall, subject to

regulation 5 of these Regulations, be for such period not exceeding three years at any one time as the local authority shall specify on making the appointment.

(5) Each local authority shall maintain a record of those persons whom they have appointed to be members of the panel established in respect of their area.

(6) Every local authority shall have regard to the number of children in their area who may become the subject of specified proceedings and the different racial groups to which they belong, in making appointments under this regulation.

GENERAL NOTE

Local authorities are to assess, interview and appoint guardians ad litem for a maximum period of three years at a time (art. 4);

Termination of panel membership

5.—(1) The local authority may terminate a person's membership of the panel at any time where they consider that he is unable or unfit to carry out the functions of a guardian ad litem or a reporting officer.

(2) Before terminating a person's membership of the panel the local authority shall—
 (a) notify him in writing of the reasons why it is proposed that his membership of the panel should be terminated;
 (b) give him an opportunity of making representations to the local authority.

(3) Where the local authority, having considered any representations made under paragraph (2)(b) of this regulation, still propose to terminate a person's membership, they shall refer the matter to a complaints board.

(4) The complaints board shall make a recommendation to the authority after taking account of any representations of the person whose membership the local authority proposed to terminate.

(5) The local authority shall consider the recommendation of the complaints board, as to termination of a person's membership and decide whether or not to terminate membership and give notice to that person in writing of their decision together with their reasons for the decision.

GENERAL NOTE

Local authorities may terminate membership to the panel if a guardian is considered to be "unable or unfit to carry out the functions of a Galro." A skeleton termination procedure is set out requiring local authorities to act in the manner of a responsible employer (art. 5).

Complaints about the operation of panels and members of the panels

6.—(1) For the purpose of monitoring the administration and procedures of the panel and the work of guardians ad litem and reporting officers in relevant proceedings each local authority shall establish a procedure for considering complaints about the operation of the panel in respect of their area, and about any member of that panel including refusal to reappoint a person to be a panel member.

(2) The local authority shall investigate any such complaint and if they cannot resolve it to the satisfaction of the person making it they shall refer it to the complaints board to make a recommendation to the authority about it in writing.

(3) Any person in respect of whom a complaint is made shall be notified by the local authority in writing of the complaint and they shall give him an opportunity of making representations to them and if the matter is referred to the complaints board they shall provide him with an opportunity to make representations to the complaints board.

(4) The local authority shall only make a decision on a complaint referred to the complaints board having taken into account the recommendation of the complaints board and they shall notify the person who made the complaint and any person in respect of whom the complaint was made in writing of their decision.

GENERAL NOTE

A new development is that local authorities are required to establish a Complaints Board with the Board considering complaints about the operation of the panel as a whole, or about any individual GALRO, including refusal to reappoint a panel member. Membership of the Board is to consist of three persons one being neither officer nor member of any Local Authority, one being involved with a different Local Authority, and the third is to be a local court clerk. An outline procedure for the processing of complaints is set out. Local Authorities will need to draw up their own detailed procedures. The Complaints Board is to make recommendations to Local Authorities concerning any complaints. The final decision, however, rests with the Local Authority whose task is also to carry out any necessary investigations into the complaint (arts. 3 and 6, Sched. 1).

Administration of the panel

7.—(1) Each local authority shall appoint a person with such qualifications and experience as they consider appropriate to assist them with the administration of the panel in respect of their area and that person shall not participate in the local authority social services functions in respect of services for children and their families (other than the administration of the panel or an inspection unit established under the Secretary of State's directions under section 7A of the Local Authority Social Services Act 1970).

(2) Each local authority shall ensure that records are kept in relation to the operation of the panel which shall include—
  (a) the name of each child in respect of whom a guardian ad litem or reporting officer is selected from the panel;
  (b) a description of the relevant proceedings in respect of which the selection is made;
  (c) the name and level of the court (whether High Court, county court or family proceedings court);
  (d) the name of any person selected from the panel and whether he has been appointed in specified proceedings or in proceedings under the Adoption Act 1976 as a guardian

ad litem, or in proceedings under the Adoption Act 1976 as a reporting officer;
(e) the date of each appointment, the date on which work started in respect of that appointment and the date on which it finished;
(f) details of fees, expenses and allowances in each case in which there has been such an appointment;
(g) the result of the proceedings in each case in which there has been such an appointment.

GENERAL NOTE

The panel administrator is to be appointed by the Local Authority, that person "shall not participate in Local Authority Social Services functions in respect of services for children and their families." Proper cases records must be kept (art. 7).

Panel committee functions

8. The local authority shall make arrangements for the panel committee to assist with liaison between the local authority in their administration of the panel and the courts in the local authority's area and to advise on—
(a) the standards of practice of guardians ad litem and reporting officers in relevant proceedings in their area;
(b) the appointment and reappointment of guardians ad litem and reporting officers to the panel, termination of their appointment and review of their work;
(c) the training of guardians ad litem and reporting officers; and
(d) matters arising from complaints concerning guardians ad litem, reporting officers and the administration of the panel (but not the investigation of particular complaints).

GENERAL NOTE

The panel administrator is likely to be involved in appointment, complaints, termination, training, financial and administrative matters, and monitoring, as well as servicing panel committees which are to be set up with functions set out in article 8.

Expenses, fees and allowances of members of panels

9. (1) Each local authority shall defray the reasonable expenses incurred in respect of relevant proceedings by members of the panel established in respect of their area and pay fees and allowances for members of such panels in respect of relevant proceedings.

(2) No expenses, fees and allowances referred to in paragraph (1) of this regulation shall be defrayed or paid by local authorities by virtue of paragraph (1) in respect of a member of a panel who is employed

under a contract of service by a local authority or probation committee for thirty hours or more a week.

General Note
Local Authorities are to meet guardians' reasonable expenses and fees in carrying out their work in specified proceedings (art. 9).

Monitoring the work of guardians ad litem and reporting officers

10. (1) For the purposes of monitoring the work of guardians ad litem and reporting officers each local authority which has established a panel in respect of their area shall—
    (a) obtain the views of the panel committee on the work of each member of the panel who has been appointed a guardian ad litem or reporting officer, and
    (b) review the work of each such member of the panel
at least once during the first year of an appointment to the panel.
(2) The results of each review shall be recorded by the local authority in writing and they shall send a copy of the results to the member of the panel to whom they relate.

Training

11. The local authority shall, having regard to the cases in which members of the panel have been or may be appointed as a guardian ad litem or reporting officer, identify any training needs which members of the panel may have and make reasonable provision for such training.

Revocation of the Guardians Ad Litem and Reporting Officers (Panels) Regulations 1983 and Amendment Regulations 1986

2. The Guardians Ad Litem and Reporting Officers (Panels) Regulations 1983 and the Guardians Ad Litem and Reporting Officers (Panels) (Amendment) Regulations 1986 are hereby revoked.

Schedule 1

Regulation 3(a)

Complaints Board

The complaints board shall consist of three persons,—
    (a) one of whom shall be a person who is neither an officer nor a member of a local authority;
    (b) another of whom shall be a person who is involved in the functions in respect of services for children and their families of a local authority which has not established the panel;
    (c) another of whom shall be a justices' clerk of a magistrates' court in the local authority's area.

Schedule 2

Regulation 3(b)

Panel Committee

1. The panel committee shall consist of at least one of the following—
   (a) a representative of the local authority;
   (b) a justices' clerk of a magistrates' court in the local authority's area;
   (c) a person who has relevant experience of child care who is neither an officer nor a member of a local authority;
   (d) a representative of the panel established under regulation 2(1) of these Regulations.
2. The panel committee shall not be chaired by a representative of the local authority.
3. The membership of the panel committee shall not consist of a majority of representatives of the local authority.
4. Appointments to the panel committee shall be for such period not exceeding three years at any one time as the authority shall specify on making the appointment.

General Note

The panel committee is not to be chaired by a representative of the local authority, and membership shall not consist of a majority of local authority representatives (Sched. 2.).

INDEX

AIDS
  medical examination, interim order
    relating to, 117
Abbreviations
  summary of, 13
Abduction
  abducted child, recovery of, 149–152
  authorised person, meaning, 150
  child in care, of, 148–149
  designated officer, meaning, 150
  responsible person, meaning, 149
Absconding child
  liberty, use of accommodation for
    restricting, 79, 82
Access
  person authorised to seek access,
    meaning, 131
Accommodating authority
  meaning, 206
Accommodation
  emergency, accommodation by police in
    case of, 138–142
  liberty, use for restricting, 79–83
  local authority, provision by,
    detention, child in, 63–64
    duties relating to, 69–74, 246–257
    general duty relating to child, 64–69
    generally, 58–63
    police protection, child in, 63–64
    remand, child on, 63–64
  meaning, 64
  near child's home, 70, 74
  prevention of removal from, 228
  secure. See Secure accommodation.
  voluntary organisation, provision by,
    163–165
  wardship jurisdiction, restrictions on use
    of, 228
Adoption
  amendments of legislation, 211–212,
    284–295
  county court, allocation of proceedings
    to, 440
  order, effect of care order on, 101
  wardship jurisdiction, restrictions on use
    of, 228–229
Adoption Act 1976
  amendments, 211–212, 284–292
  proceedings under, 12
Adoption agency
  meaning, 233
Advice and assistance
  local authority, provision by, 74–79
  person qualifying for, meaning, 75, 78
Allocation of proceedings
  Children (Allocation of Proceedings)
    (Appeals) Order 1991, 452
  Children (Allocation of Proceedings)
    Order 1991, 432–452

Appeal
  appeal period, meaning, 120
  care order, case about, 119–120
  child minding, relating to, 194–196
  Children (Allocation of Proceedings)
    (Appeals) Order 1991, 452
  day care of young children, relating to,
    194–196
  district judge, from, 469–470
  family proceedings court, to, 418–419
  family proceedings, relating to, 404–407
  High Court, to, 219–221
  magistrates' court, from, 406–407
  supervision order, case about, 119–120
Assistance. See Advice and assistance.
Assisted community home. See Community
  home.
Authorised person
  meaning, 94, 127, 131, 150

Bank holiday
  emergency protection order, duration of,
    136
  meaning, 233
Blind
  local authority, provision of services by,
    50, 55
Body corporate
  offences by, 232

Care
  children in. See Children in care.
  public law, 10–11
Care centres
  list, 442–452
Care order
  abduction of child in care, 149
  accommodation provided by local
    authority. See Local authority.
  additional procedural conditions, 94, 98
  appeal in case about, order pending,
    119–120
  application for, 93, 97
  attendance of child at hearing, 221–222
  authorised person, meaning, 94
  criminal proceedings, in, 213–214
  delay in making application, 99–100
  development, meaning, 94
  discharge, 117–119, 215
  duration of, 214–216
  effect of, 100–103, 214–216
  grounds for, 93, 97–98
  harm, meaning, 94
  health, meaning, 94
  ill-treatment, meaning, 94
  interim order, 114–117
  meaning, 94–95, 233

491

Index

Care Order—*cont.*
  residence order discharges, 35, 36
  restrictions, 94, 98
  supervision order, substitution of, 215
  variation, 117–119
Cases
  review of, 83–87
Cash
  advice and assistance provided by local authority, 75, 78
Channel Islands
  abducted child, recovery of, 152
  Children Act 1989, application of, 236
  orders, effect of, 230–231
Child abuse
  wardship jurisdiction, restrictions on use of, 229
Child assessment order
  application for, 126–130
  authorised person, meaning, 127
  meaning, 126, 233
  medical examination, submission to, 127, 130
  psychiatric examination, submission to, 127, 130
Child care training
  approved, meaning, 203
  meaning, 202–203
Child minding
  appeals relating to, 194–196
  child minder,
    meaning, 233
    requirements to be complied with by, 187–189
  domestic premises, meaning, 185
  emergency, protection of children in, 192–193
  inspection, 193–194
  offences, 196–197
  premises, meaning, 185
  registration,
    cancellation of, 190–192
    local authority, by, 183–187, 281–284
  relevant establishment, meaning, 57
  review of provision for, 57–58
  review period, meaning, 57
  reward, for, 184, 186
  Scotland, 197–198
Child of family
  meaning, 233
Children
  child, meaning, 233
  emergency protection. *See* Emergency protection order.
  financial relief with respect to, orders for, 46–47, 238–246
  jurisdiction, removal from, 44–45
  name, change of, 44–45
  parental responsibility for, 18–20
  welfare of, 14–17
Children Act 1989
  background, 9
  commencement, 13, 236–238
  consequential amendments, 237, 308–323

Children Act—*cont.*
  extent, 13, 236–238
  minor amendments, 237, 299–308
  overview, 9
  private law, 9–10
  proceedings under, 12
  public law
    care, 10–11
    day care, 11
    other care, 12
  savings, 237, 323–342
  short title, 236
  text, 127
  transitional provisions, 12, 237, 323–342
Children at risk
  refuges for, 152–154
Children in care
  abduction of, 148–149
  parental contact with, 103–107
Children in need
  co-operation between authorities, 87–88
  local authority, provision of services by, 49–55, 246–257
  recoupment of cost of providing services, 89–92, 254–257
Children's home
  meaning, 170, 233
  registered. *See* Registered children's home.
  Secretary of State, inspection by person authorised by, 198–201
  unregistered, children not to be cared for in, 170–173
Christmas Day
  emergency protection order, duration of, 136
Civil cases
  secure accommodation, provision of, 81
Co-operation
  local authorities, between, 87–88
Community home
  assisted,
    determination of dispute relating to, 158–159
    financial provisions applicable on cessation of, 161–163
    local authority, closure by, 160–161
    voluntary organisation, discontinuance of, 159–160
  conduct of, 155, 263–267
  controlled,
    determination of dispute relating to, 158–159
    financial provisions applicable on cessation of, 161–163
    local authority, closure by, 160–161
    voluntary organisation, discontinuance of, 159–160
  directions that premises be no longer used for, 157–158
  disposal,
    financial provisions applicable on, 161–163
    meaning, 162

Index

Community Home—*cont.*
  financial provisions on cessation, 161–163
  local authority,
    closure by, 160–161
    provision by, 155–157, 263–267
  maintenance of child in, 69, 71–72
  management, 155, 263–267
  meaning, 233
  premises,
    financial provisions applicable on disposal of, 161–163
    meaning, 162
  proprietor, meaning, 162
  recoupment of cost of providing services, 90
  relevant time, meaning, 162
  responsible authority, meaning, 162
  voluntary organisation,
    discontinuance of, 159–160
    provision of accommodation by, 163–165
Conditions
  children in need, provision of services for, 49, 54
  section 8 order, relating to, 42, 43
Confidentiality
  documents, of, 407, 416
Consent
  notification of, 407, 417
  parental responsibility for child, relating to, 18, 19–20
Consultation
  local education authority, with, 89
Contact order
  Contact with Children Regulations 1991, 462–464
  court's power to make, 37–41
  general principles, 41–43
  meaning, 30, 32, 233
  penal notice, attachment of, 404
  restrictions on making, 35–37
  supplementary provisions, 41–43
Contribution order
  application for, 419
Controlled community home. *See* Community home.
Costs
  family proceedings, 415–416, 475–478
  legal representative, personal liability of, 476–477
  recoupment of, 89–92, 254–257
County court
  adoption, application for, 440
  allocation of proceedings to, 439–440
  classes of, 432
  ex parte application, 363
  family proceedings. *See* Family proceedings.
  fees to be taken in, 482
  freeing for adoption, application for, 440
  High Court,
    transfer from, 439
    transfer to, 438–439
  Lambeth County Court, 440

County Court—*cont.*
  magistrates' court,
    transfer from, 436–437
    transfer to, 438
  principal registry of Family Division, 440
  transfer from one county court to another, 438
  Woolwich County Court, 440
  See also Court.
Court
  attendance of child at hearing, 221–222
  contact order, power to make, 37–41
  jurisdiction of, 216–218, 295–299
  meaning, 151, 197
  prohibited steps order, power to make, 37–41
  residence order, power to make, 37–41
  rules of, 218–219, 345–428
  specific issue order, power to make, 37–41
Court order
  private law, 10
Criminal cases
  secure accommodation, provision in, 82
Criminal proceedings
  care order in, 213–214
  legal aid, 226
  supervision order in, 213–214
Cultural background
  local authority, general duty of, 65, 68

Day care
  meaning, 56, 197, 233
  pre-school child, provision for, 55–57
  public law, 11
  recoupment of cost of providing services, 89–92, 254–257
  relevant establishment, meaning, 57
  review of provision for, 57–58
  review period, meaning, 57
  supervised activity, meaning, 56
  young child, for,
    appeal relating to, 194–196
    domestic premises, meaning, 185
    emergency, protection of children in, 192–193
    inspection, 193–194
    offences, 196–197
    person providing, requirements to be complied with by, 189–190
    premises, meaning, 185
    registration,
      cancellation of, 190–192
      local authority, by, 183–187, 281–284
    reward, for, 184, 186
    Scotland, 197–198
Defamation proceedings
  publish, meaning, 225
Delay
  care order, application for, 99–100
  supervision order, application for, 99–100
Department of Health
  guidance, 13–14
  youth treatment centres, establishment of, 203

Designated officer
  meaning, 150
Detention
  accommodation provided for child in, 63–64
Development
  children in need, provision of services for, 50, 55
  meaning, 50, 94
  reasonable standard of, 50, 55
Directions
  family proceedings, 388–392
  section 8 order, relating to, 42, 43
Disability
  disabled, meaning, 233
  local authority, provision of services by, 50, 55
  next friend,
    certain minors may sue without, 472–474
    person under disability must sue by, 470–472
  person under disability,
    meaning, 470
    next friend, must sue by, 470–472
    service on, 474
    separate representation of children, 474–475
Disability working allowance
  recoupment of cost of providing services, 90, 91
Disclosure
  emergency protection, discovery of child in need of, 146, 148
Disposal
  meaning, 162
Dispute
  controlled and assisted community home, relating to, determination of, 158–159
District health authority
  meaning, 233
District judge
  appeal from, 469–470
  misconduct, powers in relation to, 477–478
  neglect, powers in relation to, 477–478
Documentary evidence
  family proceedings, 396–399
Documents
  confidentiality of, 407, 416
Domestic court
  family proceedings court, name changed to, 216
Domestic court panel
  family panel, name changed to, 216
Domestic premises
  meaning, 185, 233
Domestic proceedings
  court's powers in, 113
  family proceedings, name changed to, 216

Education
  education authority, meaning, 198

Education—cont.
  local authority. See Local education authority.
  special educational needs, meaning, 235
  See also Local education authority.
Education supervision order
  compulsory school age, 109, 110–111
  details of, 111–112
  direction to local education authority to apply for, 408, 419
  discharge, 215
  meaning, 109, 233
  school attendance order, non-compliance with, 109, 111
  use of, 110–112, 260–263
Emergency
  police, removal and accommodation of child by, 138–142
  protection of child in, 192–193
Emergency protection order
  abduction of child in care, 149
  authorised person, meaning, 131
  contact with child, importance of, 133, 135
  discovery of child who may be in need, 146–148
  duration of, 135–138
  effect of, 130–135, 214
  Emergency Protection Order (Transfer of Responsibilities) Regulations 1991, 464–466
  extension of, 136, 138
  grounds for, 130–135
  local authority's duty to investigate, 142–146
  meaning, 233
  medical examination, submission to, 130
  person authorised to seek access, meaning, 131
  psychiatric examination, submission to, 130
  rules relating to, 154
  supplementary provisions, 135–138
Employment
  children's home, person disqualified from being employed in, 174–175
Enforcement
  residence order, of, 45–46, 416–417
England and Wales
  orders, effect of, 230–231
Entry and search
  emergency protection, discovery of child in need of, 146–147, 148
Evidence
  children, given by, or with respect, to, 222–224
  documentary, 396–399
  expert, 399–400
  hearsay,
    admissibility of, 431–432
    Children (Admissibility of Hearsay Evidence) Order 1991, 431–432
    welfare report, 29, 30
  oath, child understanding nature of, 222, 223

Index

Evidence—*cont.*
  oral, 401
  secure accommodation, relating to,
    407–408, 417
  self-incrimination, privilege against,
    225–226
Examination of child
  family proceedings, 399–400
Expenses
  panels of guardians ad litem and
    reporting officers, 488–489
Expert evidence
  family proceedings, 399–400

Family
  child of family, meaning, 233
  local authority, provision of services by,
    49–55, 246–257
  meaning, 50, 53
Family assistance order
  court's power to make, 47–49
  meaning, 233
  persons named in, 47, 48
  supervision order, replacement of, 48
Family credit
  recoupment of cost of providing services,
    89, 91
Family hearing centres
  list, 441–442
Family panel
  domestic court panel changed to, 216
  Guardians Ad Litem and Reporting
    Officers (Panels) Regulations 1991,
    483–490
Family proceedings
  amendment, 400
  answer to application, 373–374
  appeals, 404–407
  application,
    answer to, 373–374
    procedure, 360–363
    withdrawal of, 363–364
  application for leave to commence,
    358–359
  application of Rules, 353–354
  attendance at directions appointment and
    hearing, 394–396
  citation of Rules, 354
  commencement of Rules, 354
  confidentiality of documents, 407, 416
  contribution orders, 419
  costs, 415–416, 475–478
  court's powers in, 112–114
  directions, 388–392
  documentary evidence, 396–399
  domestic proceedings changed to, 216
  education supervision order, direction to
    local education authority to apply
    for, 408, 419
  evidence,
    documentary, 396–399
    expert, 399–400
    oral, 401

Family proceedings—*cont.*
  evidence—*cont.*
    secure accommodation, relating to,
      407–408, 417
  examination of child, 399–400
  expert evidence, 399–400
  Family Proceedings (Costs) Rules 1991,
    475–478
  Family Proceedings Courts (Children Act
    1989) Rules 1991, 345–428
  Family Proceedings Fees Order 1991,
    478–483
  Family Proceedings Rules 1991,
    Part IV, 345–428
    Part IX, 470–475
    Part V, 466–469
    Part VIII, 469–470
  forms, 408–410, 420–422
  guardian ad litem,
    appointment of, 374–378
    Guardians Ad Litem and Reporting
      Officers (Panels) Regulations 1991,
      483–490
    powers and duties of, 378–383
  hearing, 401–404
  interpretation, 353, 354–355
  investigation under section 37, 408, 418
  justices' clerk,
    delegation by, 419–420
    limits on power to make order, 418
  Magistrates' Courts Act 1980, application
    of section 97 of, 420
  meaning, 31, 34–35, 233
  notices and respondents, 411–415,
    422–427
  notification of consent, 407, 417
  oral evidence, 401
  parties, 367–370
  prescribed matters, 355–358
  private law, 10
  residence order, enforcement of, 416–417
  secure accommodation, evidence relating
    to, 407–408, 417
  service, 370–373
  single justice, limits on power to make
    order, 418
  solicitor for child, 383–386
  timing of, 392–393
  transfer of, 364–367
  transitional provision, 408
  withdrawal of application, 363–364
Family proceedings court
  appeal to, 418–419
  Children (Allocation of Proceedings)
    (Appeals) Order 1991, 452
  Children (Allocation of Proceedings)
    Order 1991, 432–452
  domestic court changed to, 216
Father
  parental responsibility for child,
    acquisition of, 22–25
  at the time of birth, meaning, 18, 19
  unmarried father, 18, 19
  paternity, tests to establish, 212–213

Index

Feelings of child
  local authority, general duty of, 65, 68
Fees
  Family Proceedings Fees Order 1991, 478–483
  panels of guardians ad litem and reporting officers, 488–489
Financial provisions
  Children Act 1989, under, 236
  controlled or assisted community home, cessation of, 161–163
Financial relief
  children, with respect to, orders for, 46–47, 238–246
Financial support
  Secretary of State, by, 202–203
Forms
  Family Proceedings Rules, under, 408–410, 420–422
Foster parent
  local authority foster parent, meaning, 198, 234
  meaning, 152
  number of children fostered, limits on, 171, 173, 275–277
  placement of child with, 69, 72–73
  private, person disqualified from being, 179–181
  refuges for children at risk, 152–154
  registration, 184, 186
  section 8 order, restriction on making, 35, 36
  See also Private fostering.
Functions
  meaning, 201, 233

Good Friday
  emergency protection order, duration of, 136
Guardian
  appointment of, 25–27
  disclaimer of appointment, 27–29
  guardian of child, meaning, 233
  natural guardian, concept of, 19
  residence order in favour of, 25, 27
  revocation of appointment, 27–29
  termination of appointment, 27–29
Guardian ad litem
  appointment of, 374–378
  Guardians Ad Litem and Reporting Officers (Panels) Regulations 1991, 483–490
  local authority records, access to, 124–126
  Official Solicitor acting as, 121, 124
  powers and duties of, 378–383
  representation of child and his interests, 120–124
  specified proceedings, 120, 121, 123–124
  statutory basis for service, 120–124
Guardianship proceedings
  court's powers in, 113
Guernsey
  abducted child, recovery of, 152

Guidance
  Department of Health, 13–14

Harm
  meaning, 94, 234
Health
  children in need, provision of services for, 50, 55
  meaning, 50, 94
  reasonable standard of, 50, 55
Health authority
  advice and assistance for child accommodated by, 76
  meaning, 234
  notification of children accommodated by, 206–207
  special health authority, meaning, 235
Health service hospital
  meaning, 234
Hearing
  family proceedings, 401–404
Hearsay evidence
  admissibility of, 431–432
  Children (Admissibility of Hearsay Evidence) Order 1991, 431–432
  welfare report, 29, 30
High Court
  appeal to, 219–221
  county court,
    transfer from, 438–439
    transfer to, 439
  ex parte application, 363
  fees to be taken in, 483
  principal registry of Family Division, 440
Home
  accommodation near child's home, 70, 74
  community. *See* Community home.
  maintenance of child in, 69, 72
  meaning, 171
  registered. *See* Registered children's home.
  voluntary. *See* Voluntary home.
Hospital
  health service hospital, meaning, 234
  meaning, 234
  recoupment of cost of providing services, 90

Ill-treatment
  meaning, 94, 234
Impairment
  local authority, provision of services by, 50, 55
Income support
  recoupment of cost of providing services, 89, 91
Independent school
  meaning, 171, 172, 234
  welfare of children accommodated in, 209–211
Information
  returns of, functions of Secretary of State, 203–205

Index

Inquiries
  Secretary of State, functions of, 201–202
Inspection
  child minding, 193–194
  children's homes, of, by person authorised by Secretary of State, 198–201
  day care of young child, 193–194
Interim order
  care order, 114–117
  medical examination, submission to, 115, 117, 130
  psychiatric examination, submission to, 115, 117, 130
  relevant period, meaning, 115
  supervision order, 114–117
Investigation
  local authority's duty to investigate, 142–146
  under section 37, 408, 418
Isle of Man
  abducted child, recovery of, 152
  orders, effect of, 230–231

Jurisdiction
  courts, of, 216–218, 295–299
  removal of child from, 44–45
  wardship, restrictions on use of, 227–229
Justices. *See* Magistrates' court.

Lambeth County Court
  allocation of proceedings, 440
Legal aid
  granting of, 226–227
Legal representative
  costs, personal liability for, 476–477
Liability
  costs, personal liability of legal representative for, 476–477
  parental responsibility for child, relating to, 18, 20
Liberty
  accommodation used for restricting, 79–83
Linguistic background
  local authority, general duty of, 65, 68
Local authority
  accommodation provided for child, detention, child in, 63–64
    duties relating to, 69–74, 246–257
    general duty, 64–69
    generally, 58–63
    police protection, child in, 63–64
    remand, child on, 63–64
  advice and assistance, provision of, 74–79
  child minding, review of provision for, 57–58
  children in need, provision of services for, 49–55, 246–257
  co-operation between authorities, 87–88
  community home,
    assisted, closure of, 160–161

Local authority—*cont*.
  community home—*cont*.
    controlled, closure of, 160–161
    provision of, 155–157, 263–267
  day care,
    meaning, 56
    pre-school children, for, 55–57
    provision of, 55–57
    relevant establishment, meaning, 57
    review of provision, 57–58
    review period, meaning, 57
  default power of Secretary of State, 205–206
  emergency protection order, application by, 130–135
  family assistance order, powers relating to, 47–49
  family proceedings, powers of court in, 112–114
  investigation, duty relating to, 142–146
  local authority foster parent, meaning, 198, 234
  meaning, 234
  miscellaneous functions, 92–93
  records, guardian ad litem's access to, 124–126
  recoupment of cost of providing services, 89–92, 254–257
  representations, inquiries into, 83–87
  review of cases, 83–87
  statutory duty, failure to comply with, 205–206
  voluntary organisation, duties relating to, 167–170
Local education authority
  advice and assistance for child accommodated by, 76
  appropriate local education authority, meaning, 89
  consultation with, 89
  education supervision order. *See* Education supervision order.
  meaning, 234
  notification of children accommodated by, 206–207
Local housing authority
  meaning, 234
Lord Chancellor
  Official Solicitor, duties and functions of, 121, 124
  orders, power to make, 232–233
  regulations, power to make, 232–233

Magistrates' court
  appeal from, 406–407
  county court,
    transfer from, 438
    transfer to, 436–437
  justices' clerk,
    delegation by, 419–420
    limits on power to make order, 418
  Magistrates' Courts Act 1980, application of section 97 of, 420

498

Index

Magistrates' courts—*cont.*
   privacy for children involved in proceedings, 224–225
   proceedings to be commenced in, 434
   refusal to transfer, transfer following, 437–438
   single justice, limits on power to make order, 418
   transfer from one magistrates' court to another, 435
Maintenance
   local authority, provision by, 69–74, 246–257
Material
   meaning, 224
Matrimonial proceedings
   court's powers in, 113
Medical examination
   emergency protection order, relating to, 130
   interim order, relating to, 115, 117, 130
   supervision order, relating to, 130
Mental nursing home
   advice and assistance for child in, 76
   meaning, 234
   notification of children accommodated in, 207–209
Misconduct
   district judge, powers of, 477–478
Mother
   parental responsibility for child, 18, 19

Name
   child, of, change of, 44–45
National Society for Prevention of Cruelty to Children
   authorised person, meaning, 94
   care order, effect of, 101
Natural guardian
   concept of, 19
Neglect
   district judge, powers of, 477–478
Next friend
   certain minors may sue without, 472–474
   person under disability must sue by, 470–472
Northern Ireland
   court, meaning, 151
   orders, effect of, 230–231
   recovery order, 151–152
Notice of proceedings
   meaning, 219
Notices
   family proceedings, 411–415, 422–427
Notification
   consent, of, 407, 417
   health authority, children accommodated by, 206–207
   independent school, welfare of children accommodated in, 209–211
   local education authority, children accommodated by, 206–207

Notification—*cont.*
   mental nursing home, children accommodated in, 207–209
   nursing home, children accommodated in, 207–209
   residential care, children accommodated in, 207–209
Nursing home
   advice and assistance for child in, 76
   meaning, 234
   notification of children accommodated in, 207–209

Oath
   child understanding nature of, 222, 223
Offence
   abducted child, recovery of, 149–152
   abduction of child in care, 148–149
   bodies corporate, by, 232
   child minding, relating to, 196–197
   day care of young children, relating to, 196–197
   private fostering, relating to, 182–183
Official Solicitor
   guardian ad litem, acting as, 121, 124
Oral evidence
   family proceedings, 401
Orders
   care. *See* Care order.
   Channel Islands, 230–231
   child assessment. *See* Child assessment order.
   contact. *See* Contact order.
   emergency protection. *See* Emergency protection order.
   England and Wales, 230–231
   family assistance, 47–49
   financial relief with respect to children, for, 46–47, 238–246
   Isle of Man, 230–231
   Lord Chancellor's power to make, 232–233
   Northern Ireland, 230–231
   prohibited steps. *See* Prohibited steps order.
   residence. *See* Residence order.
   Secretary of State's power to make, 232–233
   specific issue. *See* Specific issue order.
   supervision. *See* Supervision order.
Ordinary residence
   meaning, 235

Panels
   family panel, domestic court panel changed to, 216
   Guardians Ad Litem and Reporting Officers (Panels) Regulations 1991, 483–490
Parental responsibility
   any person with, 23, 24
   care order, effect of, 100, 101–102

Index

Parental responsibility—*cont.*
  child, for, 18–20
  emergency protection order, relating to, 131
  father, acquisition by, 22–25
  meaning, 20–22, 234
  parental responsibility agreement, meaning, 234
  private law, 9–10
  residence order and, 43–44
Parents
  children in care, parental contact with, 103–107
  residence order in favour of, 25, 27
  wardship jurisdiction, restrictions on use of, 229
  welfare of child, 16
Parties
  family proceedings, to, 367–370
Paternity
  tests to establish, 212–213
Patient
  meaning, 470
  See also Disability.
Penal notice
  section 8 order, attachment to, 404
Person under disability. *See* Disability.
Police
  emergency, removal and accommodation of child in case of, 138–142
  search warrant, powers relating to, 231–232
Police protection
  abduction of child in care, 149
  accommodation provided for child in, 63–64
  local authority's duty to investigate, 142–146
Pre-school child
  day care for, 55–57
Premises
  community home, no longer used for, 157–158
  domestic premises, meaning, 185
  meaning, 162, 185
Prescribed
  meaning, 219, 234
Privacy
  children involved in proceedings, for, 224–225
Private fostering
  appropriate authority, meaning, 179
  enactment, meaning, 179
  offences, 182–183
  private foster parent, person disqualified from being, 179–181
  privately fostered child, meaning, 175–177, 234
  penal notice, attachment of, 404
  welfare, 177–179
  prohibition of, 181–182
  supplementary provisions, 277–281

Private law
  court order, 10
  family proceedings, 10
  parental responsibility, 9–10
Privilege
  self-incrimination, against, 225–226
Probation officer
  family assistance order, powers relating to, 47–49
Prohibited steps order
  court's power to make, 37–41
  general principles, 41–43
  meaning, 31, 32–33, 234
  penal notice, attachment of, 404
  restrictions on making, 35–37
  supplementary provisions, 41–43
Proprietor
  meaning, 162
Protected child
  meaning, 234
Protection of children
  abducted child, recovery of, 149–152
  abduction of child in care, 148–149
  attendance of child at hearing, 221–222
  child assessment order, 126–130
  emergency protection. *See* Emergency protection order.
  local authority's duty to investigate, 142–146
  refuge for child at risk, 152–154
  regulations, 154
  rules, 154
Psychiatric examination
  emergency protection order, relating to, 130
  interim order, relating to, 115, 117, 130
  supervision order, relating to, 130
Public holiday
  emergency protection order, duration of, 136
Public law
  care, 10–11
  day care, 11
  other care, 12
Publicity
  wardship jurisdiction, restrictions on use of, 229
Publish
  meaning, 224

Racial group
  meaning, 68
Racial origin
  local authority, general duty of, 65, 68
Records
  local authority, guardian ad litem's access to, 124–126
Recovery order
  abducted child, relating to, 149–152
Refuges
  children at risk, for, 152–154
Registered children's home
  advice and assistance for child in, 76
  children's home, meaning, 170, 233

Index

Registered children's home—*cont*.
   home, meaning, 171
   maintenance of child in, 69, 71–72
   meaning, 171, 234
   persons disqualified from carrying on, 174–175
   registration, 172–173, 271–274
   regulations, 274–275
   unregistered children's home, children not to be cared for in, 170–173
   voluntary organisation, provision of accommodation by, 163
   welfare of child in, 173–174
Registered pupil
   meaning, 234
Registration
   child minding, of,
      cancellation, 190–192
      local authority, by, 183–187, 281–284
   day care of young children,
      cancellation of, 190–192
      local authority, by, 183–187, 281–284
   registered children's home, of, 172–173, 271–274
   voluntary home, of, 165–166, 267–270
Regulations
   Lord Chancellor's power to make, 232–233
   protection of children, relating to, 154
   Secretary of State's power to make, 232–233
Relative
   meaning, 234
Relevant establishment
   meaning, 57
Relevant period
   meaning, 115
Relevant proceedings
   meaning, 219
Relevant time
   meaning, 162
Religious persuasion
   care order, effect of, 100, 102–103
   local authority, general duty of, 65, 68
Remand
   accommodation provided for child on, 63–64
Reporting officers
   Guardians Ad Litem and Reporting Officers (Panels) Regulations 1991, 483–490
Representations
   inquiries into, 84, 87
Research
   Secretary of State, functions of, 203–205
Residence order
   care order, discharge of, 35, 36
   court's power to make, 37–41
   effect of, 214
   enforcement, 416–417
   general principles, 41–43
   guardian, in favour of, 25, 27
   jurisdiction, removal of child from, 44–45
   meaning, 31, 33, 234

Residence order—*cont*.
   name of child, change of, 44–45
   parent, in favour of, 25, 27
   parental responsibility and, 43–44
   penal notice, attachment of, 404
   restrictions on making, 35–37
   supplementary provisions, 41–43
Residential care home
   advice and assistance for child in, 76
   meaning, 234
   notification of children accommodated in, 207–209
Respondents
   family proceedings, 411–415, 422–427
Responsible authority
   meaning, 162, 206
Responsible person
   meaning, 234
Review period
   meaning, 57
Reward
   child minding, for, 184, 186
   day care of young children, for, 184, 186
Risk
   refuges for children at, 152–154
Rules
   court, of, 218–219, 345–428
   protection of children, relating to, 154

School
   independent. *See* Independent school.
   meaning, 235
School attendance order
   effect of, 214, 216
   non-compliance with, 109, 111
Scotland
   child minding, 197–198
   court, meaning, 197
   day care of young children, 197–198
   education authority, meaning, 198
   local authority foster parent, meaning, 198
   recovery order, 151
Search
   emergency protection, discovery of child in need of, 146–147, 148
   warrant, constable's powers relating to, 231–232
Secretary of State
   children's homes, inspection of, 198–201
   default power of, 205–206
   financial support by, 202–203
   functions, meaning, 201, 233
   inquiries, 201–202
   orders, power to make, 232–233
   regulations, power to make, 154
   research, 203–205
   returns of information, 203–205
   statutory duty, local authority failure to comply with, 205–206
Section 8 order. *See* Contact order; Prohibited steps order; Residence order; Specific issue order.

Index

Secure accommodation
  Children (Secure Accommodation) Regulations 1991, 452–461
  Children (Secure Accommodation) (No. 2) Regulations 1991, 461–462
  civil cases, use in, 80–81
  criminal cases, use in, 82
  evidence relating to, 407–408, 417
  liberty, restriction of, 79–83
  meaning, 203
Self-incrimination
  privilege against, 225–226
Service
  family proceedings, 370–373
  meaning, 235
  person under disability, on, 474
Services
  children in need, provision by local authority for, 49–55, 246–257
  recoupment of cost of providing, 89–92, 254–257
Signed
  meaning, 235
Solicitor for child
  appointment of, 383–386
Special educational needs
  meaning, 235
Special health authority
  meaning, 235
Specific issue order
  court's power to make, 37–41
  general principles, 41–43
  meaning, 31, 33–34, 235
  penal notice, attachment of, 404
  restrictions on making, 35–37
  supplementary provisions, 41–43
Specified proceedings
  guardian ad litem, representation of child by, 120, 123–124
  meaning, 121
Sunday
  emergency protection order, duration of, 136
Supervised activity
  meaning, 56
Supervision order
  additional procedural conditions, 98
  appeal in case about, 119–120
  application for, 93, 97
  attendance of child at hearing, 221–222
  authorised person, meaning, 94
  care order, substitution for, 215
  criminal proceedings, in, 213–214
  delay in making application, 99–100
  development, meaning, 94
  discharge, 117–119, 215
  education, 109–112, 260–263
  family assistance order, replacement by, 48
  grounds for, 93, 97–98
  harm, meaning, 94
  health, meaning, 94
  ill-treatment, meaning, 94
  interim order, 114–117

Supervision order—cont.
  meaning, 95, 235
  restrictions, 98
  supervised child, meaning, 235
  supervisor,
    meaning, 235
    primary duty of, 108–109, 257–260
  variation, 117–119
Time limits
  care order, appeal in case about, 120
  supervision order, appeal in case about, 120
Timetable
  family proceedings, 392–393
  section 8 order, relating to, 41, 42
Training
  approved child care training, meaning, 203
  child care training, meaning, 202–203
Trust deed
  meaning, 158

Unregistered children's home
  children not to be cared for in, 170–173
Upbringing
  meaning, 235
Urgency. *See* Emergency protection order.

Value
  children in need, provision of services for, 49, 54
Visiting
  voluntary organisation, children accommodated by, 167, 169
Voluntary home
  maintenance of child in, 69, 71–72
  meaning, 165, 166, 235
  registration, 165–166, 267–270
  regulation of, 165–166, 270–271
  trust deed, meaning, 158
Voluntary organisation
  accommodation, provision by, 163–165
  advice and assistance for child accommodated by, 76
  assisted community home, of, discontinuance of, 159–160
  controlled community home, of, discontinuance of, 159–160
  duties of, 166–167
  local authority, duties of, 167–170
  meaning, 235
  visiting children accommodated by, 167, 169

Wardship
  care order, effect of, 214
  Family Proceedings Rules 1991, 466–469
  jurisdiction, restrictions on use of, 227–229

Index

Warrant
  emergency protection, discovery of child in need of, 147, 148
  search, constable's powers relating to, 231–232
Welfare
  child, of, 14–17
  children in need, provision of services for, 49, 52
  children's home, child in, 173–174
  family proceedings, powers of court in, 112, 114
  independent school, children accommodated in, 209–211
  privately fostered children, of, 177–179
Welfare officer
  role of, 386–388
Welfare report
  court's power to call for, 29–30
  hearsay evidence, admissibility of, 29, 30
  presentation of, 29, 30
Wishes of child
  local authority, general duty of, 65, 68
Woolwich County Court
  allocation of proceedings, 440
Words and phrases
  accommodating authority, 206
  accommodation, 64
  adoption agency, 233
  appeal period, 120
  appropriate local education authority, 89
  approved child care training, 203
  authorised person, 94, 127, 131, 150
  bank holiday, 233
  care order, 94–95, 233
  child, 233
  child assessment order, 126, 233
  child care training, 202–203
  child minder, 233
  child of family, 233
  children's home, 170, 233
  community home, 233
  contact order, 30, 32, 233
  court, 151, 197
  day care, 56, 197, 233
  designated officer, 150
  development, 50, 94
  disabled, 233
  disposal, 162
  district health authority, 233
  domestic premises, 185, 233
  education authority, 198
  education supervision order, 109, 233
  emergency protection order, 233
  family assistance order, 233
  family proceedings, 31, 34–35, 233
  family, 50, 53
  foster parent, 152
  functions, 201, 233
  guardian of child, 233
  harm, 94, 234
  health, 50, 94

Words and phrases—*cont.*
  health authority, 234
  health service hospital, 234
  home, 171
  hospital, 234
  ill-treatment, 94, 234
  independent school, 171, 172, 234
  local authority, 234
  local authority foster parent, 198, 234
  local education authority, 234
  local housing authority, 234
  material, 224
  mental nursing home, 234
  notice of proceedings, 219
  nursing home, 234
  ordinary residence, 235
  parental responsibility, 20–22, 234
  parental responsibility agreement, 234
  patient, 470
  person authorised to seek access, 131
  person qualifying for advice and assistance, 75, 78
  person under disability, 470
  premises, 162, 185
  prescribed, 219, 234
  privately fostered child, 175–177, 234
  prohibited steps order, 31, 32–33, 234
  proprietor, 162
  protected child, 234
  publish, 224
  racial group, 68
  registered children's home, 171, 234
  registered pupil, 234
  relative, 234
  relevant establishment, 57
  relevant period, 115
  relevant proceedings, 219
  relevant time, 162
  residence order, 31, 33, 234
  residential care home, 234
  responsible authority, 162, 206
  responsible person, 234
  review period, 57
  school, 235
  secure accommodation, 203
  service, 235
  signed, 235
  special educational needs, 235
  special health authority, 235
  specific issue order, 31, 33–34, 235
  specified proceedings, 121
  supervised activity, 56
  supervised child, 235
  supervision order, 95, 235
  supervisor, 235
  trust deed, 158
  upbringing, 235
  voluntary home, 165, 166, 235
  voluntary organisation, 235
Young children
  day care for. *See* Day care.
Youth treatment centre
  establishment of, 203